Anonymous

Reunion of Twelfth Iowa vet. vol. infantry

Anonymous

Reunion of Twelfth Iowa vet. vol. infantry

ISBN/EAN: 9783337732233

Printed in Europe, USA, Canada, Australia, Japan

Cover: Foto ©ninafisch / pixelio.de

More available books at **www.hansebooks.com**

FIRST REUNION

—:OF THE:—

12th Iowa V. V. Infantry,

— HELD AT —

MANCHESTER, IOWA,

— ON —

Tuesday and Wednesday, April 6th and 7th, 1880.

DUBUQUE, IOWA:
TIMES PRINTING HOUSE.

1880.

FIRST REUNION
—OF THE—
12th IOWA INFANTRY.

ITS ORIGIN.

The first Re-union of the 12th Iowa Infantry had its origin in Delaware County, in December, 1879.

At an informal meeting of a few of the regiment, at Delhi, at which were present Lieut. Abner Dunham, Col. S. G. Knee, Major G. H. Morrisey and Lieut. C. E. Merriam, it was determined that a Reunion should be had, at Manchester, on the 6th and 7th of April, 1880, that being the anniversary of the battle of Shiloh.

At this meeting the following Officers for the Re-union were appointed, viz:

S. G. KNEE, President; D. B. HENDERSON, Vice President; ABNER DUNHAM, Secretary; G. H. MORRISEY, R. W. TIRRILL, C. E. MERRIAM, Executive Committee.

Then followed several meetings, at which Lieut. J. E. Simpson and others were present, with the Committee and Officers, and the Secretary issued the following Call:

TWELFTH REGIMENT IOWA VOLUNTEER INFANTRY.

DEAR COMRADE:—At a preliminary meeting of a number of the officers and members of the Twelfth Regiment, held at Delhi, Delaware County, December 27th, 1879, to consult as to the propriety of having a Reunion of the surviving members, it was unanimously resolved that such meeting should be held. At this meeting, Col. S. G. Knee, of Colesburg, was chosen President, Col. D. B. Henderson, of Dubuque, Vice President, and Lieut. Abner Dunham, of Manchester, Secretary, who, together with Major Geo. H. Morrisey, of Delhi, and Mr. C. E. Merriam, of Hopkinton, were constituted an Executive Committee, and empowered to call a meeting of the Regiment at such time and place as they should deem appropriate.

They have, accordingly, determined to have the first meeting of the Regiment at Manchester, Delaware County, on Tuesday and Wednesday, April 6th and 7th, next, at which meeting your attendance is earnestly requested.

It has seemed to those of us who have inaugurated this movement, that such a meeting of those members of the "Old Twelfth" as still survive, would be attended with much to interest us all. We ask you then to come and join your old comrades in arms, in this their first annual meeting, and in the renewal of old friendships and associations. There will be here many of the officers of the different companies, and we most earnestly desire to see every member of the Regiment present.

By order of Executive Committee,
LIEUT. A. DUNHAM,
Manchester, Iowa, January 23, 1880.   Secretary.

At a final meeting of the Officers and Executive Committee, all being present, the following Programme was adopted:

PROGRAMME.

TUESDAY FORENOON.

MEETING OF THE COMRADES AT THE TRAINS.
GENERAL HAND SHAKING.

TUESDAY AFTERNOON, 1:30 O'CLOCK,

ASSEMBLY.
ADDRESS BY THE PRESIDENT.
BUSINESS.   VISITING.

TUESDAY EVENING, 7:30 O'CLOCK,

ASSEMBLY AT CITY HALL.
PRAYER, BY REV. D. RUSSELL, 11TH N. Y. INFANTRY.
MUSIC.
WELCOME BY THE MAYOR, HON. C. SANBORN.
RESPONSE BY THE PRESIDENT.
ORATION, BY D. B. HENDERSON.
FIVE MINUTE DRILL IN THE MANUAL OF ARMS.
BY CO. C. 4TH REGT. I. N. G.
SONG.—"RALLY ROUND THE FLAG, BOYS," BY ALL.
TATTOO.

WEDNESDAY MORNING.

SIX O'CLOCK, REVEILLE.
NINE O'CLOCK, ASSEMBLY AT CITY HALL.
BUSINESS.   VISITING.
ONE O'CLOCK, P. M., BANQUET AND TOASTS.
VISITING, AND ESCORTING DELEGATES TO THE TRAINS.

Banquet at Ford's Hall.

PROGRAMME FOR BANQUET.

Wednesday, 1 o'clock, P. M.

GRACE BY REV. ALVAH DAY OF MANCHESTER.
BANQUET.   MUSIC.

"THE STATE AND THE NATION—Mutually Dependent and Independent."
Response by Major E. M. VanDuzee, of St. Paul.

"THE ARMY AND NAVY—The Safeguards of all Nations. Response by Hon. R. W. Tirrill, Manchester.

"THE CHILDREN OF THE 12TH IOWA—God Bless them! and may they live long to enjoy the Freedom that their Fathers, Living and Dead, fought to Secure." Response by Florence L. Dunham, Manchester.

"HARDTACK AND COFFEE—The Reserves from which we daily drew Nerve and Inspiration." Response by Capt. E. B. Soper, Emmetsburg.

MUSIC.

"THE GIRLS WE LEFT BEHIND US—The only Power that has made Prisoners of us all." Response by Harvey Smith, Waterloo.

"HISTORY OF THE TWELFTH IOWA INFANTRY." Capt. W. L. Henderson, Leroy, Minn.

"THE WIVES, MOTHERS, DAUGHTERS AND SWEETHEARTS OF THE TWELFTH IOWA—None Suffered More, none Complained less. Our Flag Their Flag Their Homes Our Hearts." Response by Lieut. J. E. Simpson, Dubuque.

"OUR GALLANT DEAD—The Noble Heroes who, although passed to the Shores of the Great Unknown, still Live in our Memories, and are Cherished as among the best of our number." Response by R. P. Clarkson, Des Moines.

MUSIC.—"The Red, White and Blue." Chorus by All.

COMMITTEES.

EXECUTIVE COMMITTEE.
S. G. KNEE, President.   D. B. HENDERSON, Vice President.
ABNER DUNHAM, Secretary.   D. H. MORRISEY,
C. E. MERRIAM.

RECEPTION COMMITTEE.
R. W. TIRRILL,   W. H. GOODELL,   JOHN OTIS.

DECORATION COMMITTEE.
MRS. E. ALLEN,   MRS. F. BETHELL,   MRS. A. M. SHERWOOD.
MRS. E. HOAG,   MRS. W. C. CAWLEY,
MRS. T. W. ROBINSON,   MRS. L. P. HUNT.

FINANCE COMMITTEE.
D. B. HENDERSON,   G. H. MORRISEY,   C. E. MERRIAM.

COMMITTEE OF REGISTRATION OF MEMBERS, AND RESERVED SEATS AT CITY HALL.
C. E. MERRIAM,   HARVEY SMITH,   H. S. LILLAGAR.

COMMITTEE ON TOASTS.
R. P. CLARKSON,   R. W. TIRRILL.

COMMITTEE ON BANQUET.

R. W. TIRRILL,	S. G. KNEE,	G. H. MORRISEY.
MRS. ABNER DUNHAM,	MRS. W. N. BOYNGON,	MRS. W. H. GOODELL,
" F. BETHELL,	" W. C. CAWLEY,	" H. A. MORSE.
" A. M. SHERWOOD,	" N. N. CORNISH,	" E. HOAG,
" C. E. BRONSON,	" C. H. DAY,	" L. P. HUNT,
" T. W. ROBINSON,	" E. R. CONGER,	" J. H. PRATT,
" T. W. ROBINLON,	" CHAS. BURNSIDE,	" M. BABCOCK,
" M. F. LeROY,	" H. HOYT,	" E. ALDEN,
" H. C. GRAHAM,	" E. G. RUNDELD,	" J. A. ABBOTT,
" A. O. MOORE,	" H. M. CONGER,	" A. S. BLAIR,
MISS J. KINSLEY,	MISS H. HOAG,	MISS O. MADISON,
" N. BURNSIDE,	" L. HONEY,	" L. ALLEN,
" S. BAILEY,	" N. PAXSON,	" H. TILTON,
" L. McLAIN,		

THE GREAT REUNION.

THE TWELFTH IOWA AT MANCHESTER.

The first reunion of the surviving members of the veteran 12th regiment, Iowa Volunteer Infantry, took place in this city on Tuesday and Wednesday of this week. To say it was the most successful meeting conveys the faintest idea of the occasion. From first to last it was the most inspiring and enthusiastic gathering ever seen in Manchester. After years of separation, the men who, for more than four long years had endured danger and privation, and untold suffering, who had together faced death on many a battle field, who, many of them had suffered the horrible torture of starvation and disease in Southern prison-pens, who had at last, broken in health and prematurely gray, come back to those for whom they conquered, once more found themselves face to face, and clasped hand in hand. What the emotion, what the feelings of these men must have been, words are powerless to express.

From the first hour of their arrival here, the sense of their presence and what they had done and what they endured, seemed to pervade the entire community. The people of Manchester and of the country round about, rose, as one man, to welcome the members of the old 12th and to do them honor. The patriotic fervor of the old war days seemed to be revived. The women of Manchester, especially, worked with unflagging zeal, and to their efforts, in a large measure, is due the glorious success of the reunion.

Large numbers of the buildings were adorned with flags and streamers showing the national colors, rows of flags were stretched from THE PRESS office to the Clarence House, and from Thorpe Bros. to Lawrence & Lister's, and at the entrance of the City Hall had been erected arches of evergreens, and the whole street was gay with flags of every description.

The Decoration Committee deserves the highest credit for the manner in which they performed the arduous duties imposed upon them. The walls and chandeliers of the City Hall were fairly covered with most tastefully arranged evergreens and flags, among which were hung numerous pictures and mottoes, the whole combining to make a pleasing and spirited scene. On the proscenium of the stage hung the colors of the regiment, tattered and torn by storms and rebel bullets, and they were a most forcible reminder of the trials and vicissitudes through which the brave men of the "Old Twelfth" passed while fighting the battles of the union.

In a recess in the scene at the back of the stage, was a large picture of General Grant, with a flag hanging on each side. On one side of the hall, near the stage, hung a picture of President Lincoln, and under it the words, "A government of the people, for the people and by the people." On the opposite wall was another picture of General Grant, and under it the words, "Let us have peace." In another place, surrounded by evergreens, hung a list of some of the battles participated in by the 12th Regiment. The battles named were Fort Donelson, Nashville, Spanish Fort, Vicksburg and Tupelo.

The session opened Tuesday afternoon with music by the Manchester Cornet Band," after which Col. Knee, who was booked for an address, introduced Col. J. J. Woods, the first commander of the regiment, saying that at that time it would be an insult to ask those present to listen to any other man. Col. Woods spoke in substance as follows:

MY FELLOW SOLDIERS OF THE 12TH IOWA:—I do not appear before you to perform any duty, or fill any place assigned me by your committee; but with great reluctance, and at the earnest solicitation of Col. Knee, your honored president, I consented to occupy his place. I am not large enough to fill it, but I thank him for allowing me to talk about what I please, and as long or short a time as I please.

But upon this occasion my thoughts can only wander in one direction. I am thinking of the time when, at the bugle call of our country, we came forth—farmers from their farms, mechanics from their shops, merchants from their counters, lawyers from their clients, doctors from their patients—enrolled ourselves, nearly one thousand strong, for the defense of our country. We recall the process of organization and drill; the sojourn at Benton Barracks, where death, by disease, began his inroad on our ranks; the bombardment of Fort Henry and the siege of Donelson, where our ranks were first thinned by rebel bullets. I recall the moment when Buckner, of Co. A, the first man we lost in battle, fell; how cold the following night was; how, the next day, we took the rebel rifle pits, and how, upon the third morning, the shout of triumph arose and passed from rank to rank, at beholding the white flag displayed from the rebel ramparts, and Gen. Simon B. Buckner turned over his fortifications to "Unconditional Surrender" Grant.

But oh, how vividly is pictured upon my brain the events of eighteen years ago to-day. How we remember that Sabbath morning, when, instead of being summoned by the church bell to the worship of the living God, we were summoned by the roar of cannon and the rattle of musketry to the work of carnage and death. You remember how hurriedly we formed our ranks of war and marched to the front, meeting on the way hundreds retiring to the rear with tales of woe and disaster; but you pressed forward and fearlessly took up your position in the front line of battle, and right nobly did you maintain it, repelling every charge or assault of the enemy and driving him back in confusion, until the troops upon your right and those on the left of the 8th and 14th Iowa gave way and left you to defend yourselves as best you could.

You remember how you undertook to fight your way to the rear and sent death and destruction into the ranks of the enemy until many of your comrades were killed by your side, and I and many others fell wounded on the field of battle; and the only alternative was surrender or annihilation. If all had stood their ground as you did, the disaster of that day would never have been recorded. How sadly I felt when you were marched to the rear, while I, with wounded and dead comrades, lay upon the battle field, enclosed by the foe. I recall how the rebel Gen. Hardee, after some pleasant conversation, tried to elicit from me facts in reference to our troops that might be of value to the rebel army; and how a Texas subaltern pointed a pistol at my head and threatened to blow my brains out; how I had heard rebels boast of the brave deeds they had done that day, and how they would complete the great victory the next day; how, during that night, I listened to the groans of the dying, growing less and less as time wore on, and their departed spirits returned to God who gave them. In the meantime, the shells from our gunboats were bursting around us. At length the morning dawned, the morning of the day upon which, according to their boasts of the evening before, the enemy was to complete his victory. But soon I heard them tramping to the rear, and the cry from the rear, "The cavalry are getting on our flanks!" and then the additional cry, "Buel has come!" Soon I looked forth and joyfully beheld the flag of my country waving in the breeze, and gradually approaching nearer and nearer. Oh, how my heart leaped for joy! Never did that flag look so beautiful before. It gave assurance of victory to our army. To me it was a resurrection from death unto life, for I would have died in the rebel hands had I not been rescued. It told me that I should again see home, and wife and children. It told me more: It told me that I should live to try again the gage of battle with the enemy of my country, upon other fields of action. Oh, glorious flag of my country! forever may it wave over a happy and united people.

But time would fail to recount the further history of our regiment —your release from prison, the reorganization of the regiment with diminished numbers, the capture of Jackson, the siege of Vicksburg, Tupelo, and the various other engagements in which you bore a worthy part. Suffice it to say, that in all these engagements you proved yourselves to be the bravest of the brave. On the battle fields of the South, you won imperishable renown, whether engaged in the grand charge that won the day, as at Donelson, or staying the tide of threatened disaster, as at Shiloh. In marches and in skirmishes, in sieges and assaults in attack and defense, by the heroism with which you faced death and danger in every form, by your intelligence and love of country you proved that you possessed the characteristics of true soldiers in the highest degree, and your noble achievements constitute a rich treasure in which all have an interest.

My comrades, to-day we meet together as the widely scattered members of a common household, after long years of separation. We come together under that dear old flag, dear to the heart of every member of the regiment. We come, not now at the rallying cry of battle, but to recall and contemplate the common joys, the common hopes, the common toils, the common trials and sufferings through which, as members of the same regiment we were called to pass. We come with the most grateful and tender affection for the honored dead of our regiment, whose places among us are vacant to-day, and who went to their long rest from the battle field, from the hospital, from the prison pens of the South, and, more recently, from their homes widely scattered throughout the land. They went down gloriously unto death, that the Republic might ascend up gloriously unto life. To-day we miss the light that beamed from their countenances; they are no longer among us, but—

"On fame's eternal camping ground,
Their silent tents are spread."

For them we can only shed the silent tear, and weep with the fathers and mothers, the wives and children, whose hearts overflow with sorrow for their lost loved ones.

My comrades, I have already passed the meridian of life, and am going down the western declivity, but I assure you that time has not diminished my love for liberty, or country, nor dimmed my affectionate regard for you, who, with me, spent some of your best years in their defense; and though the wounds we received and the hardships of the service, cause us some pain and affliction, we bear it all with cheerful fortitude, knowing that the necessities of the times demanded the sacrifice. And when I speak of my country, the idea in my mind is not that of any pent up Utica; it is not confined by municipal walls, nor limited by State boundaries; my country is not Ohio, though I was born there; it is not Kentucky or New York, although I was educated within their borders; it is not the noble State of Iowa, though I married my wife within her precincts, and two of my lovely children lie buried within her soil; it is not the beautiful land of Kansas, where I now dwell; but my country is where floats that glorious flag, and when for the last time I shall behold its starry folds, next to my hopes of a better life up yonder, will be the desire that my country may be great, and that union, peace and prosperity may prevail throughout all her vast borders.

And now that we have met beneath that dear old flag, grasped the hand of friendship, heard the strains of martial music, renewed our devotion to our common country, when we part I shall return to the duties and avocations of life, in my far-off Kansas home, with renewed courage and a thankful heart that I have been permitted to see your faces again.

At the conclusion of Col. Woods' address, Col. D. B. Henderson moved that a committee of five, of which Col. Woods should be chairman, be appointed by the President to prepare a plan for a permanent organization of the surviving members of the 12th Regiment, with a view to the continuation of these pleasant reunions; said committee to report Wednesday morning. Carried. The president appointed as such committee, J. D. Cole, D. B. Henderson, H. J. Playter and J. E. Simpson.

Several letters of regret were read by Secretary Dunham, which are given below.

STUTTGART, GERMANY, March 15th, 1880

LT. J. E. SIMPSON, Dubuque, Iowa.

My Dear Sir:—Through my son Otto I received your letter dated 25th of February, inquiring for my address. Therein I see - although so many years have elapsed since I was amongst you—that you still think of me. This sign of remembrance is unspeakably touching and gratifying to me. When in America, last year, it was my great wish to come once more to Dubuque and call and see any of you, but circumstances called me back to Europe.

Not to be able to be personally present at your reunion on the 6th of next month is a source of great regret to me, and therefore I beg you my dear sir, to be my interpreter on that occasion, and tell my dear brothers in arms—officers and members of the old 12th Iowa, that the days spent amongst them, the remembrance of the love and kindly feeling of all is deeply engraved in my memory as of the happiest time in my life, and neither time nor distance can ever weaken my attachment to the boys in blue.

My love to each of the dear ones present; three cheers for the dear old 12th Iowa, and the Union forever! Long life and happiness to all the remaining ones. Thoughts of regret for those called off. To you, yet especially, my expressions of regards.

Ever your old Major,
S. D. BRODTBECK.

DES MOINES, IOWA, March 30th, 1880.

ABNER DUNHAM, Secretary, Manchester, Iowa:

My Dear Sir: - Your favor of March 15th, inviting me to be present at the reunion of the 12th regiment of Iowa Volunteers, is at hand.

It would give me personal pleasure to accept, did not my official engagements prevent.

The record of the 12th Iowa illuminates a bright page in the history of the State. You did well by your country in the hour of danger, and I am heartily thankful that so many of you are spared to enjoy the blessings of peace, won by your regiment in connection with the other soldiers of the Republic's grand army.

May you each and all be spared for many years to meet around your festive board and fight your battles over, which in the days of 1861-4 were stern realities.

Thanking your committee for the invitation, and again regretting my inability to attend, I am,

Yours truly,
JOHN H. GEAR.

SPARTA, WHITE Co., TENN., April 2, 1880.

To the Members of the Twelfth Iowa Volunteer Infantry, at their Reunion, April 6th, 1880:

Comrades:—The regret I feel in consequence of my inability to respond in person to the many urgent invitations I have received from different members of the old regiment to be present at your reunion, is greater than I can well express by means of an ordinary letter. As many of you doubtless know, I am at present in the service of our old friend, "Uncle Sam," and can only leave my post by permission of those in authority. I have been confidently expecting such permission, but for some reason it has failed to reach me, and as I would have to start from here to-day in order to be with you on the 6th instant, I am compelled to send you my regrets and congratulations in the form of a letter, and must bear my disappointment as best I can, hoping that at your next reunion my efforts to be present may be rewarded with better success.

The day you have selected for your reunion could not have been more appropriately chosen, but I will not refer especially to the time of which this day is the anniversary, nor the gallant part you bore on that day, nor yet to the splendid record you made for yourselves during the war, as your orator no doubt, will say all that can be said on this subject; and all who are familiar with the history of the Iowa troops during the rebellion will agree, I think, to the claim we make that the Iowa soldiers were second to none in the world, and that the record of the 12th will compare favorably with that of any regiment sent out by the State.

According to my recollection of events it was the rule during the war, at the various entertainments of pyrotechnical displays, etc., held in the neighborhood where we chanced to be encamped or bivouacked to reserve at least a part of the front seats for the 12th Iowa; but, comrades, if I could be with you I should want to talk of something aside from our war record. I should esteem it a privilege to meet and greet you all once more, and to tell you of the love and friendship I have cherished for all of you during the years that have passed since we separated, and to assure you all that as I now look back over my life's history I find in it nothing of which I am half so proud as I am of the fact that during the dark days of the rebellion, while we each, in our humble way, sought to manifest by our actions something of the love and devotion we felt for our glorious country; that it was my privilege and honor to command for so long a time the brave, noble, generous fellows whose names are inscribed on the rolls of the 12th Iowa Infantry.

May God bless and prosper you all, and keep your hearts true to yourselves and to each other, as they were true to your country during the years when I so proudly thought and spoke of you all as "my boys."

May your reunion be a successful and happy one, and while you are having a glorious good time together, may you each have a kind thought for me, and believe me, each and all,

Your true friend and comrade,
J. H. STIBBS.

OLATHE, Kansas, March 30, 1880.
LT. A. DUNHAM, SEC'Y:

Dear Comrades:—Permit me, through you, to express my hearty approval of the reunion inaugurated by some of the members of the "old 12th," and hope it a grand success.

Nothing would be more gratifying to me than to be able to meet my old comrades and friends on the occasion of this reunion. I know it will have a tendency to awaken memories of the camp, the march and the fierce conflicts that have slept for years and have almost passed from memory. Some of those scenes are as beautiful in imagination as they were in reality, and others are sad, very sad. Many of our bosom companions, brave, noble fellows, have long since fought their last fight. It will be sad to miss them when you call the roll. I hope you will not report me "absent without leave." I always tried hard to do my whole duty. I am now on detached duty, and hope Col. Knee will excuse my absence this time, and at your next meeting I hope to be able to meet with you. I would like to grasp you all by the hand and commingle my congratulations with those who now survive of the old 12th. My good wishes attend you, and may the many noble deeds of her dead heroes be emulated and indelibly recorded in the memories of her living heroes. Living heroes, I say! for were there any in the service of our country entitled to the name, it was the bloody 12th. "Hurrah, boys, hurrah; down with the traitors and up with the stars!" Stand by our country. With kind regards for all,

Truly Yours,
S. R. BURCH,
Late Adjutant 12th Iowa Vet. Inft'y.

ST. PAUL, Minn., March 26, 1880.
LT. ABNER DUNHAM, SEC'Y., MANCHESTER, IOWA:

My Dear Sir:—I have just received back from Manchester, Minn., a letter which I wrote you on receipt of your first letter enclosing the circular announcing the reunion of our old regiment. The wrong direction, through a blunder of mine, will, I trust, serve to excuse what may have seemed to be a lack of courtesy in not replying to your letter.

I have also received your letter of the 16th inst., and have delayed in replying until now in the hope that I might see my way clear to respond favorably and accept the duty assigned to me.

I regret, however, to say, that a variety of circumstances compel me to foregoe the pleasure of meeting my old friends and comrades on the occasion referred to. I am sure you and they will not attribute this decision to a want of inclination, but will accept my assurance that nothing short of the most imperative considerations would prevent me from attending the reunion.

The recollections of my army service and the friendships then formed are cherished by me with the most lively pleasure; and I hope still at some time to renew those friendships with such as survived the perils and hardships of that period and have come safely through the vicissitudes of the years that have followed.

With my sincerest wishes that you may have a most pleasant and profitable reunion, and that arrangements may be made for similiar reunions in the future, I remain,

Very truly and sincerely yours.

E. M. VANDUZEE.

XENIA, Iowa, March 28, 1880.

LT. ABNER DUNHAM, MANCHESTER, IOWA:

Dear Comrade: Yours of the 18th ult. is received. It will be impossible for me to attend the reunion on the 6th and 7th of April. I hereby send greetings to my old comrades hoping that it may yet be my privilege to meet them once more ere death severs the ties and associations of this life.

The principles for which we gave four years of the best part of our lives are yet dear to my heart. I realize that we are fast passing away. Eighteen years more and the survivors of the 12th Iowa, who so bravely stood to their gunson the morning of the 6th of April, 1862, can be counted on one's fingers. But when we are gone, I trust that what we did on that eventful day, and what was done on every other day for the cause of the Union, will be held in grateful remembrance forever.

Your comrade,

JAS. L. THOMPSON.

NIOBRARA, Neb., April 4, 1880.

DEAR FRIEND ABNER AND THE TRIED OLD COMRADES OF COMPANY F:

The near approach of the reunion of the gallant old 12th, on the, to us, ever memorable 6th and 7th of April, which, after a lapse of eighteen years, brings up its scenes before us, prompts me to send my words of greeting, though I cannot be with you in person. As memory travels back to that quiet Sabbath morning, all the incidents seem to come up in regular order. The reveille, the roll call, the squad for the sick list, the tempting breakfast of baked beans and biscuit (which we didn't eat,) and the ominous long roll which sent us to the front to face a brave and determined foe, the roar and rattle of the musketry, and the screech of shot and shell all through that long day, the long fight against hope, which our dear old comrades made, the falling of the dead, whose lives sealed their devotion, the cries of the wounded, to whom relief could hardly be afforded, and the final closing of the scene of carnage, all go to make up a picture which we can never forget.

And now when so many years have marked their flight, and you gathered together to talk over the incidents of life in camp and on many a hard fought field, we instinctively call to mind those who cannot answer the roll call here. We will cherish their memories. I wish I could be with you. I want to see the old familiar faces and see how much they have changed since the time when we used to stand up in a row at roll call. Do you remember some of those frosty mornings, when the inexorable Orderly would get us out to say "here," and how some of us that slept too sound to gives us time to complete our toilets would rush out in undress uniform, and getting behind our file leader so the watchful eyes of said Orderly might not discover us, signify our presence and then dodge back to our tent to get a little more sleep which that everlasting drum had banished from our eyes.

When we think of all that eighteen years have brought to us of good or ill, of the change in thought or sentiment which those years have produced, the many questions that must necessarily arise for solution in a government like ours, the duty we owe it, and the duty it owes to every citizen, however humble, white or black, do we fully realize the grave issues that are looming up in the near future? Have we seen bad men coming into power, have we seen those principles which so many of your number gave their lives to establish gradually being undermined, and all that was accomplished then, now to be overthrown? If you do realize all this it does behoove us to now vote as we fought, and for all time to come to settle the question now and forever, that throughout all our broad domain no citizen of this land, however poor or humble he may be, no matter what his birthplace, color or religion, but shall have all the rights of an American, to live where he may wish to vote as he shall please, and to enjoy unmolested the fruits of his toil. Until that time comes you, dear comrades, have a work to do: and at this time when you meet together to renew the past, it seems to me not out of place to give this your thought, how to still bring our beloved country out of the bondage of sectional strife, corrupt influences, and all the evils of ignorant and wicked men. Let us all then labor for this end that we may have a country that shall be free in fact as it is in name.

And now wishing I might see you all face to face and grasp your hands, and hoping as the years go by to meet you and give you the assurance for your welfare which I feel, and that your present meeting will be full of pleasant memories in the future, I subscribe myself

One of your number, JOHN BREMNER.

BURLINGTON, Iowa, April 5, 1880.

MY DEAR COMRADES:

It is with regret that I write you. I would so much rather be present and grasp the friendly hand once more. Nothing would please me better than to be present; and I had made arrangements to that effect until to-day. Things have taken a change that prevents me, and will therefore have to content myself with anticipation, which is said to be more pleasant than participation. But be that as it may, I wish you a pleasant coming together, and that you will think of the absent ones. I know, however, they are held sacred in the memory of each.

I remain your comrade
ALBERT J. ROE.
Co. F, 12th Iowa Vet. Vol. Infantry.

ELWOOD, Iowa, April 4th, 1880.

MR. ABNER DUNHAM:

Dear Sir and Comrade of the Grand Old 12th Iowa Infantry:—Your call for a reunion of the members of the old 12th I have read. I was in hopes that I could be with you. But as I cannot be present in person, I expect to be in spirit and full harmony.

It is now eighteen years since that memorable conflict at Shiloh, where many of the 12th gave up their lives, and many more were wounded for life, while a prison hell waited for the lives of many more of the boys of the gallant Twelfth, and as I think, I ask the question, have they died in vain? and have the gallant members who lived through four years of terrible war, suffered in vain? God forbid.

And now, dear comrade, if Col. Woods is present, take him by the hand for me. Also my old captain, Major VanDuzee, and all in general, for business is such I cannot be with you. With love to all I will close. Yours, a lover of Union and Liberty.

GEORGE TESKEY,
Company I, 12th Iowa, V. I.

PEORIA, Ill., April 5, 1880.
LT. ABNER DUNAAM, Manchester, Iowa:

Dear Sir:—I regret to have to write to you that I cannot be with you to-morrow and the next day, at the reunion of the grand old 12th. I am suffering with rheumatism and cannot undertake the journey. Please remember me to all who may be present, and say that I regret very, very much that I cannot be with them.

Very sincerely your friend and comrade,
J. W. GIFT.

TELEGRAM.

DUBUQUE, April 7, 1880.
COL. S. G. KNEE:

I cannot express my disappointment at not being with the boys. Unexpectedly, important business prevented. Give my regards to the glorious old Twelfth at the banquet to-day; and for any regimental organization count me in. Hope the hardtack is better than at Donelson.

J. W. TAYLOR.

It was moved and carried to tender a vote of thanks to the old comrades who were unable to be present, for their kind letters of remembrance.

In consideration of his great age, and the fact of his being in Germany, so far away from all his companions in arms, a motion was carried that a committee of two be appointed to draft a letter to Major S. D. Brodtbeck, expressing the kind wishes of the regiment, which letter was signed by all the members present. D. W. Read and Geo. H. Morrisey were appointed as such committee.

MANCHESTER, Iowa, April 6.
Dear Major S. D. Brodtbeck, Stuttgart, Wurtemberg, Germany:—

We, the undersigned members of the Twelfth Iowa Veteran Volunteer Infantry, in reunion assembled, have just had read to us by Lieut. J. E. Simpson your kind letter, which was received with repeated cheers. We thank you for the expressions contained therein of undiminished love not only for the services of our dear old regiment, the Twelfth Iowa, but also for our glorious Union, for which we as citizens and soldiers offered our services. It does our hearts good to know that though far from us, still you give us and the cause for which we together fought so warm a place in your affection, and for which we each tender you our renewed pledge of friendship and love. We rejoice to see from your photograph, which has been passed from hand to hand, that time has dealt so kindly with you, and hoping that at some future reunion we shall have the pleasure of grasping your hand in friendly greeting. We remain, dear Major, your affectionate comrades in arms.

Signed by all the members present.

On motion, Drum Major McKee and Fife Major French were invited upon the stage to give some of their soul-stirring music, while Color Bearer Grannis held the colors of the regiment over them. At the close of this exercise, there was uproarous applause and cheering.

The Eldora Cornet Band then favored the audience with some very fine selections, and were followed by the Dubuque Battalion Drum Corps, whose spirited martial music awakened the greatest enthusiasm among the old veterans. The Dubuque Drum Corps consists of four fifes, five snares and a bass drum, and though we are no judge of this kind of music, we thought they were hard to beat.

No other business coming before the meeting, adjournment until evening was the next in order.

After adjournment, many of the old veterans remained in the hall, visiting and recalling old times, and "fighting their battles o'er again," It is needless to say that this afternoon visiting was most highly enjoyed by the old comrades in arms, who had become so widely scattered over the country, and who were now re-united for the first time since they were mustered out of service.

THE FOLLOWING IS THE ROLL OF MEMBERS PRESENT.

FIELD AND STAFF.

J. J. Woods, Montana, Kansas,
Myron Underwood, Eldora, Iowa.
W. H. Finley, Hopkinton, Iowa.
S. M. French, Denver, Colorado.
G. H. Morrisey, Delhi, Iowa.

COMPANY A.

S. R. Edgington, Eldora, Iowa.
C. M. Runkle, Eldora, Iowa.
Sumner Kemp, Alden, Iowa.
R. E. Kellogg, Alden, Iowa.
N. W. Zieger, Eldora, Iowa.
G. H. Cobb, Eldora, Iowa.
W. P. Haywood, Lyons, Iowa.
A. E. Webb, Eldora, Iowa.
Seth Macy, Marshalltown, Iowa.
Davie S. Martin, Iowa Falls, Iowa.
Tom Bell, Eldora, Iowa.
D. A. Armstrong, Liscomb, Iowa.
R. P. Clarkson, Des Moines, Iowa,
J. R. C. Hunter, Oskaloosa, Iowa.
Robert Morris, Oskaloosa, Iowa.

COMPANY B.

W. C. Earle, Waukon, Iowa.
R. Wamopler, French Creek, Iowa.
John D. Cole, Lansing, Iowa.
A. J. Rodgers, Waukon, Iowa.
H. R. Andrews, Brush Creek, Iowa.

COMPANY C.

D. B. Henderson, Dubuque, Iowa.
S. S. Blanchard, Postville, Iowa.
A. K. Ketchum, Clarion, Iowa.
H. J. Grannis, Fayette, Iowa.
Emery Clark, Elgin, Iowa.
S. Gifford, Douglass, Iowa.
Henry Clark, State Center, Iowa.
R. D. Williams, West Union, Iowa.
John Delezene, Douglass, Iowa.
F. W. Moine, Strawberry Point, Iowa.
W. L. Henderson LeRoy, Minn.
Geo. L. Durno, Springville, Io.
P. R. Ketchum, Windsor, Iowa.
D. W. Reed, Waukon, Iowa.
R. Z. Latimer, Fayette, Iowa.
G. E. Comstock Dubuque, Iowa.
G. H. Latimer, Maynard, Iowa.
N. H. Spears, Mill, Iowa.
William Hamlin, Oelwein, Iowa.
James Stewart, West Union, Iowa.
S. C. Beck, Maynard, Iowa.
H. C. Curtis, LeMars, Iowa.
Jas. Barr, Algona, Iowa.
Geo. Hazlet, Butler Centre, Iowa.

COMPANY D.

M. W. Whitenack, Waterloo, Iowa.
Hiel Hale Ft. Madison, Iowa.
E. B. Soper, Emmetsburg, Iowa.
Majr Rowan, Vinton, Iowa.
L. M. Ayers, Cedar Rapids, Iowa.

COMPANY E.

Harvey Smith, Waterloo, Iowa.
S. J. Crawhurst, Miller's Creek, Iowa.
C. V. Surfus, Bristow, Iowa,
D. Craighton, Geneva, Iowa.
J. S. Margretz, Hitesville, Iowa.
C. D. Morris, LaPorte City, Iowa.
A. B. Perry, Lester, Iowa.
John Elwell, Chicago, Ill.
Charles Cook, Lester, Iowa.
T. M. Early, Bristow, Iowa.
Thos. Demoss, Bristow, Iowa.

COMPANY F.

H. M. Preston, Fort Dodge, Iowa.
R. W. Tirrill Manchester, Iowa.
J. J. Eaton, Edgewood, Iowa.
Nelson Ralston, LeMars, Iowa.
Samuel Kaltenbach, Manchester, Iowa.
W. A. W. Nelson, Hazleton, Iowa,
Robert L. Weeden, Nugent's Grove, Iowa.
T. R. McKee, Manchester, Iowa.
Geo. Kent, Oelwein, Iowa.
Jas. F. Lee, Clay Mills, Iowa.
J. E. Eldridge Edgewood, Iowa.
Joshua, Widger, Waterloo, Iowa.
Josiah Hofhill, Wood Center, Iowa.
Ed. Corell, Greely, Iowa.
Thos. McGowan, Independence, Iowa.
H. W. Mackey, Maynard, Iowa.
Jos. S. Girton, Hazleton, Iowa.
W. H. Goodell, Manchester, Iowa.
Abner Dunham Manchester, Io.
Hiram Kaster, Manchester, Iowa.

COMPANY G.

J. E. Simpson Dubuque, Iowa.

COMPANY H.

Alex. S. McConnell, Hopkinton, Iowa. A. T. Garner, Farley, Iowa.
S. G. Knee, Colesburg, Iowa. Jas. Evans, Dubuque, Iowa.
H. J. Playter, Bristow, Iowa. D. Moreland, Earlville, Iowa.
Jos. Franks, Ward's Corners, Iowa.

COMPANY I.

M. D. Nagle, Dubuque, Iowa.

COMPANY K.

U. R. Mathis, Omaha, Nebraska, H. C. Merriam, Hopkinton, Iowa.
C. E. Merriam, Hopkinton, Iowa. Godfrey, Dolley, Hopkinton, Iowa.
P. J. Morehouse, Winthrop, Iowa.

NAMES OF WIVES PRESENT.

Mrs. G. H. Morrisey, Delhi, Iowa. Mrs. Sam'l Koltenbach, Manchester, Iowa.
" S. R. Edgington, Eldora, Iowa. " Hiram Kaster, Manchester, Iowa.
" R. P. larkson, Des Moines, Iowa. " W. H Goodell, Manchester, Iowa.
" G. L. Durno, Springville, Iowa. " J. E. Eldridge and Daughter, Edgewood, Iowa.
" Hiel Hale, Ft. Madison, Iowa.
" J. E. Simpson, Dubuque, Iowa. " T. R. McKee, Iowa Falls, Iowa.
" R. W. Tirrill, Manchester, I wa. " D. Moreland, Earlville, Iowa.
" S. J. Crawhurst, Manchester, Iowa. " Joseph Franks, Ward's Corners, Iowa.
" Abner Dunham, Manchester, Iowa. " C. E. Merriam, Hopkinton, Iowa.
" W. L. Henderson and Daughter, LeRoy, Minn. " G E. Comstock, Dubuque, Iowa.

SOLDIERS' WIDOWS.

Mrs. Wm. A. Morse, Manchester, Iowa.   Mrs. Abner Campbell, New York, N. Y.

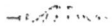

TUESDAY EVENING.

The hall was again packed at an early hour in the evening, fully one thousand persons being unable to gain admittance. After prayer by Rev. D. Russell, of the 11th N. Y. Infantry, followed by vocal and instrumental music, led by G. E. Comstock, of Co. C., Hon. C. Sanborn, the Mayor of the City, delivered the welcoming address.

MR. PRESIDENT AND GENTLEMEN OF THE TWELFTH IOWA REGIMENT:

It is my pleasant duty in behalf of the citizens of Manchester, to extend to you officially, a most hearty welcome to the hospitalities of this town, on this anniversary occasion of the bloody battle of Shiloh, in which you bore so conspicuous a part. And I welcome you, not only with all the meaning that a long time custom has attached to the ceremony of granting the "Freedom of the City" to returned conquerors, but with the added weight that should and does attach to that ancient rite, in consequence of your having been engaged in a more noble warfare than they—inasmuch, as the rescuing of your beloved land from the hands of ignoble traitors is more memorable than conquering a foreign foe.

Once again I welcome you, and trust that the memories of the duties which you have so well performed in the past, will ever be your support in the future battles of life. And I assure you that the memory of your achievements will ever be held sacred, not only by us but also by the free and liberty loving people of the entire nation.

To this Col Knee, the President, made the following happy response:

MR. MAYOR:

As President of the Reunion Association of the 12th Regiment of Iowa Volunteers, it becomes my duty to thank you, and through you, the citizens of Manchester for the kind and hospitable manner in which you have welcomed and entertained us, the surviving members of the Iowa Twelfth.

Sir, we have come together from nearly every quarter of this great nation; we have left our several vocations, in almost every sphere of life, the shop, the counter, the desk and the farm, at the instance of our comrade, your esteemed citizen, Lieut. Abner Dunham, who took the initiative step, and to whom belongs the credit for the success of this, our first reunion, and have met in your beautiful city for the purpose of reviewing in memory the vivid scenes of the march, the camp and the battle field—events that by us can never be forgotten.

Sir, we feel that it is well that we again have met, and lived over again the events of the past; but none of such events have afforded us a livelier pleasure than the fraternal manner in which you and your people have received us. You have made us feel that Manchester is true and warm hearted, and has received us with an affection akin to that with which she greeted her own boys returning from the field of strife.

And now, sir, when we separate and depart for our respective homes we will carry with us the consciousness that the happiest events of our lives took place at our reunion as the guests of the good people of Manchester. Again sir, we return you and your people our sincere thanks for your kindness and hospitality.

The President then introduced to the audience, Col. D. B. Henderson, of Dubuque, who then delivered one of the grandest, most eloquent and patriotic orations that has ever been delivered at any point since the war. His glowing tribute to the grand old Twelfth Iowa, of which he was an honored member, being a Lieutenant of Company C, until he lost a leg on Corinth's bloody field, was a grand peroration from beginning to end, and kept the audience in a continual roar of laughter and applause.

He spoke as follows:

HENDERSON'S ADDRESS.

MY DEAR COMRADES:

What words are fitting for this occasion? What can the lips say when the heart only can speak? This occasion calls up such a past, that the emotions rise like a swollen flood to drown the voice. The eye, the hand, the heart, have the only voice for this sacred hour. I would not speak to you thus formally were I permitted to consult my own heart. No! I woud rather take your hands in mine, and looking into your face, read there all that we have seen, have suffered, have lost, and have won. I would banish the voice and only feel.

There was an hour when we did not dare to feel; when we would not permit the voice to tremble. In the presence of the awful hour that first called us together; in the presence of events that over-topped human ties and human loves our lips had to be compressed to steel, our tears were turned to fire and our hearts to stone. But to-night, in the presence of the peace that we helped to secure, we may recall the sad events of the past; we may remember partings that never had a meeting; we may think of faces that cannot meet us here; and in doing all this even a tear may fall upon a soldier's cheek and leave no stain.

Is this a meeting of friends? No! It is more than a meeting of friends. Are we simply friends? We, who while smothering the tenderest emotions, sprang to arms at the same moment, rushed to encounter the same sufferings, the same dangers, and the same glories, and were inspired by the same grand motives? We, who fought under the same flag, slept in the same tent or in the same trenches, buried the same comrades and united in the same wild, rapturous, triumphant shout of victory? My God! are we only friends? We are brothers! If you have one brother you have up there and here nearly a thousand. What earthly ties can be dearer, truer, or stronger than those that bind us together? We were plighted in the face of death; we were united at the altar of liberty; our marriage bells were the voices of cannon, the groans of the dying and the last tattoo. This is the meeting of brothers, tried and true, after a parting of fifteen years.

In September, 1861, when it became apparent that the war would yield to no ninety-days attack, when it became evident that the South really intended to destroy this government—fair as it was—the men of the Twelfth Iowa hastened to Dubuque to muster into the defence of their country for the longest period that Abraham Lincoln - God bless him—asked; namely three years. Then and there, 981 officers and men pledged themselves to their country. These 981 men were not soldiers! The name soldier applies to the paid vassals of a king. But these men were not soldiers; they were citizens of the Republic, who had but one thought, that their country was in danger, and if it fell they must be buried beneath its ruins. In 1861, they came from their farms, their forges, their schools and their workshops, all with one common thought, that our country was in danger, and we had a duty to perform.

I repeat, they were not soldiers. They were patriots—patriots in all the deep, broad, thrilling meaning of that word. They did not go to fight—to kill, they went to defend, to save.

I will show you what kind of men the Twelfth was made of by telling you a story of one of its number, a private soldier.

On the 30th of May last, in the presence of eleven men of the 12th Iowa, I told this story of one of the members of the regiment, and I give it as a true one—and God knows how true it was. On the train coming here this morning, I met another who was knowing to the facts which I am about to relate. The lad I refer to was not American born. He was a simple country lad.

In September, 1861, as I was out recruiting for my company, I stopped at a farm house, and while eating dinner I was talking about the war, when this young man dropped his knife and fork, and said in broken English, "I go too." We shook hands, and were comrades from that hour. That man never failed to report for duty. Never missed a roll-call. Comrades, you all remember the march to Ft Henry, how we got wet through and had to sleep on our feet. Charley Larson, for that was this lad's name, was unfitted for duty by that march. His hands were shaking and he was as white as a sheet; and when we started for Ft. Donelson, Dr. Finley said Charley was not fit to go with us, and must stay behind. But Charley said he must go, and coming to me begged that I let him go, but I told him no, that he was not able. But when we got within sight of Ft. Donelson, who should we see coming up in the rear of his company but Charley Larson. Seeing he was bound to go, the boys took his luggage and he marched on, sick as he was, up to the breastworks of Donelson. He was not able to stand up, the Surgeon truthfully said, and yet he marched after that flag until it was carried through the abatis and planted on the inner works of Donelson. He was so weak that he trembled like a leaf shaken by the wind, and yet he fought by your sides, and sent unerring bullets to rebel hearts at Donelson.

After the carnage of Shiloh we missed Charley. We supposed that he too was a prisoner. But not so. Four days after the battle we heard of a wounded man, with a figure twelve on his cap, being in the camp of the 3d Iowa. It was Charley. The poor fellow had been struck at the terrible moment when the 12th found itself surrounded on every side by rebels and death. We carried him to his tent in our regiment, where Dr. Finley and myself worked over him for several hours trying to find the place where the bullet lodged. We at last found it in his spinal column. I watched over him, in his tent, for several nights, praying that his life might be spared us; but when he spoke, his only words were, "It's all right, it's all right." I rubbed his cold hands and begged him to tell me if he suffered. He would look steadily into my eyes and slowly repeat his only answer, "It's—all—right." Just that and nothing more. He saw I was mourning over his death; he wanted me to know and testify that he was satisfied "it was all right." Dr. Finley often came with me, and tried to save him, but it was of no avail. There came a moment when the eyes did not see me; they were looking up and away beyond all comrades here. The lips moved but uttered no sound for me, but angels heard the words, "it's all right, it's—all—right."

And such were the men who composed the rank and file of the 12th Iowa. I can't say all I would wish to of the 981 men who went in the 12th Iowa.

I want to say a few words about our original field officers. Our Colonel, who sits here among us to-night, came from his far-off home on the borders of the Indian Territory, for the especial purpose of visiting with his old comrades. Col. Woods, the brave and trained soldier, was a graduate of West Point, a man, calm, kind and true, his bosom undisturbed by an unworthy ambition; the humblest, simplest soldier never feared to address him, and always met a kind look and gentle answer, and that, too, even if the soldier forgot the formal salute. When other regimental commanders could only see stars, our Colonel's heart was full of love for his men, and he saw only stars on the flag of our glorious Union, and which he felt must be kept there. Comrade of his men, as well as commander. Such a man was Col. J. J. Woods.

Our Lt. Colonel is not able to meet with us to-night. Within the past 12 months, he has been mustered out, but if he were on earth, nothing would have kept him from this reunion. He could not handle a regiment and was in no sense a fighter, but in every sense a patriot, and lacking in no qualities that made a true man. Where Lt. Colonel Coulter is buried lies a loved comrade, a model citizen and a noble man.

Our Major—God bless the little Dutch Major—from top to toe a soldier; from heart to hand a soldier; a natural drill master. How well we all remember his "Voll in levt ving." I never had much regard for military tactics, and used to watch the Major and learn from him, instead of the books. The Major noticed this, and said to me one day: "Lieutenant, have you ever yet learned how to get the countersign from the pickets and take their gun away from them?" and I replied, "No." He said, "Come with me on the picket line to-night, and I will show you how to do it." I shall never forget that time. I have a scar on my right leg to-day, which will bear witness to the point where the Major ends and army regulations begin. [Laughter.]

Yes, we were a well-officered regiment. Our chaplain had some good streaks. Even Hart Spears would sometimes take off his hat to Chaplain Eberhart. Hart liked him because he laughed so when a conceited Lieutenant got enchered on a lone hand. And the boys would say that our Chaplain would bet higher and "stay" longer with a "bob-tail flush," than any chaplain in the Western Army. [Laughter.]

I regret to see, from your general laughter, that so many of you know the meaning of those apt army words.

I would like to say a few words about our Company officers, but there is too long a list to name them all, and none should be omitted. We had thirty line officers as free of offence as any sent from any other State. Duty, not promotion, was their ambition. They were free from petty bickerings and unseemly jealousies. As a regiment, your only quarrels were with the enemy in front of you and under arms.

Comrades, what was it that called us together in 1861? Was it gain? Was it the $13 per month? No. You had many a line officer who, when elected by his company, did not know the difference in rank or pay between a sergeant and line officer. What was it. then, that called us together? To save the republic. To save a land that was at once the cradle and throne of liberty. That you might be, in the hand of God, the thunderbolt to destroy that dark creation of hell, human slavery. That the shameful stain might be forever removed from the bright flag of freedom. That the mother—black or white—might hold her infant on her bosom without dread of separation. To make the Declaration of Independence a casket of jewels, instead of an aggregation of infamous lies. You sprang to arms to secure a strong and free government? To ensure free schools and plenty of them. To ensure equality to all and bondage for none. You found that Washington and the fathers had but half done their work, when they shook from our limbs the shackles of Britain and left untouched those that bound the slave. You found that the cursed system they left to you was destroying your country. It was everywhere with its slime, its cruelty, its corruption and its unending demands and relentless tryranny. It had gagged and throttled the great high tribunal of justice, the Supreme Court of the United States. It had planted treason in every room, bureau and department of the Executive office, while Congress, the great law-making power, was a boiling seething sea of rebellion. You saw it was high time for blood and death, and so you went.

Comrades, how I would like to retrace the path we trod. I remember how well we left Dunleith The night was cold and bitter. The Mississippi ran cold with floating ice. We were piled deep into the bare cars, and while tears were flowing on the other side, we sang the Star Spangled Banner, and sent its glorious sounds floating to the hills of Iowa. I can hear it yet. Brave and strong were your hearts That was the start you made.

From there we went to St. Louis. Who of us has forgotten it? Here we were first baptized with death. Here our brave boys fell like grain before the sickle. Almost one in every ten o" our number never got farther than St. Louis, and never returned to Iowa. In a few short weeks. 76 of our number were dead. Measles, pneumonia, smallpox—relentless allies of the South—cut through our lines. and filled a graveyard with the fallen of the 12th Iowa. We went there a young, we left there an old regiment. Then came the marching orders, and we went—many of us the rounds of the hospitals, to take our last farewell of our sick comrades. Many of you remember this. And you remember, too, the Sisters of Mercy. How they watched over and nursed our brave boys. How they fulfilled their last requests. How they promised to send to their far-off homes, the last letters, the photographs. the little keep-sakes that should soften the grief of those who mourned their death, and how faithfully those promises were kept. Amid sobs, and groans, and cries, these sisters walked their rounds watching over the suffering as though they had been their brothers indeed. I wish I had the tongue of an angel and long ages in which to speak all their praise. They were our sisters, and well we remember how gentle, kind and true they were.

At last we left St. Louis, and thence passed amid scenes that were dramas—nay, tragedies rather—of death, of danger, and of victory. To long marches, to trenches, hard tack and field hospitals. How rapidly act followed act, scene succeeded scene. To-day in the mud of Smithland, to-morrow our camp fires lighted up the beauties of Tennessee, and tens of thousands of white tents, spreading far and wide, present a picture that gives promise of peace and rest, and makes no hint of danger or of death. The next day 15,000 rebels laid down their arms, at the imperative command of "unconditional surrender." Men of the 12th Iowa you were there!

[Here the Col. told some very amusing stories, portraying the raids of the boys on the hogs, poultry, etc., which were highly relished by the boys present, they being cognizant of the facts. He continued:]

At the storming of Ft. Donelson, the 12th lost its first man in battle, Buckner, of Company A,—shot in the eye by a rebel sharp-shooter. This was before we charged. Do you remember how we gathered about the strong but quivering Buckner as he lay there our first bloody offering to freedom? No sounds escaped your lips, but oh! there were oaths registered then and there, in manly hearts, oaths that only found utterance from the musket's mouth, and amid the roar and carnage of battle. You remember the sharp-shooters of the enemy, the grape and canister that mowed our ranks, the brave men falling by the wayside. But this old flag was planted on the breastworks by the brave Grannis, and though men fell on every hand, the 12th would not yield an inch and that flag would not go down.

Yes, you were a fighting regiment. You proved it at Ft. Henry, at Donelson, at Shiloh, and at Corinth, at Jackson. Vicksburg, Brandon, Tupelo, White River, Nashville, Brentwood Hills, Spanish Fort, and twelve minor battles. You were in 28 engagements, 112 days under fire, marched 2,670 miles, always advancing, and traveled in all 13,809 miles. You lost 95 men killed in battle, had 204 officers and men wounded, and 217 died of disease. Of the 981 men who went to the field, 801 sustained some injury by battle or disease. You had 382 men captured at Shiloh, who went to rot and die in the prison hells of the South. Yet, in the face of these disasters, when your term of service had nearly expired, when your wives and children, your parents, brothers, sisters and friends were longing for your return, at the appeal of Abraham Lincoln, who said, "Boys don't leave me yet," you re-enlisted, on the 5th of January, 1864, to see your country through the storm.

Fellow citizens of Delaware county, You who are here, let me ask, do you owe these men anything? Do you know what and who these men are? They went through fire and smoke, through death and hell for you. They stood,—after three years of privation and danger and suffering—at the very doors of home, with loving wives, their old parents, and dimpled faced babes, holding out their arms and crying for joy at their near return. Yet, even then, at your call and that of their country, they turned their backs on all the delights of home, and plunged once more into danger and death:—for you. Do you know these men? Their hands are rough and hard, perhaps, but oh, how steady and true they were, when treason raised the standard of rebellion and you and your liberties were in danger. Do you know that those men were a part of that immortal Brigade at Shiloh, which with the brave 8th Iowa, held back the very centre of the rebel attack? Do you know that they mowed down regiment after regiment, and drove back column after column, not for four hours as the reports have it, but for eight deadly hours, thus giving our army night, night giving us Buell, and Buell giving us victory? They were taken prisoners, but the army was saved and victory won! Captured they were but holding their posts! Captured they were, but with their flag flying, their guns in their hands and their bullets in rebel h arts! Then followed the rebel prisons: Selma,

Taladega, Atlanta, Libby and Macon. For six months these men, honorable prisoners of war, were kept rotting and dying in rebel prisons. The guests of Southern chivalry, but rotting and dying, rotting and dying!

Ah! friends, I see before me heads of snow, that would be like the raven's wing but for sufferings that we can never know. Fellow citizens you see before you all that is left of an Iowa regiment that served for four and one-half years and never lost a single battle. It was in twenty-three engagements and was never beaten. It was under deadly fire one hundred and twelve days and its flag ever advancing. That flag is like our country torn, but HERE, like its regiment, there are but fragments left of it. But what man, what section, what king or country dare insult a shred of that torn and tattered flag! There it hangs comrades, still our flag. It is silent and torn but what glorious memories it awakens! Look at it comrades, it tells us all the past; look at it treason, it warns you for all the future!

My comrades, I could scarcely begin talking to you, and it seems as though I can not stop. I can not do you and your brave deeds justice. But let me ask you to do one thing. Do not forget your dead comrades. Their bodies lie here and there, on hill-top and in valley, but let them not be forgotten. When you would make of your boys men on whom the Republic may safely rest, tell them of your comrades dead—AND WHY THEY DIED.

When you take a ballot in your hand, and politicians ask you to manifest a spirit of compromise and conciliation, think of your dead comrades—AND WHY THEY DIED.

When an attack is made on human rights, and the exercise of that freedom which belongs to an American citizen, white or black; think of your dead comrades—AND WHY THEY DIED.

They are still with us. The thought of them remains to keep us steadfast to our country, and maintain it pure and free. One of them I will name, who was with us in every battle, on every march, by every camp fire, who sat by every sick bed, who lay in every prison and suffered from every wound, the grandest man and truest comrade of us all—ABRAHAM LINCOLN. Be his memory embalmed in our hearts forever.

And now comrades, good bye, We may not all be here at the next Reunion. A few more gatherings, and the last member of the 12th Iowa Regiment will be mustered out. But, until then, boys, Forward guide centre, March! And when the last muffled drum is sounding may some loved voice repeat over our ashes:

"On fame's eternal camping ground
Their silent tents are spread."

The proceedings of the first day were then closed with music by the Band.

WEDNESDAY MORNING.

This morning a committee of five was appointed to prepare and present a plan of permanent regimental organization ; also a regimental historian. Several letters from absent members were read, all bearing the deep regret of the writers for their inability to be present. Among them were letters from Maj. Brodtbeck, now of Stuttgart, Germany, Gov. Gear, Col. J. H. Stibbs, now of Tenn., Adj. Burch of Kansas, Maj. E. M. Van Duzee of St. Paul, J. L. Thompson of Hardin county, and J. D. Baker of Minn.

A permanent organization of the Regimental Society was effected. 110 members being present. Col. Samuel G. Knee was elected President; Capt. E. B. Soper, Vice President ; Abner Dunham, Secretary and Treasurer. It was decided to hold Reunions every four years.

D. W. Reed was appointed Historian of the Regiment, to be assisted by R. P. Clarkson and Lieutenant Cole.

R. P. Clarkson, Colonel W. C. Earl, Lyman M. Ayers, H. C. Curtiss and Colonel S. R. Edgington were selected as the Executive Committee.

Comrades Simpson and Comstock made motions for the publication of the proceedings of this Reunion, with a view to sending a copy to all members of the Regiment not present at the Reunion. These motions were amended by Colonel D. B. Henderson with a motion nominating G. E. Comstock, of Dubuque, a committee to superintend the publication of the proceedings, with instructions to mail copies to all members desiring them.

After numerous speeches by members, it was finally decided that Reunions be held every four years.

At this point the treasurer of the city of Manchester, presented in the name of the City Council, the sum of $50 towards defraying the expenses of the Reunion.

Here the old drum and fife Majors of the regiment appeared on the stand and played the same old tunes under which the regiment marched in the days of its full glory and pride, and the boys were again wild with enthusiasm.

WEDNESDAY AFTERNOON.

The tables for the Dinner were placed in the room formerly occupied by the Reform Club, over the store of L. A. Loomis. The ladies of Manchester—who never do anything by halves—had there spread a banquet that might tempt the appetite of an anchorite. The tables were decorated with evergreens and flowers, and the universal verdict was that Manchester had fairly surpassed herself in the preparation of so magnificent an entertainment. It is needless to say that, after grace by the venerable Rev. Alvah Day, the members of the glorious 12th did ample justice to the repast.

On returning to the assembly hall the beautiful poem written by J. W. Shannon, Esq., of Elkader, was read by Col. S. R. Edgington, of Eldora, who recited it with appropriate spirit and feeling. It was listened to with profound attention and challenged "cheers" and "tears" from the delighted audience. Here it is:

CHEERS FOR THE LIVING, TEARS FOR THE DEAD.

To the Twelfth Iowa Boys, at Manchester.
BY J. W. SHANNON.

Loud cheers for boys who wore the blue !
　While all our hearty welcomes brightly burn;
Loud Cheers, for girls, so sweet and true,
　That thro' sad years awaited their return.

God bless the hero's hearth and home !
　Where happy children coo on crippled knees,
And fond embrace must ever come
　Thro' rugged vet'ran's awkward empty sleeve !

God bless the CAUSE for which ye bled,
　Whilst dearest, bravest comrades nobly died,
And keep its standards far ahead
　Thro' all the teeming future's battle-tides.

The cause of slave—the cause of Man!—
　True cause of God, that breaks each shackling chain,
Whereby a king, or priest, or clan
　May manacle a hand or heart or brain.

> O, hush the voice that dares proclaim
> Ye merely "Greek 'gainst Greek" in gory feast!—
> That Donelson's and Shiloh's flame
> But shone on battle of the angry beast!
>
> Eternal honor to your names,
> In record, wreath, and cheers, and lofty song!
> Not that ye slayed for soldier fame—
> Ye stood for endless Right 'gainst monstrous wrong.
>
> Ye stood on field whose mighty sweep
> Was never matched 'neath light of rolling sun;
> God help ALL nations' hearts to keep,
> And prize, and guard the victory won.
>
> And bless our greetings once again,
> To all for whom this grateful feast is spread,
> Midst thund'ring cheers for living men
> And holy tears for all the glorious dead.

Now began the Toasts; and a rare season it was. The first Toast was:

"THE STATE AND THE NATION—Mutually Dependent and Independent."
Responded to by H. C. Curtis, of Lemars.

This was entirely impromptu, as it had been assigned to Major Van Duzee, who could not attend. He said:

It always affords me pleasure to meet my old comrades. It was a question, eighteen years ago, if we had a nation—whether we had a country. That question we debated on the battle field. Eighteen years ago we were marching as prisoners through the streets of Corinth. But the question has been settled. It is no longer a question in dispute. We are a nation, thank God. But let us not forget the cost of this nation, the price we paid for the liberty we enjoy. As we look at our banner, its tattered and torn shreds, how memory goes back over the past. What we suffered, what we endured in defending that old flag, let us never regret.

"THE ARMY AND NAVY—The Safeguards of all Nations. Response by Hon. R. W. Tirrill, Manchester.

Ever since the creation of the world, the weaker have been forced to bow in humble submission to the mandates of the stronger; the uncivilized to the civilized; the minority to the majority. This seems to be a fundamental law of our very nature:—and acting upon that grand and noble principle, "The greatest good to the greatest number," we are necessarily forced to admit the correctness of this natural law when applied to national affairs.

For the protection of our natural and individual rights, governments and nations have been formed, and the great underlying principle of all nations and governments is Law, and the absolute enforcement of that law is the only safeguard guaranteed to the people who have entered into the solemn compact of National Unity. For this safeguard, Armies and Navies have been organized, and from the early days of the Trojan war, down through the succeeding ages, the Army and the Navy have been the great power behind the throne to compel obedience to that law, without which nations fall and fade away, and with them go those individual rights, so sacredly guarded by the constitutional law of all civilized nations. Deprive us of these natural, inherent, inalienable, God given rights, which by a sense of our own intuitions wells up in the secret bosoms of brave men and true women, and to be a citizen is but to be a prisoner—bound and fettered by the iron grasp of another's will! The nobility of our birth, which makes us proud of our American citizenship, induces a spirit of patriotism which causes us, as it did our fathers, to pledge our lives, our fortunes and our sacred honor, in defense of those liberties dearer to us than life itself.

This noble spirit we inherit from our Spartan ancestry, and while it is, in every sense, commendable to the foreign or American soldier and citizen, it should not be cultivated beyond its proper sphere of usefulness—into haughtiness and pride, as exemplified in the ambition of Xerxes, Alexander, Napoleon, Cortes and others, whose individual approbation has been sought at the expense of the public good.

The Army and the Navy, the Safeguards of all Nations! Foreigners throughout all the world, and Americans alike, proclaim it, and it would be idle in me, in the space of ten minutes, to attempt to narrate from the historic page, in the old and new world, thousands of instances where the mere presence of a well disciplined Army and Navy have had even the moral force—the physical being known—to dispel the dark cloud of tyranny and despotism which has hung over an oppressed people, and enabled them to see through the misty haze into the beautiful sunlight of freedom and liberty.

That old flag, torn in fragments by rebel bullets, thrown to the breeze by those who saw it safely through in triumph from Donelson to Nashville, and carefully deposited as a memento among the archives of our noble State, would quell a second or third insurrection in South Carolina. Yet the Army and Navy are recognized as our Safeguard. But in our exalted pride for our Army and Navy, we should not forget that they are to be maintained and held only in reserve, subject to that higher power of civilization, "National Arbitration," from the lessons of which we have almost learned (although not quite) that our swords may be turned into plowshares and our spears into pruning hooks.

"THE CHILDREN OF THE TWELFTH IOWA—God Bless them! and may they live long to enjoy the Freedom that their Fathers, Living and Dead, fought to secure."

Florence L. Dunham, who was to respond to this toast, was a little Miss of scarcely six years old. She faced the immense audience bravely at first, but the sea of faces shook her courage, she hesitated, and finally burst into tears. But the audience cheered her to the echo, and not a heart but beat with sympathy for her. The verses she was to have spoken, were written for the occasion by her mother, Mrs. Abner Dunham, and are given herewith:

  I love the brave old soldier,
   With coat and pants so blue,
  With buttons bright and jaunty cap.
   And heart so bold and true;
  Who'd give his life for freedom,
   And think not of renown;
  High, high in air he'd bear our flag
   Traitors would trample down.

  Beneath this old and tattered flag,
   Its colors once so gay,
  Now torn, and dim, and stained
   With blood of many a fray.
  Beneath its glorious stripes and stars
   My papa fought with you;
  O'er him it waived in danger's hour,
   And comrades tried and true.

And when he takes me on his knee,
  I love the best to hear
The stories of his army life,
  Though oft it brings a tear;
He tells me of the dull days spent
  In sickness and in pain;
Of weary marches, long and sad,
  Through sunshine and through rain;

With aching limbs and weary heart;
  With clothes all mud and sleet;
With scarce a crumb of food or drink;
  And oh! such tired feet
Were in that long and fainting march!
  Brave comrades faltered by the way;
Each shared with each the burden,
  For many a dreary day.

And of the blood stained battle field,
  Where guns and cannons roar;
The grass, that once was bright and green,
  All red with human gore.
Where oft he's seen his comrades fall,
  And could not stop to save
Till they drove the banded traitors back;
  Then scooped a shallow grave,

And placed them there with tender hands,
  As brother would for brother,
Smoothing away the tangled locks,
  And clipping one for mother.
Sorrowing mother your lot is blessed,
  Though your treasures left are few,
Since you give for your country's good the best,
  God ever gave to you.

Then oft he'll tell of days
  That passed so slowly by,
In rebel prisons' dingy walls
  Where they were left to die.
Columbia's bravest sons, our boys so true,
  To die for want of food
And kindly care; shame, shame, traitors,
  To waist such precious blood!

I do not wonder papa loves
  His brother soldiers so;
And wishes oft his girl could be
  A soldier, brave as you;
But if she can't a soldier be,
  Or lead a soldier's life,
Perhaps, when she is older grown,
  She'll be a soldier's wife.

Soldiers, then we give you welcome;
  A royal welcome, too;
Right eagerly we'll grasp the hand
  Of those who wore the blue,
In days of darkness, dire and dread,
  To you so staunch and true,
Our all we owe, our banner bright, our country's fame;
  God bless the "Boys in Blue."

"HARDTACK AND COFFEE The Reserves from which we daily drew Nerve and Inspiration." Response by Capt. E. B. Soper, Emmetsburg.

Capt. Soper, of Emmettsburg, rose to the fourth toast. He said he was not quite so full of his subject as he had been on former occasions. Why the committee chose him to respond to this toast was a mystery to him, unless it was because he had a faculty of stowing away large quantities of those commodities. Why hardtack was so much abused he could not say, nor where it got its name. Where the "hard" came from he could understand, but where they got the "tack" was beyond his investigation. But, after all, hardtack was the soldier's friend. We were glad to have it with us, and when we had it not, we wished we had. No better or more healthy food could the soldier have than the much abused hardtack. Coming to coffee, the Captain said he would take the liberty to read a short description of coffee and its effects on the human system. The soldier needed just such a thing to sustain him. There was never an army so well fed as ours during the rebellion, and hardtack and coffee were the substantials.

Miss Verda Kelsey then sang "Is the Battle Over," Mrs. A. J. Brown playing organ accompaniment, and she sang it in a manner to call forth tumultuous applause.

On motion of Col. D. B. Henderson, Miss Kelsey was made an honorory member of the Twelfth Iowa, amid a storm of cheers, the boys shouting till it seemed the roof of the hall would be lifted off.

"THE GIRLS WE LEFT BEHIND US—The only Power that has made Prisoners of us all." Response by Harvey Smith, Waterloo.

Mr. President, Ladies and Gentlemen, Comrades of the 12th Iowa:

I feel particularly honored to-day for having been selected to respond to this toast of: The Girls We left Behind Us. I always liked the girls we left behind us, and I plead guilty to the charge of being partial to them. The State of Iowa furnished her full quota of brave soldiers and sent them to the field, but she at the same time like a good general, held in reserve a force equal to any emergency, in the loyal true hearted Girls we left behind us.

Oh, how we used to think of them, who though absent, were still to memory dear, and wish we could be with them. We used to dwell upon their kindness, and when we used to receive letters from the Dear Girls we left behind us, how we used to read them over again, and ponder over the words of cheer therein contained. Words of cheer and kindness which served to encourage us in the camp, on the march, on the battlefield, in the siege, and in the prison pens of the South. Words of hope which nerved us on to greater exertion and nobler achievements. Oh! how we used to watch for those letters. And Dear Girls we left behind us, did you think, did you know what a noble thing you were doing when you used to write those cheering letters, bright and radiant with kind words of hope and cheer? I remember oh, so well when after we had been on a long campaign and returning to where the mails could reach us, how eagerly we received the contents, and some of the Boys used to receive a great many letters addressed in a feminine hand, and when asked who their letters were from, they invariably replied, oh from my sisters and I tell you some of the boys had a great many sisters, judging from the number of letters they used to receive. Many of us carried next our hearts photographs of the Girls we left behind us. And we used to often take them out and fondly gaze on them through the mist of gathering tears. And then when at times we grew more confident, the boys would show each other the pictures they had of "the Girls we left behind us," and as we would look them over, we would ask, why who is this, John?—oh, that is my sister Mary, and then we would ask who is this, John? And he would reply, that is my sister Jane. And so it was clear through the whole list. And I tell you some of those boys had the biggest lot of grand good looking sisters I ever heard of or saw in my life. I used to think they were particularly fortunate in having so many splendid looking sisters. Oh, Dear Girls we left behind us, your thoughts were often with us, breathing prayers for our safety and success. And when the armed host moved forward to the grand assault, the loyal heart beats of the brave and true hearted Girls we left behind us kept time to our onward march. And then when the war was ended and the last armed foe surrendered and we returned home, all flushed and crowned with the laurel wreath of victory, how the Girls we left behind us met us at the gate, and proceeded to make "Prisoners of us all."

We laid our trophies at their feet and gladly surrendered unconditionally, though how they accomplished this wonderful result I never could fully determine. Perhaps I can no better describe it than in the words of the old song—

"Lovely woman is the sugar,
Spoons us poor men seemed to be,
Matrimony is hot water,
Love is like a cup of tea."

and when the whole unwritten history of this war shall be made up, and every heart throb of woe and endurance be written down—high up on the roll of fame ought to be inscribed in letters of imperishable gold, the names of the Girls we left behind us.

Mr. President, I can not close this response without an allusion to those of the Girls we left behind us, who have ere this passed from earth. Let us cherish their memory, follow their example, tread the radiant pathway of their virtues as in ascending brightness it leads us safely over the valley of shadows, to that land beyond the river.

"THE WIVES, MOTHERS, DAUGHTERS AND SWEETHEARTS OF THE TWELFTH IOWA None suffered more, none complained less. Our Flag their Flag. Their Homes Our Hearts." Response by Lieut. J. E. Simpson, Dubuque, Iowa.

Mr. President and Comrades:—This toast would have found a warm response in the hearts of the Twelfth Iowa in the days of 1861. And finds a no less hearty one to-day, among us the survivors of our noble regiment. There were but few, if any at all, who went away with us, who did not leave behind some loved one, mother, wife, daughter, sister or sweetheart, to endure and suffer the pangs and heart-aches of separation. Ours was to go, to do, to dare. We had the excitement of camp life, the frequent change of scene, and all the glitter, glory and pomp of war, to distract our attention and occupy our thoughts. But theirs was to remain at home, with their accustomed round of quiet home duties to perform, to suffer and wait.

Poets may sing, Historians may write, and the story can never be half told, of the agonizing suspense of the mothers, wives and sweethearts, of the Twelfth, eighteen years ago—as the wires brought the news of a great battle being fought on the banks of the Tennessee, of our defeat; then our victory, then came the news of the capture of our regiment. What words of mine, comrades, can convey even in a slight degree the agony and suspense of these loved ones at home? That dear old gray headed mother, who had given up her son, and in many cases her sons, that the Union might be saved; the wife who had seen her husband; the sister her brother; the sweetheart her "soldier boy"; go away to war.—(And here Mr. President, let me remark, that we in a measure forget what terrors that word war, brought with it in 1861-2, to a people unaccustomed to fighting and blood-shed.) All of this was with tears and heart-pangs. But when the news came from Shiloh, it seemed to them, and it was to many, the death knell to all their hopes. No truer words could be said than those of our toast: "None suffered more and none complained less," is equally true.

History tells us all along its pages, of woman's love and devotion; not only to her own but to her country. She has in all ages borne her full share of the hardships and burthens of war. And the women of our own dear country failed not, in its hour of peril,—faithful, fearless, devoted. They were found in the hospital, cheering all, caring for the sick and wounded. At their homes unceasing in their efforts, in collecting supplies to go forward to the front. All over our broad prairies could be witnessed scenes of patriotism and sacrifice, before which the stories of the mothers and matrons of ancient Greece and Rome pale. There are hearts turning toward us to-day—prayers of mothers and sisters, all over Northern Iowa. Comrades tell how they came to wish them a pleasant time at our Reunion, and express their continued love for the "Old Twelfth."

The mother and sister of John Stillman who fell shot through the brain at Donelson are with us in their thoughts and prayers to-day. Poor John—a noble, gallant soldier. Well I remember with comrade Rogers we carried him to the rear in hopes we might catch one last word. But within the hour, just as the last ray of the sun touched the tops of the noble oaks that formed that Southern forest, John's soul went home to the God who gave it, as pure as the snow on which he lay.

That noble Scandinavian mother, Mrs. Steen, of Winneshiek county, who, having seven sons—all good men and true,—sent six to the defense of the Union; three of whom—John, Henry and Theodore, went with us in the Twelfth. Her thoughts are with us to-day.

With what love and affection every member of the Twelfth is held by a mother like Mrs. Nelson Burdick of Decorah, who having five sons, all of them splendid specimens of "Iowa Boys" sent them all to do battle for the Union, and only two returned—Corporal Nelson Burdick, her youngest son, who died from disease and hardships incurred with you in rebel prisons, and Lieutenant A. A. Burdick, who was killed at the battle of Tupelo by a solid shot from the rebel batteries, both honored members of the Twelfth Iowa.

Such women are cemented to the Twelfth with ties that time only strengthens. And when and wherever we may meet we shall always have a place in their hearts second to none. We meet to join hands in friendly grasp. We tell of these scenes of suffering with no vain boast. We have no desire to rake up the past, nor dwell upon its struggles. With charity towards all, enjoying as we are the blessings of peace so hardly won, at such a cost of suffering both mental and physical, to the men and women of that time.

But the lesson taught cost too much, and we can not afford to have it lost. So we tell the story, that our children may learn what the Union is to us—that they may cherish it dearly, love it as warmly, and be as ready to sacrifice and suffer for it, against foes within, and without, as the men and women of 1861 did. And as we the story tell, and the lesson teach, do not let us fail to make clear to them and draw the lines distinct between loyalty and disloyalty, patriotism and treason.

Mr. President and Comrades, I know of no more fitting way to close the response to this toast, than by asking you to join me, in three hearty cheers for "The Wives, Mothers, Daughters and Sweethearts of the Twelfth Iowa—None suffered more, none complained less. Our flag their flag—Their homes our hearts."

Mrs. W. N. Boynton, then favored the audience with "The Battle Prayer," in her usual finished and effective manner, and was heartily encored, when she gave "The Star Spangled Banner," with great effect, and to the great delight of the boys.

"HISTORY OF THE TWELFTH IOWA VETERAN VOLUNTEER INFANTRY." Read at the First Reunion of the Regiment, at Manchester, Iowa, April 6th, 1880, by Capt. Wm. L. Henderson, Co. C, Leroy, Minn

Dear comrades of the Twelfth we meet again,
We call the roll and former ties renew;
We pitch our camp in quietude and peace,
At Manchester the pleasant rendesvous.

We hear again the morning reveille,
Our glorious banner once again is seen;
We eat together at the self same mess,
And drink once more from out the same canteen.

We greet each other with a friendly grasp,
We see fond welcome in each beaming eye;
Each face suggests some memory of the past,
The camp, the march, the thrilling battle cry.

We fight our battles over once again,
Resumed the march pursued with blistered feet;
Again in thought you mount the picket guard,
A silent sentinel on your lonely beat.

The Iowa Twelfth was raised with speed and care,
Throughout the Northeast counties of the State;
Hardin, Linn, Blackhawk and Delaware,
Winneshiek, Allamakee, Jackson and Fayette.

Hardin county heads the list with "A."
As stalwart boys as ever wore the blue;
Always on hand for battle, work, or play,
When mustered in they numbered ninety-two.

Then ninety men came marching from the north,
From Democratic steady Allamakee:
All hardy sons of toil and noble worth,
Those were the boys of gallant Company "B"

"C" Company left their homes in old Fayette,
To follow the destiny of their country's star;
Leaving their books, their college, and their State,
One hundred students in the art of war.

Company "D," the youthful sons of Linn,
Proud to uphold the banner of their State;
And all resolved the Union's cause must win,
A splendid Company, numbering ninety-eight.

Blackhawk county gave us Company "E,"
Who hated slavery and the rebel rag:
Ninety-four as steady honest men,
As ever fought for country and for flag.

Delaware county so generous of her sons,
Resolved to make the starry banner safe;
She, ever ready with her men and guns,
Gave ninety nine brave men in Company "F."

Winneshiek gave the Regiment, Company "G,"
Those noble sons of Scandinavian sires;
Ninety men chivalrous and free,
As ever fought for freedom's sacred fires.

Dubuque and Delaware at last combine.
And both united, gave us Company "H;"
Eighty-two brave men as ever formed a line,
Or vanquished treason in its latest ditch.

Eighty-five strong men, resolved to win or die,
Guided by duty, patriotism and reason;
Yes, Jackson county gave us Company "I."
Who struck hard blows at slavery and treason.

Delaware county gave us still another.
Company "K" came, numbering eighty four;
She bade them like the ancient Spartan mother,
Return victorious, or return no more.

Another Company merits special mention.
Familiar since the days of Roderick Dhu;
All soldiers on the war path after chickens,
Invariably belonged to Company "Q."

How fitting that in Delaware you meet.
And on her soil that war worn banner raise;
Here will the Twelfth her loyal people greet,
And tender her our grateful meed of praise.

The Regiment began its training and restraint,
Camp Union was not destitute of charms;
Those early drills were borne without complaint,
And formed a friendly brotherhood in arms.

The field and staff selected and commissioned,
Without the usual jealousy or hate;
Woods by training in the stern profession,
A better officer never left the State.

Even now, when in the peaceful walks of life,
We hear the Colonel's words without abridgment;
Fall on our ears so measured, calm, and slow,
FALL IN TWELFTH IOWA REGIMENT.

Colonel Coulter was a splendid fellow.
As brave a man as ever met the foe;
In war or peace his measured accents mellow,
Fell from his honored lips by far too slow.

Brodtbeck, by example, was a gallant soldier,
His stern commands all indicated fight;
But winter campaigns try the strongest men.
The snows of Donelson took him from our sight.

Your Chaplains, sentinels on the walls of Zion,
At times sent forth the glorious gospel cry;
Chaplains like sinners, have their hour of weakness,
When they are not just quite prepared to die.

On dress parade, when all so trim and neat,
The pride or terror of the diligent;
The report and orders never seemed complete,
Without the legend, U. E. Duncan, Adjutant.

Our Surgeons were skillful, genial and good,
Though hardened somewhat by the toils of war;
Stern Parker, Huff, and gracious Underwood,
The rugged Finley, and patient Barr.

What contrasts mark the soldier's checquered life,
Regardless of what he was, or might have been;
His training for the purpose of war,
Make men combined a terrible machine.

A change of base from Iowa to Missouri,
To Benton Barracks, where two months you staid;
The better to withstand the rebel fury,
By training in Division and Brigade.

At St. Louis, the Regiment battled with disease,
Eighty soldiers died at one fell swipe;
Death and contagion came on every breeze,
Black measles of the most malignant type,

From Benton Barracks eagerly you go,
Marching orders came extremely lucky;
Raported to General Grant at Cairo,
And camped in the field at Smithland in Kentucky.

Embarked in transports on the Tennessee.
To reach and invest Fort Henry from the land;
You arrived in time to see the rebels flee,
The cautious Johnnies dare not make a stand.

Then on to Donelson, that mysterious stroughold,
Who's rugged slopes inspired the mind with awe;
The rebel defenders, confident and bold,
Within their works and bristling abettis.

The very heavens conspired at your defeat,
Poured on your heads an avalauche of storm;
Chilled each sentinel on his cheerless beat,
And wrapped in snow, e tch sleeping soldier's form.

Yet from his wintry bed, each warrior rose.
Shook from his freezing limbs the clinging snow;
Rushed gaily up the slopes with shouts and blows,
And like a tempest swept the vanquished foe.

The rebel flag at last has disappeared.
And with it all the venom it engendered;
And in its place a pure white flag is reared,
HURRAH! HURRAH! Fort Donelson has surrendered.

The rebel cannon hush their wild alarms,
The musketry suspend its leaden showers;
THIRTEEN THOUSAND prisoners stack their arms.
And rugged Donelson at last is ours.

Even victory brought you many throes of grief,
Dear comrades dead, and absent friends who weep;
In silence, and with fitting service brief,
You left them to their last and dreamless sleep.

From Metal Landing, on the Tennesse,
Again you stem that river's rising flood;
To fill an oppointment at the Shiloh church,
And take your Sunday's baptism of blood.

Just eighteen years ago this pleasant day,
For nine long hours your deadly muskets rattle;
Firm as a rock you barred the rebel way,
Held your ground and saved the ill stared battle.

Shiloh was fought without a general head,
Its history incomplete, even to this hour;
Blundering incompetence piled up your dead,
Your manhood alone withstood the rebel power.

Unknown to the Twelfth, that on its left and right,
The foe had penetrated with slaughter dire;
Still unsupported you maintained the fight,
Engulfed in a vortex of the rebel fire.

Your Colonel wounded. General Wallace dead,
Ninety-seven soldiers wounded on the field;
Sixteen dead comrades on their gory bed,
And still the bleeding Twelfth refused to yield.

Environed and beset on every side,
By rebel hosts encompassed like a wall;
At five P. M. you ceased to stem the tide
Of battle, with the dark and bloody pall.

Your courage largely saved that field of blood,
You held the rebels from the Tennessee;
'Till Buel's troops began to cross the flood,
The Twelfth was lost, the Union army free.

Our buried comrades on the Tennessee,
For long hath slept beside its rippling waves;
And SWEETLY too, blessed MARTYRS of the free,
A Nation guards their consecrated graves

Here began your term of prison life,
Your fearful sufferings, who alas! can tell?
DEATH by STARVATION, HEARTLESS means of strife,
Your jailors seemed the very FIENDS of hell.

Still unsubdued by dead line or stockade,
Your patient courage glorified your State;
Surrounded by your gallant old Brigade,
The Eighth and Fourteenth Iowa shared your fate.

But what a fate,—surpassing all belief;
Can heaven be kind, and tardy justice lag?
Cold and exposure doth augment your grief—
Your famished bodies clothed in filth and rags

Exposed to each surly guard's revengeful mood,
The vermin infested sands your only bed;
The DIRTY CART that brought your LOATHSOME food,
Removed your BLIGHTED and UNTIMELY dead.

No ray of light to cheer the fearful gloom,
You hear some COMRADE with his latest breath,
Pray for release before the AWFUL tomb
Close round him in that CHARNEL house of death.

Humanity and progress both demand,
That this fair land may ne'er behold again;
Such willful disregard of heaven's command,
As marked the horrors of the prison pen.

Our dead in prison 'tis a sacred spot,
Where traitors laid those martyrs of the Nation;
No cause on earth could prosper with the blot
Of soldiers slain by DAMNED assassination.

Peacefully they sleep in distant Southern graves,
The land of sunshine, flowers and clinging vines;
Where summer winds like sweet Æolian harps,
Sing their sad requiem through the lonely pines.

The fragments of the troops escaping capture,
By whatsoever duties were delayed;
Were all combined without a shade of rapture,
And styled the UNFORTUNATE UNION BRIGADE.

And like unfortunates of every class,
Required to perform twice what they did before;
At guarding rations, railroad, bridge or pass,
Or doing out-post duty for the corps.

The advance was made on CORINTH under HALLECK;
A change of tactics was at once begun:
The sword was cast aside for spade and mattock,
And war was waged on the EUROPEAN plan.

After long weeks of labor in the trenches,
Great Corinth, the objective point was won;
The spoils of war were countless Negro wenches,
And one dismounted, pond'rous, wooden gun.

Halleck returned, each colored refugee,
Refused his information and assistance;
The friends of freedom stood aghast to see,
This General foster slavery and resistance.

Corinth was made the base of operations,
On Vicksburg, by the line of Holly Springs;
Vast supplies and half a million rations.
Were stored within its Fort encircled rings.

The REBELS tiring of their own provisions,
Black-strap molasses, corn, and tasteless rice;
Advanced on Corinth in three grand divisions,
Under Villpagne, Van Dorn and Price.

The Union Brigade as usual were on hand,
Marching out to meet them, a committee on deception;
To amuse the reb's and bring them to a stand,
Till Corinth was re-enforced for their reception.

To the very letter the orders were obeyed,
To form in line of battle under fire;
And meet the rebel column undismayed,
Repel his charge, then steadily retire.

All day long the rebel column charged,
And step by step you doggedly retreat;
And hour by hour the forces were enlarged,
Preparing for the rebels' sure defeat.

General Price became impatient of delay,
And urged his worried forces to the fight;
To capture Corinth 'ere the close of day,
And feed his soldiers from the stores at night.

Here for the night the rebel charge was stayed,
The darkening woods with drunken clamor filled;
Here night was welcomed by your thinned Brigade,
And here your General Heickelman was killed.

Each fifteen minutes through that autumn night,
The rebels sent their messengers of hell;
To quiet your nerves and make your slumber light,
With soldier's lullaby, a bursting shell.

The morning found both armies in their place,
And ready to unseal the book of fate;
The Union Brigade now occupied the space,
Between Forts Richardson and Robinnett.

There is a calm precedes the wildest storm,
Before the lightning's flash or thunder rattle;
Just like the calm when strong battalions form,
Sure harbinger of on impending battle.

A single gun within the rebel lines,
And all his fierce battalions were in motion;
Sons of the Southern palm, and Northern pines,
Now met to test their courage and devotion.

The rebel masses press their devious way,
Through falling timber,—difficult obstruction.
While on their ranks converging batteries play,
With marked effect and terrible destruction.

Unmindful of the cannister and shell,
And heedless of the thundering cannonade;
The rebel column staggered, stopped, and fell.
Before the volley of your old Brigade.

That glorious flag so often fell and rose,
Its very tissue singed by rebel fire;
But to the last it waved before its foes,
Upheld by the Twelfth, till all its foes retire.

For two brief hours the battle fiercely raged,
Repulsed and bleeding their recall was sounded;
The Twelfth lost THIRTY from EIGHTY men engaged,
And every commissioned officer was wounded.

The enemy lost five thousand on the field,
His rout was most disastrous and complete;
In lengthened struggles Southrons have to yield,
And PRICE as usual beat a swift retreat.

The chosen seed of Israel's ancient race,
Who once of old on heavenly manna fed;
At Corinth were found, not weeping o'er the place,
But robbing the gallant and unconscious dead.

General Grant took special notice of the crime,
But not to punish with prison house or fines;
In general orders secured at the time,
The Jews were banished from the Union lines.

By order the Union Brigade was discontinued,
The fragments ordered to their several States;
Their love of country firm and unsubdued,
Rejoiced to meet their liberated mates.

The Twelfth's surviving prisoners were exchanged,
After long months of wretched prison life;
With hated treason they were enstranged,
And doubly anxious to renew the strife.

At St. Louis the Twelfth again were re-united,
Re-organized again for active war;
Again your regimental faith was plighted,
For victory and your Nation's rising star.

The Regiment soon was ready for the front,
And anxious to respond to duty's call;
To Vicksburg you were sent to share the brunt.
And walk on foot through General Grant's canal.

The boat on which you sailed down to Vicksburg,
Was loaded with coffins for prospective dead;
For want of space, you used them for a table,
At night you used them for your bunk or bed.

You disembarked at Duckport, Louisiana,
The land of cypress swamps and alligators;
Stagnant bayous fringed with mock banana,
The home and hot-bed of rebellious traitors.

Vicksburg, majestic in its strength was seen.
The very embodiment of slumbering war;
The Mississippi only rolled between,
So very near it seemed, and yet so far.

Even in repose the silent water batteries,
Seemed conscious, active, living, sentient things;
And branching works, like human arteries,
Connecting all its fort encircled rings.

Here you beheld that wonderful display,
The Vicksburg batteries blazing like retorts;
Gloomy midnight changed to glorious day,
When Union transports passed the rebel forts.

Vicksburg was impregnable from the front,
Its capture by the Yazoo far too dear;
Captured it must be, and as was your wont,
You marched by the flank to take it from the rear.

Your progress marked war's desolating path,
Through burning ruins of sugar house and gin;
A soldier's vengeance, or a planter's wrath,
Fit sequence of secession, war and sin.

Lone chimneys stand where lordly mansions stood,
Like monumental tomb stones o'er the place;
Where prayers to heaven ascended from the good,
To CURSE the oppressors of the Negro race.

You found amusement on the weary march,
In shooting buzzards, snakes and alligators;
The sacred birds and reptiles of the South,
With characteristics like their kindred traitors.

The road to Hard Times Landing was so long,
The transports bore you to the Eastern shore;
Gaily you sung that stanza from the song,
May Hard Times Landing come again no more.

Grand Gulf was left dismantled by the fleet,
You with Sherman was ordered to explore;
The exterior line of Pemberton's retreat,
And capture Jackson with the Fifteenth Corps.

This for the Twelfth was not unpleasant duty,
As you had called at Jackson once before ;
When insults greeted you from lips of beauty,
And you had promised them to call once more.

Your second call was rather unexpected,
By rapid marching through a summer storm ;
You found the Johnnies busy cooking breakfast,
And helped yourselves without the usual form.

Some were engaged in conning o'er their books,
Some playing cards, or polishing their gaiters ;
The Twelfth found them very admirable cooks,
But very negligent and careless waiters.

The people now forgot to jeer and mock,
The Yankee soldiers at their just carouse ;
When rebel stores ascend to heaven in smoke,
Accompanied by the old Confederate house.

Railroads cut, and rebel stores consumed,
The troops with Jackson settled all their bills ;
The march on Vicksburg was again resumed,
To the music of our guns on Champion Hills.

Pemberton defeated on the Champion Hills,
Before the Thirteenth Corps falls slowly back ;
Disheartened at all those multiplying ills,
He fled to Vicksburg, when you crossed the Black.

Your army corps from Black River led the van,
Your Regiment in advance when brought to bay ;
The Vicksburg Forts with gloomy thoughts you scan,
At nine o'clock, the eighteenth day of May.

Within their works all silent and sedate,
The rebels from their battlements beholds ;
Deploying squadrons seal them to their fate,
Like anaconda in its lengthened folds.

Provisions now were very high and scarce,
For all you had from the commissariat store.
When you began the battle, march and chase,
Was three days rations twenty days before.

The value of HARD TACK now you comprehend,
Satiety and loathing are forgot :
And like the memory of an absent friend,
You prize it highest when you have it not.

Grant flushed with victory in the open field,
Propelled his army like a pond'rous sledge ;
Full on the forts, expecting them to yield,
Without the labors of a regular siege.

Vainly the columns charge with bated breath,
Entire Brigades became the forlorn hope ;
Repulsed before those giddy heights of death,
You plant your flags along the outer slope.

But not content with courage and devotion,
More victims still, for war's avenging thunder ;
Fresh Brigades were doomed and put in motion,
A noble sacrifice to McClernand's blunder.

The cruel charge was barren of results,
The bleeding soldiers uttered no reproaches;
Vicksburg could not be taken by assault,
But regular siege and gradual approaches.

For forty days you work at sap and mine,
Alternate nights is given to sleep and rest;
Alternate nights you guard the picket line,
And every duty is performed with zest.

Magnolia blossoms strew the trembling earth,
Sweet perfume by the summer breeze was spread;
Now from the field a pestilential breath,
Is wafted from our still unburied dead.

A flag of truce from every fortress tell,
The thundering batteries now are hushed and still;
Our gallant dead were buried where they fell,
Along the crest of Vicksburg's bloody hill.

Two hours armistice, both the armies meet,
On neutral ground their courtesies begin;
No boast of victory, glory or defeat,
Death and the grave make enemies akin.

The time is up, the BLUE and GRAY retire,
The signal gun is heard from near and far;
Five hundred guns resume their deadly fire,
With all the horrors of tumultuous war.

The answering batteries, through the summer nights,
Made music like a chime of pealing bells;
The arch of heaven was glorious with the lights,
Of burning fuse and bright exploding shells.

On July fourth the works were all complete,
The knell of Vicksburg was already tolled;
The garrison capitulate to escape defeat,
And thirty thousand prisoners were paroled.

The backbone of the rebel cause you broke,
The Mississippi valley now was free,
And free indeed, for not a slavish yoke
Was borne from Lake Itasca to the sea.

Johnston's army came like gallant liege,
You marched at once and met him at the Black;
He came too late to raise the Yankee siege,
You crossed the stream and promptly drove him back.

He sought at once the shelter of his guns,
At Jackson, where he fortified the place;
A useless labor lost, because he runs,
And leaves the once proud city in disgrace.

Your Regiment and Brigade was sent in chase,
A duty performed with spirit and abandon;
You changed his slow retreat, into a race,
And closed the campaign with the fight at Brandon.

Two rebel armies captured or destroyed,
For want of work your Generals thought it best;
The summer months in camp should be employed,
To build SHEBANGS, recuperate, and rest.

How tedious were those weary days in camp.
So trying to the active soldier's patience;
How deleterious to the general health,
Was HARD TACK fried in grease, the usual ration.

The CLASSIC NAME of one important RATION.
I dare not speak, for fear of punishment,
It is that part of the MATERNAL HOG,
Where juvenile swine derive their nourishment.

The summer gone with all its fading beauty,
The time for active service is at hand;
You march on Brownsville, bent on warlike duty,
Where all the reb's SKEDADDLE, or disband.

The Mississippi campaign now is o'er,
The country of armed rebels wholly free;
Transferred from Sherman to the Sixteenth corps,
You join your division at Memphis, Tennessee.

Detailed for duty never done before,
Rebuilding railroads now your thoughts employ;
You led the van as a construction corps,
As promptly as you labored to destroy.

This duty done you garrison Chewalla,
Colonel Stibb's commandant no one interferes;
There you passed a very pleasant winter,
And re-enlisted as Veteran Volunteers.

Companies "I" and "G" prepared and in platoon,
Marched to a party, through the somber woods:
The boys struck up their old familiar tune,
And ALL TO A MAN LEFT, the rebel dance who could.

Chewalla to Vicksburg you were ordered back,
On garrison duty, where one month you staid;
Protecting all the crossings of the BLACK,
Till Sherman returned from his meridian raid.

To Iowa now you went on veterans' furlough,
And reach your pleasant homes by various ways.
The brightest page your checkered lives can show,
Was that bright holiday of thirty days.

Short thirty days, a drop in human life,
Friends grasp your hand with many doubts and fears;
The blushing MAIDEN, PARENT, FRIEND, or WIFE,
Sob their good bye with eyes suffused in tears.

Still more endeared to country, home and friend,
While silent prayers like holy incense rise;
You take the field, those treasures to defend,
The soldier's love of country never dies.

The veterans meet at Davenport on time,
And soon rejoined their comrades at the front;
Where General Smith and MR. Banks combine—
Along the Red River on a rebel hunt.

Your late position is again restored,
The first division of the Sixteenth corps,
No more with musty camps will you be bored,
But marching or fighting till the war be o'er.

A. J. Smith, your dashing corps commander,
An active Vesuvius, always in eruption;
In battle he was a perfect Salamander,
His corps the very war cloud of destruction.

Your march was often fleeter than the wind,
Your path seemed blackened by the SIMOON's breath,
Your tents and baggage always left behind;
Your war cry followed by the stroke of death.

Your line of march though never trod before,
Left few inducements for a march again;
The rebels supplied your basket and your store,
And real war was never felt till then.

The natives reap the fruits of disobedience,
And the States once traversed by the Sixteenth corps;
Were ready to resume their old allegiance,
And satisfied with war forevermore.

Forrest flushed with victory over General Sturges,
And treating armed Contrabands like brutes;
His acts applauded by the rebel Burghers,
Who gloried in his fiendish attributes.

War at best is cruel and severe,
But HORRIBLE when MALICE guides the hands.
Historic justice DAMNS the dark career,
Of Forrest murdering captured Contrabands.

You marched at once to stay the cruel disaster,
Filled with contempt for such a treacherous chief;
At Tupelo you applied your usual plaster,
And punished for once this Negro killing thief.

The post of honor assigned to your Brigade,
You plainly see his motley gathering host;
In three lines deep the columns were arrayed,
You even hear their proud exultant boast.

Forrest promised his troops a very easy battle,
Another Guntown massacre he said;
Stampede the Yankees like a herd of cattle,
And feed the buzzards with their butchered dead.

With all the eloquence of an auctioneer,
He sold his Yankee wares so very cheap;
And those same Yankees cost the butcher dear,
You piled his dead in one promiscuous heap.

Forrest reforms his shattered line anew,
Grown desperate in view of probable defeat;
You meet his onset with a counter charge,
When all his lines are broken and retreat.

You taught him lessons in the art of war,
Kindly removed and dressed his wounded braves;
Foul murder leaves a more enduring scar,
Casts deeper shadows o'er the gloom of graves.

The confederate stores at Tupelo consumed,
The railroads cut and Forrest's troops defeated;
Your march on Memphis was again resumed,
With that affair at Old Town Creek completed.

At Tupelo your losses were severe,
Sixty-four in wounded, killed and missing,
Their noble deeds we honor and revere,
Their glorious death receives a nation's blessing.

Companies "A" and "F" detatched for special duty,
Guarding the whites from raiding Mamalukes;
One rosy dawn so fresh with summer beauty,
Repulsed a Brigade of General Marmaduke's.

The rebel forces full six hundred men,
Who summoned your forty veterans to yield;
Your ringing answer shook the southern glen,
They fled, and left you, masters of the field.

They also left their fallen comrades there,
Sure evidence of their disastrous flight;
Twenty dead and wounded to your care,
Human trophy's of a desperate fight.

In Mississippi other raids you made,
More foes to conquer, other fields to win;
But Forrest now avoids your dextrous blade,
And rebel provender, getting scarce and thin.

Across the Mississippi now you go,
Where rebel cavalry resistless race;
The Union horsemen being found too slow,
Smith's infantry were started in the chase.

Embarked on transports ready to explore,
The white river country, gloomy, wild and rough;
Through treacherous Bandits on its murky shore,
You disembark at rugged Duvall's Bluff.

With steady march you sweep across the State
Of Arkansas, where lawless robbers rove;
O'er barren hills, composed of rock and slate,
Through DISMAL swamp, and NASEOUS papa grove.

Across the Ozark range with rapid strides,
Where primative races sung their fetich hymns;
With scarcely space along its rocky sides,
To pitch your camp or streach your weary limbs.

Down from the hills you sweep, a compact force,
Your daily march, at night bring pleasing dreams;
Rapidly gaining on the rebel horse,
You ford or swim the rushing mountain streams.

A strange phenomenon never seen before,
Unknown in warefare's pre-existing rules;
The rapid marching of the Sixteenth corps,
From sheer exhaustion killed the patient mules.

This fact alone, retarded operations,
And frequent halts the hurried march beguile;
The dying brutes call forth your obligations,
The average loss was three mules to the mile.

By Cape Girardeau sound to Jefferson city,
You sailed, to give the weary mules a rest.
Price saw the point, and more from fear than pity,
Turned his plundering columns to the West.

You disembark without an hours delay,
And once again renew the novel chase;
Where mounted rebels try to run away;
And infantry still gaining in the race.

The enemy burn the bridges in his rear,
And to all destructive usages conform;
Which does not even check your swift career.
You swim the ice-cold Osage in a storm.

Right in the midst of war and its alarms,
The soldier being a common resident;
A halt is called, the Regiment stack their arms,
And dripping wet you vote for PRESIDENT.

You exercised the freeman's sacred right,
Without a thought of folly, fraud or vice;
With ballot and bullet both you fairly fight,
This Presidential campaign after Price,

You make a spurt and march both day and night,
While ague chills and burning fevers parch;
Before or since no record of the sight
Of Infantry sleeping while upon the march.

Across three States you chased the rebel host,
Captured all his baggage, guns and cattle:
His army scattered, broken up and lost,
His retreat was more disastrous than a battle.

Without a moment's time for needed rest,
The Sixteenth Corps was sent to Tennessee,
Where Hood on General Thomas closely prest,
When Sherman's army started for the sea.

Along the course of three Majestic streams,
Past marts of trade and silent sombre wood,
Up the Cumberland your transport streams,
Where you confront the rash, impetuous Hood.

Your landing from the boats was made in time,
Your corps its noble destiny fulfills;
Out on the centre of the Union lines
You stem the rebel torrent from the Hills.

The gallant Hood you never met before;
You only knew his fighting reputation;
His introduction to the Sixteenth corps
Broke the last link that bound his federation.

The opposing squadrons scarce their lines conform,
When from the north the wintry tempests blow,—
The wrath of heaven seemed riding on the storm,
And both the armies are engulfed in snow.

The heavenly wrath subdued the wrath of men;
War for a time the shivering hosts forego;
No shelter save the hills or wooded glen,
One hundred thousand soldiers 'neath the snow.

Scarce had the melting snow from mountain sides
Poured down its torrents to the swelling flood,
When battling armies help to swell the tide
With precious streams of gallant soldiers' blood.

A council of war by all the corps' commanders;
General Thomas granted A. J. Smith's request,—
The Sixteenth corps, those fiery salamanders,
Should strike the besieging rebel army first.

December fifteenth, ere the break of day,
The movement was begun with silent tread;
Dense clouds of vapor o'er the landscape lay,
The drowsy rebels thought you still in bed.

Like opening drama on the mimic stage
The foggy curtain lifted to the sun,
Revealing all the Sixteenth corps engaged,
And the last great battle of the war begun.

The charge was sharp, decisive and severe;
No hesitation marked the prompt advance;
No doubtful laggards lingered in the rear,
And all our flags went o'er their works at once.

Hood's veteran soldiers, brave, misguided men,
Fell back before you in disastrous rout;
While breathless you renew the charge again,
Capturing their cannon in their last redoubt.

You gathered up the captured spoils of war,
Advanced your lines till you confront your foes.
Eat your scant rations, and beneath the stars
Sank on the field of battle for repose.

Hood, staggered by the almost crushing blow,
Strong disappointment now his bosom fills,
Not one step northward now his legions go,
Besieged himself along the Brentwood Hills.

When morning broke calm and serenely bright,
Your veteran ranks were moving o'er the plain;
Full in the front and center of the fight,
You take the post of honor once again.

Wood's fourth corps was to storm the Overton's Hill,
His success or defeat, Smith's only sign:
To hurl his corps against the Brentwood Hill,
And break in pieces Hood's extended line.

By ten o'clock, with stubborn resistance,
You gain position near your watchful foe,
And wait for hours within good striking distance
For Woods to move and strike the signal blow.

You hear at last the tumult of his charge,
In quiet suspense you wait with anxious breath;
When from the hill the enemy discharge
Full on his ranks the leaden streams of death.

Vainly the soldiers strive, both white and black,
To reach the crest of Overton's fiery Hill;
Repulsed and bleeding they are driven back;
The firing cease and all the lines are still.

The calm was but the prelude to the storm;
The Sixteenth corps from their concealment rose,
Without a halt their broken lines to form;
You heedless rush on panic-stricken foes.

The rebel works became a wall of fire,
In sharp response to your resounding cry;
When veteran soldiers of a hundred battles
Break their ranks, throw down their arms and fly.

You take their batteries, arms and battle flags,
And capture prisoners, now a seething mass,
All struggling to escape beyond the hills,
Or through the defile of the Brentwood pass.

Your work in Tennessee was now completed;
You had no other contracts, jobs or leases;
You left the rebels broken and defeated,
With General Thomas gathering up the pieces.

You made a halt at Eastport, Mississippi,
Ostensibly to build your winter quarters;
But marching orders came and set you free,
And off again like roving Calmuck Tartars.

At Eastport you were short of food supplies;
The country round depleted and forlorn;
The baggage mules, your steady constant friend,
Divide with you his fodder and his corn.

You embark at Eastport through a storm of sleet,
And down the Tennessee in steamers glide,
Past former scenes of victory or defeat,
And comrades' graves that dot the river's side.

And down the Mississippi's swollen tide,
The grandest trophy of the waning war,
With not a fort or city on its banks,
But floats on high the glorious stripes and stars.

Down through the richly laden orange groves,
Through flowering shrubs and beautiful exotics,
Down where your regiment and the Sixteenth corps
Were formed by balmy breezes from the tropics.

You disembarked below the Crescent City,
Where sugar cane and orange groves abound,
Close by the buried dead of former wars
You camp on Jackson's famous battle ground.

Here you beheld the CREOLE population,
In holy frenzy o'er their sacred law;
Where masked absurdities of every nation
Were represented in their MARDI GRAS.

With orders to report at Mobile Bay,
You marched to the lake along the Newshell road;
Green fields and flowers all o'er the landscape lay;
The smoothest pathway armies ever trod.

Lake Ponchartrain you crossed in stormy weather,
High winds and chopping waves from ocean free;
Your regiment nearly foundered altogether;
Your craft was frail for such a stormy sea.

You landed on the shores of Dauphin Island,
And down to the gulf in joyous troops you go,
Where drifted sand along the sea-washed shore
Was white and spotless as the mountain snow.

Here you had oysters fresh from Mobile Bay,
And hunted shells amongst the ocean caves;
Like happy school boys on vacation day,
You bask in the sun, or plunge beneath the waves.

War with its hardships call you once again ;
To General Canby next you bring relief,
That gallant soldier who has since been slain,
The noble victim of the Modoc chief.

You cross the bay, and up the Fish river swamp,
In rear of Spanish fort to make a landing;
The rebels fall back before you and decamp,
And all arranged by previous understanding.

You land amidst the gloomy pitch pine thickets,
And march through resinous camps of pitch and tar,
Driving before you all the rebel pickets,
Who lure you on to more infernal war.

Your camps are pitched beneath the forest shade;
Your pine knot fires illuminate the scenes;
Fresh gathered branches for your fragrant bed,
You seek repose and court the land of dreams.

You emerge from the woods in front of Spanish Fort,
Begrimmed with smoke and clothing glazed with pitch.
Rebellion had reached this court of last resort,
Besieged in Spanish Fort, THEIR LAST GRAND DITCH.

The place was worthy of its reputation;
Planted TORPEDOES, nicely matched with gravel;
Four years of skillful murderous preparation,
Made Spanish Fort a hard old road to travel.

Instinctively you step with cautious tread,
EARTH, AIR and WATER, all combine and meet,
In hurling death at your devoted head,
While fiery billows roll beneath your feet.

Ten days of active work with pick and spade,
And wooden morters on your picket line;
Ten days of raining shell and cannonade,
Your zig-zag works the rebel fort entwine.

The rebels, seeing that their cause was lost,
The evacuation of the fort began;
You entered the works at midnight April ninth;
The war was over, ALL YOUR BATTLES WON.

Now, when from war and tumult you were free,
And rebel armies cease their stern commotion,
The courageous Reed and gallant Major Knee
Received their just and merited PROMOTION.

With other promotions all along the line,
Fresh from the ranks, d-void of pomp or style,
The noblest heroes of the civil war
Were the glorious veterans of the rank and file.

For one year, after all strife was over,
You served as magistrates and courts of law,
Recovering cotton and other goods in trover,
A civil bureau under martial law.

An executive and judiciary both combined,
Enforcing the law by order and obedience;
Your pardoning power was clear and well defined,
Administering to rebels the OATH of their allegience.

The accredited agents of the Freedmen's Bureau,
You protect the negroes in their sacred rights,
Enforcing contracts with their former masters,
Suppressing riots and preventing fights.

You even wore the high judicial ermine,
In causes of equity, common law or tort;
In all decisions promptly you determine,
And right or wrong a "COURT OF LAST RESORT."

Three years passed in battle and destruction,
As glorious as the ancient wars of Greece;
One year devoted to national reconstruction.
And splendid achievements in the paths of peace.

Four years devoted to your country's glory,
Four years of life beneath the forest aisles,
Four years complete your glorious warlike story,
And your long march of fifteen thousand miles.

Fourteen years of civil life is past
Without a sign or word of mutual greeting;
When to the rendezvous we come at last,
To hold this glorious regimental meeting.

This happy gathering, like a pleasant dream,
Will bless our lives, and all its joys prolong;
A glimpse of heaven with no dark veil between,
This grand exchange of sentiment and song.

"OUR GALLANT DEAD"—The Noble Heroes who, although passed to the Shores of the Great Unknown, still Live in our Memories, and are Cherished as among the best of our number." Response by R. P. Clarkson, Des Moines.

No other subject stirs up such hallowed memories, or touches so tenderly the hearts of all Iowa, and of all the homes of our whole country. The war left us a nation of desolate hearthstones, bereft of their best and brightest idols. Nearly every graveyard has its soldier graves that are objects of veneration to the whole community and will be until the generation that "fought the good fight" shall have passed away, and even their children and their children's children will cherish and annually decorate the grass-grown mounds, in praiseworthy remembrance of the heroic services of our "gallant dead" for the reunited country they died to save.

But this is a privilege that only a few enjoy. The great mass of "our gallant dead" sleep their last sleep far away from home and friends, the most of them in unknown graves, and the bones of a vast number of them lie bleaching on war-beaten trails all over the "solid South" and around all their accursed prison hells. They consecrated the rebellious land with blood too precious for such unworthy soil. Their fame is now the Nation's greatest heritage. They were of the Greeks who battled for their country's honor and will be forever entitled to the proud distinction of having fought for principles that all coming generations must make eternal or be forever unworthy of such heroic sacrifices. There must be no half way ground in history. The army that fought to preserve the whole country were patriots, and all those that opposed them were traitors, and are traitors still. The patriots are Greeks to be praised and venerated, while history will properly place the traitors on its blackest pages.

In these days when politicians are so anxious to gain popularity with the rebellious horde, it is necessary that plain words be spoken, and that treason be painted in its true colors. This is due to patriotism, and is mild punishment to traitors. We were not hired Hessians that conquered merely by superiority of numbers, but soldiers for God-given principles that could not have been defeated. It was a war for the continuation of national supremacy and honor, and Providence rightly managed the conflict, so as to eradicate grievous wrongs, that had been upheld by the nation since the formation of the government.

Nothing has struck the soldiers of the North in the last war with harder or more cruel force, than the false words of the unworthy successor of Grant—our most gallant leader in war and peace. Speaking plainly the present President of the United States, when he was exhibiting himself at Atlanta, Georgia, a few months ago, to the beaten but still defiant rebels, insulted every soldier in the Union Army, in comparing the war "to a struggle between Greeks," and in stating that we "are entitled to no special credit for having conquered the Southern Greeks." Let us, at this, our first regimental union, hurl back his false and hollow words with all the scorn that language can express. Such words should have blasted the tongue that spake them. It was the scheming trick of a political poltroon, but even the rebels were ashamed of a Northern man that would so debase himself, and none of them have ever asked the renomination to the Presidency that he was seeking to induce, while his name is execrated by all the gallant army he so foully slandered.

If this be treading on political ground it is in vindication of those who were not time servers, but soldiers whose gallant defense of undying principles placed a star on each shoulder of the foul slanderer, and whose votes elected him to the Presidency. Let us defend the gallant patriotism of our comrades, living and dead, whenever it is assailed, and teach our children to honor the living and venerate the names of "our gallant dead" and remember that their lives were given freely to perpetuate this land of liberty forever.

The statistics show that the whole number of men called into the national service during the war was 2,688,523 and that about 1,500,000 of these men were in active service; 96,089 were killed or died of wounds, and 184,331 from diseases—a total of 280,420 dead. The cost of the war to the government in mere dollars and cents was $3,098,233.078, while the different States expended, in bounties, or premiums to recruits $500,000,000. The colored troops numbered 178,975 and their loss speaks volumes for their bravery, as out of that number 68,178 perished. To these must be added that great tower of strength and will that stood at the government's helm throughout the war and was the solid rock against which the hosts of disgraceful peace and armed traitors beat in vain—the great heart and brain that guided the Ship of State through the channels filled with shoals and quicksands and died, by the hands of an assassin, just as the ship was passing the last breaker—the self-made man that was Providentially raised up from among the poor and lowly to be the Savior of the Nation, like one of old, to be the Savior of the World—the grandest and greatest among our "gallant dead"—Abraham Lincoln.

Shall it ever be said that all this blood and treasure was spent in vain? Can a nation so drenched with blood be so base as to forget the heroism of our fallen comrades that constitute this grand army that has gone on before to a realm where traitors are unknown? Better that our land should become a barren desert over which oceans should forever flow to condemn the base ingratitude and wash out all marks of such an ungrateful country's existence.

The Iowa regiments lost 3,482 killed or died of wounds; 8,482 died by disease; 6,777 were disabled by wounds and sickness, and therefore discharged, making the State's total casualties 23,295 out of a total of 66,814 three years men in the service, or considerably more than one-third the entire number. The records of the war department show that Iowa furnished 75,835 men, including those that enlisted for short terms, or went into the regiments of other States. Iowa's loss was, therefore, greater than the statistics show.

Only last Sunday I stood by the bedside of a dying Iowa soldier, and almost his last words were in "fighting his battles over again" and recounting his experience in the much dreaded Andersonville prison. He was but 16 years old when he enlisted and was at first rejected by the mustering officer, but the fire of patriotism was too strong in Thomas W. Eichelberger, of the 7th Iowa Infantry, to be thus quenched. Changing his clothes and coloring up his face to give himself a more robust appearance, he again presented himself to Lt. Chambers for examination, and not being recognized he was accepted. He was a patriotic boy, a brave soldier and a noble man. His love for his brother soldiers was strong enough to include all who were on the Union side and he took the soldier view of all controversies and always lent the helping hand to comrades in distress. Having been daily associated with him for a year past and learned to love him as a pure, noble and cherished friend, I cannot refrain from paying this brief tribute to his noble qualities in life and of the real pleasure he seemed to feel in death from the full knowledge of having served his God and his country faithfully and well.

Speaking more directly of those we knew best and loved the most, those who shared with us the regimental toils and camp, the march and the battlefield, and who are at this time and will be forever, the nearest our heart strings, and who, if such things are possible, are with us in spirit now. The Twelfth Iowa had 109 killed, or died of wounds, being over one-ninth of our entire number; 217 died by disease and 254 were discharged for disability caused by wounds or sickness, making the total casualties 580 men, over two-thirds of the number originally sworn into the service being permanently disabled during the war, and it is perhaps too true now that fully three-fourths of those who marched so gallantly forth from Camp Union with the grand old regiment are now beneath the ground. The regiment "fought like brave men, long and well," at Fort Donelson, where the heart of the North was raised from the great despondency caused by the flood of misfortunes to our armies during the disastrous campaigns of 1861 to a furore of jubilation never before witnessed on American soil, in which battle the General that the world has just pronounced the greatest living soldier, statesman and man, with less than 20,000 men, captured 17,623 prisoners, 17 heavy guns, 48 field pieces, 20,000 small arms and 3,000 horses—at Shiloh, the bloodiest battle of the war, numbers engaged considered, in which Iowa lost nearly as many men in killed and wounded as in all the other battles of the war and which was the day of blood, death and capture to our own regiment—at Corinth, Jackson. Vicksburg—where we captured 15 Generals, 31,600 soldiers, 39,000 muskets and 172 cannon, the greatest capture of men and arms from the invention of gunpowder up to that time, and which battle broke the backbone of the rebellion, opening up the Mississippi river and cutting the Confederacy in twain, at Pleasant Hill, Yellow Bayou, Lake Chicot. Simsport, White River, Tupelo, Nashville Spanish Fort, Blakely and other less noted battles, and our "gallant dead" now lie buried in nearly every State in the Union.

Shiloh was Iowa's greatest day of desolation and mourning, nearly all the Iowa regiments in the service at that time being in the battle and all of them lost men heavily. Three Iowa regiments—the Eighth, Twelfth and Fourteenth—were nearly destroyed, all the survivors of the three regiments that went on to the battle field being taken prisoners, just at the close of the first days' fight, over one-third of the Twe fth being killed and wounded. It is useless to attempt to describe the sufferings of those that died in, or of those that survived the accursed prison hells. Language cannot portray their sufferings. Suffice it to say that one-third of those that were taken prisoners died of ill-treatment or starvation, or were so physically wrecked that they were discharged and that over one-half of that gallant number that went forth to battle on that gory field, on that beautiful Sabbath morning, never reported to the regiment for duty again.

May the everlasting peace of God be with "our gallant dead." We feel with a new force, gathered here without them to-day, what a sacrifice they made, and how, God help us in our mortality, and, God bless them in their repose, we loved them then and almost worship them now. It is not the love of the mother for her child, that love transcendant, which heaven itself cannot match, but it is a love that comes first after the closest ties of kindred—a love that men sharing hardships and dangers and daring death together learn to have for each other—a love that has in its origin no selfishness, in its continuance no ingratitude, and which, please God, will have in enduring time no forgetfulness.

We cannot open our hearts to let the curious world read with garish interest of what is treasured there—the sacred memories of fast fellowship, the sacred confidences, or the lover-like friendships of the camp and the march; or, of the still more holy last confidences and last words, caught from the lips of comrades dying in battle, prison or hospital. But in this presence, here to-day, with so many of our surviving comrades around us, and with, perhaps, the spirits of "our gallant dead" hovering in benediction over us, as the phantom armies of the slain, above the clouds, were pictured as fighting in sympathy with the armies of the living on the field of Gettysburg, we may, with soldier hearts, speak here of the sharp, fresh pain we feel to-day as this scene so vividly recalls anew the dismal agony of sorrow we felt, when our cherished comrades fell by our side in the iron and leaden hail of Donelson, or, when they sank down in the red rain of death into the still redder soil of Shiloh's scarlet ground; or when they died with yet greater sufferings and still greater heroism, with even starvation and death not able to make the white lips complain, amid the grisly horrors of Montgomery, Tuscaloosa. Macon and Libby, and how with life as sweet and the future as bright and their friends as dear to them as ours are to us to-day, and with a hope for their country last in their hearts, and a smile of remembrance of the loved ones at home last on their faces, they died without a murmur, dying as heroes died—as Christ died—for others.

There is no American Valhalla—no marbled and royal palace of immortality for our American heroes slain in battle to inhabit alone—but there is reserved for them instead the nobler Valhalla of our own hearts, in which their memories and their souls are sovereign now and shall be always.

In one of the cemeteries at Washington City, a modest shaft of pure marble rise over the last couch of a young lieutenant of the navy, who with the sun of his glory and fame, hardly yet shining in its earliest morning, went down at his post in conflict. The marble bears to its hero this legend: "Here lies, given back by the sea, the body of Lieutenant Rodman, slain at his place of duty." So of our hearts to-day, comrades, and of our hearts so long as they shall beat, and of our children's hearts so long as gratitude shall teach to them its perfect lesson, it shall be said: "Here lies, given back from the carnage of the unmarked graves of Donelson, Shiloh, Corinth, Tupelo, and other gory fields, and from the unspeakable sorrows and horrors of the undistinguishable trenches of the starvation pens of Montgomery, Tuscaloosa, Macon and Libby, the imaged memory of our noble, precious, immortal Dead. An angel even could not take from our hearts, nor take out of the hearts of men to come, nor from the heart of history, the gratitude of a memory so noble, and God Himself will guard and foster it.

"Our Gallant Dead" are our greatest honors, our grandest trophies and our proudest scars. Their deaths made heroes of us all, and gave the Twelfth Iowa its proud record as a regiment baptized with fire and blood. They sacrificed home, friends and life with heroic cheerfulness, and their last good bye still lingers in the hearts and affections of the cherished idols left at home. We all recollect the last nights with loved ones. They were nights of weeping without slumber; heavy hearts left the last breakfast almost untouched, and while loving eyes were strained to catch the last sight of loved forms as they faded in the distance, outstretched hands waived Hope's benediction for a safe return.

This parting was our hardest trial. It was a struggle between patriotism and affection. Patriotism won the day, and fought the good fight till peace prevailed.

> "Ah! grander in historic glory
> Than the greatest that linger behind,
> They shall live in perpetual story,
> Who saved the last hope of mankind.
> Our oath, that till manhood has perished,
> And virtue and honor are sped,
> We'll be true to the cause they cherished,
> Eternally true, 'to our gallant dead.'"

The "Red, White and Blue" was sung by Miss Verda Kelsey with magnificent spirit, the entire assembly joining in the chorus.

CANE PRESENTATIONS.

Just now Col. Henderson arose, and stepping toward Col. Wood said:

"My Old Commander—The Twelfth Iowa Regiment has given me a new command. Their money bought this cane, and I am instructed to present it to you with these words: That as you could always lean upon them in battle, they want you by this token to know that as you pass down the western hill-side of life you may lean implicitly upon their warm heart's affections. Accept it as a token of their enduring love."

Col. Wood took the cane, trembling with visible emotion, and recovering his broken voice said:

"Col Henderson and Comrades of the Twelfth—I accept this token of your devoted love. I will retain it ever, and can never forget what it means; and if ever again the hand of treason should be raised against the flag of our country—although I may be an old man and bearing heavily on this staff—I swear by the living God! will come from my distant home to Delaware, and, raising my voice as never before, will cry out: "Fall in Twelfth Iowa; close order—MARCH! and every one of you will be found in your old places in the ranks."

The fire that burned in the Colonel's eye at Donelson was again seen at this moment, and bursts of applause greeted the regimental commander.

Maj. Reed, of Waukon, now stepped forward and took Lieut. Abner Dunham's hand and said:

"Your comrades, appreciating all you have done to bring us together in this reunion, instruct me to present you with this cane, which I do with pleasure, knowing by years of service with you how well you deserve this token of your comrades' love."

The Lieutenant took the cane and endeavored to express his thanks, but in spite of repeated efforts found his emotions too great for him. With his tears were mingled those of many of his comrades.

John F. Merry now sang "The Soldiers' Reunion" which was called for by the audience, and was warmly applauded.

On the platform was the flag of Company C presented by the ladies of the Upp-r Iowa University through the preceptress, Miss Lizzie Sorin, and which was returned to her after "this cruel war was over." Also the flag carried by the regiment at Corinth and in that battle held up defiantly before the enemy by Maj. J. D. Cole of Lansing, after he was shot through the body, and would not yield until he fell from loss of blood. And here was the regimental banner and its old flag in the hands of Lieut. H. J. Grannis, of Fayette, which had been in so many battles that it hung in speaking shreds; whose hands they never left during the war, save when in rebel prison pens a prisoner. He waived it before the audience, and said: "This is the flag we carried," quoting a line of the song just sung, "and this is the man who carried it," said Maj. Reed, pointing to Color Sergeant Grannis. Whereupon Comstock proposed three cheers for our Color Bearer who carried our colors from '61 to '66.

Col. D. B. Henderson, proposed three rousing cheers for the people of Manchester, the Eldora and Manchester bands, and the Dubuque Drum Corps, who attended in a body at their own expense, and who won great praise.

THE BROTHERHOOD OF THE REUNION.

It is with a mingled feeling of pleasure and pride that we write of the complete and gratifying success of the First Annual Reunion of the Twelfth Iowa Regiment, held at Manchester, on the 6th and 7th inst., the anniversary days of the battle of Shiloh. As a soldier in the noble old Regiment and as a participant in the glad Reunion, we write of the occasion with a heart filled with feelings such as only a soldier can appreciate. The brotherhood of comradeship in the army is as close a bond and as tender a tie as ever binds men together. Nothing so tests the manhood of men as the test of army life, and nothing so proves it. The selfishness or the unselfishness of a man is quickly demonstrated there, and the men who become friends under such circumstances of peril and proof, find in the enduring tie the noblest freemasonry of friendship capable of being formed between men. It was in memory of a friendship so sublime as this, that the survivors of the Twelfth Iowa Regiment came together in this Reunion at Manchester, fifteen years after the close of the war, and eighteen years from the time of the battle of Shiloh. In our dispatches from Manchester was told, in an incomplete way, a part of what was done at the Reunion. But no reporter could describe the heart there was in it all, nor how tender grew the strong men as they once more, after so long a separation, took each other by the hand. Only those who were there as participants can know as to that, and only soldiers can even imagine what it was.

A permanent organization was formed of the survivors of the Twelfth, and means are to be instituted to search out and gather into the membership all those who have left the State or moved to distant homes. We shall strive thus to bring together the last one of our surviving comrades, and once more stand together a united brotherhood preserving our friendships and meeting in regular anniversaries so long as any of us survive. It is a noble aspiration, and who that reveres patriotism or loves his kind will not bid it fervent godspeed?

The following short sketch of the history of the Regiment, in the Manchester Democrat, will be of interest just now in reviving in the public mind the services of this noble Regiment:

The Twelfth Regiment was mustered into the service at Dubuque in November, 1861, and in the following February took part in the battles which resulted in the capture of Fort Donelson.

Eighteen years ago to-day this Regiment occupied a central position on the battle field at Shiloh, and held their place until six o'clock in the evening, when about four hundred of them were overpowered and obliged to surrender, but not until after one hundred and thirteen of their number were killed or wounded.

For two hours before the surrender the Twelfth, with two or three other Regiments, were entirely surrounded, and in fact, contended against the entire rebel army. Those taken prisoners were exchanged, and the Regiment reorganized in time to take part in all the principal battles of the Vicksburg campaign.

The Twelfth took part in the battle of Tupelo, Miss., in July, 1864, and out of two hundred men engaged, lost sixty-three in killed and wounded. The Regiment also fought bravely at the battle of Nashville, and during its term of service did about as much fighting as any Regiment in the war of the rebellion, being in twenty-three battles and under fire one hundred and twelve days. And each of these battles brought the survivors closer to each other than before, and there are few relations in life where the bonds of friendship are stronger than those that exist between such men.

Around such a proud and precious record as this, may not the survivors of the Regiment cluster to preserve still more certainly to the future the splendid heritage of its fame!

RESOLUTIONS.

Mr. Clarkson, from the committee on resolutions, reported the following, which were adopted:

WHEREAS, The city of Manchester has placed at the disposal of the Twelfth Iowa Infantry Volunteers, for their use free of charge, the city halls, and also donated generously in cash; and

WHEREAS, The ladies of Manchester, have generously tendered said Regiment a rich and bountiful banquet, surrounded by decorations and beauties which only patriotic zeal and woman's taste could collect; and

WHEREAS, The Iowa National Guards, of this county, have spared no pains to contribute to the pleasure of this Reunion, thus bringing the soldiers of the past and the soldiers of the future warmly together; and

WHEREAS, Mr. H. L. Rann of the Manchester Press, has devoted himself and his paper to promote the interests of this gathering, refusing all compensation, and the Manchester Democrat has thrown its columns open for the interests of the Regiment, therefore, be it

Resolved, That the Twelfth Iowa Infantry Volunteers, to each and all of those who have thus kindly and generously contributed to the happiness and success of this our first Reunion, do hereby extend their sincere and heartfelt thanks, and they will ever remember the city of Manchester as a center of kindness, hospitality beauty and worth.

Resolved, That we gratefully commend the good taste of those of our number who selected Manchester as the place of meeting of this Reunion, being the city so generally celebrated for the two things we had so little of in the army—butter and eggs.

Resolved, That the mothers, wives, sisters, daughters and children of the Twelfth Iowa are members of the organization this day effected; that they are as honorably entitled to this membership as any one who fought and veteranized, and as such members they are cordially invited and earnestly requested to attend the Reunions of the Regiment.

Resolved, That we desire, in this public manner, to tender to Col. J. J. Woods, our old commander, our heartfelt thanks for coming from the extreme southern part of an adjoining State to be present with us at this our first Reunion, and for the noble and eloquent address with which he greeted us. His memory shall live with us and with the history of the Regiment while life lasts and history endures.

Resolved, That our thanks are especially due to Lt. Abner Dunham for the faithful and efficient manner in which he worked up this Reunion, resulting as it has in the most enjoyable gathering in the life time of those present. While the Reunion itself will always be remembered with pleasure, the happiness enjoyed on this occasion will always remind us of the brave and genial spirit that made possible this meeting of the kindred spirits of the Twelfth Iowa

THE ABSENT MEMBERS OF THE REGIMENT.

STAFF.

Major S. D. Brodtbeck, Highland, Ill.
Dr. C. C. Parker, Fayette, Iowa.
J. W. Taylor, Dubuque, Iowa.
N. E. Duncan, Kansas City, Missouri.

COMPANY A.

A. J. Wickham, Eldora, Iowa.
Frank C. Cromwell, Alden, Iowa.
Z. N. Miller, Spragueville, Iowa.
Samuel Walker, Maysville, Mo.
J. D. Conger, Eldora, Iowa.
B. F. Hach, Eldora, Iowa.
D. V. Ellsworth, Eldora, Iowa.
Levi Dobins, Eldora, Iowa.
G. W. Mitchell, New Providence, Iowa.
E. S. Sawin, Union, Iowa.
Job Crist, Eldora, Iowa.
Thos. H. Wilson, Iowa Falls, Iowa.
Geo. W. Moore, Maysville Iowa.
H. Creamer, Nevada, Iowa.
Wm. Mann, Iowa Falls, Iowa.
Martin Snyder, Webster City, Iowa.
Wm. Hallester, Eldorado, Iowa.
I. H. Bowers, Eldorado, Iowa.
T. H. Bailey, Eldora, Iowa.
Nathan Welch, DeWitt Ill.
Samuel Jackson, Dewitt, Ill.
M. Kidwiler, Iowa Falls, Iowa.
Wm. G. McPherson, Austin, Minn.
T. Fountain, Marshalltown, Iowa.
Geo. W. Reed, Rockport, Mo.
G. W. Rulow, South Bend, Ind.
G. H. Haskins, Marysville, Mo.
Robt. Morris, Edgewood, Ia.
Simon LeFever, Berlin, Iowa.

COMPANY B.

M. H. Pratt, Waukon, Iowa.
R. G. Pratt, Waukon, Iowa.
Hugh McCabe, Waukon, Iowa.
John Dowling, Waukon, Iowa.
Frank Klees, Waukon, Iowa.
I. D. S. Isted, Milwaukee, Wis.
L. D. Bearce, Monona, Iowa.
Geo. Hach, Preston, Iowa.
Steven Thibedo, Rossville, Iowa.
W. B. Bort, Victory, Wis.
J. P. Jackson, Harper's Ferry, Iowa.
Fred Monk, Union City, Iowa.
C. C. Ogan, Monroe, Minn.
C. Deamy, Dayton, Ohio.
A. West, Dubuque, Iowa.
Wm. P. Winter, Buffalo Fork, Iowa.

COMPANY C.

J. F. Hutchins, Minneapolis, Minn.
Wm. Quivey, Oelwein, Iowa.
John Kent, Oelwein, Iowa.
Silas Crossman, Elgin, Iowa.
Jas. Carmichael, Illyria, Iowa.
Ross Mattocks, Elgin, Iowa.
Benj. Delezene, Big Bend, Neb.
J. D. Baker, Montevado, Minn.
J. L. Mattocks, Cedar Rapids, Iowa.
Wm. L. Jordan, Wisner, Neb.
Wilson King, Wisner, Neb.
A. C. Bushnell, Waukon, Iowa.
G. W. Cook, Reno, Kan.
E. J. Abbott, West Union, Iowa.
John Strong, Mill, Iowa.

COMPANY D.

F. D. Thompson, Nevada, Iowa.
S. R. Burch, Olathe, Kan.
R. K. Soper, Martelle, Iowa.
H. C. Mooreland, Cedar Rapids, Iowa.
J. C. Dalley, Vinton, Iowa.
E. A. Batolph, Cedar Rapids, Iowa.
D. E. Steadman, Vinton, Iowa.
Francis Curren, Cedar Rapids, Iowa.
John H. Stibbs, Sparta, Tenn.

COMPANY E.

Wm. Hamilton, LaPort City, Iowa.
B. E. Eberhart, LaPort City, Iowa.
E. Sawyer, LaPort City, Iowa.
N. Shroyer, Gilbertsville, Iowa.
J. C. Jones, Geneva, Iowa.
R. L. Bird, Maysville, Iowa.
Jas. Cook, New Castle, Neb.
Silvester, Cook, New Castle, Neb.
Ezera Strong, Sioux City, Iowa.
Oliver Lichty, Waterloo, Iowa.
A. W. Myers, Shell Rock, Iowa.
Oliver Sharp, Finchford, Iowa.
M. V. B. Sunderland, Janesville, Ia.
Anthony Biler, Waterloo, Iowa.
H. F. Coon, Waterloo, Iowa.
H. J. Harrison, Washington, D. C.
G. L. Seeler, Salubi, Iowa.
C. P. Collins, Charles City, Iowa.
C. Haywood, Dysart, Iowa.
Nathan Church, Webster City, Iowa.
Charles Ochs, Ackley, Iowa.

TWELFTH IOWA V. V. INFANTRY.

COMPANY F.

G. W. Wooldridge, Elkport, Iowa.
Geo. W. Gift, Peoria, Ill.
R. C. Eldridge, Neeley, Neb.
T. C. Nellson, Hazleton, Iowa.
Jas. W. Potter, Fayette, Iowa.
H. J. F. Small, Chicago, Ill.
John Bremner, Yankton, Dakota.
A. J. Roe, Burlington, Iowa.
John Roe, Dubuque, Iowa.

COMPANY G.

Theo. Steen, Omaha, Nebraska.
Henry Steen, Hooper, Nebraska.
D. O. Aaker, Ridgway, Iowa.
G. D. Nass, Decorah, Iowa.
John O. Johnson, Decorah, Iowa.
John Steen, Wahoo, Neb.
L. D Townsley, Chicago, Ill.
Jacob Womeldorf, Decorah, Iowa.
Andrew Hulverson, Decorah, Iowa.
A. E. Anderson, Decorah, Iowa.
O. P. Rocksvold, Thoten, Iowa.
John Oleson, Thoten, Iowa.
Geo. Kirkland, Freeport, Iowa.
W. L. Windsor, Clinton, Mo.
G. W. Sharp, Frankville, Iowa.
E. V. Andrus, Decorah, Iowa.
A. A. Carey, Castulia, Iowa.
V. R. Dunn, Bonair, Iowa.
S. West, Decorah, Iowa.
Geo. Smith, Decorah, Iowa.

COMPANY H.

John Ware, Burlington, Iowa.
John VanAuda, Freemont, Neb.
W. L. C. Atkinson, Omaha, Neb.
Robert Fischel, Colesburg, Iowa.
Squire Fischel, Colesburg, Iowa.
Alfred G. Gosting, Strawberry Point, Iowa.
James M. Crosby, Epworth, Iowa.
N. E. Duncan, Kansas City, Mo.
Ed. Becket, Dubuque, Iowa.
B. A. Clark, Colesburg, Iowa.
W. H. Cock, Dubuque, Iowa.
A. J. Davis, Dubuque, Iowa.
G. S. Douglass, McGregor, Iowa.
A. C. Gilmore, Indianapolis, Indiana.
R. M. Grimes, Indianapolis, Indiana.
G. W. Hoerner, Dubuque, Iowa.
J. Shorter, Shell Rock, Iowa.
S. B. Sloan, Colesburg, Iowa.
W. S. Wisegarver, Colesburg, Iowa.

COMPANY I.

A. L. Parmer, Lincoln, Neb.
Dave Paup, Erie, Kansas.
E. B. Campbell, Armstrong Grove, Iowa.
John S. Ray, Naponee, Neb.
Warren Coats, Roseville, Ill.

COMPANY K.

E. F. Mathis, Omaha, Neb.
J. J. Brown, Ohio, Neb.
Charles D. Billings, Ohio, N
J. B. Morgan, Davenport, I

The above Roll is as nearly correct as we are at present a.. certain.

G. E. COMSTOCK,
Co. "G," 12th I. V. V. I.

Second Reunion
12th Iowa V. V. Infantry
Manchester, Iowa.

SECOND REUNION

OF THE

Twelfth Iowa V. V. Infantry,

HELD AT

MANCHESTER, IOWA,

ON

Wednesday and Thursday, May 21 and 22, 1884.

DUBUQUE, IOWA:
C. B. DORR PRESS.
1884.

Abner Dunham

Attention !!

COMRADE:

The Committee on Publication send you this pamphlet containing the proceedings of our last re-union. We send a copy to each surviving comrade whose address we have, and we hope that those who have not already paid for the book will remit to our Treasurer, G. H. Morisey, of Manchester, Delaware County, Iowa, the amount of its cost, 25 cents. All who signed our by-laws, and become members of our society, and whose names appear under Section VIII on page 10 of this book, are entitled to this copy free. We are anxious that all who can will become members of our society, and if you will send one dollar to Treasurer Morisey, and direct him to do so, he will inscribe your name on the roll, making you a member, and you will then be entitled to this book without additional cost, but unless this is done, we hope you will be able to send the 25 cents. If you know of any comrade who served in our regiment, and whose name does not appear in our book, will you be kind enough to send his name and address to our secretary,

Respectfully,

COMMITTEE.

E 507
.5
 tn I

COMMITTEES.

HALL DECORATIONS.

M. F. Le Roy,	W. C. Willson,	F. Cornish,
Harry Bradley,	Frank Smith,	B. Keller,
Mrs. S. M. Sherwood,	Mrs. Dr. N. S. Craig,	Mrs. E. M. Carr,
Mrs. Dr. C. C. Bradley,	Mrs. F. Bethel,	Mrs. P. H. Snider,
Misses Laura Doolittle,	Ella Sherman,	Sadie Hutchinson
Mattie Toogood,	Winnie Meserve,	Annie Kinnie,
Emily Seeds,	Etta Gemmill,	Minnie Work,
Lulu James,	Susie Paxson,	Nellie Flint,
	Hortense Trenchard.	

STREET DECORATION.

B. H. Keller,	A. M. Sherwood,	Thos. Toogood,
F. P. Doolittle,	Mrs. H. N. Cornish,	Mrs. W. C. Cawley,
Mrs. Enoch Allen,	Mrs. B. W. Jewell,	Miss Nellie Doolittle
Misses Mattie Dawson,	Mary Morey,	Anna McFee,
Lilly McFee,	Minnie Marvin,	Mamie Satterlee.

FROM W. A. MORSE POST, G. A. R.

R. M. Marvin,	S. E. Meserve,	A. C. Carter.

ENTERTAINMENT.

Mrs. W. C. Cawley,	Mrs G. W. Morrey,	Mrs. N. F. Lawrence
Mrs. Crawford Hutchinson,	Mrs. P. H. Snider,	Mrs. E. M. Carr
Misses Alice Willson,	Nellie Paxson.	

FINANCE.

W. H. Norris,	G. W. Dunham,	J. W. Ford,	K. M. Marvin

One hundred and fifty dollars was raised and disbursed by this committee to contribute to our happiness. The success of the reunion is largely due to the untiring energies and labors of the above named committees, also the hospitality and liberality of the citizens of Manchester in opening their hearts and homes to make us thrice welcome.

Respectfully,

COMMITTEE { J. H. Stibbs, J. E. Simpson, G. E. Comstock.

PROGRAMME.

Wednesday Forenoon.

10:00 A. M.—Meeting Comrades at trains, by W. A. Morse Post, G. A. R., led by the Eldora Silver Cornet Band.
Assembly at City Hall.   General hand-shaking and visiting.
Welcome, by Post Commander, J. B. SATTERLEE.
Response, by Col. JACK STIBBS.

12:00 M—Dinner.

2:00 P. M.—Assembly.   Street Parade, under command of Col. Jack Stibbs. All Old Soldiers invited to "Fall In."   Music.   Business.   Visiting.
Reading Letters from absent Comrades.   Singing Camp Songs and Telling Stories.

5:00 P. M.—Dress Parade.

Supper.

7:00 P. M.—Assembly.   Music.   Prayer by Rev. F. HUMPHREY, Chaplain 12th Iowa.   Words of Welcome, in behalf of the City of Manchester, by Mayor J. T. ABBOTT.   Response, by Col. D. B. HENDERSON.

ADDRESSES—20 MINUTES EACH.

"The 12th Iowa at Tupelo, Miss."—By Col. W. R. MARSHALL, of the 7th Minnesota Infantry.
"The Roll Call."—After the Battle—A Poem.—By Col. JACK STIBBS.
"What I saw at Nashville, Tenn."—By Rev. F. HUMPHREY.

MUSIC.

"The Bitter Pill at Fort Donaldson."—By Col. WM. T. SHAW, of the 14th Iowa Infantry.
"The Famous Charge of the Entire Army, May 22, 1863, at Vicksburg, Miss."—By Hon. H. C. CURTIS.

GRAND LOVE FEAST.

"The German version of Barbara Freitchie."—By Col. JACK STIBBS.
Make a Speech, Sing a Song, Tell a Story, or be reduced to the ranks. Five minutes each.   Tattoo.   Taps.   Lights Out.

Thursday Morning.

6:00 A. M.—Reveille.
9:00 A. M.—Assembly.   Music.   Business.   Report of Committees.   Visiting.

Banquet—Program.

1:00 P. M.—Grace, by Rev. F. HUMPHREY.   12th Iowa Deploy as Skirmishers!
General Engagement.   Surgeons and Drum Corps to the rear, with Ambulances and Stretchers!
2:00 P. M.—Re-assemble at Hall.

Toasts and Farewells.

Music.

I. Iowa and Our Whole Country. Their Liberties we Prize, and Their Rights we Will Maintain, with our Lives, our Fortunes, and our Sacred Honors.
Response—Gov. B. R. SHERMAN.

II. Our Brigade Commanders and Invited Guests.
Response—Capt. S. R. EDGINGTON.

III. Shiloh—The Saddest, Darkest Hour in Our History. "Fame's Eternal Camping Ground" for so many of the Best and Bravest of our number.
Response—Gen. J. M. TUTTLE.

IV. The Opposing Armies of 1861-65—Their Relations Then and Now.
Response—Col. D. B. HENDERSON.

V. Greenbacks and Graybacks—The first we could not keep with us, the last were hard to drive away.
Response—Hon. J. N. WEAVER.

VI. The Citizens of Manchester—Their Hospitality and Loyalty—Making their Homes our Homes, and our Re-union a Success.
Response—R. P. CLARKSON.

VII. Iowa at Shiloh—Heroes of the "Hornets' Nest" and "Hell's Hollow." They Held their Line of Battle throughout the day, on the memorable 6th of April, 1862 ; they sacrificed themselves, but saved the remainder of Grant's Army from capture, or entire destruction.
Response—Col. J. L. GEDDES, 8th Iowa Infantry.

VIII. "It's All Right !"—A Poem, Suggested by Charley Larson's last words to Col. Henderson.—(Page 21, pamphlet.)
Response—Hon. J. W. SHANNON.

Benediction.

Reunion 12th Iowa V. V. Infantry,

May 21st and 22d.

Wednesday morning, May 21st, dawned bright and beautiful; nature arrayed in her most gorgeous robes, was ready to welcome the heroes of war and peace. The streets and dwellings were decked with flags and wreaths, all indicating the hearty welcome Manchester was ready to extend the old 12th Iowa.

Many of the boys came the day previous, to be ready to join in all the gladness the occasion might afford them, and at train time accompanied by W. A. Morse Post, of the Grand Army of the Republic, proceeded to the depot to welcome those who should come that morning. Amid the cheers of their comrades, a large number stepped off the cars. After the hearty greetings the order to "fall in" was given and the march was made to the city hall, where the exercises were to take place.

Immediately on entering the hall, the Manchester Glee Club sang "The Battle Cry of Freedom," in splendid style. At the last verse the audience, filling the room, rose and joined in the chorus, making the old hall resound with the grand melody.

Col. S. G. Knee, President of the veteran Association, then introduced Commander J. B. Satterlee, who, on behalf of W. A. Morse Post and the citizens of Manchester, welcomed the veterans to the city. He said he had been delegated to open this skirmish, that he never was in worse condition to perform such a duty, and that all he could do, was on behalf of W. A. Morse Post and the good people of Manchester, to say "welcome! welcome! thrice welcome!"

To this Col. Jack Stibbs responded as follows:

Commander Satterlee and Comrades of Morse Post:

I have been delegated by my comrades of the Twelfth Iowa here assembled, to reply to your address, and to thank you, and through you, the citizens of Manchester, for the kind and generous welcome that has been extended us. Four years ago, our first reunion was held in your city, and after it was over there was a universal feeling among those who were present that we could never hope to receive so hearty a reception in any other place as had been tendered by your good people here. Therefore, when we came to consider the question of where to hold the reunion this year, and were assured by our Secretary, Dunham, and others here, that the people of Manchester would be glad to entertain us once more, we were selfish enough to decide to again accept of your hospitality.

We are especially pleased on this occasion to be welcomed by an association of soldiers, and particularly by the Morse Post, for he whose name you have adopted, Capt. W. A. Morse, was one of our number. A brave and gallant officer, a good citizen and a generous fellow, whom we all loved and respected. Then too, you each know what war means, and can appreciate, as only soldiers can, the feelings that have prompted us to assemble here to day. Each one of us who is here has made more or less of a sacrifice to attend this meeting, and I assure you we are prompted by no selfish motives, but are actuated simply by feelings akin to those which cause a family of children to travel from the four quarters of a continent to meet around the old family board on Thanksgiving day. This, to us as a regiment, is our Thanksgiving Day. Many of us have not met for more than twenty years, but our friendships were formed and cemented under circumstances that made them enduring, and we each feel, as the years pass that make us older, that our love and affection for old comrades is constantly growing rather than diminishing.

For myself I can say, and I am sure I but express the feelings of my comrades here, I have forgotten the disagreeable features of our service, and in thinking of the old Twelfth Iowa I try to remember only the glorious record made by the regiment, the heroic bravery so often displayed by its members, the sturdy determination so fully expressed to keep our flag afloat until the last Rebel stronghold was taken, the patient enduring of hardships and privations, and above all, the jolly fun which, despite our hard service, was always found in camp, and I come here to-day feeling that to each survivor who honorably bore the badge of the old Regiment, I want to hold out both hands and say, "Comrade, I love you." This being done, I shall feel that I have been well repaid for my visit here. We hope while here to so conduct ourselves that your citizens will be glad to see us again, but I must warn you, that it is a part of our purpose to shake off as nearly as possible the effects of the past twenty years, and for two days at least, we mean to be boys again. So do not be surprised if all we do is not in keeping with our gray hairs and wrinkled faces. Again I thank you for your welcome.

A round of hearty applause greeted this speech, showing the appreciation of the audience. "When Johnnie Comes Marching Home," was then sung by the choir with stirring effect.

During the hour devoted to this part of the program the Eldora Silver Cornet Band of 12 pieces, Det Hunter, leader, played several inspiring airs, adding greatly to the interest of the meeting.

The Hall was hung on every side, with the national colors, and decorated with evergreens and flowers, and on the wall, at the

west end were conspicuous the mottoes,—"To the Living, Cheerful Praises,"—"To the Dead, Bright Flowers—Sweet Memories."
An adjournment was announced to 2 p. m.

AFTERNOON.

At 2 p. m. took place the street parade under command of Col. Jack Stibbs, led by the Cornet Band and Co. C. I. N.G., of Manchester, commanded by J. W. Ford, after which all repaired to the hall.

Capt. E. B. Soper of Emmetsburg, read the plan for the permanent organization of the survivors of the 12th Iowa, which was as follows:

Articles of Incorporation of the Society of the Twelfth Regiment of Iowa Veteran Volunteers.

ARTICLE I.

The name of this corporation shall be the Society of the Twelfth (12) Regiment of Iowa Veteran Volunteers.

ARTICLE II.

This Society shall be composed of persons who served in and were honorably discharged from the Twelfth Regiment of Iowa Volunteer Infantry, during or at the close of the war of the Rebellion, and shall be admitted to membership in such manner as may be provided by the By-Laws of this Corporation.

ARTICLE III.

The principle place of business of this corporation shall be at Manchester, Delaware County, Iowa; but business may be transacted and elections held at any reunion of the survivors of said Regiment wherever the same may be held.

ARTICLE IV.

The purposes and objects of this corporation shall be:

1st. To institute and maintain an organization of the surviving members of the late Twelfth Regiment of Iowa Infantry Volunteers.

2nd. To cause to be prepared a roster by companies of all members of said Regiment not deceased while in the military service of the United States and to make and keep up thereon a record of the post office address, occupation and general character of all surviving members thereof, and to ascertain and record the date, place and cause of death of all now or hereafter deceased.

3d. To promote fellowship and social intercourse among the surviving members thereof by holding reunions and such other meetings as may be provided for by the By-Laws of the corporation.

4th. To look after the disabled, needy and unfortunate members thereof whether members of this Society or not and render them such aid and assistance, as may be proper in the premises.

5th. To procure funds, donations and otherwise, and to take and hold property in its corporate name for the purpose of carrying out the objects aforesaid.

ARTICLE V.

The officers of this corporation shall consist of a president, a vice president, a secretary, a treasurer and five (5) directors, who shall have the control and management of the business of the corporation, and who shall be elected at such times and in such manner as may be provided in the By-Laws of the corporation.

ARTICLE VI.

This corporation shall commence with the adoption of these articles and continue twenty years. Its indebtedness shall at no time exceed five hundred dollars and the private property of its members shall be exempt from corporate debts.

ARTICLE VII.

The names of the officers of this corporation for the first year of its existence are as follows:

President, S. R. EDGINGTON.
Vice President, D. W. REED.
Secretary, ABNER DUNHAM.
Treasurer, GEO. H. MORISEY.
Directors, S. G. Knee, J. H. Stibbs, R. P. Clarkson, John Steen. Ben. Eberheart.

The undersigned members of the 12th Regiment Iowa Volunteer Infantry during the war of the Rebellion having associated themselves for the purposes hereinbefore expressed do hereby adopt, make, sign and execute the foregoing articles of incorporation, dated at Manchester, Iowa, this 21st day of April, A. D. 1884.

E. B. SOPER,   D. B. HENDERSOM,
S. D. BRODBECK,   GEO. H: MORISEY,
R. P. CLARKSON,   J. H. STIBBS,
J. E. SIMPSON,   D. W. REED,
ABNER DUNHAM,   S. R. EDGINGTON,

State of Iowa, } Be it remembered that on the 21st
Delaware County. } day of May, A. D. 1884, before the undersigned, a notary republic, within and for aforesaid county and state, personally appeared; E. B. Soper, D. B. Henderson, Geo. H. Morisey, R. P. Clarkson, J. H. Stibbs, J. E. Simpson, D. W. Reed, Abner Dunham, S. R. Edgington, to me personally known to be the identical persons who hath signed and executed the foregoing articles of incorporation and severally acknowledged the execution of the same to be their voluntary act and deed for purposes therein expressed.

[SEAL]   Witness my hand and official seal hereto affixed at Manchester, this day and year first above written·
W. H. NORRIS, Notary Public.

They were then referred to a committee consisting of Capt. Soper, R. P. Clarkson, Col. Jack Stibbs, Maj. D. W. Reed and Maj. G. H. Morisey, who submitted the following by-laws, which were adopted:

By-Laws of the Society of the Twelfth Regiment of Iowa Veteran Volunteers.

I.

Any person who served in, and was honorably discharged from, the 12th Regiment Iowa Infantry Volunteers, may become a member of this Society by signing these By-Laws and paying to the Treasurer the sum of one dollar.

II.

All who are eligible to membership in this Society, the wives of members thereof and such persons as may be elected thereto at the time of and in the manner of electing officers of the Association, shall be honorary members of this Society, and shall be entitled to meet with and participate in all Reunions of the Society, but they shall have no vote at any election held by the Society, and shall not be subject to dues or assessments.

III.

All elections of officers, honorary members and amendments to Articles of Incorporation and By-Laws shall be by ballot. The person having the highest number of votes for any office at any election shall be declared elected.

IV.

All meetings and reunions of the Society shall be held at Manchester, Delaware County, Iowa, unlsss otherwise ordered by the Board of Directors.

V.

The Officers and Directors of the Society shall constitute a Board of Directors of the Society, and shall have charge and control of the business and affairs of the Society and shall have and exercise such powers as may be proper and necessary to carry out the objects of the organization, but they shall not levy assessments upon the members of the Society exceeding the sum of one dollar per year, and no member whose assessments are in arrear shall be entitled to vote at any election, or upon any questions.

VI.

The duties of the officers of this society shall be as follows: The President shall preside at all meetings of the society and shall also be the president of the Board of Directors. The Vice-President shall in the absence of the President perform the duties of that office. The Secretary shall likewise be the secretary of the Board of Directors. He shall keep a record of all proceedings of the society, and of the Board of Directors. He shall be the custodian of all books, papers and correspondence of the Society, and under the direction of the Board of Directors shall cause the proper rosters and records provided for by the Articles of Incorporation to be properly made and kept and shall receive therefor such compensation as the Board of Directors may deem just and proper. The Treasurer shall safely keep all funds coming into his hands by virtue of his office and pay out the same only upon orders drawn on him by order of the Board of Directors and signed by the presiding officer thereof and the Secretary. The Directors shall be elected from different companies of the regiment and shall with the officers of the Society constitute of the Board of Directors of the corporation a majority of whom shall be a quorum to transact the business of the Society.

VII.

The officers of the Society elected at the reunion of said regiment in 1884 shall hold their offices until their successors shall have been elected and enter upon the discharge of their duties. An election of officers shall be held at every reunion of the Society, and vacancies occurring by death or otherwise shall be filled by the Board of Directors.

VIII.

At the reunion in 1884 the members of each company shall organize by electing a president, a secretary and a committee of three members who shall as far practicable procure and transmit to the secretary of the Society the necessary facts and dates to enable him to make up the record of the company as required by the By-Laws and Articles of Incorporation of the Society.

W. A. Hamlin, company	C	Joseph Soper, company	D	W. A. Nelson, company	F
J. C. Kuhns,	" H	J. W. Gift,	" F	G. W. Kirkland,	" G
F. W. Moine,	" C	S. Kemp, company	A	D. W. Reed,	" C
Chas. I. Martin,	" C	Geo. Teskey, company	"I"	James Stewart, company	C
J. E. Simpson,	" G	P. R. Ketchum,	" C	M. E Muder,	" G
A. J. Rodgers,	"B"	A. E. West,	" A	A. T. Garner,	" H
W. N. Mann,	" F	G. H. Latimer,	" C	T. McGowan,	" F
F. Humphrey, chaplain.		Mrs F. Lankins, com'ny	B	H. C. Merriam,	" K
W. H Trowbridge, comp'y	D	J. W. Rich, company	E	P. J. Morehouse,	" K
E. O. Kelsey, company	C	J A. Van Anda, comp'y	H	B. E. Eberhart,	" E
J. W. Ward,	" H	D. E. McCall, company	C	John S. Ray,	" I
S. R. Burch, adjutant,		S. Kaltenbach,	" F	M. B. Goodenow, comp'y	I
Henry Steen, company	G	F. Dubois,	" D	J. S. Margretz,	" E
Geo. Kint,	" G	Geo. H. Morisey,	" H	C. V. Surfus, company	E
I. B. S. Isted,	" "B"	R. P. Clarkson,	" A	D. Conley,	" D
Joseph Franks,	" H	Mrs. R. P Clarkson, Co.	A	B. P. Zuver,	" D
J. C. Jones, company	E	John E. Kent, Company	C	P. R. Woods,	" C
D, Craighton,	" E	S. G. Knee, Lieut. Colone'.		F. M. Hamblin,	" H
J. B. Morgan,	" K	S. R. Edgington, Lieut. Col.		J. A. Light, company	H
N. J. Davis,	" I	James F. Lee, company	"F"	J. Shorier,	" H
H. S. Briggs,	" H	R. Z. Latimer,	" C	Hiram Kuster,	" F
G. A. Hauge,	" G	Mrs. W. A. Morse, comp'y	F	John Steen,	" G
John. Elwell, company	E	L. M. Ayers, company	D	John J. Eaton, company	H
John B. Thompson, com'y	G	W. W. Whitenack, comp'y	D	I. L. Jordan,	" C
H. J. F. Small, comp'y	F	Geo. W. Wooldridge,	" F	O. P. Rockswold,	" G
Anthony J. Biller, comp'y	E	Edwin Carell, company	F	R W Tirrill.	" F
W. L, Henderson,	" "C"	D. O. Aaker,	" G	Edwin A. Buttolph, Co.	D
D. W. Moreland,	" H	A E. Anderson.	" G	John F. Lee, company	F
Hart Spears, company	C	A. B. Perry,	" E	S. Gifford,	" C
H. M. Preston,	" F	James Burr, assistant surgeon		Abner Dunham, comp'y	F
C. E. Merriam,	" K	T. C. Nelson, company	F	S. M. French,	" F
A. J. Millett,	" D	Joseph S. Girton,	" F	H. J. Grannis,	" C
Sam J. Lewis,	" D	R. L. We den,	" F	Allen M. Blanchard, Co.	D
Jas, Evans,	" H	Geo. L. Durno.	" C	Eli King. company	D
H. R. Andrews,	" "B"	George H. Coob,	" A	Henry M. Bailey, comp'y	D
J. F Zediker,	" "I"	J. W. Ballinger,	" C	J. H. Stibbs,	
G. E. Comstock,	" "C"				

The Secretary then read the following letter from Col. J. J. Woods:

MONTANA, SOLIETTE CO., KANSAS, MAY 16, 1884.

Dear Dunham: — Amid the hurried duties of an active life, (for one of my age, (61) the thought just occurred to me that if I kept my promise, to wit: that if I did not attend the reunion of our old beloved 12th, you should receive a letter from me before that event, I must write before mail time. Hence without taking time to give elegance of form to my sentences, I hasten to say that I exceedingly regret that private business at home, the distance to Manchester and the expense of the trip, combine to prevent my attendance at the reunion. Say to my comrades (and the people of Manchester) that I remember, with gratitude the kindness I received from them at our last reunion, that I would be glad to meet them again face to face, press their friendly hands and look into their loving eyes, recount with them the scenes and incidents when our hearts were cemented together in the camp, the march and the fiery ordeal of battle, and with devotion to the great principles of liberty drop a silent tear together in remembrance of those of our brave comrades, who laid down their precious lives a holy sacrifice upon the altar of their country. And then probably many who were not at the last reunion will be at this one. O how I would like to greet them. By why attempt to express my feeling in words. "The heart feels most when the lips move not."

I will hurridly close by saying, if life, health and strength permit, I will make strenuous efforts to be with you at your next reunion.

Yours Fraternally,
J. J. Woods.

P. S.—I want to tell you that I had the pleasure of meeting Gen. Prentiss recently and hearing him deliver his fine address on the battle of Shiloh.

Major D. W. Reed being called for, made some remarks concerning the proposed history of the 12th Regiment. He said what was greatly to be desired was a complete list of all the men whose names had ever appeared on the muster roll of the regiment. He said such a list was in the office of the Adjutant General at Washington, and that it was possible to obtain a copy of it, as he had been informed. He had in his possession much material for that history, but, though he had addressed letters to every commissioned officer of the regiment, requesting some account of his personal service, he had been unable to get a response from a single one of them. He hoped some member of each company would prepare an account of the service of the company, and send it to the committee on the regimental history. This was the only way in which anything like a trustworthy history of the regiment could be written. He briefly reviewed the history of the regiment at Shiloh, and successfully defended it from the charge, so often made, of having been captured early in the day on that memorable 6th of April, 1862.

After which a very interesting letter from Capt. T. B. Edgington of Memphis, Tenn., was read, followed by letters from Capt. Robt. Williams of Co. E., in which he gave a graphic account of the part taken by the 12th Iowa at Shiloh and Topelo.

Then followed letters from a large number of the absent comrades in which they expressed their sorrow at their inability to attend, and sent love and kind remembrance to all who were present. Amongst these letters we note that of Capt. H. J. Playter, Adj't. Duncan, J. V. G. Price, Isaac Watkins, W. B. Kieth, J. V. Crane, Geo. Nauman, C. M. Runkle, H. W. Ross, R. E. Hamlin, R. L. Johnson, E. King, A. A. Stewart, R. C. Cowell, W. L. Winsor, J. M. Tarpening, Isaac Woodmansia, Frank Renchin, Sam'l West, Asst. Surg. Underwood, Lt. J. D. Cole, Thos. Barr, Harman Grass, H. W. Bailey, I. G. Clark, A. J. Millett, Surg. Finley, Capt. Hunter, Capt. Switzer, Maj. Vanduzee, C. A. Coon, Van R. Dunn, A. H. Graves, G. A. Houge, Lawrence Lott, Cruay Clark, J. L. Mattocks, H. F. Coon, J. P. Strong, F. J. Crowhurst, H. C. Winterstine, Oliver Sharp, W. P. Haywood, A. M. Blanchard, W. B. Bort, A. L. Palmer, C. C. Stribling.

A letter from Gen'l. John A. McArthur, who commanded our division in 1864 and 65, was read, in which he expressed his regard for the boys and wished them a glorious good time. General J. M. Tuttle, who commanded our division in 1863, sent us the following:

DES MOINES, May 26, 1884.

G. E. Comstock, Esq., Manchester, Iowa.

DEAR SIR:—I returned home from the east, last Saturday, to find your invitation and other correspondence about your 12th Iowa reunion. I would have surely been there, had I known just when it was to have come off, and regret exceedingly that I was not there; for I hear that you had an excellent time of it. Yours Truly,

J. M. TUTTLE.

Here is another letter, written to E. J. Congar, Esq., by one who was there, Capt. J. E. Simpson of Dubuque, which will show how the reunion is regarded by those who were present:

DUBUQUE, May 24, 1884.

What a good time we had at Manchester. How kind everyone was to us. God bless them all. To the 12th Iowa, the 6th and 7th of April, 1880, and the 21st and 22nd of May, 1884, are bright, green spots, ever to be kept in memory, until the last survivor is under the sod. "Three cheers for the good, kind people of Manchester." Very Truly Yours,

J. E. SIMPSON.

Many other letters were read, that were retained by the comrades, who presented them; hence the names of the writers cannot be given. The committee on publication regret that a lack of space prevents the publication in full of all letters that were received as the reading of them proved one of the most interesting and enjoyable features of the occasion.

Col. Stubbs said it was unusual to read letters from persons who were here, but he wanted to read a few lines from a letter he received from comrade S. M. French, who came 130 miles on foot through the mountains of Colorado, 65 of them on snow shoes, to be here at this reunion. The audience insisted on bringing Mr. French to the front, when they gave him three cheers that threatened to raise the roof off the building.

Everybody then joined in singing "John Brown," and everybody did it with a will.

The following committees were then appointed:

Finance.—J. W. Gift, Thos. J. Lewis, Lt. H. J. Small, Dr. Jas. Barr.
Resolutions.—Harvey Smith, R. P Clarkson, D. B. Henderson.

John Steen, Wahoo, Nebraska, was elected Treasurer, *pro tem.*, and after singing, and the announcement that there would be a dress parade at five o'clock, the session was closed.

DRESS PARADE.

This was a pleasing feature of the program. Col. Jack Stibbs was attired in the regimentals he wore when he was mustered out of the army. Since which time he had grown corpulent and the coat had grown too small, but he obviated the difficulty by the aid of strings attached to the buttons. The pants, too, fit closely; in fact the *tout ensemble* of his attire was somewhat ludicrous, but amusing to all. After the manœuvres had been gone through with in a very creditable manner, Adjutant Burch read the following:

ORDERS:

Headquarters 12th Iowa Infantry, Manchester, Iowa, May 21. General order 76. To the surviving members of the 12th Iowa:—This being the first dress parade held by our regiment for nearly twenty years, I take pleasure in congratulating you on the soldierly appearance presented by you on this occasion. When our last dress parade was held we had just finished a series of campaigns, extending over a period of more than four years, during which time we took an active part in suppressing the most formidable rebellion known in the history of the world. On returning to our homes at the close of the war we were gratified to find that our friends were satisfied with our achievements, and that all considered we had done our duty well, and to-day we are happy in knowing that the people of the great State of Iowa point with pride to the record of the Twelfth Iowa Infantry, as being second to that of no regiment ever sent from the State. For nearly two decades peace has reigned within our borders, and they who were our enemies in war are now our friends, acknowledging to the world that the cause for which we fought was just and right, and that we fairly gained the right to be styled their conquerors.

Since the war closed the surviving members of our organization, have as a whole, acquitted themselves creditably in the great battle of life, and we have here to-day a body of citizens of whom any community might well be proud. Time, with his ruthless hand, has made sad inroads in our ranks, and many an anxious inquirer after some old friend is met to-day with the crushing reply, dead. We hope that there are many parades in store for our association, but our own good sense tells us that the time is not far distant when the last remaining member of our regiment must answer to the call of "lights out." Then let us hope that when our reveille is beaten in the camp of the great Hereafter, that we may meet with hearts true and loyal, as they were when we went forth to fight our country's battles. By order of

J. H. STIBBS.
Colonel Twelfth Iowa Infantry and Brevet Brigadier General.
S. R. BURCH, Adjutant.

Special order. Headquarters 12th Iowa Infantry, No. 91, Manchester Iowa, May 21, 1884, Comrades: Nearly twenty years have elapsed since we were in active service. The statute of limitation serves as a bar to punishment for minor offenses committed during the war and our friends have generously offered us a free pardon for our youthful indiscretions, therefore I wish to admonish you that it is no longer necessary for the survivors of the regiment to deny any acts committed by them in service.

Sergeant R. P. Clarkson of Company A should no longer deny that he is the identical person who commanded the regiment's foragers, and that he did more stealing of something to eat than any man in the army.

Private Dennis Conley of Company D, should no longer hesitate to tell from whom it was he took the sow belly with which to cook his veal on the occasion when he and three others ate a whole calf in a single night.

Private Tom McGowan of Company F, should frankly admit that it was he who gathered in Mrs. Malchevey's yellow-legged chickens on the night of our arrival at Cape Girardeau in the fall of 1864.

Private Geo. Annis, of Company F, should cease to denounce as false the story that after he lost his voice in the service, he on one occasion actually took a mule by the ear and whispered profane words into it, hoping thereby to make it go faster.

Major John W. Rowan, of Company D, and Private Hart Speers, of Company C, are admonished to let up on their stories about big mules in the South, as our people are too well educated to be longer gulled with their stories about having driven mules in the army that were twelve feet high and weighed over 3,000 pounds.

Chaplain Humphrey is reminded of the fact that we can if necessary produce fifty witnesses who will swear that his horse did jump eighteen feet high and kick himself on the belly with all four feet at the same time, on the occasion of his being beset with yellow jackets in the Arkansaw Swamp, and it is folly to attempt to conceal the fact longer.

Qr. Master Morisey is hereby publicly warned that unless he ceases to deny having been present at the Major's quarters on a certain occasion when seven kegs of beer were ordered for the use of eleven persons, that the full particulars of that remarkable meeting will be published.

Other admonitions of a character similar to the foregoing, will be officially promulgated unless there is a more general disposition manifested by the survivors to state correctly their experiences in service.

We earnestly trust that this order may have a salutary effect, and even hope that it may be the means of wringing a confession from the unregener-

ate wretch who stole the Colonel's blankets in the evening of December 25th, 1864, thereby compelling him to sleep with the cook, whose name was Nicholas Johnson. We have taken pains to give the cook's name in full, in order that no false impressions may be created in the minds of those not fully conversant with the facts. By order of   J. H. Stibbs,
        Colonel 12th Iowa Infantry, Brevet Brigadier General.
  S. R. Burch, Adjutant.

The reading of the orders created considerable merriment. The veterans then broke ranks and were dismissed until even.

EVENING SESSION.

The evening session opened with a tableau, representing the "Goddess of Liberty," Mrs. W. H. Goodell making an imposing goddess. Between the three scenes of the tableau Mrs. W. C. Wilson sang, "The Star Spangled Banner" in her usual admirable and finished style. The effect of the whole was very pleasing and effective.

Pres. Knee then introduced Dr. J. T. Abbott, Mayor of Manchester, who said:

  Mr. President, Ladies and Gentlemen:
    It strikes me that this matter is somewhat mixed up, that I should be asked to welcome to our town the 12th Iowa after they have been here in full possession of our town and hearts twenty-four hours. But, to carry out the program. It gives me pleasure to welcome the 12th Iowa to Manchester. Those who arrived yesterday, this morning and this noon saw the signs of that welcome on almost every post and hanging from every window, and beaming from the face of every individual, Welcome! It was a pleasure to see comrades clasp each other by the hand, see the silent tear trickle down the cheek, hear the hearty greeting. There is a fraternal feeling amongst comrades, and it is no wonder after the associations of the past.
    "A fellow feeling makes us wondrous kind."
    There are, it seems to me, feelings among individuals as they come together at this hour such as they would experience under no other circumstances.
    I noticed at the train this morning, a soldier, who, as he stepped on the platform said, "Where is our old major; I want to see our old major," and as he discovered him, he said, "By —— there he is." His language perhaps was more expressive than elegant. Tears trickled down his cheek as he met his old comrade, and clasped him by the hand.
    In behalf of the citizens of Manchester, I welcome you to our hospitality. Some of you were here four years ago, and today. There are many more together now. They propose, or at least I propose, you shall be so well entertained upon the present occasion, you will want to come again. Again, we welcome you, 12th Iowa, to the hospitalities of Manchester.

This was greeted with the heartiest applause, which upon Col. Henderson rising to respond, was renewed and when permitted to speak, he said:

COL. HENDERSON'S ADDRESS.

Are you responding to this toast or am I? (Applause.)

The first thing that strikes my mind, Mr. Mayor, is that Manchester has chosen an excellent executive head, and that he has the good sense to see the apparent absurdity of welcoming the 12th Iowa to Manchester at this late hour. (Applause) Why the old 12th has been in the possession of the hearts and homes of Manchester during the entire day. (Applause.) But you were appointed to welcome us, and you had to do it even after we had the town captured, and right royally have you extended your generous welcome. Now they ask me to act as respondent. Dunham and Comstock got you and me into this difficulty. Dunham is such a worker himself that he makes everybody else work, and Comstock is so full of music that he didn't know any better.

Welcome to us! Yes, we have had a true, genuine, hearty, ringing welcome! Welcome was on the faces that greeted us, in the voices that shouted to us, in the hands that grasped ours. The floating flags, the generous banners, the open doors and open hearts all bade us a joyous welcome.

Beautiful girls have been hanging upon our breasts, fastening the true blue with words of welcome. (The only trouble is they ought to have taken more time for that pleasant work. (Applause.)

Yes Mr. Mayor, we have been made welcome before you or I could say anything. Welcome! Is it not a sacred word? Don't it warm the heart of the old soldier when welcome *means* welcome as it has this day?

Welcome! Four years ago, comrades, we knew that. Their hearts and their doors were thrown open. Their tables were here, yea, more than that, their tears were the only jewels we wore. Manchester—Welcome! Always sweet, tender,—and why? Because the citizens of Manchester are backed by our comrades, who know how to give and take a welcome. Keep on! Keep right on! Take and pile it up! Welcome! With all our hearts. I apologize for the remarks Mr. Mayor; but you gave me the text, and as I said, I cannot help preaching. I will retire now for some one else to follow.

Col. Jack Stibbs introduced Col. W. R. Marshall of the 7th Minnesota Infantry by saying:

I have been accorded the privilege of introducing tonight, Gen'l Wm. R. Marshall of Minnesota, who after Col. Hill was killed in 1864, commanded our brigade. Those of you who were present at Nashville, will never forget General Marshall, as he appeared while leading our brigade in the charge of the second day, and how as he dashed to the front through our ranks, he called to our regiment to follow him. He is to tell us something of what he saw at Tupelo, and I am sure that no one, not a member of our regiment, could do it better.

You remember that on the morning of the 14th of July, 1864, our regiment, together with three companies of the 7th Minnesota, were assigned a position, which proved to be the most exposed of any along the line. The remaining seven companies of the 7th Minnesota, under General Marshall, were placed in our rear to act as a support in case the rebel charge proved to be too heavy for us to withstand, but when the fight opened, I found on looking round, that General Marshall had come to the front to see for himself the effect of the charge. When our muskets had become foul from much firing, he and his men took our places for a time in front and throughout the fight he was in a position to see our every movement, therefore he is well fitted to tell of the part we took in that battle. In writing to the General, asking him to meet with us on this occasion I said to him, that I knew of no one outside our regiment whom the boys would be more pleased to see than himself, and I am sure you will all endorse this statement. I now propose three cheers for our old Brigade Commander, General Marshall.

Three cheers were given with a will after which General Marshall said:

Ladies and Gentlemen, Veterans of the Twelfth:

I feel very grateful to Colonel Stibbs for the very flattering words with which he has introduced me. To many of you I do not feel a stranger. Of the Veterans of the 12th I can say upon many a weary march and hard fought battle field I have been with them, and they with me. I esteem it one of the honors that I have been favored with the command of men as brave, gallant, and truly soldierly. It would have been no common occasion that would call me from my home to leave cares that every man has. Nothing short of this, to meet old comrades whom I met amid the dire trials of war. I feel it an honor to have the opportunity of speaking to the veterans of the 12th and the patriotic citizens who have given them so royal a welcome. It reminds me of the uprising of the people at the first call of patriotism when the old and young, women and all, with one grand patriotic impulse prepared these now grown grey veterans for that service in which they did such distinguished work for the cause of liberty.

I feel as though this were no occasion for an elaborate and extended historical sketch. I hardly feel as though I ought to detain you with a narrative of that battle. It was not so important, but it was one of the hardest fought battles of the war. I have met many who testify that in all the battles of the war they had not seen a worse.

Forrest and Chalmers and other confederate commanders, who had command of their forces in Tennessee, had been remarkably successful in their inroads over that union state. General Sturgis in the month of June, had been repulsed disastrously at Guntown. Gen. Forrest had defeated Gen. Sturgis with 4,000 men. Sturgis superior forces did not avail from his lack of knowledge on that occasion. The Red River expedition forces were on their way up the Tennessee. Gen. Sherman was camping at Chattanooga. After the disaster to Sturgis, the army having been to some extent reorganized, the 12th being in the 16th corps, reinforcements were added to retrieve the disaster to the main army under Sturgis. We marched by way of Ripley and Pontotoc. Our march would have lead us southeast to Okolona. Halting one day at Pontotoc and finding the rebels strongly intrenched our march was changed in the direction of Tupelo. On the 13th we took up our march toward the railroad at Tupelo. During the day we were attacked on the flank; the 12th were there and repulsed the rebels, inflicting a severe punishment. When some two or three miles from Tupelo we were attacked very heavily, and repulsed the enemy after a short fight. Gen. Lee had at hand a very formidable army. They thought they had before them an easy victory. They were well informed on every movement of the union army. Our command was about equal—had some 12,000 men.

They assaulted us on the morning of the 14th. The 12th under command of Colonel Stibbs, held the key to our position upon that field. It was assaulted most terribly and charge after charge made by the rebel army. It was most gallantly and bravely repulsed. The 12th bore the most deadly assault unflinchingly. I need not detain you to tell you much. Gen. Smith came to Col. Stibbs and said, he supposed he knew they were going to have heavy work, and he added "Don't you let them break that part of the line." He saw it was coming—that it would be disastrous to have the line broken. That was now the center of a horseshoe. Forrest and other confederate leaders were in this battle and they meant to accept no such result as failure. Men never fought with more determination than they did there. I talked with soldiers who had been in seventeen battles, and never saw harder fighting than there. I afterwards met one of Forrest's corps who was wounded and lost a leg, and he told me that in all Forrest's experience (he was wounded the only time during the war) he never was so severely repulsed as there. The number lost in the 12th was about in proportion to the number engaged in the battle. The 7th Minnesota lost more, but our numbers were larger in the 7th than in the 12th. We were in the Indian outbreak of 1862. Our experience was considerable but we had not seen much fighting. Our regiment was a large one. While the 12th which was engaged at Shiloh, Nashville, Vicksburg, Spanish Fort, in the Red River campaign, and other places was much depleted, it probably never was engaged in any battle in which it bore a more honorable part or held a more important position, or suffered a greater loss in proportion to the men engaged, than in this. No battle is more worthily or honorably inscribed than the battle of Tupelo. In connection with this I may mention the little grey horse I rode at Spanish Fort and Tupelo, and from which I was wounded,—that old horse is still living on my farm in Minnesota, and I would have been glad to have brought him here to-day. I apprehend there are few of the old horses living to-day. I express again veterans of the 12th my appreciation of the honor of being invited to this reunion. I hope you will have many more such happy reunions spared to you yet.

Applause testified the pleasure experienced from General Marshall's address.

Colonel Stibbs preliminary to reciting the roll call then said:

I am called on to recite a little poem which is designed especially for the benefit of the old soldiers. It may be old to many of you, but I am sure you will all agree that you never heard anything which served to bring more vividly before your minds, the recollections of a night in camp after a hard days' fight than does this little story of the "Roll Call."

In order that you may appreciate it fully, I want you to go back with me twenty years to one of the little valleys in ;the South, where we bivouacked for the night after a battle, and I can think of none more appropriate than Old Town Creek, where we camped on the evening of July 15th, 1864. What a beautiful place it was. Across on the further side was the creek, which we always expected to find near camp. This side of it in the meadow our trains were parked and here in the timber we spread our blankets for the night. None of you will ever forget the funeral we had that evening. One of Co. B's men, August Leue, was shot during the forenoon, and supposing his wound was not a dangerous one, we tried to bring him away with us, but the poor fellow died in the ambulance during the afternoon. On reaching camp, a grave was prepared at the foot of a great oak tree which stood at the roadside, and just as the last rays of the setting sun came glancing up the valley, word was sent along the line and we gathered promiscuously at the grave. There was but little form or ceremony about the affair. Only a few words and a short prayer from the chaplain and then the brave fellow was wrapped in his blanket and laid away. The grave was marked by a rough board taken from a cracker box and we left it as one more landmark to show the course of the Twelfth Iowa.

Imagine yourselves in that camp now. The busy orderly has had no time during the day to call his roll, and now as the shades of night are gathering about us, he takes advantage of the first opportunity offered to ascertain the fate of those who went with him into the morning's fight. All recognize and respond promptly to his call as it is heard down the line, "Attention! Co. 'D,' fall in for roll-call."

You all remember the greasy old roll book which was always carried in his breast pocket and in which each man's war history was recorded, and now to make the picture complete, we will suppose that a corporal stands by his side holding the stump of a tallow candle and he calls the roll:

"*THE ROLL CALL.*"

BY N. G SHEPHERD.

"Corporal Green!" the Orderly cried;
  "Here!" was the answer, loud and clear,
  From the lips of the soldier who stood near—
And "Here!" was the word the next replied.

"Cyrus Drew!"—then a silence fell—
  This time no answer followed the call;
  Only his rear man had seen him fall,
Killed or wounded, he could not tell.

There they stood in the failing light,
  These men of battle, with grave, dark looks,
  As plain to be read as open books,
While slowly gathered the shades of night.

The fern on the hillside was splashed with blood,
  And down in the corn where the poppies grew
  Were redder stains than the poppies knew;
And crimson-dyed was the river's flood.

For the foe had crossed from the other side
  That day, in the face of a murderous fire
  That swept them down in its terrible ire;
And their life-blood went to color the tide.

"Herbert Kline!" At the call there came
  Two stalwart soldiers into the line,
  Bearing between them this Herbert Kline,
Wounded and bleeding, to answer his name.

"Ezra Kerr!"—and a voice answered, "Here!"
  "Hiram Kerr!"—but no man replied,
  They were brothers, these two; the sad winds sighed,
And a shudder crept through the cornfield near.

"Ephriam Deane!"—then a soldier spoke:
  "Dean carried our regiment's colors," he said;
  "Where our Ensign was shot, I left him dead.
Just after the enemy wavered and broke.

"Close to the roadside his body lies;
  I paused a moment and gave him drink;
  He murmured his mother's name, I think,
And death came with it and closed his eyes."

'Twas a victory; yes, but it cost us dear—
  For that company's roll, when called at night,
  Of a hundred men who went into the fight,
Numbered but twenty that answered, "Here!"

After a medley by the Eldora band, which stirred up the veterans greatly, Major Reed being called said:

Comrades:

You will remember many were desperately wounded, though living, and we were obliged to leave them on the field at Tupelo. Just before marching, the 12th received orders to make a detail of men to remain with the wounded and be taken prisoners. I called upon Serg. H. R. Andrews, Co. B, to remain with the detail, Henry Winterstein of Co. I, being among the number. They came begging to be excused, asking me to call for volunteers. They didn't want to be detailed to do an act of charity. To be detailed to remain and fall into Forrest's hands was asking a good deal of a soldier. They remained and entered upon the duty. I should like to have them tell us about it.

Comrade H. R. Andrews being introduced, said:

Comrades, Ladies and Gentlemen:

This was a hard place to put a soldier. It was simply an act of charity, and the idea that my officers thought it necessary to command me to do an act of charity touched me to the quick. I asked the adjutant to call for volunteers, if none offered then we would. The adjutant promised the record should show we volunteered. It was a hard trial, the men we had been fighting were the same that committed the massacre at Fort Pillow, and so shamefully treated Sturgis' wounded, simply because they were fighting side by side with negro troops; we had negro soldiers with us. Knowing the feeling of the rebels, it was like going to certain death to voluntarily fall into their hands, but there were our comrades, bleeding, dying with none to care for them, and although we might only cool their tongues with a little water and lose our lives in the attempt, we said we would stay.

To be prepared for any emergency, I went among the men of the regiment and asked contributions of confederate money. I soon had over $4,000. This was of great use to us. All our hospital supplies were stolen the first day, after this we had only what was bought with this money. I paid five dollars each for old sheets to make bandages, two dollars each for chickens to make broth, and other things in proportion. There were sixty-three of our own, and about three hundred rebel wounded at the hospital, sixteen men had been left as nurses. I was elected ward master. About 5 P. M. of the 15th, the stragglers from the rebel army came around us, abused us, threatened us, and stole every thing they could find. Their army was going to Old Town Creek after this excitement was over. On looking about for my help Winterstein and a man from the 35th Iowa whose son was among the wounded was all I had left, the rest had gone north. All that night we then were alone with nearly 400 wounded men, some of whom were dying every hour. About 9 A. M. of the 16th, Forrest came to the hospital, and learning he had some prisoners in a building near, I asked him to let me have some of them to help. I got nine. We signed a parole not to try to escape from the hospital. A few days afterwards a rebel officer came around to send the prisoners south, and wanted us. I showed him my detail and made oath. I had had a similar detail for each of the others but the stragglers had stolen them the first day. This satisfied him and he left us.

We remained at Tupelo about three weeks, then moved the wounded to Mobile. The doctor in charge had neglected to get return transportation for us, when my detail again came in play to get us back into the department of northern Mississippi. At Meridian the officer in command would neither talk to us nor look at our papers, but hurried us on to Cahaba. There the rebel officer was more considerate. I told my story, showed my detail and again made oath that I had had the details of the other men, which were stolen from me at Tupelo, and we were soon released. Thus I succeeded in getting those nine regular prisoners released as nurses. I do not think that false oath is registered against me "up there," if it is, when I get there I shall scratch it out.

Colonel Stibbs introduced Rev. F. Humphrey, Chaplain of the Twelfth Iowa, in these words:

No more pleasant duty could have been assigned me, than that of introducing to-night our Chaplain. Owing to the fact that Army Chaplains are looked on as non-combatants and because during our war there were certain ones who thought more of their personal comfort than of the wellfare of their men, they as a class, did not receive I think, the full measure of credit that was their due, but I believe I am safe in saying that no man of the 12th Iowa ever had cause to speak disparagingly of our Chaplains.

We had first Brother Eberhart, who was famous for his war speeches, and we all loved him as a father. I had expected to meet him here to-day, but learned from his son Ben who is here, that he had been dead three years or more, though Ben says his spirit is certainly with us, and I verily believe that somewhere, from out the great world beyond the river the dear old face is looking down on us to-night, and enjoying with us the pleasures of this meeting.

After Chaplain Eberhart had been compelled to resign owing to ill health, there came to us the Rev Frederick Humphrey, who proved no unworthy successor of the one who had preceded him. He accepted as his first duty, the spiritual care of our men. Yet from the outset he recognized the fact that long prayers would not stop the flow of blood from a freshly severed artery, nor carry a canteen to the lips of a dying soldier, therefore when the long roll was beaten, he reported himself on the color line ready for work. When the bugles sounded the charge on the evening of the first day's fight at Nashville, I saw him sitting on his horse by the side of Col. Hill and I know that throughout that battle he was constantly with us, and we certainly could find no one more competent than he to tell "What I saw at Nashville."

Rev. Humphrey spoke as follows:

Mr. President, and Soldiers of the Twelfth Iowa Infantry:

I thank Col. Stibbs for his cordial introduction and flattering mention of my services in the army; and I thank you fellow soldiers, for your cheers and greeting on this occasion.

In response to "*What I saw at Nashville*," I saw thrilling deeds, splendid battle lines, heroic charges and a great national victory; but the best and noblest of all I saw men, brave men, men who for the fight had hearts of iron, arms of steel and wills to strike, who struck for country and humanity, struck Treason's army of 40,000 and made that marshalled phalanx stagger and reel under the blows of the deadly onslaught and who sent its legions broken, shattered and flying back to their "own place." Twenty years have passed, and in this reunion of the 12th Iowa Infantry here to-night, I see again the faces of many of those patriot warriors dear to my heart, whom I then saw in the smoke and flame of battle, their locks now steel-mixed by hardship then endured, and some whitened by the frosts of twenty northern winters. Here is Color-Bearer Grannis who with Clark amidst hissing iron hail planted the stars and stripes in triumph on the enemy's forefront work the 15th, and on the last wall of his line the 16th of December, 1864. Here are the familiar features of Sergeant Major Burch and Major Reed, then Adjutant, and Col. Knee then acting Major, these officers ever in the thickest of the conflict in front; and here is Brevet Brigadier General John H. Stibbs, then Colonel of the 12th Iowa, Colonel and Regiment the "bravest of the brave," handling his regiment as the engineer handles his steam engine and charging the hostile lines like a thunderbolt; and here too is our last brigade commander Ex-Governor Marshall of the gallant 7th Minnesota who led the brigade to victory after the fall of the lamented Hill. Time fails to recount the names and deeds of all the heroes who fought at Nashville and on other fields of glory, many of whom are here to-night rejoicing in the joy of this happy reunion, their hearts aglow with patriotism in memory of common sufferings for the right, their manhood ennobled by self sacrifice for their country. God accepted that bloody sacrificial offering and now you are citizens of a reunited republic the freest and happiest of all history—a republic which your valor aided in rescuing from tyranny's bottomless abyss and in re-establishing on Civil Liberty's granite rock of eternal right.

Thanks to Lieut. Dunham and others for this reunion in beautiful Manchester. How striking the contrast between the blue skies, green fields, bright suns and happy homes of Manchester in these verdal May days of 1884, and the Nashville clouds, fogs, rain, sleet, snow, ice, mud and desolation of those December days of 1864. That was the agony of war, this is the bliss of peace. The contrast turns our eyes back to those dark days and battle fields of 1864. Canby is assaulting the outworks of Mobile, waiting for A. J. Smith and the 16th corps to come and help him capture the city. With 70,000 invaders in those same December days, Sherman's eagles are feeding on the vitals of the confederacy, and swooping down on Savannah in distant Georgia. With 130,000 fighters Grant's artillery is sounding the knell of the rebellion at Petersburg and Richmond in Virginia. While these great armies of the republic are fighting on those separate and remote fields, Gen. John B. Hood with 55,000 veterans crosses the Tennessee river near Florence, marches north to kindle anew the fires of treason in that state, and if possible to advance and capture the rich towns and cities and to invade the free states north of the Ohio. To meet this invasion Thomas assembles troops from every available source. Wood's 4th corps, two divisions of Schofield's 23rd corps, 5,000 of Sherman's troops under Steedman, Wilson's cavalry corps and the 16th corps of 12,000, under A. J. Smith having aided in the route of Price, is ordered from the borders of Kansas to oppose Hood's threatened invasion. On the morning of the first of December as the ambulances were bringing into the city the wounded from the bloody field of Franklin, the 16th corps landed at Nashville. The same day Hood with 40,000 men pitched his camp on the outer heights of Nashville. And here I must say that it would afford me the highest pleasure to give an account of the movements and of the heroism of the different corps, divisions, brigades and regiments of both armies for they are full of valor and thrilling incidents, but this time and place limit me to a general account with some details of our own regiment and brigade.

Hood might attempt to enter Nashville on any one of nine turnpikes and three railways which radiated from the city between high bluffs out into the country. Across these roads, valleys and over the bluffs Thomas with 60,000 men threw up earthworks extending from the Cumberland river above Nashville around the city to the river below the turn. On the outer circle of heights beyond the lines of Thomas, Hood entrenched in choice military positions admirably located to mow down assaulting columns. His position was formidable. The northern states were alarmed. The Washington authorities were anxious. They telegraphed Thomas to fight at once. Even Grant left his Virginia battle grounds and came to Washington with the purpose of going himself to Nashville. From the 8th to the 14th rain, sleet, snow and ice paralyzed military movements. Truly the country had cause for anxiety. For Hood had 40,000 fighting men and fourteen days in which to fortify and to make his army impregnable to any force that could be hurled against him. The victory that soon followed has caused the country to overlook the magnitude of the peril at that time. Look at Hood's splendid position. With such commanding military heights, with those hills and natural bastions for the defence, support and protection of an army's lines and wings, I believe that there are few men of the 12th Iowa here who could take 40,000 men, and those heights and so fortify them in fourteen days that they could hold them against the assault of three times 40,000. Hence the uncertainty of the issue of the then pending battle. Country and government had cause for alarm. But the generalship of Thomas the Von Moltke of the American armies, and the valor of the troops dispelled doubts and alarm by the victory of the 15th and 16th of December.

On the 14th the temperature moderated and the ice melted. The morning of the 15th dense fog fills the Cumberland valley, the air is electric with the approach and opening of a great battle. Near 9 o'clock the fog lifts, drifts away and reveals the hurrying and fierce preparations for battle. Steedman opens the fight on our left by a vigorous demonstration with artillery and musketry against Hood's right. A. J. Smith with the 16th corps, its right supported and covered by Wilson's cavalry, makes the main attack on Hood,s right and steadily bends it back to the east of Charlotte and Hardin Pikes. Wood's corps form an unbroken line from Smith's left to Steedman's right. Schofield's corps forms in reserve in rear of Smith. To the east of Hardin Pike, McMillen's and Hubbard's brigades of McArthur's division with Hatch's cavalry assault and carry in heroic charges two strong forts and turn their guns on their morning friends. The third brigade of the same division, emulating its companions, prepares to storm the forts on Hillsbro Pike a half mile in advance.

In giving details of our own men, I intend no disparagement of others equally brave. The third brigade forms in double lines of battle, the 12th Iowa and 7th Minnesota in the front line, the 35th Iowa and 33rd Missouri in the second line. "Forward" is the order by Col. Hill. Then the brigade moves in quick step for some distance, descends into a depression and rests, the men lying on their faces sheltered by a rising crest before them—shot and shell shriek and burst over them—up again and forward over the crest into another depression and rest again close to the bosom of mother earth; musketry and canister hiss and whistle their sharp notes close to their heads. Yonder on the crest of a hill sixty rods distant stands the fort. Col. Stibbs said to Adjutant Reed, "Tell the color-bearers to carry the colors straight to the centre of that fort." Then in the teeth of an iron tempest from musketry and artillery at close range the brigade swept like an avalanche across the intervening space and carried the fort by storm. In the moment of victory Col. Hill shot through the head, fell from his horse. The enemy hastily withdrawing his artillery to another fort across the Pike reopens on his lost fortress filling the air with clouds of shot, shell and fragments of stone. Col. Marshall and Adjutant Reed on the wings advancing to the assault soon captured the second fort with its guns, while Col. Stibbs, mounting a captured and harnessed artillery horse reformed the brigade lines and sent notice of Col. Hill's death to Col. Marshall who as ranking officer then took command of the brigade and pressed forward after the retiring enemy till night put an end to the operations of the first day's fighting. Hood's whole line had been forced back—his right wing a distance of five miles. Thomas had handled his army with consummate skill, had kept his lines united and supported and had put nearly every man into the fight. On the 16th Steedman's and Wood's troops formed Thomas' left, the cavalry and Schofield his right and Smith his centre. Hood had now seen the error of his extended lines and from hard necessity he contracted them. He placed his wings in strong positions, his left on Overton's hill and his right on Shy's hill, fortified them and connected them by a strong line of entrenchments.

The movement of Smith's 16th corps on the 15th from Harding Pike had been five miles southeast. To face Hood's centre lines the morning of the 16th, the 16th corps wheeled to the right. Adjutant Reed tells me that he afterwards learned from prisoners, that when the rebels saw the corps wheeling by brigades they said that it was the most beautiful military evolution on the battle field that they had seen during the war and that those were troops that they had not met before.

McArthur's division of the 16th corps advanced till within musket range of Hood's central line, threw up slight breastworks and continued the fight. From that time till four in the afternoon there was a sharp constant fire of musketry and artillery.

Steedman assaulted Hood's right on Overton's hill and was driven back. Schofield pressed Hood's left and Wilson's cavalry was gaining the rear of Shy's hill. The artillery redoubled its fire and shattered the entrenchments on the heights that protected Hood's left. Its thunder crash and roll I can never forget. At 4 o'clock Thomas ordered a general charge along his whole line.

Then for a half hour the sharp, short, quick reports of musketry increases in frequency and in volume—the volley swells louder and louder till it becomes one continuous, unbroken roar—the heavy, sublime roar of a mighty tempest. The brigades of McArthur's division advance *en echelon*. McMillon's up Shy's hill, Hubbard's over the level plain and Marshall's in double lines of battle, the 12th Iowa and 7th Minnesota in front down the descending ground in the face of a Louisiana battery of four twelve pound Napoleons, they carry the enemy's entire line and capture prisoners, artillery and small arms by thousands. The charge was magnificent, the victory was complete, the result was glorious. The invasion was ended. In its results at that time while our large armies were fighting in Virginia and Georgia, the battle of Nashville and the destruction of Hood's army of invasion were momentous and decisive events in terminating the war. The first invasion of the north was attempted by Lee in 1862 and defeated on slave soil at Antietam. A second attempt by Lee was made in 1863 and defeated on free soil at Gettysburg where near 200,000 men engaged in the deadly conflict. Again the invader was defeated and driven back south of the Potomac.

A third attempt under Hood to invade the north was made in 1864. The invading host hurled itself against a wall of fire at Franklin and Nashville and staggered and fell smitten and blasted and destroyed by the flaming swords of Liberty's patriot hosts and by the lightnings of insulted Heaven. The invasion of the free north could not succeed because in His moral government of the universe, God had no further use in this 19th century for an enlightened nation whose reason for existence is human slavery with its train of wickedness. Perjury and wrong may conquer for a time, but moral truth and right have their origin, support and defence in the being of God, and in His time they will surely and certainly triumph, for the mightiest power in the universe is moral power. The triumph of the confederacy would have been a reversal of the moral order of God. God fought with us, because we fought for right. Gladly do we turn from the trials of that day to the joys of this reunion. And from this reunion we look forward in faith, hope and charity to the grand reunion under our High Captain in the Paradise of God where war shall be no more and peace and joy shall reign for ever.

The "Red, White and Blue" was then sung by Miss Carrie Toogood, in a very agreeable style, the audience taking up the chorus with great animation.

Col. Stibbs then presented to the audience, Sergeant Grannis, who carried the colors of the 12th all through the war and in every engagement. He had the old battle flag of the regiment on the stage, and the boys, as he stood with it on the platform, gathered about him and sang "The Battle Cry of Freedom" with a vim that would have scared a brigade of Johnnies.

The "exercise" put down on the program as the "Grand Love Feast" followed, and was begun by Col. Jack Stibbs, who rendered a German version of "Barbara Frietchie," an humorous production that continued the wild uproar of enthusiasm.

BARBARIE FRIETCHIE—NEW VERSION.

Id was droo der streeds of Fredericksdown,
Der red-hot zun he was shine him down,

Bast der zaloons all filt mit bier,
Der rebel vellers valked on dier ear.

All day droo Fredericksdown so fast,
Horses, und guns, und zogers bast.

Der rebel flag he shone him oud so bridt.
As if, by Jinks, he got some ridt.

Vere vas der Onion flag? Der zun
He look him down not on a von.

Up jumped dot olt Miss Frietchie den,
Zo oldt by nine score year und ten.

She grabbed up der oldt flag der men haul down,
Und fasen id guick by her nidtgown.

Den she sot by der vindow ver all could see
Dere vos non vot lofe dot flag so free.

Purty soon come ridin' up Stonewall Jack,
Sittin' from der mittle of his horse's back.

Under him brow he squint him eyes;
Dot flag! dot make him great surprise.

Halt! each veller make him sdill,
Fire? was echoed from hill to hill.

Id busted der sdrings from dot nidtgown,
But Barbarie Frietchie, she was arount.

She grabbed der flag again so guick,
Und oud of der vindow her arms did sdick.

"Obuse of you would dis olt bald head,
But leave alone dot flag!" she said.

Zo zoon, zo quick as Jack could do,
He holler him out mit a face zo blue:

"Who bulls one hair out of dat bald head,
Dies awful guick, go aheadt!" he said.

Und all dot day, und all dot night,
Till efery rebel vos out of site.

Und leave behind him dot Fredericksdown,
Dot flag he vas sthicken by dot nidtgown.

Dame Barbarie Frietchie's vork is done,
She don't forever got some fun.

Bully for her! und drop a tear
For dot old voman mitoud some fear.

Col. Henderson then introduced Harvey Smith, of Waterloo, who gave a very interesting account of his recent visit, with the late excursion, to the battlefield of Shiloh in a speech of 45 minutes, after which he called attention to the relics brought from the field, which consisted of several pieces of wood from the trees on the old battle ground, cannon balls and canister shot, old rusty bayonet, flint locks, fragments of shell, rebel bullet mould, etc, etc.

After singing by the Glee Club, and the benediction by Chaplain Humphrey, the meeting adjourned.

The Following is the Roll of Members Present.

REGIMENTAL AND FIELD OFFICERS.

James Barr, Assistant Surgeon, Algona, Iowa.
W. R. Marshall, Col. 7th Minnesota, St. Paul.
F. Humphrey, Chaplain, Fairmont, Minn.
G. H. Morisey, Major, Manchester, Iowa.

S. G. Knee, Lt. Col., Colesburg, Iowa.
J. H Stibbs, Col. & B'vt Brig. Gen. Chicago.
S. D. Brodtbeck, Major, Denver, Colorado.
J. L. Geddes, Brig. Commander, Vinton, Ia.

COMPANY A.

H. A. Cramer, Nevada, Iowa.
J. H. Bowers, Eldora, Iowa.
S. R. Edgington, Eldora, Iowa.
S. Kemp, Alden, Iowa.
G. A. Cobb, Eldora, Iowa.
B. F. Ibach, " "

W. W. Moore, Manchester, Iowa.
R. P. Clarkson, Des Moines, Iowa.
E. S. Sawin, Union, Iowa.
A. E. Webb, Iowa Falls, Iowa.
T. R. Bell, Iowa Falls, Iowa.

COMPANY B.

John Dowling, French Creek, Iowa.
J. A. Decker, Lansing, Iowa.
Geo. Ibach, Preston, Minnesota.
I. B. S. Isted, Milwaukee, Wis.

A. J. Rogers, Waukon, Iowa.
H. R. Andrews, West Union, Iowa.
W. P. Winters, Bancroft, Iowa.
Mrs. Fred Lankins, Chicago, Ill.

COMPANY C.

S. C. Beck, Waverly, Iowa.
James Stewart, West Union, Iowa.
H. B. Clark, Melburn, Iowa.
J. E. Kent, Oelwein, Iowa.
W. A. Hamlin, Plymouth, Iowa.
Samuel Conner, Maxwell, Iowa.
J. W. Ballinger, Lacy, Iowa.
S. Gifford, Auburn, Iowa.
P. R. Woods, Fayette, Iowa
Hart Spears, Mill, "
D. W. Reed, Waukon, "
P. R. Ketchum, Windsor, Iowa.
G. Hazlett, Allison, "
F. W. Moine, Strawberry Point, Iowa
A. K. Ketchum, Clarion. "
G H Latimer, Mill. "

G. W. Proctor, Laurens, Iowa.
R. Z. Latimer, Fayette, Iowa.
D. E. McCall, Calver, Kansas.
R. F. Rogers, Waucoma, Iowa.
H. J. Grannis, Flag Bearer, Fayette, Iowa.
Geo. E. Comstock, Manchester, Iowa.
C. J. Martin, Tripoli, Iowa.
E. A. Kelsey, " "
Geo. L. Durno, Springville, Iowa.
D. B. Henderson, Dubuque. "
W. L. Henderson, LeRoy, Minn.
J. L. Jordan, Bull City, Kansas.
J. H. Carmichael, Volga City, Iowa
H. C. Curtis, LeMars, Iowa.
G H. Jakway, Lamont. "

COMPANY D.

Dennis Conley, Davenport, Iowa.
W. A. Trobridge, Des Moines, Iowa.
Francis Curran, Marion, Iowa.
F. Dubois, Dennison, "
Herman Elgin, Grafton, "
W. Bomgardner, Scranton, Iowa.
B. P. Zuver, Adams, Neb
Lyman M. Ayers, Cedar Rapids, Iowa.
S. R. Burch, Olathe, Kansas.
Thomas J. Lewis, Cedar Rapids, Iowa.
J. W. Rowan, Vinton, Iowa.
James Galliger, Creete, Neb.
T. L. Prescott, Chicago, Ill.
E. B. Soper, Emmettsburg, Iowa.
Wm. W. Whitnack, Waterloo, Iowa.
Edwin A. Buttolph, Cedar Rapids, Iowa
J. H. Stibbs, Chicago, Illinois.
J. N. Weaver, Algona, Iowa.

COMPANY E.

Wm. Hamilton, La Porte City, Iowa.
E. Sawyer, " "
B. E. Eberhart, " "
J. W. Rich, Vinton, Iowa.
F. Large, La Porte City, Iowa.
David Schrack, Oelwein, "
David Craighton, Geneva, Iowa.
A. W. Myers, Shell Rock, "
C. V. Surfus, Bristow, Iowa.
J. S. Margretz, Hitesville, Iowa.
J. C. Jones, Hampton, "
A. J. Biller, Waterloo, "
A. B. Perry, Lester, Iowa.
John Elwell, 92, Ex. Building, Chicago, Ill.
T. M. Early, Bristow, Iowa.
Harvey Smith, Waterloo, Iowa.

COMPANY F.

W. H. Bucknam, Dubuque, Iowa.
W. W. Mann, Runnellsburg, Nebraska.
C. Thorn, Waverly, Iowa.
W. A. Nelson, Hazelton, Iowa.
T. C. Nelson, " "
J. J Eaton, Edgewood, "
James Trumble, Manchester, Iowa.
H. W. Mackey, Maynard, "
A. L. Manning, Dunlap, "
H. J. T. Small, 452 Wood st., Chicago, Ill.
Geo. Kent, Oelwein, Iowa.
G. W. Woolridge, Carthage, D. T.
H. M. Preston, Ft. Dodge, Iowa.
Samuel Kaltenbach, Manchester, Iowa
Joshua Widger, "
Joseph S. Girton, Hazelton, Iowa.
W. H. Goodell, Manchester, "
J. F. Lee, Clay Mills, Iowa.
Ed. Correll, Greeley, "
J. W. Gift, Peoria, Ill.
John Bremner, Yankton, D. T.
Abner Dunham, Manchester, Iowa.
Hiram Kaster, " "
R. W. Terrill, " "
R. L. Weedon, Nugent, "
S. M. French, Steamboat Springs, Colorado
John F. Lee, Council Grove, Kansas.
John Otis, Manchester, Iowa.
Thomas McGowan, Independence, Iowa.

COMPANY G.

O. P. Rocksvold, Thoton, Iowa.
G. W. Kirkland, Freeport, Iowa.
J. E. Simpson, Dubuque, "
A. E. Anderson, Calmar, "
D. O. Aaker, Ridgeway, "
John Steen, Wahoo, Neb.
M. E. Meader, Hesper, Iowa.
J. B. Thompson, Spillville, Iowa.
G. A. Hauge, Albert Lea, Minn.
Henry Steen, Oakland, Neb.
Nelson J. Davis, Berrien Springs, Mich.
Warren Wall, Nashua, Iowa.
A. Carey, Castalia, Iowa.

COMPANY H.

J. Shorter, Shell Rock, Iowa.
J. A. Light, Norfolk, Neb.
A. T. Garner, Farley, Iowa.
S. C. Fishel, Iowa Falls, Iowa.
H. S. Briggs, Marens, "
J. A. Van Anda, Fremont, Neb.
J. B. Flennikcn, Norfolk, "
D. W. Moreland, Earlville, Iowa.
James Evans, Dubuque, Iowa.
Franklin M. Hamblin, Iowa Falls, Iowa.
Edward Winch, Arena, Wis.
J. W. Ward, Burlington, Iowa.
Joseph Frank, Mamont, "
J. C. Kuhns, Manning, "
Alex. McConnell, Hopkinton, Iowa.
R. W. Fishel, Greeley, Iowa.
S. M. Jackson, Lincoln, Neb.
S. B. Sloan, Greeley, Iowa.

COMPANY I.

M. D. Nagle, Dubuque, Iowa.
M. B. Goodman, Ord, Neb.
J. S. Ray, Naponee, "
Geo. Teskey, Elwood, Iowa.
J. F. Zediker, Franklin, Neb.

COMPANY K.

Henry Waldroff, La Porte City, Iowa.
Porter Willard, Hopkinton, Iowa.
P. J. Morehouse, Masonville, Iowa.
Samuel Horn, Maynard, "
Ira D. Blanchard, Edna, Minn.
W. B. Morgan, Bloomington, Neb.
H. C. Merriam, Hopkinton, Iowa.
J. B. Morgan, Davenport, "
N. H. Baldwin, Ade, Kansas.
C. E. Merriam, Hopkinton, Iowa.

MEMBERS OF OTHER REGIMENTS.

J. A. Snyder, Co. D, 49th Wis. Manchester, Ia
J. M. Garrison, Co. B, 23d " "
G. O. Harrison, Co. K, 31st " "
Jas. Stewart, Co. G, 27th Wis., " "
H. B. Sisson, Co. K, 27th " Delaware, Ia
W. S. Jones, Co. K, 2d Wis. Cav. Manchester
J. D. Biggs, Co. G, 46th Wis. Inf. "
H. C. Eddy, Co. G, 22nd " " Winthrop Ia
C. H. Johnson, Co. D, 4th Wis. Cav. Del., Ia
R. B. Lynn, Co. D, 11th Wis. Inf. Manchester
P. A. Peterson, Co. H, 27th Wis. Inf. "
Wm. Wasson, 3rd Ind. Battery, Delaware, Ia
Eugene Hall, Co. F, 9th Iowa, Earlville, "
Jas. T. Fowler, Co. G, 9th Iowa, Greeley, "
Geo. Redhead, Co. C, 13th " Postville, Ia
Anthony Swindle, Co. I, 4th " Barryville, "
John Malven, Co. H, 5th Iowa, Greeley, Ia.
W. H. Golder, Co. B, 8th Ia., Manchester Ia
L. D. Rogers, Co. G, " Winthrop, Ia.
Jas. Shadle, Co. G, 22nd Ia., Manchester, Ia
R. M. Marvin, Co. H, 31st Ia., "
J. C. Butts, { Co. F, 37th Ia. { Dyersville, Ia.
           { War of 1812. }
H. C. Fox, Co. F, 46th Ia., Manchester, "
G. A. Odell, " " Greeley, Iowa.
S. C. Hursh, Co. G, 8th Ia., Cav. Waverly, Ia
R. G. Crawford, Co. L, 8th Ia., Cav. Hop'ton
J. H. Evans, Co. B, 4th Ia. Cav., Dyersville,
W. F. Delaney, Co. B, 4th Ia., Cav., Hazel G
Chas. Delaney, " " "
Cyrus Stoner, " " Earlville, Ia
D. K. Fox, Co. K, 4th Ia., Cav., Manchester
J. H. Peters, Lt. Col. 4th Ia. " "
B. F. Skinner, Co. G, 1st " "
S. W. Trenchard, Co. G, 1st Ia. Cav. "
G. H. Dubois, " "
A. Miller, Co. L, 1st Ia. Cav. Manchester, Ia
E. D. Smith, Co. G, 6th Ia. Cav. Forestville,
A. B. Durfey, " " " Edgewood.
C. J. Bailey, Co. " " " Manchester
Chas. Sydow, " D, 27th Iowa, Conover, Ia
I. S. Hanna, " E, " " Nugent, Ia
A. D. Hubbell, Co. F, 27th Ia., Edgewood, Ia
W. J. Millett, Co. F, 27th Ia., Manchester, Ia
R. B. Wilson, " " " "
C. O. Torrey, " " " "
Rollin Lewis, " " " "
A. J. Brown, " " " "
B. W. Kenyon, " " " Tower Hill, Ia
F. D. Smith, Co. C, 11th Vt. Masonville, Ia.
A. H. Blake, Co. F, 9th " Manchester, Ia
Henry Stiles, Co. A, 2nd " Masonville, "
S. A. Paige, Co. G, 10th " "
Wm. Williams, Co. B, 26th Mass. Manchester
S. E. Meserve, Co. K, 16th Mass., "
B. W. Jewell, Co. F, 1st Mass., "
J. C. Hadley, Sappers & Miners, 3rd Md., "
H. P. Chapman, Co. B, 16th N. H. Manch'st'r
D. G. Meader, Co. D, 6th Maine, Eldora, Ia
Allen Meader, Co. E, 26th " "
C. W. Rollins, Co. A, 22d " Delaware, Ia
Michael Duffey, Co. A, 1st Nev. Cav. Nugent
A. Knowles, Co. K, 7th Mo. Cav. Winthrop, Ia
T. J. Doane, Co. D, 70 Ind., Des Moines, Ia
D. A. Bender, " A, 120 Ind., Manchester, "
A. A. Hamlin, Co. A, 97th Ind., "
J. P. Wilson, Co. A, 103 Pa., Manchester, "
L. Smith, Co. I, 111th Pa., Cav., Forestville,
Amos Lightfoot, Co.E, 11th Pa., Cav. Man'str
Henry Hunt, Co. E, 10th Mich., Manchester
C. H. Babcock, Co F, 33d O., Masonville, Ia
A. G. Thompson, Co. D, 61st O., Manchester
G. O. Vincent, Co. E, 1st O., Bat. "
W. H. Ayers, Co. F, 103d " Delaware
John Dubois, Serg. Maj. 21st Ia., Manchester
P. S. Crosby, Co. H, 21st Iowa, "
N. S. Preston, " " Delaware.
L. S. Stone, Co. K, " " Delhi.
C. Husted, co. F, 21st Iowa, Manchester.
J. F. Merry, " K, " "
C. P. Donton, Co. K, " "
Newton Green, Co. K, 21st Ia., Hazel Green
C. Scott, Co. H, " Manchester.
Daniel H. Gregg, Co. H, 51st Ill. "
A. J. Collinge, Co. A, 39th Ill., "
C. H. Osborn, Co. K, 46th Ill., Brush Creek
Joseph Mitch, " F, 12th " Manchester, Ia
W. S. Martin, " F, 54th " "
G. M. Hickok, " I, 1st Ill. Ld. Art., "
Arthur Spare, " I, 38th Ill., "
J. R. Boardman, Co. K, 28th Ill. ,Forestville
Luther Rich, Co. E, 52nd Ill., Manchester
J. L. Chapel, " B, 74th " "
G. A. Day, Col. 91st Ill., Manchester, Iowa
C. H. Westbrook, Co. B, 8th Ill. Cav. "
A. C. Carter, Co. E, 146th Ill. Inf. Manches'tr
James McFarland, Co. H, 57th Ill. Inf, "
Henry Woodring, " C, 55th Ill. Inf. Wav'ly
Fred Glitsher, Co. I, 105th Ill. Inf.. Manch'er
Jas. O. Mayes, " I, 11th Ill. Cav., "
O. S. Fowler, Co. K, 13th Ill. Lamont
C. B. Eaton, Band' 11th Ill. Manchester, Ia
A. O. Moore, Co. F, 95th Ill., Manchester, Ia
J. W. Parker, Co. B, 46th Ill., "
A. J. Patch, Adj. 7th Minn., Dubuque, Iowa
W. R. Marshall, Col. 7th Minn., St. Paul
W. H. More, Co. H, 16th Iowa, Dubuque, Ia
C. H. Mattox, Co. H, 16th Ia., Manchester
A. J. Abbott, " C, 2nd Ia. Cav. "
Jas. Ireland, " I, " " "
John Wood, " " " "
J. B. Thompson, Co. I, " "
H. Percival, Co. C, 7th N. Y. Manchester, Ia
A. F. Loomis, Co. K, 125th N. Y. Golden, Ia
C. L. Rundle, Co. B, 94th " Earlville, Ia
Dr. C.C. Bradley, H.S., 136th N.Y. Manch'er
E. D. Allen, Co. I, 5th N. Y. Art., Earlville
J. B. Satterlee, Co. B, 44th N. Y. Manch'str
E. F Sias, Co. B, 186th N. Y. Manchester
Geo. Commerford, Co. A, 48th N. Y. "
A. J. Simpson, co. F, 13th N. Y. "
Peter Broadway, Co. A, 64th N. Y. "
J. S. L. Scott, Co. F, 121st " "
J. T. Abbott, Co. I, 185th " "
E. S. Cowles, Co. G, 7th Ia. Cav., Campton

MEXICAN WAR.

M. S. Allen, A, Mich., Sabula, Iowa.
H. D. Wood, 4th Co. Ill. Cav. Manchester
S. R. Edgington, A, 3rd Ohio, Eldora
John carr, U. S. Frigate, Savannah, Man'str

Thursday Morning.

The first business of the hour was the reports of committees.

Capt. Gift of the committee on finance reported the condition of the treasury.

Comrade Dunham moved that a committee of three be appointed by the chair who should confer with the reporter as to what matter should be prepared for publication in the proceedings of this convention. Carried and the chair appointed: Col. Jack Stibbs, G. E. Comstock and Lieut. J. E. Simpson.

Col. Stibbs here presented Mr. Jas. C. Butts of Dyersville as an old soldier of the war of 1812; that he also served in our late war of '61. He is 89 years old, wears no glasses, reads anything, was in the 37th Iowa, the grey-beards. Iowa is the only State that furnished those soldiers; boys, this is just what we are coming to; the last member of the 12th will stand up sometime.

The boys gave the old soldier three rousing cheers.

Comrade Smith of the committee on resolutions then reported the following which were adopted.

Resolved, That it is with a profound sense of appreciation that we desire to tender to the citizens of Manchester our sincere thanks for their warm and hearty reception of the members of the 12th Iowa Volunteers.

Resolved, That we will ever remember with delight this our second reunion at the beautiful city of Manchester, and as we go to our several homes, we will carry with us a happy recollection of the grand welcome and pleasant reception accorded us.

Resolved, That we as veterans and members of the 12th Iowa Volunteers, hereby extend to the officers and members of W. A. Morse Post, No. 190, G. A. R., of Manchester, our warmest thanks for their hearty, soldierly greeting and good cheer.

Resolved, That it is with a genuine sense of their hospitality to us that we wish them all long and prosperous lives, and that sometime in the near future it may be ours to return the compliment so cheerfully awarded us.

Resolved, That we extend to the members of the First Regimental Band, of Eldora, our warmest thanks for the excellent music rendered by them which has contributed so materially to the pleasure and success of this reunion.

Resolved, That we respectfully request the Congress of the United States to pass a law pensioning all disabled union soldiers who are incapacitated from providing for themselves and families, without limitation as to date of disability.

Resolved, That the 12th Iowa Infantry, in reunion assembled, emphatically protest against the removal of Gen. J. L. Geddes as Military Instructor of the Iowa Agricultural College, and request his reappointment by the board of trustees, at the earliest practicable moment.

Resolved, That our Senators and Representatives in Congress are hereby requested to use their best endeavors to amend the bill now pending Congress to pension prisoners of war, so as to include all who were confined in rebel prisons fifty days or over. Many members of the 8th, 12th and 14th Iowa, the 58th Illinois, and other Iowa, Ohio, Illinois and Missouri regiments, who were confined in rebel prisons fifty-five days at Cahaba, Tuscaloosa, and Montgomery, Ala., and Macon, Georgia, are now physical wrecks, from starvation and ill-treatment, in aforesaid prisons, but are unable to prove such facts to the satisfaction of the Pension Department. Therefore, we ask the change above mentioned, in order that justice may be done them, and sadly needed relief secured.

Resolved, That we extend to Col. W. R. Marshall, Gen. J. L. Geddes, two of our old brigade commanders, who have added so much to the real pleasure of our reunion, and to the other invited guests present, our sincere heartfelt thanks for the kindly interest they continue to take in our regimental organization. We hail them with pleasure, and shall always be pleased to meet them, and hereby extend to them a cordial invitation to attend our next and all following reunions.

Resolved, That the warmest thanks of every member of the 12th Iowa Regiment are hereby extended, together with our soldierly greeting, to the officers and members of Company C, I. N. G., of Manchester, who have so signally contributed as escort, to the pleasure and success of this reunion, and that we shall ever remember with feelings of pride, their soldierly appearance and acts.

Resolved, By the 12th Iowa Reunion Association that the Eldora Silver Cornet Band, of Eldora, Iowa, be and hereby are made honorary members of our association.

The chair appointed on motion the following as committee to nominate officers:

H. C. Curtis, Co. C.
L. M. Ayers, Co. D.
S. R. Edgington, Co. A.
J. E. Simpson, Co. G.
S. G. Knee, Co. H.

It was moved by Comrade Simpson that the secretary address a letter to Col. Woods, expressing our regret at his absence, thanks for his kindly remembrance and wishes for his welfare, with the warmest greetings of his old comrades in arms.

The chair announced a committee of ladies from the citizens who desired to give the boys as hearty a welcome as they got from Shiloh. You will be compelled to retreat and let your foes take possession of the field.

The distribution of tickets to the banquet being in order, while they were waiting, Col. Stibbs said:

WHO IS HELENE VIOLET B?

This is a question that has been bothering the minds of many of us for the past four years, and I am glad to be able to say that I am fully prepared to answer it. I am free to confess that when I first learned of this mysterious personage I was a good deal surprised, and rather sorry too, to think that a sure enough woman had served for three long years with the 12th Iowa, and I never found her out. So when we began our preparations for this reunion I determined if possible to find Miss Helene and bring her with me, and I am happy to say, that she is now present an interested listener to my story, but she is not here in the form that many expected to see, and her appearance, age, height, complexion and style of her bangs can only be guessed at.

It is a well established fact that there are persons in the world, who honestly believe that they have a dual existence, and that there dwells within them the spirit of another who accompanies them through life. Whether such a thing can be or not we have no time now to discuss, but the fact that the belief exists cannot be questioned.

Such a person served in the 12th Iowa. He was a dutiful soldier and to-day carries the scars of wounds received while manfully facing the enemy. He told me this story in confidence and therefore I am not at liberty to give names, but I can assure you that he is honest in his belief and that he has not sought to impose on us an improbable story. He claims that from his infancy he has carried with him the spirit of his sister, Helene Violet, that he is in constant communication with her, and she acts as his guide and counsellor. Warns him of impending dangers, and predicts events that are to occur. When she chooses to speak for herself, he is compelled to act as her amanuensis, and thus it happened that she made herself known to the regiment. She heard read the proceedings of our last reunion and her womanly nature was aroused and her sympathies excited by hearing of the part taken by little Florence Dunham the daughter of our worthy secretary, and she at once determined to write to her. When the soldier who represents her found what a storm of comment and curiosity her letter had provoked, he sought to conceal his connection with the matter, as he recognized that which is a reality to him, would be ridiculed by many, and as I have given you the story in full, I ask that you will make no further effort to learn the name of the soldier who represents Helene Violet B.

The reading of this little episode was warmly applauded, after which all repaired to the banquet room where an elegant repast had been prepared by the ladies of Manchester. Chaplain Humphrey having asked a blessing upon the generous fare, the boys fell to with a will and amply showed their ability to clear all before them, then in good order each reteated to make room for the reserve force which followed until all had enjoyed the feast.

AFTERNOON SESSION.

The committee on nomination of officers reported as follows:

President—Col. S. R. Edgington, Eldora,
Vice President—Major D. W. Reed, Waukon.
Secretary—Lt. A. Dunham, Manchester.
Treasurer—Major G. S. Morisey, Manchester.
Directors—Lt. S. G. Knee, Co. H, Colesburg; Gen. J. H. Stibbs, Co. D. Chicago; Sergt. R. P. Clarkson, Co. A, DesMoines; Q. M. S. John Stein, Co. G Wahoo, Neb.; Ben Eberhardt, Co. E, LaPorte.

After considerable urging and coaxing to induce Lt. Dunham to accept the position of secretary, the report of the committee was adopted, and Col. Edgington conducted to the chair. The Colonel being introduced said:

Comrades of the 12th: To the veterans I return my sincere thanks for this high compliment. I have considered myself too modest to appear before you; but it has been your pleasure to elect me your president for the ensuing year. I assure you that if I fail in aught, it will be in judgment, The heart will be right. I thank you again. I will attempt to do my duty. History says that the 12th was under fire 112 days, and I commanded the regiment more than fifty of those. What ever I may have been wanting in that, I shall be wanting in this. Again I thank you.

One of the most interesting scenes of the reunion was enacted at this time. The boys called forward "Sukey" Jackson, the old drummer, S. M. French, former fife major, and H. J. Grannis the color-bearer. The long roll, reveille, tattoo were successively called for and beaten, and at their close three rousing cheers were given for each, with three for the old flag which was held by its bearer.

The Chair then presented Capt. John F. Merry, the Gen. Western Passenger Agent of the Illinois Central, who had done much toward making the reunion a success. Capt. Merry said he felt as though he needed no introduction to this audience. There was scarcely a face that was not familiar to him. He had done what he could to ensure the success of the reunion, and was quite sure that his efforts had caused him more pleasure than they could have done anybody else. He spoke of recent visits to Vicksburg, and said a visit there would afford some idea of the grand character of a government that, while providing so liberally for the living soldiers, cared so tenderly for the dead. The Captain's short speech was warmly applauded.

The Eldora Band then played some beautiful selections, when the chairman reported that he had just been handed a receipted bill for the entertainment of the band, while here. He said this was something wholly unexpected, and was but another evidence of the warm-hearted liberality of the people of Manchester toward the 12th regiment. He assured them their kindness would never be forgotten.

The president announced as the special feature of the afternoon the toasts which were laid down in the exercises. Owing to the absence of expected guests, several changes were made; but all present highly enjoyed the following:

Hon H. C. Curtis responded to the following:

"THE FAMOUS CHARGE OF THE ENTIRE ARMY, May 22. 1863, at Vicksburg, Miss.

Mr. President, Comrades and Fellow Citizens: —

I confess to you that I am taken a little by surprise at this time, by being called upon to respond to the sentiment, "The charge of the whole army at Vicksburg, May 22, 1863." Had I been called upon to relate some amusing anecdote of the war in which we struggled together for four long, long years, to conquer the brazen enemies of our country, I would not have wondered, but to recount the deeds and the heroic valor of our noble army, on that memorable day, and place on the canvass of your imagination, those awful scenes, that we all will remember as long as we live, I say tongue cannot describe, nor pen picture, that awful struggle. The imagination staggers back, lost and powerless as we attempt to cast our eye back for twenty years on the scenes, awful yet grand and inspiring, on that bloody field.

Let us go back for moment to Grand Gulf from which point that Iowa Army of Grant started for the interior of Mississippi, the ultimate object being the capture of that strongest of all strong points, which the rebels held at that time, throughout the confederacy. We look over the history of France, and see the dashing effective campaigns of Napoleon, and wonder at the audacity of the plans of the great French General, surrounded as he was by his famous and trusty marshals.

And yet, my dear comrades, no general of ancient or modern times, went into a great campaign against such fearful odds, and discouraging circumstances as did our great general in the Vicksburg campaign. We marched rapidly to Jackson and Clinton, thus being placed exactly between two hostile armies, one of which was greater in number, and the other nearly as large as ours; but you know better than I can tell you the fighting qualities of that devoted 40,000 of which you were a part, that astonished the civilized world, with victory upon victory from the day we left Grand Gulf till Vicksburg was ours with its vast munitions of war, and thirty-eight thousand rebel prisoners.

The 15th army corps under W. T. Sherman, in which was the 12th Iowa, arriving at Jackson, after a rapid heavy march in the rain, about 4 p. m., struck I. E. Johnson's rebel army a stunning blow, destroying Jackson with vast confederate supplies while the rebels were on the full run, completely demoralized. Our army was quickly concentrated at Champions' Hill, and thrown, like an avalanche of dynamite, against the Vicksburg army under Gen. Pemberton, who quickly withdrew his fragments of torn divisions and brigades within the intrenchments of Vicksburg.

Come with me now for a moment, to our victorious army as it lay with its mighty arm stretching for six miles right and left around the doomed city. Every man that wore the blue in that devoted army, measured up to the full standard of a fighting veteran; in our rear, on Black River, was Johnson, stealthily, yet cautiously approaching us, bringing relief to the besieged garrison of Vicksburg, retreat for us was annihilation to our army; advance for our army on to the enemies works meant the loss of one brave boy in every third of our army.

During the evening of May 21, '63, prior to that famous charge, and while the army lay quiet on their arms, orders were passed around among the various commands that at the hour of one o'clock p. m., of the 22d, the enemies' lines and forts were to be stormed by a grand charge of the whole army. Little did our comrades who now sleep in heroes' graves in that field, dream that night, of the awful slaughter that awaited them, or that another twenty-four hours from that time, the whole northwest of our country would be a scene of wide spread grief and mourning. The hour came for the dreadful work, and 40,000 men plunged forward into the smoke and carnage of battle, into the jaws of death; 500 cannon belched forth their iron missiles of death. The clay clad hills of Vicksburg shook and trembled in the mighty storm of battle. The yellow earth-works of the enemy, assumed a grey appearance, as the storm of musketry, shot, shell and hand grenade rent the air, and are hurled full in the faces of our stealthily yet rapidly advancing divisions. Down steep hill sides, through brush felled and sharpened timber, now our flags were at a stand still, and now advancing on the enemy. Here and there in places our lines were on the enemies' works, and flags flying defiantly in the face of the enemy, until night threw her sombre curtains on the scene, did the work of death go on. Never did brave men fight with such desperation for the flag they love. Never did brave men strike harder for union and liberty, and yet that grand bleeding army of veterans was not discouraged, but persistently held their ground gained at such expense of heroic blood until July 4th, following, when the whole army of the confederate Gen'l. Pemberton, unconditionally surrendered, With the fall of Vicksburg, the fall of the confederacy began. The monster reptile, (Secession) was cut in two never to be united; but I have spoken too long, and will say no more.

Col. Henderson then spoke on the sentiment:

THE OPPOSING ARMIES OF 1861-65—Their relations then, and now.

At the very opening of my remarks I want to say that I hope every soldier present, though not a member of the 12th regiment, will feel, as we do, that he is a part of this reunion. (cheers) That's right comrades, I knew I was voicing the sentiment of every member of the old Twelfth. I have had my heart warmed by the greeting of these old soldiers, and I wanted to thank the good people of Manchester for not discriminating against any soldier, and for their most generous welcome to us all.

I have had some other little incidents to warm my heart: There is a man in this audience who is a real type of the true warm hearted people of this county, I shall tell you what he did; but I will not mention his name, as he requested that nothing be said of his action. He came quietly up to our treasurer and asked if he might be permitted to contribute a little to this reunion. He don't live in Manchester. He put his hand in his pocket, as he had done many a time before for the soldiers and their families, and pulled out, not cents or dimes but an X, and handed it to the treasurer. I have known him for twenty years. He was always among the first to volunteer aid to the soldiers. That is the kind of a man Charles Crocker is, (I mention no names) a representative man, one whose big heart always thrilled in sympathy with the soldiers. (applause.)

One other little incident which might seem to be personal. There are those here who are the only living representatives of those who wore the blue. For the first time we have had with us a young man, whose father we called Tom. Before the battle of Shiloh he conducted a prayer meeting in the camp of the 12th. I have been warmed to see the boy. This is his first vacation. After his father's death the little fellow took the farm and worked winter and summer. He made my heart swell with emotion when he said he never had so enjoyed himself before. Pardon me if I do not speak his name. He is like Crocker, a type of many others. I have seen the grayheaded old men of your city—and mothers and sisters, drawn here by that influence which brings children to a common hearthstone.

Now as to the opposing armies, their relations then and now. I do not need to speak of those old victories, and the armies then. I am quite sure the soldiers cannot be found who better understand those armies than the soldiers before us. You all know them well; they were great armies, both of them. History will never place two such armies face to face again. Americans all—from many states, but every one of the common family. He who says the confederate army was not brave will be laughed at by those living, and in history.

One army—that which we aided, was impelled, was elevated by patriotism. The other was blinded by sectionalism, and infuriated by passion. We knew then and now that we were right; let that never be forgotten by Americans. They know *now* that they were *then* wrong. I am glad to-day, let us accept the situation as it is.

More than this I do not think this the proper time or occasion to say. A few words as to those two armies now. Here I will not express the sentiments of all but I believe it is the honest sentiment of most of you.

Take the Union army now. How do you feel about the past? Is there bitterness about the past, boys? There *is* no bitterness in the heart of the union soldier towards the armies they opposed. We cannot afford it—cannot afford to keep up bitter feelings. My good friends, these boys fought to unite and keep united this country. We laid down many of our comrades to unite it, and we cannot afford to divide it. We fought to make it the flag of America, and we want every man to be a brother that comes under its folds. Is there bitterness in your hearts now? Let us be just, my comrades and fellow citizens. From '61 to '65 there was bitterness in many hearts. I will not venture to tell the story. You all remember those times. No one need blush for Donalson. After the capture of the rebels, one of our men, shot through the head and unable to speak, attempted to cross a low place near the landing. Standing on the other side, was a long row of captured rebels. Our boy got stuck in the mud, beside the rebel line. He extended his hand for help. One near him said harshly, "Not by a damn sight." That was one side. Right beside the wounded comrade stood another, who sprang to his aid and helped him with both hands, then said to the other, "you are a pretty soldier." The true qualities of a man will stand out any where, and every-where as Burns has said:

"A man's a man for a' that."

My friends, bitterness should no longer be in our hearts. I am seated now in a legislative body, made up largely of confederate soldiers and officers. I forget these men ever stood in battle array against me. They speak to me as kindly as I could wish. We treat each other as friends, not enemies. I do not know a member of the 12th, who would clinch his hand when another open palm is stretched out to meet it. That is the feeling of the old 12th. Now, my friends, I am not making these utterances from any mere sentiment. I have said that you were right when you fought. Forget it not. You fought to save your country. When principle demands a soldier, whether in peace or war, be a soldier. When friendship is asked, be a friend. Your motto was "Crush the opposing army." We are now comrades. Let the two armies be lost in the heart of the whole American people. These are my sentiments and yours. My good friends, there are many of you who will have no marble over your last resting place to speak for you; but the records will show you were the volunteers of the 12th. You would not exchange that little record of honor for the fame of the Cæsars, or the blood bought statue of Napoleon.

We are getting old. We have given the spring time of our life to our country. The breath of autumn comes to fan our cheeks. Soon these little flakes silvering our hair will be turned to snow. Not far distant, our reunion will be held in the tents of the immortal. Living thus let us cultivate those qualities as true citizens of America that will show we are great and generous soldiers; not for fame or blood; but that we were volunteers when called upon to save our country, and to defend it to the last.

The boys then sang "My Country, 'Tis of Thee," while standing upon their feet. Judge J. N. Weaver, of Algona responded to the toast:

"GREENBACKS AND GRAYBACKS—The first we could not keep with us, the last were hard to drive away."

As to Greenbacks, I do not know why your committee should have selected me to respond. I am incapable of handling the subject. I never *have* handled it very much. It may be that because of the intimate connection of the greenback question and a distinguished namesake of mine, you have thought appropriate to put down as a part of the program, Weaver on Greenbacks. But as distance lends enchantment to the view, I may be allowed to draw upon my imagination, so far as to say that greenbacks are a *good thing*, and actually, if I had my *choice* today, as between greenbacks and graybacks, I would take greenbacks.

I suppose graybacks are good in their place; but I have never been able in my limited investigation of the natural order and eternal fitness of things to find any plan to assign to the graybacks; I say I have not. The grayback himself seems to assume that providence has marked out a field of artillery for him, and no granger more assiduously tickles the soil of his field than did our late comrade, the grayback. There is after all I find but little of the imaginative when we come to think of the grayback, except so far as actual experience may seem to bring on the fear of impending doom. Regarding the grayback himself, "tell me not in mournful numbers life is but an empty dream." With him, "life is real; life is earnest." He is all business, and he "always carries his point;" unless he gets settled upon one of the boys, in which case he imposes that necessity upon the other fellow. Now I do not wish to offend the sensitiveness of any of the ladies present by the use of any improper or unbecoming language; but this subject warms up as I advance, and I must say, that if there is any living thing or creature of similar size on earth, that is a more absorbing subject, more insinuating, sneaking, puney, "cussed" and devilish without a rival; anything that can inflict more mortal agony and excruciating pain to the square inch, and generate a *tendency* toward profanity, more than the original grayback, I have failed to discover him, and he has failed to wake me up. Screens will defeat the designs of the mere mosquitoe. The grayback, as we had him, was every where present in spite of all obstacles. My toast says the graybacks "were hard to drive away." It may be that the committee in using the term graybacks had in mind the other kind, "the Johnnies." If that is true, I am sorry, for my interpretation has engendered a good deal of *bad blood*. But which ever was intended, that part of the toast is literally true, for they were both hard to drive away, and the 12th Iowa, many times found to their sorrow, that the Johnny grayback was hard to drive away, and many of them found themselves in the position of Paddy, in the old story, when he caught the tartar. Paddy said, "I have caught a tartar." The captain said, "bring him along then." Paddy said, "He won't come." "Then *you* come," said the captain. "Be-jabers he won't let me," said Paddy. Right there, I might add, we did have the advantage of the other grayback, for we *could* bring him with us.

I would like to say of the greenbacks, that they *were* hard to get, between pay days especially, and we couldn't keep them. They, unlike the graybacks would get away from us. We couldn't keep them. They went a good ways with us, if it didn't take long for them to go. They were then the promises written down and printed of the government we had sworn to preserve and defend, to pay us, sometime. We thought Uncle Sam's note was as good as his bond and they were, and proved so to be. If the Union had been destroyed, these greenbacks would have been worthless and valueless. If it was saved, the promise would be redeemed. The time did come when we caught the johnny tartar, and though we did not always drive him away, we did finally bring him with us, and he is here to stay. The Union was restored, the pledge of the government was made good.

In response to the sixth toast:

"**THE CITIZENS OF MANCHESTER.**--Their Hospitality and Loyalty—Making their Homes our Homes, and our Reunion a Success."

R. P. Clarkson said:

Friends and Comrades: The good people of Manchester have established themselves deeply and firmly in the hearts of every member of the Twelfth Iowa Infantry. We had such a pleasant meeting, were so kindly greeted, and so hospitably entertained at our first reunion, four years ago, that the mere mention or thought of Manchester has carried us back in imagination to the happy homes of those who so kindly greeted us and who labored so patriotically and sympathetically to make our reunion a success. Time, in its never halting rounds has brought us back to our second quadrennial, and again have the people of this beautiful city captured our hearts by their unexcelled kindness and continued great interest in all matters concerning the 12th Iowa.

Altoona, Pa., Wooster, Ohio, and Manchester, Iowa, are three places that will always live in the hearts and memories of the members of the 12th Iowa, but the first shall be last, and the last shall be first with us always. The kind treatment received from the good people of Altoona and Wooster, as we were returning from rebel prison hells, forms two of the bright links in our war history, but the unexcelled hospitality and heartfelt sympathy we have received from Manchester friends, throughout the war and at our reunions, have endeared them to us forever, and the reunions made so grandly successful mainly by their patriotic labors and cheering presence, will always be remembered as the happiest events in our regimental history.

Manchester has truly become a Mecca, to which the surviving members of the Twelfth Iowa make quadrennial pilgrimages to renew our patriotism, greet our comrades, "fight our battles o'er again," and enjoy the boundless hospitality of the cleanest and one of the most beautiful cities in Iowa. This city was the home of Company F, one of the very best companies in the Twelfth Iowa. They were a grand company of gallant men, and it gives us great pleasure to see so many of them still reported present, fit for duty and full of rations. Sadly we miss those who have joined the phantom army, and now wait the coming of the reserves in the world beyond; but nothing gives us greater pleasure than the heartfelt embraces and vigorous salutations we receive from those who still "hold the fort" at Manchester.

I voice the unanimous sentiment of the 12th Iowa in saying that the members of Company F, members of W. A. Morse Post, and all the good people of Manchester are enshrined in our hearts and memories for their boundless hospitality, happy homes, pretty ladies, bright babies and brave men. No other city has so strong a hold upon our affections and friendship. Our hearts are yours, our time is at your service, and our homes are always open to receive you. May health, happiness, and prosperity always remain with you. Think of us when you are happy and be happy all the time.

Gen. Stibbs corrected an error of Comrade Clarkson, concerning the names of places where the returning prisoners were entertained and subsequently wrote a letter on the subject which is here given in full:

CHICAGO, May 23, 1884.

R. P. Clarkson, Esq., Des Moines, Iowa:

DEAR DICK.—During the proceedings at the reunion, yesterday, I made an attempt to correct a statement of yours; but as you know, the subject proved too difficult for me to handle, and I was unable to finish my story. I regretted it sincerely, for there was a bit of inside history in what I tried to tell, that would have been new and interesting to many of our comrades.

When I was released from prison in 1862, being a captain at that time, I together with other officers of our regiment, was sent to Washington, D. C., and there furloughed for thirty days. We knew nothing, then, of the whereabouts of our enlisted men, and I went at once to visit my parents, at Wooster, Ohio. Within an hour after I reached home, I received a telegram from my brother Joe, telling me our boys were at Annapolis. Md., and asking me to come and take him from the hospital. I started on the first train, and found the poor fellow a living skeleton, debilitated beyond recognition. He died afterwards, from the effects of his imprisonment, and I am sure my comrades will approve my assertion, that no braver, better boy than he, ever shouldered a musket in defence of his country.

When I reached Annapolis, I found the boys so anxious to get nearer home, that I determined to take them west, and when It was announced that I had secured an order to take them all to St. Louis, Mo., there was a joyful shout over the good news, and every sick man who had strength enough to stand on his feet, came forth from the hospital, all insisting that they were sound as a dollar, and fully able to stand the journey west. But I soon found that I had as many as seventy-five men in the party who were too weak to sit up in their seats, and in no condition to subsist on the army rations provided.

At Baltimore we were given a supper at the Soldier's Rest, and a good, big lunch for each man to carry with him.

The next evening, in response to my telegram, the ladies of Altoona, Pa., came to our train and provided us with a bountiful supper, and the following morning I sent, from a station on the line of the P. & F. W. R. R., a telegram insubstance as follows:

"*To the President of the Ladies' Soldiers' Aid Society, Wooster, Ohio.*

I am coming on No. 4, in charge of 250 returned prisoners, many of whom are sick. Can you give us a breakfast?"

I did not know into whose hands this telegram might fall; but I felt sure it would be some one who would recognize my name, and that it would at least result in the furnishing of a breakfast for my sick men. We were but two hours' run from Wooster, when my message was sent, and there was but little time for preparation; therefore we were surprised beyond measure at the reception given by the generous people. As I learned afterwards, the merchants had closed their stores. workmen left their shops, and every body had rushed home pell mell, to gather up whatever could be found in the way of eatables.

It seemed as though the entire city had turned out to meet us. Gallons upon gallons of good, hot coffee were furnished us, together with an abundant supply of delicacies of every description and a store of substantials that lasted us throughout the remainder of our journey.

The conductor came to me and said he was already four hours late, and could not hold his train to have our men fed; but that he would carry forward and return a committee of citizens, who might be detailed for that purpose. Accordingly, fifty or more ladies and gentlemen boarded our train with their supplies, and distributed them as we journeyed on, and at Mansfield they were transferred to the east bound train and returned. This fact, no doubt, accounts for your confusion of names, and caused you to remember Mansfield as the place where we were entertained.

While at Wooster my time was fully occupied; I had but a moment in which to greet my parents, and deliver to them poor, sick Joe, and assure them that as soon as my boys were disposed of, I would be back home for a short visit, and as we were about to start I called upon a friend and said to him: "Explain to me George, the secret of this demonstration. I did not even hope for more than a breakfast for my sick men, and am amazed at this outpouring of my old friends and acquaintances. Tell me who is the President of your Aid Society?"

The answer which came to me as the train moved off, was "Your mother."

I do not wonder that the old veterans of the 12th Iowa remember with love and gratitude, the generous people at Wooster, Ohio; and I think that after reading this you will not wonder that the recollection of this affair, caused my feelings to get the better of me for a moment, when I tried to correct you yesterday. Very truly your friend,
J. H. STIBBS.

In response to the toast:

IOWA AT SHILOH.—Heroes of the Hornet's Nest and Hells Hollow. They held their line of battle throughout the day on the memorable sixth of April, 1862; they sacrificed themselves, but saved the remainder of Grant's army from capture or entire destruction.

Col. Geddes spoke as follows:

Comrades and Fellow Citizens:—In responding to the toast, "Iowa at Shiloh," I feel that this large audience is not critical, and I know it is sympathetic, I consequently feel satisfied that it will treat any shortcomings on my part with tenderness and consideration.

The name Shiloh always conveys to my mind and my heart the vibrations of a melancholy cadence which the lapse of twenty-two years had failed to eflace or even lessen: and as long as historic literature exists, it will ever be enshrouded with the glamour of heroic romance. The desperate and determined resistance made by a few isolated Iowa regiments for ten consecutive hours, to the persistent onslaught of the flower of the southern army, in self-sacrifice and patriotic devotion equals in pathos, the classic record of Spartan valor in the Pass of Thermopylæ.

In no pitched battle of the war was Iowa so largely represented as there. Eight thousand five hundred of her sons faced the foe in the cause of freedom and the Union on that bloody field, 1,200 were killed and wounded and 1,100 consigned to the tortures of a long imprisonment in the dungeons of the South. It brought desolation to thousands of happy Iowa homes, and although time may allay, it can never wholly remove the sad wounds young Iowa received there.

I do not wish in this presence to criticize the action of those great generals whom we all revere, and whose subsequent gallantry and distinguished leadership placed the martial prowess and glory of our country on the highest pinnacle of fame. But there were others on that field, that day, the 6th of April, 1862, who are entitled, as American citizens, to justice. Yes, my comrades, to exact justice. No matter how subordinate your position in that grand old army, you are entitled to all. Yes, to all that the truth will reveal, and nothing more, and you desire nothing more.

The sad result of the first day's fight at Shiloh, was caused by a combination of mistakes, arising, as the facts reveal, from culpable negligence or unfortunate inexperience; I will be charitable enough to base my opinion on the latter hypothesis. My comrades, it was a mistake, a fatal mistake, and in violation of the plainest precepts of war and stategy, to form a camp of instruction between an unfordable and unbridged river and a brave, determined and vigilant foe in close proximity, a foe alert and eagle-eyed; commanded by their most distinguished general, with subordinates of equal genius. How quickly advantage was taken of this mistake, you, my comrades, well know. Citizen soldiers, raw and green as the beautiful prairies they so lately left, were dumped promiscuously on that river landing. Thousands were led to the slaughter that morning, who had never before handled a musket or bit a cartridge. It was a mistake, my comrades, when in case of reverse, our retreat was effectually cut off by a deep, rolling river, not to have some sort of defense behind which our inexperienced men could shelter themselves in case of attack. You know, also, that there was nothing of the kind on that day. No, your own manly breasts were the defense that met the enemy in the grand swoop of their might on that defenseless camp on the banks of the Tennessee. Like a rock in a mighty, rushing torrent, you Iowa boys stood, as it rushed against, around, but never over you.

It was a mistake that the division of brave men at Crump's Landing, who with eager ears, listened to the booming of guns, at Shiloh, and knew that their comrades were hard pressed, were not brought there before the sun had set on the bloody field. Yes, my comrades, it was a mistake that cost young Iowa, her best young blood, that the division which had lain there for three weeks previous, with ample force of cavalry, should have been ignorant of the nearest road to Shiloh, six miles distant.

The time allotted me on this occasion will not permit me to discuss any more of the causes which led to the disastrous results of that battle. But this I will say, that the Second, Seventh, Eight, Twelfth and Fourteenth Iowa Regiments of Infantry, at the distance of a mile and a half from the landing, fought and held their position there from eight o'clock until near sundown; held in successful check the right center of the rebel army, and at half past five o'clock in the evening were still fighting a division of the enemy, while its main body was within four hundred yards of the Union army at the landing, with its retreat completely cut off by the river.

Now, my comrades, in view of these facts—and these are not all the facts —had that division of the rebel army not been held at bay by these regiments —and that it was held so, I need only to refer you to Gen. Ruggles' report for corroboration—had it been free to act with the rest of the rebel army at the landing before it was too dark, what I ask you would have been the fate of the crowded thousands huddled together there?

Why has there been so much said and written about the battle of Shiloh? Why, after the lapse of nearly a quarter of a century, does this interest still exist, and as the years roll by, only increase in intensity of pathos? Why is it, my comrades of "Iowa's Shiloh Brigade," you cling so fondly to the memories of that fight, and with a tenacity that throws into the shade, as it were, the many other great battles of the war in which you gallantly participated? I ask you, men of the old Twelfth Iowa, you who were always esteemed by the

Eighth Iowa boys as brothers, and whose associations together were always pleasant, why is it, when you look upon your emblazoned and tattered banner now suspended in Iowa's capitol, your eyes linger long and mournfully on that name "Shiloh?" The names of Fort Henry, Fort Donelson, Vicksburg, Jackson, Nashville, Tupelo, where you "plucked victory from the arms of defeat," and many other names are there that signal your gallant deeds? Why is it then, I ask that among all these fields that record your devotion to your country's cause you visit and would far rather visit that timber-crested hill on the banks of the Tennessee? And permit me to inquire why it is that a suffering public—as comrade, Col. Shaw, is pleased to call them — are not yet tired of what has been said and written about that memorable battle? My comrades, all these questions may be answered and are answered in a sentence containing only five words; but pregnant with immeasurable meaning—"justice has not been done." But "truth crushed to earth will rise again," and the truth about Shiloh is rising, and will yet be written, so to speak, on the canopy of high heaven, to be seen and read of all men, for all time. Justice will yet be done and after the lapse of twenty-two years is being done. Done to you my comrades, who meet here today, and done to those of our number who fell at Shiloh, and today are resting in unknown graves near that Southern river's bank.

And you, my comrades, who lately visited that sacred spot on the field of Shiloh, did you not that day, as you marched over the old familiar roads, or stooped over the graves of your departed comrades, with the crowding memories of the great past, picturing themselves on your minds, feel something of that strange, weird influence that impressed the heart of the old French soldier, who returning after long and varied services in the German wars, battle scarred, worn and weary, came on his homeward march to the banks of the Rhine which separated him from his home in beloved France? As the old soldier gazed upon his native land, his heart was filled with emotions of tenderness, as his memory recalled two loved comrades who, in the glow of youthful ardor and strength of early manhood, thirty years before, had crossed that same stream with him, and whose bones had for many years been bleaching on the battle fields of Germany. He was ferried across the river, and as his feet touched his native soil, he took the price of three fares from his purse, and said:

> Take, O boatman, thrice thy fee;
> Take, I give it willingly,
> For, invisible to thee,
> Spirits twain have crossed with me.

Did you not, my comrades, on that visit, feel conscious, like the old French soldier, of an unseen presence there, of some dear comrade of the infinite. He has gone home; has fought his last battle. His discharge has come, and his remains lie buried in an unknown grave. Yes, there were those in that grand old army bound to us by the closest ties of friendship, and there is no friendship so strong and abiding as that found in mutual suffering and danger. No union of hearts more sacred than that which is united by the heart's best blood.

> By communion of the banner,
> Battle scarred and glorious banner,
> By baptism of the banner,
> Brothers of one church are we.

"Stripes and Stars, Answer to Bonnie Blue Flag," a song composed by Col. Geddes, while in prison at Selma, Alabama, was then sung.

STRIPES AND STARS.

Answer to "Bonnie Blue Flag."

Music arranged by Henry Werner.

We're fighting for our Union. We're fighting for our trust.
  We're fighting for that happy land where sleeps our fathers' dust;
It cannot be dissevered, tho' it cost us bloody wars.
  We can not give up the land where floats the Stripes and Stars!

CHORUS.

Hurrah! Hurrah! for equal rights hurrah!
  Hurrah for the brave old flag that bears the Stripes and Stars.

We treated you as brothers until you drew the sword,
  With impious hand, at Sumpter; you cut the silver cord,
So now you hear our bugles. We come, the sons of Mars;
  We'll rally round the brave old flag, that bears the Stripes and Stars.

We do not want your cotton; we care not for your slaves;
  But rather than divide this land; we'll fill your Southern graves.
With Lincoln for our chieftain, we'll wear our country's scars.
  We'll rally round that brave old flag that bears the Stripes and Stars.

The chairman announced a ten minutes speech, on "A Soldier's Attachment," by Capt. J. F. Zediker, of Co. I, 12th Iowa. He said he had come 600 miles to attend this reunion, and it seemed as though ten minutes was a short time in which to say what he would like to say to his old comrades. The attachment of old soldiers for one another, was formed on the field, in the camp and on the march, enduring privations under the summer heats and the chill blasts of winter. Made strong by hunger and thirst, and hardships endured together; by danger and suffering; by the loss of comrades left on the battle field; by sufferings in Southern prisons. Is it a wonder that our attachment should be so strong? A few more years, and those who meet at these gatherings will be feeble and few. But let us all, while any of us are left, instill into the minds of our children, the same sentiments of loyalty and patriotism that actuated us.

The Hon. J. W. Shannon, of Dakota, then read the following poem, suggested by Charlie Larson's last words to Col. Henderson — "It's all Right."

"IT IS ALL RIGHT."

Rings voice from Orient, old, and far,
    From region battle riven:
"Sweet words earth's lovliest daughters are,
    But *deeds* are sons of Heaven!"

O men of mighty deeds! that shine
    With flaming Shiloh's glow,
We come with words, and measur'd line,
    The sweetest that we know,—

As loving "daughters," proud and true,
    To greet the "sons" whose deeds
Have wrought the nation all anew,—
    Anew have writ its creed.

We love you well! and yet how tame
    The warmth we know and feel,
Beside these friendships knit in flame
    'Midst clang of clashing steel!

We know our alien place at feast,
    Where vet'rans fire-tried,
'Neath beaming skies of golden peace,
    Live o'er with martial pride,—

The days when terror's trumpet-blast,
    Announced the lurid morn!
Whose noon, with sulph'rous cloud o'ercast;
    But presaged deadlier storm!—

Where shoulders touched, 'midst mad'ning roar,
    To close in freedom's name,
The gap where murd'rous cannon poured
    It's all-devouring flame!

Dark days when faltering line was torn,
    And bravest heart stood still;
The joy of vict'ry's sunburst born;
    The cheers that shook the hills!

The days of tramp and blist'ring toil,
    The nights of dreams of home,
On blanket wet, and crimson soil;
    Where mangled comrade moaned.

Of famine gaunt, in loathsome cage,
    Where vicious vermine tooth
Tattooed the scars of fiendish rage
    On flesh of noblest youth!

Ah! who that wrought at home may dare
    To touch the sandal's hem,
Of least who fought, and wear these scars
    Of scourge and prison den.

How soon must fade the record, rare,
    Of highest civil fame,
Beside the burning line that bears
    Dear CHARLEY LARSON'S name!

"It is all right, if Right prevail!"
  He said. So spake ye all
Who faced, with him, hell's flaming hail,
  To conquer or to fall.

It is all right with them who died.
  God knows when work is done,
Alike in peace and battle-tide,
  Where service is his own,

"It is all right, my heroes true!"
  The State proclaims today;
Though blooming boys of gallant blue,
  Fast join Time's Iron-Grays,—

Nor Time nor age can luster dim
  Of names your children bear;
Proud glory's page is writ for him,
  Whose father's name is there.

"It is all right! It is all right!"
  Aspiring masses call,
Throughout the world; "in Freedom's fight
  Ye conquered for us all!"

Oh God! who lead'st the march of man,
  Thy soldiers, sure, are these,
Who fearless fought!—who faithful stand
  In all the ways of peace.

If loving song and hon'ring cheers
  May yield the brave delight;
Let all Thy Heavens echo here,
  "*It is, dear boys, all right!*"

Then was sung, by request of a veteran, "We shall Meet but We shall Miss Him."

Capt. Simpson said he had a message for the 12th Iowa. Last Sunday he met Mrs. Nelson Burdick, of Decorah, who had five sons in the army, two in the 12th Iowa.—Corporal Nelson Burdick, her youngest son, who died from disease contracted in rebel prisons, and Lieutenant A. A. Burdick, killed at Tupelo, belonging to the 12th Iowa. She wanted Mr. Simpson to say to the boys that she loved every member of the old 12th, and that she should ever remember them with the tenderest regard

On motion of Col. Henderson, Comrade Simpson was instructed to return to Mrs. Burdick the assurance of the undiminished regard and affection of the 12th Iowa.

Col. Henderson offered the following resolutions:

Resolved,—That the thanks of the members of this reunion are due and are hereby gratefully tendered to Mrs. Kate M. B. Wiison, Mrs. A. J. Brown, Miss Carrie C. Toogood; Messrs. A. D. Brown, J. F. Merry, W. H. Norris, Geo. W. Dunham, R. G. Kennedy and Ben. Keller, for the music so wisely chosen, and beautifully rendered on this occasion.

Resolved,—That no special thanks are herein given to Comrade Comstock's inspiring efforts with the other singers, for the reason that he enjoys it so thoroughly himself, that his efforts carry their own compensation with them.

Resolved,—That we hereby tender a vote of thanks to Mrs. W. A. Morse, for use of piano, and Messrs. Torrey & Jones for organ.

Comrade Marvin stated that the number of veterans of the 12th present was 166, and a total of 300 altogether. The 12th was divided as follows: Co. A, 10; B, 7; C, 32; D, 18; E, 16; F, 28; G, 13; H, 18; I, 5; K, 10, and were enlisted from New Hampshire, Vermont, Massachusetts, New York, Pennsylvania, Indiana, Ohio, Missouri, Illinois, Wisconsin, Nevada, Iowa, Michigan. Four Mexican veterans were present and an 1812 veteran.

The ladies, for the excellent dinner furnished, were complimented by cheers and a tiger. Business ensued and it was requested that the names of the wives and daughters and mothers of comrades be sent to the secretary.

Lieut. J. B. Morgan, Lieutenant Small and Major Reed were appointed a committee to prepare a history of the Union Brigade.

Col. Henderson introduced Major Brodtbeck, who made a few happy remarks.

An incident, worthy of record, is that Mrs. E. C. Lankins came from Denver, Colorado, to attend the reunion. Mrs. Lankins was with the regiment two years. She is the widow of F. F. Lankins, Co. B, 12th Iowa, who died at Denver, Col., two years ago.

The order of exercises was then pronounced to be that each must "tell a story, sing a song or stand on his head." Col. Stibbs being called out said he wished to tell a little incident about the major. It was in January, 1862, the boys concluded to present the major with a testimony of regard. They purchased a sword and appointed the orderly sergeants, headed by Morrissey to call upon the major and present it. They made their call in the evening, passed over the sword, and it broke the old major all up. At last he said, "Boys I will ask you to haf some peer;" and calling his colored servant, he told him to go out and get some. "How much will you have," asked the servant. There were eleven of the party; the major looked them all over, sized up the crowd, and as he took their measure and his own, he said, "About seven kegs." Yes, seven kegs for eleven men.

Ben. Eberhart was called forward to exhibit himself and his "glass eye." He took up another incident of the major, when the 12th were in camp at Dubuque. Our old major liked to pick up the greenies. One day he was riding along, and met a young fellow, who awkwardly saluted him. Straightening himself up, the major frowned on him and said: "How dare you salute me?" The fellow said "I wasn't salutin' you; I was salutin' your horse." The major passed on.

H. P. Andrews said: At one time on the march, Major Vanduzee was in command. You know he was very strict. There were strict rules against foraging. This was in Missouri. While marching one day, just a few rods over a fence, Ketchum, (he was corporal) saw a chicken running along. It was too tempting. Handing his gun to a comrade, he sprang over the fence and gave chase. The major saw him and in his squeaky voice, he yelled out, "Corporal — Ketchum." Ketchum looked over his shoulder, and said, "Yes, sir," but continued the race and brought in his prize. Night came and we went into camp. Every one wondered what the major would do. We expected Ketchum would be reduced to the ranks. A summons soon came by an orderly for Ketchum to appear at headquarters. He entered the tent where the major was writing; saluted him, and at length said, "I am here, sir." "What did you mean by disobeying my order, sir?" "I did not disobey sir," said the corporal. "What do you mean?" sternly demanded the superior. "Well," said Ketchum, "you said Corporal, Ketch 'em, and I did Ketch ,em." "Go to your tent, sir," was the order, and that was all we ever heard of it.

Comrade S. R. Burch said on call for a story: Chaplains Humphrey and Bagg were riding out one day. Humphrey, you know, was a great fellow to ask questions. Well these two came to a farm house where they found an old lady, whose negative answer to every question was surprising. She "did not know." At last Humphrey asked her if "there were any Episcopalians round there. Said she didn't know. Our two chaplains turned about and were riding through the gate when the old lady called out, "Say mister, I saw the skun of one hangin' on our neighbor's shed door one day."

Chaplain Humphrey here remarked he had always noticed the name of the animal depended somewhat upon the complexion of the man who told the story.

Many other reminiscences were related by those present when the lateness of the hour forbade further indulgence.

The president announced that the next reunion of the 12th would take place in 1888, the time and place to be announced hereafter.

The meeting adjourned, pronounced to be the most enjoyable reunion ever held in Iowa or anywhere else. The vets were escorted to the train, which pulled out in the midst of a fierce storm of rain, thunder, lightning and rousing cheers from those left behind.

held, lost and won in the terrible struggle of twenty-two years ago. The most of the heavy timber on the field in 1862 has been cut off, but many of the battle-scarred trees are still standing, and with the help of these and the numerous ridges and gulleys we were enabled to fully and finally settle many long disputed points. Representatives of the Iowa Brigade composed of the Second, Seventh, Twelfth and Fourteenth Iowa, headed by Col. Shaw of the Fourteenth Iowa, mounted, Gen. Tuttle and the rest of us on foot, easily found our first line of battle, followed the line of retreat to the last desperate struggle of the Eight, Twelfth and Fourteenth Iowa, and part of Gen. Prentiss' division, where less than 4,000 men fought the three rebel divisions, of Polk, Hardee and Breckenridge, for half an hour, when our ammunition was exhausted and we made the last effort to escape in a deadly, pell mell rush across "Hell's Hollow" and were finally forced to surrender in the Third Iowa's tents just at sunset, the last heavy fighting in the first day's contest. This little band by their stubbornness in being the last to give way on the entire line, had saved the balance of the army from capture, but had sacrificed themselves. How well they fought the thousands of "unknown" graves in the National Cemetery on the bluff sadly and strongly tell. Their line of retreat, the crossing of "Hell's Hollow" and the point of capture were more thickly strewn with dead bodies than any other place in the fearful struggle. Not one-half of the number of any of the three Iowa regiments named, who so grandly marched forth to battle on that beautiful Sabbath morning, were ever reported for duty again. Their bodies rest in this beautiful cemetery and in the accursed soil around the rebel prison pens in nearly every Southern State east of the Mississippi river, and in home cemeteries, where they were laid by loving hands, from disease contracted in the rebel prison hells. But enough of sadness before remembrance drives the pencil to bitterness.

The day has been well spent by the veterans in hunting mementoes of the battle and they have generally secured a goodly number, consisting of bullets picked up from the ground or chopped out of trees, broken gun barrels, bayonets, cannon balls, shells, grape and cannister shot, etc. The whole field has been thoroughly searched and it is safe to say that thousands of pounds of relics will be carried away as highly prized treasures, to be handed down to future generations as mementoes of the hardest fought battle in the West and one of the most stubbornly contested great battles of the war.

SECOND DAY.

This had been a busy day with the excursionists in huting for relics and in exploring every portion of the old camp and battle ground. The search for relics has been highly successful, and everybody is well laden with shot and shell, canes, bullets of all kinds, bayonets, rusty gun barrels, gun caps, etc. The trees in the deadliest portion of the battle field were literally filled with bullets, and the most of the trees that were here during the battle are dead, many of them standing monuments of the deadly fray, but about an equal number have fallen to the ground and are rotting away. The excursionists have chopped into the old trees on every side, and successfully angled for the old bullets, the point of entrance into the trees being still plainly marked by a scar on the bark. In the live trees the bullets were generally found about four inches from the bark, and the rings of the growth of these trees show plainly the twenty-two years' growth since the battle. Axes and hatchets were in demand to cut the bullets out of the trees, and there are many blistered hands aboard the two boats tonight. The bullets in the dead trees were more easily secured, being readily picked out with knives or punched out with canes or sticks. The natives report that nearly all the larger trees that stood on the ground during the battle were killed by the infantry balls shot into them, and nearly every tree struck squarely by cannon shot or shells near the ground died in a few years after the battle. Many of these now cumber the ground but the larger number have been worked up into rails or utilized for firewood. The old stumps were good land marks—for nearly every soldier present had stood behind a long to be remembered tree when the bullets were flying thick and fast during some portion of the day, and those trees and stumps have been of great service in tracing out the different positions held during the day. The writer sat upon the stump of a tree today, behind which "Long Ace Wickham," of Co. A, 12th Iowa, stood sideways and loaded and fired his musket in the last desperate stand made by the 12th Iowa before their wild, but deadly rush across "Hell's Hollow," near the close of the first day's battle. While standing behind this tree Mr. Wickham was wounded and one ball made four holes in him and forty-seven holes in his clothing, but he continued to load and fire as long as the rest of us. We secured a piece of the old stump and if his eyes happen to see this letter, and he will send his present address to the Iowa State Register, Des Moines, Iowa, a splinter of the stump will be sent to him. The plowed fields yielded a vast number of musket balls and cannister shot, and all of them were quite thoroughly searched. Some of the large sixty-four pound gunboat shells, thrown by the gunboats during the night after the first day's battle were picked up near the line of battle first held by the division of Gen. Prentiss, nearly two miles from the river, and pieces of these shells were picked up on nearly all portions of the battle field occupied by the left wing of the Union army. Tonight the excursionists are well laden with relics, and it is estimated that they have picked up during the past two days 5,000 to 10,000 pounds of bullets, balls, shells, muskets, &c., and now have them on the boats. They are valuable relics, and will be handed down carefully to the children of coming generations as mementoes of the terrible battle of Shiloh.

MONDAY

Morning there was a general agreement for an Iowa reunion at the 'Hornets' Nest," the name given by the rebels to the deadly position held all day by Tuttle's brigade, and a portion of Prentiss' division. During the forenoon about one hundred men and some of the ladies visited this noted point, the majority of the men present having been in the brigade of Gen. Tuttle and the division of Gen. Prentiss. The position held by Tuttle's brigade was fully traced out, nearly every man present being able to find nearly the exact spot where he stood in ranks or laid upon the ground during the long hours of the first day's fight, previous to the retreat late in the day. The Hornet's Nest and Hell's Hollow received more attention, and were more enquired for than any other points on the battle-field, and the trees at and between these two points were chopped into all over to secure bullets. A majority of the crowd lingered about these points nearly all day, securing the necessary information to enable them to help straighten up some of the fallacies of this famous but poorly reported battle. Gen. Tuttle and Col. Shaw were thorough and searching in their examination of the field, and they hope to secure a re-survey of the battle-field by the government in order that history may be corrected, and full justice done the brave men who fought all over this portion of the battle-field, and made it famous with the best blood in their commands. There was general regret that Gen. Prentiss was not present in order that the line in front of his position could have been more fully traced out, but the different locations of Tuttle's brigade have been fully and positively identified, and coming time cannot erase them from the memory of those present to-day who were in the fight twenty-two years ago.

Shiloh church and spring were also two prominent places visited. The old church was burned down some years ago, but the water flows from the spring over a little pebbly bottomed channel in the same volume that it did during the war, and the appearance of its surroundings has not materially changed. A new church has been built on the site of the old church by the so-called "Southern Methodists," while a quarter of a mile nearer the landing a new church has been built by the so-called "Northern Methodists." This is not a well posted theological pencil, therefore it cannot tell why these churches are designated as above, but we are informed that they were so designated during and before the war.

The rebels present, during the two days have been few in number. The programme had been arranged for the citizens to give us a basket dinner at the Shiloh spring Sunday and they had agreed to do so, but the old prejudices overcame their good intentions and so they abandoned the basket dinner before we arrived. A majority of the people we saw on the battle-field were those who were Unionists during the war, many of them in the Union service, free it from that false claim, "as a nation of the free," and to place our flag on the very pinacle of fame, we must see too that our flag floats on the very pinacle of fame, we must see, too, that our flag floats from every school house in the land and that the rising generation inherits and imbibes that spirit of loyalty and patriotism which you learned during a four years of horrible and cruel war.

In no way can this be done better than by continuing these reunions. Count me in for any duty assigned and rest assured that next time I will be there. Report me this time "Absent, but accounted for."

As ever your Comrade from 1861 to 1865,
ABNER DUNHAM,
Company F, 12th Iowa Infantry.

Maquketa, Aug. 8th, 1894.
J. E. Simpson:—

Dear Sir: I will say that I. K. Crane received your circular inviting him to the reunion of the 12th at Sioux City, and he bids me say to you that it will be impossible for him to be there in the body as he can almost hear the last roll call. He has been sick all summer, and never will be able to march to the music of fife or drum in earth life more. But he will be with the boys in spirit, and if he should be freed from his suffering body will be with you in his spiritual body, free from all pain and suffering. He is suffering from dropsy, brought on through rheumatism and heart trouble. His limbs have swollen until they are bursting, and he can hardly get his breath. Still he is cheerful and wishes the old 12th a good time, and if he has answered the last roll call on earth will be at your camp fire with you. He bids me say this for him, and I close hoping and wishing you a happy time. I subscribe myself, Your friend, his wife,
MRS. I. K. CRANE.

He says read to the boys if you wish.

Dunkerton, October 5th, 1894.
Dear Secretary and Comrade:—

It is with deep regret that I sit down to inform you that I shall not be able to be with you and the boys at the reunion, and I regret it the more because I fear it will be the last opportunity I shall have of meeting with comrades. I am now nearly 72 years old. If I drew a pension as most of the boys do, I believe I should go, but times are too hard with me. Give my love to all of the boys of the noble old 12th Iowa. God bless you all. May you all have a good time together. Truly yours,
A. B. PERRY,
Company E, 12th Iowa.

No. 11 Edward Street, Chicago, Ill., Sept. 23, 1894.
Dear Comrade Simpson:—

Comrade Weaver's circular per your favor came duly to hand. If I can go to Sioux City I will, but I am getting old and shaky now, and hesitate to

ADDENDA.

We here append several interesting letters, &c., which did not properly belong with the proceedings of the reunion, but which the comrades of the twelfth will find will greatly enhance the work.

The first is by Comrade R. P. Clarkson, written to the *Iowa State Register*, giving an account of his visit to the field of Shiloh.

ON THE TENNESSEE.

APRIL 4, 1884.

At Paducah, Ky., we were kindly greeted by the mayor, city clerk, and many others, who seemed pleased to meet so many Northern people. Col. Huston, the city clerk, was a confederate, but he gallantly admits that the lost cause was fairly and honorably beaten,'and he is now an active, fighting Republican. He says that all that is necessary to enable the Republicans to carry Kentucky this fall, is for them to "make a school-house and cross roads campaign like you do in Iowa." Paducah is an active business city, and has been very much improved since the war.

We passed Fort Henry, 71 miles from Paducah, Friday night. This is the point where many of us heard the first "loud barking of the dogs of war" when they meant business. Here the gallant Commodore Foote demolished a strongly built and heavily armed fort, in less than half an hour, with his gunboat fleet, and thus opened the river to the army of the Tennessee. The heavy works on the banks of the river have been leveled down, but the fortifications on the bluff are still intact, and looked grim and defiant in the distance.

The people who gathered at the banks at every landing seemed to be of the free and easy class, too tired to work and too proud to beg. They were generally pleased to see so many "Yanks" in one crowd again and conversed freely in regard to war times and their present political and social condition. There are no school houses on the hills—not one seen by us between Paducah and Shiloh—but there are still houses in many valleys. The rich send their children to Paducah and other cities to be educated, but the only education that the children of the poor get is given them by their parents, who are almost universally illiterate. There is a splendid country along the Tennessee, and intelligence and Yankee energy would soon develop it into one of the most prosperous regions of the United States. It has splendid and boundless timber and limestone, and the soil, with proper cultivation would produce immense crops of corn, cotton, peanuts, etc. The climate is mild, as indicated by the fact that steamers run on the river the whole year. Nature has been lavishly bountiful in favors bestowed, but the inhabitants do not realize the possibilities within their grasp.

Conversation with men at the landings developed the fact that three-fourths of the men along the Tennessee were rebels. They talk very freely about war times and boast of the victories they won, but generally close up the conversation with "you 'uns were too much for we 'uns in the long run." There is still considerable hard feeling between Confederates and Unionists, as the people here call the two classes, but the strong general fear of Uncle Sam's wrath, generally keeps the rebel element in subjection. At Shipp's landing, Mr. Wm. Hawks stated that he was in a rebel regiment in the rebel center at Ft. Donnelson, and that on the evening before the fort surrendered, his brigade was double quicked to the rebel right to dislodge Tuttle, but we couldn't do it and were captured and taken to Chicago, where we were kept in prison for seven months, when we were exchanged and sent to Vicksburg, where Tuttle and bad luck again overtook us, and knowing on the night of the 3d of July that Vicksburg would be surrendered on the 4th, I slipped out between the pickets of both armies, went to La Grange, Tenn., took the oath of allegiance and remained at home during the remainder of the war." This was interesting history to the men of our party who fought under Tuttle.

Mrs. M. M. Sheldon, of Perryville, Tenn., had three sons in the Union army and two in the Confederate. Four of them were in the battle of Shiloh, two in each army. One of the sons died during the war, but four returned, and they fight their battles o'er and o'er every time they meet. They differ on politics, prohibition and all other issues, and the mother says that it seems impossible for them to agree on anything.

Mr. A. O. Montague, a farmer eight miles from Clifton, Tenn., is on the boat returning home from Paducah. He was a member of the Forty-eighth Confederate Tennessee, and talks quite intelligently on political matters. In his locality, the Democrats and Republicans are about equal in numbers, and there are no greenbackers. The state of Tennessee has a law prohibiting the sale of all intoxicating liquors within four miles of unincorporated towns, where schools are taught ten months in the year.

About midnight, April 5th, our boats tied up at Crump's Landing for the night. This landing was made famous by the inactivity of Gen. Lew Wallace during the battle of Shiloh. Wallace had 8,000 men, and was ordered by Gen. Grant to march to Shiloh by the Purdy road, on the morning of April 6. He waited until the roar of the battle roused him from his lethargy and then slowly marched out on the Purdy road. Nearing the battle field where his men were so badly needed, and which was only five miles from his camp, he countermarched to Crump's Landing, and then came up the river road. In this way he did not reach Shiloh until the first day's battle was over. If he had obeyed Grant's orders he would have reached the battle field before noon of the first day's battle, and the Purdy road would have brought him to the rear of the rebel army, which would have enabled our forces to defeat the Confederates before noon and to capture a large portion of their army. Wallace was not punished for disobeyance of orders, but he should have been shot. He has no friends in the army of the Tennessee.

Leaving Crump's Landing at 8:15 this morning, with the boats lashed together, we rounded the point below Shiloh, at 8:30; when the stars and stripes at the cemetery first floated in view, the veterans gave three cheers for the old flag, both steamers whistled vigorously and long. And the Audubon band struck up "Home Again." Reaching the old landing at 8:45 we filed off in two rows like the regulars" and marched up the hill to the cemetery, the band playing "Marching through Georgia." At the cemetery gate every head was uncovered and the procession marched bareheaded around the bluff and back to the stand which was decorated with evergreens and draped with the stars and stripes.

The exercises at the cemetery were short but impressive. The day was pleasant, warm and spring like and every veteran seemed to fully realize that he was standing among the graves of thousands of comrades who laid down their lives in defense of a country that has not proved worthy of the great sacrifice.

After the exercises were concluded there was a general hand shaking with about one hundred citizens of the vicinity and a number from Corinth, after which there was a hurried inspection of the cemetery and, then a rush of the veterans for the old camp.

The whole battle field was soon a scene of active tracing out of old camps and positions in attle, and as representatives of nearly every regiment in the fight are on the ground, there was little difficulty in tracing out the positions trust myself in a prohibition state any more. I hear the G. A. R. had a good time in Pittsburg. I didnt go—couldn't get a vacation this year from the Chicago P. O., but one week from today lets me out. My resignation here takes effect October 1st. But times are hard and money close, and I may not be able to attend at Sioux City. I have been an employe in this P. O. since 1885, and am worn out. I shall go to the Soldiers' Home---not, perhaps, to Marshalltown, but to Dayton, Ohio. I may be entitled at Marshalltown, but I was for years at the Dayton home, am on furlough from there now, and there is more going on there---printing office (I am a printer), theatre, church, etc., and six thousand inmates---see? I hope that the dear old boys will have a good time at Sioux City, and with best wishes I remain,

Your old comrade-in-arms,

ALLEN M. BLANCHARD.

Helena, Mont., Oct. 6th, 1894.

Mr. E. B. Soper, Emmetsburg, Iowa:---

My Dear Comrade: Your favor of September 28th just received, and am sorry to say that it will be impossible for me to attend the reunion at Sioux City. I am just now engaged in mining matters requiring my undivided attention. Were it not for that I would surely be with you, as you say it has been nearly thirty years since we last met, and I assure you that it is my wish to meet yourself and old comrades with a hearty shake hands as soon as circumstances will permit. Please remember me kindly to all comrades. My heart is with you if I cannot be. With the best of wishes,

I remain yours truly,

W. L. LEE.

Columbus, Ohio, Sept. 22nd, 1894.

Mr. J. E. Simpson:---

Dear Comrade: I received your circular in regard to the reunion of the old 12th. I am so far away that it is pretty hard for me to attend the reunion. Nothing would please me better than to shake the hand of every surviving member of Company I, and in fact of all the 12th. I will do my utmost towards reaching Sioux City by the 10th of next month. To tell the truth of the matter I have been under the weather pretty bad lately, and my finance is low. I wish they had made it Dubuque or some town on the east side of the state.

Please send me Sergeant Cotes' address. I know it is in South Dakota, but forgot the town. I am trying for an increase of pension. Cotes was wounded at Tupelo when I was. He and Bill Koehler and I were in Cahaba together. And please send Koebler's address. I know it is Dubuque, but don't know the number or street. If you know Capt. Sumbardo's address please send it also. I will send you a blank to fill out as to my health before I was wounded if you can remember me. The youngest member of Company I---the boy that had the preacher's suit, plug hat and all on the Tupelo ten, fifteen, and as high as twenty Union soldiers, and are so described in the Roll of Honor in the superintendent's office The states having regimental groups are Iowa, Illinois, Wisconsin, Michigan, Indiana, Ohio and Kentucky, but soldiers from all these states and in all the regiments having groups are also scattered all over the cemetery in named and unnamed graves. Iowa has three regimental groups, the Third, Twelfth and Thirteenth Iowa, each having a group in semi-circular form, the three semi-circles joining each other, with the name of the regiment cut into a tall stone in the center of its semi-circle. The group of the 12th regiment is as follows;

12th Iowa: Nos. on the 21 graves, 455 to 475. Names, Lieut. J. D. Ferguson, W. L. Paulley, T. H. Wilson, A. D. Campbell, Daniel Luther, J. P. Ayers, Jno. Bradfield, R. E. King. Thirteen unnamed graves. Eight more of the known graves of the 12th are buried in section M., and others in other sections

All sections of three of the regiments above have named graves scattered through the different sections, in addition to the above groups. This indicates bad management on the part of the superintendent in charge at the time the bodies were removed; but he is dead now, his body is buried in the cemetery and this pencil never fights a dead man. It would have been much more convenient and satisfactory if each State's dead had been in one section and the section divided off so far as possible into regimental groups.

The following is a complete list of the "known" dead of the 12th Iowa regiment interred at Shiloh cemetery, with company, date of death and place of original burial, so far as shown by the superintendent's books:

Ayers, J. P.—D. 12th Iowa, Pittsburg Landing, Tenn.
Blanchard, John D.—K. 12th Iowa, March 31, 1862, Savannah, Tenn.
Bradfield, John--E. 12th Iowa, Shiloh.
Campbell, A. D.—F. 12th Iowa, Shiloh.
Cooley, Archibald S.—12th Iowa, April, 1862, Shiloh.
Ferguson, Jason D., Lt.—D. 12th Iowa, Shiloh.
Garrison, A —F. 12th Iowa, Savannah, Tenn.
House, Nathan—C. 12th Iowa, April 6, 1862, Savannah, Tenn.
King, Reuben D.—Co. A., April 6, 1862, Shiloh.
Luther, Daniel,—Co. D., Shiloh.
Moore, Solomon W.—Co. E., March, 1862, Savannah, Tenn.
Paulley, Wm. L.—E. 12th Iowa, Shiloh.
Ricker, Jacob,—G. 12th Iowa, April 23 1862, Savannah, Tenn.
Shinkle, Marion,—I. 12th Iowa, March 31, 1862, Savannah, Tenn.
Wigton, Thos. J.—F. 12th Iowa, April 4, 1862, Savannah, Tenn.
Wilson, Thos. H.--I. 12th Iowa, Shiloh.
Herring, L. G.—G. 12th Iowa, Savannah, Tenn.

In addition to the above, Iowa is known to be largely represented in the 2,361 "unknown" graves. One-eighth of the known graves are those of brave Iowa soldiers and it is undoubtedly true that 300 to 500 more of the best and bravest men that Iowa sent to the war sleep in unknown graves in Shiloh cemetery. This will be a sad letter to many Iowa homes when read over to find a trace of a father, brother, son or friend known to be killed at Shiloh. Knowing the anxiety with which the list will be read over, great care was taken in copying from the records to get it correct, and the list above given contains the name of every 12th Iowa soldier in "known" graves in Shiloh cemetery.

The cemetery was begun in 1870, five years after the war was over. The first superintendent was Maj. Peter Jako, who died in 1870 and is buried in the cemetery. Each year thereafter until 1876, there was a new superintendent but no record was kept of their names. In September, 1876, Capt. L. S. Doolittle, of 96th Illinois, was appointed. He is still the superintendent and a first class man for the position. He receives a salary of $900 per annum and is furnished one employe at $30 per month. The government furnishes house, tools, fuel, stock, etc., everything except food and clothing for himself and family. He and his lady, formerly Miss Anna White, of Milburn, Illinois,

Cottage 9, Soldiers' Home, Quincy, Ill., Oct. 9, 1894.

Mr. J. E. Simpson and 12th Iowa:—

Dear Comrades: I received your kind invitation to attend the reunion the 10th to 12th inst.

I am very sorry I can not meet with you, but it is not possible for me to attend on account of my finances. My check will reach me too late to attend the reunion. I wish you all a good time.

Truly our ranks in the 12th Iowa are thinning and we can have but a few more reunions here, but there is a time coming when we can have a grander reunion than any of these, if we all live as faithful to our God as we did for our country, and fight the good fight of faith, we will have one of the grandest reunions in heaven we have ever had. I am trying every day to live a christian, and as I cannot be with you I request you to take a vote of the boys and report to me the number that are trying to serve God and make their home in heaven, where all is peace and joy forever. Please do this for my pleasure at least. I want to say here that I have not spent my pension at the saloon (God forbid), but I have spent it in helping to build a United Brethren church in this city and for other benevolent purposes. I want you to know that I have not squandered my money as some of the boys have done in our home.

We have thirty-eight boys in our cottage and eight of us are trying to fight the good fight of faith and gain a home in heaven. I trust the few that used to hold prayer meetings in the army are still attending and enjoying prayer meetings. If any have gone astray let them return as the prodigal of old did. We then had to fight the enemy of our country and our soul too. Now we have to fight the enemy of our soul, and that is whisky. Thousands are going to ruin every day in Quincy. This is all. Write an tell me about the reunion. How many were there? Give me their addresses and I will write to them. Love to all,

LAWRENCE LOTT
To the 12th Iowa.

Superior, Neb., Oct. 9, 1894.

Dear Comrades:—

I started to come to the reunion and got as far as Superior and I learned it would cost me full fare to come, and times are so hard and money so scarce that it is impossible for me to get there. I understood it was only half fare till I got to the depot. I am very sorry that I cannot be there. I saw A. G. Davenport this morning and he said to send his respects to all the old boys, and we hope that the next time will be able to get there.

PETER KEARNS,
A. G. DAVENPORT.

Holmes City, Douglas County, Minn., Oct. 7th, 1894.

J. E. Simpson, Norfolk, Neb.:—

Dear Comrade: Your circular of Sept. 10 duly received. I have always had an ardent desire to attend a reunion of the 12th Iowa, but the distance and financial circumstances always so far intervened. My personal appearance can therefore not be with you only by letter of regret.

Very truly,   L. LEWIS,
Late Co. I, 12th Iowa Infantry.

Magnolia, O., Sept. 12, 1894.

J. E. Simpson, Esq., Norfolk, Neb.:---

Dear Sir and Comrade: It was with mingled feelings of pleasure and regret that I perused your circular letter of invitation to attend the fifth reunion of the 12th Iowa Volunteer Infantry---pleasure that I was still held in remembrance by my comrades-in-arms, and regret that circumstances would not permit me to be present with them on that occasion. I, as well as the rest of the one time "Boys in Blue," am getting old---too old to take so long a trip, much as I would love to meet once more those with whom I bore arms during those trying years. But few more such privileges will be accorded us, but there will be a grand review beyond at which I trust we may all pass muster.

Hoping that you who are present may enjoy the meeting to the fullest, I assure you that my thoughts will be with you. Yours fraternally,

A. BROTHERS.

Soldiers' Home, Hot Springs, S. D., Oct. 11, 1894.

J. E. Simpson:---

Cannot come to reunion; not able; my best wishes to you all.

EMERY CLARK.

St. Edwards, Neb., Oct. 4th, 1894.

J. E. Simpson, Norfolk, Neb.:---

Dear Comrade: It is with the deepest regret that this will have to substitute my personal attendance at this reunion of the 12th Iowa.

I shall be with you in spirit and with my best wishes for the happiness of the comrades of the old 12th Iowa, hoping you will have a pleasant time. I will bid you good bye until our next reunion. Yours truly,

W. H. ELLISON,
Company K, 12th Iowa V. V. I.

Ponca, Oct. 9, 1894.

Comrades of the 12th Iowa:—

It is with the deepest feelings of regret that I write you of my inability to be present with you at this, your fifth reunion. I have anticipated great pleasure in meeting with you once more, but hard times presses me so closely, and not being a pensioner, I am unable to be present. My wife, who is a member of the Woman's Relief corps sends kind greetings and many regrets, that she cannot be with you.

were very kind to us and did all in their power to aid all in search of the graves of friends or information. No registry of visitors was kept for some time after the cemetery was opened. The first name registered was Nov. 14, 1870, and only 181 names were registered up to May 9, 1876. The total number of visitors registered up to evening of April 7, 1884, saw 2,617.

The saddest feature about the cemetery is the fact that nearly the entire number of dead comrades of the regiments that were captured, except those who were killed early in the day in the first day's fight, "sleep their last sleep" in "unknown" graves. The 8th, 12th and 14th Iowa regiments, all of which were captured at the close of the first day's fight, are but slightly represented by known graves in the cemetery, and this is also true as to other captured regiments. The dead of these regiments were scattered on the line of battle, along the line of retreat, where they made the last desperate stand in their efforts to break the enemy's line after we had been surrounded, and piled in continuous heaps across "Hell's Hollow." Owing to the scattered condition of the dead, their comrades left in regimental camps could not find their bodies after the battle was over, and so they were buried in the long and shallow trenches, hundreds in a trench, by soldiers detailed to bury the dead.

Another important feature is brought out by this fact. In case of the captured regiments there was no one to report the casualties for these regiments after the battle was over, and so the number of killed in those regiments is given in all the printed reports only for the known dead found on the field. In case of the 12th Iowa the official report gives the number of killed in this regiment as "10," when it is positively known by those of the regiment who were captured that the number of killed and mortally wounded in this regiment was nearly one hundred. Company A alone had seven killed and two mortally wounded, who died the next day, and very few of this company escaped death or wounds. Company A. lost more men than any company in the regiment, but the loss to the other companies was very heavy. This is true history, but it was too late to correct the official reports after the captured were released from the rebel prison hells, and the official records still perpetuate the false reports as first made, thus belittling the brave men, who were the only troops that held their original line of battle all day, and whose stubborn resistance was all that saved the entire army from destruction.

The first and last place with the veterans was the cemetery. We went to it sad in heart and came away with increased sorrow. Twenty-two years had not lessened the love for the brave comrades buried here in a rebellious soil conquered and consecrated by the best and bravest of our number. They sacrificed home, friends and life with heroic cheerfulness and with a hope for their country last in their hearts, a smile of remembrance of loved ones at home last on their faces, they died without a murmur, dying as heroes die—as Christ died—for others. Did they die in vain? Let the history of the next twenty-five years answer.

We left their silent and the greatest part of them "unknown" graves in silence and unutterable sorrow, bowed down with grief this pencil cannot express. No other nation in the history of the world ever had such noble warriors, and no other nation ever came so near giving up all the fruits of their brave struggles, undying devotion and self-sacrificing valor. The American Nation has proven itself unworthy of such heroic sons, and branded itself with infamy and dishonor. Even the muddy waters of the Tennessee sluggishly wash the base of their last resting place in its course to the northwest, and toward the desolated homes of nearly all our honored dead who are buried on its banks, as if in wild mockery of the phantom army being unable to rise from their shroudless, coffinless graves and take up their line of march in the same direction. Oh, the bitterness that sorrow drove deep into the hearts and minds of their living comrades as they took their last look upon their graves. Language cannot express it, thought cannot fathom it, and comprehension cannot compass it. Every veteran came away from these mute graves in the green woods of Tennessee thinking less of his government, less of the American people, and more of th   gratefulness of republics than ever before. No army of equal intelli   ce, devotion and valor can ever be enlisted in this nation again until her ople have forgotten how the fruits of the last war have been thrown aw , how treason has been rewarded, and how loud-mouthed rebels now boast their treason in the halls of the American Congress.

Who Saved the Day at Shiloh.

The following, written by Col. Geddes, and taken from the *Iowa State Register*, will be exceedingly interesting to members of the 12th and 14th Iowa:

On the near approach of the twenty-third anniversary of the battle of Shiloh I feel that the time has arrived when simple justice may be done the brave men who stood by their colors and country so heroically on that bloody day.

For twenty-two years I, for one, have keenly felt that the heroism of three devoted Iowa regiments has never been candidly acknowledged by the authorities, nor the far-reaching consequences of their patriotic devotion fully appreciated. I will therefore answer your question, "Who Conquered at Shiloh?" by stating without fear of contradiction, and with the opportune assistance from Confederate reports of that battle, now for the first time published by the War Department, that Iowa conquered at Shiloh!

How often have we recalled to our memories that timber-crested hill, so sacred to us all as the resting place of many a dear comrade, and soon to be visited again by some of the survivors, drawn as it were by some wierd and all-pervading influence to the spot, which for these many years they have longed to tread once more.

These three Iowa regiments—the Eighth, Twelfth and Fourteenth—defended a position all that day of so much importance to our army, that had it been carried by the rebels, even as late as 3 o'clock in the afternoon, the high bluffs of the Tennessee would not have had a Union soldier to shelter.

Permit me to quote from the official reports of a few of the Confederate officers who, with their commands, engaged these three Iowa regiments, and who describe the position they held so vividly that most of our surviving comrades who may read this cannot fail to recognize the historic spot. On page 483, Vol. X: War of the Rebellion, Col. R. S. Gibson, commanding First Brigade, Ruggles' division, reports as follows:

"The position alluded to was a densely wooded hill, surrounded by a ravine." Again, on page 480, he says: "The brigade moved forward in fine style, marching through an open field under a heavy fire, and half way up an elevation covered with an almost impenetrable thicket upon which the enemy was posted; on the left was a battery opened that raked our flank, while a steady fire of musketry extended along the entire front. Under this combined fire our line was broken and the troops fell back, but they were soon rallied and advanced to the contest. Four times the position was charged and four times the assault proved unavailing. The strong and almost inaccessible position of the enemy, his infantry well covered in ambush, and his artillery skillfully posted and efficiently served, was found to be impregnable to infantry alone. We were repulsed." Again, on page 483, he continues: "I had sent Mr. Robert Pugh to the General after the first assault, for artillery, but the request was not granted, and in place of it he brought me orders to advance again on the enemy. In the execution of this order we charged repeatedly, as described, and were repulsed."

In this connection I will quote from my own report, written in a rebel prison twenty-two years ago, and found in the same document, on page 166: "About 1 p. m. General Prentiss placed a battery in position immediately in front of my regiment. The precision of its fire, which was directed by the General in person, made great havoc in the advancing columns of the enemy. It therefore became an object of great importance to them to gain possession of the battery. To this end they concentrated, and hurled column after column on my position, charging most gallantly to the muzzles of the guns."

For the purpose of still further corroborating the rebel testimony, I quote from Col. W. T. Shaw's report, on pages 153-4, made after his return from prison: "I now perceived a large force of the enemy approaching from the left and front, and immediately reported the fact to Col. Tuttle, who, at my request, sent me a couple of brass six-pounders, which were nearby. These I got into position just in time to receive the enemy. They advanced with the most desperate bravery, the brunt of the attack falling upon the Eighth Iowa, by whom it was most gallantly borne." I have good authority for saying that the firm resistance of the center at that time was the chief means of saving our whole army from destruction.

In identifying the topography of this important position held by these three Iowa regiments, I would call attention to the report of Col. J. J. Woods, of the Twelfth Iowa, on page 151. With the precision of a trained officer he thus describes the position: "The Eighth Iowa was on the left of the Fourteenth, forming an angle to the rear with our line. An open field lay in front of our right. Dense timber covered our left, a small ravine immediately behind us. Again and again did he attack us. We repulsed every attack and drove him back in confusion."

Now compare with the foregoing the report of Capt. E. M. Dubroca, commanding the Thirteenth Louisiana Regiment of Col. Gibson's brigade, page 491: "Our loss in crossing the field was very heavy. We were ordered to the right to charge the enemy, who were lying in ambush at the foot of the hill, entirely hidden from us by a dense undergrowth, which screened their position. 'There is a time when patience ceases to be a virtue.' We were forced to fall back and form anew. And a second and third time we returned to the charge, leaving on the field some of our brave soldiers."

Also compare the report of Col. J. F. Fagan, commanding First Arkansas, Gibson's brigade, Ruggles' division, on page 488. He says: "It was about noon, the turning point of the day and the turning point of the battle. Upon the edge of a wheat.field, to the right of the field last mentioned, the regiment, with the whole brigade, was drawn up in line of battle, and marching directly to the front, across a field, entered a dense thicket of undergrowth, which led down to a ravine and a hill beyond. Here we engaged the enemy three different times, and braved a perfect rain of bullets, shot and shell Three different times did we go into that valley of death, and as often were forced back."

Sufficient, I think, has been stated to prove, beyond controversy, two important facts. First, the position these three devoted regiments occupied during the battle of the 6th of April, 1862, and the terrible character of the conflict sustained. Much more can be gleaned from the rebel reports in further corroboration of these facts, but your precious space warns me to desist. I will only notice two important points. First, the time these three Iowa regiments were captured, and second, the result of their heroic resistance. How often have our brave boys been pained on hearing the oft-repeated mean and flippant remark, "O, you were captured in the morning at Shiloh," and by many who never dared approach the foe near enough to be captured. What a legacy to a weeping wife when the news of the bloody conflict sped over the lines to our homes, "Your husband was taken prisoner with his regiment without fighting." The true state of the case could not be ascertained, for no witness was there but those concerned.

In regard to the time of capture I will quote from the report of Col. B. L. Hodge, Nineteenth Louisiana Infantry, page 493: "Again we advanced into the little farm, and again when midway the clearing, the enemy opened fire upon us. Again we pressed on to the fence directly in front of his ambuscade. Here we remained exposed to his merciless fire for over half an hour. I may be permitted to add, sir, that this formidable position of the enemy, after having withstood the repeated attacks of various regiments, was only carried at last by a charge on the right flank, supported by a battery on the left. After the enemy were driven from this stronghold, we, with several brigades, moved toward the river. It was then nigh sunset."

COMPANY A.

Armstrong, B. A..............................Liscomb, Iowa.
Bowers, I. H......................Eldora, Hardin Co., Iowa.
Bird, G. M...Ill.
Bell, Thos. R...............................Iowa Falls, Iowa.
Brother, A......................................Arlington, Ohio.
Brown, S. B..................Jewell City, Jewell Co., Kansas.
Congar, J. D............................Eldora, Hardin Co., Iowa.
Clarkson, R. P.....................Des Moines, Polk Co., Iowa.
Cromwell, T. C....................................Oakland, Iowa.
Combes, E. C..............................Dewalls Bluff, Ark.
Cobb, G. H...........................Eldora, Hardin Co, Iowa.
Crist, Job...................................Marshalltown, Iowa.
Dobbins, Hiram..............................Jewell Co., Kan.
Dobbins, Levi....................Eldora, Hardin Co., Iowa.
Edgington, S. R......................Eldora, Hardin Co, Iowa.
Edgington, T. B............No. 18 Madison St., Memphis, Tenn.
Ellsworth, D. V....................Eldora, Hardin Co., Iowa.
Fountain, Francis..
Glass, Carl......................Dayton, (Mill Home,) Ohio.
Haskins, G. H..................................Marysville, Mo.
Haywood, W. P......................................Lyons, Iowa.
Hunter, J. R. C..............................Webster City, Iowa.
Hobbs, Jas. C. H...................Peru, Nemaha Co., Neb.
Iback, B. F...........................Eldora, Hardin Co., Iowa.
Jackson, Sam'l..Oregon.
Kidwiler, M..Mo.
Kemp, Sumner.......................................Alden, Iowa.
Kellogg, R. F..Alden, Iowa.
Lefever, Simon....................................Bolekow, Mo.
Macy, Seth...................................Des Moines, Iowa.
McPherson, W. G..
Moore, G. W....................................Maryville, Mo.
Moore, W. W................Manchester, Del. Co., Iowa.
Miller, Zabina...
Mann, William..............Steamboat Rock, Hardin Co., Iowa.
Mitchell, G. W............................Lawn Hill, Iowa.
Martin, D. S.................................Iowa Falls, Iowa.
Parish, Wm..
Richards, Wm..
Reed, G. W.....................................Yarkie, Mo.
Runkle, C. M..............................Plankenton, Dak.
Rulo, G. W......................................South Bend, Ind.
Richards, Joseph..................................Boone, Iowa.
Sprague, K. S...................................Fremont, Neb.
Sawin, E. S......................................Union, Iowa.
Wilson, T. H................................Iowa Falls, Iowa.
Walker, Sam'l........................Dewitt, Carroll Co., Mo.
Welsh, Nathan..
Wickam, A. J...................................Eagle City, Iowa.
Webb, A. E..........................Eldora, Hardin Co. Iowa:
Zieger, J. W.........................Eldora, Hardin Co., Iowa.
Zieger, N. W........................Eldora, Hardin Co., Iowa.

COMPANY B.

Andrews, H. R. .... West Union, Iowa.
Beurce, Corp. L. B 37 .... Castane, Iowa
Bathen, Robt. .... Rossville, Iowa
Bort, Com. Wesley B. .... Viroqun. Wis
Borgee, 1st Lieut. J. B....supposed to be dead, Salt C'k., P. O., Ills
Baily, Geo. N. .... St. Paul, Minn
Bailey, W. F. .... St. Paul, Minn
Bort, James. .... Died in Lansing, Iowa
Bort, A, K. .... Decorah, Iowa
Cole, 2d Lt. J. D. .... Lansing, Iowa
Decker, Adam. .... Lansing, Iowa
Deeny, Cornelies........... Died at Soldier Home, Milwaukee, Wis
Dowling, John. .... French Creek, Iowa
Dowling, Thos. .... Rossville, Iowa
Earle, Capt. W. C. .... Waukon, Iowa
Engelhorn, Corp. Matthew .... Kansas
Ettle, Geo. .... Waukon, Iowa
Encion, E. A. .... Glenwood, Dak
Fry, Henry B. .... Pa
Ferguson, Bradnor. .... Pa
Goodykoontz D. F. ....
Hulstis, Jos. H. .... Waterville, Iowa
Hansom, Capt. W. R. .... Dead
Iback, 1st Serg. George. .... Preston, Minn
Isted, Ibach F. .... Milwaukee, Wis
Iverson, Knud. .... Lansing, Iowa
Iback, Serg. George. .... Preston, Minn
Jackson, 1st Lt. Jos. P. .... Village Creek, Iowa
Klees, Frank. .... Rossville, "
Larsen, Aslak. .... Preston, Minn
McCabe, Hugh. .... Waukon, Iowa
McGuirn, Bryan. .... Freeport, Ills
Monk, Fred. .... Eitzen, Minn
McClintock, James. .... Rossville, Iowa
Ogan, C. C.. .... Sibley, Iowa
Pratt, Marcellus H. .... Waukon, Iowa
Pratt, R. C. .... Waukon, Iowa
Rogers, Serg. Maj. Altheris J. .... Waukon, Iowa
Russell Chas. .... Brooklyn, Mo
Sargent, Richard B. .... Kansas, Kan
Sjodin, Peter. .... Died
Sanner, Mick F. .... Rossville, "
Spaulding, Josiah D. .... Dead
Smith, S. C. .... North McGregor, Iowa
Thibedo, Stephen. .... Waukon, "
Upstrom, Serg. John. .... Worthington, Minn
Wampler, Robt. .... Waukon, Iowa
Winter, Serg. W. P. .... Algona, Iowa
White, Elisha J. .... Died
Winter, Rufus B. .... "
Woodmanon, Isaac. .... Rossville, Iowa

COMPANY C.

Capt. Wm. W Warner,........died Memphis, Tenn., Dec. 12, 1863.
Capt. Geo. W. Cook,.....................Medicine Lodge, Kan.
Capt. David W. Reed, (Major 12th Iowa)...........Waukon, Iowa
Capt. Wm. L Henderson,............................Leroy, Minn
1st Lt. David B. Henderson, (Col. 46th Iowa).......Dubuque, Iowa
1st Lt. Henry J. Grannis,...........................Fayette, Iowa
2d Lt. Aaron M. Smith,........died South Bend, Ind., Jan. 1st, 1883
1st Sergt. Jer F. Hutchins, (Capt. Co. E. 12 Ia.) ...Minneapolis, Minn.
Sergt. Gilbert Hazlett,............................Allison, Iowa
Sergt. Emery Clark,...............................Estelline, Dak
Sergt. Jas. Stewart,...........................West Union, Iowa
Sergt. Phineas R. Ketchem,........................Windsor, Iowa
Sergt. Philo R. Woods,............................Fayette, Iowa
Sergt. Frank W. Moine,....................Strawberry Point, Iowa
Corp. David Connor,........died of wounds, Nashville Jan. 5, 1865
Corp. Thomas Henderson,............killed Shiloh, April 6, 1862
Corp. Sam'l. F. Brush,..............died Macon, Ga., Oct. 31, 1862
Corp. Geo. L. Durno,...........................Springville, Iowa
Corp. Jas. Barr,(Asst. Surg. 12th Iowa)..............Algona, Iowa
Corp. Daniel D. Warner,...........died Macon, Ga., Sept. 10, 1862
Corp. John W. Bysong,...........................West Point, Neb
Corp. Joseph D. Baker..........................Montivedo, Minn
Corp. Geo. E. Comstock.........................Manchester, Iowa
Corp. Henry C. Curtis,.............................Lemars, Iowa
Corp. John A. Delezene,......................Rock Rapids, Minn
Corp. Wm. H. Jordan,........................Cheney, Wash. Ter
Corp. Amos K. Ketchum,............................Clarion, Iowa
Corp. John F. Kent,...............................Olewein, Iowa
Corp. Wilson King,................................Emerick, Neb
Musician Sumner Hartshorn,..................... died in Mich—
Abbott, Edward J..............(Rover, no permanent residence)
Ayers, James I........................died Macon, Ga. Oct. 3, '62
Adams, Edward..................died Fayette, Iowa, Dec. 20, '71
Beck, Sam'l C....................................Waverly Iowa
Blanchard, S. S................................died Postville, Iowa
Ballinger, John W................................Lacey, Iowa
Brown, Albert..........re-enlisted in 9th Iowa Cavalry, killed by
            accident at Hickory Plain, Ark. Dec. 24th, '64
Brown, John T...
Brown, Geo....................................Woodstock, Ill
Burroughs, Geo. A.............................Douglass, Iowa
Bowers, Wm. H.............................Limestoneville, Pa
Barton, Alvah H...
Baker, Miles................died Nov. 19, '67, Eden Iowa
Bushnell, Abner C......................died Pueblo, Col. Jan. '82
Beadle, Henry.....................died Macon, Ga. Aug. 9, 62
Brown, Addison L....................deserted from Selma Ala
Barr, Henry ....Tama Co., Iowa

Becktell, David T................................ Volga City, Iowa
Barnes, James (Transfer from 27)................................
Brant, Allen (Transfer from 27)................... Fairbanks Iowa
Benjamin, Nathan (drafted)................. ....
Bennefield, Wm. (substitute)....................................
Browsley, Wm. (drafted)...
Chase, Thos. H....................... died St. Louis, March 28, '62
Clark, Henry.................................. Melbourne, Iowa
Connor, Felix...... .... died St. Louis, Jan 14, '62
Connor, Sam'l......... .... Maxwell, Iowa
Connor, Daniel.................... died St. Louis, Mo. Jan. 14, '62
Card, Silas B...
Crossman, Silas................... died Elgin, Iowa April 14, 1881
Clawson, Elijah..................... died St. Louis, Mo. Ian. 10, '62
Carmichail, Jas. H.............................. Volga City, Iowa
Carrington, Chas............. .... Mitchell Co
Comstock, Frank................................... St. Louis, Mo
Canfield, Theron P. (27th Iowa)............... Buffalo Grove, Iowa
Davis, Jay C...... .... Wisconsin
Davis, Andrew J........................... Berian Springs, Mich
Delezene, Benj........................ ..... Republic City, Neb
Dawson, John (27th Iowa)..
Forbes, David..
Forbes, William......................... died St. Louis, Jan. 2, '62
Grannis, Geo. W............. Missing at Shiloh, never heard from
George, Henry............... died of wounds Md. City, May 2, '62
Gifford, Simeon.................................... Auburn, Iowa
Gillam, Ezekel D. (27th Iowa)...................................
Hood, Alonzo F........................ died St. Louis, Jan. 31, 62
Hazlett, John B................. .... Howard, Dakota
Hamlin, Wm. A................................... Plymouth, Iowa
House, Nathan................... died Savannah, Tenn. April '62
Hill, John W...
Hill, Benj. J. (drafted)..
Hendershot, Thos................................. Plainview, Neb
Henkee, Martin (drafted)............. died Memphis, April 17, '64
Henselbecker, Henry (drafted)..................... Bluffton, Iowa
Hamlin, Lyman S............................... Fairbanks, Iowa
Hinkel, Edward C. (drafted)..................... Winfield, Iowa
Husted, Jacob M..
Henderson, James A. (27th Iowa)................ Cherokee, Iowa
Jordan, Isadore L............................ Bull City, Kansas
Jaques, Luther................................ Fairbanks, Iowa
Jones, Henry......................... died St. Louis, Jan. 17, '62
Jones, Geo. M. (drafted)...
Jordan, Daniel M.......... killed Rockdale, Texas, Nov. 10, 1881
Jewell, Jas E. (27th Iowa).......................................
Jackway, G. H. (27th Iowa)..................... Lamont, Iowa
Kelley, Artemas..

Kent, Wm A..Dallas, Wis
Kelsey, E. A..Tripoli, Iowa
Lewis, Leroy...........................died St. Louis, Jan. 3d, 1863
Lattimer, Robt. Z.....................................Fayette Iowa
Lattimer, Geo. H..Mill, Iowa
Larson, Chas.........................killed at Shiloh, April 6, 1862
Lyons, Wm. A....................................West Union, Iowa
Little, Jas..
Lott, Lawrence..................................Kampeska, Dak
Munger, Albert P........................Cowlitz, Wash. Ter
Mattocks, Jason L...............................Minneapolis, Minn
McCall, Daniel E................................Culver, Kansas
McCall, John W...................................Brownville, Neb
McIntyre, Thos. J...............died Vicksburg. Feby. 26th, 1865
Mattocks, Ross.......................................Wadena, Iowa
McElvain, John..............................died McLeansboro, Ill
Muchmore, Stephen D. (27th).........................
Martin, Chas. I. (27th).........................Tripoli, Iowa
Pendleton, Chas. E................killed Shiloh, Apr. 6, 1862
Patterson, Sam'l. W (27th)..........................
Proctor, Geo. W (27th)..........................Lawrens, Iowa
Pitts, James (drafted)...........................London, Kan
Prichet, John L. (drafted).........................
Quivey, Wm. W................................Humboldt, Iowa
Quivey, John...................died Oct. 4, 1862, Macon, Ga
Russell, Granville............died Feby. 17, 1862, St. Louis, Mo
Rodgers, Reuben F..............................Waucoma, Iowa
Rodolph, John J......................................
Rockwell, Wm. R. (drafted).........................
Spears, Niles H..Mill, Iowa
Simar, Willard E...................died Macon, Ga., Oct. 10, 1862
Smith, Jacob R.......................................
Smith, Norton T................killed Vicksburg, May 22d, 1862
Smith, Henry C..............died May 3d, 1863, Millekins Bd. La
Siegman, Charles..............died Anapolis, Ma., Oct. 27, 1862
Stone, Sam'l ;..................died Anapolis, Ma., Oct. 3d, 1862
Stone, Daniel....................................Waucoma, Iowa
Sykes, Orvis..Freeport, Ill
Spears, Daniel H............died Sedalia, Mo., Nov. 12, 1864
Sherbone, Daniel.....................................
Strong, John P....................................Schuyler, Neb
Sprowls, John..
Saulsbury, John......................................
Tatro, August..................................Clermont, Iowa
Utter, Albert...................................Sycamore, Ill
Verdin, Isaiah..
Williams, Rodolphus..........................West Union, Iowa
Wallace, Charles...............died July 9, 1863, Hospt. Boat
Warner, Walter B.................................Clermont, Iowa
Wait, Van Buren................deserted St. Louis, April, 1863

COMPANY D.

Stibbs, John H.............Room 92, Govt. Building, Chicago, Ill.
Soper, E. B...................... ....Emmetsburg, Iowa.
Prescott, T. L. 1123 Lexington Ave, corner S. W. Ave., Chicago, Ill.
Ayers, Lyman M...........................Cedar Rapids, Iowa.
Buttolph, Edwin A...........................Cedar Rapids, Iowa.
Baumgardner, William..........................Scranton, Iowa.
Burch, Sylvester R................................Olathe, Kansas.
Bailey, Edwin H.....................Fredonia, Wilson Co., Kan.
Bailey, Henry W.....................Kirkeman, Shelby Co., Iowa.
Blanchard, Allen M...Room 58, 171 E. Randolph street, Chicago, Ill.
Barr, Thomas..................................Shellsburgh, Iowa.
Burch, John W................................Olathe, Kansas.
Blood, Alvarro C...
Brown, Angus, M..
Clark, John M............................Cedar Rapids, Iowa.
Conley, Dennis................ ....Davenport, Iowa.
Cowell, James L.........Marengo, Columbia Co., Washington Ter.
Clark, Chas. W................... ....Cedar Rapids, Iowa.
Curren, Francis....................................Marion, Iowa.
Clark, Isaac G........ ....Dennison, Iowa.
Cowell, Robert C........ ....Guthrie Center, Iowa.
Clemans, Nick, alias Chas. Ransom ....Smith Center, Kansas.
Dailey, James C......... ....Cherokee, Iowa.
DuBois, Ferdinand................................Denison, Iowa.
Ellgen, Harmon......................Grafton, Worth Co., Iowa.
Ferner, James D...................................Nevada, Iowa.
Flint, Samuel H.............No. 2, S. 3d Ave, Leavenworth, Kansas.
Gephart, Perry.......... ....Chicago, Ill.
Grass, Harmon................................Fargo, Dak. Ter.
Gallagher, James........ ....Crete. Neb.
Howard, William C......... ....Chelsea, Iowa.
Hale, Neil....................................Tucson, Arizona.
Holler, Irdill W..
Johnson, Robinson L............................Bayard, Iowa.
King, Eli..Washington, Kan.
Lanagan, James............................Odel, Gage Co., Neb.
Luther, John...................................St. Joseph, Mo.
Lewis, Thos. J............................Cedar Rapids, Iowa.
Lee, Wm. L............................ ....
Lumbert, John B......................... ....
Little, James H............................. ....
Martin, Richard S............ ....
McIntyre Alpheus.................... ....
Moorehead, Chas. L.......... ....Cedar Rapids, Iowa.
Millett, Allen J..............................Hastings, Neb.
Morrow, B. Frank............................Almena, Kansas.
Maryatt, O. H.................................Red Cloud, Neb.
Minor, David W....................Arcata, Humboldt Co., Cal.
Moorhead, Homer C................,........Cedar Rapids, Iowa.

Price, Nathan G...Jewell City, Kansas.
Price, J. V. George..................Mountain Grove, Wright Co., Mo.
Pangborn, Howard.........Palouse, Whitman Co., Washington Ter.
Rowan, John W...Vinton, Iowa.
Ross, Henry W..Red Cloud, Neb.
Renchin, Frank.........................Bloomington Prairie, Minn.
Ross, Jesse H...Cedar Rapids, Iowa.
Steadman, Dudly E...Vinton, Iowa.
Scott, Josiah...Shellsburgh, Iowa.
Soper, Roswell K..Estherville, Iowa.
Sartwell, Joseph O...Marion, Iowa.
Steward, Aaron A..Carthage, Mo.
Sivets, Daniel...
Tarpenning, James M..South Bend, Neb.
Thompson, Frank D..Nevada, Iowa.
Trowbridge, Wm H..........701 S. E. 5th street, Des Moines, Iowa.
VenEmman, Wm. M..........Grand View, Douglass Co., Dak. Ter.
Whittam, John J...............care J. N. Whittam, Cedar Rap. Iowa.
Wagner, Jasper..Center Point, Iowa.
Whiteneck, W. W...Waterloo, Iowa.
Weaver, John N...Algona, Iowa.
Zuver, B. P...Adams, Gage Co., Neb.

Stibbs, Joseph...died July 16th, 1866, at Wooster, Ohio, of abscess of back contracted in rebel prisons..........................
Blackburn, Joseph M..died April 20, 1862, near Shellsburg, Iowa, of desease on account of which discharged........................
Breman, Patrick..died Sept. 17th, 1873, at Hot Springs, Arkansas, of disease of lungs and liver...............................
Craft, James died July 3d, 1863, of disease on account of which discharged.
Baumgardner, Samuel died June, 1877, at Vinton, Ia, of consumption
Doolittle, Washington A. died July 21, 1880, at Watkins, Benton Co., Iowa, of Bright's desease, resulting from chronic diarhea and lung difficulty..
Doleshall, Wencil. died Aug. 31, 1873, at Cedar Rapids, Iowa.....
Frees, James P...died April 5, 1862, at Cedar Rapids, Iowa, of pneumonia..
Frees, Andrew J. killed June 30, 1873, at Cedar Rapids, by B. C. R. & N. Ry. Cars...
Gilchrist, Wm. B..died at Shellsburg, Iowa, of disease on account of which he was discharged.....................................
Lutz, Wm. B..died Oct. 31st, 1877, at Cedar Rapids, Iowa, of old age and general debility......................................
Martin, Ebenezer B..died Dec. 28th, 1868, at Cedar Rapids, Iowa, of consumption..

NOTE.—Any one knowing the addresses of those not given, or of their death, will confer a favor on Co. D., by addressing E. B. Soper, Emmetsburg, Iowa.

COMPANY E.

Boone, R. G............Scott, Mahaska County, Iowa
Biller, Anthony............Waterloo, "
Beckwith, W. H............Parkersburg, Iowa
Boylan, Thos............Stocton, Brooks County, Kansas
Bird, E............Winterset, Madison county, Iowa
Bird, R. L............Maysville "
Belton, James............Edgewood, Clayton county, "
Collins, Chas. P............Charles City, Floyd county, "
Cook, Charles............Lester, Blackhawk county, "
Creighton, David............Geneva, Franklin county, "
Crowhurst, Seth J............Salem, McCook county, Dakota
Cook, Joseph............New Castle, Dixon county, Nebraska
Cook, John J............No. 318 South 4th St., E. D. Brooklyn, N. Y
Cook, Adolph............
Coon, H. F............died Oct. 1884, Waterloo, Iowa
Church, Nathan............Webster City or Eagle Grove, "
Demoss, Thos............Bristow, Butler county, "
Ellwell, John............4340 Emeret Ave. Chicago
Eberhart, Ben............LaPorte City, Blackhawk county, Iowa
Early, T. M............Bristow, Butler county, "
Graham, Jacob............Davenport, Scott county, Iowa
Hamilton, Wm............LaPorte City, Black Hawk county, "
Hayward, C. B............Dysart, Tama county, "
Harrison, H. J............Interior Department, Washington, D. C
Jones, John C............Geneva, Franklin county, Iowa
Large, F. A............LaPorte City, Black Hawk county, Iowa
Myers, A. W............Shell Rock, Butler county, Iowa
Margret, J. S............Hittesville, Butler county "
Morris, C. D............Worthing, Dakota
Minium, David............Big Grove, Pottawatamie county, Iowa
McCall, Daniel............Culver, Ottowa county, Kansas
Ochs, Charles............Ackley, Hardin county, Iowa
Perry, A. B............Lester, Black Hawk county, Iowa
Reed, Zeff............Fredonia, Louisa county, Iowa
Rich, J. W............Vinton, Benton county, "
Surfus, C. V............Bristow, Butler county, Iowa
Stewart, Joal A............Oregon City, Oregon
Sunderlin, M. V. B............Janesville, Bremer county, Iowa
Seeber, G. L............Sabula, Jackson county, "
Schrack, David............Lester, Black Hawk county, "
Switzer, C. R............Lewis, Cass county, "
Sharp, Oliver............Finchford, Blackhawk county, "
Smith, Harvey............Waterloo, Black Hawk county, "
Sawyer, E............Enterprise, Black Hawk county, "
Shumaker, John W............Waterloo, Black Hawk county "
Shroyer, Nathaniel............Tainter, Mahaska county, "
Strong, Ezra............Sioux City, Plymouth county, "
Talbot, Allen E............Orleans, Indiana
Williams, (Capt.) Robt............Van Couver, Washington Ter
Watkins, Isaac............Crawfordsville, Montgomery county, Indiana
West, D. F............Theon, Wash. Ter

COMPANY F.

Ainsworth, J. E.	Missouri Valley Junction, Iowa
Annis, Geo. W.	Lanark, Carroll county, Ill
Bremner, John	Yankton. Yankton county, Dakota
Buckman, Wm. H.	Dyersville, Dubuque county, Iowa
Brown, Eugene	Brush Creek, Fayette county, "
Correll, Ed.	Greeley, Delaware county, "
Coolidge, F. W.	Rawlins, Wyoming Ter
Coolidge, O. E.	Central City, Nebraska
Dunham, Abner	Manchester, Delaware county, Iowa
Dahl, John A.	Silver Creek, "
Eldridge, J. E.	Hepler, Crawford county, Kan
Eldridge, R. C.	Niagara Falls, N. Y
Eaton, John J.	Edgewood, Clayton county, Iowa
French, S. M.	Denver, Colorado
Girton, Jos. S.	Hazleton, Buchanan county, Iowa
Goodell, Wm. H.	Manchester, Delaware county, "
Gift, J. W.	Peoria, Ill
Grice, A. J.	Doniphon, Hall county, Neb
Halthill, Josiah.	Wood Center, Clayton county, Iowa
Hasbrouck, Daniel H.	Prairie Creek, Union county, Oregon
Kaltenbach, Sam'l.	Manchester, Delaware county, Iowa
Kaltenbach, L. P.	San Bernardino, California
Kent, George	Olewein, Iowa
Kaster, Hiram.	Manchester, Clayton county "
Kirchner, Mike.	
Lee, Jas. F.	Clay Mills, Jones county, Iowa
Lee, John F.	Council Grove, Morris county, Kansas
McGowan, Thos.	Independence, Buchanan, county, Iowa
Mackey, H. W.	Maynard, "
Manning. A. L.	Dunlap, Harrison county, "
McKee, T. R.	Blunt, Dakota
Manley, R. L.	
Mann, Wm. W.	Ranelsburg, Hall county, Neb
Nelson, W. A. W.	Hazleton, Buchanan county, Iowa
Nelson, T. C.	Hazleton, Buchanan county, "
Otis, John Sr.	Manchester, Delaware county, "
Preston, H. M.	Ft. Dodge, Webster county, "
Potter, Jas. W.	Fayette, Fayette county. "
Peasley, R. H.	Kansas
Ralston, Nelson.	Lamars, Plymouth county, Iowa
Roe, A. J.	Burlington, "
Small, H. J. F.	452 SoWood St., Chicago, Ill
Steen, C. C.	Minneapolis, Ottowa county, Kansas
Schneider, Justus	Rosewell, Miner county Dak
Stribling, C. C.	Clifton, Tenn
Tirrell, R. W.	Manchester, Delaware county, Iowa
Thorn, Chris.	Waverly, Bremer county, "
Tibbetts, W. F.	Cheney, Sedgwick county, Kansas
Weeden, R. L.	Nugents Grove, Linn county, Iowa
Widger, Joshua.	Manchester, Delaware county, "
Wooldridge, Geo. W.	Elkport, Clayton county, "
Wandall, A.	Volga City, Clayton county, "

COMPANY G.

C. C. Tupper, died Benton Barracks, Jan., '62
L. D. Townsley, Mapiml Durango, Mexico
J. F. Nickerson, died in rebel prison.
J. E. Simpson, Dubuque, Iowa.
A. A. Burdick, killed at Tupelo.
A. E. Anderson, Calmar, Iowa.
O. C. Thorson, died at Eldorado, Iowa.
R. A. Gibson, died U. S. service.
J. H. Womeldorf, Neleigh, Neb.

G. O. Hanson, died at Decorah.
W. L. Winsor, Clinton, Mo.
T. Steen, died at Omaha.
A. W. Erit, died in service.
J. O. Johnson, Mabel, Minn.
N. B. Burdick, died at Decorah.
R. Hard,
G. W. Sharp, Fargo, Dakota.

Andrus, E. V. Decorah, Iowa.
Anderson, A. Albert Lea, Minn.
Anderson, G. Rothsay, Minn.
Anderson, A. M., died of wounds rec'd Corinth.

Aker, D. O., Ridgeway, Iowa.
Anderson, Peter
Anderson, E.

Brown, J. H. died at Decorah.
Bowers, A., died in Ohio.

Ballard, Strawder

Crane, John
Crowell, J. M.
Connolly. C. died at Somerville, Mass.
Christopherson, C Hartland, Minn.

Clark, J. M.
Cutlip, J.
Coon, C. A. Sabinal, Texas.
Carey, A. A. died at Castalia, Iowa.

Dunn, Van R, Dewitt, Neb.

Davis, N. J. Berrian Springs, Mich.

Engbertson, E.
Eastonson, G, died at Mound City, Iowa.

Ellsworth, W, D. died in Benton Barracks.

Fuller, A. S. Lyons, Dakota.
Fuller, A   "   "

Fladmark, S. M. M,

Green, L. D.
Gilbertson, O. Benton, Minn.
Gulbranson, A. Rothsay, Minn.

Gorhamer, O. H. died at St. Louis, '62.
Gilbert, L. died at Keokuk.

Hanson, Ole
Hulverson, A. Decorah, Iowa.
Hall, Giles
Houge, G. A. Albert Lea, Minn.
Hanson, Hans. Lake Park, Minn.
Hanson, Halver, Sheldon, Dakota.

Hanson, Claus
Hall, Austin, died at St. Louis, '63,
Helgerson, G. died at Nashville, '64.
Harris, F. W.
Hand, Andrew J.

Johnson, H. E. Alexandre, Minn.
Johnson, Henry 1st. died at Huntsville, '62.
Johnson, Henry 2d.

Jenson, A. died Sept. '63 in Miss.
Johnson, A. died at Greensville, La., '65.
Johnson, N. O.

Kittleson, C, B. died in Minn.
Kittleson, G.

Kirkland, G. W. Freeport, Iowa.

Larson, Hover, died at Savannah, Tenn.
Larson, John

Larson, Peter
Low, Lewis L.

Manson, J.
Montgomery, Wm. V.
Madinn, D, L.
Maloney. J. died in field.
Miller, S. lives in California.
McCabe, C. Sherburne, Minn

McCalley, P. died at Hesper.
McLoud, S.
Miller, O. D. Stuart, Neb.
Meyer, C.
Meader, M. E. Hesper, Iowa.
Moe, Peter

Nass, G. H. Woodside, Iowa.

Nelson, Swen

Oleson, O.
Oleson, O. G. killed at Shiloh.
Oleson, J. died at Thoten, Iowa.

Oleson, E.
Oleson, Ammon. died at Memphis.
Oleson, A. H.

Pollock, Joseph, mustered out at Selma, '65.
Pierce, Fletcher

Palmer, R. lives in Neb.
Peterson, N. died at Camp Woods, '63,

Romberg, L. O. died at Chewalla, '64.
Ricker, J. died at Savannah, '62,
Raucha, Fred. Skidmore, Mo.

Raucha, Ed,
Rocksvold, O, P. Thoten, Iowa.
Ryerson, F,

Smith, I. K. Baraboo, Wis.
Simmons, R. Lake Park, Minn.
Staples, C. J. died at Frankville, Iowa.
Steen, John, Wahoo, Neb.
Steen, Henry, Oakland, Neb.
Smith, G. M. died at Decorah, Iowa.
Sernson, S. A. killed at Tupelo, '64.

Skinner, C. died '63, steamer Crescent.
Skinner, F. Forest City.
Simmison, Nels.
Severson, Nels.
Stalim, Lars. L.
Simmons, John.
Slattery, Thomas.

Tinke, J.
Thompson, A. K.
Taylor, W. H, H.
Thompson, J. B., Speilville, Iowa.

Thompson, T., Lincoln Center, Kansas.
Torgenston, M. died '65, at Montgomery.
Tobinson, Andrew.
Thoryson, Andrew.

Wright, C. F.
Wheeler, Horace.
Wait, W. Nashua, Iowa.

Wold, L. T., died at Vicksburg, '63,
West, S., Red Cloud, Neb.
Wiley, Wm., died at St. Louis, '63.

COMPANY H.

Atkinson, W. L. C.....................................Omaha, Neb
Briggs, U. I..Marcus, Iowa
Brown, Tom....................................Jewell City, Kansas
Benedict, R. W......................................Jessup, Iowa
Becket, Ed...Dubuque, Iowa
Benedict, John W...............................Plum Creek, Neb
Carrie, John G.............................Butte City, Montana
Crist, John W............................Central City, Dak. Ter
Clark, B. A.......................................Colesburg, Iowa
Crosby, J. M.........................Pukwana, Brule county, Dak
Cox, W. U......................Alta, Buena Vista county, Iowa
Duncan, N. E..................................Kansas City, Mo
Evans, James.....................................Dubuque, Iowa
Fishel, S. C......................................Iowa Falls, Iowa
Fishel, S. K..............................Fort McGinnis, Montana
Fishel, Robt.......................................Greeley, Iowa
Franks, Joseph.....................................Lamont, Iowa
Flenniken, J. B.............................Battle Creek, Neb
Grimes, R. M......................................Kearney, Neb
Gilmore, A. C................................Indianapolis, Ind
Gosting, Alfred G.........................Strawberry Point, Iowa
Horner, Geo.......................................Dubuque, Iowa
Hamblin, R. E.....................................Arcadia, Ohio
Henry, Philip......................................Greeley, Iowa
Jackson, S. M......................................Lincoln, Neb
King, Wilson.......................................Emerick, Neb
Kuhnes, J. C.......................................Manning, Iowa
Knee, Sam'l G....................................Colesburg, Iowa
Light, Robt..Bernett, Neb
Light, Joseph.....................................North Fork, Neb
Langslou, Aaron I..transferred from Co. D 27th Ia to Co. D 12 Iowa
Mason, John S..................................Worthington, Iowa
Moreland, C. D.W..................................Earlville, Iowa
McConnell, Alex S................................Hopkinton, Iowa
McCune, W. U...................................Emmetsburg, Iowa
Nawman, Geo....................................North Platt, Neb
Playter, H. J..................................Washington, D. C.
Smith, Thomas................................Turkey River, Iowa
Shorter, James..................................Shell Rock, Iowa
Sloan, S. B..Greeley, Iowa
Trumble, James................................Manchester, Iowa
Winch, Edward......................................Arena, Wis
Wisegarber, Wm..................................Oneil City, Neb
Ward, John.......................................Burlington, Iowa
VanAnda, John.....................................Fremont, Neb

COMPANY I.

Brown, J..............
Crane, I. K................Maquoketa, Jackson Co., Iowa
Coates, Joseph Warren................................Dakota
Campbell, E. B.....................Armstrong, Grove Co., Iowa.
Davenport, A. S.....................Superior, Douglas Co., Neb
Eddie, Thos. C.........................Atwood, Rawlins Co., Kan
Eddie, Alex...........................Atwood, Rawlins Co., Kan
Fry, Wm. L.........................Scranton, Green Co., Iowa
Goodnow, M. B ....Ida, Valley Co., Neb.
Hatfield, Augustus..............................Jersey City, N. J.
Hardin, J............................Monmouth, Jackson Co., Iowa
Nagle, M D... ....Dubuque, Dubuque Co., Iowa
Nims, Weed.........................Bellevue, Jackson Co., Iowa
Perkins, J-H..................... ....Scatte, Washington, Ter
Palmer, A. L............................Sciatt, Washington Ter
Ray, John S..Naponee, Neb
Rolf Marion......................Maquoketa, Jackson Co., Iowa
Sumbardo, C. L. (captain)....................Minneapolis, Minn
Starbuck, Wm................................Lake Preston, Dak
Smith, Henry...................Maquoketa, Jackson county, Iowa
Teskey, George. ....Elwood, Clinton county, Iowa
Thompson, Jas. L..................Perry, Dallas county, Iowa
Van Duzee, E. M. (Maj.).................. ....St. Paul, Minn
Vanhook, Sam'l.................Maquoketa, Jackson county, Iowa
Wintersteen, Henry...............................Monmouth, Ill
Wilson, T......................Maquoketa, Jackson county, Iowa
Wood, Joel....................Maquoketa, Jackson county, Iowa
Wells, A. Charles..............Maquoketa, Jackson county, Iowa
Zediker, Jas. F. (Capt.)............Franklin, Franklin county, Neb

COMPANY K.

Brooks, John.....................
Blood, Geo. W.....................
Brown, J. J..................Bloomington, Franklin county, Neb
Billings, Chas. D...............Bloomington,   "   "   "
Billings, Abram..Luzern N. Y.
Blanchard, Thos.....................LeMar, Ottowa county, Kan
Barden, Henry A..........................
Baldwin, Newton.......... ....Ada, Ottowa county, Kan
Church, P..........................Arborville, York county, Neb
Dolley, Godfrey.................. Hopkinton, Delaware county, Iowa
Deutsher, Albert.................Nat Home, Dayton county, Ohio
Ellison, H................................. Neoma, Neb
Freeman, Richard.................Spencer, Midona county, Ohio

Horn, Sam'l..................................Colesburg, Iowa
Keith, W. B.........................Precept, Kerwin county, Neb
Kemp, Wm..................................Kirwin, Kan
Merriam, H. C.................Hopkinton, Del. county, Iowa
Merriam, C. E...................   "   "   "   "
Mathis, W. R.................King and Decater sts., Omaha, Neb
Mathis, E. R....................   "   "   "   "
Morgan, J. B......................Davenport, Scott county, Iowa
Morehouse, P. J...................Masonville, Del. county, Iowa
Mosher, Alvin...
Morgan, Wm. B...............Bloomington, Franklin county, Neb
McConnell, Alex S................Hopkinton, Del. county, Iowa
Mickey, Isaac...................Waukon, Allamakee county, Iowa
Myers, Jos. A...Dead
Phillips, C. E.......................Tekamah, Burt county, Neb
Robinson, Alonzo...................Albion, Boone county, Neb
Webb, Laurence.................Cedar Rapids, Linn county, Iowa
Willard, Porter H..................Hopkinton, Del. county, Iowa
Waldroff, Henry........Laporte City, Black Hawk county, Iowa

NAMES OF WIVES AND CHILDREN PRESENT.

Miss Blanche Knee,
Mrs. A. J. Rodgers,
" Geo. S. Durno,
" D. W. Reed,
Miss Minnie Reed,
Master Reed,
Mrs. E. B. Soper,
" Wm. Henderson and daughter,
" J. E. Simpson,
" H. R. Andrews,
" P. R. Woods,
" H. J. Granule,
" R. Z. Lattimer,
" P. K. Ketchum,
" James Stewart,
" James Barr and two daughters,
" G. H. Morisey,
" Abner Dunham and daughter Florence,
" A. A. Moore,
" Fred Lankins,
" John Otis,
" R. W. Terrill,
" G. E. Comstock,
" R. P. Clarkson, and daughter,
" J. J. Eaton,
Mrs. D. W. Moreland,
Miss May Moreland,

Master Chas. Moreland,
Mrs. J. F. Zediker and Infant,
" W. W. Mann,
" J. Franks,
" A. J. Millett,
Miss Lewis Co. B,
Mrs. H. A. Lewis,
" Robt. Fishel,
" O. P. Rocksvold,
" John Bremner and son,
" S. Fishel,
" S. R. Edgington,
Miss Webb,
Mrs. J. N. Weaver,
" J. W. Gift,
" J. A. Vananda,
" Hiram Kaster,
" W. W. Moore,
" L. Lewis,
" C. E. Merriam,
" Geo. Kent,
" Joe. Girton,
" W. A. Morse,
Master Alfred E. Comstock,
" Merton E. Comstock,
" Willie W. Comstock.

ELDORA SILVER CORNET BAND.

J. D. Dunter, Leader.
Geo. H. Lewis, 1st. E Cornet.
A. S. Richards, 2d. E Cornet.
Ed. Whitney, 1st. B. Cornet.
Geo. B. Speers, Solo Alto.
E. A. Hudson, 1st. Alto.

F. J. Stallsmith, 2nd. Alto.
J. W. Peisen, 1st. Tenor.
A. Meader, Baritone.
D V. Meader, Tuba.
M. W. Moir, Small Drum.
Harry B. Shilling, Bass Drum.

M. W. Moir, Sec.
Eldora, Iowa.

The band were made honorary members of the Association (see resolution page 32) and omitted there by error.

COMMITTEE ON REGISTRATION AND HISTORY.

Co. A.

Capt. A. E. Webb, Eldora, Iowa.
Lieut. B F. Ibach, " "
Sergt. R. P. Clarkson, DesMoines, Iowa

Co. B.

Lieut. John D. Cole, Lansing, Iowa.
Sergt. Major A. J. Rodgers, Waukon, Iowa.
H. R. Andrews, West Union, Iowa.

Co. C.

Maj. D. W. Reed, Waukon, Iowa
Capt. W. L. Henderson Leroy, Minn.
Lieut. H J Grannis, Fayette, Iowa

Co. D.

Capt. E. B. Soper, Emmetsburg, Iowa
B. P Gouber, Adams, Neb.
Edwin A Batolph, Cedar Rapids, Iowa.

Co. E.

Harvey Smith, Waterloo, Iowa.
John C. Jones, Geneva, Iowa.
J. S. Margretz, Hittesville, Iowa.

Co. F.

Capt. John Bremner, Yankton, Dak.
W. A. Nelson, Hazleton, Iowa.
Abner Dunham, Manchester, Iowa.

Co. G.

Capt. J. E. Simpson, Dubuque, Iowa.
D. O. Anker, Ridgeway, Iowa.
O. P. Rocksvold, Thoten, Iowa.

Co. H.

Col S. G. Knee, Colesburg, Iowa.
Ralph Grimes, Kearney, Neb.
W. J. Playter, Washington, D. C.

Co. I.

Capt. J. F. Zediker, Franklin, Neb.
Wm L. Fry, Scranton, Iowa.
Geo. Tesky, Elwood, Iowa.

Co. K.

Lieut. J. B. Morgan, Davenport, Iowa.
Sergt. C. E. Merriam, Hopkinton, Iowa.
Sergt W. R. Mathis, (King and Decatur Sts,)
Omaha, Neb.

ERRATA.

On page 3, in the Hall Decoration Committee read, *Mrs. A. M. Sherwood* for Mrs. S. M. Sherwood; Read, *Winnie Work* for Minnie Work. In the Entertainment Committee read *Mrs. G. H. Morisey* for Mrs. G. W. Morrey. In Finance Committee read *R. M. Marvin* for K. M. Marvin.

On page 11 third line from bottom, read *Tupelo* for Topelo.

On page 30, fourth line, read *G. H. Morisey* for G. S. Morisey.

Poem on page 43 should have the name of the author *J. W. Shannon* inserted.

Page 46, ninth line, read *H. R. Andrews* for H. P. Andrews.

To the Roster of Co. F., page 68, add the names of David S. Godfrey, Jasper Mo., L. C. Bush, Lexington, Iowa.

THIRD REUNION

—OF THE—

TWELFTH IOWA

Veteran Volunteer Infantry,

—HELD AT—

WATERLOO, IOWA,

1888

ATTENTION, COMRADES!

It has been determined that we will send a copy of the proceedings of our last reunion to each surviving comrade whose address we have. And we hope that those who have not already paid membership fees or dues, will remit said dues of one dollar, or send twenty-five cents, the cost of said pamphlet, to the undersigned treasurer of the association at Algona, Iowa. All who signed our by-laws and became members of our association, whose names appear on page 46 of this book, are entitled to a copy free of charge.

We are anxious that all who can will become members of our society, and if you will send one dollar to the treasurer and direct him to do so, he will inscribe your name on the roll making you a member, and you will be entitled to this book without additional cost. Unless this is done we hope you will send the 25 cents.

Comrades let us not forget each other. Help a little in the good work. If you know of any comrade who served in our regiment whose name does not appear on our book, or whose address is changed, be kind enough to send his name and address to Capt. E. B. Soper, Emmetsburg, Iowa.

By order of Executive Committee.

    JAMES BARR, Treasurer,
      Algona, Kossuth Co., Iowa.

THIRD REUNION

———OF THE———

12TH IOWA V. V. INFANTRY,

———HELD AT———

WATERLOO, IOWA,

THURSDAY and FRIDAY, APRIL 5TH and 6TH, 1888.

MANCHESTER, IOWA:
Manchester Press Steam Job Print.
1888.

EXPLANATORY.

In the preparation of this pamphlet, the Committee have labored under many disadvantages, all of which have had a tendency to delay its issue.

Those who have not had the trial, know but little of the annoyance and immense labor required in the preparation of a pamphlet of proceedings of any deliberative body, in the absence of matter which should have been prepared and kept at the time of meeting.

Many of the speeches were extemporaneous, and our Secretary not being able, with all his other duties, to keep accurate minutes of the proceedings, and there being no short hand reporter provided, the Committee found themselves almost entirely without the proper data from which to make up this pamphlet.

They were therefore compelled to commence a system of correspondence with the comrades who favored the Association with impromptu remarks, asking them to furnish as nearly as possible what they said, so as to enable us to prepare something worthy of publication. Some replied, sending us the required matter, for which we take this opportunity to express our sincere thanks, others replied, saying that it was impossible for them to recollect what they said upon various subjects; others, that owing to important and pressing business engagements, it was impossible for them to comply; and others for some reason unknown to us did not reply at all.

We regret exceedingly, not only on our own account, but on account of all the comrades and all the readers of this pamphlet, that we have been unable to procure some matter that we have considered almost indispensable, notably among which was the excellent address of welcome by our late Governor, the Hon. B. R. Sherman.

R. W. TIRRILL,
G. H. MORISEY, Committee.
A. DUNHAM.

COMMITTEES.

Committee of Arrangements.

B. R. SHERMAN, Chairman.
J. H. LEAVITT,
J. W. KRAPFEL,
G. E. LICHTY,
J. E. WYANT,
WM. THOMPSON,
W. W. WHITENACK,
C. D. BECKER,
H. A SARGENT,
G O. SNOWDEN,
R. P. FOWLER.

FRANK NEELY,
S. M HOFF,
I. VANMETER,
C. D. WANGLER,
F. E. CUTLER,
A. J. EDWARDS,
H. H. SAUNDERS,
W. M. SINDLINGER,
DR. G. J. MACK,
C. W. MULLEN.

Finance Committee.

GEORGE O. SNOWDEN,
W. W. WHITENACK,

H. H. SAUNDERS,
J. E. WYANT.

Printing Committee.

B. R. SHERMAN,

I. VANMETER.

Hall and Rendezvous Committee.

R. P. FOWLER, West Side,

C. D. WANGLER, East Side

Hotel and Transportation Committee.

J. H. LEAVITT.

Banquet Committee.

A. J. EDWARDS,
S M. HOFF,
F. NEELY,
W. M. SINDLINGER,
C. B. STILSON,
MRS. THOMPSON,
MRS. MEADOWS,
MRS SNYDER.

H. A. SARGENT,
W. W. WHITENACK,
WM. THOMPSON,
G. E. LICHTY,
MRS. WHITENACK,
MRS. ALBEE,
MRS. HOFER,

Music Committee.

F. E CUTLER,
DR. ARTMAN,
MR. BENTLY.

C. O. BALLIETT,
F. C. PLATT,

Invitation and Toast Committee.

C. W. MULLEN,
F. NEELY.

B. R. SHERMAN,

PROGRAM--FIRST DAY.

Meeting of Executive Committee.   Music.
Called to Order by Col S. R. Edgington, President of the Reg'tl Association.
Prayer.
Appointment of Committees on Resolutions, Finance, next Reunion, etc.
Reading of letters from absent comrades.
Report of Historical Committee, by D. Reed.
Discussion and further action in regard to Regimental History.
Miscellaneous Business.   Short talks on call.

EVENING.

Camp Fire.   Music.
Address of Welcome.   Response by Col. S. R. Edgington.
Why We Hold Reunions—Response by S. R. Burch.
Music.
The "Hornets Nest Brigade." Their valor saved the World's Greatest Commander.—Response by T. B. Edgington, of Memphis, Tennessee.
Was the War Worth the Sacrifice? One Country, One Flag, and More Stars. Response by D. B. Henderson, of Dubuque.
Home when the Boys were Away. The Dark Days of '61 to '65.—Response by Mrs. R. W. Tirrill, Manchester, Iowa.
The Broom Stick Mightier than the Sword. It always Rules the Infantry. Response by D. W. Reed, Waukon, Iowa.
Music.
The Iowa Soldiers' Home. A Grateful State proudly acknowledges her indebtedness.—Response by B. E. Eberhart, La Porte City, Iowa.
"Co. Q." Always ready for Duty and Double Rations—Response by P. R. Ketchum, Winslow, Iowa.
Music.
The Citizens of Waterloo. Your Patriotism and Hospitality will live in our memories forever.—Response by J. H. Stibbs, Chicago.
Song—"Marching Through Georgia."   All sing.

PROGRAM--SECOND DAY.

Music.   Called to order.   Prayer.
Committee Reports.   Election of Officers.
Miscellaneous Business.   Short Talks by Everybody.
Music.   Parade.   Banquet at Turner Hall.
Toasts and Responses at West Side Opera House.
The Folks at Home.—Response by Rev. J. O. Stevenson, Waterloo.
Music.
The Army Chaplain.—Response by Rev. C. S. Percival, Waterloo.
Music.
The Sacrifices for the Union.—Response by Col. W. P. Hepburn, Clarinda.
Music.
"Hard Tack."—Response by H. C. Hemenway, Cedar Falls.
Music.
"The Girl I Left Behind Me."—Response by C. W. Mullan, Waterloo.
Music.
The Heroism of the War.—Response by Col. D. B. Henderson, Dubuque.

REUNION
OF THE
12TH IOWA V. V. INFANTRY,
APRIL 5th & 6th, 1888.

The third reunion of the surviving members of the old 12th Iowa Volunteer Infantry, was held at Waterloo, Iowa, Thursday and Friday, April 5th and 6th, 1888, and was attended by about 170 of the Veterans, many of whom were accompanied by their wives and children.

The city of Waterloo had donned her gala dress for the occasion, and as the old comrades arrived from different sections of the country, they were greeted at the depots by the proper committees and escorted to the Opera House, where registration was in order and hand-shaking and renewals of old times were indulged in.

The forenoon of the first day was given to the greeting of comrades, renewing the old friendships and fighting the old battles over again.

Among the numerous tasty decorations with which the city abounded, the most notable was that on the Logan House corner, it being a monument about fifteen feet high and placed on a base in imitation of stone, the inscription on the monument being as follows:

HORNET'S NEST BRIGADE.—12TH IOWA VET. VOL. INFANTRY.

FIELD AND STAFF.

Colonel—J. J. Woods.
Major—S. D. Brodtbeck.
Quartermaster—J. B. Dorr.
Asst. Surgeons { W. H. Finley.
{ M. Underwood.
Lieut. Col.—J. P. Coulter.
Adjutant—N. F. Dungan.
Surgeon—C. C. Parker.
Chaplain—A. G. Eberhart.

Under this was the following list of battles in which the regiment took part:

Fort Henry, Fort Donelson, Shiloh, Corinth, Siege of Corinth, Jackson, Vicksburg, Black River, Jackson, (Second), Brandon, Tupelo, White River, Nashville, Holly Springs, Spanish Fort.

The other two faces of the shaft were devoted to the records of the several companies, showing the counties where they were recruited and the original commissioned officers, as follows:

Co A, Hardin county, Captain, S. R Edgington; 1st Lieut., A. E. Webb; 2d Lieut., G W. Moir; 92 men.

Co. B, Allamakee county. Captain, W. C. Earl; 1st Lieut., L. H. Merrill; 2d Lieut., J. H. Borger; 90 men.

Co C, Fayette county Captain, Wm. Warner; 1st Lieut, D. B. Henderson; 2d Lieut, A. M. Smith; 100 men.

Co. D, Linn county Captain, J. H. Stibbs; 1st Lieut., J D. Furguson; 2d Lieut., Hile Hale; 98 men.

Co. E, Blackhawk county. Captain, W. Haddock; 1st Lieut, J. Elwell; 2d Lieut., R. Williams; 94 men

Co. F, Delaware county Captain, J. E. Ainsworth; 1st Lieut., J W. Gift; 2d Lieut, W. A. Morse; 99 men.

Co G, Winneshiek county. Captain, C. C. Tupper; 1st Lieut., L. D. Townsley; 2d Lieut, J. F. Nickerson; 90 men.

Co. H, Dubuque county. Captain, H. J. Playter; 1st Lieut., R. Fishel; 2d Lieut, L W. Jackson; 82 men.

Co. I, Jackson county Captain, E. M. Van Duzee; 1st Lieut., J. J. Marks; 2d Lieut., A. L Palmer; 85 men.

Co. K, Delaware county. Captain, I. G. Fowler; 1st Lieut., L Webb; 2d Lieut., J. J. Brown; 84 men

Total number, 981 men. Number of miles marched, 15,000.

Near the base of the monument was a brass mountain howitzer captured by Co. D, at Selma, Alabama.

THURSDAY AFTERNOON.

At one o'clock the executive committee met at the Opera House and proceeded to the transaction of such matters as were ready for their consideration.

Upon the completion of the business before the executive committee, the association having convened, together with a large outpouring of the citizens of Waterloo, the assemblage was called to order by Col. S. R. Edgington, president of the regimental association, who introduced Rev. Dr. C. S. Percival, Chaplain of the 12th N. Y. Cavalry during the war, who opened the exercises with prayer.

The first order of business being the appointment of committees, the president made the following appointments:

On Resolutions—R. W. Tirrill, R. P. Clarkson, J. E. Simpson, John N. Weaver and E. B. Soper.

On Finance—J. W. Gift, J. H. Stibbs, B. E. Eberhart, John Cole and J. F. Zediker.

On Officers for next Reunion—D. W. Reed, W. W. Whiteneck, R. W. Tirrill, J. E. Simpson and P. R. Woods.

The secretary then proceeded to read the following letters and telegrams from absent comrades:

MONTANA, KANSAS, March 11, 1888.

Mr. W. W. Whiteneck—Dear Comrade:—Your letter reached me several days ago, but as it did not state when the reunion was to be held, I delayed answering until I ascertained the time. The probability is that I shall attend, but I cannot be certain yet whether I shall be able to do so or not. I feel much obliged to you and other members of the regiment for the kindness you have heretofore shown me, and the interest taken to have me present at the reunion. I assure you it would afford me great pleasure to meet again my comrades of the old 12th. Yours, truly, J. J. WOODS.

LOS ANGELES, CAL., March 26, 1888.

My Dear Col Edgington:—Received yours of 21st ultimo Accept my thanks for the welcome invitation. You can be assured that nothing would give me more pleasure than to be able to meet you and our dear boys once again, but it will be impossible for me to attend next reunion

Please give my love and hearty greetings to "every one" of the good old boys of the 12th. "May they all prosper and enjoy life and be able to celebrate yet many reunions," is my toast and my most earnest wish and prayer.

Affectionately, your old comrade and Major, S. D BRODTBECK.

P. S.—I could not write to you earlier, because my dear wife, my companion for nearly fifty years, was ill, and yesterday was laid in her eternal resting place on earth, and is waiting for me in heaven, where I hope to meet her and all my dear comrades.

HOUSE OF REPRESENTATIVES,
WASHINGTON, D. C. February 21, 1888.

Major D. W Reed,—Waukon, Iowa. My dear friend:—Yours transmitting notice of our next 12th Iowa reunion is just received. That is one of the reunions I will not miss if it is possible for me to be there. Of course that must be subordinate to my public duties, but if possible I will be there, and I authorize you to say so to any inquiring friends. Very truly yours, D. B. HENDERSON

HOUSE OF REPRESENTATIVES,
WASHINGTON, D. C., March 19, 1888.

Col. S. R. Edgington, Eldora, Iowa. My dear Colonel:—I find that I must come to you to perform a painful duty, and that is to say that there is but little hope of my being able to attend our next reunion. With the tariff battle coming on, with the presidential fight impending and the immense work that it is now imposing upon me, together with my current official duties, I do not see how it will be possible for me to spare the time to go to Waterloo.

I write you this now so that you may make further preparations for speaking, as there is not one chance in ten of my being able to attend.

It hurts me to write this conclusion, for I have no gathering of any kind that I look forward to with as sincere pleasure as I do the reunion of the old 12th Iowa Infantry.

Remember me kindly to all the comrades at the reunion, and please make it clear to them that it is through no fault of mine that I am not with them. Your friend and comrade, D. B. HENDERSON.

ST. PAUL, MINN, April 4, 1888.

Col. S. R. Edgington. My dear friend:—I have tried to plan to attend the reunion of our old regiment, but an attack of nervous prostration, which puts me under the doctor's care, prevents. Be kind enough to present my warmest greetings to all who are present, and express my regrets at being unable to join in the pleasant exercises of the reunion. Very truly, E M. VAN DUZEE.

ST PAUL, MINN, April 4, 1888.

Capt. J. F. Zediker. My dear friend:—Yours of 28th ult. received. I am very glad to hear from you and to know of your success in this life and hope of a better life beyond. I have, in the last few years, received several cards and circulars from you, but do not remember of receiving any letter to which I have not responded.

It would give me much pleasure to meet my old comrades and take them by the hand. I presume they have changed in outward appearance so that I should fail to recognize many of them, as they, doubtless, would hardly know me. I am bearing some of the marks of time, but my spirit is still young. I cherish very pleasant memories of the companionships of our service, and should enjoy talking over old times and renewing old friendships. But I am to be disappointed again. I am now under the doctor's care for nervous prostration I had hoped to be able to attend this reunion, as circumstances have prevented my attending the others. I shall hope, another year to be present. Give my kindest regards to all members of company I, who are at the reunion, and my best wishes for their future welfare. I shall be glad to hear from you often. Very truly. E M. VAN DUZEE.

BERRIEN SPRINGS, MICH., April 3, 1888.

Abner Dunham, Manchester, Iowa. Dear comrade:—I received your notice of the third reunion of the 12th Iowa Infantry, which takes place at Waterloo on the 5th and 6th of April, of that grand old regiment I love so well; and when I read the notice, as follows: "Time is thinning our ranks, and we who are left, must step to the front, and so long as possible keep our lines unbroken," it makes me think back twenty-five years ago, of the hardships, sufferings, pain and distress, we incurred together in the war and prison dens. Company G boys will remember I am the boy who made my escape from Memphis Sunday morning, but was recaptured at Germantown, and sent south. I had made all arrangements to meet with you, but will not be able to for the reason that I am taken with a very bad cold. Please remember me to all of the dear comrades, and especially to all of the company G boys I hope to be with you at your next reunion. I am fraternally,
NELSON J DAVIS, Late Co. G, 12th Iowa Infantry.

DENVER, COLORADO, April 1, 1888.
To Members of the 12th Iowa in Third Reunion Assembled:

Dear Comrades:—Until within a few weeks, I had fully intended to be with you at Waterloo, but my business is such that I cannot leave without greater loss than I can afford. I regret exceedingly that it is so, for I know from former experience what a good time you will have I can imagine you now, as I write, and your dear old faces are as plainly before me as on *dress parade*. Oh, how the old memories crowd themselves on my mind, and my pen is unequal to the task of putting them on paper. As I sit here thinking, I see Dunham, (God bless him) and Morisey, and Comstock, and Grannis, and Reed, and Knee, and—well, I see you all, and here's my hand, shake, boys, my heart is with you, if my body is absent. Here I am, crying like a baby.

You all know the effort I made four years ago to be with you, so I think it not necessary to assure you of my loyalty, and as you grasp each other by the hand, and the eyes moisten, and you live over again "The Days of Auld Lang Syne," just give me a kindly thought, for I will be with you in spirit.

I wish you a royal good time, and may God bless you. Yours until the Grand Review. S. M. FRENCH, Late Principal Musician 12th Iowa,
2911 Lafayette St, Denver, Colorado.

WAHOO, NEBRASKA, April 4, 1888.

Capt. J. E. Simpson, Waterloo, Iowa. My dear old friend:—For the last four years I have indulged the hope and expectation to be with you at Waterloo this time, and not until last evening did anything transpire to prevent me from going. I am so very sorry. Please present my compliments and regrets to Col. Edgington and all inquiring friends and comrades, and assure them that the fire of love for country, flag, and the old regiment burns just as bright as ever on my heart's altar. The camp, march and field are remembered with melancholy pride, and at the bier of the daughter of the regiment—Miss Florence Dunham—I drop a silent tear, in token of the untimely departure of one so promising and universally beloved. Hope you will have a pleasant, enthusiastic meeting. I have but one favor to ask at your hands at this time, which is, when Sergt.—Lieut. Grannis appears upon the stage with the old war-worn, tattered and torn colors, give one long, loud shout for your absent friend and comrade, JOHN STEEN.

PIEDMONT, WEST VIRGINIA, March 19, 1888.

Dr. James Barr, Algona, Iowa. My Dear Doctor:—Yours of the 14th inst., enclosing a call to the third reunion of the 12th Iowa V. V. Infantry is just received. To be allowed to meet those noble men once more would be a delight, but to do so this year will be impossible. I am sorry to hear of the death of the wife of Comstock, and of the daughter of Dunham. They have gone home. We, too, at no distant day shall be mustered out. While in the service let us hold the fort. And I well know that you will and the veteran lieutenant and the color-bearer of a hundred fields will always stand to the colors in the front in the thickest of the fight.

My health compelled me to leave the northwest for a warmer climate. Since I came here it has improved, yet I have to use my forces with a care and prudence to which I was a total stranger before I entered the army.

I trust and hope that you will have a jubilant reunion at Waterloo, like that we had at Manchester. Give my love to the veterans whom I honor and respect, and I hope a country saved by their valor will acknowledge its obligation to their heroism by giving them some assistance in the way of pensions to meet the needs of declining years—assistance which is justly due but can never pay back the health, strength and life which they gave to their country. With kind remembrances to your family, your friend,

F. HUMPHREY.

BIG RUN, JEFFERSON COUNTY, PA., March 29, 1888.

To the Members of the 12th Iowa Infantry:

It is with extreme regret that I can not, under existing circumstances, be present at the reunion on the 5th and 6th of April, (much as I would like to be there). My best wishes are with the boys. Hoping you may all have a pleasant and enjoyable time, I remain, W. H BOWERS,
Company C, 12th Iowa Infantry.

DAVENPORT, IOWA, April 4, 1888.

To my old Comrades of the 12th:

Comrades:—I am very sorry I cannot be with you at your reunion; circumstances over which I have no control prevent me from meeting my old comrades. I know it would be a great pleasure to me, but it can't be helped, so the next best I can do is to report by letter, so put me down on the rolls as present, anyhow.

I extend to one and all of my old comrades, the right hand of friendship; let those that are absent think of those that are present, and those that are present remember those that are absent; all as brothers, for brothers we are always, aye and ever. Wishing you all such a good time as only a reunion can bring to the old heroes of a hundred fields, and the best men that ever trod a continent, I am now as heretofore, your comrade,

(Shake, every one.) DENNIS CONLEY, "D," 12th Iowa V. V. I.

VANCOUVER, W. T., March 21, 1888.

Benjamin E. Eberhart. My dear friend and comrade:—I was much pleased to receive your favor inviting me to come and join in the third reunion of the dear old 12th Iowa. I have long wished for the pleasure to be at one of its reunions, to once more see and greet my brave and gallant old comrades. But I am sorry to say that I cannot possibly avail myself of the happy privilege to do so at the coming reunion, owing to the absence of my commanding officer on detached duty until April 30th, current. I have charge of the issuing of all the military stores at this ordnance depot to every Post in the department, as the same is required. I have had charge of that duty ten years, hence in the absence of my commanding officer, I cannot be spared from my duty. I have pending in Congress a bill for my special retirement, with seventy-five per cent of pay and allowances, which, if it passes, I will be free and at liberty to go where and when I please, and if such shall be my good fortune, and I be alive when the next reunion is held, I promise

to be there if possible. It will be but a few times that it can be possible but for a lucky few to so meet, owing to the most having been mustered out and joined the great silent majority, their deaths hastened in most cases from physical infirmities engendered in the terrible ordeal of that long and cruel war for the preservation of our loved nation. When I think of the patriotism and sacrifices which alone impelled the brave union soldiers to voluntarily imperil their lives in defense of their loved country, and the inestimable blessings secured to the nation through their unconquerable valor, and considering the plethoric condition of the national treasury, with such vast amount of treasure lying idle and kept out of the business circulation of the country, I feel aghast at the refusal by the governing power of prompt recognition of the claims of the nation's defenders as petitioned by the G. A. R. committee, and the first settled among them should be the claims of the prisoners of war, to reward them as it best and only can for the outrageous and inhuman treatment which they endured at the hands of their brutal captors. Ben, with all your sad misfortune to get so seriously wounded at the battle of Shiloh by that grape shot which went under the bridge of your nose and lodged in the socket of your right eye, and which necessitated sending you to the rear for medical treatment, you thereby was certainly saved from the tortures of the confederate prison hells. Ben, I shall never forget your forcible and impious exclamation, when I first picked you up and relieved you of your sword and revolver. No, luckily you was left a very narrow margin for life, and your face was very bloody from your wound. I surely thought your end had come, but that meaning exclamation dispelled that gloomy thought, and I concluded that you would get well. Oh, how rejoiced I would be, if present, to hear repeated by the comrades the old, old stories of glory and suffering we shared in common together I hope that our sturdy old friend and comrade, D. B. Henderson, will be present with you to enthuse the boys. The boys must keep him in Congress to champion their cause and interest. I am highly pleased that Waterloo (the old headquarters of company E,) is selected for the occasion, as it is the most central place for the majority to reach that could be selected, and I feel well assured that you will receive a cordial welcome and hospitable treatment. I beg of you to express for me my sincere love and regard to every comrade of the old regiment. I hope that it will be a happy and profitable meeting. I am,
Your friend and comrade, ROBERT WILLIAMS.

LAKE FOREST, LAKE COUNTY, ILLS., April 1, 1888.

Dear Comrade:—I was very glad to hear from you, and also from Gen. J. H. Stibbs, and I am very sorry that I cannot be one of your number at the reunion. My whole heart is with you; it is so that I cannot possibly get away; please give my best wishes to all of old company "D." I will write you a good letter when I hear from you again. Give my best respects to little Captain J. H. Stibbs; tell him I will write to him very soon. So good bye; from your old friend and comrade PERRY GEPHART.

HAZELTON, IOWA, April 4, 1888.

Dear Comrades and Soldiers:—I regret that I cannot be with you, but under the circumstance it is impossible to be there. I have been sick for some time, and am not able to come, but I hope that you will have a good time, and maybe the next reunion I will be able to come. I am in hopes so, at least. I will close by sending my best wishes to you all.
Your Comrade, JOSEPH S. GIRTON.

LOUISVILLE, KY., April 1, 1888.

Dear Dunham:—It is with feelings of regret that I announce my inability to attend the reunion on the 5th and 6th. I had looked forward to the meeting with no little anxiety, but since I left home measles broke out in the family of my next door neighbor, and I fear that my children and wife have been exposed, not one of them ever having had them. Say to the boys for me, that I regret very, very much that I can't be with them, for if there is a people on earth—outside of kin—I truly love, it is the members of the old 12th. It is true our associations were short, but long enough to seal our love for one another to eternity. Tell the boys I think of them often, and especially never do I wander over the beautiful grounds of the cemetery at Pittsburg, but what the days of more than a quarter of a century ago, the 6th of April, and the faces of the dear boys who stood around me on that memorable day, are brought vividly back. And when I pass over these grounds and read the names of our fallen comrades, some of whom I can remember, my heart grows sick. Tell Justice Schneider, if he is alive and present, that I remember him well, and would be glad to hear from him, as would I also from any of the boys. I hope yet to pay you all a visit, and am nearly sure that I will do it at some day not far distant. Should I defer the matter for twenty-five or thirty more years, age will be creeping on us and we would not seem ourselves.

Accept my sympathy for your last sad bereavement—the loss of your daughter. I again entreat you to remember me kindly to the boys.

I am, truly, C. C. STRIBLING.

LINCOLN, NEB., April 3, 1888.

Dear friends of the 12th Iowa Infantry Volunteers:—I had thought up to date I surely should be with you on this great occasion, but as duty compels me to stay at home I must sacrifice the pleasure it would afford me to be with you all to-day. My mother has been sick for two years, and for the last six months has been bed fast, so that it is impossible for me to leave her, therefore my absence from you is unavoidable, but you may rest assured my thoughts are with you all, and I hope you will have a glorious reunion, and that all that are at this reunion may live to celebrate a good many more. With the very kindest regards to all, I remain, yours as ever,

F. F. LANKINS, Co. B, 12th Iowa V. I.

PORTERVILLE, KANSAS, April 2, 1888.

Dear Mr. Dunham, and other friends:—I am reminded that the 5th and 6th of April is drawing near, and that many of the old 12th Iowa will meet in reunion. I have still pleasant remembrance of the reunion at Manchester, eight years ago. I wish to be remembered to all of the friends, particularly company F. Tell them that while sunny Kansas is not paradise, I cannot help, as I look out on the green trees and flowers and sunshine to-day, wishing they might have as pleasant a day for the reunion as to-day is here.

Hoping that you may all have a pleasant time, and the camp-fire may have plenty of rails, I remain, with kindest regards,

ALICE F. ELDREDGE LAMBDIN.

And I think I belong to the 12th Iowa.

ST. PAUL, MINN., April 4, 1888.

Abner Dunham, Sec'y, Waterloo, Iowa:

Dear Sir:—I wrote Capt. Reed, when I received notice of the reunion of the Veteran Twelfth Iowa, at Waterloo, on the 5th and 6th, that I surely would be there. At the last hour I find, with regret, that I cannot, without undue sacrifice, leave home and business. Please make my cordial greeting to the men of that noble regiment, with whom I was so pleasantly associated in the army, and express my sincere regret that I cannot be with them. God bless them, one and all. Sincerely yours, WM. R. MARSHALL.

VINTON, IOWA, April 1, 1888.

Abner Dunham, Sec'y 12th Iowa Infantry Association:

My Dear Comrade:—I deeply regret that sickness in my family prevents my attendance with the comrades in the Third Regimental Reunion, and the more so, because of the thinning in the ranks which must take place by the inevitable muster-out between this time and the next reunion. That the Third Reunion may be in every way satisfactory, is the earnest wish of

COMRADE J. W. RICH, Co. E, 12th Iowa.

DES MOINES, IOWA, April 3, 1888.

Col. S. R. Edgington, Eldora, Iowa. My dear Colonel:—Yours of 27th ultimo inviting me to attend the meeting of your gallant old regiment—the 12th Iowa—on Shiloh day at Waterloo, received. I regret exceedingly that other engagements will prevent my going, for nothing would give me more pleasure than to meet with the brave men who stood like a wall of fire in front of the enemies of our country, on that memorable day, and who so potentially aided in making the Iowa soldier and the "hornets' nest" a name to be proud of and a reward to be envied.

My kind regards to the boys, and may you all live to see many returns of this anniversary of the great battle of Shiloh, in which they took so distinguished and honorable part. Truly your friend, J. M. TUTTLE.

UNION STOCK YARDS, CHICAGO, ILL., April 5, 1888.

Abner Dunham—Secretary Soldiers' Reunion:—I have looked forward to the meeting of to-day with great pleasure, but circumstances prevent my being with you. Give my regrets to comrades. JOHN ELWELL.

YANKTON, D. T., April 5, 1888.

Abner Dunham—Secretary 12th Iowa Association:—With kindest greetings to the dear old Twelfth. JOHN BREMNER

Major D. W. Reed, chairman of the committee on the history of the regiment, then made the following report:

To the Comrades of the 12th Iowa Infantry:

Your committee on Regimental History beg leave to report as follows:

At our reunion four years ago, your committee reported progress, and suggested, that to make the history as complete as it ought to be, sub-committees should be appointed by each company to collect and arrange such matters of interest peculiar to each company as ought to be preserved. Such committees were appointed, and their names published on page 73 of minutes of your last reunion. It was also suggested at that time that personal sketches of lives of commissioned officers at least, be procured for the history. Very soon after said reunion your committee notified the chairman of each of these sub-committees of their appointment, and urged their co-operation in the work of making the history a faithful record that would preserve to our children the events in the service of a gallant regiment.

To give some direction to this work and make it as nearly uniform as possible, your committee suggested that company histories should cover the following particulars at least:

I. When and where organized and by whom recruited.

II. When ordered into camp; date of arrival at camp.

III. Date of muster into United States service.

IV. Sketch of life of each commissioned officer, with enlistment, promotion, wounds, special service, etc.

V. Record of battles, campaigns, scouts, marches, skirmishes, etc., by company, especially when detached from regiment.

VI. Matters of special company interest, and worthy of record, such as individual acts of gallantry, incidents of camp, etc

VII. As complete roster of company as possible, showing each man's enlistment, wounds, promotion, death, discharge, etc.

Failing to receive responses to these requests, personal letters were written to other members of committees, until responses have been received from several companies, and others have agreed to have the work done.

Comrade J. S Margretz was first to respond with a very complete history of company "E." Comrade Soper responded with a chapter of history of company "D" This company divided the work among different members of their committee, and are doing thorough work. Comrade J. D. Cole, from his very complete diary kept during the war, was able to put company "B" in splendid shape. Comrades Col. Edgington and Clarkson have vouched for the work of company "A," but have not handed it in. Comrade Bremner—company "F,"—asks further time to complete his work. Companies "G" and "H" are without a promise from any one to undertake the work. Comrades Zediker and Teskey have assured us that company "I" would be attended to. Comrade Morgan—company "K"—chairman of committee, assures us that it is impossible for him to give sufficient time for this work, and others of the company have not replied to letters sent.

Your committee has also endeavored to obtain some personal items of *Regimental* Officers, relying upon sub-committees to arrange such items of company officers.

From the office of Adjutant General U. S. A., and other sources, we were able to obtain the desired items in regard to Col. Woods. From comrade M. P. Mills, who married the daughter of Lieut. Col. Coulter, we are promised a sketch of the Lieutenant Colonel's life. Major Brodtbeck could not be persuaded to put himself on record, but by appealing to his daughter, Mrs. Wymetal, of Denver, Colorado, we were able to secure a complete record of his service in the Prussian army, etc. Mrs. Dr. Huff has said that as soon as she can get at the doctor's papers she would give her personal attention to the matter. Several others are on file, others are promised and only one or two have refused outright, though several have required considerable urging. These personal sketches are, we are sure, just such items as the comrades will desire to know and have preserved in permanent form. Your committee has been very much interested in these sketches and histories, and hope other officers now living, and friends of those deceased, will surely see that all these items are furnished.

The sub-committee on history of Union Brigade have not reported their work. This gallant band of much abused, imposed upon-soldiers should not be neglected. Some of the best fighting of the war was done by these same men. In addition to these personal sketches and company histories, your committee has procured full sets of Adjutant Generals' reports of the State of Iowa, and have prepared references to all mention made of the regiment, from which to copy such matter as may be of interest. They have also made quite lengthy extracts from official reports of the battles in which the regiment was engaged, as published in official records of the rebellion, including reports of confederate officers commanding the troops opposed to the 12th Iowa on different fields. We find these reports very interesting, especially of such battles as Shiloh, for by these, at least, we are able to prove that the "Hornets' Nest Brigade" did not surrender in the morning without firing a gun, but that they fought the whole rebel army and surrendered only when the day was spent and the battle won. Nearly every confederate officer on the field that day, from corps commander to the last colonel, claims the honor of having taken part in the final action which broke Grant's line at five o'clock p. m., and that they were present when Prentiss surrendered.

These reports, of themselves, if put in shape for ready reference, will prove, without a lingering doubt in any mind, that the 2d, 7th, 8th, 12th, and 14th Iowa, comprising the "Hornets' Nest Brigade," held the key to the position on the field of Shiloh twenty-six years ago to-day, and held it against the combined attack of twelve whole brigades and the Crescent regiment; that after twelve unsuccessful charges in which these forces literally broke themselves to pieces on our line, Gen. Ruggles admits that he found it impossible to break the line by direct assault with infantry, and sent his staff to collect all the artillery to his left, and names eleven batteries and a section which he brought to a commanding position in our front and concentrated the fire upon our position while he sent infantry to attack the flanks.

It was, according to these reports, only after the extreme rebel left commanded by Gen. Pond, had driven Sherman and McClernand back, and by a continuous right wheel had, in *rear* of "Hornets' Nest," met the forces of Chalmers, who had on the right driven back Stewart and Hurlbut, and this brigade was enclosed in a circle composed of the whole rebel army and exposed to the concentrated fire of Ruggles' artillery, that they were forced from the position assigned them in the morning.

All this matter now on hand should be properly arranged, and as soon as reports are all in, should be printed. Your committee urge immediate action by those who have not completed the work intended, forgetting, if need be, our natural modesty in preparing these sketches, remembering that we work not for ourselves but for our children and the generations to come after us.

You know, comrades, that our record, especially at the battle of Shiloh, had been so misrepresented that it seemed for a while that we should never recover from the effects of the untruthful reports first published by some reporter never nearer the battlefield than Cairo. But these misrepresentations are being corrected as true history is written, and we have only to preserve these facts and proofs which we now have, to be able to place before the world a record which shall challenge comparison with any in the proud galaxy of Iowa regiments, of which it can truthfully be said, not one had a stain upon its banner.

Let us then, comrades, give this matter our earnest attention and complete the work at once, realizing that each successive reunion finds our ranks greatly depleted, and those who can furnish items desired will soon have received their final discharge from the active duties of life.

Respectfully submitted, D. W. REED,
                                       R. P. CLARKSON, } Committee.
                                       J. D. COLE,

Short talks were indulged in by the comrades present on this subject matter, when, upon motion, the report of the committee was accepted and adopted

Comrade J. E. Simpson then offered the following:

Mr. President and Comrades:

"Allow me to call your attention to a matter that I think important and proper. It is this: That there should be appointed, some one from each company, whose duty it shall be to ascertain all the dates, facts and circumstances connected with the death of those of their respective companies, who may die between the time of our holding our reunions. For instance, to illustrate, since our last reunion I am informed of the death of two of our comrades, of company "G," Archibald A. Carey, who was with us at our last reunion, and at that time his face showed that death had marked him for its own. He said to us on dress parade, that it would be the last time he would meet with us. His prediction proved true. Honest, upright, a great sufferer, never a well man since our bitter experience at Benton Barracks, in the winter of 1861. Slowly and surely he passed away, surrounded by his family and friends, near Castalia, Iowa. O. D. Miller, another of our comrades, has died; a plain, simple man, who did every duty well, one of those soldiers who was always prompt to say, "I will go, orderly." Away off in Nebraska he had taken him a homestead For years he had been a patient sufferer, never complaining, never regretting that he went to the defense of the Union. A comrade of good standing in his G. A. R. Post at Stuart. His widow writes me, as he drew near his end he had an intense longing to see some one of his old comrades. His heart went to those with whom he had camped, marched, fought and toiled, and his dying thoughts were of them.

Now, my dear comrades, it does seem to me that this is a matter of importance and should be carefully attended to. One after another we shall drop away, and certainly our organization ought to take note of the little incidents and surroundings of the last sickness and death, and have it announced at these reunions."

Acting upon the suggestion of the foregoing the president appointed the following from each company:

Company A—R. P. Clarkson,   Company F—R. W, Tirrill,
        "   B—J. D Cole,   "   G—J. E. Simpson,
        "   C—D. W. Reed,   "   H—J. A. Van Anda,
        "   D—J. H Stibbs,   "   I—J. F. Zediker,
        "   E—J. W. Shoemaker.   "   K—J. B. Morgan.

The balance of the afternoon was given to general talk by the comrades, reminiscences and story telling, and after a general love feast was adjourned to meet again at the camp fire in the evening.

EVENING SESSION.

The camp fire in the evening was held at Brown's Opera House, the building being filled to its utmost capacity, many being unable to gain admission. The Waterloo cornet band enlivened the occasion with its sweet strains of music, and the several responses to the different toasts were interspersed with choice and appropriate songs by the Glee Club of the city, whose presence added much to the festivities of the occasion.

Ex-Gov. B. R. Sherman then took the stand, and delivered an appropriate and feeling address of welcome. It was wholly extemporaneous, and no draft of it can be obtained.

Col. S. R. Edgington, president of the association, responded in the following feeling speech:

Mr. President—Ladies and Gentlemen:

On behalf of my comrades of the 12th Iowa, I thank you more than I have words to express for your kind words of welcome, so beautiful and so complimentary. I want to say to the good people of Waterloo, that we are glad to be here in your beautiful and patriotic city, that gave to the 12th Iowa regiment the brave and fearless company "E," whose comrades touched elbows on many a bloody battle field.

We remember your loyalty and devotion to the flag in our struggle for liberty and union, and how nobly your heroic sons volunteered and filled up the ranks and left for the front and field of battle.

Waterloo is noted for her hospitality to the boys who wore the blue. The city is handsomely built on both banks of the beautiful Cedar river, whose waters flow onward to the Mississippi and down to the sea.

Away back in 1861, when Waterloo was not as large and beautiful a city as it is to-day, I brought my company (A) over from Hardin county by teams, for the purpose of taking the cars for our camp at Dubuque. What a change since 1861. Then there were but few inhabitants and but one railroad. Now you are of many railroads and many thousands of inhabitants.

Many of you will remember that about the close of the war many of our citizens were much troubled about what would become of society, when the veterans were all mustered out. It was a matter of grave apprehension to many of our people, especially among those who were not truly loyal to our country and flag, that when this great, grand army, who had saved the liberty of our people, were mustered out and turned loose on society, murder, arson, and all manner of crimes would be committed by the old vets. How wild were such imaginations. When the army was mustered out and the veterans laid aside the musket and the sword, and returned again to their farms, their work-shops and all other peaceful avocations, society stepped up to a higher plane of civilization. My experience and observation is that our veterans are our best citizens.

Your speaker has served in two wars and my observation is that any man who was not a good citizen, was worthless as a soldier. A good soldier always makes a good citizen, wherever his lot may be cast.

When we think of who is most entitled to praise for saving the union, we do not think of our great generals and brilliant commanders—all honor to them and their noble deeds—but rather do we think of the brave men who carried their muskets, that stormed the trenches of Donelson and Vicksburg, who stood like walls of living flame at Shiloh and Gettysburg; and of the men who carried their muskets and one hundred rounds of cartridges and marched under Sherman from Atlanta to the sea.

These old veterans we have with us here to the gratitude of every American citizen. The men who carried and the men who followed that dear old flag. These are the men who, in 1861, put pleading love aside, unclasped the dimpled hands of prattling babes fast locked about their necks, parted from wife and child because their country called. Boys who forced back their tears, forsook a father's house and the happy home group, the loved maiden and the joys of youth, and with mother's kisses warm on their lips went to the field of battle, following their flag.

When in my dreams, or when my mind dwells on army days and I think of those killed in battle or died in hospital, or were starved to death in southern prison hells, I seem to hear something saying, "Comrade, we are in a fairer land than earth; we are in and enjoy a realm where the rainbow shines brightly evermore; where the sun, moon and stars are spread out before us like islands, great and small, on the broad ocean of eternity; here traitors never come and treason is unknown. We leave robes of blue, for robes of gray are not used here."

I do not endorse the attitude of our government towards the prisoners of war, nor have the survivors of rebel prison hells received justice from the government that they deserve. It seems to m· they have not. The prisoners were allowed to suffer and die by thousands as a military necessity for the suppression of the rebellion. Our government was not willing to give man for man in exchange, and at the close of the war thousands of sick and feeble prisoners were discharged to die or to be nursed back to life at their own expense. Men who left home and loved ones and endured without a murmur the privations of camp and field. Men who stood unmoved amid the storms of leaden hail. Yes, brave, honorable and true men who never turned their backs on friend or foe. These are the men who composed the Union army. These are the men who saved our country and flag.

No other country on the face of the earth could have survived and come through so fierce a war with her territory intact, with the rights and liberties of all her people maintained. None other but this our own Columbia, "the land of the brave and the free."

These veterans of the 12th Iowa Infantry were in twenty-three battles. They were under the rebel fire 112 days. They marched during their term of service—four years and three months—2,670 miles. They traveled by water and land 13,809 miles. Total number of casualties, 582. Total number killed in battle, 95. Total number died of disease, 217. Total number discharged for disease and wounds, 247. They were first in the fight and last to leave the field. They suffered in southern prison hells for more than six months.

This short historical sketch is given for the benefit of those who have grown up since the war, that they may better know what the old veterans did to save our country and flag from the traitors' grasp.

Comrades of the grand old 12th Iowa, veterans of twenty-three hard fought battles, behold that dear old flag again,

> With its stars and its stripes, and the red white and blue,
> So dear to the hearts of all loyal and true;
> The banner of our Union, the flag of the brave and the free,
> On hill top or in valley, or down by the sea.

In peace or in war all hail to the flag of my country wherever it waves!

On behalf of my comrades of the 12th Iowa, who have come here from all over the state of Iowa, and many of them from other states, I thank you again for your kind words and acts of welcome. It would be difficult to convey to you our deep feelings of appreciation for the hearty and cordial manner in which you have approved that welcome by your appearance in such large numbers and for this splendid reception.

In response to the toast, "Why We Hold Reunions," comrade S. R. Burch responded as follows:

Beloved Comrades—Ladies and Gentlemen:

"Why we hold reunions," is a question easily answered by any member of the dear old 12th. But comrades, just why I've been selected to respond to the interrogatory I'm at a loss to know, when we have such a multitude of orators to draw upon to do this part of the work of our reunions; work I say for the reason what would be a very great pleasure for some of our comrades, who are by profession, and who possess natural and acquired gifts for imparting to others rich gems of thought, clothed with beautiful language, which is food for the intelligent mind, while I might labor and burn the midnight oil and yet fail to say anything of very great interest. But as I am detailed to perform this duty, I shall attempt to give a few reasons why we hold reunions.

We come together once in four years, to grasp the warm hand of him who many times during that terrible war did so many things to make us love each other as members of the same household. It must be a hard heart that would not cement to that of his comrade who stood side by side with him in the ranks at Pittsburg Landing, twenty-six years ago to-morrow. You, comrades, all remember as though it were but yesterday, the beautiful, bright Sabbath morning, when we were preparing our camp and equipments for Sunday morning inspection, when we heard in the distance a rumbling sound as of thunder, and instead of the drum corps playing "The girl I left behind me," for the assembly of the companies for inspection, the long roll was sounded from the colonel's quarters, which brought forth the boys from their tents, partly clad and with bated breath and hearts beating quicker, some with musket in parts for cleaning, others at a brook a little way off washing and searching for something they had not lost—graybacks; but in less time than it takes to tell the story the companies were formed; boys who were not able to answer to the roll-call a short hour before were now in the ranks to answer "here" when their names were called. The color-bearer (you all know him) took position and the companies were quickly formed to his right and left; now the rebel artillery was belching forth fire and smoke, and the rattle of musketry grew thicker and thicker, when the colonel's clear voice rang out, "battalion, right face, forward, double quick, march." When we had gone but a short distance we met hundreds of wounded and frightened soldiers, wild with excitement and fear, coming from the front, who admonished us not to go out there for we would all be killed. If you will not mention it I will tell you that we too were badly scared, but our officers undaunted led the way and we followed on. We met the victorious enemy who had driven in our exposed regiments, and now began the conflict, terrible in carnage and blood; beloved officers fall mortally wounded; a brother pierced with a rebel bullet; a dear comrade falls, then another and another; on, on, throughout the long day the battle raged fiercer and more terrible; repeatedly did the enemy mass his forces and charge our line, which we hurled back as often as they came, inflicting terrible loss. This position the enemy denominated, "The Hornet's Nest." When the rattle of musketry grew fainter and fainter and farther away, both on the right and on the left, our flanks are driven in; our battle line is broken; the enemy came up in our rear, when more fierce than ever (if possible) the battle raged till the sun was nearly down; now being surrounded and cut off from our forces by overwhelming numbers, what did we do, surrender? No. The rear rank faced to the rear and opened fire upon the foe—who soon realizing our fearful execution, charged our position from both front and rear. Many, very many of our brave boys fall bleeding and dying, and we who so miraculously escape the bullet, were destined to a more deplorable calamity, that of being overpowered and taken "prisoners of war," to be incarcerated in the prison pens of the south to be placed in the custody of a Wertz, to starve and die.

Comrades, we who survive those terrible ordeals, meet together once in four years to tell our wonderful stories of hardships endured, and greet each other. These are some of the reasons why we hold our reunions. Dear friends, do you wonder why we hold reunions? What I have told you is but a small part, one day's experience as it were. I have told you of but one battle in which we were engaged. We might tell you of the suffering from the cold storm and hard fighting at Donelson; the fierce and unsuccessful charges on the strong fortifications of Vicksburg, the capture and recapture of Jackson, of the battles of Corinth, Tupelo, Nashville and Spanish Fort. The long and weary marches in all kinds of weather, on short rations; then it was unsafe for a chicken to crow or a pig to squeal. Friends, do not think for a moment that we had no fun in the army, for the inventive ingenuity of the Yankee so proverbial, from the force of circumstances was brought into requisition, and it would take hours to tell of the many little incidents happening to break the monotony of camp life; and now we love to meet and refresh our memories of the past and renew our acquaintance. Time is fast changing the raven hair to snowy locks—the bloom of youth to furrowed cheeks and wrinkled brow.

When I take part in camp-fires and sham battles now and then,
These war-like reproductions call to mind the gallant men
Who marched and bivouacked with us; still we look for them in vain—
We can tell you of their valor, of their records free from stain.

They were strong and hopeful when from home they marched away;
Soon to learn each soldier's duty was comprised in to "obey."
Very few knew of the heartache 'neath the uniforms of blue;
Some did call us over loyal when to homes we bade adieu.

Even thoughtless words were spoken of the bravest volunteer—
Why enlist, if ties were binding, or if homes were very dear?
Smile upon them brave old soldiers, ask them of the mystery,
Why men sacrificed their life-blood for the boon of liberty.

Then we little thought of honors intervening years have brought;
We were thinking of our country and the lessons patriots taught.
Should the old flag be disfigured—lessened by a single star?
Never! for brave men revered it, both in peace and time of war.

Fierce and long the bitter contest; those were anxious months and years;
We can never reproduce them, never reproduce the tears;
Rank and file can shoulder rifles, epaulets be worn again,
But no regiment can muster *old time* officers and men.

Vain the roll call, vain the bugle, till the last loud trumpet sounds,
There will be the grand reunion on the new plantation grounds;
If the martyred soldiers trusted last in Him who bore the cross,
Their's the gain, and yet while grieving we had counted it but loss.

The last to fall was Gallegher, of D., soon all will be laid to rest;
But down through future ages will live brave Logan's request,
That the graves of fallen comrades, on the 30th day of May,
Be strewn with flowers as tokens of remembrance on that day.

And when we hold reunions could we muffle the drums somewhat!
Lest the widowed and the orphaned think their loved ones are forgot.
And don't forget to battle for the principles of right;
'Twill keep the banner waving and the nation's record bright;
For with north and south united, other nations yet will see,
Our moral conflicts but enhance our love of liberty.

"The Hornets' Nest Brigade." Their valor saved the world's greatest commander.

The response to this toast had been assigned to comrade T. B. Edgington, of Memphis, Tennessee, but not being present the following letter was read from him:

MEMPHIS, TENN., April 1st, 1888.

Comrades of the 12th Iowa:—Circumstances have prevented my attendance at your reunion. It has been my great desire to attend this reunion, not only because I would meet my old comrades, but because the reunion is to take place among the hospitable people of Waterloo, Iowa, a people whose hospitality to our comrades of the Old Twelfth was as honest and heartfelt as were the hospitalities extended to us by the people of Altoona, Pennsylvania, on our return from military prisons, when the living skeletons that crowded the train, found themselves suddenly surprised and overwhelmed with substantial food and dainty delicacies, steaming hot as it came fresh from the kitchens of their mountain homes, to be dispensed by the hands of fair maidens amid smiles and tears. While I cannot be present at the reunion in the flesh, you will find me there in spirit.

For myself I will say that time has laid his hand upon me so gently that I still consider myself "one of the boys," yet my step may not be so elastic as when I was the file leader of the regiment, and my spirits may not be so buoyant as when we scaled the breastworks of Donelson.

Finding myself unable to attend the reunion, it was my purpose to write out my response to the toast assigned me, but I have not been able to do so.

Referring, however, to the subject matter of the toast, there never has been any doubt in my mind but that the valor of the "Hornets' Nest Brigade" saved the Union army from defeat at the battle of Shiloh.

The Southerner, to this day, believes that Gen. Beauregard should have pressed on and followed up the success of the confederate army and closed the work of the day with a complete defeat and capture of the Union army.

No one can vindicate the good generalship of Gen. Beauregard so well as members of the "Hornets' Nest Brigade," who laid down their arms with us at 6 o'clock p. m., on Sunday, April 6, 1862. Albert Sidney Johnson, their commanding general, had fallen that day. The stubborn resistance and final capitulation of the "Hornets' Nest Brigade" had thrown the enemy's center into almost inextricable confusion. Beauregard found the disciplined army of an hour before, an army of fragments, a howling mob, which had forgotten the errand for which it came, in the exultation of a partial victory.

The reorganization of the confederate army so as to make an onward movement that night was a physical impossibility to any new commander who should step into the shoes of that great general, Albert Sidney Johnson.

History will vindicate the sound judgment and good generalship of Gen. Beauregard, while it places the blood-bought laurel wreaths on the "Hornets' Nest Brigade," which held the overwhelming enemy in check until night and Buell came.

The attack on Shiloh was made under the direction of the authorities at Richmond. Their plan was to demolish Grant's army before Buell's army could form a junction. Thereupon they would capture or destroy our transports and gunboats; when this was done they would fall upon Buell's army, west of Columbia, Tennessee, cut off its communications and destroy or capture it; when this was once done there was nothing south of the Ohio river that could resist the victorious confederate army, and it would have become an army of invasion.

The battle of Shiloh was fought when the nation was smarting under the humiliation of the Bull Run defeat, when the cry of "*On to Richmond,*" had entered upon its second season of disappointment, when the voice of the copperhead was heard in the land. If the South had been successful in its plans for the destruction of Grant's and Buell's armies, who can say that the Union would not have perished? The probabilities are strongly that way. A reaction in public sentiment after such a series of signal defeats would probably have demanded terms of peace at the cost of the nation's life. If this be so, then has not the valor of the "*Hornets' Nest Brigade,*" not only saved the "world's greatest *commander,*" but has it not saved the world's greatest *nation?* These are questions that we will submit for your consideration. If you cannot solve them, posterity will form its own unbiased conclusions. History doubtless will point its index finger at the "*Hornets' Nest Brigade,*" as one of the agencies which was indispensable to the nation's life.

With cordial greetings for the survivors of the old 12th, and Co. "A," in particular, I am, as ever, your old comrade,   T. B. EDGINGTON.

"Was the War Worth the Sacrifice." One country, one flag and more stars.

Col. D. B Henderson was to have responded to this toast, but as his congressional duties detained him at Washington, Capt. E. B. Soper was called upon to fill his place. As no reporter was present to take his remarks, which were extemporaneous, we are unable to give but a synopsis, as follows:

"He first considered the money cost of the war to the Federal government, and used illustrations to give some idea of the immense treasure expended, and estimated that the cost to the Southern States, with the property destroyed by the ravages of war, fully equaled expenditures of the North—to which should be added the loss of life, the unmeasured suffering on battlefields and in hospitals, of the sick and wounded, the tears and heartrending anguish of wives, mothers and sisters, and all the miseries of the bloody and long continued strife, the immeasurable sum total of which constituted the sacrifices the war cost. Against this he put, the country preserved as a unit—four million slaves made free, their masters and the white people of the slave states likewise made free, the better feeling existing between the sections resulting from the changed condition in the new South, and the mighty strides made in educating the whole people up to a better comprehension of the worth of our institutions by the severe schooling of the war; all these and others were brought forward, considered and illustrated at some length, and the audience then left, by the speaker, to decide whether the war was worth what it cost."

"Home When the Boys Were Away." The dark days of 1861 to 1865.

This toast was eloquently responded to by Mrs. E. J. W. Tirrill, wife of comrade R. W. Tirrill, of Co. "F," in the following manner:

"The time had come, when brothers must fight and sisters must pray at home."

These familiar lines from an old army song, bring the long past to our very doors. Again the drum and fife are heard in our streets; the recruiting officer is abroad in our land; they are raising liberty poles in every town prominent or obscure, and speeches full of the spirit of '76 are kindling an enthusiasm none too soon. Young America is present, and understands the situation, and from that time henceforth the love of liberty and regard for the stars and stripes are a part of his education. It is well to mention these days either in song or story; thus may they learn that a government builded ever so well, must needs be kept in repair Therefore, I can but think it profitable to sometimes look back.

The presence of these flags with their inscriptions, their folds bearing the honored stamp of service, the memories they recall naturally take us back more than a quarter of a century, when the grandest family of States on the globe could name its traitors. But an all-wise Providence had not forsaken us, and if the god of battles allowed the fetters of war with their devastations to enfold us for a time, was it not that great good should result to us, as a people, in obliterating from this unity, more than two centuries of bond service?

There are hundreds of volumes of histories of the war and its times, of both public and private life, but what of the unwritten history of the loyal women of our nation, during those terrible years, from '61 to '65, and where is there one that regrets any sacrifice for such a cause? When our fathers, husbands and brothers went forth to face the enemy did we say with the Roman matron, " bring back thy sword or come not back to us?" No; but "Go, and when duty is done, if there is body enough left to contain the soul, we'll welcome you home."

Thus they went, with our prayers, and heaven's blessing as a guiding star.

Did our hands assist them when preparing for departure? They will tell you. Did we do the best we could when they were gone? I will tell you. We must remember that times were different in Iowa then from now. Most of us lived on farms, and the State was comparatively new, and if our brothers, too young to join the army, needed us to help husk the corn, we went, and continued to go till all was gathered. We did most of our housework in the evenings, and mended our gloves for next day's husking, for our hands were not accustomed to out-door toil. But the emergency of the case developed new capabilities; how much we could do that we little dreamed of before. If our help was wanted "in the field where the sugar cane grew," there we could be found. If the house called for paint, we painted it. If the grove required pruning, it was done. Or when the oxen were yoked and the younger brothers were starting for the timber four or five miles away, did we ever go with them to keep them company, to add cheer to labor? They could tell you; for fuel must be had, for the terrible northern winter was before us with its deep snows and desolation. Thus we managed, and hunger was kept from the door and comforts were not altogether wanting. Have we forgotten how the drifting snows would delay the trains, and days would pass and no news from the seat of war? And after a battle where our 12th Iowa added a glorious page to theirs and Iowa's history, can we tell the first news the papers brought for us "missing;" but the sequel told us not forever. And for some the missive read, "right arm gone," and for others, "dead!" Alas, how many mothers, wives, sisters and sweethearts, watched for the letter that never came. Three years since I stood by my soldier brother's grave in the National cemetery near New Orleans. There, with thousands of others, away from their kindred, where—

> Graceful palms and clinging vines,
> Waving moss and Southern pines,
> Seem like sentinels, ever watching
> Where they sleep.

If there is any hallowed ground on this continent, is it not the last resting place of our boys that wore the blue? Not only in the North were we helping with our relief societies, but when news came of a battle, and nurses were wanted, where were many of our women found? If Europe had her Florence Nightingale, we had many,

> "Whom the wounded blest for their tender care,
> And named them as saints in their evening prayer,
> Kissing their shadows, did they fall
> Across their pillows from off the wall."

Nameless the price of their labors! Never, this side of the silent city, will they their just reward receive.

All this is past, and no wonder we were victorious and the stars and stripes yet live—for God and the women were for us. There have been times in the history of our country when the Administration looked not upon the soldier with contempt; he was honored with positions of trust. Is it so to-day? Do not former traitors sit in high places and laugh from their vantage ground? Yet we are not disheartened nor faithless, believing that the autumn of 1888 will name a chief magistrate whose love of country and loyalty to the government may be assured by his regard for all faithful Union soldiers. In conclusion let me say, if I for one moment forget what the dear old flag cost, I have only to look at three pictures. They are not framed, they are forever on memory's walls. The first, our national cemeteries. The second, our boys as they were sent home from hospitals and battle fields, with limbs gone or useless, with sightless eyes and health forever wrecked. If angels ever weep, here is fitting occasion for their tears. The third and last, a picture where the eye of pity would be dimmed with horror and the hand of the artist be powerless—Libby and Andersonville.

"The Broomstick Mightier than the Sword." It always rules the infantry.

Major D. W. Reed responded to this toast in the following happy manner:

Mr. President, Comrades, Ladies and Gentlemen:—

To me has been assigned "The *Broomstick* Mightier than the Sword. It Always Rules the Infantry." I confess that this is not the first time, by any means, that the Broomstick has been assigned to me. But how the committee discovered that I was especially well informed about the subject is more than I can tell.

We know from experience that the sword is the most inoffensive of the weapons of war. We know that it never "hewed the way to the gulf," that Wellington and Napoleon did not "measure swords at the battle of Waterloo," that it was not the "flaming sword of Sheridan that drove Early from the valley," that bayonets even were more terrible in story than in actual use, and never won the battles of Gettysburg or the Wilderness, but that powder and balls from musket and cannon's mouth were the effective agents in winning battles.

Nevertheless, the sword, by common consent, has come to be the representative of the *executive* power of man.

In like manner the *pen*, of itself, has never been a mighty agent in controlling the nations of the earth, but the brain, the thoughts of man, have been symbolized by the pen, and ever since the foundations of the first government were laid, there has been a contest between these great forces that together control the actions and thoughts of men, and "which is greater, the pen or the sword," has been discussed in school, on the rostrum and in legislative halls, in every age of the past, and the illustrous examples of Alexander, Frederick the Great, Napoleon and Washington, who formed Empires and established Republics at the head of armies, have been contrasted with that of Cicero, Bacon, Franklin and Jefferson, who by their philosophy taught the principles on which those Empires and Republics were founded, and wrote the laws which governed and sustained them.

In our own time we *still* have the discussion, as to which was greater, the immortal pen of Lincoln that wrote the emancipation proclamation declaring freedom to four million slaves, or the all-conquering sword of Grant that executed that decree and struck the shackles from the last bondsman in this land and made our nation what it had so long professed to be, *free*, without a stain upon its banner.

Thus through all ages these two instruments representing the powers which *men* wield have been contending for supremacy, and the arguments, like equal weights in evenly balanced scales, have held the matter in equal poise. A simple contest, *man* contending against *man*.

It has been reserved for a committee of the 12th Iowa to introduce a new element into the controversy, and woman's influence in the governmental affairs of the world has been proposed under the symbol of the Broomstick.

Now, I know, and some of you know, that the broomstick is by no means woman's only weapon of offence and defence. The bald-heads before me— especially those of some of the committee—remind me that they possibly had in mind some more efficient weapon when they proposed this toast, but dared not attack it themselves. But, comrades, from my experience I can give you some valuable advice. Hide the poker, call a truce on hot water and hair-pulling, buy a soft-handled broom for your wife—for, like the sword, it is a harmless weapon; a little arnica heals the wounds, and is cheaper than hair restoratives.

Yet, comrades, while the broomstick is least to be feared of woman's weapons, it has come to be a symbol of woman's influence in controlling the affairs of government. And from the time when Cleopatra and Josephine, by their influence, ruled the men who commanded the armies, to our own time, when our patriotic women, Spartan like, sent their husbands, brothers and sons, to the field to do battle for their country, and with their broomsticks gallantly held in check the copperheads in the rear, woman has gradually arisen under the civilizing influences of the Christian religion, from a position of slavery to one where she has taken her place by the side of man in every avenue of public life; and it is really a question worthy our discussion whether woman does not to-day wield a mightier influence in executing the laws than does man. In the great reforms she has surely shown her ability and willingness to grapple with the serious questions of State and National government, and has won for herself a place on man's level, at least in executing the laws, and fully his equal with the pen, with which she has created the public sentiment that has made the laws. And as she in her proper sphere has the moulding and directing of the infant mind, whether it be to wield the pen or the sword, she has undoubtedly proven her ability to rule not only the infantry, the cavalry and artillery, but kings, emperors, presidents and the world. We therefore acknowledge the broomstick mightier than the sword, and gladly yield to woman that all-powerful emblem of her influence and authority, and promise never again to dispute its supremacy, even with the sword.

"The Iowa Soldier's Home." A grateful state proudly acknowledges her indebtedness.

This toast was responded to by comrade Ben. E. Eberhart, of Co. "E," now quartermaster at the Soldiers' Home at Marshalltown:

Who of you, my comrades, does not still remember the soldiers' homes of 1861 to 1865, the homes that we left when we took up arms in defense of our country, and when weary with marching we wrapped ourselves in our blankets and slept, and saw in our dreams the faces of loved ones at home? Or on the lonely picket post how the thoughts would wander back to the North, and how we endeavored to picture a dear mother, loving wife and children, or sweetheart, and we wondered what they were doing; how we laid plans for the future, as to what we would do if we were spared to return to the loved ones at home; and, finally, when the war was ended and we were permitted to lay aside the habiliments of war and again resume those of peace, with what zeal each took up that which had been laid aside four long years before, fully determined to make up for the time that we had lost in the peaceful pursuits of life. All this we well remember. Some of you have succeeded, but many have failed, through no fault of their own. They started on the march as zealously as any, their hopes and aspirations were as great as yours, but disabled by wounds and disease they were unable to keep up with their comrades and finally fell out of ranks and became stragglers, and many became homeless and destitute, some took refuge in the National Homes and others found their way to the poor house.

Through the medium of the G. A. R., the Iowa Legislature was informed of the needs of these comrades, and a bill was passed by the 21st General Assembly appropriating $100,000 to build a State Soldiers' Home. The Governor appointed six comrades, with that staunch and ever faithful friend of the soldier, Gen. J. M. Tuttle, at the head, as a board of Commissioners to superintend the erection, and as trustees of the Home.

The site selected is a high piece of ground just northwest of the city of Marshalltown, on the banks of the Iowa River. The grounds consist of 128 acres, about twenty of which are beautiful grove. The building is of brick and stone, is 218 feet front with wings 120 feet deep, and four stories high It cost $63,700 and was dedicated on the 30th of last November and opened for the reception of inmates on the 1st day of December. On the lower floor are the Q. M. and commissary department, kitchen, dining rooms, smoking and bath room, and laundry. The next floor above is the chapel, hospital, headquarters, library and reading rooms, ladies' and gentlemen's reception rooms, commander's living rooms and three sleeping rooms. The two stories above are sleeping rooms. The sleeping apartments are large dormitories containing from 16 to 24 beds. They are furnished with single iron bedsteads, woven wire springs, cotton mattresses, pillows, sheets and blankets. Each inmate has a wardrobe large enough to contain all of his effects.

The accommodations are ample for 300 inmates. The entire building is heated by steam and lighted by gas. Although in no sense an applicant for the place, Col. Milo Smith, of Clinton, Iowa, was the unanimous choice of the commissioners for the position of commandant. Col. Smith was Colonel of the 26th Iowa Infantry, is a capable business man, and seems to be peculiarly adapted for the position. He demands obedience to the rules adopted for the health and comfort of the inmates, but with that degree of kindness and consideration that commands the respect of all.

The inmates pass the time smoking, playing cards, checkers, dominoes, and kindred games, telling old army experiences, and, in fact, holding one continuous camp-fire, always ready and willing to favor and assist comrades more decrepit than themselves, evincing at all times that comradeship understood by none but the volunteer soldier.

There, my comrades, are gathered in a comfortable home over 130 old veterans, who with arms of iron and fingers of steel helped to fill the breach on many a contested field; who climbed the giddy heights of Lookout Mountain, charged the slippery slope with Grant at Vicksburg, marched with Sherman from Atlanta to the sea, rode with Sheridan in the Shenandoah Valley, fought among the blood-spattered tombstones of Gettysburg, and helped us save the day in the "Hornets' Nest" at Shiloh; who gave their health freely for the preservation of national unity and for the old flag. Comrades who have lost their haversacks in the march of life, but who are no longer homeless or destitute, but will be the welcome guests of a grateful State until the long roll shall beat and they shall answer to their names as members of that Grand Army above, commanded by the Great Captain of the universe.

"Co. Q." Always Ready for Duty and Double Rations.

Comrade P. R. Ketchum responded as follows:

Comrades, Ladies and Gentlemen:

Most people have a very mistaken idea of the character of Co. Q. They seem to be of the opinion that Co. Q were the roughs of the army. Friends, this was not the case. A soldier who was always ready for duty and double rations, was a good soldier; and Co. Q, always ready for duty, was composed of the very best soldiers in the Union army. Co. Q was also the largest company in the army. It was composed of companies, regiments, brigades, divisions, and whole army corps belonged to company Q. There was one corps in particular, comrades, it may be some of you remember them; they used to be known as "Old Smith's Guerillas." They were always ready for duty

If they were ordered to charge and take a battery, they took it; if they were ordered to charge the enemy's works, they took them; if they were ordered to hold a position on the field of battle, they held it. Company Q seldom got what the boys used to call "a soft snap," (doing garrison duty or something of that kind.) No, their services were too valuable for duty of that kind. They were always at the front, or on the march. You remember, comrades, that on some of our marches, the commissary used to cut our rations down to one-half, and sometimes less. It was just so in company Q; but that made no difference to them. If our commissary was unable to furnish the required rations, the southern confederacy had to. Co. Q was always ready for duty when they were compelled to draw rations from the southern confederacy. This, however, they never resorted to when it was not a military necessity. Company Q never did anything by halves. After they had served about two years they could see by the way things were progressing, that the war could not be brought to a close in another year; they began to think of re-enlisting, and when the proposition was made to those old battle-scarred veterans to re-enlist, every man in company Q enlisted. They were going to see the rebellion put down, and the government restored, and they did it. The war could not have been brought to an honorable close without the aid of company Q. They had the best officers that ever wore soldier straps; they never saw the boys do anything wrong. Upon one occasion, after a hard day's march in the State of Mississippi, the day had been hot and the roads dusty, company Q was very tired and hungry, as they had been on half rations for several days; they had filed off of the road to go into camp. The Colonel had taken his position in front of the regiment, was casting his eye up and down the line to see if each company was in position and ready to stack arms; one of the boys saw a luscious looking porker only a few rods away; he stepped out of the ranks a few paces, covered Mr. porker with his musket, hesitated a moment, cast his eye at the Colonel to see if he was going to reprimand him or give him the order to fire; the Colonel seemed to be waiting for something, so the comrade fired; he fell back, took his place in the ranks, and the Colonel gave the command, stack arms. In a short time Col. Stibb's darkey was frying some nice slices of ham, and if the Colonel had been asked where that ham came from, he would have known no more about it than the Czar of Russia.

Company Q could always be depended upon. On one occasion a detachment of company Q, consisting of the 16th corps, had been ordered to Nashville, Tennessee, to reinforce Gen. Thomas against Gen. Hood. They arrived there on or about December 1st, 1864, the day after the battle of Franklin, one of the hardest fought battles of the war. Gen. Schofield's retreating army was arriving, and taking a position around the city of Nashville; great excitement prevailed in the city; the citizens were of the opinion that Gen. Hood would be in possession of the city before night. This detachment of company Q was disembarked and marched to the front, took a position where there had been some hastily made rifle pits. During the afternoon General Thomas asked Gen. Smith if he felt satisfied that his men could hold his part of the line. Gen. Smith replied, "If it were not for the rifle pits, all hell could not drive my men from their position." As I said before, company Q never did anything by halves. I will have to tell you of an incident that took place down in Tennessee; it was after Gen. Hood had been driven from Nashville, and company Q had followed him for about ten days, over worse roads than were ever seen in Iowa; on December 24, 1864, went into camp, with orders that they would not move the next day; that being the case they proposed having a Christmas dinner, and they had one, and a good one, too. Quite late in the afternoon on that Christmas day a farmer came into camp and enquired for headquarters. Company Q was always civil to strangers; he was very politely directed to the headquarters of Gen. A. J. Smith, the commander of the 16th corps, who listened very attentively to all the grievances the farmer had to relate in regard to boys taking his pigs, chickens, turkeys, etc., when the General gravely asked, "did they take all you had?" The farmer replied, "no, they did not take all I had, but they took a heap o' 'em." "Then it was not my boys," said the General, "you will have to go somewhere else for redress." The boys just loved that old white-haired General. They thought a good deal of all their officers, without, it may be, rare exceptions, and the officers thought a great deal of their men. Company Q often had very strict orders against foraging, even when they thought it a military necessity. Upon one occasion they were on a march in Missouri; rations, as usual on a march, were scarce; as soon as they had gone into camp one night, a captain had been out to get rails for a bed, and as he came back, said, "there is a fat calf in that pasture." That's all that was said, and the captain had veal for supper. Company Q was always ready for duty and double rations. It was company Q that saved Gen. Grant and his army at Shiloh. It was company Q that led Gen. Sherman to the sea. It was company Q who put down the rebellion and saved the nation; and the little remnant that is left of them to-day, are among our best citizens, and are still battling for right and justice.

"The Citizens of Waterloo." Your patriotism and hospitality will live in our memories forever.

This toast was responded to by Col. J. H. Stibbs, in a very appropriate manner, a copy of which we have been unable to procure.

The concluding of the camp-fire was the singing of "Marching Through Georgia," by the audience.

FRIDAY MORNING.

This is the anniversary of the battle of Shiloh, and as the boys who composed part of the "Hornets' Nest Brigade" on that memorable day, greeted each other in the morning, they naturally referred to the contrast between that day and this, and then began the telling of incidents both laughable and sorrowful.

The exercises of the forenoon were held in Goodman's Opera House, on the west side of the river, and the president called the association to order promptly at 9 o'clock.

After prayer had been offered the association first proceeded to the selection of a place for the holding of the next reunion.

The committee appointed for this purpose then reported through comrade J. E. Simpson, whose home is now at Norfolk Neb., as follows:

Mr. President and Comrades:

Your committee would like to have an expression from the regiment as to the time and place of holding our next reunion. It has been suggested that it be held at Sioux City, and I favor that. There are a large number of the regiment scattered through Nebraska, Dakota, Kansas, and States and Territories west that it would accommodate very much to have our next reunion at that point.

I have no authority from anyone to extend the hospitality of that city, but I know a number of the citizens, and from what I know of them and their mode of receiving visitors to their beautiful city, I have no hesitation in saying to you that if you will locate our next reunion there, Sioux City will give you a warm and hearty welcome.

Come over on the Missouri slope, see our beautiful country, our immense farms, our great Missouri, and we will show you, from the bluffs of your state, a glimpse, like the man of old at the promised land of Nebraska. It will be as a new book opened up unto you, who have always lived on the Mississippi.

I plead not in behalf of us, who are here at this reunion; we shall be at the next reunion if we live, place it where you may, but I appeal in behalf of your comrades who are living north, south, and west of Sioux City. To many of them it has been impossible to meet with you in the past, on account of the long distance to be traveled and the expenses to be incurred. Come over and meet us half way, test the hospitality of the "Corn Palace" city of the West. Don't be afraid but what you will be welcome, and I pledge you that every comrade living west of the Missouri, will be present at the reunion in 1892, at Sioux City; though their pockets be not filled with much gold or silver, you will find their hearts to be as large as their farms, and none of them have less than a quarter section.

In urging this I do not forget our good, warm-hearted friends at Manchester. We are simply going visiting, and then we will come home again, for after our pleasant and happy meeting in 1880 and 1884, Manchester will ever remain as a home to the 12th Iowa.

I now move you, Mr. President, that the next reunion of our regiment be held at Sioux City, Iowa.

The claims of Sioux City were strongly urged by the comrades from the West, and much discussion followed, when the following telegram was read from Mayor Cleveland, of that city:

SIOUX CITY, IOWA, April 6, 1888.

To John Weaver and D. D. McCunn, Members 12th Iowa:

Will do all we can to make things pleasant for you.
J. CLEVELAND, Mayor.

Upon a vote being taken the comrades from the east gracefully refrained from voting and allowed those from the west to satisfy their own preferences in the matter, and accordingly Sioux City was selected on the first ballot.

Comrade John N. Weaver, of company D, feelingly urged the claims of Sioux City, and it might not be out of place to here append his letter to Secretary Dunham, after his return home, on the subject:

SIOUX CITY, IOWA, April 8, 1888.

Lt. A. Dunham, Manchester, Iowa:—My Dear Sir and Comrade:—

Don't entertain any misgivings about the kindly reception of the old 12th at Sioux City. I urged the claims of Sioux City specially in behalf of the boys in Nebraska and elsewhere, who had followed the "Star of Empire," and because I *knew* Sioux City would *always* do the "square thing" by the soldier. Our people are well pleased and will welcome you.

Very truly and fraternally,
JOHN N. WEAVER.

We also add his letter to the *Sioux City Journal*, on the subject, under date of April 10, 1888:

To the Editor of the Journal:—The next reunion of the 12th Iowa Infantry, four years hence, being fixed to be held at Sioux City, will you indulge me by publishing in reference to it a little that may be of interest to you, the citizen soldiers and citizens of the city generally.

The first quadrennial reunion of the old Twelfth (of which I had the honor of being a member) was held eight years ago, at Manchester, Iowa. Steps were then taken and effected four years later, at our second reunion, by which the survivors of the regiment are incorporated under the laws of the State. You, having been a soldier, can appreciate, perhaps, the pleasure of meeting the boys who stood "shoulder to shoulder" in the same regiment and companies during the war—"drank from the same canteen"—stood by each other when sick, wounded or in prison. While I entertain the kindliest and most brotherly feeling toward every soldier of '61 to '65, yet for genuine enjoyment I believe there is nothing so cheers the heart of the soldier as to meet those of his own regiment and company with whom he shared the same hardships, trials, dangers, hard tack and "sow belly," and with whom he personally became acquainted and learned to love during the dark days "that tried men's souls." Every one can relate some story or joke about his comrade that not only interests the boys of his regiment but every listener.

The selection of Sioux City was made for the next reunion specially for the convenience of the members of the regiment who have followed "the star of empire" since the war, and have located in Nebraska, Kansas, Dakota and Northwestern Iowa. These "boys" involuntarily looked to Sioux City as the most accessible point to effectuate such a purpose, and, though I had not conferred with our people, I knew and felt that from the well-known hospitality of Sioux City people I was entirely safe in "inviting" the next reunion to the Corn Palace city, I being the only representative present from Sioux City at our reunion last week at Waterloo, and assuring "the boys" they would receive a royal welcome.

Our practice has been at these reunions to have a "headquarters" at one of the hotels, and the rest of the "boys" distribute themselves at the hotels *ad libitum* "at reduced rates." We do not "camp out," but hold our meetings in a suitable hall, where everybody is free to go and is gladly received. We have been royally received at Manchester and Waterloo at our former meetings, but I believe Sioux City will witness the grandest reunion of them all.

We have plenty of oratorical ability on the part of the regiment to speak for it, among whom I might mention Col. Henderson, of Dubuque, as one. For story telling, Col. "Jack" Stibbs, of Chicago, is a distinguished representative of the regiment. I mention these names as only an indication of the fun that may be expected. We have other formidable rivals for even these.

We have the best ability in Sioux City in these respects to meet the boys of the Twelfth half way. Respectfully, JOHN N. WEAVER.

The committee appointed to nominate officers for the next reunion then reported the following:

President—Major D. W. Reed, of Waukon, Iowa.

Vice President—J. N. Weaver, of Sioux City, Iowa.

Secretary—Capt. E. B. Soper, of Emmetsburg, Iowa.

Treasurer—Dr. James Barr, of Algona, Iowa.

Executive Committee—The above officers with addition of J. E. Simpson, of Norfolk, Nebraska.

Upon motion the report of the committee was adopted and the foregoing duly declared elected for the next reunion, and Major D. W. Reed was conducted to the president's chair, and duly acknowledged his thanks in a very short and appropriate speech.

Comrade R W. Tirrill, chairman of the committee on resolutions, then reported the following:

Resolved, That we extend to the citizens of Waterloo our heartfelt thanks for their genial hospitality and hearty greetings extended us, and for the kindly interest taken to make our reunion so successful, and to add to our comfort while in their beautiful city.

Resolved, That we greatly appreciate the attendance of so many fellow comrades at this, our third reunion, and that we bid our absent comrades all hail in the battle of life, with an earnest hope that they will fight a good fight and go down into the last ditch with the colors flying.

Resolved, That we are unalterably in favor of pensioning all disabled Union soldiers without reference to date of disability. This we ask as a matter of justice to the disabled soldiers and as a lesson to future generations that a strong government of the people realizes its indebtedness to those who so heroically sacrificed home and friends to save the government in its weakness.

Resolved, That we deeply sympathize with Comrade Dunham and family in their sad bereavement through the recent death of their loved daughter, Florence L. Dunham, who was adopted as the daughter of this regiment at our first reunion. A bright, loving and dutiful daughter on earth, she now waits with kindred spirits gone before to welcome us to the life beyond the borderland of earthly troubles.

Resolved, That the heartfelt sympathies of this association be extended to comrades Knee and Comstock in the sad loss of their affectionate and beloved wives, since our last reunion. May their pathway be so brightened through the balance of their days that the irreparable loss they have sustained may be lightened upon them.

Resolved, That our sympathies are also extended to sister Rebecca Otis, who mourns the death of her husband, John Otis, late of Co. F, and whose noble work in the hospitals during the war will ever be remembered by the surviving members of the 12th Iowa. May her pathway be easy through life.

Resolved, That we gratefully appreciate the fostering care of the people of Iowa in their efforts to provide for disabled soldiers by the erection of the Iowa Soldiers' Home, at Marshalltown, and we respectfully ask a sufficient appropriation by the Legislature now in session to complete everything necessary for the comfort of the inmates and maintenance of the Soldiers' Home during the current biennial period.

The report of the committee was adopted by a rising vote.

A committee composed of Comrades R. W. Tirrill, G. H. Morisey, and Abner Dunham was selected to publish the proceedings of the reunion in pamphlet form, and to send copies to all members of the regimental association who have paid up their quadrennial dues of $1.00 each.

The hour for dinner having arrived, the meeting was adjourned to convene promptly at 1:30 in the afternoon.

Friday Afternoon.

Upon being called to order Comrade J. E. Simpson then submitted the following eulogy:

Mr. President and Comrades:

The sad and painful duty has been assigned to me of announcing to you the death of the "Daughter of our Regiment," Florence L. Dunham, at her father's home, in Manchester, Feb. 24, 1888, of typhoid fever.

Those of you who were present at our first reunion, at Manchester, eight years ago, will remember the little girl, then only about eight years old, who came out on the platform and commenced to recite a poem, written by her mother, the wife of our beloved comrade and most worthy secretary, Abner Dunham, commencing, "I love the brave old soldier." How pretty and interesting she looked. Glancing up and seeing the great sea of faces she became embarrassed, burst into tears, touching every heart present. Some warm hearted comrade sprang up and moved she be adopted as "The Daughter of the Regiment," and it was carried by a unanimous and hearty vote.

Those who were with us four years ago will remember the beautiful, sprightly girl, who had a warm hearty hand-shake and welcome for each 12th Iowa man present.

"THE MANCHESTER PRESS," in announcing her death in the columns of that paper, speaks in words and tones that found a response in the heart of each one of us, as follows: "Last week, when we went to press, it was thought that Florence Dunham was improving, with a fair chance for recovery. But the next morning her disease took an unfavorable turn, and Friday evening, the 24th of February, after most intense suffering, she was released from worldly pains and troubles. Her death, so sudden and unexpected, will bring sorrow to many outside her immediate circle of friends. All over Iowa, and in distant states, there are those who will grieve at the news of her decease. The members of the Twelfth Iowa, who attended the first reunion of the regiment in this city, will remember the sweet-faced, modest little girl, who stood upon the platform and recited the poem written for the occasion, in a manner which captivated all hearts. Since that time, Florence Dunham had been the veritable "Child of the Regiment." And in every corner of the land, wherever one of the veterans of the Twelfth Iowa is to be found, there will be found a sincere mourner for the loss of the fair girl who was loved by all. Just at the threshold of womanhood, that she should thus be taken from family and friends, from a life in which she delighted, and in which she gave promise of happiness and usefulness—all seems hard to bear. The funeral took place at the house, on Sunday, conducted by Rev. B. M. Amsden, and notwithstanding the bitter weather, was largely attended."

Darling sweet Florence, just budding into womanhood, looking with pleasant anticipations to this coming reunion and the meeting with the old veterans of her regiment, to whom she bid fair in time to come, when our members grow less, to become a veritable daughter indeed. God has seen fit to take her to himself. Members of the 12th were there to meet her on the other shore. She will be there to welcome us as we, one after the other, answer the last "roll call" to be "mustered in" to that better land, where kindred spirits can meet and mingle, not as here, years apart and for a few passing hours and then separate, but for all time to come.

Beautiful loving daughter, we bid thee farewell until we meet.

To our beloved comrade and his dear wife we tender our most heartfelt sympathies and mingle our tears with them in this hour of affliction and sorrow. The light has gone from their home. We bow in humble submission to the fiat of Him who gave and taketh away.

The balance of the afternoon to the time of parade was given to short speeches and story-telling by comrades Simpson, Grannis, Henderson, Helen Viola, VanAnda, Zediker, Woods, Thompson, Nagle, Gift, Soper and others.

At 5 o'clock the comrades were formed in line for a grand parade, there being 160 of the old veterans in the ranks by companies, and proceeded to march through the principal streets to the grounds, where they were formed in line for a grand dress parade, when the following order was read by adjutant Burch:

Headquarters, 12th Iowa Infantry, Waterloo, Iowa, April 6, 1888.
General Order No. 99, to the Surviving Members of the 12th Iowa.

Four years have elapsed since our last dress parade, and it is with pleasurable emotions that I again am able to congratulate you upon your soldierly bearing upon this occasion—not only this, I am proud of your achievements as a regiment in the dark days which "tried men's souls," proud that where duty called the old 12th was always ready to go, and went; that you through all your services conducted yourselves as true soldiers in camp, on the march and in the field—proud that you made your glorious record, not as those choosing the profession of arms as such, but as intelligent men and citizens stepping to the front when the question of the perpetuity of our nation arose. And leaving the pursuits of peace and becoming soldiers for the purpose of maintaining the Union of the States at the cost of business, health or life itself, if need be—intending if you survived the struggle to return to the peaceful pursuits of home. For more than four years you did your duty and performed deeds of daring and valor and endured hardships such as pen cannot describe, nor artist paint, nor poet picture. Your record stands forth without a stain to mar its enduring grandeur and its glorious fame. Surely these considerations should fill me and all of us with pride. But you have performed still greater achievements. When the war was over you returned to your homes and as if by magic the brave soldier of the old 12th of yesterday becomes the true high-minded citizen of to-day. It is your highest glory that not only did you do your duty during the time you were soldiers of the great war for the union, but that, when the war was over and you had resumed the arts and ways of peace, your record as citizens of our great nation has been as glorious as that you made as soldiers in the long dark days of the rebellion. You to-day are among the sovereigns of this great government of the people and for the people, and *your* voices and votes have done as much in moulding the moral sentiment that characterizes and promotes our political future as did your deeds of valor and your endurance during the dark hours of war. You have assumed and occupied your several stations in life as citizens since the war. You have so acted and conducted yourselves as to stand honored and respected, not only as soldiers, but as men of character, respectability and prominence, as citizens.

It is a pleasure to know that each and all of you are engaged in honorable pursuits, and that the record of each of you since the war, when examined makes as proud a showing of respectability and honor as did the record of your splendid military achievements in the old 12th Iowa.

J. H. STIBBS, Late Colonel 12th Iowa V. V. I.,
S. R. BURCH, Adjutant.   Brevet Brig. Gen'l.

After the dismissing of the parade, it being then about 6 o'clock, the comrades repaired to the Turner Hall, where a most excellent banquet was in waiting for them, prepared by the ladies of the Woman's Relief Corps, No. 15, of Waterloo, and to which all did ample justice.

Friday Evening.

The closing exercises of the reunion took place in the evening at the Opera House, which was again filled to overflowing by the citizens of Waterloo. Ex-Gov. Buren R. Sherman presided over the deliberations, and after a few complimentary remarks to the regiment proceeded with the program.

"The Old Folks at Home," was earnestly responded to by Rev. J. O. Stevenson, of Waterloo, who was in Scotland when the rebellion began, and his description of the sympathy of the Scotch capitalists, who were for the south, and of the laboring people, who were for the north, was extremely interesting.

"The Army Chaplain" was responded to by the venerable Rev. Dr. C. S. Percival, Chaplain of the 12th N. Y. Cavalry, during the war, and he told the veterans more about Chaplains in half an hour than most of them realized throughout the whole war.

H. C. Hemenway, of Cedar Falls, was expected to be present to give his ideas on "Hard Tack," but being unavoidably absent, Major D. W. Reed was drafted on short notice, and he speedily showed his familiarity with the subject.

"The Girl I Left Behind Me," was eloquently responded to by C. W. Mullin, of Waterloo, who clearly detailed the experience and feelings of every veteran present toward the only power which has ever conquered the whole Union army.

Col. J. H. Stibbs then delivered his new version of "Barbara Frietchie," amidst a storm of applause, and by particular request we publish it herewith:

BARBARIE FRIETCHIE—NEW VERSION.

Id was droo dar streeds of Fredericksdown.
Der red-hot zun he was shine him down,
Bast der zaloons all filt mit bier,
Der rebel vellers valked on dier ear.
All day droo Fredericksdown so fast,
Horses, und guns, und zogers bast.
Der rebel flag he shone him oud so bridt,
As if, by jinks, he got some ridt.
Vere vas der Onion flag? Der zun
He look him down not on a von.
Up jumped dot olt Miss Frietchie den,
So oldt by nine score year und ten.
She grabbed up der oldt flag der men haul down,
Und fasen id guick by her nidtgown.
Den she sot by der vindow ver all could see
Dere vos non vot lofe dot flag so free.
Purty soon come ridin' up Stonewall Jack,
Sittin, from der mittle of his horse's back.
Under him brow he squint him eyes;
Dot flag! dot make him great surprise.
Halt! each veller make him sdill,
Fire? was echoed from hill to hill.
Id busted der sdrings from dot nidtgown,
But Barbarie Frietchie, she was arount.
She grabbed der flag again so guich,
Und oud of der vindow her arms did sdick.
"Obuse of you would dis olt bald head,
But leave alone dot flag!" she said.
Zo zoon, zo quick as Jack could do,
He holler him out mit a face zo blue;
"Who bulls one hair out of dat bald head,
Dies awful guick, go aheadt!" he said.
Und all dot day, und all dot night,
Till efery rebel vos out of site,
Und leave behind him dot Fredericksdown,
Dot flag he vas sthicken by dot nidtgown.
Dame Barbarie Frietchie's vork is done,
She don't forever got some fun.
Bully for her! und drop a tear
For dot old voman mitoud some fear.

Short story-telling was then indulged in by comrades and others present, when the exercises were drawn to a close and the reunion adjourned to meet at Sioux City, four years hence.

Excellent music and singing interspersed the proceedings of the evening and as the comrades departed for their several homes they were profuse in their praises of the treatment accorded them by the citizens of Waterloo.

The only regrettable circumstance connected with the reunion was the absence of Col. D. B Henderson, Hon. W P. Hepburn, Col. J. J. Woods, Major S. D. Brodtbeck, and others who were expected to be present and take part in the proceedings.

IN MEMORIAM.

DEATH OF COL. S. R. EDGINGTON.

Col. S. R. Edgington, of Eldora, Iowa, died at his home in Eldora, Iowa, May 20, 1888. Col. Edgington was a gallant soldier of two wars—the Mexican war and the war of the Rebellion. He served in an Ohio Regiment during the Mexican war. Soon after that war he moved to Eldora, Iowa, where he resided nearly forty years. In the pioneer days of Hardin county the Edgington log cabin was one of the most hospitable homes in Iowa, and all the early settlers of that region remember many kindnesses extended to them by Colonel and Mrs. Edgington. The Edgington log cabin was one of the first buildings erected in Eldora, and it was occupied as a store and a residence until the advent of saw mills and brick yards, when separate buildings were erected. Col. Edgington continued in merchandise until the war broke out in 1861, when he organized Company A of the 12th Iowa Infantry, and joined that regiment at Dubuque. Soon after the battle of Shiloh, in which battle he commanded the regiment after Col. Woods was wounded, he was promoted to Major, and some months after was promoted to Lieutenant-Colonel of the regiment, which rank he held when mustered out. The greater part of the time since the war he had been the proprietor of the principal hotel at Eldora. For some months previous to his death he had been afflicted with some disease of the kidneys. At the reunion of the 12th Iowa Infantry at Waterloo, April 5th and 6th, 1888, he was President of the Regimental Association and was feeling quite poorly, but none anticipated that he would be called away in such a short time. Talking of future reunions, he said: "Comrades, we will continue having our reunions every four years while we live, and when we die we will have unending reunions in Heaven." He was a splendid officer, a genial comrade and a steadfast friend. His death will be a sad loss to his numberless friends in Hardin county, to his comrades of the 12th Iowa Infantry, and to the state and country.

The Following is the Roll of Members Present.

Regimental and Field Officers.

Colonel—J. H. Stibbs (Brev. Brig. Gen.) Chicago, Illinois.
Lieut. Colonel—S. R. Edgington, Eldora, Iowa.
  "   "   S. G. Knee, Colesburg, Iowa.
Major—D. W. Reed, Waukon, Iowa.
Adjutant—S. R. Burch, Olathe, Kansas.
Asst. Surgeon—James Barr, Algona, Iowa.
Quartermaster—George H Morisey, Manchester, Iowa
  "   H. C Morehead, Cedar Rapids, Iowa.
Serg. Major—A. J. Rodgers, Waukon, Iowa.

Company A.

S. Kemp, Alden, Iowa.
W. W. Moore, Manchester, Iowa.
D. S. Martin, Iowa Falls, Iowa.
Seth Macy, Des Moines, Iowa.
R. S. Kellogg, Dows, Iowa.
G. H. Cobb, Eldora, Iowa.
R. P. Clarkson, Des Moines, Iowa.
Thos H. Wilson, Robertson, Iowa.
S. R. Ferree, Belle Plaine, Iowa.

Company B.

Lt. John D Cole, Lansing, Iowa.
J. H. Butts, Cherokee, "
R. G. Pratt, Storm Lake, "
R Bathen, Riceville, Iowa.
Thos Dowling, Rossville, Iowa.
W. P. Winters, Bancroft, "

Company C,

S. C. Beck, Waverly, Iowa.
J E. Kent, Belle Plaine, Iowa.
P. R. Woods, Fayette, "
G. Hazlett, Allison "
A. K. Ketchum, Clarion, "
R. Z. Latimer, Fayette, "
E A. Kelsey, Tripoli, "
W. L. Henderson, LeRoy, Minn.
Hart Spears, West Gate, Iowa.
S. Gifford, Douglass, "
C. J. Martin, Horton, "
J. W. Bysong, West Point, Nebraska.
James Stewart, West Union, Iowa.
J W. Ballinger, Lacy, "
P R. Ketchum, Windsor, "
F W. Moine, Strawberry Point, Iowa.
G. H Latimer, West Gate, Iowa.
H G. Grannis, Flag Bear, Fayette, Ia.
Geo. L. Durno, Springville, Iowa.
W. A. Kent, Dallas, Wisconsin.
I W. King, Emrick, Nebraska.
J. P. Strong, Schuyler, "
L. S. Hamlin, Oelwein, Iowa.

Company D.

Lyman M. Ayers, Cedar Rapids, Ia.
Thos. J. Lewis, "   "   "
Edwin A. Buttolph, " "   "
J. W. Clark, "   "   "
Thomas Barr, Shellsburg, "
A. J. Millett, Hastings, Nebraska.
H. W. Bailey, Kirkman, Iowa.
E. D. Steadman, Vinton, "
J. W. Rowan, Vinton, Iowa.
E. B. Soper, Emmettsburg, Iowa.
Wm. W. Whiteneck, Waterloo, "
J. N. Weaver, Sioux City, "
J. W. Burch, Olathe, Kansas.
Josiah Scott, Shellsburg, Iowa.
Harman Grass, Fargo, Dakota.
A M Blanchard, Chicago, Illinois.
W. C. Howard, Chelsea, Iowa.

Company E.

Wm. Hamilton, La Porte City, Ia.
F. A. Large, "   "   "
David Craighton, Geneva, "
C. V. Surfus, Bristow, "
J. C. Jones, Geneva "
A. B. Perry, Dunkerton, "
C. B. Hayward, Mooreville, "
R L. Bird, Yuma, Colorado.
C. R. Switzer, Lewis, Iowa.
H. J. Harrison, Waterloo, Iowa.
E. Sawyer, La Porte City, Iowa.
David Schrack, Oelwein, "
A W. Myers, Shell Rock, "
J. S. Margretz, Hitesville, "
A. J. Biller, Waterloo, "
B E. Eberhart, Marshalltown, Ia.
J. W. Shoemaker, Waterloo, "
N. J. Shroyer, Taintor, "
C. D. Morris, Worthing, Dakota
M. V. Sunderlin, Janesville, Iowa.

Company F.

W. A. Nelson, Hazelton, Iowa.
J. J. Eaton, Edgewood, "
Geo. Kent, Oelwein, "
Joshua Widger, Manchester, Iowa.
J. W. Gift, Peoria, Illinois.
Hiram Kaster, Manchester, Iowa.
Thos. McGowan, Independence, Ia.
J. E. Eldredge, Walnut, Kansas.
H. Olmstead, Independence, Iowa.
T. C. Nelson, Hazelton, Iowa
H. F. Mackey, Maynard, "
H. M. Preston, Ft. Dodge, Iowa.
J. F. Lee, Clay Mills, "
Abner Dunham, Manchester, Iowa.
R. W. Tirrill, " "
T. R. McKee, Dell Rapids, Dakota.
A. J. Roe, Burlington, Iowa.

Company G.

G. W. Kirkland, Freeport, Iowa.
Warren Wait, Nashua, "
Van R Dunn, De Witt, Nebraska.
J. E. Simpson, Norfolk, Nebraska.
A. H. Groves, Decorah, Iowa,
A. S. Fuller, Lyons, Dakota.

Company H.

J. Shorter, Shell Rock, Iowa.
J. A. VanAuda, Fremont, Neb.
Franklin M. Hamblin, Iowa Falls, Ia.
Joseph Frank, Lamont, Iowa
S. M. Jackson, Lincoln, Neb.
W. H. McCune, Ruthven, Iowa
David Jones, Monona, "
Wm Royse, Atlantic, "
Wm. Shorter, Shell Rock, "
J. A. Light, Norfolk, Nebraska.
J. B. Flenniken, Norfolk, Neb.
J. W. Ward, Burlington, Iowa.
R. W. Fishel, Greeley, "
S. B. Sloan, " "
W. H. Cox, Alta, "
J. G Currie, Butte City, Montana.
J W. Crist, Central City, Dakota.

Company I.

M. D Nagle, Dubuque, Iowa.
J. F. Zediker, Franklin, Neb.
J. W. Coates, Talcott, Dakota.
W. L. Fry, Scranton, Iowa.
J. F. Butlers, Moorville, Iowa.
D. D. McCollum, Sibley, "
Geo Teskey, Elwood, Iowa
E. B. Campbell, Armstrong Grove, Ia
M. McDermott, Epworth, Iowa.
J. L. Thompson, Franklin, Neb.
M. B. Goodnow, Ord, "

Company K.

Henry Waldroff, La Porte City, Ia.
Ira D. Blanchard, Crookston, Minn.
C. E. Merriam, Hopkinton, Iowa.
C E. Phillips, Blair, Nebraska.
W. R. Mathis, Omaha, "
P. J. Morehouse, Masonville, Iowa.
H. C. Merriam, Coggon, "
J. M. Beckner, Charles City, "
Ike Mickey, Waukon, "

Roster of Members of the 12th Iowa V. V. Infantry, so far as known, at the time of this Reunion.

Field and Staff.

Colonel—Jackson J. Woods, Montana, Kansas.
" —J. H. Stibbs, Chicago, Illinois
Lt. Col.—S. R. Edgington, Eldora, Iowa.
" —S. G. Knee, Colesburg, "
Major—S. D. Brodtbeck, Los Augeles, California.
" —E. M. Van Duzee, St. Paul, Minn.
" —D. W. Reed, Waukon, Iowa.
Surgeon—C. C. Parker, Fayette, Iowa.
" —Myron Underwood, Eldora, Iowa.
Asst. Surg.—W. H Finley, Franklin, Nebraska.
" —James Barr, Algona, Iowa
Adjutant—N. E. Duncan, Dubuque, Iowa.
" —S. R. Burch, Olathe, Kansas.
Quartermaster—G. H. Morisey, Manchester, Iowa.
" —H. C Morehead, Cedar Rapids, Iowa.
Chaplain—Frederick Humphrey, Fairmount, Minn.
Hospital Steward—C. H. Hobbs, Peru, Nebraska.
" " —J. J. Walker, De Witt, Missouri.
Com. Sergt.—James Evans, Dubuque, Iowa.
Sergt. Major—A. J. Rodgers, Waukon, "
Drum Major—T. R McKee, Dell Rapids, Dakota.
Fife Major—D. S Martin, Iowa Falls, Iowa
" " —S. M. French, Denver, Colorado.

Company A.

Armstrong, B A Liscomb, Iowa.
Bird, G M Illinois.
Brother, A Arlington, Ohio.
Cougar, J D, Eldora Hardin Co., Ia.
Cromwell, T C Oakland, Iowa.
Cobb, G H Eldora, Iowa.
Dobbins, Hiram Jewell Co , Kan.
Edgington, S R Eldora, Iowa.
Ellsworth, D V Eldora, "
Ferree, S R Belle Plaine, Iowa.
Haskins, G H Marysville, Mo.
Hunter. J R C Webster City, Ia.
Iback, B F Eldora, Iowa.
Kidwiler, M Missouri.
Kellogg, R E Dows, Iowa.
Macy, Seth Des Moines, Iowa.
Moore, G W Maryville, Mo.
Miller, Zabina
Mitchell, G W Lawn Hill, Iowa.
Parish, William
Reed, G W Yarkie, Missouri.
Rulo, G W South Bend, Indiana.
Sprague, K S Fremont, Nebraska.
Wilson, T H Robertson, Iowa.
Welsh, Nathan
Webb, A E Eldora, Iowa.
Zieger, N W Eldora, Iowa.

Bowers, I H Eldora, Hardin Co., Ia.
Bell, Thos. R Iowa Falls, Iowa.
Brown, S B Jewell City, Kansas.
Clarkson, R P Des Moines, Iowa.
Combes, F C Dewalls Bluff, Ark.
Crist, Job Marshalltown, Iowa.
Dobbins, Levi Eldora, "
Edgington, T B Memphis, Tennessee.
Fountain. Francis
Glass, Carl Dayton (Mill Home) Ohio.
Haywood, W P Lyons, Iowa.
Hobbs, Jas. C H Peru Nebraska.
Jackson, Samuel Oregon.
Kemp, Sumner Alden, Iowa.
Lefever, Simon Bolekow, Missouri.
McPherson, W G
Moore, W W Manchester, Iowa.
Mann, William Steamboat Rock, Ia.
Martin, D S Iowa Falls, Iowa.
Richards, William
Runkle, C M Plankinton, Dakota.
Richards, Joseph Boone, Iowa.
Sawin, E S Union, Iowa.
Walker, Samuel Dewitt, Missouri.
Wickam A J Eagle City, Iowa.
Zieger, J W Eldora, Iowa.

Company B.

Captain Willard C Earle..Waukon, Iowa.
" Watson R Hanscom..............................died— "
1st Lieut. L H Merrill ....died, Montgomery, Ala., May 29, 1862.
"   J H Borger..................died, Salt Creek Station, Illinois.
"   J P Jackson.........................Village Creek, Iowa.
2d "   J D Cole..................................Lansing, "
Sergt Maj A J Rodgers...............................Waukon, "
1st Sergt George Ibach............................Preston, Minn.
Sergt. J D Spaulding..................................dead.
"   Elias Repp......................
"   D Harbaugh..................died at Macon, Ga., Oct. 15, 1862.
"   Henry Fry.............,.......................Pennsylvania.
"   W P Winter................................Bancroft, Iowa.
"   John Upstrom........................Worthington, Minn.
"   R B Sargent...Kansas.
Corp'l H Goodrich........................
"   M J Roe........................ died at Macon, Ga., Sept. 29, 1882.
"   F E Hancock...........died at Annapolis, Md., Oct. 27, 1862.
"   Stephen Thibeda.............................Waukon, Iowa.
"   Robert Wampler............   "   "
"   Aslak Larson..............................Preston, Minn.
"   Fred Monk..................................Eitzen, "
"   L D Bearce.............................Castana, Iowa.
"   M Engelhorn......................   ....Kansas.
"   W B Bort.................................Viroqua, Wis.
Wagoner E J White............. ....died at French Creek, Iowa.

" Augustus H West,   Andrews, H R West Union, Iowa.
Adams, O F   Bailey, Geo. N St. Paul, Minn.
Bailey, W F St. Paul, Minn.   Beisel, J B died Lansing, Ia. Feb. 25,'64
Brock, Gustavus   Bryant, J L " Macon, G., Sept. 25, '62
Butts, J H Cherokee, Iowa.   Bathen, Robert Riceville, Minn.
Barnhart, Amos L (died May 4, 1864) Bort, A K Viroqua, Wisconsin
      (Memphis, Tenn.) Bort, M Jas died at Lansing, Iowa.
Burnum H   Burlingame, O D Chicago, Illinois.
Calico, Geo. d'd St. Louis, Jan. 7, '62. Candee, George
Churchill, L B   Castellar, Frank
Decker, Adam Lansing, Iowa.   Deeny Cornelius (died Milwaukee, '64
Dodge, Ansel H deserted 1861   (at Soldiers' Home.
Dowling, John French Creek, Iowa. Dowling, Thomas, Rossville, Iowa.
Edwards, Isaac   Ettle, George, Waukon, Iowa.
Erickson, E A Glenwood, Dakota. Feidt, John
Ferguson, B Pennsylvania.   Goodykoontz, D F Boone, Iowa.
Griffin, Lawrence—deserted.   Greenup, E T d'd July 18, '64, Memphis
Hawkins, Hiram   Hanson, Jens d'd Oct 5, '62, Macon, Ga.
Hanson, O d'd Jun. 30,'62, Atlanta, Ga. Huestis, J H Waterville, Iowa.
Hughes, John died St Louis, Mo. Hannan, Lawrence, died July 28,
Husted, Jacob M died July 29,   1864, Cairo, Ill.
      1864, Memphis, Tenn. Isted, I B S Milwaukee, Wisconsin.
Iverson, Knud Lansing, Iowa. Jennings, D P
Jones, Henry   Johnson, Lewis
King Chas d'd Oct. 12, '62, Macon, Ga. Klees, Frank Rossville, Iowa.
Kuck, Henry "   10, "   "   " Knudson, Hans
Kleven, Sam " Aug 24, "   "   " Lankins, F W died in Nebraska.
Lene, August killed, Tupalo,   Lewis Edward
      Miss., July 15, 1864. Larson, Kensil
Larkins, Rees N   Maynard, W M died Sept. 6, 1863,
McCabe, Hugh Waukon, Iowa.   Vicksburg, Miss.
McKay, Frank   McGuire, Brian, Freeport, Illinois.
Miner, Jasper J died Dec. 24, 1861, McClintock, James Rossville, Iowa.

McDonald, James .... St. Louis, Mo.
Noyes, Alonzo
Nye, G F d'd Nov. 6, '63, Lansing, Ia.
Ogan, Chas C Sibley, Iowa.
Oleson, Barchart
Peterson, Bore
Patterson, Jas. W died of wounds
    July 24, '64, Memphis, Tenn.
Peck, John P
Pratt, W H Spokane Falls, W. T.
Porter, John B
Russell, Charles, Brooklyn, Mo.
Sohn, Jno. d'd Dec. 21, '62, St. Louis.
Schiffhauer, Rich
Scott, Jos d'd Oct 31, '62, St Louis
Stillman, John J killed Feb 13,
    '62, Fort Donelson, Tenn.
Smith, Ira J
Thayer, Jesse
Woodmansee, Isaac Rossville, Ia.
White, Wm. M d'd June 30, '62,
    . Macon, Ga
Winter, Rufus—dead.
Walcott, Daniel H died Nov. 23,
    '65, Talladega, Ala.

Mann, Ansel E—dead.
Noyes, Charles H died Aug. 7,
    1862, Macon, Ga
Oleson, Ole
Oleson, John Spring Grove, Minn
Perry, Edwin R died Nov 6, 1862,
    Annapolis, Vd.
Peck, Ira E d'd July 16, '62, Macon, Ga
Peck, Simon " Sept. 24. " " "
Plank, Levi Lake De Funiak, Florida.
Pratt, R G Storm Lake, Iowa.
Roe, Charles E
Stack, Thos. d'd Jan. 11, '62, St. Louis
Sjodin, Peter—dead.
Stecker, William
Stortz, Joseph
Smith, S C North McGregor, Iowa.
Sanner, Michael F Rossville, Iowa.
Thronsen, Knud died June 30,
    '62, Atlanta, Ga.
Wood, Edwin W
Wood, Stephen
Wilber, Robert
Winter, Francis A killed July 14,
    '64, Tupelo, Miss.
Warberg, Ole B Spring Grove, Minn.

NOTE.—Total number of Company, 132; of whom reported dead, 42; disability during service, 30; from wounds, 4; wounded in action, 35; taken prisoners April 6, 1862, at Shiloh, Tenn , 56; killed in action, 3.

Company C.

Capt. Wm. W Warner................died at Memphis, Tenn., Dec. 12, 1863.
" Geo. W. Cook.......................................Medicine Lodge, Kansas,
" David W Reed, (Major 12th Iowa)....................Wankon, Iowa,
" Wm L Henderson..Leroy, Minn.
1st Lt. David B. Henderson, (Col. 46th Iowa)..............Dubuque, Iowa.
" Henry J Grannis......................................Fayette, "
2d Lt. Aaron M Smith..............died at South Bend, Ind , Jan. 1, 1883.
1st Sergt. Jer. F Hutchins, (Capt. Co. E, 12th Ia.).........Minneapolis, Minn.
Sergt. Gilbert Hazlett....................................Allison, Iowa.
" Emery Clark......................................Estaline, Dakota.
" James Stewart....................................West Union, Iowa.
" Phineas R Ketchum................................Windsor, "
" Philo R Woods....................................Fayette, "
" Frank W Moine....................................Strawberry Point, "
Corp. David Connor..............died of wounds, Nashville, Jan. 5, 1865.
" Thomas Henderson...................killed at Shiloh, April 6, 1862.
" Samuel F Brush.............died at Macon, Ga., Oct. 31, 1862.
" Geo. L Durno.....................................Springville, Iowa.
" James Barr, (Asst. Surg. 12th Iowa)...............Algona, "
" Daniel D Warner..............died at Macon, Ga., Sept. 10, 1862.
" John W Bysong....................................West Point, Neb.
" Joseph D Baker...................................Montivideo, Minn.
" George E Comstock................................Manchester, Iowa.
" Henry C Curtis...................................Lemars, Iowa.
" John A Delezene..................................Rock Rapids, Minn.
" William H Jordan.................Cheney, Washington Territory.
" Amos K Ketchum...................................Clarion, Iowa.
" John E Kent......................................Belle Plaine, "
" I W King...Emerick, Neb.
Musician Sumner Harfshorn........................died in Michigan.

Abbott, Edward J (rover, no permanent residence-
Beck, Sam'l C Waverly, Iowa.
Ballinger, John W Lacey, "
Brown, John T
Brown, George Woodstock, Ill.
Burroughs, Geo A Douglass, Iowa.
Barton, Alvah H
Bushnell, Abne r C d'd at Pueblo, Col., Jan. 1882
Barr, Henry Tama county, Iowa.
Barnes, Jas. (transfer from 27.)
Benjamin, Nathan (drafted)
Bennefield, W m. (substitute)
Chase, Thos. H d'd St. Louis, Mar. 28, '62
Connor, Felix d'd " " Jan. 14, '62
" Daniel " " " " " "
Crossman, Silas" Elgin, Ia Apr 14, '81.
Carmichael, Jas. H Illyria, Iowa.
Comstock, Frank St. Louis, Mo.
Davis, Jay C Wisconsin.
Davis, Andrew J Berrian Spring, Mich.
Dawson, John (27th Iowa)
Forbes, Wm. d'd St Louis, Jan. 2, '62.
George, Henry died of wounds M'd City, May 2, '62.
Gillam, Ezekiel D (27th Iowa)
Hazlett, John B Howard, Dakota.
House, Nathan died at Savannah, Tenn., April, 1862.
Hendershot, Thos. Plainview, Neb
Henselbecker, Henry (drafted) Bluffton, Iowa.
Hinkel, Edward C (drafted) Winfield, Iowa.
Jordan, Isadore L Bull City Kan
Jaques, Luther Fairbanks, Iowa
Jones, Geo. M (drafted)
Jewell, James E (27th Iowa)
Jackway, G H (27th Ia.) Lamont, Ia.
Kent, William A Dallas, Wis.
Lewis, Leroy d'd St. Louis, Jan. 3, 63.
Lattimer, George H West Gate, Ia.
Lyons, William A West Union, "
Lott, Lawrence Kampeska, Dak.
Mattocks, Jason L Minneapolis, Minn.
McCall, John W Brownville, Neb.
Mattocks, Ross Wadena, Iowa.
McElvain, John d'd McLeansboro, Ill.
Martin, Chas. I (27th) Horton, Ia.
Patterson, Samuel W (27th.)
Proctor, Geo W (27th) Lawrens, Ia.
Prichet, John L (drafted.)
Quivey, Jno d'd Oct. 4, '62, Macon, Ga.
Rodgers, Reuben F Wancoma, Ia.
Rodolph, John J
Spears, Niles H West Gate, Iowa.
Smith, Jacob R
Smith, Henry C died May 3, '63, Milliken's Bd. La

Ayers, Jas L d'd Macon, Ga., Oct 3, '62.
Adams, Ed d'd Fayette, Ia., Dec 20, '71.
Blanchard, S S died at Postville, Iowa.
Brown, Albert re-enlisted in 9th Iowa. Cav., killed by accident at Hickory Plain, Ark., Dec. 24, 18 4
Bowers, Wm H Limestoneville, Pa.
Baker, Miles d'd Nov. 19, '67, Eden, Ia.
Beadle, Henry d'd Macon, Ga. Aug. 9, '62
Brown, Addison L deserted, Selma, Ala
Becktell, David T Volga City, Iowa
Brant, Allen (transfer from 27) Fairbanks, Iowa.
Browsley, Wm. (drafted)
Clark, Henry Melbourne, Iowa.
Connor, Sam'l Maxwell "
Card, Silas B
Clawson, Elijah d'd St. Louis, Jan. 10, '62
Carrington, Chas. Mitchell county.
Canfield, Theron P (27th Ia.) Buffalo Grove, Iowa.
Delezene, Benj Republic City, Neb.
Forbes, David
Grannis, Geo. W missing at Shiloh, never heard from.
Gifford, Simeon Douglass, Iowa.
Hood, Alonzo F d'd St. Louis, Jun 31, '62
Hamlin, Wm A Plymouth, Iowa.
Hill, John W
Hill, Benj J (drafted)
Henkee, Martin (drafted) died at Memphis, April 17, 1864.
Hamlin, Lynam S Oelwein, Iowa.
Husted, Jacob M
Henderson, James A (27th Iowa) Cherokee, Iowa.
Jones, Henry d'd St. Louis, Jan. 17, 62.
Jordan, Daniel M killed at Rockdale, Texas, Nov. 10, 1881.
Kelley, Artemas.
Kelsey, E A Tripoli, Iowa.
Lattimer, Robert Z Fayette, Iowa
Larson, Chas. killed Shiloh April 6, '62.
Little, James
Munger, Albert P Cowlitz, W. T.
McCall, Daniel E Culver, Kansas.
McIntyre, Thos. J died at Vicksburg, Feb 26, '65.
Muchmore, Stephen D (27th.)
Pendleton, Chas. E killed Shiloh, April 6, 1862.
Pitts, Jas. (drafted) London, Kansas.
Quivey, Wm W Humboldt, Iowa
Russell, Granville died Feb. 17, '62, St. Louis, Mo.
Rockwell, Wm. R (drafted).
Simar, Willard E d'd Macon, Oct. 10, '62
Smith, Norton T killed at Vicksburg, May 22, '62.
Siegman, Chas d'd Annapolis, Oct. 27, "

Stone, Sam'l d'd Annapolis, Oct. 3, '62. Stone, Dan'l Wauconna, Iowa.
Sykes, Orvis Freeport, Illinois, Spears, Dan'l H d'd Sedalia, Nov. 12, '64
Sherbone, Daniel Strong, John P Schuyler, Neb.
Sprowls, John Saulsbury, John
Tatro, August Clermont, Iowa. Utter, Albert Sycamore, Ill.
Verdin, Isaiah Williams, Rudolphus, West Union, Ia
Wallace, Chas. d'd July 9, '63, Hos- Warner, Walter B, Clermont, Iowa.
    pital Boat. Wait, Van Buren deserted St. Louis,
                                                      April, 1863.

Company D.

Stibbs, John H.....................Room 88, P. O. Building, Chicago, Ill.
Soper, E B.....................................Emmetsburg, Iowa.
Prescott, T L............1123 Lexington Ave., cor. S. W. Ave., Chicago, Ill.
Ayers, Lyman M Cedar Rapids, Ia. Buttolph, Edwin A Cedar Rapids, Ia.
Baumgardner, Wm Eldora, Iowa. Burch, Sylvester R Olathe, Kansas.
Bailey, Edwin H Fredonia, Kan. Bailey, Henry W Kirkman, Iowa.
Blanchard, Allen M Chicago, Ill. Barr, Thomas Shellsburg, "
Burch, John W Olathe Kansas. Blood, Alvarro C
Brown, Angus M Sioux City, Iowa. Clark, John M Cedar Rapids, Iowa.
Conley, Dennis Davenport, " Cowell, James L Marengo, W. T.
Clark, Chas W Cedar Rapids, " Curren, FrancisMarion, Iowa.
Clark, Isaac G Omaha, Neb. Cowell, Robert C Guthrie Center, Ia.
Clemans, Nick alias Chas, Ran- Dailey, James C Cherokee, Iowa
    som, Smith Center, Kan. DuBois, Ferdinand, Denison, Iowa.
Ellgen, Harmon Graiton, Iowa. Ferner, James D Nevada, "
Flint, Samuel H Leavenworth, Kan. Gephart, Perry Lake Forest, Ill.
Grass, Harmon Fargo, Dakota. Howard, William C Chelsea Iowa.
Hale, Neil Tucson, Arizona. Holler, Irdill W
Johnson, Robinson L Sanford, Neb. King, Eli Washington, Kansas.
Lanagan, James Odel, Nebraska. Luther, John Norton, Kansas.
Lewis, Thos J Cedar Rapids, Iowa. Lee, William L Helena, Montana
Lambert, John B Little, James H
Martin, Richard S McIntyre, Alpheus
Moorehead, Chas L Cedar Rapids, Ia Millett, Allen J Hastings, Neb
Morrow, B Frank Almena, Kansas. Maryatt, O H Red Cloud, Neb.
Minor, David W Arcata, Cal. Moorehead, Homer C Cedar Rapids Ia
Price, Nathan G Jewell City, Kan. Price, J V Geo Mountain Grove, Mo.
Pangborn, Howard Palouse, W. T. Rowan, John W Vinton Iowa.
Ross, Henry W Red Cloud, Neb. Renchin, Frank Bloomingt'n Pra., Min.
Ross, Jesse H Red Cloud, Neb. Steadman, Dudley E Vinton, Iowa.
Scott, Josiah Shellsburg, Iowa. Soper, Roswell K Estherville, "
Startwell, Joseph O Marion, Iowa. Steward, Aaron A Carthage, Mo.
Sivets, Daniel Sublett, Mo. Tarpenning, 'as M Northville, Tenn.
Thompson, Frank D Nevada, Iowa. Trowbridge, Wm H Des Moines, Ia.
VanEmman, Wm M Grand View, Dak. Whittam, John J Cedar Rapids, Ia.
Wagner, Jasper Center Point, Iowa. Whiteneck, W W Waterloo, Iowa.
Weaver, John N Sioux City, " Zuver, B P Adams, Nebraska
Stibbs, Joseph—died July 16, 1866, at Wooster, Ohio, of abscess of back, contracted in rebel prisons.
Blackburn, Joseph .—died April 20, 1862, near Shellsburg, Iowa, of disease on account of which discharged.
Breman, Patrick—died Sept. 17, 1873, at Hot Springs, Arkansas, of disease of lungs and liver.
Craft, James—died July 3, 1863, of disease on account of which discharged.
Baumgardner, Samuel—died June, 1877, at Vinton, Iowa, of consumption
Doolittle, Washington A—died July 24, 1880, at Watkins, Benton Co., Iowa, of Bright's disease, resulting from chronic diarrhœa and lung difficulty.
Doleshall, Wencil—died August 31, 1873, at Cedar Rapids, Iowa.
Frees, James P—died April 5, 1862, at Cedar Rapids, Iowa, of pneumonia.
Frees, Andrew J—killed June 30, '73, at Cedar Rapids, by B C R & N R'y cars.

Gilchrist, Wm B—died at Shellsburg, Iowa, of disease on account of which he was discharged.
Lutz, William B—died Oct. 31, 1877, at Cedar Rapids, Iowa, of old age and general debility.
Martin, Ebenezer B—died Dec. 28, '68, at Cedar Rapids, Ia., of consumption.
Gallagher, James—died Jan. 31, 1886, at Crete, Neb, of Bright's disease.

NOTE.—Any one knowing the addresses of those not given, or of their death, will confer a favor on Co. D, by addressing E. B. Soper, Emmetsburg, Iowa.

Company E.

Boone, R G Scott, Iowa.
Beckwith, W H Parkersburg, Ia
Bird, E Winterset, Iowa.
Belton, James Edgewood, Iowa.
Cook, Charles Lester,   "
Crowhurst, Seth J Salem, Dakota.
Cook, John J Brooklyn, New York.
Coon, H F d'd Oct. '84, Waterloo, Ia.
Demoss, Thomas Bristow, Iowa.
Ellwell, John Chicago, Illinois.
Early, T M Bristow, Iowa.
Hamilton, Wm La Porte City, Ia.
Harrison, H J Waterloo, Iowa.
Large, F A La Porte City, Iowa
Margretz, J S Hittsville, Iowa.
Minium, David Big Grove, Iowa.
Perry, A B Dunkerton, Iowa.
Rich, J W Vinton,   "
Stewart, Joel A Oregon City, Ore.
Seeber, G L Sabula, Iowa.
Switzer, C R Lewis,   "
Smith, Harvey Waterloo, Iowa.
Shumaker, John W Waterloo, Ia.
Strong Ezra Sioux City, Iowa
Williams, (Capt.) Robt Vancouvre, W T

Biller, Anthony J Waterloo, Iowa.
Boylan, Thomas, Stockton, Kan.
Bird, R L Yuma, Col.
Collins, Chas P Charles City, Iowa.
Creighton, David Geneva,   "
Cook, Joseph New Castle, Neb.
Cook, Adolph
Church, Nathan, Webster City or Eagle Grove, Iowa.
Eberhart, Ben Marshalltown,   "
Graham, Jacob Davenport,   "
Hayward, C B Mooreville,   "
Jones, John C Geneva,   "
Myers, A W Shell Rock,   "
Morris, C D Worthing, Dakota.
Ochs, Charles Ackley, Iowa.
Reed, Zeff Fredonia, Iowa.
Surfus, C V Bristow,   "
Sunderlin, M V B Janesville, Iowa.
Schrack, David Oelwein,   "
Sharp, Oliver Finchford,   "
Sawyer, E La Porte City,   "
Shroyer, Nathaniel Taintor,   "
Talbot, Allen E Orleans, Indiana.
Watkins, Isaac Crawfordsville, Ind.
West, D F Theon, W T.

Company F.

Ainsworth, J E Mo. Valley Junc. Ia.
Brenner, John Yankton, Dak.
Brown, Eugene Brush Creek, Ia.
Coolidge, F W Rawlins, Wyom'g T.
Dunham, Abner Manchester, Ia.
Eldridge, J E Walnut, Kansas
Eaton, John J Edgewood, Iowa.
Girton, Joseph S Hazelton,   "
Gift, J W Peoria, Illinois.
Halfhill, Josiah Wood Center, Ia.
Kaltenbach, Sam'l Manchester, "
Kent, George Oelwein,   "
Kirchner, Mike
Lee, John F Council Grove, Kan.
Mackey, H F Maynard, Iowa.
McKee, T R Dell Rapids, Dak.
Mann, Wm W Ranelsburg, Neb.
Nelson, T C Hazelton, Iowa,
Preston, H M Ft Dodge, Iowa.
Peasley, R H Kansas.
Roe, A J Burlington, Iowa.

Annis, Geo W Lanark, Illinois.
Buckman, Wm H Dyersville, Iowa.
Correll, Ed Greeley,   "
Coolidge, O E Central City, Neb.
Dahl, John A Silver Creek, Iowa.
Eldridge, R C Niagara Falls, N Y.
French, S M Denver, Colorado.
Goodell, Wm H Manchester, Iowa.
Grice, A J Doniphon, Nebraska.
Hasbrouck, Dan'l H Prairie Creek, Ore
Kaltenbach, L P San Bernardino, Cal.
Kaster, Hiram, Manchester, Iowa.
Lee, James F Clay Mills, Iowa.
McGowan, Thos. Independence, Ia.
Manning, A L Dunlap, Iowa.
Manley, R L
Nelson, W A Hazelton, Iowa.
Olmstead, H Independence, Iowa
Potter, Jas. W Fayette, Iowa.
Ralston, Nelson Lemars,   "
Small, H J F Chicago, Illinois.

Steen, C C Minneapolis, Kansas.
Stribling, C C Clifton, Tenn.
Thorn, Chris. Waverly, Iowa.
Weeden, R L Nugent's Grove, Ia.
Wooldridge, Geo W Elkport, "
Schneider, Justus Rosewell, Dak.
Tirrill, R W Manchester, Iowa.
Tibbetts, W F Cheney, Kansas.
Widger, Joshua Manchester, Iowa.
Wandall, A Volga City, "

Company G.

C C Tupper, d'd Benton Bar. Jan.'62.
L D Townsley, Mapima Durango, Mex.
J F Nickerson, d'd in rebel prison.
J E Stimpson, Norfolk, Neb
A A Burdick, killed at Tupelo.
A E Anderson, Calmar, Iowa.
O C Thorson, d'd at Eldorado, Ia.
R A Gibson, died U S service
J H Womeldorf, Neleigh, Neb.
Anderson, A Albert Lea, Minn.
Anderson, G Rothsay, "
" A M d'd wounds rec'd Corinth.
Brown, J H died at Decorah.
Bowers, A died in Ohio.
Clark, J M
Cutlip, J
Coon, C A Sabinal, Texas.
Carey, A A died at Castalia, Iowa.
Davis, N J Berrian Springs, Mich.
Ellsworth, W D d'd Benton Barracks.
Fuller, A S Lyons, Dakota.
Fuller, A " "
Gorhamer, O H d'd St. Louis, '63.
Gilbert, L died at Keokuk.

Groves, A H Decorah, Iowa.
Hulverson, A " "
Hall, Giles
Houge, G A Albert Lea, Minn.
Hanson, Hans. Lake Park, "
Hanson, Halver Sheldon, Dak.
Jenson, A d'd Sept '63, in Miss.
Johnson, A d'd Greensville, La., '65.
Johnson, N O
Kirkland, G W Freeport, Iowa
Larson, Hover d'd Savannah, Tenn.
Larson, John
Manson, J
Montgomery, Wm V
Madinn, D L
Maloney, J died in field.
Miller, S lives in California.
McCabe, C Sherburne, Minn.
Nass, G H Woodside, Iowa.
Oleson, O
" O G killed at Shiloh.
" J died at Thoton, Iowa.
Pollock, Jos must'd out at Selma, '65.
Pierce, Fletcher
Romberg, L O d'd at Chewalla, '64.
Ricker, J died at Savannah, '62.
Raucha, Fred Skidmore, Mo.
Smith, I K Baraboo, Wis.
Simmons, R Lake Park, Minn.
G O Hanson, died at Decorah.
W L Winsor, Clinton, Mo.
T Steen, died at Omaha.
A W Erit, died in service.
J O Johnson, Mabel, Minn.
N B Burdick, died at Decorah.
R Hard.
G W Sharp, Fargo, Dakota.
Andrus, E V Decorah, Iowa.
Aker, D O Ridgeway, "
Anderson, Peter
Anderson, E
Ballard, Strawder
Crane, John
Crowell, J M
Connolly, C d'd at Somerville, Mass.
Christopherson, C Hartland, Minn.
Dunn, Van R Dewitt, Nebraska.
Engbertson, E
Eastonson, G d'd at Mound City, Ia.
Fladmark, S M M
Green, L D
Gilbertson, O Benton, Minn.
Gulbranson, A Rothsay, "
Honson, Klaus
Hanson, Ole
Hall, Austin, d'd at St. Louis, '63.
Helgerson, G died at Nashville, '64.
Harris, F W
Hand, Andrew J
Johnson, H E Alexandre, Minn.
Johnson, Henry 1st d'd Huntsville, '62.
" " 2d
Kittleson, C B died in Minnesota.
Kittleson, G
Larson, Peter
Low, Lewis L
McCalley, P died at Hesper.
McLoud, S
Miller, O D Stuart, Neb.
Meyer, C
Meader, M E Hesper, Iowa.
Moe, Peter '
Nelson, Swen
Oleson, E
" Ammon died at Memphis.
" A H
Palmer, R lives in Nebraska.
Peterson, N d'd at Camp Woods, '63.
Raucha, Ed.
Rocksvold, O P Thoton, Iowa.
Ryerson, F
Skinner, C d'd '63, steamer Crescent.
" F Forest City.

Staples, C J d'd at Frankville, Ia.
Steen, John Wahoo, Neb.
Steen, Henry Oakland, Neb.
Smith, G M died at Decorah, Ia.
Seruson, S A killed at Tupelo, '64.
Tinke, J
Thompson, A K
Taylor, W H H
Thompson, J B Speilville, Iowa.
Wright, C F
Wheeler, Horace
Wait, W Nashua, Iowa.

Simmison, Nels.
Severson, Nels.
Stalim, Lars L
Simmons, John
Slattery, Thomas
Thompson, T Lincoln Center, Kan.
Torgenston, M d'd '65, at Montgomery.
Tobiason, Andrew
Thoryson, Andrew
Wold, L T d'd at Vicksburg, '63.
West, S Red Cloud, Neb
Wiley, Wm. died at St. Louis, '63.

Company H.

Atkinson, W L C Omaha, Neb.
Brown, Tom Jewell City, Kan.
Becket, Ed Dubuque, Iowa.
Currie, John G Butte City, Mon.
Clark, B A Colesburg, Iowa.
Cox, W H Alta, "
Evans, James Dubuque, "
Fishel, S K Ft McGinnis, Mon.
Franks, Joseph Lamont, Iowa.
Grimes, R M Kearney, Neb.
Gosting, Alfred G Strawberry Pt., Ia.
Hamblin, R E Arcadia, Ohio.
Hamlin, F M Iowa Falls, Iowa.
Jones, David, Monona, "
Kuhnes, J C Manning, "
Light, Robt Bernett, Nebraska.
Langslou, Aaron l transferred from
    Co. D, 27th Ia. to Co. D, 12th Ia.
McConnell, Alex. S Hopkinton, Ia.
Newman, Geo. North Platt, Neb.
Royse, Wm. Atlantic, Iowa
Shorter, James Shell Rock, Iowa.
Sloan, S B Greeley, "
Winch, Edward Arena, Wis.
Ward, John W Burlington, Iowa.

Briggs, U I Marcus, Iowa.
Benedict, R W Jesup, Iowa.
Benedict, John W Plum Creek, Neb.
Crist, John W Central City, Dak.
Crosby, J M Pukwana, "
Duncan, N E Kansas City, Mo.
Fishel, S C Iowa Falls, Iowa.
    " Robert W Greeley, Iowa.
Flenniken, J B North Fork, Neb.
Gilmore, A C Indianapolis, Ind.
Horner, Geo. Dubuque, Iowa.
Henry, Philip Greeley, "
Jackson, S M Lincoln, Neb.
King, Wilson, Emerick, "
Knee, Samuel G Colesburg, Iowa.
Light, Joseph A North Fork, Neb.
Mason, John S Worthington, Iowa.
Moreland, C D W Earlville, Iowa.
McCune, W H Ruthven, "
Playter, H J Washington, D C
Smith, Thomas Turkey River, Ia.
Shorter, Wm. Shell Rock, Iowa
Trumble, James Manchester, Ia.
Wisegarber, Wm O'Neil City, Neb.
VanAnda, John N Fremont, "

Company I.

Austin, N E Andrew, Iowa.
Butters, John F Mooreville, Iowa.
Brown, J
Buchanan, James Tama, Iowa.
Coates, J W Talcott, Dakota.
Campbell, E B Armstrong Grove, Ia.
Cobb, Edgar C Keokuk, Iowa.
Davenport, A G Superior, Neb.
Eddie, Thos. C Salina, Kansas.
Fry, Wm. L Scranton, Iowa.
Hatfield, Augustus Jersey City, N J.
Hendricks, Wm. Winterset, Iowa.
Kennedy, Sam'l L Cedar Rapids, Ia.
Markham, W H Hawkeye, Kansas.
McCollum, D D Sibley, Iowa
McDermott, Michael, Epworth, Ia.
Nims, Weed Maquoketa, Iowa.
Palmer, A L Seattle, W T.
Ray, John S Naponee, Neb.
Sumbardo, C L (Capt.) Ramsey, Minn.

Austin, Marion, Staplehurst, Neb.
Belknap, Albert Scribner, "
Bintner, Wm Brayton, Iowa.
Crane, I K Maquoketa "
Campbell, Thos. Humboldt, Iowa.
Cobb, Wm A Walla Walla, W T.
Devine, John Dubuque, Iowa
Dupray, Wm H Storm Lake, Ia.
Eddie, Alexander Greshumptom, Kan.
Goodenow, M B Ord, Nebraska.
Harding, James Baldwin, Iowa.
Kohler, Wm. Dubuque, "
Kerns, Peter Reubens, Kansas.
McKinley, James Maquoketa, Iowa.
McCarron, W F Athens, Tenn
Nagle, M D Dubuque, Iowa.
Perkins, J H Seattle, W T.
Paup, David A Sac City, Iowa.
Rolf, Marion Maquoketa, Iowa
Starbuck, Wm. Huffman, Dakota.

Smith, Henry Maquoketa, Iowa.
Thompson, Jas. L Franklin, Neb.
Vanhook, Sam'l Maquoketa, Iowa.
Wilson, T Maquoketa, Iowa.
Wilson, John F Fulton, "
Yeley, George Clinton, "
Teskey, George Elwood, Iowa.
Van Duzee, E M (Maj.) St. Paul, Minn.
Wintersteen, Henry Monmouth, Ill.
Wood, Joel Maquoketa, Iowa.
Wells, Charles A Sabula, "
Zediker, Jas. F (Capt.) Franklin, Neb.

Company K.

Brooks, John
Brown, J J Bloomington, Neb.
Billings, Abram Luzern, N Y
Barden, Henry A
Beckner, J M Charles City, Iowa.
Church, P Arborville, Nebraska.
Deutsher, Albert Nat. Home, Ohio.
Freeman, Richard Spencer, "
Keith, W B Precept, Nebraska.
Merriam, H C Nugent, Iowa.
Mathis, W R Omaha, Nebraska.
Morgan, J B Davenport, Iowa.
Mosher, Alvin
McConnell, Alex S Hopkinton, Ia.
Myers, Joseph A — dead
Robinson, Alonzo Albion, Neb.
Willard, Porter H Hopkinton, Ia.
Blood, George W
Billings, Chas. D Bloomington, Neb.
Blanchard, Thos. Le Mar, Kansas.
Baldwin, Newton Ada, Kansas
Blanchard, Ira D Crookston, Minn.
Dolley, Godfrey Hopkinton, Iowa.
Ellison, H Neoma, Nebraska.
Horn, Samuel Colesburg, Iowa.
Kemp, Wm. Kirwin, Kansas.
Merriam, C E Hopkinton, Iowa.
Mathis, E R Omaha, Nebraska
Morehouse, P J Masonville, Iowa.
Morgan, Wm B Bloomington, Neb.
Mickey, Isaac Waukon, Iowa.
Phillips, C E Blair, Nebraska.
Webb, Laurence Cedar Rapids, Ia.
Waldroff, Henry La Porte City, Ia.

The following is a list of the Members who paid their Dues at Waterloo, Ia.

James Barr,
A J Rogers,
George H Cobb,
John D Cole,
P R Wood,
John M Clark,
Homer C Morehead,
Edwin A Butolph,
E D Steadman,
Charles R Surles,
H J Hanson,
M V Sunderlin,
E P Sawyer,
H Koster,
Joe Franks,
J W Crist,
James S Thompson,
W R Mathis,
S R Burch,
J W Gift,
C E Merriam,
A B Perry,
Hart Spear,
Robert Buthen,
F M Hamlin,
Gilbert Hazlett,
Josh Widger,
J C Jones,
J Shorter,
Jerry Margretz,
Thomas J Lewis,
Mr. and Mrs. R P Clarkson,
S G Knee,

W H McKuhne,
John A VanAnda,
R E Kellogg,
C J Martin,
J B Flannigan,
I W King,
Maj. Rownu,
E A Kelsey,
W A Kent,
J A Light,
A S Fuller,
Harmon Gross,
Thomas Farr,
Robert Z Latimore,
H W Bailey,
B E Eberhart,
J N Weaver,
S W Jackson,
A J Roe,
S Fort Slonu,
M B Goodnow,
Col. Edgington,
E B Soper,
George Terkey,
Captain Simpson,
George H Morisey,
A Dunham,
D D McCallum,
R W Ferree,
Robert W Fishel,
Seth Macy,
Col. Stibbs,

George D Durno,
A H Groves,
George W Kirkland,
P R Ketchum,
C D Morris,
S Kemp,
J W Conts,
James F Lee,
John F Lee,
F W Moine,
Michael McDermott,
J W Ward,
J F Campbell,
Thomas McGowan,
James F Zediker,
A J Biller,
H J Graunis,
E B Campbell,
James Stewart,
L Myers,
Josiah Scott,
A K Ketcham,
W H Cox,
Thomas Dowling,
Thomas C Nelson,
John Ballanger,
A W Blanchard,
John Kent,
D W Reed,
Charles R Switzer,
S D Brodtbeck,
Daniel Sivets.

Names of Wives and Children Present.

Mrs. S R Edgington, Eldora, Iowa.
Master Bertram Barr, Algona, Iowa.
Mrs. R P Clarkson, Des Moines, Iowa.
" A J Rogers, Waukon, Iowa.
Miss Minnie A Reed, Waukon, Iowa.
Mrs. C J Henderson, LeRoy, Minn.
" E J Lewis, Cedar Rapids, Iowa.
" E B Soper, Emmetsburg, Iowa.
Master E B Soper, jr., Emmetsburg, Ia.
Mrs. L M Ayers, Cedar Rapids, Iowa.
" Alex Myers, Shell Rock, Iowa.
Master Ralph A Dunham, Manchester, Ia.
Mrs. R W Tirrill, Manchester, Iowa.
Master E W Knee, Colesburg, Iowa.
Mrs. C E Merriam, Hopkinton, Iowa.

Mrs. James Barr, Algona, Iowa.
" G H Morisey, Manchester, Iowa.
" S Kemp, Alden, Iowa.
" D W Reed, Waukon, Iowa.
Master Herbert Strong, Schuyler, Nebraska.
Miss Gussie Henderson, LeRoy, Minn.
Master Mac Lewis, Cedar Rapids, Iowa.
Miss Rubie Soper, Emmetsburg, Iowa.
Master E H Soper, " "
Mrs. B E Eberhart, Marshalltown, Iowa.
" Abner Dunham, Manchester, Iowa.
" George Kent, Oelwein, Iowa.
" J J Eaton, Edgewood, Iowa.
" R W Fishel, Greeley, Iowa.

The following surviving members of the original band of the regiment were present at this reunion:

D. S. Martin—Fife Major.
Sewell Jackson—Fifer.

Truman McKee—Drum Major.
W. H. McCune—Bass Drummer.

FOURTH REUNION

— OF THE —

TWELFTH IOWA

Veteran Volunteer Infantry,

— HELD AT —

SIOUX CITY, IOWA,

May 18th and 19th, 1892.

NORFOLK, NEB.
PRESS OF THE DAILY NEWS.
1892.

Attention Comrades!

It has been determined that we will send a copy of the proceedings of our last reunion to each surviving comrade whose address we have. And we hope that those who have not already paid membership fees or dues, will remit said dues of one dollar, or send twenty-five cents, the cost of said pamphlet, to the undersigned treasurer of the association at Algona, Iowa. All who signed our by-laws and became members of our association, whose names appear on page — of this book, are entitled to a copy free of charge.

We are anxious that all who can will become members of our society, and if you will send one dollar to the treasurer and direct him to do so, he will inscribe your name on the roll making you a member, and you will be entitled to this book without additional cost. Unless this is done we hope you will send the 25 cents.

Comrades let us not forget each other. Help a little in the good work. If you know of any comrades who served in our regiment whose name does not appear on our book, or whose address is changed, be kind enough to send his name and address to J. E. Simpson, Norfolk, Nebraska.

By order of Executive Committee.

JAMES BARR, Treasurer,
Algona, Kossuth Co., Iowa.

FOURTH REUNION

— OF THE —

TWELFTH IOWA

Veteran Volunteer Infantry,

— HELD AT —

SIOUX CITY, IOWA,

May 18th and 19th, 1892.

NORFOLK NEB.
PRESS OF THE DAILY NEWS
1892

OFFICERS OF THE SOCIETY.

MAJOR D. W. REED, President,
   Suite 814, Chamber of Commerce, Chicago, Ill.
J. N. WEAVER, Vice President, Bolton Block, Sioux City, Iowa.
J. E. SIMPSON, Acting Secretary, Norfolk Nebraska.
DR. JAMES BARR, Treasurer, Algona, Iowa.
   The above officers being the Executive Committee.

The following members are a committee, each for his own company, to report the deaths of their comrades who may pass away, reporting the time and place of death and such details of interest that may appear, to the members of the Regiment when next they meet in reunion.

This is a very important duty and one that should be well attended to.

Co. A, R. P. Clarkson, Des Moines, Iowa.
Co. B, J. D. Cole, Lansing, Iowa.
Co. C, D. W. Reed, Suite 814, Chamber Commerce, Chicago, Ill.
Co. D, J. H. Stibbs, Rooms 88, P. O. Building, Chicago, Ill.
Co. E, J. W. Shumaker, Waterloo, Iowa.
Co. F, R. W. Tirrell, Manchester, Iowa.
Co. G, J. E. Simpson, Norfolk, Neb.
Co. H, J. A. Van Anda, Fremont, Neb.
Co. I, J. F. Zediker, of Nebraska State Journal, Lincoln, Neb.
Co. K, Dr. J. B. Morgan, Davenport, Iowa.

Comrades who know or learn of any deaths of the members of the Regiment should report the facts to the proper member of the above Committee.

Abner Dunham

REUNION

⮞OF THE⮜

12th Iowa Veteran Volunteer Infantry.

MAY 18 & 19, 1892.

Explanatory.

DEAR COMRADES:—We think it best to commence the proceedings of our reunion by the circular letter sent you May 21st. It explains all the circumstances fully and gives the names and addresses of those who were present. There was a resolution passed by unanimous vote of all present that the present organization be continued until our next reunion; and all the officers and committees be requested to continue in the discharge of their respective duties.

Also another resolution that J. N. Weaver and J. E. Simpson be a committee on publication of these proceedings.

Also that R. W. Tirrel, J. H. Stibbs and Wm. L. Henderson act as committee on resolutions.

One of the pleasant little episodes of our reunion was the visit from M. Deal, Esq., of Bucyrus, Ohio, who chanced to be in Sioux City and heard of our meeting, came and gave us a very interesting talk. Living at Gettysburg at the time of the battle, he and his brother, were the first civilians over the field after the great battle and what he saw and heard at the time, he told to us. He contributed liberally to our contribution to the sufferers of the flood, for seeing with our own eyes the extent of the loss and suffering, the comrades present put together their mites, and sending the same by the hands of Comrade

Weaver, who returned with the following very handsome acknowledgment:

SIOUX CITY, May 19, 1892.

To the Veterans of the 12th Iowa:—

I have the honor to acknowledge your contribution to the flood sufferers by the hand of Judge Weaver and beg to thank you kindly in behalf of the citizens of Sioux City. Fraternally yours,

MORRIS PIERCE, Mayor.

Weighed down with the cares of the hour and the constant demands upon him night and day Mayor Pierce found time to come and say a kindly word to us on Thursday evening.

One thing we was all agreed upon and that was the character and quality of the music rendered for us by the K. P. Band of twenty instruments. Quiet and modest and always ready, they gave to us those good old tunes that carried us back to our soldier days, and brought the camp, the march and the field of thirty years ago back to us most vividly.

Also that Col. Woods and Col. Edgerton's histories be made a part of and published in these proceedings.

Comrade Andrews, of Co. B, offered the following resolution: Resolved, that it is the sense of this meeting that our next reunion be held within the next two years at Sioux City, Iowa. After discussion, carried, with the understanding that this was the sense and feeling of those present, and the whole matter be left to the Executive Committee for their action after hearing from the absent comrades.

There has been a large number of letters received from comrades and there are a few coming yet in answer to the circular letter of May 21st. The large majority say Sioux City and 1894, for our next meeting. This is a matter your Executive Committee will duly consider and act upon in due time.

We desire to call your attention to the *call of your treasurer*, Dr. James Barr, Algona, Iowa, for funds. Comrades must keep in mind postage and printing must be paid for, and we are now publishing these proceedings with less than half the cost in the treasury, trusting comrades will promptly remit their dues.

Your committee desires to say that under the rules governing the railroads of the country that reduced fares cannot be had for regimental reunions except in the state where held or the regiment was raised, hence we cannot get reduced fares only for the state of Iowa.

We regret our proceedings were so short and incomplete, but the facts and circumstances have all been told to you. We have done the best we could and trust our work will be received by you in the spirit we send it out. With love and kind greetings to you all, and wishing we may all meet at our next reunion and have a regular love feast of good things, we remain, Yours Truly,

JOHN N. WEAVER,
J. E. SIMPSON.

SIOUX CITY, IOWA, MAY 21, 1892.

To the Members of the 12th Iowa Infantry, Greeting:

We who succeeded in getting to Sioux City in time for our Fourth Quadrennial Reunion, the18th and 19th of May, found, at the hour of assembling, this beautiful city overwhelmed with an unprecedented flood, rendering hundreds homeless and thousands waiting for shelter.

Of course, Wednesday forenoon, nothing could be done but shake hands and commence to register. In the afternoon it was deemed best to give up any attempt at a regular programme and simply visit, enlivened by the fine music of the band and cheering strains of the fife and drum by comrades French and McKee, and anxiously waiting hour by hour, hoping that other comrades, whom we knew were en route, would be able to get here. Evening was spent much the same way.

Thursday morning came bright and clear, and although the city was full of excitement, and every one's attention, both hands and heart, was turned to the duties of the hour, we met and resolved ourselves into an old-fashioned, Methodist love feast, in which every man, woman and child present, from Company A. to Company K. inclusive, was called upon for a speech, a song, a dance or a recitation, and just like all members of the old 12th, every one responded without hesitation. Enthusiasm grew, hearts melted, cares for the time being were thrown away and we had a good time; interspersed with all this were dispatches coming in every hour from comrades delayed en route, letters from absent ones were read, the Shubert Quartette and the K. P. Band (20 instruments), whose selections were of the very best kind and pleased every one here, at frequent intervels enlivened the occasion added much to the enjoyment.

Thursday night brought Gen. J. H. Stibbs, who had forced his way through (after a forty-eight hour march) from Des Moines. He took hold at once and entertained us with his pleasant remarks, a number of fine recitations and some amusing stories. All this time, remember we were hoping and expecting the comrades, who were detained at different points, would come in and share with us the pleasures of the occasion. Some of the comrades had to leave Thursday night, but a great bulk of them resolved to remain over Friday in hopes that others might come.

Friday morning came with a snow storm, amounting almost to a blizzard, something almost unprecedented at this season, adding to the general distress and misery in the city and damping down our enthusiasm till we got together, when, amid the inspiring sound of the fife and drum we continued our love feast, and soon the same warm, kind feelings were expressed and seen.

Friday afternoon we appointed a committee on resolutions, resolved to continue our organization with the same officers as at present, till the next reunion, requesting them to perform all the duties and act in the premises as their good judgement decided. There was a general and full expression that our next reunion must be held within the next two years. The idea of holding it in Chicago during the World's Fair was not favored, comrades fearing that, under the excitement and novelty of the surroundings, it would be impossible to enjoy what again has been clearly demonstrated to be the main object of reunions of the 12th Iowa, to-wit: to visit with each other and among ourselves.

The citizens of Sioux City, have expressed a warm and earnest desire that the next reunion might be held here. And it is but fair to say that the larger share of those present were of that mind. Our old home, Manchester, was warmly spoken of and many hearts turned that way. After very full discussion and expressions of opinion, the whole matter was left to the discretion of the Executive Committee, after hearing from the members of the regiment in response to this letter, which is sent to every living member known.

We now ask of you, dear comrades, on receipt of this letter.

(1) To send your membership fee of $1.00 to Dr. James Barr, Treasurer, Algona, Iowa, so we can publish the proceedings of this reunion which will largely consist of letters and telegrams received, corrected rosters of the companies up to date, with Post Office address; also a personal history of Col. Woods, that we feel warranted in saying every man, woman and child connected with the 12th Iowa will read with pleasure and profit, it being a detailed history from his boyhood, written by Major Reed and revised by the Colonel himself, before his death. Also a full biographical notice of Col. Edgerton, and a notice of the death and the incidents thereof, of comrades who have died since 1888. Every pains will be taken to publish these proceedings as soon as possible and a copy mailed to every member who has paid his dues.

(2) We want you as soon as you get this letter and have carefully thought over the subject, to drop a postal card to the secretary, indicating where you want the next reunion held, and when you want it held. On the receipt of these answers they will be carefully collated and laid before the Executive Committee for their consideration and action in calling our next reunion. From the expression of those who were present and those who started or intended to come, we are fully satisfied that, if there had not been some unforeseen calamity, as did happen, we would have had the largest, one of the most enthusiastic reunions that the 12th Iowa ever had.

It is due to the citizens of Sioux City to say, that, acting conjointly with comrade J. N. Weaver, they provided for us a good hall, one of the best bands in the state(20 instruments), solely at our disposal during the reunion, paid printing expenses, amounting to over $30.00, so that practically, the expenses of the reunion, excepting the individual ones of the comrades, were fully provided for by the citizens of Sioux City. They also had made elaborate preparations in connection with the reception of the boys, to decorate and place the city in holiday attire in honor of the occasion, which was only prevented by the unprecedented storm and wind occurring at that time, which rendered it wholly impossible to make any decorations on the streets or buildings in the city.

They had also, in connection with the Woman's Relief Corps, made full arrangements to give the boys a royal banquet the evening of the 9th, which, with the full concurrence and approbation of the comrades present, was abandoned, and the funds provided for that purpose diverted to the relief of the suffering and hungry of the city, so rendered by the flood.

Three large boat clubs, with elegant boat club houses and many boats at Riverside Park, on the Big Sioux River, which is beautifully located and the best pleasure resort, with facilities for boating, had prepared to throw open their boat houses, and tender for our use, their boats for the pleasure of the occasion, free.

The Electric Railway line, leading from the business part of the city to Riverside Park, a distance of about 4 miles, had made a rate for the boys to this pleasant resort of one fare for the round trip.

A Reception Committee, consisting of twenty-five comrades and twenty-five citizens, provided with appropriate badges, were ready to receive the comrades and do them every favor, which was only prevented by the unprecedented flood. Do not fail to answer this letter. We are, Respectfully and fraternally yours,

D. V. Ellsworth	Company A	Newman Grove, Neb.
D. A. Armstrong	"	Zearing, Iowa.
R. M. Runkle	"	Plankinton, So. Dakota
Mrs. C. M. Runkle,	"	"
John P. Peck	"	B
John Upstrom	"	Sioux Falls, " "
Hiram R. Andrews	"	Turkey River, Iowa.
Mrs. H. R. Andrews	"	"
John E. Kent	"	C Belle Plaine, Iowa.
W. A. Kent	"	Barron, Wis.
Mrs. W. A. Kent and child	"	"
I. W. King	"	Emerick, Neb.
J. W. Bysong	"	West Point, Neb.
J. B. Hazlett	"	Sioux Falls, So. Dakota.
J. L. Jordan	"	Alton, Kan.
W. L. Henderson	"	Riceville, Iowa.
Georgia Henderson	"	"
Mrs. Maude Ramsey	"	"
P. R. Woods	"	Fayette, Iowa,
Mrs. E. O. Woods	"	"
R. R. Soper	"	D Estherville, Iowa.
Mrs. R. R. Soper	"	"
Wm. M. Van Eman	"	Grand View, So. Dakota.
J. H. Stibbs	"	Chicago, Ills.
A. M. Blanchard	"	11 Edward Street, Chicago.
A. A. Stewart	"	Carthage, Mo.
J. D. Fernner	"	Nevada, Iowa.
F. D. Thompson	"	"
*L. M. Ayers	"	Cedar Rapids, Iowa.
John N. Weaver	"	Sioux City, Iowa.
Mrs. J. N. Weaver	"	"
Miss Katie Weaver	"	"
Miss Daisy Weaver	"	"
Miss Flora Weaver	"	"
Miss Cora Weaver	"	"
John V. G. Price	"	D Mountain Grove, Mo.
Mrs. John V. G. Price	"	"
B. P. Zuver	"	Adams, Neb.
Mrs. B. P. Zuver	"	"
Master B. P. Zuver	"	"
B. E. Eberhart	"	Marshalltown, Iowa.
C. D. Morris	"	Worthing, So. Dakota.
J. P. Cook	"	Ponca, Neb.
Mrs. J. P. Cook	"	"
Miss Laone Cook	"	"
S. J. Crowhurst	"	Salem, So. Dakota.
Sylvester Cook	"	Iona, Neb.
R. W. Terrill	"	F Manchester, Iowa.
Mrs. R. W. Terrill	"	"
Nelson Ralston	"	Canton, So. Dakota.
F. W. Coolidge	"	Shoshone, Idaho.
Mrs. F. W. Coolidge	"	"
T. R. McKee	"	Denver, Col.
Isaac Johnson	"	Pleasanton, Kan.
S. M. French	"	Denver, Col.
J. E. Eldridge	"	Stark, Kan.
John Bremner	"	Yankton, So. Dakota.

Peter Moe...............	Company G	.............Springfield, Minn.
Ole Gilbertson...........	"	" ....Gilchrist, Minn.
Samuel West...	"	" ....Red Cloud, Neb.
Mrs. Samuel West...	"	" ....
Henry Steen.............	"	" ....Belgrade, Neb.
J. E. Simpson...........	"	" ....Norfolk, Neb.
Mrs. Mary A. Simpson...	"	" ....
Lars L. Stallem..........	"	" ....Sioux City, Iowa.
*A. H. Groves........... ..	"	" ....Decorah, "
*G. H. Nass.............	"	" ....
A. S. Fuller,.............	"	" ....Sioux Falls, So. Dakota.
Joseph A. Light..........	"	H ....Norfolk, Neb.
Mrs. J. A. Light........	"	" ...." "
J. B. Fleniken	"	" ....Battle Creek, "
J. A. Van Anda..........	"	" ....Fremont, "
Mrs. J. A. Van Anda.....	"	" ...." "
Master Van Anda........	"	" ...." "
J. W. Ward.............	"	" ....Burlington, Iowa.
J. M. Crosby............	"	" ....Yankton, So. Dakota.
Master Roy Crosby......	"	" ...." "
Wm. H. Dupray.........	"	I ....Sioux City, Iowa.
Mrs. Wm. H. Dupray....	"	" ...." "
Master Wm. Dupray.....	"	" ...." "
E. C. Cobb	"	" ....Keokuk, "
John S. Ray.............	"	" ....Naponee, Neb.
Master J. S. Ray........	"	" ....
D. D. McCullum.........	"	" ....Sibley, Iowa.
Wm. Koehler............	"	" ....Dubuque, "
Mrs. Wm. Koehler.......	"	" ...." "
J. F. Butters.............	"	" ....Sioux City. "
Mrs. J. F. Butters........	"	" ...." "
Miss O. P. Butters.......	"	" ...." "
Miss Stella Butters......	"	" ...." "
O. B. Goodenow..........	"	" ....Ord, Neb.
W. R. Mathis............	"	K .....2536 Decatur St., Omaha.
E. R. Mathis.............	"	" ......1100 4th Av. Council Blfs.
Alonzo Robinson.........	"	" ....Cedar Rapids, Neb.
W. H. Ellison............	"	" ....St. Edwards, Neb.
Charles Rademacher.....	"	" ....Sioux City, Iowa.

*Arrived after adjournment.

JOHN N. WEAVER, President.
                    Sioux City, Iowa.
J. E. SIMPSON, Secretary,
                Norfolk, Nebraska.

The following verses were composed and written by the talented and beautiful young daughter of our Comrade J. N. Weaver, under the inspiration and spirit of the occasion. We know comrades will appreciate the sentiments so kindly and beautifully expressed by our fair young comrade:

THE GALLANT TWELFTH.

Ye comrades of the Gallant Twelfth,
    Who fought long years ago,
Your hair grows gray, and fails your health,
    Your steps are getting slow.

But brightly gleams your honest eye
  When telling o'er once more
The stirring tales of gallant deeds,
  From '61 to '4.

The worthiest people in the land,
  Are you, who bravely fought
To save the gallant stripes and stars,
  And a great success you wrought.

And furthermore, I here would say
  That your numbers, howe'er few.
Deserve the best that can be had,
  Three cheers for the boys in blue.
                  —Flora B. W.
May 20, 1892.

None of the comrades present will forget how pleased we all were on the evening of the second day to greet the smiling face of Gen. J. H. Stibbs, who, after a "forced march" of two days and nights at last got to us. His kindly words and his cheerful ways was as a gleam of sunshine amid the gloom, and his rendition of

"Decoration on the Place,"
"Old Man Jim,"
"Only Room in the Procession for but One Flag,"
"Down to Washington,"
"Barbara Fritche,"
"Snyder's Ride,"
"Marion Coming Home,"
"The Man with the Musket," and
"Two Opinions,"

will linger in the memories of those who heard him for many a long year.

Comrade J. W. Shumaker, Co. "E," reports as died since our last reunion: Comrades A. Myers, of Shell Rock, Iowa; J. E. Jones, Geneva, Iowa, and James Demoss. The dates of death and details he was unable to get.

Mrs. C. E. Phillips, of Blair, Neb., writes of the death of our comrade and her husband, late Co. "K." She says in his last sickness he often spoke of his old comrades of the 12th Iowa, in words of affection and kindness. He was with us at Waterloo and she speaks of how much he enjoyed the reunion there.

Since our last reunion "Taps" have sounded for our Comrade E. V. Andrus, Co. "G," Decorah, Iowa. He was a brave, loyal soldier, who did every duty well. Peace and rest has come to him at last. He lies with many of his comrades in the beautiful cemetery "on the hill" in full sight of the "Upper Iowa Valley" he loved so well.

TALCOTT, S. D., May 3, 1892.

D. W. Reed.

MY DEAR COMRADE:—As the time for the next reunion draws near, I take the liberty to send you the following, as it is possible you might not be aware of all the facts:

About the time of our reunion at Waterloo, Iowa, Sergt. Emery Clark, of Co. "C" 12th Iowa Infantry, died at the Black Hills, S. D.

You will doubtless remember that he was severely wounded, having both jaw bones broken at the battle of Tupelo, Miss., July 14, 1864. He was picked up on the field where he had fallen, unconscious, and kindly cared for by our hospital corps. On July 15 he was taken prisoner with the other wounded of that battle, remained at Tupelo for about a week when all were taken to Mobile, Ala., where they arrived about July 25. On the surrender of Forts Gaines and Morgan to Com. Farragut, all wounded prisoners were removed to Castle Morgan prison, at Cahaba, Ala. He was a prisoner at that place until Nov. 23, 1864, when he started for Charleston, S. C., to be exchanged—an agreement having been entered into for the exchange of 1,000 sick. On the day of his arrival at Macon, Ga., en-route for Charleston, Gen. Sherman, on his glorious "march to the sea," had cut the road to Charleston. Sergt. Clark was therefore imprisoned at Macon for a short time, when all the prisoners at that place were sent to Andersonville. He was confined at that notorious prison until the close of the war and was released at Jacksonville, Fla., April 29, 1865.

It is customary to lavish praise on those who, like the 12th at Shiloh the "Hornet's Nest," withstand the desperate attacks of the enemy and call their conduct heroic, and rightly too, but what shall we say of the conduct of Sergt. Clark who daily endured the pangs of a slow starvation while almost rotting with scurvey in Southern prison pens yet remained unfalteringly true to the old flag, not yielding to the temptation daily offered, nay, urged upon him, not even when it seemed that his life depended upon it. Such conduct marks a heroism in a man beside which the facing of the enemy in the field pales into insignificance.

Not many are called upon to suffer as much for their country as Comrade Clark suffered for his. Let us hope and trust that the God of battles will deal mercifully with him and with us all, and that when the last trumpet shall sound, he may, with all of the old 12th Iowa, be found on the "right side" as he was in the hour of our country's danger.

I give you these facts concerning Comrade Clark, as with a single exception—Comrade Kohler, of Co. "I"—I am the only one of the 12th Iowa who was with him all the time of his second imprisonment. You can make such use of them as you desire. I do not know the date nor place of his death, but am assured of the truth of the statement that he died about the time given. I am your old comrade,

J. W. COTES,
Late of Co. "I," 12th Iowa.

MARSHALLTOWN, IOWA, May 21, 1892.

J. E. Simpson, Norfolk, Nebraska.

DEAR COMRADE:—I was under the impression while at the reunion that one of the 12th boys had died at the home. Upon my arrival here this a. m. I looked the matter up and found that Able C. Gilmore, of Co. "H," 12th Iowa, died December 18th, 1891, and that his body was sent to Indianapolis, Ind., to his wife, Elizabeth Gilmore.

Yours truly, B. F. EBERHART.

The following sketch of our late comrade and president of our association, Col. S. R. Edgington, was prepared and written at the request of your committee by the Rev. C. F. McLean, of Eldora, Iowa, brother-in-law of our late comrade:

OBITUARY OF COL. S. R. EDGINGTON.

Col. Samuel R. Edgington was born near Mansfield, Richland county, Ohio, May 12, 1827, and died at Eldora, Iowa, May 20, 1888, having thus reached the 62nd year of his age. He was the son of Judge Jesse Edgington. His youth and early manhood were chiefly spent at the old Edgington farm homestead in Richland county, Ohio, where he was born and where his grandfather had settled many years before, having purchased the land of the United States government. The military instinct early showed itself in his enlistment for the Mexican war when he was eighteen years old. He was away from home attending college at the time and volunteered with others, joining the Ninth Ohio Infantry, under Col. S. R. Curtis. After doing good service in the Mexican war he returned with his regiment to Ohio and was honorably discharged.

May 8th, 1849, he was married to Miss Lois Beal, in Richland county, Ohio.

In the fall of 1852 he came with his wife to Iowa and in the following spring settled in Hardin county, same state, and were among the first families that located at Eldora, the county seat. Here the family have since resided and here the three sons of the Colonel were born and grew to manhood's estate.

Shortly after he came to Eldora, Col. Edgington engaged in the mercantile business and continued in the same until 1861. That year he responded a second time to his country's call and enlisted for three years or during the war of the Rebellion. He soon raised the first company of soldiers for the 12th Iowa Volunteer Infantry and was immediately, and by unanimous vote, elected captain of the same. Company "A" was composed mostly of Hardin county young men and as brave and splendid a lot of soldiers as ever marched to the field of strife.

The regiment camped a while at Dubuque and then at St. Louis. Then came the advance southward. Then came Fort Henry, Donalson and Shiloh, the two last among the greatest and bloodiest battles of all history. There were terrible experiences for fresh recruits, but our men of the 12th Iowa made a glorious record for themselves on those fields. Said Col. Edgington in his speech at the reunion at Des Moines, Oct. 1887, referring to the famous Iowa "Hornet's Nest Brigade" and its conduct at Shiloh, April 6, 1862: "These veterans are not unknown. Their deeds of heroism at the battle of Shiloh are the admiration of every city of our own state and nation. For ten long hours they held their battle line and saved the day until night and Buell came. History has not done full justice to these brave men. Three of these regiments, the 8th, 12th and 14th, were captured by the rebel army that day just as the sun was hiding behind the western horizon, April 6th, 1862. They endured their captivity and suffering like grand heroes for seven long months, without a murmer, in the prison hells of the South. But the grandest heroes of that bloody day at Shiloh and the "hornet's nest" and "hell's hollow" were those who died fighting when surrounded by such fearful odds." One point made by Col. Edgington in the above extract was this, that while his brigade sustained the first terrible onslaught of the rebel host in the early morning of that eventful day they held their own all day and were not captured until nightfall, whereas the impression has been given that they were captured and hurried off the field before noon. Some time during the struggle at Shiloh, Col. Wood, of the 12th, was stricken down and Col. Edgington assumed command and fought bravely with his men until obliged to surrender to superior numbers.

He and his two younger brothers, all of the same company, passed weary months of prison life in the South and the youngest of the three was brought home to die.

Some time after the exchange of prisoners the 12th Iowa was reorganized at Davenport and proceeding to St. Louis was there re-joined by S. R. Edgington, now regular commissioned Major and afterwards Lieutenant-Colonel. The regiment was soon ordered to Vicksburg and participated in the whole of that memorable siege. At Brandon, at Raymond and twice at Jackson, Miss., they took an active part with their commander and made this series of battles so successful in determining the fate of the rebellion. A comrade relates this incident in the Dubuque Times: "The day that the 12th Iowa arrived at Jackson, Miss., on their way to Vicksburg, they were ordered to lie down some distance outside of the confederate works. They did not have a Brussels carpet to recline upon but instead a very damp piece of ground. It had been raining three days before the regiment reached Jackson and Col. Edgington, who knew that the boys were tired and would as lief charge as not, rode out in front of the regiment with the brave Gen'l Mower and in about ten minutes came back saying "Boys we can take those works and not half try." Then old Gen'l Mathias gave the order to charge and the yell that those wet Northern boys gave was enough to scare even the ghosts of the Southern confederacy. We took those works—it was no trouble—and after a day or two we went on to Vicksburg."

The Col. was a man of few words and seldom if ever was heard to refer to his own achievements in the war, but enough is known to justify the remark that he never flinched from duty as a soldier and never required his men to face any danger where he did not lead the way himself. In all probability not a few bold exploits and dangerous skirmishes in which he engaged have never been recorded save in the memory of his war associates.

In 1863 he was honorably discharged and returned to his home in

Eldora, Iowa, thereafter to cultivate the arts of peace and to build up the interests of society. He never forgot his old comrades but always delighted to mingle with them in their reunions and recount the stirring incidents of the war. He was high authority on military law and jurisprudence. He had thoroughly studied this difficult subject, especially in its application to army discipline. A well informed army man who was with him much of the time during the service and has since become a prominent and successful lawyer, says that Col. Edgington was the best posted man in such matters that he knew of in the volunteer army. He was frequently consulted on this subject and became a sort of encyclopedia of military law. The Colonel was not in sound health much of his time after his discharge from the service. Doubtless the exposure of the camp and the field predisposed his system to a complication of disorders that culminated in diabetes and ended his life. But he never complained of his affliction and always spoke cheerfully to those enquiring after his health. He refused to take to his bed almost to the last and not until he was unable to help himself. His record is made up and his history is with us. He has left to the world the example of a brave and honorable man whose memory all would do well to cherish.

Mr. President and Comrades:

To me has been assigned the painful duty of announcing in this formal and public manner the death, since our last reunion, of our Colonel Joseph Jackson Woods, at his home at Montana, Kansas, September 27th, 1889. As soon as I received word that I was expected to perform this duty, I at once wrote the family of Col. Woods and received in reply the following letter from his daughter Miss Carrie Woods, that I now read to you.

Parsons, Kas., Feb. 24, 1892.

Lieut. J. E. Simpson, Norfolk Nebraska.

Dear Sir: Your letter of the 8th inst. asking for data in regard to the events of my beloved father's life, etc. was (after some delay) received.

I send you a manuscript sketch of the important events of his life, which we found among his papers after his death. The manuscript was written by some one, we know not whom, and was sent to my father for correction. It was to be published in a history of his regiment, or of Iowa Colonels or some such book. All we know about it is that my father told my mother that he had received the sketch but had not yet felt able to correct it. Perhaps you can find out at the reunion who wrote it. If you can, please deliver it to him and notify us. I have made a copy of it. Father had corrected a part, if not all of it, which will be seen by the pencil markings and certain interlinings which I recognize as his writing.

After his service in the Kansas Legislature my father devoted his time to farming and stock raising, and took no part in active public life with the exception of making political and temperance speeches occasionally. He was also a notary public and a member of the school board for a great number of years.

In 1888, the Union Labor politicians lauding their doctrines, so destructive to the principles of government, throughout the state, so aroused my father's indignation that he spent much time and energy in making speeches for the cause of Republicanism, and, we fear, shortened his life thereby.

Below is an extract copied from a newspaper which refers to his presence at a congressional convention held at Fredonia, Wilson county, in 1888:

"The first delegate on the ground was Col. J. J. Woods, of Montana. He got in Tuesday at noon, ahead of everybody.

Col. Woods was a West Point graduate and a Lieutenant in the "old army." At Shiloh he commanded an Iowa regiment, was badly wounded, and was among those captured with the division of General Prentiss. Though old in years and quite feeble, he made one of the most earnest, patriotic and eloquent speeches delivered in the convention."

Many times he spoke endearingly of the "Boys" of the 12th and particularly when the time came around for the annual reunion of the regiment. He prized his cane very highly.

When appeals for aid in securing pensions came to him he always did what he could to assist, but many times expressed regret that he could not remember the facts desired.

Though not united with any church, his religious belief was Unitarian, and he read many Unitarian works during the latter years of his life.

During the last five years of his life he was in feeble health. He was a constant sufferer from chronic diarrhœa, which he contracted during the service. He retained his mental vigor to the last.

In the summer before his death he bought a home in Parsons, twelve miles from Montana, and was preparing to move to it to enjoy the sunset of life in rest from labor.

He returned one evening from a drive to Parsons very sick and suffered intensely for three days. He had hemorrhage of the bladder and suppression of the kidneys, and afterwards blood poisoning set in. Through all of his sickness he was patient and cheerful, and at times even humorous. He hoped to live but was ready for death if it must come. For several days before his death he was almost constantly delirious, and fought again the battles of the war.

He died, apparently without pain, after an illness of ten days, on the morning of the 27th day of September, 1889. He was buried in the beautiful cemetery of Oakwood at Parsons, Kansas, a part of which is set apart and nicely arranged for the graves of the soldiers.

The Grand Army of the Republic, of which he had been a member, performed the burial service.

I can think of nothing more of particular interest, though it would take many pages to recount his many good and noble deeds; and the loss to his family and friends occasioned by his death, words cannot express.

I send best wishes to the surviving comrades.

Yours respectfully, CARRIE WOODS.

Thus I found my work already done and by an abler pen than mine, and reviewed by the Colonel himself before his death. I am sure this personal history of our beloved Colonel, written with so much care by the historian of our regiment, Major D. W. Reed, when made a part of the proceedings of this session, will be read and treasured by you around your firesides and in your homes, and will be a lesson, well to teach your children and their children, of a noble, true, good man, who, from early youth, without the advantages of birth or fortune, won the love and esteem of all with whom he came in contact with, and did every duty, in all the positions in which he was placed, well and faithfully. A tower of strength to those with whom he came in contact, with a stern, rigid integrity, a love of principle and right, he never faltered nor hesitated for a moment to do and to say what he deemed to be the right. Modest, diffident almost to a fault, never pushing himself forward or making any claims for himself, but performing every duty given to him with ability, no wonder he soon won the love and esteem of those who knew him. Every man and officer of the regiment, as they came to know him, learned to love and respect him. Those of us who were present at our first reunion at Manchester twelve years ago, remember with pleasure his visit to us then, and our pleasure to find, when he commenced to talk to us, he was an eloquent speaker, his burning words are still ringing in our ears, when accepting our gift of a gold headed cane, he spoke of leaning on it in his declining years, and turning to our battle torn flags to our right, he said: "If rebel hands are again raised against that dear old flag, I will come back from my far distant Kansas home and standing on the prairies of Delaware county, I will raise my voice as never before, and give the command, "Fall in 12th Iowa," and every one of the survivors will respond to my cry in defense of the Union and our dear old flag."

Our beloved commander is resting, his work is done, he has but gone before. We must quickly follow. "Taps" will soon sound for us all, and we answer to the "roll call" for the last time.

And now my dear comrades I commend you to the history of this truly good man who was our Colonel. Of him in his lifetime could have been truly said:

"His words are bonds, his oaths are oracles,
"His love sincere, his thoughts immaculate,
"His tears pure messengers sent from his heart,
"His heart as far from fraud as Heaven from earth.

J. E. SIMPSON.

OBITUARY OF COL. JOS. JACKSON WOODS.

Colonel Joseph Jackson Woods was born on the 11th day of January, 1823, on a farm in Brown county, Ohio. His ancestors came from Ireland but were not of the Irish race. Some of them were in Londonderry during the famous siege of that place in 1689.

His grandfather, James Woods, came to America in the year 1773, and settled in Pennsylvania where the father of the subject of this sketch, Samuel Woods, was born in that same year, 1773. James Woods was engaged during a part of the Revolution in furnishing supplies to the army. The mother of Joseph Jackson Woods was born in

Ireland in 1785, and came to America at the age of six or seven years. Her maiden name was Ritchey. Joseph was the youngest son that arrived at mature age of a numerous family, his father being at the time of his birth fifty years old, and having been in his prime a man of more than average ability among the farming class to which he belonged, but while Joseph was yet young his father became a physical, financial and mental wreck, so that at the age of ten years Joseph was thrown upon the world to succeed by his own resources, and went with an older brother, John, just then married, to Rush county, Indiana, where they settled in the dense forest.

He remained in Indiana two years and then returned to Ohio and lived with his relatives until he was fourteen years old, when he was apprenticed to Joseph Parish (late private secretary to President Grant to sign land patents) in Felicity, Clermont county, Ohio, to learn the saddler's trade.

In his early boyhood while at school, which was but a small part of the time, he learned rapidly, being in advance of other children of his age. He never attended the public schools after his thirteenth year.

He served five years apprenticeship with Mr. Parish, working for his board and clothing, and became very proficient in the trade, working in the winter season until 9 o'clock p. m. five nights of the week, he had but little time for mental culture, but fortunately his cousin, Dr. Allen Woods, about this time married a Miss Whipple, of Vermont, a lady of fine culture, who, becoming interested in young Woods, proposed to become his private tutor. Under this arrangement, by improving every spare moment, he completed a course of arithmetic, English grammar, geography and obtained a fair knowledge of history from books kindly loaned from the library of Dr. J. M. Woods.

At expiration of his apprenticeship the Rev. Mr. Ervine, Presbyterian minister and graduate of Ohio State University, informed young Woods that as he was about to review his Latin and Greek studies, he would willingly take a pupil and give instructions in these branches free of charge as a more thorough method of making his review. Under this arrangement young Woods pursued his studies seven months, working mornings and evenings in the saddlery shop to pay his board. The first Methodist college established in America was located at Augusta, Ky., seven miles from Felicita, Ohio. It was under the joint patronage of the Ohio and Kentucky conferences of the M. E. church, each conference entitled to keep at the college a certain number of students free of tuition, these to be selected by the presiding elders of the various districts from worthy young men of limited means. The Rev. W. H. Roper, presiding elder of the district, gave young Woods the appointment, and he entered the freshman class in that institution the same year. Although free tuition was provided he found it difficult to provide for board, clothing and books. Therefore, by advice of Dr. Woods, he applied for an appointment to

U. S. Military Academy at West Point to take the place of U. S. Grant who would graduate the following June.

His principal recommendations were from Hon. Alonzo Knowles, the leading Democratic politician at Felicita, Ohio, and Jesse R. Grant, Whig, then of Bethel, Ohio. There were several competitors for the appointment and Dr. Danns, member of Congress, declining to make a selection, sent the papers to the war department, where the appointment was given to Woods and he entered the academy in June, 1843. Seventy-five were appointed to this class; thirty-eight graduated in 1847. Woods standing No. 3 in his class. During the last year at West Point he was assistant professor as well as student. July 1st, 1847, he received his appointment as 2d Lieutenant in first regiment U. S. Artillery. The war with Mexico was at its height and he was ordered to New York harbor to drill and organize recruits for the war, where he remained until October 10th, when out of these recruits Companies L and M, 1st Artillery were organized and Lieutenant Woods was ordered to proceed with said company to Vera Cruz, Mexico, and there join his Company C, to which he had been assigned, in Northern Mexico.

The command sailed from New York, October 10th, on the ship "Empire." The weather was boisterous and after four days of invisible sun the ship ran upon a coral reef entirely covered by water, breaking a large hole in the vessel, when she settled down and broke in two. They were, by captain's reckoning fifty miles from shore, but upon its partially clearing off they perceived a small uninhabited island called Fowl Key about one-half a mile distant, and daylight brought to view Abaco, the largest of the Bahama group, at a distance of about five miles. Wreckers came to the assistance of the ship, and about 10 o'clock a. m. they landed the soldiers on Fowl Key, where they remained one week. Vessels were then procured to take a part of the command to Charleston, South Carolina; the balance with Lieutenant Woods was taken to Nassau, New Providence, since famous as the rendezvous for rebel cruisers. Remaining here eight days he then, in company with Lieut. Morris, sailed for Charleston, where they remained at Fort Moultrie until December 25th, 1847, when they again sailed for Vera Cruz in the ship "Republic," sent out from New York for that purpose.

On 1st of January, 1848, as they were entering port of Vera Cruz, a terrible norther struck the vessel, carrying them out to sea. They finally landed January 5th, and found that a majority of the regiment to which the command was assigned was on garrison duty in the city, but Co. C, to which Lieut. Woods had been assigned, was in Northern Mexico. Woods was therefore transferred to Co. M and assigned to duty with the regiment at Vera Cruz. In the month of May he had the yellow fever and was very sick. About August 1st, 1848, peace having been declared Vera Cruz was evacuated and our troops immediately imbarked for New York. Companies L and M took passage upon the screw-propeller "Massachusetts."

In October, 1848, Woods was promoted to 1st Lieutenant, and November 10th, 1848, embarked on board "Massachusetts" with companies L and M for Oregon to quell disturbances recently arisen there in which Dr. Whitman and a number of other Missourians had been murdered. The expedition was under the command of Brevet Major Hatheway and Lieut. Woods was his quarter master and commissary. These were the first U. S. troops ever in Oregon. On the passage about January 1st the ship put into port at Rio Janeiro, Brazil, and remained several days, giving the officers an opportunity of seeing the city. Imperial gardens, where all tropical fruits were growing, the ferneries, and other places of interest. Lieut. Woods was taken through the convent of the monks of St. Bernardine and was present at imperial chapel when the Emperor and Empress partook of midnight mass, the going out of the year of 1848.

Sailing from Rio Janeiro, they passed near Falkland Island and entered the Strait of Magellen with Patagonia on the right and Terre del Fuego on the left and were one week on the strait, sailing only by daylight and such distances as would insure good harbors by night. There were two convict settlements on the strait and some Indians. The officers enjoyed frequent rambles on the shore. At Valparaiso, Chili, they were shown specimens of gold recently taken from newly discovered gold mines of California. The next point made was Sandwich Islands, where they arrived in fifty-two days and remained eight days. They were constantly feted by the king as theirs was the first steamer ever seen by him. The officers gave the queen and king an excursion on board the steamer, accompanied by the royal retinue. The expedition reached the mouth of the Columbia river, May 9th, 1849, six months out of New York and having sailed 22,000 miles. They proceeded up the river ninety miles to Fort Vancouver, then headquarters of the Hudson Bay company, situated on the north bank of the Columbia river in what is now the state of Washington. Here Co. L. to which Woods now belonged, landed, and Co. M were ordered to Puget Sound.

In spring of 1850 Lieut. Woods with Co. L was removed to Astoria, near the north of the river, and from this point Lieut. Woods, with two white men and two Indians, attempted to find a practicable wagon road from Astoria to the plains across the coast range of mountains. They found the task more difficult than was anticipated, and the party came near starving to death, living for some time on such provisions as they could find in the woods upon the mountains.

At another time Lieut. Woods went in a row boat with the collector of the port of Astoria and a detail of men in the evening, to sieze a ship for violating the revenue laws. They ran along side the ship as she lay at anchor near the mouth of the river. The collector tried to climb the ladders hanging over the side, but failed, when Lieut.

Woods and one man-mounted the ladders and reached the deck when ropes were cut by ships crew. The ladders fell into the collectors boat and he pulled for shore, leaving the Lieutenant on board, but calling back to him that he would come for him in the morning. The ship hoisted anchor and immediately put to sea. The collector procured a pilot boat, armed with a canon, and gave chase, but after a few hours pursuit and firing a few shots the pilot boat gave up the chase. After a tedious run the ship put into a recently discovered bay in the northern part of California called Humbolt Bay, where several vessels were loading with timber for San Francisco. On one of these the Lieut. procured passage to San Francisco, and from there secured passage to Astoria, where he arrived after an involuntary absence of six weeks.

In April, 1851, Lieut. Woods was ordered with a detachment of men to the Dalles of the Columbia, east of Cascade range, where, in the heart of the Indian country, he commanded a small post for eighteen months, the only military post at the time and he the only commissioned officer between the Cascade mountains and Fort Laramie.

In September, 1852, he returned to Fort Vancouver, which had now become a large post and headquarters of the 4th U. S. Infantry, and at which place was then stationed several men since famous in history, among them U. S. Grant.

In February, 1853, Lieut. Woods received orders to report to the superintendent of recruiting service in New York City. He sailed on the 10th of February and reached his destination via San Francisco and Panama.

In June, 1853, he received leave of absence and visited Iowa and bought land in Clinton and Jackson counties. On October 15th, 1853, he resigned his commission in the army and removed to his lands in Iowa.

In September he married Miss Kezia Hight in Jones county, Iowa. He resided on a farm in Jackson county, Iowa, until the rebellion broke out, when he tendered his services to the governor of Iowa and was commissioned Colonel of the 12th Iowa Infantry, October 23d, 1861.

From the organization of the regiment to the siege of Vicksburg, the history of the 12th Iowa is Col. Wood's history; during that time he was never absent from his command while they were in the field as an organization, except for a short time when he commanded the brigade to which the 12th belonged. He was always the same quiet self-possessed commanding officer, yet possessing so little of "show" usual in officers of the regular army, but he attracted attention only by true merit.

He was with the regiment in its first move from Dubuque to St. Louis, always present and carefully watching the interests of his men, seeing them thoughtfully provided for during the epidemic of measles and pneumonia at St. Louis. His persistent effort secured their equipment with the best arms then known in the service, the Enfield rifle. He was with them in their first camp at Smithfield and rode calmly at their head during the effort to reach the rear of Fort Henry in time to capture the fleeing enemy. He shared the same hardships as his men, at Donaldson lying in the snow and sleet without blanket or fire, and charged bravely at their head when the final assault was made and received from Col. Cook, commander of the brigade, especial mention for his efficient and gallant services.

At Shiloh he carefully formed his regiment along the old road, and behind the old fence, and having, as he says, received personal instruction from General Grant to "Hold that position at all hazards," he held it until the enemy had driven back the troops of Sherman on the right and Hurlburt on the left, thus leaving the 12th Iowa entirely surrounded. Yet undismayed and perfectly cool, we heard his command as if on parade, "12th Iowa, about face! Commence firing!" and turning found a line of the enemy drawn up in our rear but they were soon broken by our fire, then his command, "By the left flank, double quick, march!" and the first line of the enemy was passed, only to encounter the second. At this point Col. Woods received two wounds in quick succession, one in the leg, the other in the wrist, so being dismounted he fell into the enemy's hands and was assaulted by some Texas troops with the design of taking his life, but being at that moment recognized by Gen. Hardee with whom he had been acquainted at West Point and in the regular army, he was given a special guard, and his orderly permitted to remain with him. The Col. spent the night on the ground where he fell, exposed to the fire of our gun boats and the drizzling rain. Gen. Prentiss, present at the time of the surrender and taken prisoner with the rest, speaks in highest terms of the conduct of Col. Woods, and says: "To the persistent fighting of these four regiments, 8th, 12th and 14th Iowa, and 58th Illinois, holding the ground against such fearful odds is due the failure of Beauregard to drive our forces into the river." Gen. Tuttle, in his official report says: "Col. Woods, of the 12th Iowa, particularly distinguished himself; he was twice wounded and captured and when the enemy was driven back on Monday he was re-captured."

When our forces advanced on Monday morning Col. Woods was recaptured and his wounds dressed.

He was soon after sent North and was immediately detailed on recruiting service, remaining on such duty until his regiment was exchanged, January, 1863, when he immediately took the field again and was soon ordered with his regiment to join Gen. Grant in the field in front of Vicksburg.

Reporting with his regiment at Duckport, La., April 14th, 1863, he was assigned to the command of the 3rd Brigade, 3rd Division of the 15th Army Corps. His Brigade consisted of the 8th, 12th and 35th Iowa Regiments.

About May 5th he was relieved of the command of the Brigade by

Col. Mathias, of the 5th Iowa, and returned to the command of his regiment, which he retained during the campaign in the rear of Vicksburg including the battle of Jackson.

On June 1st he again assumed command of the Brigade, and retained the command of the Brigade or Division during the remainder of the time of service; his service as commander of the 12th Iowa ceasing June 1st, 1863.

While in command of the 3rd Brigade, 3rd Division, 15th Army Corps, he served in the siege of Vicksburg, his Brigade, after June 22nd, being stationed along Black river, where very heavy guard and patrol duty was kept until July 4th, when he crossed Black river, and on the 10th formed his Brigade on the left of the main road, and within range of Jackson, Miss.

On the 15th of July Gen. Tuttle reported sick, and Col. Woods was assigned to the command of the 3d Division of the 15th Army Corps. On the 16th he moved his Division to the right and relieved Gen. Osterhaus from a position on the front. On the 17th the rebels evacuated Jackson and a few days after the Division returned to Black river, when it went into camp July 25th, Col. Woods remaining in command of the division until relieved by Gen. Asboth some time in October, 1863.

Col. Woods returned to the command of the 3rd Brigade, and November 7th, 1863, was ordered to Memphis, Tenn., and his Brigade assigned to posts along the railroad from La Grange to Corinth, where they had frequent skirmishes with the enemy.

January 29th, 1864, he was ordered with his Brigade to Black river, Miss., where they were on duty during Sherman's Meridian Expedition.

May 2nd the 3rd Division having been transferred and been designated as the 1st Division of the 16th Corps, was re-organized, the 3rd Brigade composed of the 12th and 35th Iowa, 7th Minnesota, and 23rd Missouri, commanded by Col. Woods; 1st Division, commanded by Gen. Mower, left wing of 16th Army Corps commanded by Gen. A. J. Smith.

During the summer they made two expeditions from Memphis to the interior and on July 13th, 14th and 15th, 1864, fought the battle of Tupelo, Col. Woods brigade doing most of the fighting and receiving great credit for efficient services.

Col. Woods commanded his Brigade through Arkansas and Missouri in what was known as the Price Raid. At St. Louis, Missouri, Gen. Mower was transferred to Sherman's army at Atlanta, and Col. Woods was assigned to command of Division about October 13th, 1864, and commanded the Division from Jefferson City, during the march to Kansas City and Harrisonville and returning to Sedalia when Gen. McArthur assumed command and Col. Woods returned to command of Brigade.

He commanded the Brigade again during that march through the storms of snow and rain, fording rivers floating with ice, returning to St. Louis, where he arrived Nov. 15th, his Brigade had marched within thirty days 543 miles and within sixty days, 879 miles, and since June 16th, 1409 miles.

At St. Louis Col. Woods was mustered out of service, having served more than the whole term of enlistment, and having filled with credit many important positions, always with acceptability and with honor. He richly deserves, for his services, the recognition which has often been accredited to less merit and more persistent effort for self.

His muster out was deeply regretted by all his old comrades and especially by the men whom he had so often led and who had learned to appreciate the unassuming and quiet, but brave and generous Col. Woods. In the book entitled, "Iowa Colonels," has the following: "Col. Woods has a slender stooping form, brown hair, a light complexion and mild blue eyes. He is in appearance and in fact the most unassuming of Iowa Colonels. He speaks slowly and kindly, and was accustomed to give commands with great coolness and deliberation and was never known, even under the hottest fire, to vary in the least the deliberation or the modulation of his orders. He had none of the style or austere manners of the regular army officer, and while very familiar and easy of approach by his subordinates, yet he was a good disciplinarian, and the men soon learned that he possessed great worth as a commanding officer: and while the bravest and willing to lead his regiment to the severest contest yet he was devoid of all rashness that would sacrifice his men without good reason. His services merited recognition at Washington which he never received; but with him, modesty blocked the wheels of ambition. I doubt not that it would be impossible to find any of his superior officers who will say that Col. Woods ever sought promotion or recognition at their hands in any way but by a faithful and earnest discharge of his duties on whatever command he was placed."

After his muster out he removed from the farm, where he had lived when he enlisted, to Maquoketa, where he, in company with W. F. McCarrow, purchased the "Maquoketa Excelsior," and Woods became the editor of that paper and McCarrow the local editor.

In the fall of 1867 Woods sold his interest and moved upon his farm in Clinton county, Iowa, but in 1868 he returned to Maquoketa and McCarrow having failed to make his payments on the paper and Woods, having to pay the loss, he took the whole paper and published it until May, 1869, when he removed to Montana, Kansas. He bought a farm adjoining the town and entered, with all his usual thoroughness, into the business of farming and stock raising.

In 1871 he was on the Board of Visitors at West Point, appointed by U. S. Grant.

In the fall of 1871 he was one of the three Commissioners, appointed by the Secretary of the Interior, to appraise the Cherokee neutral lands in the Indian Territory, west of the 96th meridian.

He was appointed by the president as Receiver of the Humbolt Land District, but declined the appointment. The same fall he was elected to the Kansas Legislature which convened in January, 1872. In March, 1872, he was appointed by the Governor one of the Regents of the State University.

He was a member of the Legislature in 1875, and chairman of the committee on Ways and Means.

He was an earnest Republican in politics and, although known to his comrades as a man of few words, he became quite a prominent political speaker, and took a very prominent part in the campaigns of the state, including that of 1888.

During his service he had contracted chronic diarrhœa, from which he never recovered, and from which he suffered severely, and continually grew worse until September 27th, 1889, when he died at his home in Montana, Kansas, of hemorrhage of the bladder and blood poisoning. He was buried in Oakwood cemetery, in Parsons, Kansas, the Grand Army of the Republic conducting the services at his burial.

His wife and five children survive him.

The following letters were received at different times and by different persons and will, without doubt, be read with pleasure by you all, breathing as they do the spirit of love and kindly feeling that exists so strongly between old comrades:

CHICAGO, May 25th, 1892.

My Dear Simpson:

Yours informing me that fifty of the comrades of the regiment succeeded in reaching Sioux City, is received. I am glad to know that even that number were present, and that you had such an enjoyable time together.

The reports from so many others who were on the road, and the complete arrangement for our reception by the good people of Sioux City assures us that, but for the floods, the fourth reunion would have been a grand success.

I regret the disappointment which so many of the boys have experienced, and realize very keenly how severe these disappointments have been to them because I felt them myself and all the more keenly, perhaps, because it had been my good fortune to be with the boys in all their marches and engagements from 1861 to 1866, and at all former reunions. If my telegrams were received you know of my various delays by wrecks and washouts and that I finally reached Manilla Junction, only to find further progress utterly impossible.

You know so well the great pleasure I had anticipated in meeting the comrades again that you can in some measure appreciate the feeling with which I was compelled to turn back, knowing that the long looked for pleasure of this reunion must be indefinitely postponed.

I heartily approve of your suggestion to publish proceedings and hand you herewith the letters of regret received by me. I will, however, be impossible for me to furnish "a synopsis of what I would have said to the boys." If I could have looked into their well-known faces and grasped their strong right hands, in that hearty fraternal greeting known nowhere outside the comradeship of the army, the inspiration might have given me fitting words of greeting which cannot be produced under the depressing influences of the failure to meet them. You may tell the boys, however, that nothing less than the total destruction of all the railroad bridges in the country will prevent my presence with them at our next reunion where I hope to meet every one of those who tried to get there in 1892, as well as all other members of the regiment.

The only report I could have made of "deaths in Co. C since last reunion" would have been to mention *reported* death of Sergt. Emery Clark and to have stated that the only information I have concerning said death is contained in a letter to me from Sergt. Coates of Co. "I" who was very severely wounded and, like Sergt. Clark, left on the field at Tupelo. His letter contains such a beautiful and touching tribute to Comrade Clark that I submit it as my report, endorsing its sentiment most heartily, regretting that I am unable, after earnest effort by letters to members of his family and others, to give a more complete report of the facts concerning the death of this worthy soldier who was left for dead on the field of Tupelo, but survived his wounds and a long imprisonment at Andersonville, to die under the folds of the flag he so loyally defended and within a quiet home provided for the care of worthy soldiers.

As a report on "Regimental History" I respectfully refer to report published in proceedings of 3rd reunion on pages 12 and 13. The whole matter is exactly as then reported except that companies "G" and "H" have furnished very complete and acceptable histories of those companies. I earnestly desire that the other companies who have not completed their histories, upon the plan suggested in said report, should do so at once.

With the exception of these Company Histories from a few companies, and some personal sketches which were desired, the material for the history is all arranged, and it only remains for the association to say what shall be done with it. I have the matter in shape so that it could have been submitted and a chapter or two read if desired in order that the members might be able to judge of the accuracy of the detail, and be the better able to determine what they desired to do.

The whole matter will of necessity lay over until next reunion. In the meantime I shall be glad to receive the other contributions promised for the work, all of which will be put away in a safe place, where it may be had when the association desires to use it, or for reference by future generations, should any of our children desire to know what the Twelfth Iowa did actually do towards suppressing the rebellion. Very truly and fraternally yours,

D. W. REED.

HOUSE OF REPRESENTATIVES U. S.,
WASHINGTON, May 8, 1892.

Col. James E. Simpson, Norfolk, Nebraska.

MY DEAR COMRADE: Your kind letter of the 13th of March, asking me if I could not be at our reunion on the 18th and 19th to write something for the old comrades of the 12th, was received. I have been too busy to give this request earlier attention. In letters to Comrades Barr and Reed I have said some things which they may feel like reading to the boys.

What can I say to them through you? Don't they all know how I feel, and how intensely sorry I am that I can not be with them? To go to Sioux City and return would consume more than a week, and we are right in the midst of the preparation of our appropriation bills, a work that I can not desert, for, as you know, I am the senior of the minority, therefore a duty rests with me that I cannot shirk. I sometimes feel as though I would break and run, anyhow, to get out there with you.

Four years ago I was kept away from the same cause, and I am getting heart-hungry to see the old faces. Do you know, Mr. Simpson, that the older we grow the more we are to each other. The rising generation can only catch a faint impression of the great period of '61-'5; they do not, they can not, however good of heart and keen of principles, realize and appreciate what the 12th Iowa and their comrades of the Grand Army of the Republic went through. This we must have patience with. Sometimes things are said and done towards the old soldier that "hurt me to the quick," and stir up anger that I would wish to have sleep; things more than cruel are said and done, but I thank my God that all this comes from but a very few. The great body of the American people, old and young, appreciate the mighty deeds of the soldiers of the Union, sympathize with them, and are ready by every kindness to do them justice. The statute books of our country attest the appreciation and generosity of the Nation. Let us not be unmindful of these things. Sometimes, perhaps, we ask too much, and exhibit too much our self-appreciation of what we did. The little button on the lapels of our coats is a modest thing, but it tells of a mighty history; let us imitate its modesty. We will thus impress ourselves and our deeds upon the memories of the people.

Tell the boys from me that their country is not unmindful of their acrifices and their sufferings, and that the great act of June 27, 1890, which carried so many blessings into so many homes will not be the last one, but that as our needs increase and our weaknesses develop, the country, ever on the alert, will enlarge its heart for the good of us all, and those in whom we are interested more than in ourselves.

I wish that I could be with you all for the handshake, the laugh, the story and the tearful eye. There is no music to me sweeter than the broken voice of affection as comrade meets comrade. I can look down yet upon the 12th Iowa, into their dear faces as I spoke to them last, and see the eyes all moist with affectionate recollections, eyes that scarcely flinched when death was marshaling in front of them. I wish I could see them again. I hope to—most of you, although death's cruel sickel is moving with horrid rapidity among our ranks, and reducing the numbers that attend our reunions.

In conclusion, comrade, let me wish for you all a joyous time at the reunion. Throw care to the winds, and give yourselves up to a happy period. You all deserve it. To each and all, with their relatives, their wives and children, I send the affectionate greetings of a sincere friend and comrade. Very kindly yours,
D. B. HENDERSON.

LOS ANGELES, CAL., April 21, 1892.

Major J. E. Simpson, Secretary of Executive Committee 12th Regiment Iowa Veteran Volunteers, Norfolk, Nebraska.

DEAR SIR: Received yours of March 13th, with your kind invitation to attend reunion of the glorious old 12th Iowa. I would so gladly be with you, my dear comrades, but it is impossible this time and I must therefore content myself in living over in memory the meeting at Manchester in 1884, which I so much enjoyed with you. Hoping that yet many of the old boys may answer roll call on May 18, 1892, and that you may have a good and happy reunion, I remain with kind greetings and good wishes to you dear ones all,

Affectionately, your old Major,
S. D. BRODTBECK.

LANSING, ALLAMAKEE CO., IOWA, May 17, 1892.

Dear Friend and Comrade Simpson:

It is now more than thirty years since you and I met every morning at orderly's call, and yet how vivid seem the memories of those times. How much pleasure it would give me to meet you and our old comrades once more. I defered writing to you until the last moment, thinking I might be able to come, but circumstances beyond my control have denied me that pleasure. Not even the tempting offer of certificate of disability from Surgeons Finley and Underwood have dispensed the mundane difficulties in the way.

I received the returned letters of Co. "B" but have been unable to relocate them. Comrade Isted left Milwaukee some time ago and went to Portage, Wis., and I have been informed that since he has moved west. Comrade Sanrice I hear is at Roseville, in this county. Comrades J. H. Huestis and Chas. Ogan have joined the great majority. Comrade John Dowling informed me that he had intended coming, but the loss of his home by fire prevented. Of the ninety-seven men who left Lansing in 1861, but Knud Iverson and myself are still left in the city.

And now dear comrade although the fates prevent my bodily presence, I shall be with you in spirit, and with my best wishes for the happiness of yourself and the dear comrades of the old 12th, I am

Yours in fraternity, charity and loyalty,
JOHN D. COLE.

OMAHA, May 17, 1892.

To Maj. D. W. Reed, President, or J. E. Simpson, Secretary, 12th Iowa Reunion:

COMRADES: Mrs. Hobbs and I are here enroute for Sioux City. The railroad agent here discourages our going on, as the floods are endangering the possibility of ever getting through. You all know the disappointment this brings us, the long waited for reunion. If this is in any way general I trust you will arrange for a reunion in the near future. I have prepared a paper on Hospital Department, bringing it with me, but now am unable to get it to you. Will have it before you on next occasion of our coming together, which, may God grant. Be assured, dear brothers, of my endearing love for all that ever marched and fought as 12th Iowans, and every dear boy that enrolled at Camp Union. Yours affectionately,

J. C. H. HOBBS,
MRS. C. E. HOBBS.
1441 G Street, Lincoln, Nebraska.

LINCOLN, NEB., May 16, 1892.

Gen'l J. H. Stibbs, Sioux City, Iowa:

MY DEAR GEN'L: Nothing would please me better than to meet you and the boys of the gallant 12th Iowa, but my office duties this week are such it is out of the question to leave. God bless you all.

Very truly, H. C. MCARTHUR.

THOTEN, IOWA, May 17, 1892.

J. E. Simpson, Acting Sec'y of the Society, 12th Iowa, Sioux City, Iowa:

DEAR COMRADE: It is with the deepest regret that this will have to substitute my personal attendance at this 4th reunion of the 12th Iowa. As nothing but a serious sickness in the family could have kept me at home, I am sorry to inform you that my wife being now in a very critical condition, suffering from heart disease, thus making it an impossibility for me to be with you. But, dear friends, I am with you in my mind if not in person, and hoping you will have an exceedingly good time at your meeting I will close with my best respects to all the "boys." Truly yours,

O. P. ROCKWOLD,
Late Member of Co. "G," 12th Iowa.

PARSONS, KANSAS, May 14, 1892.

Mr. J. E. Simpson, Norfolk, Neb.:

DEAR SIR: Your letter cotaining two badges and an invitation to attend the reunion of the 12th Iowa Infantry at Sioux City, was received this morning. Having previously received two printed invitations my conscience smote me when I remembered that in the rush of daily duties I had failed to acknowledge their receipt. I assure you it was not indifference that caused the neglect. Great pleasure it would give my mother, who is yet with us but no longer enjoys good health, my brother, and each of my three sisters, as well as myself, to be present with you and look into the eyes and clasp the hands of those noble men who held such a warm place in the heart of our beloved husband and father.

My mother says that she well remembers when the "boys" marched up to the quarters at Benton Barracks and received their new guns, what a fine regiment they were, and not long after when my father came home wounded, how often he would mourn for his "noble boys" in rebel prisons.

Though none of us can be with you in person we will all be there in heart and spirit. The badges you so kindly sent will be worn by my mother and myself during the time of the reunion, in honor of the regiment, and I will also make mine the subject of an object lesson to the young children in my school room at that time and endeavor to instill in their youthful minds a genuine love for our country and a feeling of respect, honor and reverence for the gallant soldiers who so bravely defended and preserved the nation.

My mother, brother and sisters unite with me in wishing for the surviving comrades of the noble 12th Iowa Infantry a pleasant, joyful reunion and many peaceful happy years at the sunset of life.

Very respectfully, CARRIE WOODS.

MEMPHIS, TENN., May 10, 1892.

Captain J. E. Simpson, Norfolk, Nebraska:

MY DEAR SIR: The circular sent out by you inviting me to the fourth quadrennial reunion of the 12th Regiment of Iowa Infantry volunteers is received.

It is a matter of profound regret to me that I am unable to attend that reunion in consequence of the fact that I am now engaged in the trial of appeal cases in the Supreme Court of the State at Jackson, Tennessee, where I will be more or less engaged during the remainder of this month.

The absence of so many comrades who have crossed over the river would make the occasion one of sadness rather than pleasure to me. Among those who have left us to return no more is my brother, Col. S. R. Edgington, who presided at the last reunion.

I want, if possible, to meet the survivors of the "old 12th" once more and renew the friendships of the past.

From the organization of the 12th until the battle of Shiloh, I was the file leader of the regiment. The regiment dressed on my button and it took its step from me. My step is just as elastic now as it was at Camp Benton, Fort Henry, Donelson and Shiloh.

My heart goes out to the survivors of the "old 12th" and I hope they may have a good time at the reunion at Sioux City, Iowa, on May 18th and 19th.

Permit me through you, to express to the survivors of the 12th my high appreciation of them individually and collectively.

Your old comrade, T. B. EDGINGTON.

WASHINGTON, D. C., April 19, 1892.

J. E. Simpson, Esq., Norfolk, Nebraska:

DEAR COMRADE: Some time since I received from you an invitation to the 4th quadrennial reunion of the 12th Iowa Infantry, to be held at Sioux City, Iowa, May 18 and 19, 1892.

I very much regret that it will be impossible for me to be present with the boys on that occasion. I expect to go to Iowa next fall, which renders my going this spring out of the question. I hope you will have a pleasant time and I further hope to meet some of the 12th Iowa boys at the gathering of the G. A. R. hosts which will assemble in this city this summer.

My address is 1921 6th Street, Northwest, Washington, D. C., and the latch string is always outside.

Be pleased to present my warmest regards to all who may be present.

Fraternally yours,
H. J. PLAYTER,
Capt. Co. "H" 12th Iowa Infantry.

KANSAS CITY, MO., May 6, 1892.

J. E. Simpson, Norfolk, Nebraska:

DEAR COMRADE: Your circular calling on the boys of the glorious old 12th Iowa Infantry, to meet in Sioux City, Iowa, May 18 and 19, to hand. I would have replied sooner but was trying to arrange so that I could tell you I would be there, but I find it will be impossible. Nothing in this world would give me more pleasure than to meet once more with those that are left of our regiment, for I have more than a brotherly love for each and every one of our regiment, be they dead or alive. Give my kindest regards to all the boys; tell them my heart is with them if I am not there in person. My health is poor. Shall be pleased to hear from you or any of the boys at any time. Should any of you ever come to this city don't fail to call and see me.

Your old comrade and friend,
N. E. DUNCAN.

DAVENPORT, IOWA, March 20, 1892.

J. E. Simpson:

DEAR COMRADE: Yours of recent date containing notice of the death of Com. Phillips, received. I am grieved to hear of his death. He was a good soldier and a good man. I return you the card in order that it may be reported at the reunion, and hope some one else of "K" Co. can be found to fill the place assigned to me, which I was not aware of till the receipt of your circular of a few weeks ago. I am so remote from all members of the company and regiment that I hear nothing of what has happened to any of them. Again, although I regret to say it, I do not expect to be able to attend the reunion. I have a matter coming before our state encampment G. A. R. which meets only a few days before that compels me to attend that meeting and it will be absolutely impossible for me to spend the time for both, meetings at one time, which would have to be the case. I was greatly in hopes of attending this reunion and having another good visit with "the boys," and regret exceedingly that I cannot. Kindly remember me to them, and express my hope that all may live to see several more reunions of the regiment. Sincerely yours,

J. B. MORGAN.

BERRIEN SPRINGS, MICH., May 12, 1892.

J. E. Simpson, Norfolk, Nebraska:

DEAR COMRADE AND COMRADES: My intentions have been to be present with you the 18th and 19th, hence seeking to have an old fashioned camp visit together once more as the old vets love each other, but I write this note to you to let you know I cannot be present with you this reunion, but will try and be present the next reunion of our old regiment. Kindly remember me to all of our "boys" and your family. I am your comrade,

N. J. DAVIS.

SPRING VALLEY, MINN., May 13, 1892.

Greetings to the Comrades of the 12th Iowa Vet. Vol.:

I had hoped to have been one of the number to attend the 4th quadrennial reunion at Sioux City, it being the first time I have had the pleasure of knowing the date, but it is impossible, as our W. R. C. convention meets in our city about the same time and cannot leave, but feel like saying, "God bless the comrades that are left of the 12th Iowa." There is nothing sends the blood coursing through my veins equal to the name of that regiment, perhaps owing some to the acquaintances I formed among them while on my visit in the south, but more particularly the many acts of kindness shown me after the death of my husband, A. A. Burdick, who fell in defence of his country.

Accept the best wishes of one who is interested in all comrades that are left and I trust this reunion will be one of the bright spots in your life for "time and tide" waiteth for no man.

Respectfully in F. C. & L.,

MRS. JENNIE STURDIVANT.

President Burdick W. R. C. No. 38, Auxiliary to Burdick Post No. 3, Spring Valley, Minn.

ST. JOHN'S RECTORY, HOME-DE-GRACE, MD., March 21st, 1892.

MY DEAR DOCTOR: Your letter of the 18th inst. came this morning. Your worthy self and the 12th I. V. V. Inft. awake the slumbering thoughts of times, deeds and scenes, which seem to be vanishing from material sight and hearing in the past, yet living and bright in thoughts and sight in memory's palace halls. Your committee's circulars for the "fourth quadrennial reunion" is admirable. To meet the comrade patriots once more would be a joy and delight. Yet there will be sad thoughts awakened by so many vacancies in the regiment caused by death. But our captain is the Prince of life. "Dust thou art, to dust returneth," was not spoken of the soul. God's blessings on the veterans of the 12th Iowa Infantry.

For me to be at Sioux City, May 18 and 19, will be impossible. I heartily thank you for your letter and circular. Remember me kindly to the veterans and to your own family. We march under one captain, a few more suns, a few more bivouacs, then the reunion on the "further shore." Yours for God and country,

F. HUMPHREY.

Under severe regime my health in this climate has improved.

ST. PAUL, MINN., May 14, 1892.

Dear Major Reed:

I will be in Chicago on the 18th or 19th. You doubtless will be gone to the 12th Reg. Reunion. I am sorry not to have time to go too. Please give a cordial greeting to the members for me. I cherish altogether pleasant memories of my association with the veterans of the regiment and shall always esteem it an honor to have commanded so soldierly a body of men. Perhaps I will find time to write a brief note of regret and greeting to you at Sioux City.

Yours truly,   W. R. MARSHALL.

ST. PAUL, MINN., May 20, 1892.

Judge J. N. Weaver, Sioux City, Iowa:

MY DEAR SIR: Major Van Duzee and myself started for Sioux City last Tuesday night: we got as far as Heron Lake, when our train was turned around and we returned to St. Paul. We were very much disappointed that we could not meet the "boys"; however, from all reports that I hear from Sioux City, I fear that our reunion was close on to a failure. I hope, however, that you have only adjourned it for one year. Have the kindness to write me and tell me all about what you did and when the adjournment was to. Yours respectfully,

AL. J. RODGERS.

DES MOINES, IOWA, April 26, 1892.

Mr. J. E. Simpson, Secretary 12th Iowa Regimental Association, Norfolk, Nebraska:

DEAR COMRADE: I very much regret being compelled to write you that it will be an impossibility for me to be present at the regimental reunion to be held at Sioux City next month. Therefore, I write you while there is still time for some other member of Co. A to be placed on the program to report for that company, and would suggest Capt. A. E. Webb, or Lt. D. V. Ellsworth, both of Eldora, Iowa, for that duty.

Trusting that you will have an interesting and joyful reunion, and hoping that you are and yours are well and happy, I am as ever

Always yours,   R. S. CLARKSON.

WASHINGTON, D. C., May 5, 1892.

D. W. Reed, President of the 12th Iowa Association:

MY DEAR MAJOR: I regret very much my inability to be with you on the occasion of our fourth reunion and can only express to you, and through you to my comrades of the dear old 12th, my great disappointment in not being able to be present and to participate in the warm greetings each will receive from every comrade, to join in and add my little mite of pleasure to that of those whose love for each other is welded together with a fire more fervent, a band more firm, than that of almost any other, not excepting the ties of kindred. We learned to bear with each other and sink our little differences, social and political, when standing in solid phalanx when the bullets of the enemy swept down to death our brother or our mess-mate; when on the long weary march; many times when a piece of fat hog and an army cracker was the sweetest morsel we had ever eaten. These bands are stronger and more enduring than those iron ones with which Wertz bound four of us together for eight days and nights, when in prison at Tuscaloosa, Ala., for displaying the flag for which we fought. I will refrain from alluding further to the past, with which you are all so familiar, and confine my thoughts to the present, hoping that you all enjoy good health and enough of the blessings of this life to be happy. But, dear comrades, I am sensible to the fact that many of you are suffering from the effects of your exposure in camp life and from the ravages of disease contracted during the years you gave to your country's cause. I am happy to say, beloved comrades, that I have reasonably good health and must certainly retain some of my youthful appearance as many question my claim to having been in the army, of which fact proof is unnecessary to you. I am again in the service of Uncle Sam, at a fair salary, and am not anxious for a discharge. Hoping to meet many of you here at the National Encampment of the G. A. R. and that you will have a most glorious and happy time at this reunion, I am, Yours devotedly,

S. R. BURCH.

The following telegrams which were received and read at the reunion will serve to show how comrades were trying to get to Sioux City:

FORT DODGE, IA., May 18, 1892.

To J. N. Weaver:

This wing of the 12'h Iowa has been temporarily repulsed. Repulse may become a rout. Superintendent says does not think we can get through; track reported washed out in several places between here and Sioux City. There is not one in party who feels like praying. A, Wilson and wife, Kemp, C. Moine and wife, Stuart, Lattimer, Grannis. Ballinger, Hazelette; D, Ayers; E, Schack, Church; T, Dunham, Tom and Wayne, Nelson, Cooldridge, McGowan, Preston; H, Fischel, Horner; I, McDermott, and Nagle. Answer here.

C. E. MERRIAM.

HERON LAKE, MINN, May 18, 1892.

To Judge J. N. Weaver:

We are storm bound here. Can't you send us an ox team.

VAN DUZEE AND RODGERS.

SIBLEY, IA., May 18, 1892.

To Mr. President and Comrades:

Can not advance; must retreat. Sorry to say a 12th Iowa man ever retreats but no other show. Kind regards to all.

ED H. BAILEY,

And Scott. Barr, Hartwell, Buttolph, Lewis, Mareph.

SHELDON, IA., May 18, 1892.

To J. E. Simpson:

Dr. Barr six others here; since last night dozen more at Worthington and Sibley. Any boys there? E. R. SOPER.

RIDGEWAY, IA., May 18, 1892.

To Major D. W. Reed:

Comrades, greeting to you all. Co. G most of all.

ANTON E. ANDERSON,
D. O. AKER.

PERRY, IA., May 18, 1892.

To Judge J. N. Weaver:

Delayed by a wreck. Will be there sometime today.

J. H. STIBBS.

To Color Bearer Granis, Veteran:

LEMARS, IA., May 18, 1892.

Trains not running; cannot get down; must see the boys. Can't reunion be postponed?
H. C. CURTIS.

To 12th Reg't Reunion, 412 5th St.:

SIOUX FALLS, S. D., May 19, 1892.

Will come tomorrow if you are in session. Answer soon.
J. B. HAZELET.

To John N. Weaver:

MANILLA, IA., May 19, 1892.

Wire me here if I shall make further effort to reach you.
D. W. REED.

To Headquarters 12th Iowa Reg't:

ROCK VALLEY, IA., May 19, 1892.

DEAR COMRADES: Owing to the high waters am unable to reach you. Respects to you and yours in F. C. L. T.
P. R. KETCHUM.

To J. N. Weaver:

STERLING, NEB., May 18, 1892.

Cannot get there in time on account of washouts.
PETER KEARNS.

To J. N. Weaver:

LEMARS, IOWA, May 20, 1892.

Sick in bed since Tuesday or would have walked down; must come by first train. Have all brave boys go to the Garretson till I can come at my expense. Tell Grannis and Reed to keep Co. C. till tomorrow. Put me down for twenty-five dollars to Sioux City sufferer's fund.
H. C. CURTIS.

To Maj. D. W. Reed:

DENVER, COL., May 17, 1892.

Greeting to all; I am with you in spirit. God bless you and yours.
Yours under the flag.
ELIZABETH A. SOBIN.

LETTERS FROM COMPANY "D."

The following is an abstract of the letters received from comrades of Co. D, in response to letters of Capt. E. B. Soper, urging their attendance at the Sioux City reunion:

Capt. Hiel Hale, deputy warden of U. S. penitentiary at Yuma, Arizona, said: "I very much regret that I cannot be at the reunion. I have been looking forward to this grand rally of the survivors of Co. D and the 12th Iowa with great anxiety, and thought all along that I would be there but find it impossible to get away from my duties. It is impossible for me to tell you how great to me the disappointment is and so will not attempt it. Remember me kindly to them all. May the reunion be a great success and may the blessings of the Great Commander rest upon all the survivors and at last when their earthly

campaign is ended, may they one and all hear His command to enter into the kingdom prepared for them, is the prayer of
Your friend and comrade, HIEL HALE.

The Cedar Rapids contingent wrote from Sibley the 19th, as follows: "We left Cedar Rapids at 12:30 the 17th and ran to Iowa Falls O K, then trouble began. Rain and wind laid us out at nearly every station, but arrived at Sibley 5:30 p. m., the 18th, and found trains on the C. St. P. M. & O. abandoned, and no prospects of an advance movement but very good prospects of our retreat being cut off. Being members of a regiment that never retreated we hate to set an example but must. All of us so wanted to see old Co. D comrades but can't this time. Words will not express our regrets."

HOMER C. MOREHEAD,
EDWIN H. BAILEY,
CHAS. W. CLARK,
JO N W. ROWAN,
JOSEPH O. SARTWELL.
EDWIN A. BUTTOLPH,
THOMAS BARR,
THOMAS J. LEWIS.
JOSEPH SCOTT.

Lieut. and Adjutant Sylvester R. Burch writes from Washington, D. C.: "The program of the 12th Iowa reunion with your note thereon was forwarded to me by my wife. She still remains in Olathe, Kan. I am again in the employ of "Uncle Sam." After I had completed my supervisor's work of the eleventh census I was ordered here and remained in that work until the first of last September, when I resigned and was appointed an auditing clerk in the department of agriculture division of accounts which I like very much. The salary is sufficient to make a good living. There are only three in my family; my daughters are both married, one living in Olathe and the other at Lake Charles, La. I am now 50 years old and grandfather, but my age is more frequently placed at 40 than 50 and my health is quite good. I can only get 30 day leave of absence in each year and am compelled to use that attending to some business at my old home and will have to forego the pleasure of visiting my old comrades, every one of whom I love."

Wm. Baumgardner writes: "I still stop at Scranton, Iowa, and if I am alive and well you will see me at the reunion at Sioux City. I hope to see all the old comrades once more for soon our days are short."

Edwin H. Bailey writes: "If nothing happens more than I now know of I shall be with you at the reunion at Sioux City, May 18th and 19th."

Henry W. Bailey writes: "I will be at Sioux City on time."

Dennis Conley writes: "Yours of the 17th at hand and in reply to your kind invitation and offer I will have to say, nay. I find it will be impossible for me to come as I have employment and can't leave; must attend to what I am doing and take the best care I can as I am placed at a disadvantage ever since that "Tupelo affair." The older I get the more I worry over my loss—*my great loss*. I am the only one that feels it sorely. I can see and feel the difference between the day I enlisted and the day I was discharged if nobody else can. Again thanking you for your kind offer I am as heretofore, Your comrade,

DENNIS CONLEY.

James L. Cowell writes: "I am in receipt of your request to attend the reunion at Sioux City for which I am thankful but am sorry to say that it is impossible. My finances are in such shape that it would not be good policy for me to leave at this time and my health is such that I don't think I could stand the journey. I would like very much to see the old boys once more but fear that I will not unless I get better. I hope to come to Iowa during the fair at Chicago and will if my health permits. I send my love to all the comrades and hope they will have a good time. While I can't be with you in person I will in heart. I am now living in the city of Walla Walla, and all communications for me should be sent to this place."

Robert C. Cowell writes: "Yours of the 15th at hand. Will say in reply that I shall try to come. I want to see the boys once more."

Ferdinand Dubois writes: "I received your letter today and was pleased to hear from you. I am going to try hard to be at the reunion and answer to roll call with the balance of Co. D. I hope to see all the boys there. I failed to be at the last reunion but hope not to miss this one."

Mrs. Harmon Grass writes: "Yours of the 15th at hand and in reply will say that I guess that Mr. Grass will be at the reunion. He wanted me to tell you that he did not think he could come this time, but I told him that I would tell you that he was coming and I think when the time comes he will go. I hope that you will all have a grand time for I think you all deserve it. I had hoped that we might both go this time, as doubtless many will be there I used to know, whom it will be my last and only chance to see but if both cannot leave I will be the one to stay. Hoping again that you may have a happy reunion, I am. Respectfully yours,

MRS. HARMON GRASS.

Irdill W. Holler writes from California: "I received your letter some time ago but having been very busy neglected answering. It is impossible for me to come and join you at Sioux City for financial reasons. I would like to come but there is no possible show. Give my regards to the boys."

John Luther writes: "Please excuse my tardiness in not writing sooner. The reunion of the 12th Iowa will be a rare treat for the old boys. If possible I will be with you. I am coming—coming—coming. Hip—hip—now everybody."

William L. Lee writes: "Your favor of recent date came duly to hand. I fully appreciate your kindness but I cannot give you a positive answer concerning my presence at the reunion at present but will say, however, that I will surely be present if it is possible to leave at that time. The spring and summer months are the busy season with mining people. I have several new enterprises on hand and cannot tell just how my absence at that time might effect myself and those interested with me but will write again as soon as I can answer definitely. I have been laid up with la grippe and rheumatism since the middle of February and have not yet fully recovered, perhaps on account of living so much on the mountains at an altitude of 8,000 feet." Later he writes: "After the receipt of your last letter I began immediately to prepare to attend the reunion of the old 12th Iowa at Sioux City, but having gone up into the mountains too soon after leaving the hospital my rheumatism came back on me and I am again under the doctor's care at Helena. I fully appreciate your efforts to get the boys together and would like the best in the world to meet you all once more but it will be impossible to do so at this time."

James H. Little, formerly Co. K 1st Iowa, and afterwards Co. D and Co. K 12th Iowa, writes: "I am more than happy to hear from you and would love to be where I could see you all. You are the first comrade I have received a scratch of a pen from since the close of the war. I often think of you all and wonder if I can ever see any of my old command again. I have forgotten none of you and never will. I would come to the reunion if I was able, but am not. I want to end my days among them. I have no family; they are all dead. But when you meet a Co. D or K man tell them old Jim Luther is still on deck. My address is Mt. Carmel, Ills. Please put this in your paper or some paper where the 12th Iowa will see it."

David W. Minor writes: "I received your notice of the 4th reunion of the 12th Iowa and in reply would say that I have long wished for the pleasure of being at one of them and of once more seeing and greeting my brave and gallant comrades. But I am sorry to say that I cannot possibly avail myself of the opportunity afforded by the coming reunion. It would give me much pleasure to meet my old comrades and take them by the hand. I have no doubt they have changed in outward appearance so that I should fail to recognize many of them as they doubtless would me. I am bearing some of the marks of time but my spirit is still young. I am unchanged, however, in the spirit of respect and brotherly love for all comrades of the 12th, and especially Co. D, from Capt. Jack down to Buttolph at the switch end of the company. I cherish many pleasant memories of the companionships of the service and should greatly enjoy talking over old times and renewing old friendships, but as I cannot be with you please give my love and hearty greetings to everyone. May they all prosper and enjoy life and live to enjoy yet many more reunions and may God be with you all till we meet again."

Nathan G. Price, on April 28th, wrote: "I will be with you at

Sioux City. Have no time to write now. Sixteen hours per day, at hard work. Take the will for the deed." But on May 15th: "It is with much disappointment and regret that I am compelled to ask you and the boys to accept this sheet as a substitute for myself at your reunion. I have worked hard to be able to be with you and one week ago I was sure of being one of you. But nature has interfered with storms and floods and wrecked my fields and plans and rendered it entirely impossible for me to leave. * * * Now Capt. and boys all! There are none of you who want me at the reunion any worse than I want to be there. None of you have worked harder to be there than I have. No one is to blame. I hope and trust that I may be the only one absent. And, bad as I feel about it, I hope each and all of you feel worse than I do. Indeed it would be a satisfaction for me to know that there was not a dry eye over my absence. But if there are even two wet eyes, dry them, wipe them quick and enjoy the pleasure of being in the company of those who are not absent. Let each give the other a kindly glance, a shake and a greeting for me and after the reunion when all have gone home I want you each and all to write to me. If I can't see you I would like to hear from you and not of you. I fear this will be our last chance of seeing each other. I hope not. I am so greatly disappointed this time that I have no expectation of ever being with you, but if I do remember that as long as I live I am

N. G. PRICE, of Co. D."

J. V. Geo. Price writes: "If the Lord is willing and nothing happens my wife and I will meet you at Sioux City in May."

Henry W. Ross writes: "I will be at Sioux City May 17, 1892, no preventing providence. Look for me."

Frank Reuchin, who was so fearfully and cruelly shot at Shiloh after the surrender by a drunken rebel, writes: "I have received your kind letter and read the proposition you offer. My thanks for your kindness. It makes my heart beat faster when I hear or read that you boys think so much of me and would like to see me. I would like to see them all as I have not seen any of them for twenty years. It is not so much a matter of money with me, as money is not so close, but business matters: and besides I am not very well at present and could hardly stand the trip. I think I will take a trip to Iowa this fall and try to see some of the boys. Now when you see the boys tell them my heart and hand is with them always and that I hold them in love and friendship ever. If it was in my power to help any one of them in distress I would do it with all my heart. I am proud that I have defended the American flag—the stars and stripes and I am willing to lay my life down for our country—my adopted country. I am proud to be a citizen of the United States, the best country in the world and I am not sorry that I got crippled defending the flag. I tried to do my duty as a soldier and as a citizen and I have no doubt all of the boys of the 12th have done the same. I hope you will all enjoy yourselves and while having a good time think of me a little."

Mrs. Chas. Ranson, whose true name was Nicholas Clemans and who deserted from Co. D, and who for some time resided at Smith Center, Kan., that her husband died in the insane hospital at Topeka, Kan., Oct. 7, 1887, of appoplexy of the brain and asking for assistance in securing a pension.

Daniel Livets writes: "Dear Comrade: I got your invitation to the reunion and would like to come and see you all once more, but I can't, for my health will not permit. Give my love to all the boys and tell them that I should like to be with them and hope they may have a good time."

Joseph Wagner, whose P. O. address is Borne City, Ind., among other things, writes: "When I left the 12th Iowa Inft. at St. Louis I went direct to Columbus, Ohio, and there enlisted in in Co. F, 11th Ohio Cav., and went directly back to St. Louis and after a few days at Benton Barracks was sent up the Missouri river by steamer to Fort Leavenworth and from there sent across the plains to New Mexico. Served three years and thirty-one days in the territories mostly, and was mustered out at Ft. Larimie, July 22d, 1866. In 1868 was married to a farmer's daughter in Morrow county, Ohio, and have four children, one son and three daughters. Have drifted around considerably since the war. Tried it awhile in Mo.; got sick of the country and went north of Cedar Rapids four miles and tried farming for six years; made my fortune and then came here: bought property and expect to end my days here. This is a great summer resort on banks of Silver Lake. Would like awful well to be at the reunion at Sioux City and renew acquaintances with comrades of the 12th. Presume that Stibbs is not very anxious to see me, but I don't hold any grudge. That little difficulty is forgotten years ago."

John Watrobeck, Cotterville, Mo., writes: "Comrade Soper: I have received your welcome letter. You have made great pleasure to me to hear from old comrades once more. Thank God that some of our boys are still living. I would like to be with you in your encampment but I am sick and worn out. I will be 70 years old on May 10, 1892, and could not stand the trip. I would like to see you. Hope you will enjoy yourselves and think of me. I will remember you all. You ask of my brother, Enos Watrobeck. He died in Tenn. in 1863 and my brother George the same year in Virginia. My two brothers died for the Union."

B. P. Zuver and E. A. Buttolph wrote numerous letters and did everything in their power to get the boys out.

A SHORT HISTORY OF CO. D's LITTLE CANNON, BY SOME OF THE FELLOWS WHO WERE THERE.

During the late unpleasantness while our regiment was stationed at Selma, Alabama, some of Co. "K" boys while prowling around an old foundry found a small brass Howitzer and walked off with it to their quarters. There they mounted it on sticks, directed it towards Co. D's quarters, with the remark that if Co. D did not do this and that they would fire on us and often went through the motions to show how they would do the act. It was great amusement for Co. K but no amusement for Co. D, and must be put to an end. John J. Whittam and William L. Lee planned to steal the gun. John W. Burch, of the "Methodist mess," was fond of lecturing the boys for their delinquencies and for a joke on him got him to go with them. "Only a joke on Co. K." They chose the late hours of a dark night to do the deed, which, like other dark deeds committed by John and Bill, proved successful. The cannon was taken to Lieut. King's tent and hid under his bunk. Co. K never mistrusted, or at least said nothing, as to where the cannon was or who "faked it." Next day it was decided that it would be a grand scheme to send the gun home to Cedar Rapids as a momento of Co. D for all time to come, so Burch and others made a box, put in the cannon and loaded it into John W. Rowan's wagon. John was regimental teamster. John had charge of the gun a short time—long enough though to give him the idea that he stole the gun and that he was sole owner, and he still imagines that he is the man. Soon thereafter the regiment was ordered to be discharged and started for home. The cannon was then put into Homer C. Morehead's mess chest. He was quartermaster and brought the gun to Davenport, Iowa. From there it was sent by freight to Cedar Rapids and put in charge of Post 88 G. A. R. Later it was given to the city provided that the city would mount it in good style. It was mounted temporarily on a pair of front wheels of a light wagon and stood around in old sheds for a long time, the city not offering to mount it as agreed to. One night Capt. Hiel Hale and Ed A. Buttolph and other men got a wheelbarrow and took it to Ed's, where it was for over a year. During the campaign of 1868 it was brought out and mounted on the same old wheels. October 3d there was a grand parade and barbecue. A squad of G. A. R. men acted as artillery men; Buttolph as powder monkey. In a grove northeast of town was the grand stand. The little gun was away at a safe distance firing salutes. Had fired some six or eight shots when the recoil of the gun broke the carriage all to pieces and the gun flew to the rear end over forty feet, landing between Buttolph's feet who was sitting on the ammunition box. No one hurt; fun spoiled. The next day the outfit was taken to a blacksmith shop for repairs. Could do nothing unless the gun was there so it was left, under protest. "Oh, it will be safe, etc., etc." The proprietor of the shop was a strong democrat. That night the gun was taken and a lot of angry men was around all day—yes, for days after. The proprietor was arrested and held to court, an attorney hired, who afterwards settled the case without consulting the men that had the gun in charge, Hale and Buttolph. Many were the surmises as to the location of the gun, places were searched and men on the lookout at all times but not a whisper could be heard but that it was acted upon, but all without avail. Often when any doings was to go on it was rumored that the gun would be brought out and company D boys and friends would lay for it. Many oaths were sworn that no one should ever fire that cannon without our consent. Time passed. 1884 Cleveland was elected president. The democrats were to have a grand ratification at Cedar Rapids; amunition bought and fixed for the little cannon which was to be brought out and fired for a democratic victory. Again Hale and others of company D and friends was on the lookout and many old G. A. R. men, regardless of politics, swore that if the democrats undertook to fire that gun it would be over their dead bodies. The night of the blowout came: excitement was at blood heat. More than one man in that crowd carried arms. The old blacksmith shop had a number of spies watching it, and all was sure of a row and eager and ready for it. It put me in mind of war times just before a battle. Angry words were uttered but none came to blows. The old army boys were used to such scenes and were cool. The cannon was not brought out and a good deal of chaff was fired at the democrats for cowardice, and it was some time before all was quiet, until the spring of '85. Then the question was up again. A railroad man was having his horse shod at the same shop. In stamping a horse broke a hole in the floor and he reported he saw the cannon under the floor. There had been so many false rumors that not much notice was taken of the last rumor, and all was quieting down when one morning in March, 1888, the cannon was found in the alley near the shop from which it was stolen, the night of October 4th, 1868. The news flew and great was the excitement. It was wrapped in an old gunny sack, as the railroad man reported. Pinned to it was a note, as follows:

"Taken from John Mehan's shop about twenty years ago. Returned to the same place by the only surviving member of the abductors. Cleveland is president and the little cannon has slept long enough. It is to be hoped that it will be better guarded in the future. The parties who removed the same have never been referred to in connection therewith." "OLD CANNON."

It is still a secret as to who the parties were. No man could handle it easily alone. It was taken to the police station and laid in the window where it was viewed by many, then turned over to Col. T. Z. Cook Post G. A. R. They have a temporary carriage and use it only for G. A. R. purposes. It may find a rest in the lodge room.

RANDALIA, IOWA, May 20, 1892.

J. N. Weaver, Sioux City, Iowa:

DEAR COMRADE: You are probably aware by telegram sent from Ft. Dodge that it was not my fault that I did not meet you on the 18th or 19th. It was with many regrets that we abandoned the expedition and retreated to our homes. I wrote Comrade Reed that I would be there or bust. Well, I'm not busted but the Illinois Central was and I am home again safe and sound, but not so with Comrade Latimer, who, on jumping off street train here yesterday fell and bruised himself considerably but not seriously.

We enjoyed ourselves at Ft. Dodge as only old "boys" can under such unfavorable circumstances. We have as yet heard no report from the Sioux City branch of our association, whether you organized, what you did, and when and where we shall make the next attempt to meet. We left Ft. Dodge about 3 p. m. the 18th, before we had any news from you, but upon arrival at Independence found that you had remembered us by instructing agent to return us at one-third fare. Many thanks. I presume we should not have enjoyed ourselves very well had we been there, surrounded as you were by the excitement and sorrow of others. Yours in F. C. and L.

H. J. GRANNIS.

HANOVER, ILL., May 5, 1892.

J. E. Simpson, Sec'y, Norfolk, Neb.:

MY DEAR COMRADE: I have been looking forward with a great deal of pleasure to meeting the boys at Sioux City on the 18th inst., but circumstances oblige me to sail from New Orleans on that date, to settle an estate at Honduras, C. A. Remember me kindly to the comrades and particularly to Co. "A." I very much regret my inability to be with you. Yours in F. C. and L.,

E. C. COOMBS,
Late Company "A."

HESPER, IOWA, June 3d, 1892.

Mr. J. E. Simpson:

DEAR COMRADE: I received your very welcome letter and have had time to consider it well. I am of the same opinion as the rest of you in regard to having our reunions oftener. I should say have them as often as once every two years. We are all growing old and as the years roll on time is making its inroads in our ranks and the time is coming when we shall meet the last enemy and he will conquer, and then there will be no more meetings for us here on earth. I am extremely sorry that we could not have all got together at Sioux City this spring but fate was against us, although we had a good time at Sheldon. There were Dr. Barr and wife, Capt. Soper and wife, Sergt. Winters and wife, Gilbert Ness, Mage Bowen, A. H. Groves, myself and wife, making a nice company.

You mentioned Chicago to be the next place for our reunion. I think it would not be a suitable place as there would be so much to see and it would have a tendency to mar the benefit we aim in our reunions. I speak for myself alone. You also mentioned Sioux City for our next. If the citizens wish it I think it but right they should have the first chance, they went to so much trouble and expense to make this one pleasant and agreeable for us.

P. S.: My wife and I send our best wishes to you and family.

From your old friend and comrade,

M. E. MEADER.

SPEILVILLE, IOWA, May 12, 1892.

Dear Friend and Comrade, J. E. Simpson:

Your invitation received. I am sorry to say that I am not able to be present, as I have been sick all winter. I am now so that I can walk on crutches from one room to the other. I hope all the boys of the 12th will have a joyful time. My best regards to you all.

Your comrade, J. B. THOMPSON.

PRECEPT, FURNAS CO., NEB., May 7th, 1892.

Dear Comrade Simpson:

I received the announcement 12th Iowa reunion. Many thanks for it. I regret very much that circumstances prevent me from meeting with the comrades at Sioux City. I will send one dollar to become a member of the association. I would like to ask Col. Stibbs if he still has that silver mounted revolver that the Confederate officer tried to make him give up when we were taken prisoners at Pittsburg landing. The officer hit him over the head with his sword and drew back to hit him again, but the Col. kept the revolver.

Your comrade,
W. B. KEITH, Co. "K."

HITESVILLE, BUTLER CO., IOWA, May 20, 1892.

J. E. Simpson, Sec'y, Norfolk, Neb.:

DEAR COMRADE: We old vets here feel very much disappointed in our reunion. We left home Tuesday morning, 17th, for Sioux City; got delayed on the road and the washout got us so we could not get there; was within four miles of Le Mars and could get no farther; got home yesterday. There was on the train the following 12th Iowa boys and their families:

Myself and wife, of Co. E, Hitesville, Iowa.
C. V. Surfus and wife, Co. E. Bristow, Iowa.
J. W. Rich and wife, Co. E, Vinton, Iowa.
David Creighton, Co. E, Geneva, Iowa.
P. H. Morehouse, Co. K, Masonville, Iowa.
W. H. McCune, Co. H, Ruthven, Iowa.

I thought I would write this to let you know that we done the best we could to get there, and was very much disappointed in not getting there.

Now we do not like to wait four years for a reunion: would it not be a good idea to try and all meet at Storm Lake, June 16, 17, 18 and 19, when the Northwestern Soldier's Association have their camp fire. But at least, all I have talked with do not desire to have the reunion put off very long. I hope those of you that did get to Sioux City did have a good time. We telegraphed to you at Sioux City from Ramsen but could not get you before we left to go back to Cherokee. We thought we could go by Sheldon but could not. I remain,

Respectfully your old comrade,
J. S. MARGRETZ,
Late of Co. "E" 12th Iowa V. V. Inft.

COLUMBUS, OHIO, July 14, 1892.

Mr. Simpson:

DEAR SIR: I received one of your letters today relating to the reunion at Sioux City, last May, from Gen. Stibbs. I did not know he was in Chicago until I saw his name in the newspaper. I am willing to hold the next reunion wherever the boys say. I have never been to one so I am in the dark in that respect. I was the youngest private soldier in the 12th; I belonged to Co. I. I was wounded at Tupelo, Miss., July 1864; I could not be taken back to Memphis, so I was left in the hands of the Rebs. I never seen the 12th after that. I had a cousin, Mike Nagle, living in Dubuque. He belonged to Co. I. Do you know his address? I see old Bill Kohler's name in your letter; he and I were in prison together. You bet your bottom dollar, old comrade, you let me know when and where the next reunion will be held and if I am walking around on top of earth I will be there. Write and let me know all the particulars.

Your friend and comrade,
JOHN DEVINE,
Arcade Hotel. Co. I, 12th I. V. V. I.

SPENCER, OHIO, May 12th, 1892.
Comrades of the 12th, and Especially of Co. K:

I have always had an ardent desire to attend the reunion of my old regiment, but distance, business or other hindering circumstances have always so far intervened and I have always promised myself from year to year, that the next I would surely go. So that as I see another opportunity go by, I feel an added disappointment and have made up my mind to put in appearance anyhow, if only by a letter of regret. Boys, I am there in spirit and send, Hail! and farewell. When the pipes are lighted think of Your old comrade

RICHARD FREEMAN.

ELWOOD, IOWA, May 11th, 1892.
D. D. McCollum, Sibley, Iowa:

Dear Sir and Comrade of Co. "I" 12th Iowa: For the past year I have been looking forward to our reunion with gladness and made preparations to be there and be one of you. But today changes have occurred to prevent my being present. I therefore send greetings to all old comrades of the 12th, from Gen. Stibbs down to that popular private, Ed Buttolph. Your comrade,

GEO. TESKEY.

MANCHESTER, IOWA, July 29th, 1892.
Capt. J. E. Simpson, Norfolk, Nebraska:

DEAR FRIEND AND COMRADE: Yours of the 25th inst. received. Always pleased to hear from you; wish I could meet you oftener that it is our privilege to shake. I will acknowledge that I received all circulars and printed matter relating to the 4th quadrennial reunion of our old 12th Iowa regiment at Sioux City. While that enjoyable event did not fully materialize it was not however the fault of our very efficient executive committee, and as to the time and place when and where we should hold our 5th reunion I am very willing to leave all that matter to our executive board. I am satisfied they will make no mistake. I am pleased to learn from you that the proceedings at Sioux City are to be compiled and printed. I know from past experience that it is quite a task but the boys will be quite thankful. I am glad that a carefully written biography of Col. Wood's life is to appear in connection with the proceedings of the reunion at Sioux City. Dr. Barr had the distribution of our copies of the 3d reunion at Waterloo. I presume he has some copies still on hand; if you will write him I think he can and will furnish you with some copies. If you find the doctor cannot furnish them let me know and I will skirmish around among the boys here and see if I cannot find you a few copies. I am pleased to learn that your health is fairly good. My condition is no worse than it has been for the past few years. The survivors of our regiment residing here are well. Please remember me kindly to Mrs. Simpson and bear in mind that the love you express for me is heartily reciprocated by me. While I remain

Very truly yours, GEO. H. MORRISEY.

GILA BEND, ARIZ., May 5, 1892.

To the Executive Committee of the Quadrennial Reunion of the Twelfth Iowa Vet. Vol. Inft.:

COMRADES: I have received your circular and the supplementary thereto in due time, and it created such a feeling of homesickness that it will be impossible for me to write my regrets, as is usual, but will say instead that when roll is called some comrade—Sargeant Eldredge.—will say here at my name for I shall be with you, if in spirit only. My health has been so poor for a long time that it will be impossible to bring this crippled old body of mine so far. First, because it would cost too much and second, it would be a severe test on these old rheumatic bones. If Gen. J. H. Stibbs will let me know his address I would like to communicate with him or in fact, any and all of the members of the regiment with whom I am acquainted. At least one certainty remains for me. I shall meet you all when the clarion notes of the bugle is heard from beyond. Very truly yours,

LUTHER WALTENBACH,
Late Co. "F" 12th Reg't Iowa Vol. Inft.

VINTON, IOWA, May 23, 1892.

J. E. Simpson, Sec'y 12th Iowa Ass'n, Norfolk, Neb.:

DEAR COMRADE: In company with four others, I was caught in the storm of Tuesday night, May 17-18, and failed to get to Sioux City. Our train stopped at Remsen, a little east of Le Mars. We tried to flank the flood from Cherokee, but failed, so returned home. It was a great disappointment to us.

I suppose there are some dues to be paid. I am ready to pay mine as soon as the amount is known, I would like a badge such as I suppose was prepared for the 4th reunion. If you have a spare one please send it. Very truly,

J. W. RICH,
Co. "E" 12th Infantry.

Interesting letters were received before and at the time of the reunion from comrades. Space and want of time will prevent our printing them in full, and with many others received in answer to the circular letter of May 21st, all breathing a spirit of love and tenderness towards comrades and memories of the past thirty years ago—that tells the story that while years have brought gray hairs and bowed forms—the hearts beat warm and loving yet. We note as follows:

Abram Billings and wife, Luzerne, N. Y.
Chas. McCabe, Sherburne, Minn.
W. A. Lyon, West Union, Iowa.
Mrs. A. J. Millett, 512 Burlington Ave., South Hastings. Neb.
A. Brothers, Magnolia, Ohio.
G. A. Hauge, Albert Lea, Minn.
N. J. Davis, Berrien Springs, Mich.
S. J. Crowhurst, Salem, S. D.
W. M. Van Ernan, Grandview, S. D.
G. W. Kirkland, Freeport, Iowa.
S. Cook, Ionia, Neb.
A. Tobiason, Windom, Minn.

P. R. Woods, Fayette, Iowa.
James P. Cook, Ponca, Neb.
J. Watrobeck, Cotterville, Mo.
J. H. Shumaker, Waterloo, Iowa.
J. Belton, Batavia, Minn.
Geo. H. Cobb, Eldora, Iowa.
I. W. King, Emerick, Neb.
J. F. Zedeiker, care Nebraska State Journal, Lincoln, Neb.
W. R. Mathas, Omaha, Neb.
Hans Hanson, Lake Park, Minn.
S. Kemp, Alden, Iowa.
C. G. Russell, Brooklyn, Mo.
W. H. Cox, Blaine, Iowa.
J. W. Cotes, Talcott, S. D.
D. W. Ballinger, Lacey, Iowa.
W. H. McCune, Ruthven, Iowa.
Frank Renchin, Blooming Prairie, Minn.
N. H. Baldwin, Ada, Kan.
Ezra Strong, National City, Cal.
Wm. L. Fry, Scranton City, Iowa.
Geo. Nauman, North Platte, Neb.
Ira D. Blanchard, No. 1917 Jefferson St., Duluth, Minn.
H. Ellgen, Bolan, Iowa.
James Shorter, Shell Rock, Iowa.
C. E. Merriam, Hopkinton, Iowa.
A. H. Groves, Decorah, Iowa.
Peter Moe, Springfield, Minn.
A. B. Perry, Dunkerton, Iowa.
Zeph Reed, Fredonia, Iowa.
J. Halfhill, Wood, Iowa.
S. C. Fishel, Iowa Falls, Iowa.
S. W. Norris, Maquoketa, Iowa.
E. Engbretson, Aastad, Minn.
T. J. Lewis, 383 First Ave., West Cedar Rapids, Iowa.
L. D. Morris, Worthing, S. D.
F. C. Nelson, Hazleton, Iowa.
John Bremner, Yankton, S. D.
D. V. Ellsworth, Newman Grove, Neb.
C. M. Runkle, Plankinton, S. D.
G. Hazlet, Allison, Iowa.
L. H. Maupsen, Franklin, Neb.
R. D. Williams, West Union, Iowa.
J. D. Cole, Lansing, Iowa.
F. S. Sawin, Union, Iowa.

RESOLUTIONS ADOPTED BY THE SOCIETY OF THE TWELFTH REGIMENT OF IOWA VETERAN VOLUNTEERS BEFORE ADJOURNMENT.

Before the Twelfth Iowa adjourned its reunion Friday evening the resolutions committee, consisting of R. W. Tirrill, J. H. Stibbs and W. L. Henderson, reported the following resolutions, which were unanimously adopted:

Resolved, That we greatly appreciate the attendance of so many of our fellow comrades at this our quadrennial reunion under such unfavorable circumstances, and while many were enroute unable to reach us, owing to high water and washouts, yet the frequent and warm heartfelt congratulations extended over the wires from the various points of their temporary rendezvous thrilled us with an electrical enthusiasm which seemed to unite us more firmly in the bonds of one common brotherhood.

Resolved, That we heartily sympathize with the people of Sioux City in the sad calamity, through an unprecedented flood, which so suddenly and completely overcame them on the morning of our first meeting; and while we are fully aware of the preparations being made to give us a royal welcome and heartily extend to us hospitalities commensurate with the usual warmheartedness of Sioux City enthusiasm, yet we commend the diversion of that same spirit of enthusiasm, wonderfully intensified, in the direction of charity unsparingly administered to their unfortunate fellow-citizens.

Resolved, That the thanks of the association are due Comrades John N. Weaver and J. E. Simpson for their untiring efforts in the great work of preparation and their devoted zeal during all of our meetings.

Resolved, That we extend our thanks to the K. P. band for their excellent music rendered under a reduced rate, and to the Schubert quartette for their thrilling songs voluntarily rendered.

Resolved, That we extend our warmest thanks and a rekindling of our old-fashioned brotherly love to comrades T. R. McKee and S. M. French for a rehearsal of those same old battle songs, the reveille, tattoo, "The Girl I Left Behind Me," and the long roll from the same old identical fife and drum that followed us from Camp Union to the gulf.

Resolved, That we deeply deplore the great loss we have sustained by the death of our Comrades and Col's J. J. Woods and S. R. Edgington. That we heartily sympathize with their families, in their sad bereavement and we shall ever hold in greatful remembrance their noble qualities—as faithful soldiers, loving comrades and honored citizens.

Resolved, That in the death of our Comrades Sergt. Emery Clark, Co. "C," A. C. Gilmore, Co. "H," C. E. Phillips, Co. "K," E. V. Andrus, Co. "G," A. W. Myers, J. C. Jones and James Demoss, of Co. "E," and other dear comrades whose names we have been unable to obtain and at present must leave among the great unknown. We one, each and all reminded of the sure and gradual depletion of our ranks and that the loving hand of the Great Father is ever open to receive us at the bivouac of the eternal camping ground. That we sincerely sympathize with all the families of our deceased comrades and we shall ever hold in sacred remembrance their loving qualities as comrades, their undaunted courage as soldiers, and their unswerving fidelity as honored citizens.

Roster of Members of the 12th Iowa V. V. Infantry, so far as Known at the time of this Reunion.

FIELD AND STAFF.

Colonel—J. H. Stibbs, Room 88 P. O. Building, Chicago, Ill.
Lt. Colonel—S. G. Knee, Colesburg, Iowa.
Major—S. D. Brodtbeck, 113 South Broadway, Los Angeles, Cal.
Major—E. M. Van Duzee, St. Paul, Minn.
Major—D. W. Reed, Suite 814 Chamber of Commerce, Chicago, Ill.
Surgeon—C. C. Parker, Fayette, Iowa.
Surgeon—Myron Underwood, Eldora, Iowa.
Ass't Surgeon—W. H. Finley, Franklin, Neb.
Ass't Surgeon—James Barr, Algona. Iowa.
Adjutant N. E. Duncan, care U. S. Custom House, Kansas City. Mo.
Adjutant—S. R. Burch, Olathe, Kansas.
Quartermaster—G. H. Morrisey, Manchester, Iowa.
Quartermaster—H. C. Morehead, Cedar Rapids, Iowa.
Chaplain—Frederick Humphrey, Fairmount, Minn.
Hospital Steward—J. C. H. Hobbs, 1441 G Street, Lincoln, Neb.
Hospital Steward—J. J. Walker, De Witt. Missouri.
Com. Sergt.—James Evans, Dubuque, Iowa.
Sergt. Major—A. J. Rodgers, St. Paul, Minn.
Drum Major—T. R. McKee, Room 102, Boston Bl'k, Denver, Col.
Fife Major—D. S. Martin, Iowa Falls, Iowa.
Fife Major—S. M. French, Room 102, Boston Bl'k, Denver, Col.

COMPANY A.

Armstrong, B A, Liscomb, Iowa.
Bird, G M, Illinois.
Brother, A, Magnalia, O.
Congar, J D Eldora Hardin Co, Ia
Cromwell, T C, Oakland, Ia
Cobb, G H, Eldora, Ia.
Dobbins, Hiram Jewel Co, Kan, R
Ellsworth, D V, Newman Grove. Nebraska
Ferree. S R, Belle Plaine, Ia
Haskins, G H, Maryville. Mo
Hunter. J R C, Webster, Ia
Iback, B D, Eldora, Ia
Kidwiler, M, Mo
Kellogg, R E, Dows, Ia
Bowers, I H Eldora, Ia
Bell, Thos R, Iowa Falls, Iowa
Brown, S B, Jewell City, Kan
Clarkson, R P, Des Moines, Ia
Combes, E C. Hanover, Ill
Crist, Job, Marshalltown, Ia
Dobbins, Levi, Eldora, Ia
Edgington, T B, 18 Madison St Memphis, Tenn.
Fountain. Francis
Glass, Carl. Dayton (Mill Home) O
Haywood. W P, Lions, Ia, R
Hobbs, J C H.1441 G St,Lincoln.Neb
Jackson. Samuel. Oregon
Kemp. Sumner, Alden, Ia

TWELFTH IOWA V. V. INFANTRY.   49

Macy, Seth, Des Moines, Ia
Mann, A J, Perry, Ia
Moore, G W, Maryville, Mo
Miller, Zabina
Mitchell, G W, Lawn Hill, Ia
Parish, William
Reed, G W, Yarkie, Mo
Rulo, G W, South Bend, Ind
Sprague, K S, Fremont, Neb, R
Wilson, T H, Robertson, Ia
Welsh, Nathan
Webb, A E, Eldora, Ia
Zieger, N W

Lefever, Simon, Bolekow, Mo
McPherson, W G
Moore, W W, Manchester, Ia
Mann, Wm, Steamboat Rock, Ia, R
Martin, D S, Iowa Falls, Ia
Richards, William
Runkle, C M, Plankinton, Dak
Richards, Jos, Boone, Ia, R
Sawin, E S, Union, Ia
Walker, Samuel, Dewitt, Mo, R
Wickam, A J, Eagle City, Ia
Zieger, J W, Eldora, Ia

COMPANY B.

Captain Willard C Earle.............................Waukon, Iowa
" Watson R Hanscom.............................. died "
1st Lieut L H Merrill...........died, Montgomery, Ala., May 29, 1862
" J H Borger....................died, Salt Creek Station, Ill.
" J P Jackson....................... Village Creek, Iowa
2d Lieut. J D Cole.......................................Lansing, "
Sergt Maj A J Rodgers..............................St. Paul, Minn
1st Sergt Geo Ibach......................................Preston, Minn
Sergt. J D Spaulding...dead
" Elias Repp ....
" D Harbaugh....................died at Macon, Ga., Oct. 15, 1862
" Henry Fry ....Pennsylvania
" W P Winter.....................................Bancroft, Iowa
" John Upstrom.................403 4th Street, Sioux Falls, S D
" R B Sargent..Kansas
Corp'l H Goodrich................................
" M J Roe....................died at Macon, Ga., Sept 29, 1882
" F E Hancock..............died at Annapolis, Md., Oct 27, 1862
" Stephen Thibeda..Waukon, Iowa
" Robert Wampler..................................
" Aslak Larson.......................................Preston, Minn
" Fred Monk...Eitzen, "
" L D Bearce..Onawa, Iowa
" M Engelhorn...Kansas
" W B Bort..Viroqua, Wis
Wagoner E J White................ ....died at French Creek, Iowa

Wagoner Augustus H West
Adams, O F
Bailey, W F, St Paul, Minn

Brock, Gustavus

Butts, J H, Cherokee, Ia
Barnhart, Amos L.
   died May 4 '64, Memphis, Tenn
Burnham, H
Calico, Geo,died St Louis, Jan 7 '62
Churchill, L B
Decker, Adam, Lansing, Iowa
Dodge, Ansel H, deserted 1861
Dowling, John, French Creek, Ia
Edwards, Isaac
Ericksen, E A, Salem, Dak
Ferguson, B, Akron, Ia

Andrews, H R, West Union, Ia
Bailey, Geo N, St Paul, Minn
Beisel, J B, died Lansing, Ia,
   Feb 25, 1864
Bryant, J L, died Macon,
   Ga., Sept 25, '62
Bathen, Robt, Riceville, Minn
Bort, A K, Viroqua, Wis
Bort, M Jas, died at Lansing, Ia
Burlingame, O D, 193
   South Water St. Chicago, Ill
Candee, Geo
Castellar, Frank
Deeney, Cornelius, died Milwaukee '64, at Soldiers' Home
Dowling, Thos, Rossville, Iowa
Ettle, George, Waukon, Iowa
Feidt, John

Greenap, S H, Motley, Minn
Griffin, Lawrence, deserted
Hawkins, Hiram
Hanson, O, died June 30, '62,
  Atlanta, Ga
Hughes, Jno, died St Louis, Mo
Husted, Jacob M, died July 29,
  1864, Memphis, Tenn
Iverson, Knud, Lansing, Ia
Jones, Henry
King,Chas, d'd Oct 12 '62,Macon,Ga
Knuck, Henry " 10 '62,
Kleven,Sam Aug 24 '62, "
Lene, August, killed, Tupalo,
  Miss, July 15, 1864
Larkins, Rees N
McCabe, Hugh, Waukon, Iowa
McKay, Frank
Miner, Jasper J, died Dec 24, '61
McDonald, James
Noyes, Alonzo
Nye, G F, d'd Nov 6, '63,Lansing,Ia
Ogan, Chas C, Sibley, Ia
Oleson, Barnhart
Peterson, Bore
Patterson, Jas W, died of wounds
  July 24, '64, Memphis, Tenn
Peck, John P, Plankinton, S D
Pratt, M H, Spokane Falls, Wash
Porter, John B
Russell, Chas, Brooklyn, Mo
Sohn, Jno, d'd Dec 21, '62, St Louis
Schiffbauer, Rich
Scott, Jos, d'd Oct 31, '62, St Louis
Stillman, Jno J, killed Feb 13
  '62, Ft Donelson, Tenn
Smith, Ira J
Thayer, Jesse
Woodmansee, Isaac, Rossville, Ia
White, Wm M, died June 30
  '62, Macon, Ga
Winter, Rufus, dead
Walcott, Daniel H, died Nov 23
  '65, Talladega, Ala
Warberg,Ole B,Spring Grove,Min R

Goodykoonts, D F, Boone, Iowa
Greenup, E T, died July 18,
  1864, Memphis, Tenn
Hanson, Jens, died Oct 5, '62,
  Macon, Ga
Huestis, J H, Waterville, Ia
Hannan, Lawrence, died July 28
  1864, Cairo, Ill
Isted, I B S, Milwaukee, Wis, R
Jennings, D P
Johnson, Lewis
Klees, Frank, Rossville, Ia
Knudson, Hans
Lankins, F W, died in Nebraska
Lewis, Edward
Larson, Kensil
Maynard, W M, died Sept 6
  1863, Vicksburg, Miss
McGuire, Brian, Freeport, Ill, R
McClintock, Jas, Rossville, Ia
Mann, Ansel E, dead
Noyes, Chas H, died Aug 7
  1862, Macon, Ga
Oleson, Ole
Oleson, Jno, Spring Grove, Minn
Perry, Edwin R, died Nov 6, '62
  Annapolis, Md
Peck,Ira E, d'd J'y 16, '62,Macon,Ga
Peck,Simon,d'd Sept 24, " "
Plank, Levi, Lake De Funiak, Fla
Pratt, K G, Storm Lake, Ia
Roe, Charles E
Stack,Thos, d'd Jan 11, '62, St Louis
Sjodin, Peter, dead
Stecker, Wm
Stortz, Joseph
Smith, C S, North McGregor, Ia
Sanner, Michael F, Rossville, Ia, R
Thronson, Knud, died June 30
  '62, Atlanta, Ga
Wood, Edwin W
Wood, Stephen
Wilber, Robert
Winter, Francis A, killed July
  14, '64, Tupelo, Miss

NOTE:—Total number of Company, 132; of whom reported dead,
42; disability during service, 30; from wounds, 4; wounded in action,
35; taken prisoners April 6, '62, at Shiloh, Tenn., 56; killed in action, 3.

COMPANY C.

Captain Wm Warner.............died at Memphis, Tenn, Dec 12, 1863
" Geo W Cook, R.......................Medicine Lodge, Kan
" David W Reed (Major 12th Iowa)
  Suite 814, Chamber of Commerce, Chicago, Ill.
" Wm L Henderson.............................Riceville, Iowa
1st Lieut David B Henderson, (Col 46th Iowa)........Dubuque, Iowa
" Henry J Grannis.............................Randalia, Iowa
2d Lieut Aaron M Smith........died at South Bend, Ind, Jan 1, 1883

1st Sergt Jer F Hutchins, (Capt. Co E. 12th Ia)..... Minneapolis, Minn
Sargent Gilbert Hazlett..Allison, Iowa
" Emery Clark, dead..............................Estaline, Dak
" James Stewart...........................West Union, Iowa
" Philo R Woods................................Fayette, Iowa
" Phineas R Ketchum, R.........................Windsor, Iowa
" Frank W Moine.......................Strawberry Point, Iowa
Corporal David Connor..........died of wounds, Nashville, Jan 5, 1865
" Thomas Henderson.............killed at Shiloh, April 6, 1862
" Samuel F Brush............died at Macon, Ga. Oct 31, 1862
" Geo L Durno................................Springville, Iowa
" James Barr, (Ass't Surg 12th Iowa)............Agona, Iowa
" Daniel D Warner............died at Macon, Ga. Sept 10, 1862
" John W Bysong...............................West Point, Neb
" Joseph D Baker................................Montividio, Minn
" Geo E Comstock..............................Manchester, Iowa
" Henry C Curtis................................Lemars, Iowa
" John A Delezene..........................Rock Rapids, Minn
" William H Jordion..............................Cheney, Wash
" Amos K Ketchum.................................Clarion, Iowa
" John E Kent..................................Belle Plaine, Iowa
" I W King...Emerick, Neb
Musician Summer Hartshorn........................Dundee, Musician
Abbott, Edward J, Santa Anna, Cal   Ayers, J L, d'd Macon, Ga, Oct 3, '62
Beck, Samuel C, Waverly, Iowa   Adams, Ed, d'd Fayette, Ia. Dec 20, '71
Ballinger, John W, Lacey, Iowa   Blanchard, S S, died at Pottsville, Ia
Brown, John T   Brown, Albert, re-enlisted in 9th
Brown, Geo, Woodstock, Ill, R   Iowa cav., killed by accident at
Burroughs, Geo A Douglas, Iowa   Hickory Plain, Ark, Dec 24, '64
Barton, Alvah H   Bowers, Wm H, Limestoneville, Pa
Bushnell, Abner C, died at   Baker, Miles, d'd Nov 19, '67, Eden, Ia
    Pueblo, Col. Jan. 1892   Beadle, Henry, d'd Macon, Aug 9, '62
Barr, Henry, Tama county, Iowa   Brown, Addison L, des'ed Selma, Ala
Barnes, Jas. (transfer from 27)   Becktell, David T, Volga City, Ia
Benjamin, Nathan, drafted   Brant, Allen, transfer from 27
Bennefield, Wm, substitute   Fairbanks, Iowa
Chase, T H, d'd St Louis Mar 28, '62 Browsley, Wm, drafted
Connor, Felix   "   Jan 14, '62 Clark, Henry, Melbourne, Ia, R
Connor, Dan'l   "   "   Connor, Sam'l, Maxwell, Ia
Crossman, Silas, died Elgin, Ia   Card, Silas B
                    April 14, 1881 Clawson, Elij. d'd St Louis Jan 10, '62
Carmichael, Jas H, Illyria, Iowa   Carrington, Chas, Mitchell county
Comstock, Frank, St Louis   Canfield, Theron P, 27th Ia.
Davis, Jay C, Wis   Buffalo Grove, Iowa, R
Davis, A J, Berrian Spring, Mich   Delezene, Benj, Republic City, Kan
Dawson, John, 27th Iowa   Forbes, David, Elgin, Ia
Forbes, Wm d'd St Louis Jan 2, '62 Grannis, Geo W, missing at Shi-
George, Henry, died of wounds   loh, never heard from
          M'd City, May 2, '62   Gifford, Simeon, Douglass, Ia
Gillam, Ezekiel D, 27th Iowa   Hood, Al'zo F, d'd St Louis, Jan 31, '62
Hazlett, John B, Sioux Falls, S D Hamlin, Wm A, Crawford, Neb
House, Nathan, died Savannah   Hill, John W
          Tenn, April, 1862   Hill, Benj J
Hendershot, Thos, Plainview, Neb   Henkee, Martin, died at
Henselbecker, Henry, Bluffton, Ia   Memphis, April 17, 1864
Hinkel, Edward, Winfield, Iowa   Hamlin, Lyman S, Oelwein, Ia
Jordon, Isadore L, Alton, Kan   Husted, Jacob M
Jaques, Luther, Crawford, Neb   Henderson, Jas A, 27th Iowa,
Jones, Geo M, drafted   Cherokee, Iowa
Jewell, Jas E, 27th Iowa   Jones, Henry, d'd St Louis Jan 17, '62

Jackway, G H, 27th Ia, Lamont, Ia
Kent, Wm A, Barron, Wis
Lewis, Leroy, d'd St Louis, Jan 3, '63
Lattimer, Geo H, West Gate, Ia
Lyons, Wm A, West Union, Ia
Lott, Lawrence, 1249
    Hempshire St, Quincy, Ill
Mattocks, Jason L, Minneapolis
  " Ross, Wadena, Iowa
McCall, Jno W, Nemaha, Neb

McElvain, Jno, d'd McLeansboro, Ill
Martin, Chas I, 27th, Horton, Ia
Patterson, Samuel W, 27th
Proctor, Geo W, 27th, Lawrens, Ia
Prichet, Jno L, drafted
Quivey, Jno, d'd Oct 4,'62, Macon, Ga
Rodgers, Reuben F, Waucoma, Ia

Rodolph, John J
Spears, Niles H, West Gate, Ia
Smith, Jacob R, Ft Smith, Ks
Smith, Henry C, died May 3,
    '63, Miliken's B'd, La
Stone, Sam'l, d'd Annapolis Oct 3,'62
Sykes, Orvis, Freeport, Ill
Sherbunie, Daniel
Sprowls, John
Tatro, Aug, Clermont, Ia
Verdin, Isaiah, C
Wallace, Chas, died July 9, '63,
    Hospital Boat

Jordon, Daniel M, killed at
    Rockdale, Tex, Nov 10, 1881
Kelley, Artemus
Kelsey, E A, Tripoli, Ia
Lattimer, Robt Z, Fayette, Ia
Larson, Chas, killed Shiloh Apr 6, '62
Little, James
Munger, Albert P, Cowlitz, Wash, R
McCall, Daniel E, Culver, Kan
McIntyre, Thos J, died at
    Vicksburg, Feb 26, '65
Muchmore, Stephen D, 27th
Pendleton, Chas E, killed
    Shiloh, April 6, 1862
Pitts, Jas, drafted, London, Kan
Quivey, Wm W, Pierce, Neb
Russell, Granville, died Feb 17
    '62, St Louis
Rockwell, Wm R, drafted
Simar, Wil'rd E, e'd Macon, Oct 10,'62
Smith, Norton T, killed at
    Vicksburg, May 22, 62
Siegman, Chas, d'd An'apolis Oct 27"
Stone, Dan'l, Waucoma, Iowa
Spears, D H, d'd Sedalia, Nov 12, '64
Strong, John P, Schuyler, Neb
Saulsbury, John, Ivanhoe, Kan
Utter, Albert, Sycamore, Ill
Williams, Rudolph, West Union, Ia
Warner, Walter B, Clermont, Ia
Wait, Van Buren, deserted
    St Louis, April, 1863

COMPANY D.

Roster of the Survivors of Co. D, 12th Regiment Iowa Volunteer Infantry, revised and corrected by Capt. E. B. Soper, Sibley, Iowa:

Col John H Stibbs, room 88, P O building, Chicago, Illinois
Capt Hiel Hale, Yuma, Arizona
Capt E B Soper, Emmetsburg, Ia
Capt John M Clark, Cedar Rapids, Iowa
Lieut Homer C Moorhead, Cedar Rapids, Iowa
Lieut Eli King, Washington, Kan
Lyman M Ayers, Cedar Rapids, Ia
Edwin A Buttolph, Cedar Rapids, Iowa
William Bumgardiner, Scranton, Iowa
Sylvester R Burch, Olathe, Kan
Edwin H Bailey, Freedonia, Kan
Henry W Bailey, Kirkman, Iowa
Allen M Blanchard, No 11 Edward St, No division, Chicago, Ill
Thomas Barr, Shelsburgh, Iowa
John W Burch, Cedar Junction, Johnson county, Kansas
A C Blood

Thomas J Lewis, Cedar Rapids, Ia
William L Lee, P O box 844, Helena, Montana
Bentley Luse, West Liberty, Iowa
Jas H Little, Mt Carmel, Illinois
Richard S Martin
Alpheus H McEntyre
B Frank Morrow, Georgetown, Custer county, Nebraska
O H Maryatt, Del Norte, Rio Grande county, Colorado
David W Minor, Arcata, Humboldt county, California
Nathan G Price, Jewel City, Kan
J V George Price, Mountain Grove, Missouri
Theodore L Prescott
Howard Pangburn, Palouse, Whitman county, Washington
Dennis C Quigley, Plover, Iowa
John W Rowan, Vinton, Iowa
Henry W Ross, Campbell, Franklin county, Nebraska

Angus W Brown
Hiram F Cooper, Littleport, Iowa
Dennis Conley, Davenport, Iowa
Jas L Cowell, Walla Walla, Wash
Charles W Clark, Cedar Rapids, Ia
John M Carson, Grinnell, Iowa
Isaac G Clark
Robert C Cowell, Bayard, Guthrie county, Iowa
James C Daily, Thayer, York county, Nebraska
Ferdinand Dubois, Charter Oak, Iowa
Harmon Elgin, Bolen, Worth county, Iowa
James D Ferner, Nevada, Iowa
Samuel H Flint, care Buffalo Glucose Co, Leavenworth, Kan
Perry Gephart, Lake Forest, Cook county, Illinois
Harmon Grass, 816 Seventh South St, Fargo, North Dakota
Irdill W Hollar, Forestville, Sonoma county, California
Robinson L Johnson, Sanford,
Keya Paha county, Nebraska
John Luther, Norton, Norton county, Kansas
Frank Renchin, Blooming Prairie, Minnesota
Jesse H Ross, Villa Park, Colorado
Dudley E Stedman, Vinton, Iowa
Josiah Scott, Shellsburgh, Iowa
Roswell K Soper, Estherville, Ia
Joseph O Sartwell, Marion, Iowa
Aaron A Steward, Carthage, Missouri
Daniel Sivetts, Sublett, Adair county, Missouri
J M Tarpenning, Northville, Cumberland county, Tenn
Frank D Thompson, Nevada, Ia
William H Trowbridge
William M Ven Emmon, Sioux Falls, South Dakota
John J Whittam
Jasper Wagner, Rome City, Nobles county, Indiana
William W Whiteneck, Waterloo, Iowa
John Watrobek, Cottersville, St Charles county, Missouri
John J Wyatt, O'Clair, Wisconsin
John N Weaver, attorney at law Sioux City Iowa
Byron P Zuver, Adams, Nebraska

DEATHS REPORTED SINCE LAST REUNION.

Francis Curran, died near Marion, Iowa, Oct. 30th, 1890, from old age and general debility.

Nick Clemens, alias Charles Ransom, died in insane asylum at Topeka, Kan., October 7th, 1887, from appoplexy of the brain.

James Galliger, died at Crete, Neb., January 31, 1886, of Bright's disease.

William C. Howard, died at Chelsey, Iowa, January 10th, 1891, of consumption.

James Lannagan, died at Fontanelle, Iowa, February 4th, 1885. Disease unknown.

John B. Lambert, killed by running away of team and being thrown from wagon, in California, early in the seventies.

Allen J. Millett, died November 28th, 1888, at Hastings, Nebraska, apoplexy.

COMPANY E.

Boone, R G. Scott, Ia, R
Beckwith, W H, Parkersburg, Ia
Bird, E, Winterset, Ia, R
Belton, Jas, Batavia, Todd Co, Minn
Cook, Chas, Lester, Ia, R
Crowhurst, Seth J, Salem, Dak
Cook, J P, Ponca, Neb
Coon, H F, d'd Oct '84, Waterloo, Ia
Demoss, Thos, Bristow, Ia
Elwell, John, Chicago, Ill
Early, T M, Bristow, Ia
Biller, A J, Waterloo, Ia
Boylon, Thos, Stockton, Kan
Bird, R L, Yuma, Col.
Collins, C P, Charles City, Iowa
Creighton, David, Geneva, Ia
Cook, Joseph, New Castle, Neb
Cook, Sylvester, Ionia, Neb
Church, Nathan, Webster City or Eagle Grove, Ia
Eberhart, Ben E. Marshalltown, Ia
Graham, Jacob, Davenport, Ia

Hamilton, Wm, La Porte City, Ia
Harrison, H J, Waterloo, Ia
Large, F A, La Porte City, Ia
Margretz, J S, Hittsville, Ia
Minium, David, Big Grove, Ia, R
Perry, A B, Dunkerton, Ia
Rich, J W, Vinton, Ia
Stewart, Joel A, Oregon City, Ore
Seeber, G L, Sabula, Ia
Switzer, C R, Lewis, Ia
Smith, Harvey, Waterloo, Ia
Shumaker, John, " "
Strong, Ezra, National City, Cal
Williams, Capt Robert, Vancouvre, Wash
Hayward, C B, Mooreville, Ia
Jones, John C, Geneva, Ia, dead
Myers, A W, Shell Rock, dead
Morris, C D, Worthing, Dak
Ochs, Charles, Ackley, Iowa
Reed, Zeff, Bard, Louisa Co, Ia
Surfus, C V, Bristow, Ia
Sunderlin, M V B, Janesville, Ia
Schrack, David, Oelwin, Ia
Sharp, Oliver, Finchford, Ia
Sawyer, E, La Porte City, Ia
Shroyer, Nathaniel, Tainter, Ia
Talbot, Allen E, Orleans, Ind
Watkins, Isaac, Crawfordsville, Ind
West, D F, Theon, Wash

COMPANY F.

Ainsworth, J E, 307 Merchants Nat'l B'k B'g, Omaha, Neb
Bremner, John, Yankton, S D
Brown, Eugene, Brush Creek Iowa
Coolidge, F W, Sho Shone, Idaho
Dunham, Abner, Manchester Iowa
Eldridge, J E, Stark, Kansas
Eaton, John J, Edgewood, Iowa
Girton, Joseph S, Hazelton Iowa
Gift, J W, 900 Main St, Peoria, Ill
Halfhill, Josiah, Wood Center, Ia
Kaltenbach, Sam'l, Manchester, Ia
Kent, George, Oelwein, Ia
Kirchner, Mike
Lee, John F, Council Grove, Kan R
Mackey, H F, Maynard, Iowa
McKee, T R, Room 102 Boston Bl'k, Denver, Col
Mann, Wm W, Ranelsburg, Nebraska, R
Nelson, T C, Hazelton, Iowa
Preston, H M, Ft. Dodge, Iowa
Peasley, R H, Kansas
Roe, A J, Burlington, Iowa, dead
Annis, Geo W, Lmark, Illinois
Buckman, Wm H, Dyersville Ia
Correll, Ed, Greeley Iowa
Coolidge, C L, Central City, Neb
Dahl, John A, Silver Creek, Ia, R
Davison, Wm, Siam, Ia, R
Eldridge, R C, Niagara Falls, N Y
French, S M, Denver, Col Room 102, Boston block
Goodel, Wm H, Manchester, Ia
Grice, A J, Doniphon, Neb
Hasbrouck, D H, Prairie Cr'k, Ore, R
Johnson, Isaac, Pleasinton, Kan
Kaltenbach, L P, Gila Bend, Ariz
Kaster, Hiram, Manchester, Ia
Lee, Jas F, Clay Mills, Ia
McGowan, Thos, Independence, Ia
Manning, A L, Dunlap, Ia, R
Manley, R L
Nelson, W A, Hazelton, Ia
Olmstead, H, Independence, Ia
Potter, Jas W, Fayette, Ia
Ralston, Nelson, Canton, S D
Small, H J F, Chicago, Ill

COMPANY G.

C C Tupper, d'd Benton Bar Jan '62
L D Townsley, River Forest, Cook county, Ill
J F Nickerson, d'd in rebel prison
J E Simpson, Norfolk, Neb
A A Burdick, killed at Tupelo
A E Anderson, Decorah, Iowa
O C Thorson, d'd at Eldorado, Ia
R A Gibson, died U S service
J H Womeldorf, Neligh, Neb R
Anderson, A, Albert Lea, Minn
Anderson, A M, d'd wounds rec'd Corinth
G O Hanson, died at Decorah
W L Winsor, Clinton, Mo
T Steen, died at Omaha
A W Erit, died in service
J O Johnson, Hesper, Iowa
N B Burdick, died at Decorah
R Hard
G W Sharp, Fargo, Dakota, R
Andrus, E V, Decorah, Iowa, dead
Aker, D O, Ridgeway, Iowa
Anderson, Peter
Anderson, E
Ballard, Strawder

Brown, J H, died at Decorah
Bowers, A. died in Ohio
Clark, J M
Cutlip, J
Coon, C A, Sabinal, Texas
Carey, A A, died at Castalia, Iowa
Davis, N J, Berrian Springs, Mich
Ellsworth, W D, d'd Benton Barracks
Fuller, A S, Sioux Falls, S Dak
Fuller, A, " "
Gorhamer, O H, d'd St Louis, '63
Gilbert, L, died at Keokuk
Groves, A H, Decorah, Iowa
Hulverson, A, " "
Hall, Giles
Houge, G A, Albert Lea. Minn
Hanson, Hans, Lake Park, Minn
Hanson, Halver, Sheldon, Dak
Jenson, A. d'd Sept '63 in Miss
Johnson, A,d'd Greensville, La, '65
Johnson, N O
Kirkland, G W, Freport, Iowa
Larson. Hover, d'd Savannah. Ten
Larson, John, Lacqui Parle, Minn
Manson, J
Montgomery, Wm V
Madinn. D L
Maloney, J. died in field
Miller, S, Yoyaima Bay, Oregon
McCabe, C, Sherburne. Minn
Nass. G H, Woodside, Iowa
Oleson, O
Oleson, O G, killed at Shiloh
Oleson, J, died at Thoton. Iowa
Pollock, Jos, must'd out at Selma '65
Pierce, Fletcher
Romberg. L O, d'd at Chewalla '64

Ricker, J, died at Savannah, '62
Raucha. Fred, Skidmore. Mo
Smith, I K, Baraboo, Wis. R
Simmons. R. Lake Park, Minn
Staples, C J, d'd at Frankville, Ia
Steen, John, Wahoo, Neb
Steen, Henry Belgrade, Neb
Smith, G M, died at Decorah Iowa
Sernson. S A, killed at Tupelo, '64
Tinke. J
Thompson, A K
Taylor, W H H
Thompson, J B, Speilville, Iowa
Wright, C F
Wheeler, Horace. Algona. Iowa
Wait. W. Nashua. Iowa, R
Wold, L T, d'd at Vicksburg. '63
West. S. Red Cloud. Neb

Crane, John
Crowell, J M
Connolly, C, d'd at Somerville, Mass
Christopherson. C, Hartland, Minn
Dunn, Van R, Dewitt, Nebraska
Engbertson, E, Aastad, Minn
Eastonson. G, d'd at Mound City, Ia
Fladmark, S M M
Green, L D
Gilbertson, O, Gilchrist. Minn
Gulbranson, A, Rothsay. Minn
Honson, Klaus
Hanson. Ole
Hall, Austin. d'd at St. Louis, '63
Helgerson, G, d'd at Nashville. '64
Harris, F W,
Hand, Andrew J.
Johnson, H E. Evansville, Minn
Johnson, Henry, 1st, d'd Huntsville, 62

Johnson, Henry, 2d, d'd Huntsville, 62
Kittleson, C B, Norway Lake. Minn
Kittleson. G
Larson, Peter
Low. Lewis L
McCalley, P, died at Hesper
McLoud. S
Miller, O D. Stuart. Neb, dead
Meyer, C
Meader, M E. Hesper. Iowa
Moe, Peter, Springfield, Minn
Nelson, Swen
Oleson, E
Oleson. Ammon, died at Memphis
Oleson, A H, Egge, S D
Palmer, R. lives in Nebraska
Peterson, N, d'd Camp Woodss. '63
Raucha, Ed
Rocksvold, O P. Thoton, Iowa
Ryerson, F, Ashby. Minn
Skinner, C, d'd '63, steamer Cresent
Skinner, F. Forest City, R
Simmison, Nels
Severson, Nels
Stalim, Lars L. Sioux City, Iowa
Simmons, John, Flandreau, S D
Slattery. Thomas
Thompson. T. Lincoln Center, Kan
Torgenston, M, d'd '65 at Montgomery
Tobiason, Andrew, Windom. Minn
Thoryson, Andrew, Crastad, Minn
Mrs. Jennie Burdick Sturdevant, Spring Valley. Minn
Wiley, Wm, died at St. Louis, '63

COMPANY H.

Atkinson, W L C, Omaha, Neb
Brown, Tom, Jewel City, Kansas, R
Becket, Ed. Dubuque, Iowa
Currie, John G, Butte City, Mon. R
Clark, B A, Colesburg, Iowa
Cox, W H, Blaine, Iowa
Evans, James, Dubuque, Iowa
Fishel, S K, Ft McGinnis, Mon
Franks, Joseph, Lamont, Iowa
Grimes, R M. Kearney Neb
Gosting, Alfred G, Strawberry Pt, Iowa
Hamblin, R E, Arcadia, Ohio
Hamlin, F M, Iowa Falls, Iowa
Jones, David, Monona, Iowa
Kuhnes, J C, Manning, Iowa, R
Light, Robt, Tilden. Neb
Langslon, Aaron I, transferred from
    Co D, 27th Ia to Co D, 12th Ia
McConnell, Alex S, Hopkinton, Iowa
Nauman, Geo, North Platte, Neb
Royse, Wm, Atlantic, Iowa, R
Shorter, James, Shell Rock. Iowa
Sloan, S B, Greeley, Iowa
Winch, Edward, Arena, Wis
Ward, John W, Burlington, Iowa
Struthers, Craig. Neb

Briggs, U I, Marcus. Iowa
Benedict, R W, Blackhawk, S D
Benedict, John W, Lexington, Neb
Crist, John W, Central City, Dak
Crosby, J M, Yankton, S D
Duncan, N E, Custom House, Kansas City,
Fishel, S C. Iowa Falls, Iowa
Fishel, Robert W, Greeley, Iowa
Flenniken, J B, Battle Creek, Neb
Gilmore, A C, Indianapolis, Ind—dead
Horner, Geo, Dubuque, Iowa
Henry, Philip, Greeley, Iowa
Jackson, S M, Lincoln, Neb. R
King, Wilson, Emerick, Neb
Knee, Samuel G, Colesburg, Iowa
Light, Joseph A, Norfolk, Neb
Mason, John S, Worthington, Iowa
Moreland, C D W, Earlville, Iowa
McCune, W H, Ruthven, Iowa
Playter, H J, Washington, D C, 1921
    6th St N W
Smith, Thomas, Turkey River Iowa
Shorter, Wm, Shell Rock, Iowa
Trumble, James, Manchester, Iowa
Wisegarber, Wm, O'Neil City, Neb
Van Anda, John N, Fremont, Neb

COMPANY I.

Roster of survivors of Co. I, 12th Iowa V. V. Infantry, corrected by Judge McCallum, Sibley, Iowa.

Austin, N. E. Andrew, Iowa
Allen, Eugene, Cedar Rapids, Iowa
Austin, Marion, Staplehurst, Neb.
Brintner, Wm. Brayton, Iowa
Brown, J.   Unknown
Butters, John F. Sioux City Iowa
Buchanan, James, Tama, Iowa, R
Belknap, Albert, Scribner, Neb., R
Benhka, Frank, Guttenberg, Iowa
Campbell, E. B. Armstrong Grove, Iowa
Campbell, Thos. Humboldt, Iowa
Cobb, Edgar C. Keokuk, Iowa
Cobb, Wm. A. Walla Walla, Wash.
Coates, J. W. Talcott, S. D.
Crane I. K. Maquoketa, Iowa
Davenport, A. G. Superior, Neb.
Devine, John, Columbus, Ohio
    Care Arcade Hotel
Dupray, Wm. H. Sioux City, Iowa
Eddie, Thomas C. Salina, Kansas, R
Fry, Wm. L. Scranton, Iowa
Goodnow, M. R. Ord, Neb.
Hatfield, Aug. Jersey City, N. J.
Harding, James. Baldwin, Iowa
Hendricks, Wm. Winterset, Iowa
Jenkins, Alonzo, not known.
Johnson, Hans, not known.

Nagle, M D, Dubuque, Iowa
Nims, Weed, Maquoketa, Iowa
O'Niel, Andrew, not known.
Palmer, A L, Seattle, Wash.
Paup, David, Sac City, Iowa
Paup, Seth, not known.
Perkins, J H, Seattle, Wash.
Pasech, Lorenso, Postville. Iowa
Ray, John S, Naponee, Neb.
Reardon, John, not known.
Rolf, Marion, Maquoketa, Iowa
Schoepf, John, died Oct. 24, 1884 at Marysville Kansas
Swank, John, Muscatine, Iowa
Sumbardo, C L, St. Paul, Minn.
Starbuck, Wm, Huffman. Iowa
Smith. Henry, Maquoketa, Iowa
Schmidt, John. not known.
Sherburn, Dan, died at Selma Ala. 1865.
1st Leut. Thompson, Jas L, Franklin, Iowa
Teskey, George, Ellwood, Iowa
Van Hook, Samuel, not known.
Van Duzee, E M (Maj.), St. Paul, Minn.
Wells, Chas A, Sabula, Iowa
Wilson, T, Maquoketa, Iowa
Wilson, J F, Fulton, Iowa

TWELFTH IOWA V. V. INFANTRY.

Kennedy, S L. Cedar Rapids, Iowa
Kohler, Wm. Dubuque, Iowa
Kerns, Peter, Reubens, Kansas
Lewis, Lewis, Home City, Minn.
Lewis, Peter, Lund, Wis.
Markham, W H, Hawkeye, Kan
McKinley, Maquoketa, Iowa
McCarron, W F, Athens, Tenn.
McCallum, D D, Sibley, Iowa
McDermont, Mike, Epworth, Iowa

Williams, S, Atlantic, Iowa
Williams, Sidney, Colfax, Ill.
Wintersteen, Henry, Monmouth, Ill., d'd '84 of disease contracted in Rebel pris.
Weaviness, Mike, not known.

Wood, Joel, not known.
Yeley, George, Clinton, Iowa
Zediker, Jas F (Capt), Lincoln, Neb, care State Journal.

COMPANY K.

Brooks, John
Brown, J J, Bloomington, Neb
Billings, Abram, Luzern, N Y
Barden, Henry A,
Beckner, J M, Charles City, Iowa
Bugbey, S M, 1012 5th St. North Minneapolis, Minn
Church, P, Arborville, Neb
Deutsher, Albert, Nat. Home, Ohio
Freeman, Richard, Spencer, Ohio
Gilchrist, J N, Durham, Iowa
Keith, W B, Precept, Nebraska
Merriam, H C, Nugent, Iowa
Mathis, W R, Omaha, Neb
Morgan, J B, Davenport, Iowa
Mosher, Alvin
McConnell, Alex S, Hopkinton, Iowa
Myers, Joseph A—dead
Robinson, Alonzo, Albion Neb, R
Willard, Porter H, Hopkinton, Iowa

Blood, George W
Billings, Chas D, Bloomington, Neb
Blanchard, Thos, Le Mar, Kansas
Baldwin, Newton, Ada, Kansas
Blanchard, Ira D, Crookston, Minn
Davis, W N, Des Moines, Iowa
Dolley, Godfrey, Hopkinton, Iowa
Ellison, W H, St. Edwards, Neb
Fuller, O T, Webster Grove, Mo
Horn, Samuel, Colesburg, Iowa
Kemp, Wm, Kirwin, Kansas
Merriam, C E, Hopkinton, Iowa
Mathis, E R, Omaha, Neb
Morehouse, P J, Masonville, Iowa
Morgan, Wm B, Bloomington, Neb
Mickey, Isaac, Waukon, Iowa
Phillips, C E, Blair, Neb—dead
Webb, Laurence, Cedar Rapids, Iowa
Waldroff, Henry, La Porte City, Iowa.
Young, A S, Nashua, Iowa

NOTE:—Comrades whose names are followed by the letter "R" have had their mail returned from post office given.

Attention, Comrades!

It is desirable that all changes of post office address and all deaths of members of the regiment be reported to the secretary promptly by any comrade having knowledge of the same, for use in our next reunion and in compiling the next roster.

J. E. SIMPSON, Secretary,
Sept. 24th, 1892. Norfolk, Neb.

FIFTH REUNION

—OF THE—

TWELFTH IOWA

VETERAN VOLUNTEER INFANTRY,

—HELD AT—

SIOUX CITY, IOWA,

OCTOBER 10, 11, 12, 1894.

NORFOLK, NEB.
PRESS OF THE DAILY NEWS.
1894.

Attention, Comrades!

It has been determined that we will send a copy of the proceedings of our last reunion to each surviving comrade whose address we have. And we hope that those who have not already paid membership fees or dues, will remit said dues of one dollar, or send twenty-five cents, the cost of said pamphlet, to the undersigned, treasurer of the association, at Manchester, Iowa. All who signed our by-laws and became members of our association, whose names appear on page — of this book, are entitled to a copy free of charge.

We are anxious that all who can will become members of our society, and if you will send one dollar to the treasurer and direct him to do so, he will inscribe your name on the roll making you a member, and you will be entitled to this book without additional cost. Unless this is done we hope you will send the 25 cents.

Comrades, let us not forget each other. Help a little in the good work. If you know of any comrade who served in our regiment whose name does not appear on our book, or whose address is changed, be kind enough to send his name and address to Abner Dunham, Secretary, Manchester, Iowa.

By order of Executive Comittee.

R. W. TIRRILL, Treasurer,
Manchester, Iowa.

FIFTH REUNION

OF THE

TWELFTH IOWA

Veteran Volunteer Infantry,

—HELD AT—

SIOUX CITY, IOWA,

OCTOBER 10, 11, 12, 1894.

NORFOLK, NEB.
PRESS OF THE DAILY NEWS.
1894.

Yes, again we see the forms and hear the voices of those who finished life's battles and went home long years ago; but I am wandering in the past.

In the living present I see before me men that have traveled many weary miles to attend the Reunion of the Veterans of the gallant Twelfth Iowa Infantry. Year by year the ranks are thinning out, but the members that remain continue to close up and move forward to meet the assaults of Father Time, and the reunions are more highly prized as the years go by. A few years more and this organization must become a thing of the past.

Among those who are permitted to attend this meeting, I note many men of honored name, men who have won fame on the bloody fields of war and on the great battlefield of life.

My friends, the people of Sioux City bid you a most hearty welcome. They have a warm place in their hearts for the veterans who saved the Union. Your comrades of this city who bore an honorable part in the same great conflict from 1861 to 1865, extend to you a comrade's welcome, and you very well know what that implies. It shall be our pleasure to make your stay pleasant and profitable. We owe the Twelfth Iowa a debt of gratitude for their liberal assistance, both in money and service, at the time the great flood swept down upon us a few years since while they were in session in this city.

Even the banquet feast was given up to feed the sufferers. Deeds like that shall ever live.

Representing the city government, I tender you the utmost freedom of the city with all that goes to enhance your pleasure. In fact we are aware that the city is besieged by a veteran army and we surrender unconditionally and cast ourselves upon the mercy of our captors, but before you shall have completed the campaign upon which you have now entered, we shall endeavor to outflank you in a manner that will convince you that we have a wide-awake, progressive people and comrades as true as ever entered the ranks, and that have proven themselves true soldiers in the business of life and efficient at a reunion, camp fire, banquet or any other place that a veteran ought to be found.

We have institutions in our city which we point to with some degree of pride and possibly you may find some of them of interest to you. Have a good time, such as old soldiers know how to have. Ask any comrade or citizen to assist you and you will find them both willing and competent. I hope this reunion will prove so enjoyable that you will ever look back to it as a very bright spot in the journey of life.

One by one we are dropping from the ranks; doubtless some that are here today will fail to respond to roll call at the next reunion of the Twelfth Iowa, but will have answered to the roll call of the Great Commander of earth and heaven and fallen into line with comrades long since mustered out by the shafts of the enemy. Well, soon we shall all be over there and our earthly cares and business will have passed into other and younger hands; but let us fight our battles faithfully and manfully, living true to our God, our fellow men and ourselves, and then we shall have a joyful reunion at the grand review on heaven's eternal camping ground.

In the absence of Major Reed, president, Comrade Weaver, vice-president, introduced Comrade R. W. Tirrill of Manchester, Iowa, who, when the applause that followed Mayor Fletcher's remarks had ceased, took the floor and responded in a beautiful address. After thanking the people of Sioux City for the hospitality extended to the old comrades assembled he paid a beautiful and impressive tribute to the friendship which had existed between them during the long time since they had first met in battle to defend the stars and stripes. There were many of the old comrades whose lips quivered and whose handkerchiefs were used freely to wipe away the tears when Mr. Tirrill reminded them of those who had fought side by side with them and who gave up their lives on the field of battle for the love of their country.

Mr. Tirrill's speech was followed by hearty applause.

J. N. Weaver and J. E. Simpson also made short addresses, after which the meeting adjourned to 7:30 o'clock.

At the close of Comrade Tirrill's response, Comrade Weaver read the following telegram from our beloved President:

Chicago, October 9th, 1894.

Hon. John N. Weaver:—

Notice of my father's death just received. I cannot come.

D. W. REED.

And Comrade Simpson read the following letter:

Chicago, October 9th, 1894.

Friend Simpson:—

In your last letter you remind me that I had said that nothing but sickness or death should keep me away from this reunion. I little thought when I said that that it would be just that alternative which would keep me away.

This morning when I came to the office all ready to take the train for Sioux City I found a letter awaiting me saying that father was very sick. I delayed one train and directed my sister to wire me any changes. At 2 o'clock the sad words came "Father is dead." I go at once to Lansing where he died. You understand the matter fully and must explain to the boys how I desired to meet them again.

I enclose a few memorandas I had made in regard to history, including an estimate for printing. Do as you think best with it. I have Regimental part completed and think it would be of interest, but the times are hard for its publication. Perhaps a committee to devise ways and means would be well. Had I reached Sioux City I would have had manuscript with me.

D. W. REED.

And then bore testimony of the high personal standing and integrity of Father Reed, who he had known since 1856. On motion of Comrade Andrews that a message of condolence and love be sent to Comrade Reed, the following was sent:

Major D. W. Reed, Waukon, Iowa:—
    The Twelfth Iowa sends love and sympathy to you and yours.

SIMPSON,
TIRRILL,
STEEN,
Committee.

Since then the following letter was received from Comrade Reed:

Chicago, November 1st, 1894.

My Dear Simpson:—
    Yours of the 30th ult. just received. The very kind and sympathetic telegram from the Twelfth was received at Waukon, as we returned from the cemetery after laying father away in his final resting place beside mother. I should have been glad to acknowledge its receipts and to have told the boys how highly I appreciated their kind and thoughtful remembrance of me at such a time, but as it was too late to answer then and reach them altogether I must tell them when I see them together again, which I hope to do in 1896.

    I received from you three numbers of Sioux City Journal, October 4th, 5th and 6th, but no paper since nor anything concerning the reunion, except a few words with French, who is now in the city. Am very glad to know that you had such a pleasant meeting. French says the best of all the reunions, so I may congratulate you on its success.

The following message on motion was sent:

Major S. D. Brodtbeck, 113 South Broadway, Los Angeles, Cal.:—
    The old Twelfth Iowa in reunion send love and greetings to you.

SIMPSON,
TIRRILL,
STEEN,
Committee.

On the return home of Comrade Simpson he found a delayed express package, sent to the Regiment, containing a photograph of the dear old Major in full uniform, as we remember him at Camp Union, Dubuque, 1861. Also a beautiful shield—red, white and blue—the work of his own hands. These will be sent to Secretary Dunham for our next reunion. And with the package came this letter:

Los Angeles, Cal., Oct. 2nd, 1894.

My Dear Comrades:—
    On looking over my papers lately I found a daguerreotype, taken at Camp Union, Dubuque, in fall of 1861. It vividly brought back to me many scenes and faces I know are gone, are no more on this earth, and all others as well as mine, bear the imprint of 33 additional years.

    Believing that it may give my comrades of the old Twelfth a pleasing reminiscence of their first acquaintance with me and their first experience of camp life, I herewith send you a copy of said daguerreotype. I regret that I cannot meet you personally this time. My love and regards to you all.

Sincerely your comrade,
S. D. BRODTBECK.

However much we may regret the receipt of these tokens of love and memory in time for our reunion, yet the circumstances goes to show the love we have and thoughtful care for each other so marked among the survivors of the old Twelfth. The dear old Major away off on the distant shores of the Pacific, having only had the regular formal notice sent to him of our reunion, had us in mind; while we in reunion on the banks of the Missouri, were thinking of him and sending him a message of love. God bless him, was the prayer of every comrade present.

On motion of some thoughtful comrade the notes kept at the time fail to show by who a message was sent as follows:

To the Thirty-fifth Iowa Muscatine, Iowa, in Reunion Assembled:—

The Twelfth Iowa in reunion sends greetings.

SIMPSON,
TIRRILL,
STEEN,
Committee.

To which the following response was received:

Muscatine, Iowa, October 11, 1894.

To Secretary Twelfth Iowa Infantry:

The Thirty-fifth Iowa Infantry in reunion assembled at Muscatine returns greeting of Twelfth Iowa Infantry.

R. D. BODMAN,
Secretary.

Major Reed in his letter speaks of certain rough notes and memorandum he encloses. They are inserted here for the information of comrades who will answer them by letter to Reed. A good deal of information on these subjects was drawn out in the informal talk and discussion that took place, in which Comrades McCabe, Butters, Fuller, Meader and Briggs and others took part.

Inquire—

Who was on right flank of the Regiment on the march from Pontotoc to Tuple July 13th?---was captured and escaped.

Name of steamboat to which Regiment was transferred from the Minnehaha, while on way home on Veteran furlough? Did a boat convey Regiment to Davenport?

There were captured at Jackson, Miss., July 11, '63, Q. M. Morrisey, Corpls. Cook, Co. E; Isted. Co. B; Comstock, Co. C; Coolredge, Co. F; Briggs Co. H; Thos. Smith, Co. H. Reports all say: "Q. M. and seven men." Who was the other fellow?

These will be found in the appropriate place in other proceedings.

Comrade Van Anda reported the death of Comrade Gillman about three years ago, also the deaths of Comrades Hunt and Hammond. Comrade Anderson made some remarks on the cause of the division of the Twelfth Iowa on the road from Pontotoc to Tupelo. Comrade Batters explained difference of opinion.

On motion a business meeting was called for first thing after dinner tomorrow. Motion to adjourn until 9 o'clock a. m., the 11th.

Letters were then read from Comrades Williams, Zediker, Barr, Hansen, Grannis, Kent, Millett, Kirkland, Cook, Shoemaker, Morgan, Wisegarber, Duncan, Devine, Hartshorn, Clarkson, Blanchard, Perry, Farpenning, Johnson, Van Eman, Koltenbach, Mrs. Crane and Mrs. Pettitt. On motion of Comrade Fuller that our programme for tomorrow be to call the roll from Co. A on, and that each comrade's wife or child present be requested to respond in five minute speeches, sing a song, or tell a story, or be put out of the room, carried. Motion to adjourn.

Evening session opened with song, "We are Coming Father Abraham," led by Comrade Eldridge with Miss Weaver at the piano. Mr. Hunt sang, "The Drummer Boy of Shiloh," that brought the applause of those present. Then came the sad duty of reading the death notices of comrades since our last reunion.

On meeting the morning of the 11th Comrade Weaver at 9:30 called the reunion to order and the reading of the obituary notices of deceased comrades that appear elsewhere in this report, and the reading of letters from absent comrades was continued. Love feast began and was engaged in by all, being one of the marked features of our last two reunions, all present being convulsed with laughter at some well timed story; and again melted to tears at the recital of some sad scene or striking incident. On the arrival of Comrade D. B. Henderson who was received with cheers and tokens of delight on every hand, a fifteen minute recess was had to shake hands and rejoice together over this happy meeting. During a greater part of the forenoon Comrade Henderson kept the old soldiers in good humor by telling some of his comical war stories. He was requested to speak, and responded with a short but eloquent speech. He was heartily applauded and the comrades were so taken with his words that he was scarcely allowed to conclude. Comrade S. G. Knee read with due and solemn care and emphasis, as if at the front of the regiment he so ably commanded, the following order:

Special Orders }   Head-quarters Dist. West Tenn.,
No. 17.   }   and 3d seperate Brigade Dep't of Tenn.
                    Memphis, Tenn. January 18th, 1866.

5. Quartermaster property to the valuue of Seven Hundred and Twenty (720.00) Dollars, for which Captain C. F. M. Norcross, A. Q. M., is responsible, having been appropriated and used by men of the 12th Iowa Veteran Volunteer Infantry without authority, it is hereby ordered that the amount be assessed upon the officers and men of said regiment and charged against them upon the final Pay Rolls.

Brevet Lieutenant Colonel Knee is charged with the execution of this order.

By Order of Brevet Major General J. E. Smith.

WM. W. M. CAMMON,
Captain & A. A. G.

Comrade Knee explained that, believing the order to be unjust and in error, he pocketed the same and had kept it all these long years, and now presented it for the consideration of the Regiment. On motion the thanks of the Regiment were returned to Comrade Knee for pocketing this order for so long a time and the Quarter Master General requested to go to the D— for his bill. On motion adjourned to 2 p. m.

Called to order by Comrade Weaver at 2:30 p. m. Opened with song, "Marching Through Georgia." Reading letter from Comrade Jack Stibbs explaining his absence. The business meeting opened by Comrade Simpson saying if he could have his way, his advice to the comrades present would be to vote to hold the next reunion at Manchester in 1896, and that they make choice of Abner Dunham secretary, and R. W. Tirrill treasurer, and gave his reason from a business point of view why they should do this. And quoting from his first address at the third reunion at Waterloo in 1888, when urging the next reunion to be held at Sioux City. He said: "We are simply going visiting and then we will come home again, for after our pleasant and happy meetings in 1880 and 1884, Manchester will ever remain as a home to the 12th Iowa." Motion by Comrade Soper that a committee of three be appointed to select officers for the association. Carried. Comrades Soper, Van Auda and Nagle were appointed as such committee. Motion by Comrade Andrews that our next reunion be held at Manchester in 1896, the particular time in said year to be decided by the officers of the association. Carried by a unanimous vote. Committee reported the following named comrades as officers: President, H. C. Curtis; vice-president, John Steen; secretary, Abner Dunham; treasurer, R. W. Tirrill; executive committee, H. J. Grannis, M. D. Nagle and J. E. Eldridge. Report approved and said committee declared elected. On motion the following comrades were appointed a committee on resolutions: Tirrill, Knee and Henry Steen. Comrade Eldridge sang his camp meeting song, "I feel Like, I Feel Like, I Feel," being joined by the whole crowd in a general march around and hand shake, and adjourned to 8 p. m.

The reunion was called to order by Comrade Weaver at 8. p. m., who introduced Comrade Geo. D. Perkins of Sioux City, as chairman of the campfire, and the following is what the Sioux City Journal said of the affair:

The feature of the reunion of the Twelfth Iowa Infantry now being held in this city was the campfire at the armory last night. It was a typical meeting of the veterans, and there was that atmosphere of warm, good feeling, comradship, charity, and all which lingers in the memory of suffering, valor and deeds of patriotism, such as is only to be found in gatherings of this character. The armory was filled, the best people of Sioux City being in the audience, and the campfire proved an occasion so pleasant that it will long be rememberd by those who participated.

About 100 members of the old Twelfth Iowa are in attendance at this reunion, and it is said that not more than 400 of the members of the gallant old regiment are still living. The attendance, therefore, seems a remarkable one, when it is remembered that the veterans, who as boys and young men enlisted in the eastern part of the state, a majority of them in Dubuque, are now scattered all over the country.

The regimental feeling in the Twelfth was strong during the war, and it is strong in the remaining regiment now. This was eloquently shown in the meeting last evening, and war, more than ever to appreciate the bonds of comradship which are welded in camp and field.

The ladies of the W. R. C. were interested visitors. The meeting was called to order shortly after 8 o'clock by Comrade J. N. Weaver. Rev. Marc Darling, Rev C. H. Strickland, Rev. H. D. Jenkins, Geo. D. Perkins and Hon. D. B. Henderson took seats at the right of the president's table. Comrade Weaver in a brief speech called upon Geo. D. Perkins to preside over the meeting. Mr. Perkins arose and welcomed the comrades of the Twelfth Iowa Infantry in substance as follows:

"Comrades of the old Twelth Iowa: I can assure you that I have in my charge the voice of the people of Sioux City to welcome you here and to extend to you one and all the hearty wishes of our people. In the present year of 1894 you can look to the struggles of the battles you have fought and say, as the years are slipping fast away, that you are proud of the fact that you are members of the grand old Twelfth Iowa." After paying a tribute to to the soldiers Mr. Perkins concluded by calling on the vocal talent of the association to sing.

After the "Battle Hymn of the Republic" had been sung, a letter from Maj. Reed was read stating that he was unable to attend the meeting on account of the death of his father. Comrade J. E. Simpson responded with a brief but eloquent speech in response to Mr. Perkins, and was greeted with applause.

Rev. Marc W. Darling on being introduced said this was not the first time that he had been mixed up in a programme of the blue and the gray. He remembered some other occasions which were not so pleasant, and when it was mentioned to him that he should take part in such programme he felt a shiver run down his spinal column. He was not one of those who believed that there is no difference between the blue and the gray, but it was not a difference of conviction nor of courage.

Rev. C. H. Strickland was then introduced as a representative of the other side of the controversy. He mentioned the fact of his entering the army of northern Virginia early in 1861 and remained with it until the federal armies relieved him in 1865. When he first enlisted he remembered to have felt afraid that the federal army would get away before he had a chance to get at it, but before the war had progressed far, he changed his mind. He contended that the confederate soldiers never had any personal feeling against their northern enemies, but were sincere in their beliefs, and showed their sincerity on more than twenty-five battle fields. He recalled the circumstances of his own surrender to the Second Iowa cavalry while that regiment was skirmishing down in the south looking for a man named Jeff Davis. There are some men down south who still want to fight, but they are men who didn't do any fighting the other time. For one, he was thankful that the war had ended as it did.

Rev. H. D. Jenkins spoke briefly, recalling incidents in connection with the war. He remembered a short time ago installing a new minister, and there were gathered around the young man at that time six Presbyterian ministers who were old soldiers. Sometimes in these gatherings he didn't know whether he was attending a Grand Army meeting or a meeting of the presbytery.

Col. D. B. Henderson then addressed "the boys" around the imaginary campfire with caracteristic eloquence, and with that rare depth of feeling which shows the source of the love which his old comrades bear for him. Col. Henderson most touchingly described his search for the graves of his old regiment on the battle field where they fell, and mentioned that when he found the grave of his brother Tom it was the first time he had known where the poor boy's remains lay. Among other things he said:

"War is a terrible thing. The reason we were there was not because we loved our section best, but because we loved the union." He had occasion not long ago to look up some figures pertaining to the war. From 1861 to 1865 the number of soldiers who enlisted was exclusive of reinlistments 2,128,-948. The number enlisted for three years was 2,037,742. The number of officers killed during the war was 4,142, enlisted were 62,916, with a total killed 67,058, while 297,058 died of wounds and disease This brings the total dead from immediate battle causes to 364,116. The total of enlistments in the union army was 2,234,911, the dead 1,054,911, leaving about 1,180,000 still living. There is another statement which tells a sad, sad story. The number admitted to the hospitals from April, 1861, to June 30, 1866, was 5,825,480, and the number of deaths in the confederate prisons was 30,212. Let those who sneer at our pension rolls keep that number in their minds.

"From statistics furnished by the government it is shown that about 27,000 survivors are lined down every year. Let me implore you that the reunions of the future may be reunions of broad minds and warm hearts.

"I don't care for war. The causes that led up to it form a problem that no human mind, however broad, can solve, and I often feel like the man who remarked, in being presented with a pair of twins, that he 'wouldn't take $1,000,000 for the ones he had, but that he wouldn't give a 10-cent piece for another pair.' "

Mr. Henderson was glad, however, to see the wounds healing between the two great sections and that the men who fought under two flags were now uniting under one cause as well as beneath the folds of the stars and stripes. He spoke of the hospitality of the confederate soldier, and remarked that in recent years he had often been thrown into their society. He did not wish his comrades to forget the issues of the war, for they will grow with the passing of the ages; but now that the graves have closed and the smoke of battle has cleared away, the old soldier should teach his children the meaning of the flag.

Col. Henderson related an incident of his experience during the last congress to show the prejudice of some of the democratic members. He said he was astonished to learn one morning that the name of an old Independence, Iowa, soldier whom he had appointed as one of the door keepers of the house, had been dropped from the pay rolls. The man had done brilliant service in the war, and had become too infirm from maimed limbs and ailments brought on from causes begun in the war to work on his farm. Mr. Henderson bethought himself of an experiment. He submitted a bill appointing the old soldier to the position of assistant doorkeeper of the house. I was no sooner read than it was vigorously opposed by an Iowa member who gave as an excuse for his antagonism that the republicans should have nothing whatever with the appointments. The democratic majority in the house was 43, the most of whom were ex-confederates. He went among these urging his claims for the union soldier benefit, and despite the opposition of the Iowan the bill was passed by a majority of eighteen.

He closed by saying that "the reunions of the heart will be all the sweeter and more beneficial when they are also reunions of the mind."

The old camp fire song known as "I Feel Like" was then introduced, and every member of the Twelfth Iowa present "turned in" the chorus with a will, and there was no doubt that it was sung as only soldiers can.

Mrs. Mary A. Widner recited a beautiful piece of her own composition with a patriotic sentiment running through it. When she had finished many a soldier's eye was glistening with as many tears.

Miss Effie Steen, of Lincoln, was introduced by Comrade Simpson for a recitation. "In '61", said Mr. Simpson, "six young Norwegian boys left their log cabin in Winneshiek county and went to the war. Three of them are in their graves, and this young lady is the daughter of one of them—Theodore Steen of Company G, Twelfth Iowa Infantry."

Miss Steen then recited a sweet poem entitled "The Whistling Regiment." Perhaps it was the effective work of the elocutionist, or better still, the thought of the brave man whose daughter she was; but somehow, as the beautiful expressions of the piece were caught by her auditors, there were many weeping eyes ere her work was completed.

Hon H. C. Curtis, of LeMars, made a brief speech. He said, among other things, that as he looked along the line of the illustrious men of other nations he was prouder that he fought under the old flag of our country.

Capt. Lathrop made a little talk and the humor of the boys was at once awakened to its utmost. He remarked that unless one has seen a man scared in battle he has never seen a real live coward. To back his assertion he told about a man who lost no time in getting away when a skirmish began, and when reproved by his superior officer for his conduct broke down, and bawled lustily: "You may talk about flying your flags from the school houses and make all the fuss you want about it, but you will never know what a flag means until you see it in the center of an army—a target for the shell and shot of the enemy who are bent upon cutting it down."

Geo. D. Perkins said the soldiers had acquired steady habits, and among other things that of retiring at a seasonable hour as one of the most commendable. He then stated that the announcements by Comrade Simpson would close the meeting.

Mr. Simpson said that the meeting today would be held at 9 a. m. as a love feast. Companies H, I and K, as well was the staff of the regiment, are yet to hear from.

When Vice-president John N. Weaver called the lovefeast of the Twelfth Iowa Infantry to order yesterday morning, being the closing day of the session, and began by saying that he had been criticised for omitting from Thursday night's programme the prayer by Rev. Dr. Jenkins. "I had rather hear Mr. Jenkins talk for five minutes," he said, "than to hear him pray for two hours."

Then Comrade Simpson arose and said: "My dear comrades, I cannot allow this reunion to close without bearing witness as well as I can, having been in a position to know whereof I talk, to the unselfish, unswerving devotion of our comrade, John N. Weaver, who, as our vice president and resident officer here, has had to carry the load of the work of preparation and arranging for our two reunions—the inability of our president to get here two years ago on account of the great storm—and now kept away by the death of his father, has put on Comrade Weaver the whole load of presiding at both of our reunions. His unfailing courtesy, his watchful care, his unremitting work, early and late, never flagging or halting, the weary miles of walking and hours of anxious care to make our reunions a success, I know have been appreciated fully by you one and all. Brought in contact with him before and after our meetings here I have learned to love and admire the man and bear this most willing testimony to the care and efficiency he has discharged the duties enforced upon him by you and in your behalf say to him 'Well done thou good and faithful servant.' "

Comrade Weaver responded in a few words saying he was glad to have been of service to his comrades towards whom one and all he had the most heartfelt love and respect. If any thing he had done had added to their pleasure and comfort he was fully rewarded for any work or labor done by him, that these two reunions had been pleasant to him, bright spots in life's pathway long to be remembered and treasured by him. Thanking them for the honor conferred on him and the kindness and forbearance shown toward him.

Those comrades who were obliged to leave on account of train time were requested to stand up so comrades could go around and shake hands and say good bye. With many a "God bless you" with tears and hearty hand shakes we bade good bye to several comrades.

Then Comrade John Steen arose and said:
"Mr. President, Ladies and Comrades:
"I accept the position to which I have been elected and most sincerely

thank you for this honor and confidence. As a tribute of respect and gratitude so richly merited, has been paid to our friend and Comrade Judge Weaver, our retiring vice president, by Comrade Simpson, for the excellent manner he has at all times discharged the duties of vice presient of this our beloved association and for the success of this reunion, I desire to move a vote of thanks to our retiring acting secretary, James E. Simpson, for his untiring energy and self-sacrificing devotion to the best interest of every member of the old Twelfth Iowa and the splendid success of this enjoyable gathering. I had the honor as well as pleasure of serving with Comrade Simpson in the war, and know something of the cordial warm-hearted nature, and his dedication to principle, duty and friend, how he forgot self to serve others. I well remember when company G was organized at Decorah, Iowa, in the early fall of 1861, when he might have gone out with the company as its captain, as its first lieutenant, as its second lieutenant. When the election of officers took place, he, with his usual magnanimity of soul, made every nomination from the position of captain down, and himself was satisfied with the position of first sergeant. He was a strict disciplinarian, but just and kind, and to no one does company G owe its debt of gratitude for being able to take its proud position among the splendid companies of our magnificent regiment, more than to our active, generous, noble and brave Simpson.

"Since the war no one of the brave boys of the regiment, save possibly one, have been more honored, and filled positions of greater public trust than he. Having held positions whose hundreds of thousands, yea, millions, of dollars of public funds, passed through his hands and every cent properly accounted for, we love him and we are glad to have him with us today. I am pleased to think that at our reunion at Manchester two years hence, he will be relieved from all burdens as an officer in this association and that he will have an opportunity to visit among his comrades, a pleasure of which he has been deprived at our last two reunions, owing to the active duties devolved upon him during these meetings. I now, Mr. President, take great pleasure in moving by a standing vote that the thanks of our comrades be tendered to Comrade Simpson for his uniform kindness and courtesy to all, for his untiring devotion to duty as the acting secretary of this association, and for the active part he has taken in making this, our fifth reunion, a decided success."

The motion was seconded by Henry Steen with a statement that he most heartily concurred in every word his brother John had said.

On motion of Comrade Tirrill a vote of thanks be extended to Comrade Simpson, amended and accepted, that the remarks of Comrade Steen be reduced to writing and published in our proceedings. Carried by a unanimous rising vote.

Comrade Simpson replied feelingly, and said what he had done had been prompted by feelings of love. His voice trembled as he spoke and tears were in his eyes. All the members of the regiment in the room were on their feet in a moment eager to shake the hand of their fellow, and many there were whose eyes were moistened by tears as they received, perhaps, the last warm hand clasp.

About this time a number of the comrades seemed to be troubled with what has been called at our reunions "lump in the throat," and to relieve the same nothing has been found more efficacious than Comrade Eldridge's song, "I feel like, I feel," and a general handshake all around.

Comrade Andrews, speaking of taking an early train for home, said he was not so old that he could not go half a mile in an hour, and his train did not leave for an hour. His talk was replete with army pleasantries.

Col. S. G. Knee of Colesburg, who was mustered out a commanding officer of the regiment, said he could not make a speech, but he would go home with the memory of the fifth reunion of the Twelfth Iowa in Sioux City as the pleasantest of his life. He closed by reciting James Whitcomb Riley's beautiful poem, "My Trip to Washington."

Comrade W. H. McCune made a short speech, relating anecdotes of army life.

"Bob" Fishel of Greely followed. He said that for the first time in his life he was called by name at the fifth reunion and his hand shaken by members of the regiment whom he did not remember. He said nobody loved his associates better than he loved what was left of the Twelfth Iowa, and he thanked the officers for the courtesies shown him.

Comrade J. A. Light of Norfolk was called upon. He said he could not make a speech, but he intended to meet with the boys every year as long as he lived.

Comrade "Hank" Briggs of Marcus related a funny incident of the war and then returned to the sober side of the soldier's life, and a lump gathered in his throat. He finished by saying he wished he could control his feelings so he could speak like the other boys.

Col. Knee, who was sitting at his elbow, shouted: "A tear on a soldier's cheek is no disgrace."

Comrade Van Anda of Fremont followed with a fund of army reminiscences. He said his thoughts were ever of his dear old comrades, the boys of the Twelfth.

President elect H. C. Curtis, of LeMars, came in at this juncture, and Vice-president Weaver relinquished the chair. Upon taking his seat Mr. Curtis said:

My Comrades and Fellow Citizens:—

I thank you from the bottom of my heart for the high and proud honor you have conferred on me in electing me president of this association, there are many of you who are better qualified than I to serve in this capacity, but I assure you I will do all I can to serve you faithfully my dear old comrades. I would rather be with you and those of your family where I can once more, after a separation of nearly thirty years, look into your honest brave faces and see the men with whom I fought for one flag and one Union for more than four long years, than be where Grover is today. At our next reunion at

Manchester two years hence let us all who are then living be there, and let no comrade fail. And as to our regimental history which is now ready for publication let me say, this should have been done twenty years ago. Let us get right at it and have our deeds of valor plainly printed upon the historic press where our children and our children's children can read it in years to come. And for me I have pledged to Comrade Simpson and Judge Weaver the sum of $100 toward the expenses of so doing. Again I thank you for this high honor.

Mrs. J. A. Van Anda made a patriotic little talk moving the entire party to tears, and her son J. Albert Van Anda recited some beautiful verses.

James Crosby, of Yankton, was wheeled to the front in his carriage. He said he had a speech all prepared last night, but Comrade Van Anda's snoring knocked the whole business out of his head. "I keep a hotel at Yankton," he said, "and a Twelfth Iowa badge is good for a week's board any time."

Comrade W. W. Quivey of Pierce, Neb., stated that this was his first reunion, but he did not propose that it should be the last.

The roll was called down the entire line of the regiment, and army speeches were delivered with the feeling which only a soldier can know. Each speech was brightened by sallies of wit, and the occasion was one of tender good feeling, with sad memories softened by time, and joy promoted by the fellowship of old and dear comrades, with whom every man present realized he cannot have many more meetings of this kind.

Comrade Andrews spoke of the Tupelo raid and the drum he could no longer play. Comrades Campbell, Butters and Dupray spoke well and feelingly, their remarks bringing smiles and tears. Comrade Goodenow telling of sleeping with the body of Comrade Buckner of company A, the first man killed in battle out of the regiment, and never discovering the fact until the next morning. Comrades Kohler and McCallum spoke.

Comrades Campbell, Butters, Dupray, Goodenow A resolution was passed extending the sympathies of every member of the regiment present to Comrade McCallum, who was present, but suffering too much pain to make more than a few remarks. Several of the comrades present bore testimony to the high personal standing and brave loyal service of Comrade Judge McCallum. Vice-President Weaver spoke in terms of the highest regard of him. So also did Comrade Curtis. Comrades Thompson and McDermott spoke. Comrade M. D. Nagle recited that beautiful poem, "Gettysburg." Then Comrades Ray, Bitner, Rev. O. C. Butters, son of Comrade Butters, so well remembered by comrades present two years ago, for his ringing words of burning eloquence, spoke a few words of cheer and love, followed by Comrade Morehouse.

Mrs. John Steen, Comrade Carrington and wife, and Comrade Nelson followed with remarks, when it was resolved that it is the wish of the regiment present that Comrade Nelson be appointed door keeper in the "Celestial City." When on motion we adjourned to 2 p. m.

The afternoon meeting was called to order at 2 p. m., and Temporary

Chairman Weaver introduced Mrs. Hill, widow of Col. H. G. Hill, of the Thirty-fifth Iowa,, who was killed at Nashville. Mrs. Hill came forward and all the members of the Twelfth shook her hand warmly in turn.

Comrade Weaver said there was a movement on foot to place the portrait of Col. Hill on the soldiers' monument to be erected at Des Moines. On motion the following resolution was passed by a unanimous rising vote:

"Resolved, That it is the earnest wish and request of the survivors of the Twelfth Iowa, in reunion here assembled, that the portrait or medallion of Sylvester G. Hill, late colonel of the Thirty-Fifth Iowa, who lost his life while so gallantly leading our brigade at the battle of Nashville, Tenn., be placed upon the Iowa soldiers' monument, to be erected at Des Moines, along with other distinguished and deserving ones who so willingly yielded up their lives that our country might live."

It was then resolved that a printed copy of the resolution be forwarded to Miss Cora B. Weed, secretary of the Iowa Soldiers Monument association at Muscatine.

Comrade Tirrell paid a glowing tribute to the late Samuel J. Kirkwood. He said the grand old man was well remembered as a brilliant soldier, and his cheering words to the solders in the hospitals often made them, in thought at least, well and hopeful.

The following resolution was passed by a standing vote:

"Resolved, That the comrades of this association remember with pride our old war governor, Samuel J. Kirkwood, late deceased, whose inspiring words on the rostrum, as well as in camp and hospital, during the dark days of 1861 to 1865 were a benediction to every Iowa soldier, as well as every true and loyal heart."

The committee on resolutions, composed of the following, Henry Steen, S. G. Knee and R. W. Terrill, reported the following, which were adopted by a standing vote:

"Resolved, That the thanks of this association are due to Mayor Fletcher, the city council, and to Companies H and L, of the Fourth Iowa National Guard, for the free use of their neat and commodious hall and reception room during our three days' session, and especially do we extend our thanks to the city of Sioux City for its generous hospitality so kindly and enthusiastically extended to us through its able mayor.

"Resolved, That this association extend its hearty thanks to Hon. Geo. D. Perkins for the able and efficient manner in which he presided at our enthusiastic 'camp fire' on Thursday evening, and also do we extend our thanks to the Rev. M. W. Darling, sergeant Company K, One Hundred and Fifty-fourth New York infantry so ably representing the 'Blue;' to Rev. C. H. Strickland, late captain Company C, Third Georgia battalion, so ably and graciously representing the 'Gray;' also to Rev. H. D. Jenkins who so completely welded the link that bound the two comrades heart to heart, and in imitation of the spirit of 'our Master' joined in holy wedlock the two great factions rent asunder by a question forever buried beneath the clash of glittering steel and smoke of battle.

"Resolved, That the association appreciates the great effort made by our dear comrade and fellow associate, Col. D. B. Henderson, who, in his crippled condition has met with us and with his usual inspiration filled us with enthusiasm and love commensurate with his great heart. We love to think of him as he is always called, 'the soldiers' friend,' the defender of his character and protector of his rights. We love his cheerful greetings, admire his stalwart, straightforward, manly bearing, and are proud of his achievements in the national congress.

"Resolvd, That the warm sympathy of every comrade of this association is extended to our worthy comrade and efficient president, Maj. D. W. Reed, who, by reason of the death of his father, was prevented from meeting with us at this wonderfully interesting reunion.

"Resolved, That we extend to the members of the grand army post of this city our thanks and high appreciation of their valuable service during our three days' session, such service having contributed materially to our successful reunion.

"Resolved, That the thanks of this association are due to our worthy and able vice-president, John N. Weaver; our efficient and faithful secretary, James E. Simpson, for their untiring efforts and great labor, by them so cheerfully performed, in making this reunion a grand success.

"Resolved, That we extend our hearty thanks to the Sioux City Journal and press of the city for the close attention they have given our meetings and for the voluntary publication of our proceedings."

Love feast contiñued, and Miss Effie Steen, Mrs. Mary A. Simpson, Mrs. Judge Weaver and Miss Weaver made remarks when called upon. Mrs. Col. S. G. Hill returned thanks to the Twelfth Iowa for their resolution. Comrades Crowhurst and Butters spoke, and Comrade Weaver made the suggestion that hereafter when comrades were notified of the time and place of reunion, they notify the secretary that they are coming. This was adopted.

James A. Henderson, of Cherokee, made the final speech of the lovefeast. He said he was not like the boy who ran away from home to go to the army and then ran away from the army to get home; but it wasn't because he didn't want to. Many of us are poor in houses and lands, and many more, God knows, are poor in health; yet, while we may suffer for want of these things, we gave every property owner in the United States a clear title to all he has on earth.

He turned to the humorous side and said that when many sheaves of wheat near the battle field were opened a chicken's head fell out. This was one of the failings of the boys who were forbidden to forage by their superior officer, who at the same time gave them the wink.

He concluded by saying "There are a few people so bankrupt in patriotism as to sneer at some of you as paupers, because you draw pensions. You may be poor in this world's goods, and poor indeed in health, but you ought to feel richer than Croesus, in the thought that you saved millions for others and perfected the title to every foot of land within the confines of this republic. A few people may belittle your worth now, but all the people of all the ages yet to come will do justice to the men who baptized this land in their own blood in the name of liberty and an imperishable union."

He then said on behalf of Col. Henderson that he regretted being unable to attend today and bid them all good bye until the next reunion.

Comrade Hayward of Moville didn't attempt to make a speech, but he said that if the hereafter were to be won by hard fighting the boys of the Twelfth Iowa could push their way clear into the pearly gates.

Comrade Curtis closed the love feast by saying that the next time the Twelfth Iowa held a reunion, and if he were president, he would endeavor to have the meeting place so far away from a horse race that no intimation of such an affair could reach it.

Secretary Simpson read letters of regret from A. H. Groves, of Decorah, Iowa, and B. Frank Morrow, of Georgetown, Neb., and William L. Henderson, of Cresco.

The secretary read reports from various members of the regiment who had been requested to supply a histoy of each individual company, as well as the regiment. Assurance has been recieved that the work is in faithful hands, and an effort will probably be made to issue a book before the next reunion.

President Curtis thought the Twelfth Iowa was behind in the publication of its history. Some of the regiments had their record printed twenty years ago, and to get it started volunteered to contribute $100 to the work.

This offer produced some little discussion, and no definite action was taken.

Comrade E. B. Campbell of Company I, and wife came to Sioux City to attend this reunion. Soon after her arrival she made a misstep, fell and broke her arm. On motion.

"Resolved, That the heartfelt sympathies of all comrades are hereby extended to Comrade Campbell and wife in their affliction, caused by her accident, and trust she will have a speedy recovery."

Comrade French of Denver, closed the meeting with a poem entitled "Only One Flag." The veterans were deeply interested, for it touched a familiar chord in all their hearts. And right here is the proper place to say that much of the interest and success of this reunion is due to Comrade French, not only for his music, but the work he did in keeping the notes of the proceedings and assisting the officials. Weighed down with sorrow and grief at the death of Comrade McKee, brought forth to his mind—by this reunion—with unselfish love he devoted himself, early and late, to the interest of his comrades.

Secretary Simpson read a poem composed by Mrs. Abner Dunham, of Manchester, dedicated "To the Boys of the Twelfth Iowa." It was full of pretty sentiment, and was enthusiastically received.

And so the meeting closed. The "good bys" and "God bless you" were tearfully said, and the warm clasp of the hand told better than words of the love that the fragment of the Twelfth Iowa bear each other.

The following is the account of our reunion as written by Comrade Nagle for the Dubuque Daily Times, October 14, 1894:

The reunion of the Twelfth Iowa, which was held at Sioux City this week, is a thing of the past—only a pleasant memory. It was a complete success in all respects, and to make it such the people of Sioux City contributed their part in an unstinted manner. The address of welcome by Mayor Pierce was full of cordiality and was heartily appreciated by the vets. The response by Comrade Tirrill, of Manchester, was in keeping with his well known reputation as an orator and polished speaker, and it was evident that in his selection for the response no mistake was made. Judge J. N. Weaver of Sioux City, who was a member of Company D, of the Twelfth, and vice-president of the association, presided in the absence of Major Reed, the president, the death of whose father on the day set for the opening of the reunion, prevented his attendance. Judge Weaver delivered a short but highly appropriate address to the veterans, welcoming them to Sioux City and promising them all the attention possible. Time has silvered his locks, but the fire of other days was in his eye as he stood face to face with he men who had gone through scenes of strife and blood with him thirty-three years ago. The reports of the officers and routine business occupied most of the forenoon, and the greater part of Wednesday afternoon was devoted to miscellaneous business. The number registered was ninety-eight, and several of these were accompanied by their wives and children.

At the evening session the names of those who had passed over to the last bivouac were read by a representative of the respective companies and each announcement was followed by eulogistic remarks. A solemn stillness pervaded the hall during the performance of this sad duty, and many were the gray-haired veterans who wiped away a tear. Of the little band of survivors now constituting Company I, death stilled the hearts of two—W. H. Markham and I. K. Crane—two men who left the service with an unblemished record. In all about fifteen had died since the last reunion at Waterloo, and among these was Comrade Hoerner, of this city, who was a member of Company H. Comrade Van Anda, of Nebraska, who served with him, paid a glowing tribute to his memory. Each speaker did likewise for the departed veteran whose demise he anounced; and thus simple but eloquent tribute was paid by those who loved them, to those who went out in their young manhood and fought and died for their country.

Col. Henderson arrived Thursday morning, and an hour later was escorted into the Armory hall, where the veterans were in session. The boys were having a little "experience meeting" at the time, when a "step" different from that which had heretofore been heard in the hall was heard and attracted general attention. On catching sight of the new-comer, Col. Simpson cried out, "Boys, there comes Col. Henderson!" All heads were turned toward the door, and just as the colonel was about to enter the hall the veterans rose en masse and gave such cheers and tigers as had never before been heard in Sioux City from the same number of men. The cheering continued for fully three minutes, during which time the colonel stood in the large doorway, leaning on his crutches, while down his cheeks came the diamonds of love sparkling a responsc to the ovation of the men who idolize him. It was a picture that could not be transferred to canvas because no artist could do it justice. The colonel was then escorted to a seat beside the presiding officer, and after the lumps had left his throat he spoke to the boys for about an hour. He spoke of the gallant record made by the Twelfth. His remarks were in a conversational tone, and as he proceeded he referred to many things in connection with the history of the regiment. At times the boys would feel tears welling up in their eyes, and again they would be cheering as though they were in the charge. The colonel said he knew the veterans would never forget what the preserving the nation meant, and he also knew that they would not fail to teach their children how to be patriotic and liberty-loving men and women. He urged that all the veterans who had wives and children should bring them to the next reunion to be held at Manchester, which was the "mother of the Twelfth."

The afternoon was devoted to expeience meeting, which was highy interesting.

The principal event of the reunion was the campfire Thursday evening. The hall was crowded to its utmots capacity and the number present could not have been less than 2,000, including all the Dubuquers who had come to attend the races. Among these were Sheriff Phillips, Alphonso Matthews, William O'Hern, M. J. Mulgrew, Tom McNear nad Ollie Rhomberg. They knew that the colonel was to be the principal speaker and they let other appointments go in order to be present and hear their distinguished fellow townsman. The program for the evening was a grand one. It included an address of welcome by Congressman George D. Perkins, who was very felicitous in his brief but eloquent remarks; an address on "The Blue," by Rev. Mr. Darling, and another on "The Grey" by Rev. Mr. Strickland, the former serving in a Pennsylvania and the latter in a Georgia regiment. Each spoke in a humorous vein and frequently "brought down the house." Mr. Strickland said that when he enlisted he was in a hurry to get to the front, fearing that the war would end before he could have a chance to annihilate the "Yanks;" but he got to the front, and if he remembered correctly, he was often in "a hurry to get to the rear." He was glad that the war ended as it did. The cause he had battled for had been shown to be wrong, and he was proud now that there was but one flag in this country. He created great merriment by saying that he never hated a "Yank" so badly that he would refused to take the proffered canteen when it contained "spiritual consolation.." Mr. Darling's remarks were frequently interrupted by applause. Rev. Mr. Jenkins, the "chaplain" of the occasion, was introduced and made some happy remarks.

All the speeches were interspersed with music, and after the audience had finished their "March through Georgia," Col. Henderson was introduced.

As he arose to take a seat on the side of a table, the ovation of the afternoon, only on a much larger scale, was repeated. He made an address, and the closest attention was given him throughout. It was not a set speech, but one that was inspired by the occasion and his surroundings. It was in part an eloquent admonition that the principles for which the soldiers had battled must be preserved, if freedom were to be preserved in the nation He spoke of the fraternal feeling that had been so eloquently spoken of by Mr. Strickland, as existing between the old soldiers of both sides, and closed by declaring that the unselfish devotion of the Union soldiers had saved the country.

Following came short speeches by Col. Simpson of Norfolk, Neb., formerly of Dubuque; Hon. H. C. Curtis of Le Mars; John Steen of Wahoo, Neb.; Col. Sam Knee of Colesburg; Judge Weaver; Lieut. Thompson of Franklin, Neb.; Comrade Tirrill of Manchester, and a splendid recitation by Miss Steen of Wahoo, Neb., whose father offered up his life for his country, being as Col. Simpson said, "one of six brothers who left their home near Decorah to fight for the Union," only three of whom came back.

The reunion was a grand success—the veterans made it such themselves, and it will prove to have been one of many pleasant recollections.

The newly elected officers of the association for the ensuing two years are as follows:

President—H. C. Curtis, Le Mars, Ia.

Vice President—John Steen, Wahoo, Neb.

Secretary—Abner Dunham, Manchester, Ia.

Executive Committee—H. J. Grannis, Randalia Ia.; M. D. Nagle, Dubuque; J. E. Eldridge, Stark, Kas.

The officers are ex-officio members of the executive committee.

There were fifteen members of Company I present, as follows: J. L. Thompson, Franklin, Neb.; William Bintner, Brayton, Ia.; David Paup, Sac City, Ia.; J. S. Ray Naponee, Neb.; William Du Pray, Silver City; John F. Butters, Sioux City; D. D. McCallum, Sibley, Ia.; William Fry, Scranton, Ia.; William Koehler, and M. D. Nagle, Dubuque; M B. Goodenow, Burwell, Neb.; E. B. Campbell, Armstrong, Ia.; J. T. Campbell, Humboldt, Ia.; J. W. Coates, Talcott, S. D.; M. McDermott, Epworth, Ia.

Friday afternoon the boys "put up a job" on Sergeant Coates and calling him into an ante-room, where they had assembled, unknown to him, presented him with a gold-headed ebony cane. It bore the inscription "From Company I, Twelfth Iowa, to J. W. C." Sergeant Coates was shot through the lung at the battle of Tupelo, and, with Comrade Koehler, fell into the hands of the enemy and remained in Andersonville about ten months. He was a noble soldier—one who was never found wanting when duty called; and it was with pride and pleasure that the boys present presented him with a very slight token of their esteem.

Col. Simpson, secretary of the association, was one of the principal veterans present, and with the other retiring officers, Major Reed, Judge Weaver and Dr. Barr, did excellent but unrewarded work and aided materially in making the reunion a success.

Comrade Curtis, the new president, is one of the leading citizens of Le Mars, and was a model soldier.

Col. Sam Knee, of Colesburg—one of nature's noblemen—was a conspicuous figure at the reunion. The boys have a great stock of love for Col. Sam; also for Lieut. "Bob" Fishel, who wouldn't be known to the boys if you should call him Robert.

Fife Major French, who said he had done more "blowing" for the regiment than any other man in it, came all the way from Denver to blow the "Girl I Left Behind Me," and other tunes.

"I Feel Like, I Feel Like, I Feel," was admirably rendered by Comrade Eldridge. The hymn has twenty-eight verses made up entirely of "I feel like."

The citizens of Sioux City, the military companies and the retiring officers received votes of thanks.

The Company I boys were sorry that Capt. J. F. Zediker was unable to be present. He was a true soldier.

Comrade H. R. Andrews, who volunteered to go to Andersonville and take care of the wounded, was in attendance. He was a hero.

Capt. Soper will publish a history of Company D and it will be a good one.

A fine poem, dedicated to the Twelfth, was composed and read by Mrs. Capt. Dunham.

Hurrah for Manchester in 1896!

The parting scenes at the close of the reunion were sad, and tears glistened in the eyes of the old Boys in Blue as they bade one another good-bye---some never to meet again on earth. With bowed heads the veterans left---some toward the setting sun, some toward the frozen north; more in the direction where smiles the God of day, and more where the soft southern zephyrs kiss the diamond dew drops from the heart of the rose.

The following is the verses written by Mrs. Abner Dunham of Manchester as read at the reunion. On motion of Comrade Steen a vote of thansks was returned to Mrs. Dunham, and the verses to appear in our proceedings:

TO THE TWELFTH IOWA.

O, comrades true, who wore the blue,
  Again we greet you here;
And yet our thoughts go wandering back,
  Far back full many a year.
Once more we're in the jolly camp,
  And voices swell with song,
The jest goes round, the laugh rings out,
  Each comrade bears along
His part of story, song or jest,
  And fun and frolic reign,
So we forget the weary days
  And we are boys again.

Again we're on the battle field
  With comrades falling fast;
We've only time to give a sign
  And we go rushing past.
We glad would stay to soothe their pain
  And close the glazing eye,
To fold the hands o'er loving breast
  And give the last good bye,

Bear from them still some message dear,
  Some token of their love;
Yet we can only leave them there
  With their just God above.

And now we're on the weary march
  With tired feet and sore,
We plod along through dust and mud,
  And wish the war was o'er;
Then some one starts some good old song
  And steps grow quick and fast;
Our every heart throb keeps the time;
  The march is o'er at last.
The fires are built, the canteen filled,
  And each one bears a hand;
No loiterers now around the camp
  When supper must be planned.

We stretch our limbs and try to rest,
  Our brains are busy still;
With home and all the loved ones there
  Thoughts will not stop at will.
We're just a great big homesick boy,
  Our hearts are grieved and sore---
Some want a sister, mother, wife
  And some a sweetheart more.

We brush a hand across our eyes
  And heave a heavy sigh;
We wish for once we were a girl---
  Then we would dare to cry.
But tired at last, our eyelids close,
  And dreams come stealing o'er.
The war is done and joyful news,
  We're home again once more;
We sleep and rest and dream fond dreams,
  Forget the weary days.
We're happy children now at home---
  That home so far away.

Now, comrades, comes another scene,
  We're standing by the bed
Of some loved comrade true and brave,
  Who ere the morn lies dead.
We hear the last fond good-bye,
  The little keep-sakes given,
The soul of one so pure and good
  Has winged its flight to heaven.

Poor, homesick boy, so loved and lost,
    Some hearts will bleed today,
For this dear husband, father, son,
    Or lover dead today.
O! War so cruel, price so dear,
    That's paid to blot the sin
Of treason, foul and traitorous name,
    And Union still to win.
They paid the debt that made all free,
    The black as well as white,
They washed in blood our royal flag
    And wiped out treasons blight.

O'er all the land our flag still waves,
    The red, the white, the blue;
No land more free, no laws more just,
    Saved by our boys so true,
And once again while hand grasps hand
    And hearts are full of praise,
We feel the old joy stealing back---
    The love of other days.

Mrs. M. A. Widner of Leeds, Iowa, who in war times was a Winneshiek county girl at Hesper, Iowa, read the following verses of her own composition. They were listened to with pleasure and received with applause. She was heartily thanked by the comrades:

OUR GREY-HAIRED BOYS IN BLUE.

Oh! Grey-haired boys who donned the blue
    So many years ago,
And marched away from life and love
    To free the southern foe.

And after long, long toil and pain
    In home and country borne,
Come halting back with death-thinned ranks
    And bodies maimed and torn.

Oh boys in blue, we welcomed you
    With glory's crown of bay,
And tidal waves of gratitude
    Broke at your feet that day.

The twice freed land your valor won,
    Her honor pledged to you,
That to her war worn, suffering sons
    She would give succor true.

But years have come and gone, and you
    With weary step and slow,

Have taken up your last long march
　To meet life's latest foe.

But, brothers, in your shortening lives,
　Oppressed with many cares,
You stand, in honor, far above
　Proud statecraft's millionaires.

Who, holding that high place and power,
　Made possible by you
And built upon your brothers graves
　Find naught that they can do.

More pleasing than, like moles to delve,
　Mid records old and gray,
That, happily they may filch from you
　Your forty cents a day.

But if to you their niggard act
　Long poverty assures,
Let them to their golden millions clasp,
　A million hearts are yours.

For Columbia's loyal daughters,
　Still to their colors true,
Love honor, and the boys
　Who wore the army blue.

　　The following is the memorandum spoken of by Major Read in his letter published elsewhere, that he was going to bring to the reunion and make arrangements about, and had to send to the secretary. There was more or less talk by comrades about the publishing our regimental history. All were in favor of having it done, but thought the times were too hard and close to try to raise the means now. Comrade Soper declared his intention to publish the history of Company D as prepared by him if he had to do it at his own expense. Comrade Curtis said he would respond to a draft for $100 any time he was called upon to help pay for the regimental history. The whole subject was laid over to the next reunion.

　　To complete regimental history wanted the company histories from:
Company A--No provisions.
Company D---Partly furnished.
Company F---Promised by Dunham.
Company I---Promised by Coates.
Company K---Promised by Merriam.
Personal sketches:
Maj. E. M. Van Duzee---Likely get it with Company .
Lieut. Col. Coulter---Promised by Mills.
Lieut. Col. Knee.
Dr. Finlay.
Q. M. H. C. Morehead---Likely get it with Company D.

The committee on regimental history request of every surviving member of the rgeiment that each comrade shall for himself examine the published reports of the adjutant general of Iowa for years 1863 to 1866, inclusive, as to his own personal record of enlistment, re-enlistment and casualities; and also the roster as published at our last reunion, and report by letter to D. W. Reed, 814 Chamber of Commerce, Chicago, Illinois. Every error or omission of any kind that you find in your own record, or that of any comrade, even to mispelling of a name, giving full particulars. Be sure you are right before making report.

The adjutant general's reports are to be seen in each court house in Iowa, and most of public libraries.

Chicago, Oct. 9th, 1894.

D. W. Reed, Esq., City---Dear Sir: We will do the composition of a "Regimental History," size of type page $37_8 \times 67_8$, in brevier type, and furnish you 800 copies, 700 pages, printed in black ink on 25x38, 50-pound, S. & C. tint paper, like enclosed sample and bind in cloth, plain edges, No. 25 beveled boards, enameled end sheets, one leaf xx gold stamped on back, not headbanded, size of trimmed page 6x9, 800 copies for $1,200.00.; 1,000 copies, $1,260.00.

In the above you are to furnish stamp for back cover, or we will furnish same and charge you extra cost, which will be but a few dollars.

Hoping to be favored with your order, which will receive prompt and careful attention, we remain Yours very truly,

W. B. CONKEY COMPANY.

Members and Visitors.

List of comrades and relatives registered at the Fifth Reunion of the Twelfth Iowa Veteran Volunteer Infantry:

Thos. H. Wilson	Company A	Robertson, Iowa.
I. H. Bowers	Company A	Eldora, Iowa.
C. M. Runkle	Company A	Plankinton, South Dakota.
Sumner Kemp	Company A	Alden, Iowa.
W. P. Winter	Company B	Bancroft, Iowa.
Thos. Dowling	Company B	Rossville, Iowa.
Frank Klees	Company B	Rossville, Iowa.
Robert Wampler	Company B	Waukon, Iowa.
John Dowling	Company B	Rex, Iowa.
Hugh McCabe	Company B	Waukon, Iowa.
H. R. Andrews	Company B	Turkey River, Iowa.
John D. Cole	Company B	Lansing, Iowa.
Mrs. John D. Cole		Lansing, Iowa.
L. D. Bearce	Company B	Onawa, Iowa.
G. Hazlet	Company C	Allison, Iowa.
I. W. King	Company C	Emerick, Nebraska.
J. W. Ballinger	Company C	Lacey, Iowa.
J. W. Bysong	Company C	West Point, Nebraska.
Mrs. J. W. Bysong		West Point, Nebraska.
Miss Anna Bysong		West Point, Nebraska.
Miss Adelia Bysong		West Point, Nebraska.
Thos. Hendershot	Company C	Plainview, Nebraska.
H. C. Curtis	Company C	LeMars, Iowa.
D. B. Henderson	Company C	Dubuque, Iowa.
W. W. Quivey	Company C	Pierce, Nebraska.
Chas. Carrington	Company C	Rock Branch, Iowa.
Mrs. Chas Carrington		Rock Branch, Iowa.
J. A. Henderson	Company C	Cherokee, Iowa.
Herman Ellgin	Company D	Bolen, Iowa.
H. W. Bailey	Company D	Manning, Iowa.
Jno. N. Weaver	Company D	Sioux City, Iowa.
Mrs. M. M. Weaver		Sioux City, Iowa.
Miss Daisy Weaver		Sioux City, Iowa.
Miss Kate Weaver		Sioux City, Iowa.
Mrs. Flora (Weaver) Ashford		Winnebago, Nebraska.
Ferd. Dubois	Company D	Charter Oak, Iowa.
Mrs. S. C. Dubois		Charter Oak, Iowa.
William Bumgardner	Company D	Scranton, Iowa.
J. W. Rowan	Company D	Vinton, Iowa.

M. H. McElroy	Company D	Percival, Iowa.
E. B. Soper	Company D	Emmetsburg, Iowa.
R. K. Soper	Company D	Estherville, Iowa.
Mrs R. K. Soper		Estherville, Iowa.
C. V. Surfus	Company E	Bristow, Iowa.
David Creighton	Company E	Geneva, Iowa.
J. S. Margretz	Company E	Hittsville, Iowa.
C. B. Hayward	Company E	Mooreville, Iowa.
Sylvester Cook	Company E	New Castle, Nebraska.
R. E. Cook, (Son)		New Castle, Nebraska.
R. L. Bird	Company E	Hampton, Iowa.
S. J. Crowhurst	Company E	Salem, South Dakota.
C. D. Morris	Company E	Canton, South Dakota.
Mrs. C. D. Morris		Canton, South Dakota.
R. W. Tirrell	Company F	Manchester, Iowa.
Mrs. R. W. Tirrell		Manchester, Iowa.
Thos. McGowan	Company F	Independence, Iowa.
F. W. Coolidge	Company F	Sho Shone, Idaho.
Mrs. F. W. Coolidge		Sho Shone, Idaho.
Nelson Ralston	Company F	Canton, South Dakota.
Joshua Widger	Company F	Manchester, Iowa.
L. C. Bush	Company F	Kalona, Iowa.
Ed Correll	Company F	Greeley, Iowa.
J. E. Eldridge	Company F	Stark, Kansas.
S. M. French	Company F	Denver, Colorado.
John Bremner	Company F	Yankton, South Dakota.
W. A. Nelson	Company F	Hazelton, Iowa.
J. E. Simpson	Company G	Norfolk, Nebraska.
Mrs. Mary A. Simpson		Norfolk, Nebraska.
O. P. Rocksvold	Company G	Thonton, Iowa.
Mrs. A. O. Anderson (daughter)		Inwood, Iowa.
A. O. Anderson		Inwood, Iowa.
M. E. Meader		Hesper, Iowa.
Mrs. Louisa Meader	Company	Hesper, Iowa.
A. S. Fuller	Company G	Maryville, Missouri.
John Steen	Company G	Wahoo, Nebraska.
Mrs. John Steen		Wahoo, Nebraska.
Miss Effie Steen		Lincoln, Nebraska.
Lars L. Stalim	Company G	Sioux City, Nebraska.
A. E. Anderson	Company G	Decorah, Iowa
John Simmons	Company G	Flandreau, South Dakota.
Henry Steen	Company G	Lyons, Nebraska
Mrs. Henry Steen		Lyons, Nebraska.
G. H. Ness	Company G	Washington Prairie, Iowa.
W. H. McCune	Company H	Ruthvan, Iowa.
R. W. Fishel	Company H	Greeley, Iowa.
R. E. Hamblin and Son	Company H	Findley, Ohio.
J. A. Light	Company H	Norfolk, Nebraska.
J. B. Flenniken	Company H	Battle Creek, Nebraska.
David Jones	Company H	Taconie, Iowa.
J. R. Shorter	Company H	Shell Rock, Iowa.
H. S. Briggs	Company H	Marcus, Iowa.
J. N. Van Anda	Company H	Fremont, Nebraska.
Mrs. J. N. Van Anda		Fremont, Nebraska.
J. Albert Van Anda		Fremont, Nebraska.

Mrs. J. R. Shorter...Shell Rock, Iowa.
W. H. Cox ....Company H.......................Alta, Iowa.
J. M. Crosby.................Company H............Yankton, South Dakota.
Mrs. J. M. Crosby.......................................Yankton, South Dakota.
Agnes Briggs ....Marcus, Iowa.
S. G. Knee..................Company H................Colesburg, Iowa.

E. B. Campbell.............Company I..................Armstrong, Iowa.
John F. Butters............Company I..................Sioux City, Iowa.
Rev. O. P. Butters..Sioux City, Iowa.
Miss Stella Butters...Sioux City, Iowa.
Mrs. Elsie (Butters) Faulkner ....Sioux City, Iowa.
Mrs. Annie (Butters) Thomley...............................Sioux City, Iowa.
W. H. Dupray..............Comany I..................Sioux City, Iowa.
Mrs. Charlotte Cuyley ....Sumner, Washington.
M. B. Goodenow............Company I...................Ord, Nebraska.
J. W. Cates................Company I...........Talcott, South Dakota.
W. L. Fry..................Company I..................Scranton, Iowa.
J. T. Campbell ....Company I....................Unique, Iowa.
D. A. Paup.................Company I..................Sac City, Iowa.
Wm. Koehler...............Company I..................Dubuque, Iowa.
D. D. McCallum............Company I....................Sibley, Iowa.
Jas. L. Thompson..........Company I..............Franklin, Nebraska.
Mike McDermott............Company I..................Epworth, Iowa.
M. D. Nagle...............Company I.................Dubuque, Iowa.
J. S. Ray, 10 in family...Company I.............Naponee, Nebraska.
Wm. Brinter...............Company I..................Brayton, Iowa.

P. J. Moorehouse..........Company K..................Masonville, Iowa.

VISITORS.

W. F. Ramsey, Co. I, 2nd Iowa Cavalry.
S. P. Adams, Co. C., 45th Illinois Infantry.
W. F. Scott, Co. I, 9th Cavalry.
Alex. Crassan, Co. C., 8th Ohio Infantry.
James Leith, Co. I, 18th Wisconsin Infantry.
O. P. Welding, Co. K, 17th Illinois Infantry.
Geo. Hann, Co. M, 2nd Iowa Cavalry.
James Jackson, Co. K, 21st Iowa Infantry.
D. J. Spencer, Co. G, 5th Wisconsin Volunteers.
H. W. Chase, Co. H, 96th New York Volunteers.
T. C. Prescott, Co. H, New Hampshire Infantry.
H. D. Jenkins, Co. A, 35th P. V. M. ——(?.)
Marcia M. Lothrop, Sioux City, Iowa.
Mrs. J. R. Haines, W. R. C. No. 9, Marshalltown, Iowa.
Mrs. Carrie Arge, Sioux City, Iowa.
Mrs. Martha Weaver, Sioux City, Iowa.
Mrs. Laurena Leitch, Sioux City, Iowa.
Mrs. Mary A. Adams, Leeds, Iowa.
W. H. McFarland, Co. P, 5th Wisconsin ——(?.)
Theo. C. Wather, Co. I, 1st O. V. L. A.
Geo. W. Wakefield, Co. F, 41st Illinois Volunteers.
Geo. D. Perkins, Co. B, 31st Iowa Infantry.
Mrs. A. Bassett, Sioux City, Iowa.
Joseph E. Spencer, Co. H, 33rd Illinois Veteran Volunteer Infantry.

Mustered Out.

Now comes the sad and painful duty of making a record of those of our dear comrades who have passed over the river and gone to their home since our last reunion. Here is what the loving pen of Comrade Clarkson says in the Des Moines Register of

COMRADE MYRON UNDERWOOD:

Dr. Myron Underwood, of Eldora, was found dead in his bed last Sunday morning. We have had over a third of a century's personal acquaintance with Dr. Underwood, and the notice of his sudden death touched a tender chord in a heart and memory that have so many friends on the other shore. He was a leading physician, surgeon and citizen of north central Iowa. He came to Hardin county as a young physician seeking a location, some thirty-five years ago. Soon afterward he was appointed the assistant surgeon of the Twelfth Iowa Infantry, a position he filled with a capability and fidelity that made him one of the most popular surgeons in the army, and afterwards in the state. At the close of the war he returned to Eldora. He was elected state senator from Hardin and Grundy counties in 1885, to fill the vacancy caused by the death of Lieut. Gov. Eastman, and rendered faithful and efficient service to his constituents and the state, but refused to accept further political honors on the ground that his patients had the first right to his services.

Dr. Underwood was still a young man, but his health had been impaired by nearly four years of hard service and privations in the army, and by the exposure to all kinds of weather physicians are compelled to endure who are called to ride or drive over the country at all hours of the day and night for over a third of a century. He was faithful and sympathetic with his patients, and considered it his duty to go wherever and whenever called. We knew him best as the assistant surgeon of the Twelfth Iowa infantry, where his knowledge and skill should have the credit of saving the lives and easing the pains and sufferings of many comrades. He took great pride in the regiment and had a personal acquaintance with every member. Flag Day was an inspiration to him and he hoped to be here on that interesting occasion. A comrade reported last week that he would not have to come to Des Moines if Dr. Underwood had not urged him to come, and he was surprised on arrival to find that the doctor was not present. The doctor was probably not feeling well enough to come himself, but bravely refrained from making any mention of his illness while urging other comrades to attend. So they go. Every day and nearly every hour calls some Iowa veteran to join the comrades gone on before, but they cross the river of life bravely and meet the future with all the heroism in which they dared death in the rain of shot and shell in 1861-65.

Eldora, Aug. 13.—Special: Dr. Myron Underwood, a leading physician and prominent citizen of this county, was found dead in his bed yesterday morning at 8 o'clock, having expired during the night of heart disease. The doctor was county coroner several years ago and it was in this capacity that he secured the ill will of the notorious Rainsbarger gang and was shot at by them and his life threatened. He was instrumental in exterminating the gang and became noted in his fight against law breakers. He represented Hardin and Grundy counties in the state senate in 1886, filling out the unexpired term of the late Governor Eastman.

Dr. Underwood was a prominent citizen, whose loss was not confined to Hardin county alone. His professional life was a constant devotion to duty and no call at his door for assistance, whether made by the rich man or the penniless beggar, was ever left unanswered. He was a man of untiring energy, prominent in all works of charity and the upbuilding of town and county. In his death Eldora loses a worthy citizen, humanity a friend, his family a father ever kind and indulgent. A widow and five children are left to mourn his loss.

Myron Underwood was born at Montville, Geauga county, Ohio, Aug. 7, 1833, where he lived until he was 12 years of age, when he moved with his parents, Jonas and Mary Underwood, to McHenry county, Ill. His literary education was received in common schools and at Mount Morris, Ill. He began the study of medicine with Dr. Hager of Marengo, Ill., in 1855. In May, 1859, he came to Hardin county, locating first at Steamboat Rock, moving to Eldora in July, 1860. In the first dark days of civil strife he considered it a duty to offer his services in defense of the flag. He was commissioned as assistant surgeon of the Twelfth Iowa Infantry serving until final discharge in Oct., 1865. He was united in marriage in 1861 to Miss Sophia A., daughter of John Ellis, who located in this county in 1856.

COMRADE D. V. ELLSWORTH.

Eldora (Ia.) Ledger, Nov. 24.—The remains of D. V. Ellsworth, formerly of this city, but lately of Newman Grove, Nebraska, arrived here on last Friday night, accompanied by relatives and friends, where the body lay in state until Sunday at 2 p. m., when it was taken to the Congregational church, where the funeral services were conducted under the auspices of Edward C. Buckner Post, G. A. R., of which order he was a member, led by Rev. E. Kent, of that church. The services were impressive and had a tendency to bring to memory many scenes of the long ago. After services at the church the remains were taken to the cemetery east of town, and there laid to rest by the former comrades in arms.

At a regular meeting of Emerick Post No. 313, Department of Nebraska,

G. A. R., the following preamble and resolution were adopted by an unanimous vote of the Post:

"Whereas, It has pleased the Great Commander of the Universe to call from our midst into the grand encampment over the river our esteemed comrade, D. V. Ellsworth,

"Therefore, Be it resolved that in the departure of Comrade Ellsworth we are called upon to mourn the loss of an energetic and useful citizen, a kind neighbor, a faithful and indulgent husband and father, a true and genial comrade, ever ready to champion the cause of a fellow comrade in distress, and a brave, noble and persistent defender of our country in her time of need.

"Resolved, That we extend our heartfelt sympathy to his bereaved wife and his now fatherless children. May God keep them and bless them is the prayer of the remaining members of Emerick Post No. 313, Department of Nebraska." J. H. SWEITZER,
HENRY NYE, S. V. C., Adjutant.
Acting P. C.

Thus has passed away a brave soldier, a good citizen, an honest man, a loving husband and kind and indulgent father. When I say that he will be missed I fail to express the sense of loss that his family and the community at large has sustained.

Deceased was born May 23, 1840, in Potter county, Pennsylvania, the fourth child of a family of six children. He removed with his parents to Eldora, Iowa, in 1854, where his father still lives hale and hearty at the age of 82 years. In the fall of 1861 he enlisted as a private in Co. A, 12th Reg't., Iowa Volunteers, and was honorably discharged and mustered out as first lieutenant of same company and regiment after a service of three years, three months and 23 days. Jan. 16th, 1865, he was married to Saloma Bowman, who, with three children the fruit of such marriage, still survive him. From the time of his marriage in 1865 until May, 1887, he lived in Eldora and vicinity and successfully farmed, was railway conductor, revenue assessor and druggist. In May, 1887, he moved with his family to Newman Grove, Nebraska, where he engaged in the law business, in which he was actively engaged at the time he was taken with his last illness. About three weeks ago he was taken with chills and although he kept about his business for a day or two he was finally obliged to give up and take to his bed. At this time an old kidney trouble, which had bothered him at times while in the service, set in and blood poisoning ensued, from which he could not rally.

Deceased was a member of Emerick Post, G. A. R., and also of Newman Grove Camp No. 1,513, M. W. A., and both organizations did all that could be done to soothe his dying bed and comfort his afflicted family. The remains were taken to Eldora, Iowa, for interment after service under the auspices of the G. A. R. and M. W. A. at this place.

Rev. W. E. Kimball of Madison delivered an appropriate and touching address, after which the two societies and his old neighbors and friends bore him to the train and we bade a final farewell to the mortal part of D. V. Ellsworth.

As a business partner and neighbor I knew deceased well during the last six years of his life and I am glad to be able to testify to his kindness of heart, his unbounded generosity, undaunted courage and persevering industry. As a lawyer he was energetic and honest, as a neighbor he was accommodating and considerate, as a parent he was indulgent and kind, as a husband faithful and affectionate. His bereaved family have the heartfelt sympathy of the entire neighborhood and while we join them in mourning their bereavement as our common loss we console ourselves with the thought that he is at rest.

W. T. S.

Daniel V. Ellsworth's home at Newman Grove, Neb.

A TRIBUTE TO MY ABSENT FRIEND.

(By J. B. Long Madison, Neb.)

Dan Ellsworth's gone! he rests in peace
   Within his dark and narrow grave,
But honors to his name won't cease
   While homes are blest he helped to save;
He was a soldier true and brave
And member of the G. A. R.,
Not one more kindly did behave
Than he to comrades since the war

But now he is removed too far
   Beyond the reach of friendship's tie;
Nor sun, nor moon, nor distant star,
   Will shed their light to guide his eye;
What pity 'tis that some to die
And absence veils their pleasant face,
While those who knew them grieve and sigh
Beause none else can fill their place.

Ellsworth, my friend! if I could trace
   The heaven where spirits live in bliss,
Or know that endless time and space
   Were occupied by souls we miss,—
As I have heard the bullets hiss
And dared grim death in days of yore,
I might resign a scene like this
To be near thee forever more.

The following names of members of Company B were handed in at our reunion who had died, and since our last meeting no additional information has been received up to time of going to press:

J. H. Huestis, died at Waterville, Iowa, 1894.

Bradner Ferguson, died at Soldiers' Home, Marshalltown, 1894.

Charles Ogan, died in California some years ago.

COMRADE B. P. ZUVER.

Byron P. Zuver died at his residence in Adams, March 1, 1893. Death resulted from a complication of lung and brain trouble resulting from la grippe. Solomon Zuver and Julia Ann Kerns, who were married in Wayne county, Ohio, in 1839, were the parents of five children, of whom Byron P. Zuver was the eldest, and all of whom are now dead with the exception of our esteemed citizen Geo. W. Zuver.

Mr. B. P. Zuver was born Nov. 8th, 1840, in Wayne county, Ohio, thus making his age at the time of his death 52 years, 4 months and 13 days.

After the removal of the family to Iowa, he attended the common schools and finished his school education at Western college, in Linn county, Iowa. He was the possessor of an active mind, which he continued to develop.

He had been a member of the county board of supervisors, held numerous other offices and had been for a number of years a member of the school board. At the time of his death and for a number of years, he had been one of the most efficient postal clerks in his division. In all of these positions his faithful services were a credit to him.

He enlisted in Company D, 12th Iowa Infantry, being the first to enlist from his county. His army record is long and honorable, being in the service 4 years and 8 months. He was in the battles of Shiloh, Fort Donaldson and Fort Henry, which were but fragments of his active army life. He was a prisoner and after being paroled rejoined his regiment. He with his regiment was mustered out of service Jan. 20th, 1866. He has written a very complete history of Company D, 12th Iowa Veteran Volunteers, and was appointed a member of the regimental historical committee. After the war he returned to Macon City, Iowa. Later he engaged in the hotel business, at Waterloo, Iowa, from which place he came to Nebraska, and took a homestead in Hooker township, July 17th, 1867. In Nebraska he became acquainted with Miss Nancy Adams, a daughter of J. O. Adams, the veteran pioneer and the man for whom our town was named. Six children were born to them, three of whom have gone on before, and three with Mrs. Zuver remain to mourn his loss. We shall miss him. We have lost a man, a manly, noble man. The town will miss him in every enterprise, charitable, social, political, or financial. The G. A. R. will have one vacant chair which will never be filled, and the vacancy of which they will never cease to feel, but we believe they will have a comrade who will place a light in the window of the temple on the other shore to guide them home. The A. F. & A. M. have lost a brother here but "Hope looks beyond this vale of tears" to a fraternity eternal. The church will miss him, his support, his influence, his encouraging words and noble character. Scores of us will miss a personal friend, his kind words, friendly acts, sympathy, encouragement and good cheer. The writer feels the loss of a true friend whose many kind acts and cheering words we shall never forget. His family has sustained a great loss, and we extend our sympathy, sharing as far as may be in their sorrow by keen sense of our own loss, and a full appreciation of their far greater loss. Funeral services were held at the M. E. church Wednesday at 3 o'clock, and were conducted by Rev. M. C. Smith of Grafton, the A. F. & A. M. and G. A. R., joining in the ceremonies.—The Adams (Neb.) Globe, March 24, 1893.

COMRADE THOMAS BARR.

Thomas Barr was born in the state of Ohio, on the 10th day of August, 1839; came to Cedar county, Iowa, with his parents in 1846, and thence removed to Benton county, Iowa, in 1848, and lived in Benton county the remainder of his life, except during his term of service.

Thomas Barr enlisted at Shellsburg, Benton county, Iowa, in Company D, Twelfth Iowa Infantry Volunteers, about the first day of October, 1861, and was a model soldier. At the battle of Shiloh, April 6th, 1862, he received a severe gun shot wound in the thigh, and with the rest of the command was taken prisoner, but was recaptured on the following day, when the advance of our lines covered the ground lost the day before. He was sent to hospital and sufficiently recovered to return to his company, then in the Union brigade, in the early autumn of 1862 was at the battle of Corinth, in the Union brigade, and was present in all the battles and skirmishes the Twelfth Iowa was engaged in after that time. He did not re-enlist and was up Red River with A. J. Smith's command and at the battle of Pleasant Hill with the other non-veterans of the Twelfth in the 35th Iowa Infantry. At the expiration of his three year's enlistment, he was mustered out, by reason of expiration of term of service and returned to his home in Benton county, where, on the 29th day of December, 1864, he was married to Amy D. Bickell. He left surviving his widow and four children, all grown up and married. He died December 27th, 1892, at his home on a farm near Sellsburg of paralysis.

Thomas Barr was a large, strong, vigorous man; was never in hospital or disabled from duty except on account of wounds received in battle. He was a quiet man, brave, unflinching and always ready for duty, never grumbling, and his death will be very much of a surprise to, and sincerely regretted by all of Company D. He was present at the reunion at Waterloo and appeared to be in vigorous health.

COMRADE T. R. M'KEE.

News came here on Tuesday that Major Truman R. McKee had died at the home of his brother in Chicago, Monday, January 8th, 1894, and that the remains would reach here for burial Tuesday evening. They arrived on the 7:55 train and were taken in charge by the G. A. R.

To most of our citizens the news came as a surprise, but to those who had an intimate acquaintance with the deceased it was to them an event not altogether unexpected. Those who knew him best were aware of the existence of a disease that had troubled him for long years and from which death would come at almost any moment. The biographical sketch is very meagre for want of materials.

Truman R. McKee was born in Watertown, New York, in 1828, and was 65 years old in May, 1893. His boyhood days were spent in Sacket's Harbor, New York. He spent a few years on the lakes as a sailor in company with his brother in his younger days. It is said that a fall from the mast of the Hornet, a vessel commanded by his brother, laid the foundations of the disease that finally ended his earthly existence. After giving up the vocation of a sailor Mr. McKee came west and was a citizen of Minnesota for a while and also of Iowa and finally came to Dakota and settled in our city, where he lived until the death of his wife, which occurred in the month of February, 1892, since which time he has been in various places, but most of the time in Chicago. Mr. McKee enlisted in Company F, 12th Regiment, Iowa Volunteers, at the outbreak of the war in 1861 as a drummer. He was in the battle of Shiloh, which occurred April 7th, 1862, and beat the long roll that called the forces together on that memorable occasion. He was mustered out of service the 28th day of April, 1862, for disability.

Mr. McKee enlisted in the army of his divine Lord and Master over nine years ago and became a "good soldier of Jesus Christ" and proved himself to be an honored and consistent member of the Methodist Episcopal church till the time of his death, when he received from the Great Captain and Bishop of our souls his promotion to membership in that grander army, of whose numbers the poet sings:

> "Soldiers of Christ, well done;
> Thy glorious warfare is past,
> Your battles fought, the victories won,
> And thou art crowned at last."

The funeral occurred at the M. E. church at 1 o'clock p. m. Wednesday, which was conducted by Rev. W. J. Hyde in a short but appropriate sermon.

The remains were laid away beside his wife in the Dell Rapids cemetery. There was no relative present except his brother, with whom the major stayed while in Chicago. There is no need of saying anything about Mr. McKee's social and moral character, for he is endorsed by the entire community for honesty and integrity.---Dell Rapids Exponent, Jan. 12, 1894.

COMRADE HIRAM KASTER.

The funeral services of Hiram Kaster were conducted by Rev. W. E. Adams, at the home of the deceased's family, some four miles southeast of Manchester, at 2 o'clock p. m. April 3. Before the hour a large crowd had gathered at the house, the most of them unable to get within hearing of the services. About 80 teams were in the procession that followed Mr. Kaster to his last resting place, facts that speak louder than words of the esteem in which he was held by his neighbors and many friends. His loss is deeply felt by the afflicted family, who have the sympathy of all who know them The following obituary was read at the service:

Hiram Kaster was born in Mercer county, Pa., July 13, 1843, and was a son of Sealey and Mary (Shilling) Kaster. When Hiram was eleven years of age his father came to Delaware county, and his youth and manhood were spent on Spring Branch. In September, 1861, soon after the opening of the civil war, and when only 18 years of age, he enlisted as a private in Company F, 12th Iowa Volunteer Infantry, and served till June, 1862, when he was discharged for disability incurred during his term of service. The principal engagement in which he took part during the time of his serivce, was at Fort

Donelson. He was in minor engagemnets, and saw a great deal of hard service in marches, and in camp during the winter of 1861-62. December 25, 1864, he married Miss Hannah Pierce, also of Spring Branch, and a niece of Mrs. Matt Brayton. Hiram Kaster died at his home in Milo township, Saturday, April 1, 1893, being at the time of his death 49 years, 8 months and 18 days old. At Fort Donelson he contracted the disease which made him so great a sufferer all these years and finally resulted in his death. He leaves a wife, three daughters and one son, also three brothers, one sister and an aged mother, besides many friends to mourn his loss. A loyal soldier, a faithful friend, a good son and brother, the kindest of husbands and fathers has gone to his rest, and the world is better for his having lived in it.

COMRADE JAMES CUTLIP.

At a regular meeting of Jo Mower Post No. 111, G. A. R., Department of Minnesota, held in their hall in Pine Island, Minn., September 7, 1892, the following resolutions were adopted:

"Whereas, It has pleased an all wise Providence to remove from our post by death, our comrade and neighbor, James Cutlip, formerly a member of Company G, 12th Iowa Infantry, and of the greater loss suffered by those who were nearest and dearest to him; therefore be it

"Resolved, That it is but a just tribute to the memory of the deceased to say that in sorrowing for his removal from our Post, we mourn for one who was in every way worthy of our respect and regard.

"Resolved, That we sincerely sympathize with his family in their affliction, and we bow to the ordering of him who 'doeth all things well.'

"Resolved, That this testimonial of our heartfelt sorrow and sympathy be forwarded to the family of the deceased and that a copy be furnished the Pine Island Record for publication."

F. HAGLER,
J. D. HASTINGS,
F. JEWELL,
Committee.

COMRADE DRENGMAN OLESON AAKER.

Aaker—At his home in Ridgeway, on the 30th ult., Hon. D. O. Aaker, aged 53 years, 6 months and 1 day.

Mr. Aaker was born in Norway in September, 1839, but came to America with his parents when only nine years old. They first settled in Waukesha Co., Wis., but in 1854 they came to Iowa and located at what was then a promising point (now defunct) in the corner of Madison and Lincoln townships, called Burr Oak Springs. When the war of the rebellion broke out Mr. Aaker promptly enlisted with Capt. Tupper in Company G of the 12th Iowa Volunteer Infantry. He served through the war and was a good soldier. In 1869 he married Christina Eleffson, who bore to him Lena, John Theodore, Adolph Oscar, and Drengman Casper, all of whom survive him.

Always active in politics and public affairs, he held numerous local offices, and in 1880 ran for clerk of the courts against Myron J. Harden, but was defeated. In the following year he ran for representative in the Iowa general assembly, was elected and re-elected two years later, making a creditable record for himself. In 1885 he ran for senator and was beaten by T. W. Burdick.

When Ridgeway was started he moved to the new town and engaged in the lumber trade. Later he became a member of the mercantile firm of Galby & Anker. For a time prosperity attended them, but they were doing business on a falling market, ten years later the wheat blight struck this region, and their debtors, unable to pay, moved away to the Dakotas and elsewhere, leaving the firm stranded financially. From this Mr. A. never recovered.

Socially and personally always genial, more than usually intelligent, "D. O." was always popular when before the people. He had his faults, as all have. His antagonisms were all political and not personal; and the grave covers them all with a mantle of love and oblivion. Peace to his ashes.

The funeral services were held Monday, a large concourse attending. Messrs. L. L. Cadwell, P. McCusker, R. F. Greer, John Harmon, C. L. Holcomb and O. A. Anderson of Col. Hughes' Post, attended as pall bearers for their deceased comrade.

COMARDE JOHN B. THOMPSOM.

John B. Thompson, a veteran of the 12th Iowa, died at or near Spilville, Sunday, and was buried Tuesday.

Comrade Thompson was a member of Company G, loved and respected by all his comrades. He passed away at his home near Spilville, Winneshiek county, Iowa, in the spring of 1894.

COMRADE STEPHEN B. MILLER.

The follwing was cut from the Yaquina Post, published at Toledo, Oregon, February 24th, 1894, and tells of the death of one of Company G, whose personal record during the war showed as much courage and bravery as any member of the regiment; of great strength and endurance; always ready for duty. He never knew what fear was. He was a soldier every inch of him. "Peace to his ashes."

Stephen B. Miller, a notice of whose decease appeared in the Post of the 17th. inst., was born in New York, in May, 1841, and consequently was 52 years and 9 months old on the day of his death.

His parents emigrated to Iowa and settled in Winneshiek county, where he was raised. At the breaking out of the late war he joined Company G of the Twelfth Iowa Volunteers. Sometime after his enlistment he was taken prisoner and incarcerated in Libby prison. A few months thereafter he was paroled and returned to his company in the field. About nine months thereafter he was again captured and thrown into that vile den, Andersonville prison, with others were sujected to the most inhuman cruelties and nearly starved to death. With hope and life almost gone, a terribly emaciated body and broken constitution he with others was released from Andersonville prison and sent to a hospital for medical treatment. After several months he regained strength enough, and by his own earnest solicitation he was returned to his regiment, where he served honorably to the end of the war. Steve, as he was familiarly called by his fellow soldiers, was known in his regiment as a brave, true soldier, and a generous worthy comrade. He was a blacksmith by trade, and worked for the O. P. company about eight years. He was always of an industrious turn, and from his prison confinement—from the effects of which he never fully recovered—he failed from year to year, until finally tuberculosis consumption and general debility carried him to an untimely grave.

He leaves a wife and two small chidren to mourn his loss. Mr. Miller was known on the Bay as a kind, indulgent father, a good provider, and a peaceful conscientious citizen. He was buried at Corvallis in Odd Fellows' cemetery, under the auspices of the Grand Army of the Republic. May his soul rest in peace. COMRADE.

COMRADE WILLIAM HOERNER.

Dubuque (Iowa) Daily Journal, Aug. 27, 1894: Another man who went forth at the call of his country has answered the last roll call, and is now a member of that Grand Army that has passed to the other shore. William Hoerner is his name, and he died Sunday morning at Finley hospital, to which place he had been taken a few days ago. Wounds and other injuries received in the army were the cause of his death. At the time of his demise he was about 60 years of age, but he looked much older, owing to continued ill health occasioned by his wounds. Mr. Hoerner was a native of Geramny, but came to this country about forty-five years ago and had been a resident of Dubuque for about forty years. At the breaking out of the war he enlisted in Company H, 12th Iowa Infantry, and served all through the struggle and remained in the service until 1866, when the regiment was mustered out. He was a brave and gallant soldier, and, with the writer of these lines was a member of the color-guard of the regiment. He was in all the great battles in which the regiment was engaged—Forts Henry, Donelson, Shiloh, Jackson, Vicksburg, Tupelo, Nashville and others—always bearing himself with honor and credit. At the expiration of his term he returned to Dubuque and shortly afterwards established an apiary in the upper part of the city, conducting it and gaining a meagre livelihood until the effects of his wounds, together with the infirmities of age, broke down his health; when, through the influence of Col. Henderson the poor old veteran was granted a small pension. Comrade Hoerner was never married. He was recognized by all who knew him as a man of honor and integrity. He was so constituted that he could not do an unmanly act. His sense of honor was as keen as that of the knights of the days of chivalry, and there is not a member of the old 12th alive to-day who will not heave a sigh of deep regret when they learn of "Billy" Hoerner's death. He was our comrade in the days when the flush of youth was on his cheek and before the hand of time had wrinkled our brow.

We knew him in the glad morning of life when he shouldered his musket and went forth to preserve the integrity of the stars and stripes. We saw him on the field of death, but he did not waver. We saw him faint from wounds, but he did not murmur. We saw him in the prison pen, but he was cheerful. We saw him throughout over four years of war and always knew him to be a soldier and a man. Like so many thousands of other soldiers he has passed into the dreamless sleep. Time has supplanted his raven locks with their silver, and the elastic step of youth had given place to the decreped pace of age. Death had no terrors for him. In the mellow sunset of an honored life he passed into the valley of the shadow and fell asleep at the sound of the taps of Death. He was a member of Hyde Clark post and will be buried under its auspices at 2 o'clock tomorrow afternoon in the soldier's lot.

> Green be the turf above thee,
> Friend of our youthful days;
> None knew thee but to love thee,
> None named thee but to praise.

He was a member of Halcyon Encampment No. 1, and Harmony Lodge No 2, I. O. O. F.

COMRADE EDWARD BECKETT.

Dubuque Daily Globe-Journal, Oct. 23, 1894: A letter received here yesterday announces the death of Capt. Edward Beckett, who passed away at the National Soldiers' Home at Leavenworth, Kas., last Thursday, and whose interment took place the following Friday evening in the cemetery connected with the home. Captain Beckett, when he was here about two months ago on a furlough from the home, was in very poor health and said then that he soon expected to be with the boys on the other side. He had been in very poor health for several years and was patiently awaiting the final summons.

Captain Ed. Beckett was born in Center Grove and at the time of his death was about 52 years of age. His father, Edward Beckett, Sr., who is still a resident of Center Grove, came to this country from England when quite a young man and engaged in mining, and the son also followed this occupation until the breaking out of the war. Captain Beckett received a good common school education, and when the call for 75,000 troops was issued by President Lincoln, in 1861, he enlisted as a member of the old Governor's Greys and served with the famous First Iowa Inafntry during its three months term of service.

When the Twelfth Iowa was being organized in this city, a few months after he had returned home, Captain Beckett took an active part in the organization of Company H, and was made a sergeant. . He served with distinction and was severly wounded in two different battles. He was by nature a soldier, and at the termination of the war enlisted in the regular army and served five years, returning home at the expiration of his term of service. In 1874, when Captain Dan Duane and others were forming the Dubuque Rifles, Captain Beckett became a member of the company and rendered such valuable assistance that he was elected first lieutenant and on the appointment of Captain Duane as colonel of the then Fourth regiment, Lieutenant Beckett was promoted to the captaincy. He was a thorough soldier and a fine drill master and took great pride in having a fine company, which, it will be readily admitted, the Rifles were under the leadership of Duane and Beckett respectively, both having been through the war.

Captain Beckett was a man who never shirked duty, no matter how dangerous it might be, and he was held in high regard by every member of the Twelfth Iowa. He was in the same company with the late G. W. Horner, who passed away last August, and fought at Donelson, Shiloh, Tupelo, Vicksburg, and all the other great battles in which the regiment too part. He is now a member of the grand army on the other side of the line of time. His death will be sincerely regretted by all who knew him, and especially old comrades-in-arms. His was a true and loyal heart. He loved the old flag and fought gallantly to preserve all that it symbolizes. He went out in his young manhood and gave the best years of his life to his country. He is now sleeping in an honored soldier's grave in the bosom of the land his valor helped to save; and all his old comrades will drop a tear when they learn that brave Ed. Beckett is no more. He was a member of Hyde Clark Post.

COMRADE W. H. MARKHAM.

W. H. Markham was born in Cattaraugus county, N. Y., and moved to Iowa, and when the dark clouds of war made their apperance he thought it his duty to go and defend that dear old flag; and on October 14th he volunteered in Company I, 12th Iowa Infantry; was taken prisoner at the battle of Shilo, Tenn., and for several months suffered the indignities of prison life; was exchanged and returned to his regiment and participated in all its engagements, in all its long and weary marches, and in February, 1866, he was mustered out of the service and returned home with the seeds of disease so firmly planted in his system that it was impossible to eradicate them. He moved to Wisconsin, and in 1885 he came to this county, thinking that the climate and in the pure light air he might regain his health. Since that time he has been our constant friend, a kind neighbor beloved by all, one who was always ready to extend the hand of charity. He was a man of more than ordinary ability, a true christian. He died on the morning of Aug. 9th. His death was no surprise. He had no fear of death and when it came it was but a transition, for he passed away as serenely as a child asleep.

He was a member of the E. E. Kimball Post, G. A. R., and was buried by the order he loved so well, assisted by the ladies of the G. A. R. The wreaths of flowers, the silken flag across his breast and the long procession plainly indicated that he had many friends. The funeral service was very impressive and painfully showed that we would all soon answer to the last roll call.

No encomium is too high, no honor too great for such a soldier. Without the incentive or the motive which controls the officer, who hopes to live in history without the hope of reward actuated only by a sense of duty and patriotism. However much of credit and glory may be given and probably justly given to the leaders of the struggle, history will yet award the main honor where it is due—to the private sodier—who, without hope of reward, with no other incentive than a conscientiousness of rectitude has encountered all the hardships and has suffered all the privations. Our comrade will be missed by all who knew him. Praxitites, the great sculptor, sought to perpetuate the smile of his beloved on marble lips, believing that art could do what love denied. No art, no cunning chisel, no undying marble are needed here. We shall indeed never again feel the warm grasp of our noble comrade, nor be glad in his sunny smile, nor drink in the deep lights of his discourse. But sweet memories of his generous nature, of his chivalrous bearing, of his devotion to principle, of his boundless love for his country, of his fidelity will survive. He was his own biographer, and his own sculptor, for he made his life a part of the undying history of his country and engraved his image in the hearts of his countrymen.   H. G. PATTERSON.

COMRADE ISAIAH K. CRANE.

Isaiah K. Crane, the son of Solomon and Elizabeth (Mills) Crane, was born in Washington, Sullivan county, New Hampshire, February 28, 1820. His earliest years were spent on the farm. In 1843, Miss Olive Heald became his wife. She died in 1855, leaving two chlidern, John H., and James C., both residents of this city. Soon after the death of his wife Mr. Crane came to this state and engaged in farming until the war broke out, when he heeded his country's call and enlisted as a member of Company I, Twelfth Iowa Infantry. He was present at Fort Henry, Fort Donelson, Shiloh the Siege of Vicksburg, the Red River expedition under General Banks, etc., serving his country faithfully and well for three years and three months. After the war Mr. Crane resumed farming in this county, and on February 13, 1865, was united in marriage to Miss Margaret Angeline Smith of De Witt, who survives him and who enjoys the proud distinction of being able to trace her ancestry to the noble Robert Bruce, of Scotland. Her father, Robert L. Smith, was the first abolitionist, to his honor be it said, of Clinton county. I. K. Crane, the subject of this sketch, died at his home in this city on Tuesday morning, August 21, 1894, of dropsy of the heart. At the age of 18 he became a member of the Baptist church and until his death, or more than fifty-six years, lived a sincere, upright christian life. If he made mistakes, and all men do, they were of the head and not of the heart, and it is the universal verdict of all who knew him well that he was one of nature's noblemen. What higher title can any man have or desire. He was honest, generous and patriotic. By his second wife he leaves two sons, R. Edward and S. Bird, both of whom as well as the other two, John H. and James C., were present at the funeral, which was held at the Buckhorn church, under the auspices of A. W. Drips Post, of which he was an honored member, and was one of the largest of the many large funerals which have been held in that neighborhood. More than ninety teams were in the procession. Dr. Heald pronounced the funeral discourse, a fitting eulogy to the departed. The remains were laid to rest in the adjoining cemetery, of which deceased has been sexton for nearly thirty years.

COMRADE DAVID S. GODFREY.

David S. Godfrey, Company F, 12th Iowa, died at Wier City, Kansas, sometime in the fall of 1887.

COMRADE A. C. GILMAN.

Comrade A. C. Gilman, Company H, 12th Iowa, died at the Soldiers' Home, Marshalltown, Iowa, December 18th, 1891, at the age of sixty-three years, of capilary bronchitis. His body was shipped to Insdianapolis, Ind., for burial. Here is what Comrade Van Anda says of him:

Fremont, Neb., Nov. 15th, 1894.

Dear Comrade Simpson: I have just received from the Iowa Soldiers' Home commander the announcement of the death of our old comrade, A. C. Gilman. One by one the boys are laid away, and when A. C. passed from this life a good soldier was absent, but accounted for. I am unable to give an extended account of him. I have not met him since '63 and know nothing of him except as a soldier. He was generally respected, always ready to do his duty and in all respects a model soldier.

Respectfully,   J. A. VAN ANDA.

COMRADE FRANK M. HAMLIN.

Comrade Frank M. Hamlin of Company H, 12th Iowa, died at his home in Iowa Falls, Iowa, April 29th, 1890, aged 57 years. Comrade Van Anda says of him:

I can only remember him as a bold boy and one that we could rely upon under every circumstance---one of those bold boys that we like to think of. But he is serving in the great army on the other side. We can go where he is, but he cannot come to us. May he rest in peace and be among those who are in the G. A. R. above.   Respectfully,

J. A. VAN ANDA.

COMRADE JAMES S. DUPRAY.

James S. Dupray, 5th sergeant Company I, 12th Iowa Volunteer Infantry, was born in Franklin, Venango county, Penn., in 1814. Enlisted in the 12th Iowa September 27th, 1861; discharged in 1862 account of disability; received in line of duty at Pittsburg Landing; died in Monroe county, Iowa, December 6th, 1876, from disease contracted in the service of the government.

Some comrade at the reunion handed in the following memorandum of deaths in Company E, with a promise that the date of deaths and other information would be sent soon. None has been received as this goes to press:

COMRADE JOHN ELWELL.

Lieut. John Elwell of Company E, 12th Iowa, died at Chicago, Ill.

COMRADE JOHN C. JONES.

John C. Jones of Company E, died at his home near Geneva, Iowa.

COMRADE THOMAS DEMORSS.

Thomas Demorss of Company E, died at his home near Briston, Iowa.

COMRADE ALEXANDER MEYERS.

Alexander W. Meyers of Company E, died at his home ta Shell Creek, Iowa.

Communications.

The following letters were received at different times and by different persons, and will, without doubt, be read with pleasure by you all, breathing as they do the spirit of love and kindly feeling that exists so strongly between old comrades:

Manchester, Iowa, Oct. 27th, 1894.

Dear Comrade Simpson:—

Yours of 23rd inst, came yesterday. I note what you say about getting out proceedings of the 5th reunion and think that you had better prepare the same and have them printed, for no one not present can begin to do it justice. Another reason is that as now situated it is impossible for me to do it on account of the county building a new court house, and I am crowded in temporary quarctrs in a room about 14 feet square and have not the room to do the work required in the office. Hope, however, to get moved in the new quarters about January 1st, when I will have fine quarters with plenty of room and good light, providing, of course, that the people on the 6th of November say by their vote that I may occupy them. Am so glad the reunion proved such a success. I almost cried when the boys started from here that I was unable to go.

The people here feel complimented that the boys are to come here again, and will give them a royal reception. They feel nearer to the old 12th than any other regiment, and no other who has held reunions here have had as good times as ours. We must work for a good representation of the families of the comrades next time, and would suggest that you put something in the proceedings that will set them to thinking about it and making perparation to that effect. I send you a paper with account of death of Ed. Beckett Compay H, who has died since reunion. Mrs. D. joins in kindest regards to you and Mrs. S. In haste, Your comrade, ABNER DUNHAM.

Chicago Ill., Oct. 10th, 1894.

My Dear Judge:—

Although I have been writing to Butters and yourself, telling of the difficulties in the way of my going to Sioux City, and of the probabilities of my being unable to attend the reunion, I have had a sneaking notion in my mind all of the time, that despite all obstructions I would find some way to cut loose at the last minute, and be with you, and last week at Council Bluffs I told Gen. Henderson and others that I would certainly show up on the morning of the second day, but I find now it is impossible for me to go. I have a number of important matters on hand that are demanding attention, and to cap the climax I have been subpoenaed before the court in a case now pending, and in which my presence is essential. I Cannot express in words the regret I feel over this matter. It is the pride of my life that I had the honor to command the 12th Iowa, and with each succeeding year I think of my old comrades with increasing love and fondness. God bless the dear old boys. Give them my love and kindest greetings, and the assurance that if the good Lord will spare my life I will use my best endeavor to be with them at the next reunion.

I trust your reunion may prove a success in every sense, and that the occasion may be counted a notable one in the history of our organization. Belive me, Very truly your friend and comrade,
J. H. STIBBS.

Manchester, Iowa, Nov. 15th, 1894.
Dear Comrade Simpson:—

Yours of 23rd ult., telling me of my being selected as secretary of our regimental association, and also of the decision of the association to return "home" at next reunion, is received. While I doubt the wisdom of the choice of its secretary it is a compliment of which I feel proud, and while incompetent to perform the duties satisfactorily to myself, be assured I will do my best.

I hope every comrade will at once begin preparations to come, for a warm reception awaits us. I feel warranted in saying that none have a bigger place in the hearts of the people of Manchester than the 12th Iowa. This I know from expressions heard on every side, both before and since the decision to return.

Let every comrade as far as they can bring their wives and children, and for them to prepare to take part in our exercises which for our children will be a great school in patriotism—a branch in their education we should do all in our power to advance.

Hoping to meet everyone of the "old boys" and their families in '96,
I am your comrade, ABNER DUNHAM.

Roseburg, Oregon, Oct. 5th, 1894.
Hon. J. N. Weaver:—

Dear Comrade: It is with keen regret that I write it is impossible to be with you and the comrades at the Sioux City reunion of our good regiment. I missed the last because of the storm. Before I missed none. And they were always like going home as I met the comrades. It is a great disappointment that I cannot at this time grasp the hand and look into the eyes and see away beyond the grey hairs and faltering step, see the boy in blue with raven locks and elastic step. And then the talk of bygones, the friendly interest in our present conditions, etc. I am proud of the 12th Iowa and its record. And as I stand on my doorstep and look out over the valley of the Umpqua and see the stars and stripes floating over the Oregon Soldiers' Home, I feel proud that I wore the blue and now the bronze button, and today count on my loyalty to that flag and American institutions in the fullest sense of the word. We bespeak you great happiness, and no flood to mar the hour. We hope yet to meet you in reunion. But let us so live, that living or dying, we be still brave soldiers and ready for the great reunion with the brave who have gone before. Fraternally yours,

JAMES BARR.

P. S.—enclosed one dollar for membership fees for myself. J. B.

Cresco, Iowa, Oct. 10th, 1894.

T. G. Henderson, Sioux City, Iowa:—

Dear Nephew: Your telegram was received in due time and I found it impossible to get away just now. It is the busy season in the grain business, and I have to be here more or less every day. I might have got away for one day, but the distance would require three or four days. Very sorry I could not meet with my old comrades. When I got your telegram I thought of sending Gussie to represent me at the reunion, as she has attended all of them. But I found that our agent had no instructions as to special rates for the reunion for a distance over 200 miles. But you will understand that my inclination leads me to your city, but my finances tell me to go slow.

There is no place my dear Tom where I would like to go at present better than to your city, and make my stay with your family, for I well know the sincerity of your invitation. With kind regards to your wife and all our friends and comrades who may be with you,

I remain your affectionate uncle.

W. L. HENDERSON

Iowa City, Iowa, Oct. 9, 1894.

J. E. Simpson, secretary 12th Iowa Infantry Association, Sioux City Reunion:—

My Dear Comrade: The undersigned was one of the storm-bound at the time of the regular reunion two years ago and was unable, even by flanking the flood, to reach Sioux City in time to meet the comrades. I had therefore fully intended to be with you at this October meeting, but circumstances make it impossible, to my great disappointment. I realize that we shall not many times more look in each other's faces and grasp each other by the hand, and I therefore hope a good number of the regiment will be there to enjoy the privilege—the last opportunity for some of the members doubtless. Be assured that the absent in body will be present in spirit. Please inform me of my dues to the association and send me a badge, if possible.

Fraternally, J. W. RICH,

Co. E, 12th Iowa Infantry.

Des Moines, Aug. 20, 1894.

Mr. J. E. Simpson, Norfolk, Neb:—

My Dear Comrade and Friend: Replying to your favor August 15th, I sent you a copy of the Weekly Register Saturday, which contains the principal details of the ceremonies of Iowa's Battle Flag Day. It was a great day, and we all regretted that you and the other absent comrades were not present.

I fear that a mistake was made in calling the 12th Iowa reunion this fall. The boys talked it over when here on Flag Day, and the unanimous opinion was that the times are too hard for them to attend the reunion. I cannot attend for the reason that the campaign will be then in its hottest stage, but I will be there in spirit and hope that the comrades who do attend will have a splendid time. I had a short editorial on Dr. Underwood's death and army service, which you will find on the first page of the Register I sent you Saturday. He was a good man, and you will well remember how sympathetic he was with our boys during their ills and wounds of the war period.

Mrs. Clarkson joins me in kindest regards.   Ever Yours,
R. P. CLARKSON.

Comrade J. E. Simpson, Secretary, etc., and all the Comrades of the old 12th Iowa Infantry:—

My Dear Comrades: I cannot express my regrets at not being able to meet with you at this our 5th regimental reunion. I have always thought that I would never let one of our reunions pass without being present. It seems, however, "that man proposes, but God disposes." You will recollect that at our last, that I, together with a number of comrades, were unable to get farther than Ft. Dodge on account of the terrible floods, and now I am again compelled by public duties to abandon the long cherished hope of at this time again taking the hand of those dear comrades of the camp, the march, the battle field, and of the prison hells, whose memory I cherish with the fondest recollections.

Ah, dear comrades, ours was a great work, a work that future generations will appreciate even more than the present, a work that we at the time could not fully comprehend, and now (although we are old, played out soldiers) can but partially realize the stupendous conflict and the far reaching effects of which we as individuals each was a factor in accomplishing. Although all was not done that might have been, yet we can be proud of the record that the 12th Iowa was never called upon for a duty, not performed.

Time flies and we, the boys of 1861, are growing old and soon must pass from the stage of action and leave the great work so well begun in the hands of our children and our children's children.

It seems but yesterday that we beardless boys shouldered the musket to forever silence that incomprehensible principle of "State Rights." What that cost us is well shown as the roll is called by the answer of more than one half of our original number, killed in battle, died in prison, died of wounds, died of disease, while a large per centage of the survivors report "unfit for duty" on account of the wounds received in battle, and of disease contracted while in line of duty.

Yes, we are growing old, but our work is not done. While we helped to make this the greatest nation on the face of the globe, while we helped to free it from that false claim, "as a nation of the free," and to place our flag on the very pinacle of fame, we must see too that our flag floats on the very pinacle of fame, we must see, too, that our flag floats from every school house in the land and that the rising generation inherits and imbibes that spirit of loyalty and patriotism which you learned during a four years of horrible and cruel war.

In no way can this be done better than by continuing these reunions. Count me in for any duty assigned and rest assured that next time I will be there. Report me this time "Absent, but accounted for."

As ever your Comrade from 1861 to 1865,
ABNER DUNHAM,
Company F, 12th Iowa Infantry.

Maquketa, Aug. 8th, 1894.

J. E. Simpson:—

Dear Sir: I will say that I. K. Crane received your circular inviting him to the reunion of the 12th at Sioux City, and he bids me say to you that it will be impossible for him to be there in the body as he can almost hear the last roll call. He has been sick all summer, and never will be able to march to the music of fife or drum in earth life more. But he will be with the boys in spirit, and if he should be freed from his suffering body will be with you in his spiritual body, free from all pain and suffering. He is suffering from dropsy, brought on through rheumatism and heart trouble. His limbs have swollen until they are bursting, and he can hardly get his breath. Still he is cheerful and wishes the old 12th a good time, and if he has answered the last roll call on earth will be at your camp fire with you. He bids me say this for him, and I close hoping and wishing you a happy time. I subscribe myself,   Your friend, his wife,
MRS. I. K. CRANE.

He says read to the boys if you wish.

Dunkerton, October 5th, 1894.

Dear Secretary and Comrade:—

It is with deep regret that I sit down to inform you that I shall not be able to be with you and the boys at the reunion, and I regret it the more because I fear it will be the last opportunity I shall have of meeting with comrades. I am now nearly 72 years old. If I drew a pension as most of the boys do, I believe I should go, but times are too hard with me. Give my love to all of the boys of the noble old 12th Iowa. God bless you all. May you all have a good time together.   Truly yours,
A. B. PERRY,
Company E, 12th Iowa.

No. 11 Edward Street, Chicago, Ill., Sept. 23, 1894.

Dear Comrade Simpson:—

Comrade Weaver's circular per your favor came duly to hand. If I can go to Sioux City I will, but I am getting old and shaky now, and hesitate to trust myself in a prohibition state any more. I hear the G. A. R. had a good time in Pittsburg. I didnt go—couldn't get a vacation this year from the Chicago P. O., but one week from today lets me out. My resignation here takes effect October 1st. But times are hard and money close, and I may not be able to attend at Sioux City. I have been an employe in this P. O. since 1885, and am worn out. I shall go to the Soldiers' Home---not, perhaps, to Marshalltown, but to Dayton, Ohio. I may be entitled at Marshalltown, but I was for years at the Dayton home, am on furlough from there now, and there is more going on there---printing office (I am a printer), theatre, church, etc., and six thousand inmates---see? I hope that the dear old boys will have a good time at Sioux City, and with best wishes I remain,

Your old comrade-in-arms,
ALLEN M. BLANCHARD.

Helena, Mont., Oct. 6th, 1894.

Mr. E. B. Soper, Emmetsburg, Iowa:---

My Dear Comrade: Your favor of September 28th just received, and am sorry to say that it will be impossible for me to attend the reunion at Sioux City. I am just now engaged in mining matters requiring my undivided attention. Were it not for that I would surely be with you, as you say it has been nearly thirty years since we last met, and I assure you that it is my wish to meet yourself and old comrades with a hearty shake hands as soon as circumstances will permit. Please remember me kindly to all comrades. My heart is with you if I cannot be. With the best of wishes,

I remain yours truly,
W. L. LEE.

Columbus, Ohio, Sept. 22nd, 1894.

Mr. J. E. Simpson:---

Dear Comrade: I received your circular in regard to the reunion of the old 12th. I am so far away that it is pretty hard for me to attend the reunion. Nothing would please me better than to shake the hand of every surviving member of Company I, and in fact of all the 12th. I will do my utmost towards reaching Sioux City by the 10th of next month. To tell the truth of the matter I have been under the weather pretty bad lately, and my finance is low. I wish they had made it Dubuque or some town on the east side of the state.

Please send me Sergeant Cotes' address. I know it is in South Dakota, but forgot the town. I am trying for an increase of pension. Cotes was wounded at Tupelo when I was. He and Bill Koehler and I were in Cahaba together. And please send Koehler's address. I know it is Dubuque, but don't know the number or street. If you know Capt. Sumbardo's address please send it also. I will send you a blank to fill out as to my health before I was wounded if you can remember me. The youngest member of Company I---the boy that had the preacher's suit, plug hat and all on the Tupelo raid---Jack Stibbs, our colonel, remembers that? I remember, you bet. The damn thing came near being the cause of putting my light out.

Your friend and comrade till death,

JOHN DEVINE,
Room 31, 152½, North High street.

Kansas City, Mo., Sept. 29th, 1894.

Captain J. E. Simpson, Norfolk, Neb.:—

Dear Comrade and Friend: Your very kind circular notifying me of the reunion of the grand old 12th Iowa to hand sometime ago. I have delayed answering up to this time, thinking I could make some arrangement to be with you, but I find it will be impossible for me to be there, as I have had no employment since April 1st; have been sick all the time. It is just as much as I can do to walk around, and am entirely out of funds. God only knows what I am to do. There is nothing on this earth that would give me more pleasure than to be once more with all the old comrades of the gallant 12th Iowa that are still left on this earth. Give all the comrades my very kindest regards and best wishes; tell them I hope we shall all meet hereafter in a better world than this. I sometimes see Comrade Comstock who runs between here and St. Louis on the Mo. P. railroad. I shall be pleased to hear from you often. Respectfully, your comrade and friend,

N. E. DUNCAN,
No. 3029, Locust street.

Mount Hill, Ill., Sept. 25th, 1894.

Dear Comrade Simpson:—

I received your letter some time ago. I am sorry to say to you and 12th Iowa comrades that I can't be with you this time. I have sold my farm at O'Neill, Holt county, Neb., and bought a farm in Jefferson county, southern Illinois. I have bought me a fruit farm. I came here the first of August and I am well pleased with my new home. We are all well and the family like their new home. Tell the boys if they come down here next June, 1895, I will give them a job of picking strawberries. I have 10 acres to pick if there is no bad luck. I have nine hundred Ben Davis apple trees and a nice peach orchard, and one hundred bearing cherry trees, blackberries and raspberries. All kinds of crops are good here and lots of improved farms for sale; prices from $10, $15, $20 to $30 per acre, and very healthy. Read this letter to the boys of Company H, 12th Iowa Infantry. WM. S. WISEGARBER.

Randalie, Oct. 5th, 1894.

Jno. N. Weaver, Sioux City:—

Dear Comrade: Your circular of Sept. 12th lies before me; have reserved reply hoping I might be able to "report at roll call Oct. 10," but unless something wholly unexpected occurs I shall be one of the worst disappointed "boys" of the 12th Iowa, for I assure you, soldier gatherings are my special enjoyment, most particularly so the "boys" that permitted me to be a non-combatant for more than four years, and you cannot imagine how hard it is to say, "cannot be with you next week." I am not very old, nor gray-headed, but must be getting childish, for the tears spring to my eyes now that I have written it.

Can I better express my sincere regret? In the language of Col. Henderson: "A reunion of the 12th Iowa is a reunion of brothers, and a meeting of brothers without me is, to me, cruel." In the same letter the colonel writes that he is "shaping matters so as to be at Sioux City."

Oh, dear! must I yield the enjoyment of the eloquence of Henderson, the irrepressible anecdotes of Stibbs, the whole-souled greeting of Reed and Knoe, the warm "shake" of yourself and every comrade of the regiment, who may be so happy as to be there? And the old drum corps with their music that revived us so on so many weary marches. To the old color guard, who so bravely surrounded me with fixed bayonets that I dare not show the white feather, and every member of the gallant 12th, I send most fraternal greeting, and with that song prayer, "God be with you till we meet again," I am yours with sincere regret, H. J. GRANNIS.

Waterloo, Iowa, Oct. 7th, 1894.

A heart-full greeting to all my dear old comrades of the old 12th Iowa, who will assemble and meet together for a grand and glorious old handshaking and good visit at Sioux City. Oh, how I regret that I cannot be with you in the flesh, as I most assuredly will be in spirit. This has been an off year for me, having been out of employment for about half the time. I am financially out of condition to incur the expense of the vacation and as I can now secure employment for a month or more I must improve the opportunity of securing the necessary means to procure for my family the comforts of life for the on-coming winter, hence I must make this great personal self-denial and sacrifice. I sincerely hope there will be a goodly number of the old boys come together. I say old boys, for when we were together in the old 12th we were boys indeed, and it is as such I wish always to remember and think of them.

I regret to think that there are many of the boys who met here in Waterloo six years ago and answered to the roll call, now answer on the other side of Jordan. I do not know how all the companies have fared, but relentless death has claimed three of the members of Company E. I have to report, and without cause or date, the death of John C. Jones, Alexander Myers and John Ellwell. All were present at the meeting here except Comrade Ellwell, whom I have met but once since the war. He died in Chicago and was buried in Elmwood cemetery of this city February, 1892, this having been his place of residence when he enlisted in the company as first lieutenant.

I do not now remember how the membership in the association is kept up. Are the dues payable at each meeting of the regiment or is there but one payment for all time? Please inform me by letter in this regard.

I would like a copy of the report of the proceedings of the meeting, as I presume there will be a goodly number of them printed for distribution among the boys. I sincerely hope there will not be such uproar amongst the elements as there was two years ago, which seemed almost like a conspiracy against the old 12th Iowa to prevent a meeting. There are three members of the 12th residents of this town, viz: H. J. Harrison, Co. E; W. W. Whiteneck, Co. D, and your sadly disapointed comrade who had lotted on a grand old time at this meeting. But again I say I hope a goodly number of the old boys will meet together and have a jolly, happy time, and the blessing of a kind and beneficient Providence rule o'er all.

Your sorely disappointed comrade, in F., C. and L.,

J. W. SHUMAKER.

Freeport, Oct. 7, 1894.

Dear Comrade James E. Simpson:---

I regret very much that I cannot meet you and the rest of the boys at Sioux City, as I have a little three-year-old girl to take care of and no one to look after my things here. Give my regards to the comrades.

Yours truly in F., C. and L.

G. W. KIRKLAND.

In this I send $1.00 for my dues.

Davenport, Iowa, Sept. 30, 1894.

J. E. Simpson:---

My Dear Comrade: I find it will be impossible for me to meet with the boys at their reunion Oct. 10 to 12. I would be pleased though if you will remember me to them one and all. I will be with them in thought if not in person. Sincerely yours, J. B. MORGAN.

Lake Park, Minn., Oct. 1, 1894.

Jno. N. Weaver, Vice-President Regimental Association 12th Iowa Inantry, Sioux City, Iowa:---

Dear Sir and Comrade: I am sorry to inform you that I will be unable to attend the reunion at Sioux City, Oct. 10th to 12th next. With the best wishes for the success of the reunion, I am, Fraternally,

HANS HANSON,
Late 12th Iowa Infantry.

Decorah, Iowa, Oct. 10th, 1894.

J. E. Simpson, Secretary:---

Dear Comrade: I am very sorry that I have to write you in place of seeing you in person, but unforseen circumstances is the sole cause. I was called away up north on important business and did not return until today. Knowing that you have an interesting and happy gathering I wish I was with you, but my heart is with you. Greet me to the boys. God bless you all! Your comrade and friend,

A. H. GROVES.

Georgetown, Custer county, Nebraska, Oct. 6th, 1894.

John N. Weaver, Sioux City, Iowa:---

Mr. President, Dear Comrade: I have received circular notice and invitation to the reunion of the old 12th Iowa, for which I am thankful to you for. I have worked hard ever since the last reunion with the firm intention to meet my old comrades at the next reunion (this one), but I regret wtih pain and disappointment to say it will be imppossible for me to be with you this time. We have had the past season the worst drouth failure ever witnessed, and we have been having a succession of failures here; three drouth failures, and once I was completely wiped out by hail, so that I have had but one crop out of five. My health has been poor, so that I have been constantly under medical treatment, so that I need not add that my financial circumstances are such as to prevent me from having the long hoped for handshake, and hearty greeting I have so much longed for. And I assure you that it has not been neglect or indifference that has caused my delay in writing a few words so that if I cannot be present in person I will be there in spirit, but a lameness of my right arm and hand prevents me from holding a pen so I can write more than a few words at a time. But I hope by the next reunion to be able to meet you all. Tell the boys I have forgotten none of them, and never will. And through you I send my hearty greeting and love to all.

Your comrade,
B. FRANK MORROW.

Denver, Col., No. 406 16th street, Oct. 8, 1894.

Greeting to the 12th Iowa veterans. I had hoped to be one of the members to attend the reunion of the noble 12th Iowa at Sioux City. There is nothing that sends the blood coursing through my veins equal to the name of this regiment. Accept the best wishes of one that is interested in all comrades that are left, and I trust this reunion will be one of the bright spots in your life. It has only been my pleasure to meet with you once and that was in 1884, if I mistake not, at Manchester. As you all know F. F. Lankins had been dead about one year at that time. His death occurred in Denver, Col., August 17th, 1883. And I see a good many of the boys have answered to the roll call for the last time. Hoping you will all enjoy this reunion, believe me, I should so much love to be with you, but as it is impossible this time, will be next time, I think, hope to, at least, and if any of the 12th should come to Denver, nothing would be of more pleasure to me than for them to come and see me. Hoping to hear good reports from you soon, I am as ever. Your true friend and comrade,

MRS. J. W. PETTEE, nee Lankins.

P. S.---My present husband was a member of the 57th Illinois regiment.

Manchester, Iowa, Aug. 10h, 1894.

J. E. Simpson, Secretary 12th Iowa Infantry Reunion:---

Dear boys of the 12th: Though absent am with you in spirit; fond greetings; God be with you until our next reunion.

GEO. H. MORRISEY.

Cottage 9, Soldiers' Home, Quincy, Ill., Oct. 9, 1894.
Mr. J. E. Simpson and 12th Iowa:—

Dear Comrades: I received your kind invitation to attend the reunion the 10th to 12th inst.

I am very sorry I can not meet with you, but it is not possible for me to attend on account of my finances. My check will reach me too late to attend the reunion. I wish you all a good time.

Truly our ranks in the 12th Iowa are thinning and we can have but a few more reunions here, but there is a time coming when we can have a grander reunion than any of these, if we all live as faithful to our God as we did for our country, and fight the good fight of faith, we will have one of the grandest reunions in heaven we have ever had. I am trying every day to live a christian, and as I cannot be with you I request you to take a vote of the boys and report to me the number that are trying to serve God and make their home in heaven, where all is peace and joy forever. Please do this for my pleasure at least. I want to say here that I have not spent my pension at the saloon (God forbid), but I have spent it in helping to build a United Brethren church in this city and for other benevolent purposes. I want you to know that I have not squandered my money as some of the boys have done in our home.

We have thirty-eight boys in our cottage and eight of us are trying to fight the good fight of faith and gain a home in heaven. I trust the few that used to hold prayer meetings in the army are still attending and enjoying prayer meetings. If any have gone astray let them return as the prodigal of old did. We then had to fight the enemy of our country and our soul too. Now we have to fight the enemy of our soul, and that is whisky. Thousands are going to ruin every day in Quincy. This is all. Write an tell me about the reunion. How many were there? Give me their addresses and I will write to them. Love to all,

LAWRENCE LOTT
To the 12th Iowa.

Superior, Neb., Oct. 9, 1894.
Dear Comrades:—

I started to come to the reunion and got as far as Superior and I learned it would cost me full fare to come, and times are so hard and money so scarce that it is impossible for me to get there. I understood it was only half fare till I got to the depot. I am very sorry that I cannot be there. I saw A. G. Davenport this morning and he said to send his respects to all the old boys, and we hope that the next time will be able to get there.

PETER KEARNS,
A. G. DAVENPORT.

Holmes City, Douglas County, Minn., Oct. 7th, 1894.
J. E. Simpson, Norfolk, Neb.:—

Dear Comrade: Your circular of Sept. 10 duly received. I have always had an ardent desire to attend a reunion of the 12th Iowa, but the distance and financial circumstances always so far intervened. My personal appearance can therefore not be with you only by letter of regret.

Very truly,
L. LEWIS,
Late Co. I, 12th Iowa Infantry.

Magnolia, O., Sept. 12, 1894.

J. E. Simpson, Esq., Norfolk, Neb.:—

Dear Sir and Comrade: It was with mingled feelings of pleasure and regret that I perused your circular letter of invitation to attend the fifth reunion of the 12th Iowa Volunteer Infantry—pleasure that I was still held in remembrance by my comrades-in-arms, and regret that circumstances would not permit me to be present with them on that occasion. I, as well as the rest of the one time "Boys in Blue," am getting old—too old to take so long a trip, much as I would love to meet once more those with whom I bore arms during those trying years. But few more such privileges will be accorded us, but there will be a grand review beyond at which I trust we may all pass muster.

Hoping that you who are present may enjoy the meeting to the fullest, I assure you that my thoughts will be with you. Yours fraternally,
A. BROTHERS.

Soldiers' Home, Hot Springs, S. D., Oct. 11, 1894.

J. E. Simpson:—

Cannot come to reunion; not able; my best wishes to you all.
EMERY CLARK.

St. Edwards, Neb., Oct. 4th, 1894.

J. E. Simpson, Norfolk, Neb.:—

Dear Comrade: It is with the deepest regret that this will have to substitute my personal attendance at this reunion of the 12th Iowa.

I shall be with you in spirit and with my best wishes for the happiness of the comrades of the old 12th Iowa, hoping you will have a pleasant time. I will bid you good bye until our next reunion. Yours truly,
W. H. ELLISON,
Company K, 12th Iowa V. V. I.

Ponca, Oct. 9, 1894.

Comrades of the 12th Iowa:—

It is with the deepest feelings of regret that I write you of my inability to be present with you at this, your fifth reunion. I have anticipated great pleasure in meeting with you once more, but hard times presses me so closely, and not being a pensioner, I am unable to be present. My wife, who is a member of the Woman's Relief corps sends kind greetings and many regrets, that she cannot be with you.

Hoping nothing will occur to mar the happiness of your reunion I wish you all an enjoyable time, and may God's blessing rest upon you all.
I am fraternally yours in F. C. and L.,   JAMES P. COOK,
Company E, 12th Iowa.

Gila Bend, Ariz., Aug. 14th, 1894.
J. E. Simpson, Secretary Reunion Committee:—

Dear Sir: In reply to your circular of the 5th inst. will say that it will be very doubtful if I can enjoy the pleasure that a meeting with you all, the survivors of the glorious old 12th, would give. However, should it become possible you may rest assured I will be on hand. I can only say that I will write you later. Be sure and send me list of all who attend, should I not be there.   Very truly, etc.,   L. KALTENBACH.

Barron, Wis., October 9th, 1894.
To my Comrades of the 12th Iowa:—

It is a disappointment to have to pen these few lines of regret at not being able to be with you. When I received the circular letter of Comrade J. N. Weaver, for I did not receive the first circular, I expected to be with you today; but my son, who is my helper in this office, was taken very sick a few days ago. So it is impossible to get away. Hoping you may have a very pleasant reunion and a large gathering is the wish of Mr. and Mrs. W. A. Kent.

P. S.—Some of the comrades present may remember that my wife asked the comrades to sign their names in her album two years ago at the reunion. We would like a list of the names present, so we can add them.

Comrade Weaver, I will send you a paper containing the write up of our town by an Iowa man—of course it will be well done.
Yours in F., C. and L.,   W. A. KENT.

Crab Orchard, Cumberland Co., Tenn., Aug. 14, 1894.
J. E. Simpson, Norfolk, Neb. :—

Dear Comrade: I received yours of August 1, 1894, sending me an inviation to be present at the 12th Iowa reunion at Sioux City, Oct. 10, 11 and 12. There is nothing that would please me so well as to meet the old boys and have a good handshake, for I know that we would have a magnificent time, and it hurts me to think that it will be impossible for me to be there. I am so far away and haven't got much to go on in this world, but I want you when you go there and meet the boys to tell them of me, tell them that I am living in the state that we done some pretty hard fighting in war times. Tell them if they haven't all enlisted under the bloodstained banner of King Emanual to enlist now, and we will make a good fight, and we will meet in that great fort on high. You will have a good time at Sioux City and may the Lord bless you all. Yours in F., C. and L.,
M. TARPENNING.

Let me hear from you after the reunion.

TWELFTH IOWA V. V. INFANTRY.   61

                                    Pleasanton, Kan., Aug. 26, 1894.
Comrade Simpson:—

In reply I will say I received notice of our reunion to be held at Sioux City, Oct. 10 to 12, and will say that I will try to be there, but it is unfortunate for us living in Kansas, as we can get no rates. But I shall be there I think. No more at the present. I remain as ever,

Your comrade and friend,   ISAAC JOHNSON,
                                        P. O. Box 181.

                                    Rea, Mich., Aug. 11th, 1894.
Dear Comrades:—

Your communication at hand. I am sorry that poor health and want of means will keep me from attending your reunion. Believe me, my heart is with our boys, and I remember with pleasure all of the 12th Iowa. I have the drum on which I played at Fort Henry and Shiloh. Yours ever,
                                    SUMNER HARTSHORN.

                                    Vancouver Barracks, W. T., Sept. 28th, 1894.
Jno. M. Weaver, Vice President 12th Iowa Association, Sioux City, Iowa:—

My Dear Sir and Comrade: I write you this to acknowledge my receipt of two circular letters---one from Comrade Capt. J. E. Simpson at Norfolk, Nebraska, dated August 1st, 1894, and the other from yourself---both inviting all the comrades to attend the fifth reunion of the old 12th Iowa at your fair city on Oct. 10 to 12, at which time the Inter-state fair will be held there.

I hereby return my sincere thanks to Capt. Simpson and yourself for the favor of the notices. But I greatly regret to have to inform you that it is utterly impossible for me to avail myself of the great pleasure that it would give me to meet with friendly greeting all the old comrades of the gallant old 12th Iowa at Sioux City at the time designated. Incident to recent general orders from the secretary of war, discontinuing the ordinance depot at this station, (and at which place I am stationed on duty) and for the shipment of all the military stores, ammunition, etc., as soon as practicable to the Benicia Arsenal, Benicia, Cal., my services are now and will yet be at the date of the reunion pressingly needed to prepare the stores for shipment. So you can easily perceive that I have my hands full of business at the present time.

Notwithstanding the comrades are now well advanced in years, and almost 30 years has elapsed since the government ceased to need their services and they returned to their homes to engage in their various pursuits in life, and many are scattered far distant apart throughout our great country. But they still continue strongly animated with their old patriotism and a loving devotion of comradeship, likened to a sort of free masonary of peace and good will among all the members, one for another. God bless every member is my earnest wish. And I fondly trust that kind providence will favor me to meet with them at the next reunion. I have but one year and a half longer to serve until I will be placed on the honored roll of the retired list of the army with a liberal pay for my support. Yours in C., F., L.,

ROBERT WILLIAMS,
Late Capt. Co. E, 12th Iowa Infantry Vounteeers.

Please send me a copy of the proceedings, and also the reigmental history if completed, and state the price and I will forward you the money as soon as I receive them. R. W.

Lincoln, Neb., Oct. 7th, 1894.
Maj. D. W. Reed, President, Sioux City, Iowa :—

My Dear Major, and all the brave Comrades of the Gallant 12th Iowa: The time is near at hand for our fifth reunion, and I see no way for me to be present with you. It gives me pain and sadness to think that I must be deprived of so great a pleasure, but financially I am unable to respond. But I assure you that my heart is with you, my sympathies are with you, and I most earnestly hope that your meeting together will be a joyous one.

As I grow older I seem to be drawn nearer and nearer to the boys who wore the blue from '61 to '66, and more and more do I admire and prize and appreciate the grand old flag we held aloft on many a hard fought field, and for which we offered our lives as a sacratice again, and again, to prevent treason's hand from tearing away one single star from its field of azure blue. No name so dear, or that sends up such a thrill to my heart as "Old Glory." Ah! it's the flag of my country; the flag of our Union; the emblem of liberty, and may God bless and protect, and keep her "afloat in the skies till time shall be no more," is the response of every liberty-loving, loyal, patriotic citizen of our great nation.

Comrades, when I am laid away in the narrow tomb, I want no broadcloth robes—I care little for flowers—but I do want to be draped with the precious folds of "Old Glory," entwined about either arm, and her untarnished stars about my neck and on either shoulder. I want my loyal sons to look for the last time upon their sire in this robe of loyalty and patriotism, to impress their hearts with a lasting lesson of love to country and devotion to its flag.

Yes, give me "Freedom's Starry emblem, boys," to be my winding sheet. Let my soul take its flight from the star-robed clay ,below to its celestial home amidst the stars above.

And now old comrades I must bid you good-bye. I so much wish I might meet you all once more and grasp again the loyal hands that carried the deadly steel into the thickest of the fight, but I fear I cannot. One by one, like autumn leaves, we are falling, seared by the frosts of time.

May God deal kindly with you all and each of you deal kindly with yourselves, by being as loyal to your God as you have been to your country, is the heartfelt desire of your old comrade.

JAMES F. ZEDIKER,
Formerly of Co. I, 12th Iowa Infty.,
34 Q St., Lincoln, Neb.

Roster of Members.

Roster of members of the 12 Iowa V. V. Infantry, so far as known at the Time of This Reunion.

FIELD AND STAFF.

Colonel—J. H. Stibbs, Room 88, P. O. Building, Chicago, Ill.
Lt. Colonel—S. G. Knee, Colesburg, Iowa.
Major—S. D. Brodtbeck, 113 South Broadway, Los Angeles, Cal.
Major—E. M. Van Duzee, St. Paul, Minn.
Major—D. W. Reed, Suite 814 Chamber of Commerce, Chicago, Ill.
Surgeon—C. C. Parker, Fayette, Iowa.
Ass't Surgeon—W. H. Finley, Franklin, Neb.
Ass't Surgeon—James Barr, Roseburg, Ore.
Adjutant—N. E. Duncan, No. 3029 Locust St., Kansas City, Mo.
Adjutant—S. R. Burch, Olathe, Kansas.
Quartermaster—G. H. Morrisey, Manchestor, Iowa.
Quartermaster—H. C. Morehead, Cedar Rapids, Iowa.
Chaplain—Rev. Frederick Humphrey, St. John Rectory, Havre de Grace, Md.
Hospital Steward—Rev. J. C. H. Hobbs, Salem, Neb.
Hospital Stewart—J. J. Walker, De Witt, Missouri.
Com. Sergt.—James Evans, Dubuque, Iowa.
Sergt. Major—A. J. Rodgers, Corner 28th St. and Wabash Ave., Chicago, Ill.
Fife Major—D. S. Martin, Iowa Falls, Iowa.
Fife Major—S. M. French, Denver, Col.—Leader the Geo. W. Cook Drum Corps, No. 3050 Downing Ave.

COMPANY A.

Armstrong, B. A., Liscomb, Ia.
Bird, G. M., Illinois.
Bowers, I. H., Eldora, Ia.
Cougar, J. D., Eldora, Hardin Co., Ia.
Cromwell, T. C., Oakland, Ia.
Cobb, G. H., Eldora, Ia.
Dobbins, Hiram, Jewel Co., Kan.
Edgington, T. B., 18 Madison St., Memphis, Tenn.
Glass.
Hunter, J. R. C., Webster, Ia.
Hobb, Rev. J. C. H., Salem Neb.
Jackson, Samuel, Oregon.
Kellogg, R. E., Dows, Ia.
Brother, A., Magnalia, Starke Co., O.
Bell, Thos. R., Iowa Falls, Ia.
Brown, S. B., Jewell City, Kan.
Clarkson, R. P., Des Moines, Ia.
Combes, E. C., Hanover, Ill.
CCrist, Job, Marshalltown, Ia.
Dobbins, Levi, Eldora, Ia.
Ferree, S. R., Belle Plaine, Ia.
Fountain, Francis.
Haskins, G. H., Maryville, Mo.
Haywood, W. P., Lyons, Ia.
Ibach, B. D., Eldora, Ia.
Kidwiler, M., Mo.
Kemp, Sumner, Alden, Ia.

Macy, Seth, Des Moines, Ia.
Mann, A. J., Perry, Ill.
Moore, G. W., Maryville, Mo.
Miller, Zablma.
Mitchell, G. W., Lawn Hill, Ia.
Reed, G. W., Yarkie, Mo.
Rulo, G. W., South Bend, Ind.
— Runkle, C. M., Plankinton, S. D.
Sawin, E. S., Union, Ia.
Welsh, Nathan.
Webb, A. E., Eldora, Ia.
Zieger, N. W., Eldora, Ia.

McPherson, W. G., Millbank, S. D.
Moore, W. W., Manchester, Ia.
Mann, Wm., Steamboat Rock, Ia.
Martin, D. S., Iowa Falls, Ia.
Parish, William.
Richards, Jos., Boone, Ia.
Richards, William.
Sprague, K. S., Fremont, Neb.
— Wilson, T. H., Robertson, Ia.
Walker, Samuel, De Witt, Mo.
Wickman, A. J., Eagle City, Ia.
Zieger, J. W., Eldora, Ia.

COMPANY B.

Captain Williard C. Earle..Waukon, Ia.
Captain J. P. Jackson...Village Creek, Ia.
— Second Lieut. J. D. Cole...Lansing, Ia.
Sergt. Major A. J. Rodgers, Corner 28th St. and Wabash Ave., Chicago, Ill.
First Sergt. Geo. Ibach...Preston, Minn.
Sergt. Elias Repp
Sergt. Henry Fry...Penn.
— Sergt. W. P. Winter...Bancroft, Ia.
Sergt. John Upstrom..403 4th St., Sioux Falls, S. D.
Sergt. R. B. Sargent...Kansas.
Corp'l. H. Goodrich
Corp'l. Stephen Thibeda..Waukon, Ia.
— Corp'l. Robert Wampler...Waukon, Ia.
Corp'l. Aslak Larson..Preston, Minn.
Corp'l. Fred Monk..Eitzen, Minn.
— Corp'l. L. D. Bearce..Onawa, Ia.
Corp'l. M. Englehorn...Kas.
Corp'l. W. B. Bort..Viroqua, Wis.

Adams, O. F.
Bartlett, F. C., Denver, Col.
Bailey, W. F., St. Paul, Minn.
Brock, Gustavus.
Burnham, H.
Churchill, L. B.
Candee, Geo.
Decker, Adam, Lansing, Ia.
— Dowling, John, Rex, Ia.
Ericksen, E. A., Salem, S. D.
Feidt, John.
Goodykoonts, D. F., Boone, Ia.
Iverson, Knud, Lansing, Ia.
Jones, Henry.
Johnson, Lewis.
Knudson, Hans.
Lewis, Edward.
— McCabe, Hugh, Waukon, Ia.
McKay, Frank.
McDonald, James.
Ogan, Chas. C., Sibley, Ia.
Oleson, Barnhart.
Peterson, Bore.
Peck, John P., Plankinton, S. D.
Pratt, M. H., Spokane Falls, Wash.

— Andrews, H. R., Turkey River, Ia.
Bailey, Geo. N., St. Paul, Minn.
Bathen, Robt., Riceville, Minn.
Bort, A. K., Viroqua, Wis.
Burlingame, O. D., 1938 Water St., Chicago, Ill.
Castellar, Frank.
— Dowling, Thos., Rossville, Ia.
Edwards, Isaac.
Ettle, George, Waukon, Ia.
Greenap, S. H., Motley, Minn.
Hawkins, Hiram.
Isted, I. B. S., Milwaukee, Wis.
Jennings, D. P.
Klees, Frank, Rossville, Ia.
Larkins, Rees N.
Larson, Kensil.
McGuire, Brian, Freeport, Ill.
McClintock, Jas., Rossville, Ia.
Noyes, Alonzo.
Oleson, Ole.
Oleson, John, Spring Grove, Minn.
Porter, John B.
Plank, Levi, Lake de Funiak, Fla.
Pratt, R. G., Storm Lake, Ia.

Russell, Chas., Brooklyn, Mo.
Schiffbauer, Rich.
Smith, Ira J.
Stecker, Wm.
Thayer, Jesse.
Woodmansee, Isaac, Rossville, Ia.
Warberg, Ole B., Spring Grove, Minn.
Wert Augustus H. West

Roe, Charles E.
Stortz, Joseph.
Smith, C. S., North McGregor, Ia.
Sanner, Michael F., Rossville, Ia.
Wood, Edwin W.
Wood, Stephen.
Wilber, Robert.

NOTE:—Total number of Company, 132; of whom reported dead, 42; disability during service, 30; from wounds, 4; wounded in action, 35; taken prisoners April 6, '62, at Shiloh, Tenn., 56; killed in action, 3.

COMPANY C.

Captain Geo. W. Cook..Medicine Lodge, Kan.
Captain David W. Reed (Major 12th Iowa)
                Suite 814, Chamber of Commerce, Chicago, Ill.
Captain Wm. L. Henderson..Cresco, Ia.
First Lieut. David B. Henderson (Col. 46th Iowa)..............Dubuque, Ia.
First Lieut. Henry J. Grannis..................................Randalia, Ia.
Mrs. J. W. Pettee (Nee Lankins)...............No. 406 16th St. Denver, Col.
First Sergt. Jer F. Hutchins (Capt. Co. E . 12th Ia.)....Minneapolis, Minn.
Sergt. Gilbert Hazlett..Allison, Ia.
Sergt. Emery Clark. (put in Co. B, Soldiers' Home).......Hot Springs, S. D.
Sergt. James Stewart..West Union, Ia.
Sergt. Philo R. Woods..Fayette, Ia.
Sergt. Phineas R. Ketchum.....................................West Union, Ia.
Sergt. Frank W. Moine....................................Strawberry Point, Ia.
Corp'l. Geo. L. Durno...Springville, Ia.
Corp'l. James Barr (Ass't. Sergt. 12th Ia.)..................Roseburgh, Ore.
Corp'l. John W. Bysong.......................................West Point, Neb.
Corp'l. Joseph D. Baker.....................................Montividio, Minn.
Corp'l. Geo. E. Comstock.......................................Fayette, Ia.
Corp'l. Henry C. Curtis..Lemars, Ia.
Corp'l. John A. Delezene..................................Rock Rapids, Minn.
Corp'l. William H. Jordon...................................Cheney, Wash.
Corp'l. Amos K. Ketchum.......................................Clarion, Ia.
Corp'l. John E. Kent..Belle Plaine, Ia.
Corp'l. I. W. King..Emerick, Neb.
Musician Sumner Hartshorn...................................Dundee, Mich.

Abbott, Edward J., Garden Grove, Cal
Beck, Samuel C., Waverly, Ia.
Ballinger, John W., Lacy, Ia.
Brown, John T.
Brown, Geo., Woodstock, Ill.
Burroughs. Geo. A., Douglas, Ia.
Barton, Alvah H.
Barr, Henry, Tama County, Ia.
Carmichael, Jas. H., Illyria, Ia
Comstock, Frank, St. Louis, Mo.
Clark, Henry, Melborne, Ia.
Connor, Samuel, Maxwell, Ia.
Davis, Jay C., Wis.
Davis, A. J., Berrian Spring, Mich.
Forbes, David, Elgin, Ia.
Gillman, Ezekiel D., 27th Ia.
Hazlett, John B., Sioux Falls, S. D.
Hendershot, Thos., Plainview, Neb.

Barnes, Jas. (transfer from 27).
Benjamin, Nathan, drafted.
Bennefield, Wm., substitute.
Bowers, Wm. H., Limestoneville, Pa.
Becktell, David T., Volga City, Ia.
Brant, Allen, (transfer from 27)
                              Fairbanks, Ia.
Browsley, Wm., drafted.
Card, Silas B.
Carrington, Chas., Rock Branch, Ia.
Canfield, Theron P., 27th Ia.,
                              Buffalo Grove, Ia.
Dawson, John, 27th Ia.
Delezene, Benj., Republic City, Kan.
Gifford, Simeon, Douglas, Ia.
Hill, Benj. J.
Hamlin, Lyman S., Oelwein, Ia.
Husted, Jacob M.

Henselbecker; Henry, Bluffton, Ia.
Hinkel, Edward, Winfield, Ia.
Hamlin, Wm. A., Crawford, Neb.
Jordon, Isadore L., Alton, Kan.
Jaques, Luther, Crawford, Neb.
Jones, Geo. M., Drafted.
Kelsey, E. A., Tripoli, Ia.
Lattimer, Geo, H , West Gate, Ia.
Lyons, Wm A., West Union, Ia.
Lattimer, Robt. Z., Fayett, Ia.
Mattocks,Jason L., Minneapolis, Minn.
Mattocks, Ross, Wadena, Ia.
McCall, John W., Nemaha, Neb.
Martin, Chas. I , 27th, Horton, Ia.
Patterson, Samuel W., 27th.
Proctor, Geo. W , 27th, Lawrens, Ia
Rodgers, Reuben F., Waucoma, Ia.
Rodolph, John J.
Spears, Niles H , West Gate, Ia.
Smith, Jacob R., Ft. Smith, Ark.
Sykes, Orvis, Freeport, Ill.
Sherburne, Daniel.
Utter, Albert, Sycamore, Ill.
Williams, Rudolph, West Union, Ia.

Henderson, Jas A., 27th Ia ,
       Cherokee, Ia.
Hill, John W.
Jewell, Jas, E., 27th Ia.
Jackway, G. H., 27th Ia., Lamont, Ia.
Kent, Wm. A., Barron, Wis.
Kelley, Artemus
Little, James.
Lott, Lawrence, Soldiers' Home,
       Quincy, Ill.
Munger, Albert P., Cowlitz, Wash.
McCall, Daniel E , Culver, Kan.
Muchmore, Stephen D., 27th.
Pitts, Jas., Drafted, London, Kan.
Pricket, John L., Drafted
Quivey, Wm, W., Pierce, Neb.
Rockwell, Wm. R., drafted.
Stone, Daniel, Waucoma, Ia.
Strong, John P., Schuyler, Neb.
Saulsbury, John, Ivanhoe, Kan.
Sprowls, John.
Tatro, Aug., Clermont, Ia.
Verdin, Isaiah C.
Warner, Walter B , Clermont, Ia.

COMPANY D.

 Roster of the Survivors of Company D, 12 Regiment Iowa Volunteer Infantry, revised and corrected by Captain E. B. Soper, Emmetsburgh, Iowa:

Col. John H. Stibbs..................... Room 88, P. O. Building, Chicago, Ill.
Captain Hiel Hale .... Yuma, Ariz.
Captain E. B. Soper... ....Emmetsburg, Ia.
Captain John M. Clark.................................... ?........Springfield, Ia.
Lieut. Homer C. Moorhead .... Cedar Rapids, Ia.
Lieut. Eli King ....Washington, Kan.

Lyman M. Ayers, Cedar Rapids, Ia.
Edwin A. Buttolph, Cedar Rapids, Ia.
William Bumgardiner, Scranton, Ia.
Sylvester R. Burch, Olathe, Kan.
Edwin H. Bailey, Freedonia, Kan.
Henry W. Bailey, Kirkman, Ia.
Allen M. Blanchard, Soldiers' Home,
    Dayton, O.
John W. Burch, Cedar Junction,
    Johnson county, Kan.
A. C. Blood.
M. H. McElroy, Percival, Ia.
Thomas J. Lewis, Cedar Rapids, Ia.
William L. Lee, P. O. box 844,
    Helena, Mont.
Bentley Luse, West Liberty, Ia.
Jas. H. Little, Mt. Carmel, Ill.
Richard S. Martin.
Alpheus H. McEntyre.
B. Frank Morrow, Georetown,
    Custer county, Neb.
O. H. Maryett, Del Norte,
    Rio Grande county, Colo.

Isaac G. Clark.
Ferdinand Dubois, Charter Oak, Ia.
Herman Elgin, Bolen,
    Worth county, Ia.
James D. Ferner, Nevada, Ia.
Samuel H. Flint, care Buffalo,
    Glucose Co., Leavenworth, Kan.
Perry Gephart, Lake Forest,
    Cook county, Ill.
Herman Grass, 816 7th S. St.,
    Fargo, N. D.
Irdill W. Hollar, Forestville,
    Sonoma county, Cal.
Robinson L. Johnson, Sanford,
    Keya Paha county, Neb.
John Luther, Norton,
    Norton county, Kan.
Frank Renchin, Pratt.
    Steel county, Minn.
Jesse H. Ross, Villa Park, Colo.
Dudley E Stedman, Vinton, Ia.
Josiah Scott, Shellsburg, Ia.

TWELFTH IOWA V. V. INFANTRY.

David W. Minor, Arcata, Humbolt county, Cal.
Nathan G. Price, Jewel City, Kan.
J. V. George Price, Mountain Grove, Mo.
Theodore L. Prescott.
Howard Pangburn, Palouse, Whitman county, Wash.
Dennis C Quigley, Plover, Ia.
John W. Rowan, Vinton, Ia.
Henry W. Ross, Campbell, Franklin county, Neb.
Angus W. Brown.
Dennis Conley, Davenport, Ia.
Jas. L. Cowell, Walla Walla, Wash.
Charles W. Clark, Cedar Rapids, Ia.
John M. Carson, Grinnell, Ia.
Robert C. Cowell, Bayard, Guthrie conty, Ia.
James C. Daily, Thayer, York county, Neb.
Roswell K. Soper, Estherville, Ia.
Joseph O. Startwell, Marion, Ia.
Aaron A. Steward, Carthage, Mo.
Daniel Sivetts, Sublett, Adair county, Mo.
J. M. Tarpenning, Northville, Cumberland county, Tenn.
Frank D. Thompson, Nevada, Ia.
William H. Trowbridge.
William M. Ven Emmon, Norfolk, Neb.
John J. Whittam.
Jasper Wagner, Rome City, Nobles county, Ind.
William W. Whiteneck, Waterloo, Ia.
John Watrobek, Cottersville, St. Charles county, Mo.
John J. Wyatt, O'Clair, Wis.
John N. Weaver, attorney at law, Sioux City, Ia.
Hiram F. Cooper, Littleport, Ia.

COMPANY E.

Boone, R G., Scott, Ia.
Beckwith, W. H., Parkersburg, Ia.
Bird, E., Winterset, Ia.
Belton, Jas, Batavia, Todd county, Minn.
Cook, Chas., Lester, Ia.
Crowhurst, Seth J., Salem, S. D.
Cook, J P., Ponca, Neb.
Early, T. M., Bristow, Ia.
Hamilton, Wm., La Porte City, Ia.
Harrison, H. J., Waterloo, Ia.
Large, F. A, La Porte City, Ia.
Margretz, J S., Hitesville, Ia.
Minium, David, Big Groves, Ia.
Perry, A. B., Dunkerton, Ia
Rich, J. W., Iowa City, Ia
Stewart, Joel A., Oregon City, Ore.
Seeber, G. L., Sabula, Ia.
Switzer, C. R., Lewis, Ia.
Smith, Harvey, Waterloo, Ia.
Shumaker, John, Waterloo, Ia.
Strong, Ezra, National City, Cal.
Shaver, W C., Utter, Mo.
Williams, Captain Roberts, Vancouver, Was.
Biller, A. J, Waterloo, Ia.
Boylon, Thos, Stockton, Kan.
Bird, R. L., Yuma, Cal.
Collins, C. P , Charles City, Ia.
Creighton, David, Geneva, Ia.
Cook, Joseph, New Castle, Neb.
Cook, Sylvester, New Castle, Neb.
Church, Nathan, Webster City or Eagle Grove, Ia.
Eberhart, Ben. E., Marshaltown, Ia.
Graham, Jacob, Davenport, Ia.
Hayward, C. B., Mooreville, Ia.
Morris, C. D , Canton, S. D.
Ochs, Charles, Ackley, Ia.
Reed, Zeff, Bard, Louisa County, Ia.
Surfus, C. V., Bristow, Ia.
Sunderlin, M. V. B , Janesville, Ia.
Schrack, David, Oelwin, Ia.
Sharp, Oliver, Finchford, Ia.
Sawyer, E , La Porte City, Ia.
Shroyer, Nathaniel, Tainter, Ia.
Talbot, Allen E., Orleans, Ind.
Watkins, Isaac, Crawfordsville, Ind.
West, D. F., Theon, Wash.

COMPANY F.

Ainsworth, J. E., 714 1st. Ave., Council Bluffs, Ia.
Bremner, John, Yankton, S. D.
Brown, Eugene, Brush Creek, Ia.
Coolidge, F. W., Sho Shone, Ida.
Dunham, Abner, Manchester, Ia.
Davison, Wm., Siam, Ia.
Annis, Geo. W., Lanark, Ill.
Buckman, Wm. H., Dyersville, Ia.
Correll, Ed., Greeley, Ia.
Coolidge, C. L., Central City, Neb.
Dahl, John A., Silver Creek, Ia.
Eldridge, J. E., Stark, Kan.
Eldridge, R. C., Niagara Falls, N. Y.

Eaton, John J., Edgewood, Ia.
French, S. M., leader G. W. Cook Drum
  Corps, 3050 Dowling Ave., Denver, Col.
Goodel, Wm. H., Manchester, Ia.
Halfhill, Josiah, Wood Center, Ia.
Johnson, Isaac, Pleasinton, Kan.
Kent, George, Oelwein, Ia.
Kirchner, Mike.
Lee, John F., Council Grove, Kan.
Mackey, H. F., Maynard, Ia.
Mann., Wm. W., Ranelsburg, Neb.
Nelson, T. C., Hazelton, Ia.
Preston, H. M., Ft. Dodge, Ia.
Peasley, R. H., Kansas.
Steen, C. C., Minneapolis, Kan.
Stribling, C. C., Clifton, Tenn.
Thorn, Chris, Waverly, Ia.
Tibbetts, W. F., Cheney, Kan.
Weeden, R. L., Nugents Grove, Ia.
Woolridge, G. W., Elkport, Ia.

Girton, Joseph S., Hazelton, Ia.
Gift, J. W., 900 Main St., Peoria, Ill.
Grice, A. J., Doniphon, Neb.
Hasbrouck, D. H., Prairie Creek, Ia.
Kaltenbach, Sam'l., Manchester, Ia.
Kaltenbach, L. P., Gila Bend, Ariz.
Kaster, Hiram, Manchester, Ia.
Lee, Jas. F., Clay Mills, Ia.
McGowan, Thos., Independence, Ia.
Manning, A. L., Dunlap, Ia.
Manley, R. L.
Nelson, W. A., Hazelton, Ia.
Olmstead, H., Independence, Ia.
Potter, Jas. W., Fayette, Ia.
Ralston, Nelson, Canton, S. D.
Small, H. J. F., Chicago, Ill.
Schneider, J., Rosewell, S. D.
Terrill, R. W., Manchester, Ia.
Widger, Joshua, Manchester, Ia.
Wandall, A., Volga City, Ia.

COMPANY G.

L. D. Townsley, River Forest,
  Cook County, Ill.
J. E. Simpson, Norfolk, Neb.
A. E. Anderson, Decorah, Ia.
Anderson, Peter.
Anderson, E.
Clark, J. M.
Coon, C. A., Sabinal, Tex.
Christopherson, C., Hartland, Minn.
Dunn, Van R., Nebraska.
Fuller, A. S., Maryville, Mo.
Groves, A. H., Decorah, Ia.
Gilbertson, O., Gilchrist, Minn.
Hall, Giles.
Honge, G. A., Albert Lea, Minn.
Hanson, Hans, Lake Park, Minn.
Hanson, Halver, Sheldon, S. D.
Johnson, Nels O., Duluth, Minn.
Kirkland, G. W., Freeport, Ia.
Kittleson, G.
Larson, Peter.
Manson, J.
Montgomery, Wm. V.
Madinn, D. L.
McCabe, C. Sherburne, Minn.
Nass, G. H., Washington Prairie, Ia.
Oleson, O.
Oleson, A. H., Egge, S. D.
Palmer, R., Nebraska.
Raucha, Fred., Skidmore, Mo.
Ryerson, F., Ashby, Minn.
Smith, I. K., Baraboo, Wis.
Simmons, R., Lake Park, Minn.
Steen, John, Wahoo, Neb.
Steen, Henry, Lyons, Neb.
Simmons, John, Flandreau, S. D.

J. O. Johnson, Hesper, Ia.
R. Hard.
G. W. Sharp, Fargo, N. D.
J. H. Womeldorf, Neligh, Neb.
Anderson, A., Albert Lea, Minn.
Ballard, Strawder.
Crane, John.
Crowell, J. M.
Davis, N. J., Berrian Springs, Mich.
Engberston, E., Aastad, Minn.
Fladmark, S. M. M.
Green, L. D.
Gulbranson, A., Rothsay, Minn.
Honsom, Klaus.
Hanson, Ole.
Harris, F. W.
Hand, Andrew J.
Johnson, H. E., Evansville, Minn.
Kittleson, C. B., Norway Lake, Minn.
Larson, John, Lacqui Parle, Minn.
Low, Lewis L.
McCloud, S.
Meyer, C. Highland, Ill.
Meader, M. E., Hesper, Ia.
Moe, Peter, Springfield, Minn.
Nelson, Swen.
Oleson, E.
Pierce, Fletcher.
Raucha, Ed.
Rocksvold, O. P., Thoton, Ia.
Skinner, F., Forest City, S. D.
Simmison, Nels.
Severson, Nels.
Stalim, Lars L., 208 Bluff St.,
  Sioux City, Ia.
Slattery, Thomas.

TWELFTH IOWA V. V. INFANTRY.   69

Tinke, J.
Thompson, A. K.
Taylor, W. H. H.
Wright, C. F.
Wheeler, Horace, Algona, Ia.
Wait, W., Ida, Mo.
West, S., Red Cloud, Neb.

Thompson, T., Lincoln Center, Kan.
Tobiason, Andrew, Windom, Minn.
Thoryson, Andrew, Crastad, Minn.
W. L. Winsor, Clinton, Mo.
Mrs. Jennie Burdick Sturdevant,
                Spring Valley, Minn.
Young, Anna S., Nashua, Ia.

COMPANY H.

Atkinson, W. L. C., Omaha, Neb.
Brown, Tom, Jewel City, Kan.
Benedict, John W., Lexington, Neb
Clark, B. A., Colesburg, Ia.
Cox, W. H., Alta, Ia.
Duncan, N. E., Custom House,
                Kansas City, Mo.
Fishel, S. C., Iowa Fall, Ia.
Fishel, S. K., Ft. McGinnis, Mont.
Franks, Joseph, Lamont, Ia.
Gosting, Alfred G., Strawberry Pt., Ia.
Hamblin, R. E., Findley, Ia.
Jackson, S. M., Lincoln, Neb.
King, Wilson, Emerick, Neb
Light, Robt., Tilden, Neb.
Light, Joseph A., Norfolk, Neb.
Mason, John S., Worthington, Ia.
McConnell, Alex. S., Hopkinton, Ia.
Nauman, Geo., North Platte, Neb.
Royse, Wm., Atlantic, Ia.
Struthers, Craig, Neb.
Shorter, James, Shell Rock, Ia.
Sloan, S. B., Greeley, Ia.
Van Anda, John N., Freemont, Neb.
Wisegarber, Wm., Walnut Hill, Ill.

Briggs, H. S., Marcus, Ia.
Benedict, R. W., Blackhawk, S. D.
Currie, John G., Butte City, Mont.
Crist, John W., Central City, S. D.
Croosby, J. M , Yankton, S. D.
Evans, Joseph, Tipton, Mo.
Evans, James, Dubuque, Ia.
Fishel, Robert W., Greeley, Ia.
Flenniken, J. B, Battle Creek, Neb.
Grimes, R. M., Kearney, Neb.
Henry, Philip, Greeley, Ia.
Jones, David, Taconic, Ia.
Kuhnes, J. C., Manning, Ia.
Knee, Samuel G., Colesburg, Ia.
Langston, Aaron J, transferred from
  Co. D, 27th Ia. to Co. D, 12th Ia.
Moreland, C. D. W., Earlville, Ia.
McCune, W. H., Ruthven, Ia.
Playter, H. J., 1921 6th St. N. W.,
             Washington, D. C.
Smith, Thomas, Turkey River, Ia.
Shorter, Wm., Shell Rock, Ia.
Trumble, James, Manchester, Ia.
Winch, Edward, Arena, Wis.
Ward, John W., Burlington, Ia.

COMPANY I.

Austin, N. E., Andrew, Ia.
Allen, Eugene, Cedar Rapids, Ia.
Austin, Marion, Staplehurt, Neb.
Brintner, Wm., Brayton, Ia.
Brown, J., unknown.
Butters, John F , Sioux City, Ia.
Buchanan, James, Tama, Ia.
Belknap, Albert, Freemont, Neb.
Behnke, Frank, Guttenberg, Ia.
Clark, Frank, Humboldt, Ia.
Campbell, E B. Armstrong, Ia.
Campbell, Thos., Humboldt county.
               Unique, Ia.
Cobb, Edgar C., Keokuk, Ia.
Cobb, Wm. A., Walla Walla, Wash.
Cotes, J. W., Talcott, S. D.
Davenport, A. J., Superior, Neb.
Dupray, Wm. H., 2630 Adel St.
             Sioux City, Ia.
Devine, John J., room 31,
  152½ N. High St., Columbus, O.
Eddie, Thomas C , Pueblo, Colo.

McKinley, James, Maquoketa, Ia.
McCarron, W. F., Athens, Tenn.
McCallum, D. D., Sibley, Ia.
McDermont, Mike, Epworth, Ia.
Nagle, M. D., Dubuque, Ia.
Nims, Weed, Maquoketa, Ia.
O'Niel, Andrew, not known,
Palmer, A. L , Seattle, Wash.
Paup, David, Sac City, Ia.
Paup, Seth, not known.
Perkins, H. J., Seattle, Wash.
Poesch, Lorenso, Postville, Ia.
Ray, John S., Naponee, Neb.
Reardon, John, not known.
Rolff, Marion, Maquoketa, Ia.
Swank, John M., Muscatine, Ia.
Sumbardo, C. L., St. Paul, Minn.
Starbuck, Wm, Oldham, S. D.
Smith, Henry, Maquoketa, Ia.
Schmidt, John, Lincoln, Neb.
Thompson, Jas. L., Franklin, Neb.
Teskey, George, Ellwood, Ia.

Eaton, T., Maquoketa, Ia.
Fry, Wm., Scranton, Ia.
Goodenow, M. B., Ord, Neb.
Hatfield, Aug., Munipan 235 Com., Jersey City, N. J.
Harding, James P., Baldwin, Ia.
Hendricks, Wm., Winterset, Ia.
Jenkins, Alonzo, not known.
Johnson, Hans, not known.
Knodt, Chas., Postville, Ia.
Kennedy, S. L., Cedar Rapids, Ia.
Hohler, Wm., Dubuque, Ia.
Kerns, Peter, Reubens, Kan.
Lewis, Lewis, Holmes City, Minn.
Lewis, Peter, Lund, Wis.

Van Hook, Samuel, (Hospital for Insane) Independence, Ia.
Van Duzee, E. M. (Maj.), St. Paul, Minn.
Wells, Chas. A., Sabula, Ia.
Wilson, T. J., Maquoketa, Ia.
Wilson, J. F., Fulton, Ia.
Wolcott, Alden E., Lynxville, Wis.
Williams, S., Atlantic, Ia.
Williams, Sidney, Colfax, Ill.
Weaviness, Mike, not known.
Ysley, George, Clinton, Ia.
Zediker, Jas. F.(Capt.),324 N. 34th St., Lincoln, Neb.

COMPANY K.

Brooks, John.
Brown, J. J., Bloomington, Neb.
Billings, Abram, Luzern, N. Y.
Barden, Henry A.
Beckner, J. M., Charles City, Ia.
Bugbey, S. M., 1012 5th St. N., Minneapolis, Minn.
Church, P., Arborville, Neb.
Deutsher, Albert, Nat. Home, O.
Freeman, Richard, Spencer, O.
Gilchrist, J. N., Durham, Ia.
Keith, W. B., Precept, Neb.
Merriam, H. C., Nugent, Ia.
Mathis, W. R., Omaha, Neb.
Morgan, J. B., Davenport, Ia.
Mosher, Alvin.
McConnell, Alex. S., Hopkinton, Ia.
Robinson, Alonzo, Albion, Neb.
Willard, Porter H., Hopkinton, Ia.

Blood, George W.
Billings, Chas. D., Bloomington, Neb.
Blanchard, Thos., Le Mar, Kan.
Baldwin, Newton, Ada, Kan
Blanchard, Ira. D., Crookston, Minn.
Davis, W. N., Des Moines, Ia.
Dolley, Godfrey, Hopkinton, Ia.
Ellison, W. H., St. Edwards, Neb.
Fuller, O. T., Webster Grove, Mo.
Horn, Samuel, Colesburg, Ia.
Kemp, Wm., Kirwin, Kan.
Merriam, C. E., Hopkinton, Ia.
Mathis, E. R., Omaha, Neb.
Morehouse, P. J., Masonville, Ia.
Morgan, Wm. B., Bloomington, Neb.
Mickey, Isaac, Waukon, Ia.
Webb, Laurence, Cedar Rapids, Ia.
Waldroff, Henry, La Porte City, Ia.
Young, A. S., Nashua, Ia.

SIXTH REUNION

OF THE

TWELFTH IOWA

VETERAN VOLUNTEER

INFANTRY.

HELD AT

MANCHESTER, IOWA.

NOVEMBER, 11TH. AND 12TH.

1896.

E 507
.5
12th I

REUNION

OF THE

Twelfth Iowa Veteran Volunteer Infantry

NOVEMBER, 11TH, AND 12TH., 1896.

The 12th Iowa Infantry, that gallant regiment of the famous "Hornet's Nest Brigade," held its sixth annual re-union at Manchester, Iowa, November 11th and 12th, 1896. The closeness of the times, illness and distance, prevented many of the comrades from attending, but what was lacking in numbers was more than made up in enthusiasm. The veterans began coming in on early morning trains of the 11th, and the scene at the depot was a jovial one. The morning and afternoon sessions were held at the Universalist church and little was done beyond the exchange of reminiscences and a general "visit." The registration of members present and collection of money to defray the expense of the publication of the usual pamphlet were attended to in the afternoon, in the way of business.

Letters of regret at their inability to be present were read from comrades who are scattered over the vast empire from the Missouri to the Pacific. They came all the way from Oregon, Washington, California and other states in the land of the setting sun, all expressing heartfelt wishes for the success of the reunion.

The reports of the officers were read, showing the organization to be in a flourishing condition.

Among the letters of regret was one from Comrade French, a resident of Colorado, who, in order to be present at a former reunion, traveled 150 miles on snow shoes and waded a river filled with floating ice. This comrade was the regiment's chief musician, who, on innumerable occasions when the boys were tried and weary from marching struck up on his fife "The Girl I Left Behind Me," or some other tune that recalled to the boys the loved ones at home and caused them to fill the magnolia-scented woods of the south with their loud hurrahs.

There was one present who had never missed a battle or a skirmish—the man who carried the flag of the 12th in the battles in which it took part—Henry J. Grannis, of Vandalia, Fayette county. The flag was displayed, draping the president's desk. It, too, was an old veteran, and if it could speak it would say that no braver man than Grannis ever held his country flag. He had a most remarkable career. He carried the regimental flag all through the struggle, and through many of the bloodiest battles, and, strange to say, never received a scratch —the records in the war department showing no similar record of a colors-sergeant.

In the evening the court room was the scene of festivities. By eight o'clock the room was well filled with an interested audience, which was called to order by H. C. Curtis, of Le Mars. The old flag of the 12th was again draped in full view of the audience, and at one side of it was a large picture of the late Col. S. G. Knee, a lamented member of the regiment. The camp-fire exercises were opened by the singing of "Marching Through Georgia," led by Comrade Comstock, of Fayette, in which the audience joined. Rev. R. D. Parsons of the M. E. church, gave the invocation, and was followed by Ralph Dunham, fifteen years old, son of Comrade Abner Dunham, who delivered a patriotic and cordial address of welcome. He paid a glowing tribute to the old 12th, and closed amid hearty applause.

The response by Comrade H. C. Curtis was well received, and recalled the troublesome days of 61-65. Mr. Curtis spoke of the sacrifice made by the veterans of the war, and remembered enthusiastically in his address the boy soldier, Wm. McKinley. The appreciation of the members of the regiment, he said, for the courtesies shown them while in Manchester, was deep and sincere.

The audience sang "When Johnny Comes Marching Home," led by Mr. Comstock. Gen. J. H. Stibbs, of Chicago, stirred the risibilities of the listeners in the delivery of a comic sketch, "The Man Who Carried the Gun." He was obliged to give another—"Me and Jim," and would not be let off until he had recited a clever sketch by James Whitcomb Riley. General Stibbs has the charm of naturalness, and was heard with great pleasure.

At this point, Comrade Dunham spoke feelingly of the absence from the reunion of the late Col. Knee and Comrade Nagle of Dubuque read a poetic tribute to the memory of the dead veteran.

In Memoriam Col. S. G. Knee.

Comrade, soldier, sleep in peace,
    Sleep the sleep that knows no waking;
A nobler soul ne'er found release
    From earthly pangs, from earthly aching.
Sleep, hero, sleep, in honor's grave,
Beneath the flag you fought to save—
Yes, fought with heart so true, so brave.

Nor would I call thee back again
    To this cold earth of pleasures fleeting;
For thou art where the heavenly strain
    Is mellowed with the heavenly greeting.
Thy duty it was nobly done,
In honor's way thy life was run—
Thou hast the crown of laurel won.

Thy comrades brave will mourn for thee,
    Though soon with thee they'll all be sleeping;
Soon they'll sail the shoreless sea,
    Leaving kindred spirits weeping.
In the bivouac of the dead,
With thee, they'll find a soldier's bed,
Where each will rest his weary head.

Friend of our young manhood's days,
    Thou are only gone before us;
No more we see life's morning rays,
    But length'ning shadows creeping o'er us.
Rest where the brave and gallant rest,
With Freedom's sod above thy breast—
Thy heart was true; it stood the test.

                     —M. D. NAGLE.

"Yes, We Will Gather at the River" was then sung, led by Comrade Comstock, and there were many in the audience who wiped away a tear. Mr. Frank Knee, the colonel's son, who was present, was then introduced and received with applause.

Major D. W. Reed, of Evanston, Ill, was then called on to give a sketch of the work of the Shiloh National Park Commission, of which he is secretary, and to tell of the appearance of the battle ground at the present day. He said the bill providing for a National Park at Shiloh originated with a 12th Iowa boy, the gallant Col. D. B. Henderson, to whose efforts the success of the Commission is in main attributable. The Park will embrace 3,000 acres, the idea being to restore the field to its condition in the time of war. Major Reed said that the roads have been but slightly changed, but that a thick growth of jack-oaks had grown over much of the field, the removal of which occasions much labor. The National Cemetery at Shiloh contains the graves of 4,000 Union soldiers, two-thirds of whom are unknown. Twenty-two bodies from the ranks of the 12th are there buried, only five of whom are known. His remarks were extremely interesting and at their conclusion he answered several questions from those present. A request was made that Gen. Stibbs give a sketch of the journey of the 12th from Annapolis to St. Louis, upon return from prison, which he did in a graphic manner. It was found that there were fourteen members of the regiment present who were among the three hundred who took the trip.

"The Battle Cry of Freedom" was the next song, after which Mrs. R. B. Raines of Independence, a niece of H. C. Curtis of Company C, gave two very interesting recitations, being heartily applauded. Comrade Dunham called on Judge E. P. Seeds of Manchester for a few remarks which were given in the speaker's ever welcome, patriotic and eloquent style. Judge J. N. Weaver of Sioux City, a member of Company D, followed the Judge in a few timely words, after which Comrade Comstock gave in brief the history of the flag of the 12th Iowa. Gen. Stibbs enlivened affairs with a few well told camp-fire stories. After a song, adjournment was made for the evening.

Another meeting of the reunion was held on the morning of the 12th in the Universalist Church. The following officers were elected for the ensuing year: President, Abner Dunham; vice president, H. J. Grannis, Fayette; secretary, H. C. Curtis, Le Mars; treasurer, Major D. W. Reed, Evanston, Illinois; executive committee, G. E. Comstock, John Steen, C. E. Merriam. LeMars was settled upon as the place for the next regular reunion, in the year 1900. In two years from this fall the 12th will meet at Pittsburg Landing on the battlefield of Shiloh. Below we give the names of the members of the regiment, together with those of their wives or daughters in attendance upon the reunion in Manchester.

Company A.

W. W. Moore, Manchester.

Company B.

John D. Cole and wife, Lansing.

Company C.

C. Hazlett, Allison.
N. H. Spears, Westgate.
D. W. Reed, Evanston, Ill.
J. W. Ballinger, Lacy.
R. Z. Latimer and wife, Fayette.
P. R. Ketchum, Hawkeye.
H. C. Curtis, Le Mars.
W. A. Kerr, Barron, Wisconsin.
G. E. Comstock, Fayette.
H. J. Grannis and daughter, Randalia.
James Stewart, Anamosa.
Geo. L. Durno and daughter, Springville.

Company D.

T. J. Lewis, Cedar Rapids.
Edwin A. Buttolph, Cedar Rapids
Dennis Conley, Davenport.
S. R. Burch, Washington, D. C.
J. H. Stibbs, Chicago, Ill.
H. C. Morehead, Cedar Rapids.
John Rowen and wife, Vinton.

L. M. Ayers, Cedar Rapids.
J. N. Weaver, Sioux City.
W. W. Whiteneck, Waterloo.

Company E.

B. E. Eberhart, Marshalltown.
J. S. Margratz, Hitesville.
David Craighton, Geneva.
Sylvester Cook, Newcastle, Neb.
A. B. Perry, Fayette.

Company F.

H. M. Preston, Ft. Dodge.
Thos. W. Nelson, Hazleton.
H. W. Mackey, Fayette.
Joshua Widger, Manchester.
Abner Dunham, Manchester.
R. W. Tirrill, Manchester.
J. J. Eaton, Edgewood.
Wm. Schneider, Ft. Madison.
G. W. Wooldridge, Edgewood.
J. W. Potter, Edgewood.

Company G.

J. E. Simpson, Norfolk, Neb.
John Steen, Wahoo, Neb.
M. E. Meader and wife, Hesper.

Company H.

Jas. A. Light, Norfolk, Neb.
H. J. Playter, Washington, D. C.

A. T. Garner, Farley.
R. W. Fishel, Greeley.
G. H. Morisey, Manchester.
J. Shorter, Shell Rock.

W. D. Nagle, Dubuque.
Wm. Keohler, Dubuque.
M. B. Goodnow, Ovel, Nebraska.
Henry Smith, Maquoketa.

Company I.

Company K.

Wm. H. Dupray, Sioux City.
S. L. Kennedy, Cedar Rapids.
E. C. Cobb, Keokuk.

N. H. Baldwin, Ada, Kansas.
C. E. Merriam, Hopkinton.

SEVENTH REUNION

OF THE

TWELFTH IOWA

VETERAN VOLUNTEER

INFANTRY.

HELD AT

DUBUQUE, IOWA.

JUNE 4TH. AND 5TH.

1901.

E 507
.5
12th I

REUNION

OF THE

Twelfth Iowa Veteran Volunteer Infantry.

JUNE 4TH. AND 5TH. 1901.

The veterans of the Twelfth Iowa Infantry met for their Seventh reunion at Peterson's Hall, Dubuque Iowa, June 16, 1901, with a much larger attendance than was expected. The meeting was called to order by President Abner Dunham of Manchester, who stated why the reunion had not been held before, his explanation meeting with the hearty approval of those present. G. E. Comstock, the secretary, was at his desk and the meeting got down to business in short order.

The veterans present with wives and other female relatives, registered as follows:

Company A.

Thomas H. Wilson, Robertson.
C. E. Coombs, Hanover, Ill.
G. H. Cobb, and Lient. C. M. Runkle, Eldora.
Mrs. C. E. Coombs.

Company B.

George Ibach, Preston, Minn.
W. P. Winter, Bancroft, Iowa.
R. Wampler, Waukon.
D. F. Goodykoontz, Boone.
John M. Dowling and Hugh McCabe, Waukon.
Aslack Larson, Preston, Minn.
Frank Klees, Rossville.
C. E. Roe, Waterloo.
Adam Decker, Lansing.
Mrs. R. Wampler, Miss Winter.

Company C.

Maj. D. W. Reed, Evanston, Ill.
Mrs. D. W. Reed, Evanston, Ill.
Hart Spears, Westgate, Iowa.
S. C. Beck, Waverly.
Mrs. S. C. Beck, Waverly.
Lieut. H. J. Grannis, color bearer Randalia, Iowa.
G. Hazlet, Allison.
Lawrence Lott, Soldiers' Home, Marshalltown.
R. Z. Latimer and G. E. Comstock Fayette.
G. P. Latimer, Westgate.
James Carmachiel, Volga.
Emery Clark, Woodbine.
W. A. Lyons, Marshalltown.
E. C. Tatro, Castalia.
Sim Gifford, Waucoma.

Company D.

Capt. E. B. Soper, Emmetsburg.
William Baumgardner, Scranton.
Adjutant S. R. Burch, Washington, D. C.
W. W. Whitenack, Waterloo.
Mrs. W. W. Whitenack, Waterloo.
Lieut. Homer C. Morehead and Ed A. Buttolph, Cedar Rapids.
John N. Weaver, Sioux City.
John W. Rowan, Vinton.
Dennis C. Quigley, Mallard.
Gen. J. Stibbs, Peoria.
Josiah Scott, Shellburg.

Company E.

J. S. Margretz, Kesley.
J. W. Rich, Iowa City.
D. Craighton, Lonera.
C. V. Surfus, Bristow.
R. L. Bird, Hampton.
T. M. Earley, Dumont.
Joe Franks, Lamont.
David Schrack, Oelwein.

Company F.

R. W. Tirrell, Manchester.
G. W. Woolbridge, J. J. Easton, Edgewood.
Lieut. Abner Dunham, Manchester.
W. A. Nelson, Tom C. Nelson, Hazelton.
Mrs. R. W. Tirrell, Mrs. Thomas Elder.
Mother Otis, Nurse.
George Kent, Oelwein.
W. H. Mac'ey, assigned from 27th Iowa.
Jno. Litscher, Dubuque.

Company G.

O. P. Rockswold, Thoten, Iowa.
W. Kirkland, Freeport.
G. H. Hess, Washington Prairie, Iowa.
M. E. Mender, Hesper.
Mrs. M. E. Meader.

Company H.

Capt. Bob Fishel, Manchester.
S. B. Slcan, Greeley.
H. S. Briggs, Marcus.
Tom Smith, Cassville, Wis.
S. C. Fishel, Iowa Falls.
A. T. Gainer, Farley.
James Evans, Dubuque.

William Cox, Alta.
Mrs. Robert Fishel, Mrs. S. B. Sloan, Mrs. S. C. Fishel.
P. Hannah, Bellevue.

J. C. Buchanan, S. L. Kennedy, Cedar Rapids.
M. D. Nagle, William Koehler, Dubuque.
George Teskey, Elwood.
Mrs. T. J. Wlison.

Company I.

J. T. Campbell, Unique.
Henry Smith, Maquoketa.
George Yeley, Clinton.
T. J. Wilson, Maquoketa.
J. F. Butters, Sioux City.
M. C. McDermott, Placid.

Company K.

P. J. Morehouse, Manchester.
Isaac Mickey, Waukon.
Godfrey Dolley, Coggan.
E. C. Merriam, Hopkinton

Mrs. Kane delegate to the meeting of the W. R. C. and Miss Bauer were also present with the Twelfth Iowa ladies, as was also Clad Fishel of Iowa Falls.

A committee on program was appointed, consisting of Major Reed, Capt. Soper and J. W. Rich, and they reported one for the afternoon and next morning.

Major Reed, secretary of the Shiloh National Park Commission gave a very interesting description of the battlefield of Shiloh. He said the battle was the most sanguinary of any fought during the civil war, when the number of men engaged on both sides were taken into account. The total number was 101,000, the confederates having several thousand more than the union army. The Twelfth Iowa lost two officers and eighteen men killed, which, with the wounded and missing ran the total loss up to 409. Eighty members of the regiment died in prison. Major Reed gave a very interesting account of the work done by the National Commission on the battlefield He said that the original condition of the field had been preserved to such an extent that the improvements that had been made had not interfered with the positions held by the several regiments, and that there were twenty-five miles of good gravel roads—better roads than those of Gettysburg. Mayor Reed's remarks were of a historical character and were highly enjoyed by the veterans, who frequently applauded.

Captain Soper, Chairman of the Iowa Shiloh Commission, spoke with reference to the regimental and state monuments which are to be erected saying that there were eleven of the former to be erected to mark the positions held by the regiments from Iowa. Each of these would cost $2,000, and the state monument $25,000 The regimental monuments would be of uniform height and design. He exhibited drawings of both monuments. The state monument, which is to be 75 feet high, will be erected on the site of Gen. Wallaces's headquarters, would be of Barry granite, and the regimental will be of the same material. The regimental will consist of four pieces, the whole weighing between thirty and forty tons, and nine feet, eleven inches in height. On the front will be the following inscription: "Iowa—Twelfth Regiment Infantry. First Brigade, Second Division." On the rear will be a large bronze tablet giving the names of those killed and who died of wounds received at Shiloh and those missing and never heard of. The monument will be in every way worthy of the Twelfth.

Capt. Abner Dunham, who represented the Twelfth on the commission of Iowa organizations that were at Vicksburg during the seige, gave a very interesting description of the work done by the commission. He spoke of the present condition of the ground occupied by the Twelfth and other regiments. He said among other things that the Twelfth was not placed on the investment line. He said he had a hot time with Capt. Reed as to the position of the guns of the Second Iowa battery, which were in advance of the speaker's company but which Capt. Reed maintained were not. He tried to convince the Captain but could not do so. Every member of the regiment knows Capt. Dunham is correct in the statement he made, and that, if the Twelfth was not on the line of investment, as much at it was possible to be, it was not at Vicksburg, at all. It was supporting the battery. With reference to the state monument, which would be a splendid one, the speaker said he had the refusal of the site occupied by Grant's headquarters; or, if this was not satisfactory, the monument could be placed on a knoll near the headquarters.

The veterans met again on the morning of the 5th and the location of the Twelfth's Vicksburg monument was briefly discussed. Then a resolution was adopted, the substance of which was that Commissioner Dunham exercise his judgment in having the monument located; in other words, the location selected by him will have the approval of the regiment.

A number of letters from comrades unable to be present were

then read and ordered filed.

Judge Weaver of Sioux City was called on and addressed the veterans briefly and aroused much enthusiasm. He was heartily applauded.

Gen. J. H. Stibbs, the last colonel of the regiment and who was breveted for gallant service, recited two fine poems, bearing on the war, and the applause was liberal. The general's heart is as young as it was in '61.

Comrade Decker, with a little piece of birch bark, gave some selections and the sound could not be distinguished from that of a fife. He was roundly applauded.

The following officers were elected: President, Abner Dunham, Manchester; secretary, G. E. Comstock, Fayette; treasurer, D. W. Reed, Evanston, Ill.

The place of holding the next reunion was left to the officers.

It was decided to publish a pamphlet of the proceedings of the reunion and a roster of all or as many as can be correctly obtained of the regiment. Any member of the Twelfth knowing his address is not known to the secretary is requested to send same to that officer, G. E. Comstock, Fayette.

In the afternoon the regiment, as a complete organization, with four of its field officers present and every company represented, under its own flag, borne by its own gallant color-bearer, Grannis, and commanded by its last colonel, General Stibbs, joined the parade of the Grand Army of the Department of Iowa and made, without doubt, its last march as a regiment. After the parade the regiment returned to the hall and said "Good-bye until we meet again."

EIGHTH REUNION

OF

THE

TWELFTH IOWA

VET. VOL. INFT.

DEDICATION
OF
LINCOLN MONUMENT
AND
HENDERSON STATUE

AT

CLERMONT, IOWA

JUNE 19 AND 20

1903

Reporter Publishing House, Fayette, Iowa.

Eighth Reunion

OF

Twelfth Iowa Vet. Vol. Infantry

Dedication

Lincoln Monument and
Col. Henderson Statue

Clermont, June 19-20, '03.

Reporter Publishing House,
Fayette, Iowa.

PREFACE.

In the preparation of this work, your Committee of the "Whole House" (your humble servant) on the "State of the Union" having under consideration the publishing of a pamphlet of the proceedings of Dedication of Lincoln Monument, Henderson Statue, and Reunion of 12th Iowa Veteran Volunteer Infantry and fulfilling treaty stipulations with various "kickers" and for other purposes, depose and say: I have no apologies to offer, or favors to ask; I have done the best I could under the circumstances, and no one will ever know what they were.

We take this opportunity to express with great pleasure our sincere thanks for the courtesies extended us by Miss Beulah Wright, Department of Expression, Upper Iowa University for her superb rendition of "The Man Without a Country." To Miss Stella Spears of Westgate, Iowa, daughter of Comrade Hart Spears for her beautiful selection and rendition of song. Also to Mrs. Prof. Chas. D. Neff of U. I. U. for rendering so effectively that old time war song, "The Flag of our Union." To the Abernathy G. A. R. Post of West Union for the tender and use of their tents for our reunion, and especially to the noble, generous and unexcelled Ladies of Clermont for their most elegant banquet which only required the "Countersign", "Twelfth Iowa", to admit to the "King's Royal Feast."

To the Fayette Band and Drum Corps for their soul stirring music, taking special pains to render some of our old time marches and quick steps, much to the pleasure and satisfaction of all the "Boys." Also to the Dubuque Times Publishing Company, Sioux City Journal, Hon. Sidney A. Foster, of the Royal Mutual Life Ins. Co., Des Moines, Iowa, for the use of half tone cuts. To Capt. J. E. Simpson for his cheerful and encouraging letter—"Go slow and keep cool"—when I was up to my eyes in work. To Col. D. B. Henderson for his "Jack up" letter which made me so hot it singed my hair.

I kept right on "sawin' wood", "going slow", and "keeping cool," and here's your "wood pile" and "the man who carried a gun" from '61 to '65. Awaiting the pleasure of Your Excellency, I have the honor to renew the assurances of my high consideration for all Comrades of the Twelfth Iowa.

Your Humble Servant and Committee of the "Whole House,"
G. E. COMSTOCK, Sec.

Eighth Reunion, - Dedications.

INVITATION.

Clermont, Iowa, April 1, 1903.

G. E. Comstock, Sec'y. of 12th Iowa Vet. Vol. Inft. Reunion Ass'n.

At a meeting of the Clermont Soldiers' Monument Association held last evening, the following resolutions were unanimously adopted:

Resolved:—That the Secretary of the C. S. M. Association be and is hereby instructed to extend a very cordial invitation to the Twelfth Iowa Vet. Vol. Inf. Reunion Ass'n. to hold their reunion here on June 19th and 20th. Also

Resolved:—That the Association have charge of the dedicating of the Henderson Statue. Also it was suggested that you advise us what action you would be pleased to have us take in making suitable preparation for the day and occasion. By order of the

Clermont Soldiers Monument Association.
A. H. Loomis, Sec'y.

THE CALL.

Headquarters Twelfth Iowa Veteran Volunteer Infantry Reunion Ass'n.
Fayette, Iowa, May 15, 1903.

Dear Comrades:

At a meeting of your Executive Committee, called by the President, to take into consideration the possibility of a reunion, it was decided to accept the proposition made to our association by the Clermont Soldiers' Monument Association, of Clermont, Iowa, to hold our reunion at Clermont, June 19 and 20, 1903, at the time of the dedication of the Lincoln monument and Col. D. B. Henderson statue.

Ex-Governor and Mrs. Larrabee, and citizens, of Clermont, propose, and very much desire, to entertain, free of cost, all of the 12th Iowa that may be pleased to come and they are preparing to make it a grand success.

Ex-Governor Larrabee has placed us under lasting obligations by conferring on our regiment the distinguished honor of dedicating the Henderson statue.

Hon. J. P. Dolliver has consented to deliver the address on that occasion. (See program herewith enclosed.)

Once more, boys of the 12th, "Rally round the flag" and make the best effort of your lives to be present, and I am sure you will feel doubly repaid. Respectfully,

G. E. Comstock, Sec'y.

EIGHTH REUNION

Dedication Program.

FRIDAY, JUNE 19.

2 p. m. Assemble at Lincoln monument.
Music by West Union cornet band.
Invocation, Rev. M. S. Rice, pastor M. E. church, West Union.
Song, Clermont Glee Club.
Presentation of Lincoln monument by Hon. Wm. Larrabee Jr.
Address by Mayor J. H. Fheelan.
2:30 p. m. Assemble at Henderson statue.
Unveiling statue by Miss Helen Larrabee.
Presentation of statue to 12th Iowa for dedication by Victor Dolliver.
Address by Maj. D. W. Reed.
Reading Miss E. A. Sorin's address on presentation of flag to Co. C, 42 years ago, by Miss Beulah Wright, U. I. U.
Song, "Flag of Our Union" by Mrs. Professor Chas. Neff, U. I. U., with chorus.
3:00 p. m. Assemble at Pavilion.
Music by Fayette cornet band.
Address, Col. D. B. Henderson.
Vocal Music.
Address, Hon. J. P. Dolliver.
Music by U. I. U. band and drum corps.

Reunion Program.

Sunset salute. Lowering the flag.
Music, Fayette drum corps.
7 p m. Assemble in Pavilion.
Music by U. I. U. band.
Invocation, T. J. Bassett, President U. I. U.
Vocal music by Miss Stella Spears of West Gate.
Address of Welcome, A. H. Loomis, of Clermont.
Response, Hon. R. W. Terrill of Manchester.
Music.
Reading, "The Man Without a Country," Miss Beulah Wright, Department of Expression, U. I. U.
"Shiloh, as seen today," P. R. Woods.
Love feast—Opened by Col. Jack Stibbs, followed by ten minute talks by comrades.
Reading of letters from absent comrades.
12 p. m. Midnight tattoo.

SATURDAY, JUNE 20.

Sunrise salute, six o'clock reveille.
8 a. m. Assemble at headquarters.
Martial music.
Address, Lieut. Abner Dunham, President.
10 a. m. Business meeting.
10:30 a. m. Offering of resolutions, singing songs, telling stories, visiting, love feast and good time for all.
12 m. Adjourn. Goodbye.

GEO. E. COMSTOCK, Sec.

At Clermont.

In the beautiful little town of Clermont, Iowa, nestled down among the hills surrounding it, (distinguished as the home of Ex-Gov. Larrabee) over six thousand people assembled, in recognition of the Dedication of Lincoln Monument, Col. D. B. Henderson Statue, and Reunion of the Twelfth Iowa Veteran Volunteer Infantry. Dark clouds, which hovered overhead during the early morning, failed to keep the people of Fayette county from coming to these exercises. From early morning till noon farmers came to the city, while the trains brought many others. The town was beautifully decorated with flags and bunting while the pavillion, from which the addresses were made, was beautifully and artistically decorated. The citizens turned out en masse, there was a great crowd present.

The Monument to Abraham Lincoln, the first unveiled, stands directly opposite the Rock Island depot. It can be plainly seen by all who pass through the town, as well as by the citizens of the place. A little park has been fitted up in military style, ornamented with a cannon brought from the old battlefields. The heroic statue stands on a base and pedestal of granite.

There are four tablets representing scenes of the war of the rebellion. Two of these are of general subjects and two apply directly to Clermont. One represents the surrender. Grant and Lee seated at a table with noted generals of both sides standing back of them. It is a striking group. The other general group represents an action in Mobile bay. It represents Farragut in the rigging and Lieutenant Dewey, now the admiral, in command of a gun squad.

The two home subjects are quite as striking as the others. One represents Thomas Henderson, of Co. C, brother of Col. Henderson, leaving home to go to war. The other is a large group representing Captain Warner, of Clermont, and his company, C of 12th, in battle; Dr. Lewis, also of Clermont, caring for the wounded and Gen. Sherman on horseback, is seen in the background.

All of the work is highly artistic and substantial. The statue is the creation of Geo. E. Bissell, of New York. The Henderson statue is the work of Massy Rhind, a sculptor, who came to this country from Scotland, before the world's fair and who has since made a prominent place for himself in the east. His work has been praised by the ablest art critics.

Monument and Statue.

After music by the band, prayer by Rev. M. S. Rice, of West Union, and more music by the local chorus, Ex-Governor Larrabee, in a few well chosen words, presented the monument to the people of Clermont and the public generally. The response was made by Mayor J. H. Sheehan. Music by the chorus closed the exercises here.

The company immediately moved to the Henderson statue, the chorus furnishing the opening music, after which Miss Helen Larrabee, youngest daughter of the Ex-Governor, unveiled the statue.

Mr. V. M. Dolliver, of Fort Dodge, on behalf of Governor Larrabee and his family, presented the statue of Colonel Henderson to the town of Clermont, after which the dedication ceremonies were given into the hands of the Twelfth Iowa Regiment.

Upon the statue was draped two flags, on either arm. On the right hung the flag of Company C, made by Miss E. A. Sorin (then preceptress) and the young ladies of the Upper Iowa University and presented to Company C. It was carried by H. J. Grannis, our Regimental Color Bearer, and was, by him, the first union flag planted on the breast works of Ft. Donelson, where Lieut. D. B. Henderson fell, seriously wounded in the throat, while leading his men in this fierce charge. On the left hung that historic emblem, the flag of Company K. Surgeon Finley of our regiment, says: "I saw that flag go down three times in that 'pot metal hell' and as often come up again." (See history of Co. K flag in this book).

It was in this fearful, hotly contested battle of Corinth, Miss., where Lieutenant D. B. Henderson again fell, this time loosing his left leg, and this is why this flag hung on that same side with the crutch. Is it any wonder, that when we recall all this, after the lapse of over forty years and when we again meet as comrades, that the "tear will unbidden start"? The interest still continued when Major D. W. Reed, of Co. C, who had received a severe wound at Shiloh, which the flag on the right arm represented, and was also in the Corinth battle, under lead of the flag on the left, arose and made the following remarks:

Maj. Reed's Address.

Gov. Larrabee, I have been requested by my comrades, of the 12th Iowa, to dedicate your generous and gracious gift and in their behalf to attempt in feeble words to express the gratitude we feel toward you for thus placing in living bronze and enduring granite this splendid testimonial to a superb Iowa soldier and that soldier an honored member of our regiment.

As the veil fell away there was revealed three objects that at once attracted my attention and filled me with emotions that are hard to control and impossible for me to describe in words. First, I beheld a perfect representation of one who was my schoolmate and classmate; our comrade and friend, and has, for over forty years, been the personal friend, not only of the members of our regiment, but of every soldier who wore the blue; one who has filled to the utmost the highest ideal of what a scholar, soldier and statesman should be and has by personal merit risen to the second highest place in the nation and has filled every station with honor to himself and his constituents, without a stain upon his character. It was a happy thought of yours, Gov. Larrabee, to select this ideal soldier, this member of the 12th Iowa as a representative and place his statue on the monument that shall for all time adorn this beautiful city, and then ask us to dedicate it.

Next, I see "Our Flag" and the sight carries me back forty two years to the Upper Iowa University where, in the summer of 1861 the students organized a company for drill, calling themselves "University Recruits" under a resolve that: "When our services are needed, we will drop our books to fight our country's battles." At the head of that company stood two men who have been today signally honored: William W. Warner and David B. Henderson. After drill September 15, 1861, Captain Warner read the call of President Lincoln for 300,000 men, and suggested that in his opinion the time had come to put our resolution to the test. At a meeting in the Chapel that afternoon twenty three students signed enlistment papers and directed Captain Warner to offer their services to the government for three years, or during the war. The ladies of the University, full of patriotic zeal and devotion to their country, fashioned with their own hands, a beautiful flag, embroidering on its folds the words "University Recruits" and gave it to the company with these patriotic words:

"Take our flag. Proudly, confidently, we commit it to your keeping. We do not bid you guard it, we know it is safe in your hands. As you have been proud to live under it, if death be your lot, may you die under its folds, and may God protect and prosper you as you defend your colors."

Upon the organization of the 12th Iowa regiment, the University recruits became Company C and "Our Flag" became the regimental colors. It received its first baptism of fire at Fort Donelson, where it was carried in triumph over the works, but left a trail of wounded in its path, among them Lieutenant Henderson and W. B. Warner, of Clermont. The bright folds of this flag waved at Shiloh, over that stubborn line at the "Hornets' Nest," from early morning until night, inspiring its defenders with heroic courage that enabled them to resist the repeated charges of the enemy. The "Army of the Tennessee" was saved but those who contributed most to prevent its defeat, sacrificed themselves and were compelled to surrender and see their flag carried from the field, a trophy of war. That was indeed a dark day for the 12th Iowa. Of 489 present for duty on the field, 479 were killed, wounded or missing. Only ten escaped the casualties of battle and they were engaged with the surgeon in caring for the wounded. But the most to be regretted feature of that disaster was the report, sent out by newspaper correspondents, that the regiment was surrounded and captured in their tents in the morning. There were few left to dispute the story and the report gained such credence, before the prisoners returned, that many accepted the statement as true. The ladies of the C. L. U. were among the first to find the true history of the surrender and we hear them in a June oration, saying:

" I honor to those who fought and fell around the flag at Shiloh. Nobly did they wrestle with the foe, but as the day wore away, kind heaven for one moment averted her face, the enemy rallied around the lessened members and our school mates were prisoners. Our flag was wrested from the grasp of those who prized it dearer than life. We tender our sympathy to those, who, enduring the fate of war, tarry beneath a southern sky; and bid them remember that captivity which comes with honor is true liberty. It is true that the flag that waved us adieu from yonder hill is ours no longer, but the spirit whose utterance it was, is as free as the air of our prairies and we but wait the word to fling forth to the breeze again:

'The stars for our heroes,
The stripes for our foes.' "

Upon the return of the prisoners the fair hands that fashioned the first flag, made this beautiful flag, an exact duplicate of the first, and presented it to the company. It is the flag that was used as regimental colors at Spanish Fort and has been present at every reunion of the regiment, still borne by the loyal, gallant hands of Henry J. Grannis, who carried our colors so bravely on every one of our battlefields.

But I see another flag, as it floats now from the arm of the statue, almost as inspiring as the other. It is the flag of Co. K, and was carried by the Union Brigade at Corinth. Around it the 12th Iowa rallied, and in that fierce melee lost, in killed and wounded, half the number engaged on the field. Three color bearers in succession went down and the flag was, for a moment, in the hands of the enemy, but its defenders rallied, and in a hand to hand conflict rescued it and placed it in the hands of Sergeant Cole of Co. B, who was soon shot through the body, but crawled to the rear, bearing the flag with him, stained, as you see, by his blood. The enemy was repulsed, but around that blood stained banner lay half our number, among them our own loved Henderson.

If it was intended to arouse all our enthusiasm, to fill our hearts too full for words, no better devise could have been planned, than to drape those flags around the statue of our loved comrade and then unveil them before our eyes.

In this year 1903, our regiment has been highly favored. The state of Iowa has erected at Shiloh a beautiful monument, which will tell to all future ages the story of its heroic struggles. And here at Clermont, the home of so many of its former members, has been erected this beautiful statue to tell to coming generations something of the honorable life and service of one of our comrades; that shall inspire our children and children's children to acts of patriotism, and to the study of the history of the country, and of a regiment that took an active part and did gallant service for our country.

And now my comrades, in the name of those of our number who shed their blood in defense of these colors; of those who died that our country might live, and of those living still pledged to equal sacrifice, if necessary, to keep our flag afloat, we dedicate this statue as a memorial, that shall stimulate the people of Clermont, of all future generations, to emulate the example of our comrade in all his gallant service for his country.

Comrades, join me, once more as of old, in three cheers for Gov. Larrabee.

Following Major Reed's address, Miss Beulah Wright, of the Department of Oratorical expression of U. I. U., stepped forth in the beauty of young womanhood, with her soul filled full of patriotic fire, and in the most effectual manner reproduced the flag presentation speech of Miss Sorrin, delivered to Co. C, September 15, 1861.

At the close of Miss Wright's reading, Mrs. Chas. D. Neff touchingly rendered "The Flag of Our Union", all joining in the chorus, lead by G. E. Comstock of Fayette, who led the same song sung at the presentation of the flag when the hoary heads now bowed with age were the brave and gallant boys who enlisted in their country's cause from old Upper Iowa. Some of these boys came from far off states, one, P. R. Ketchum, from Idaho.

At a signal, the cannon brought by the boys from Fayette, to do honor on this occasion, boomed forth thirteen times, as a salute to the flag, Lincoln monument, and Henderson statue, thus closing the services at the Henderson statue. The sea of interested spectators moved to the pavilion, where two very large tents, joined together as one, furnishing a seating capacity of some four thousand, was packed full. Senator Dolliver and Col. Henderson were orators of the day (See both addresses reproduced in this book.)

Among those of note who were upon the platform, were Hon. and Mrs. Larrabee, Hon. and Mrs. Henderson, Senator Dolliver and wife, Hon. G. N. Hougen, of the fourth district, Col. John F. Merry of Dubuque, Hon. J. H. Sweeney, of Osage, Col. Rood, of Mt. Vernon, Hon. S. B. Zeigler and wife, our beloved Col. J. H. Stibbs, Chicago, our venerated and much loved surgeons, Dr. C. C. Parker, first, Dr. W. H. Finley, first Ass't., Maj. D. W. Reed, Maj. Geo. H. Morrisy and wife, Hon. R. W. Terrill and wife, Lieut. Dunham and wife, Geo. E. Bissell of New York, sculptor of the Lincoln statue, and Mrs. Rebecca Otis, who served as nurse from '61 to '65, being now in her 77th year.

Col. Henderson arose, greeted by a tumult of applause and made remarks as follows:

Col. Henderson's Speech.

Mr. President, comrades and friends: To me this is a sacred day and a more than sacred occasion. I see before me men of the old Twelfth Iowa. This is our reunion. I see before me the faces of several survivors who were in old company C, assembled and enlisted in this county of Fayette, but the dear, bronzed faces of the living call up the equally dear faces of the dead. The events of life are our mile-stones, and he who has not such marks has not a life in which it is important to record its events. Clermont is one of my mile-stones; Fayette county is another dear old Henderson prairie; in this township, is another; the 12th Iowa and all of its men, is another. Standing here I recall my third war meeting, held in this village in September, 1861, to gather fighting men for company C of the 12th. It was held in some hall in this town. It would take a poet to describe that night, the historian cannot do it justice. We enlisted that night twenty-three men for war, picked out of the simple farm homes of this vicinity. I can recall many of the faces, outside of company C, that were at that meeting. Every eye contributed tears of patriots and friends. Whenever a man was enlisted cheers were given; the old flag was carried around the room and each man as he enlisted marched after it as the cheers of the people rent the air. I recall the face of Governor Larrabee, who tried to enlist at that and another time, but was denied that honor, because of a physical defect in one eye. I recall the dear faces of the honored parents of our beloved Captain Warner of company C and his sisters too were there, patriotic angels of the Republic and our beloved hostess of this occasion, Mrs. Governor Larrabee was there, leading in our glorious songs. Her father and mother, Captain and Mrs. Appleman were there, the first a hero of the seas; the second, and both, early pioneers, laboring for the benefit of our fields and the up-building of our great state. I can see Steadman & Stough the merchants; dear old John Hosford was with us then, and is with us now, age not dimming the warmth of his noble heart and unvarying friendship for the soldier of the Republic. We recall Ben Agard, afterwards a soldier and now in Heaven. We recall the bright-eyed Loomis, now the husband of Captain Warner's oldest sister, a man ever true to the highest duties of life, and Father Dibble was with us, and it seems to me that the citizens of this locality, far and near, were with us, with one heart for all of us, and one voice for the songs and life of our country.

One hundred and four men who wished to join company C went with us to Dubuque to muster, and after physical examination by the surgeon, 98 were found able and qualified for battle. After service in many battles; after volunteering for a second term, and after the war was ended, 38 remained, who assembled at the Upper Iowa University, the place of original enlistment. The young hero and patriot, Wm. W. Warner was brought home in his coffin and sleeps now near where we are assembled. My own brother Thomas was shot through the heart in the "Hornet's Nest" at Shiloh and sleeps today among the immortal dead by the noiseless waters of the Tennessee. Of all that we enlisted in Clermont, very few survived, but it fills me with joy to see so many of the survivors of the old Twelfth Iowa here. They have come "from near and from far" for this meeting, making another great mile-stone in our travels through life. It is heart-warming to see so many of those dead heroes' children here; there are, however, but few survivors of that sacred band of old citizens, who cheered the boys to war, to victory or death, at that little war meeting in 1861.

To me, and to many of us here, everything has a sweet memory and is stamped with battle history. There stands the mill, owned at one time by "Jack Thompson," and afterward and for a long time, by our dear William Larrabee. The Turkey River running by, many of us have fished in, swimmed in, and it's ancient music is still in our hearts. There is no ravine around here that is not made sacred by the memory of dear homes, beloved homes, Irish dances, American dances, Norwegian dances, spelling schools, singing schools, and above all debating schools. These surrounding woods contain memories and sacred stories which will ever be dear to most of those here now and on this very occasion, when Governor Larrabee is doing so much for this Fayette county and his friends. Let it not be forgotten for I believe that, in the people of Clermont, he ever has had and has now a generous, honest and enthusiastic constituency.

When we consider what has been done, and is being done in Clermont, you will agree that it is a great mile-post in the life of Governor Larrabee, and his surrounding friends.

WHAT HAS HE DONE?

My friends, it would be easier to answer the question: What has he failed to do? Turn your eyes to yonder square, where we have this day dedicated, through his precious gift, that splendid bronze statue to Abraham Lincoln. It is, as it ought to be, heroic in size; his duplicate has not yet been produced in our country. He gave his life to liberty, and no Union army, regiment or company, failed to recognize him as a comrade. Washington was the father but Lincoln was the preserver of our country. Yonder statue is by one of America's greatest sculptors. What a perpetual lesson for our people? Orator, statesman, poet, lawyer, law maker, our chief executive, martyr! His life presents a field that will ever be rich to the historian, the artist and the patriot. Governor Larrabee, you have done much that is good, but I believe that presenting this statue, is one of your greatest acts.

TWELFTH IOWA INFANTRY.

I must make a few observations, especially to my old comrades and friends of the Twelfth Iowa Infantry. The history of your state and country will show that no truer body of men entered the United States service during the Civil War. Its history is a part of the bloody history from which was evolved the final and sacred establishment and preservation of our Republic. On its great deeds I may not dwell, for history contains all that can be written of a regiment. I wish I could pen to-day the unwritten history of the old Twelfth Iowa; the early glowing heart of our patriotic boys when they left home to save their beloved land; the agonies, the tortures of the battle field; the never-to-be-truly-told story of the hospital; the sufferings of that great body of our comrades, known under the names of father, mother and friends; the unmarked graves, and, oh, if I could tell it, and make the world know it, that peculiar shout, almost a yell that followed the victorious struggle of our men. I will not leave that story for the painter or the poet, to sculptor or historian; it is buried with our dead and still remembered and cherished by our living. It was a part of the grand old Army of the Tennessee, whose commanders were Grant, Sherman, McPherson, Logan and Howard, a part of an army that never lost a single battle during the great civil war, and whose survivors are assembled here.

It would be cruel for me to name one of that regiment and at the same time omit a single name. I superintended the burial of thirteen dead comrades at Shiloh, and they are now in the National Cemetery there with a monument in the center of a half-circle, telling briefly who were buried there. It is sweet to see that the sister of dear, dead, Captain Warner, the wife of Mr. Loomis, has made her home our home on this occasion, her table our table, but all of the rest of Captain Warner's family have passed beyond and are with our departed comrades now.

You will pardon me if I refer to a letter written me, on the 21st of April, 1903, from 279 Henrietta Court, Passadena, California. It was written by a true member of company C, I must put it so. It is from Miss E. A. Sorin. In closing she said:

"One thing I forgot to say that I *must* not forget.

"I want you to bear my greeting of loving remembrance to company C."

Would you like to hear a word or two about that dear woman? She was Preceptress of the Upper Iowa University at the time of our first war meeting, and saw twenty-two of the old students enlist for the 12th. Our enlistment roll was short, we did not know just what was required for an enlistment roll. Here are the closing words:

"We drop our books to fight our country's battles."

While some of the faculty were frightened at the injury to their school, this dear woman, one of the faculty, never flinched, but her voice, her tears, and her prayers, went with us from first to last, and her love message I have just delivered. A Southerner born was she, but never for an instant was she other than faithful to the flag of her whole country.

STATUE OF D. B. HENDERSON.

Touching this bronze statue of myself. I can, should, and will be brief. I am grateful to Governor Larrabee for permitting my old regiment to conduct the unvailing and the dedication of this statue of myself. It is the product first, of Governor Larrabee's own brain and heart; the details of the work were all born of his brain. Personally, I feel a delicacy about the appearance of a crutch, but Governor Larrabee was the historian, and would have it there as a part of the monument. I am glad to note that my old comrades, with one voice, approved of this feature of the monument. Second, heroic in size, it is the product of one of America's great sculptors, Mr. J. Massey Rhind of New York, like myself, born in Scotland, and I know, like myself, ardently loving his adopted country and its great history. The statue tells its own story. But, oh! how glad I am to learn from your lips, my dear comrades and friends that, Governor Larrabee and the artist have faithfully told the story it is intended to represent. It stands in the street, where, with horses, cattle, bluejeans and bare-feet, I have often gone while a boy, discharging the simple duties of a farmer's life.

You who know me best, can measure the depths of my gratitude, and my inability to tell you what is in my heart to-day.

WILLIAM LARRABEE.

GOVERNOR LARRABEE.

I will be pardoned, I know, for saying a few words about Hon. William Larrabee, my boyhood and lifelong friend, but whether you approve or not, I am going to say some things of this great man; something of his work; something of his life; something of his heart, and something of his great character. When I first knew this man, he was hardly more than a boy, leading the work on his brother-in-law's farm in Clayton county, the farm of the Hon. E. H. Williams, whose noble wife still survives him, and who in addition to service on the district bench, became a member of the Supreme Court of Iowa, and whose farm is still enjoyed by his widow and his children. It is just across the line from Fayette county, situated in Clayton county. Many a time in youth I have bound grain by the side of William Larrabee, and I must admit that he could bind a bundle of grain about as quickly as any man I ever knew, and we had more than one test of our skill. Subsequently, he bought that mill down there in Clermont, and it was the boast of the farmers that they could send a load of wheat to Larrabee's mill by their younger children and know absolutely that they would get every cent they were entitled to. Without compensation this Connecticut yankee taught the first singing school on Henderson Prairie; the noble woman, his wife, and I were among his first pupils. He was a constant attendant upon the Henderson Prairie debating school, meeting us at the old stone school house, and here he partly developed the wonderful mind that has so enriched his state. Thoroughly educated in Connecticut, this young yankee at once took a front rank, as a leader, thinker and worker in our community. None of his old neighbors fell in battle without his looking up and ascertaining the condition of the surviving members of the dead soldier's family. His heart was ever open, and his purse ever free to those who needed help. Pardon me, if I say that, on my return from war, minus a leg, he moved without telling me, to have me appointed Commissioner for the Board of Enrollment for this district, and brought my commission to me while lying on my back after the amputation on my father's farm. With years of industry he has acquired a competency, but no man can truthfully say that there is a soiled dollar in his pocket. The accumulations of his able brain and untiring energy are as clean as his soul. His pen has contributed to the literary works of his time, not fiction, but the solid treatment of great questions. He was sixteen years in the State Senate of Iowa, the recognized leader of that body; twice he was the honored Governor of Iowa, and left a record as such Governor, which the most noble and patriotic may well follow as an example. From his birth he was a tireless worker; integrity was stamped upon his soul; each member of his family is a credit to Governor and Mrs. Larrabee, for both have lived together, worked together and are thought of and loved as one. Let me briefly resume. He has ever been my friend, loved and was loved as a brother; singing teacher, refusing compensation; a constant attendant of a vigorous debating society; a loyal friend of his Government and of its defenders; a beautiful neighbor; a patron and promoter of art, and I should add, has now a splendid bronze statue of General Grant, which at present stands at his old home in Clermont, the production of a great sculptor, which will be duly erected here; an honest miller wise and tireless farmer, a broad-minded and successful law maker; a member of the State Board of Control, where he mapped out the course his successors should pursue; an uncompromising patriot; an advocate of a sound, stable, and generous currency; a great Governor of a great state, his influence has been felt in the state, in the Nation, and in his beautiful home.

IN CONCLUSION.

I propose three cheers for Governor Larrabee, his accomplished wife, and to all of the citizens of Clermont. (Three cheers and a tiger given with wild enthusiasm.) And now, my friends, with gratitude to you who have come so far to spend this day with us, and with an affection which I hope will grow with life, I will bid each and all a kind good-bye.

COL. D. B. HENDERSON.

Senator Dolliver's Address.

Senator Dolliver, who delivered the principal address of the day, was given an ovation when he arose to speak. His oration was an eloquent effort. Touching at length on the character and achievements of Col. Henderson his address made a marked impression. He said:

Members of the 12th Iowa and Fellow Citizens:—The honor of taking part in the exercises of this day is one which I sincerely appreciate. I thank the veterans of the Twelfth Iowa for their invitation to speak a few words about their old comrade whose statue they have dedicated amid these scenes of his early manhood, among the neighbors and friends who have followed his career with affection and pride all the days of his life.

The erection of these monuments, one to the great President, and the other to a typical volunteer soldier, is an act thoroughly characteristic of the honored citizen to whose public spirit the people of Iowa owe this generous contribution to the higher life of the commonwealth. It was not the privilege of Governor Larrabee to serve in the ranks of the army in the field, though he organized a company and tendered his own service. But from the outbreak of the rebellion to the surrender at Appomattox, his patriotic heart was with the enlisting regiments, encouraging them by words of cheer, caring for their families while they were away, and in after years proving by unnumbered acts of kindness his right to the place he has always held in the gratitude and good will of the surviving veterans.

Few men in the history of our state have served the people with such distinction in the various offices which he has occupied. He has shown the most complete devotion to public interests and has discharged his duties with an eye single to the welfare of the community. He has not needed the pomp and ceremony of official station; for his counsel and guidance in the management of all public business, have never been more acceptable or more valuable than since he has occupied the position and exercised the rights of a private citizen.

In other times as interested travelers pause on their journey through this beautiful valley to look upon these impressive figures, commemorating names famous in our annals as a people, they will not forget the unpretentious citizen, conspicuous for more than a generation in the affairs of the state, who has enriched the community with such an enduring legacy.

Their erection has in it a significance somewhat deeper than at first appears. They are a witness or rather they preserve the testimony of one who has done his full part in the material development of the state, that the time has come for the people of Iowa to turn aside from the pursuit of business, to consider the place in our scheme of popular education which belongs to the ornaments of grace and beauty. It foreshadows the approach of that public opinion which will attract into the homes of our people, and into all our public institutions the influences of the finer arts, and at last make the state, already the abode of wealth and culture, a contributor in a still larger sense to the real assets of the world.

It is a pleasure to all of us that the sculptor whose genius created the statue of Lincoln which we have dedicated today, is present on the platform, and I take great pleasure in presenting Mr. Bissell, who has come all the way from his home in New York, to join in the exercises of the day. He is not only a great artist but was a good soldier in the Union army.

(Senator Dolliver at this point brought Mr. Bissel forward amid hearty enthusiasm in which the whole audience shared.)

Senator Dolliver continued:

Now that the thread of my discourse has been interrupted, I will say another thing. The author of the Henderson statue is not here, but there is one here who has had as much to do in shaping the character and moulding the career of Colonel Henderson as the artist had in giving form and stature to his image in bronze. I ask the Twelfth Iowa to salute Colonel Henderson's wife—the woman who has shared his honors, and helped to carry his burdens.

(Senator Dolliver at this point escorted Mrs. Henderson to the front of the platform, the whole audience rising and following the members of the old regiment in three rousing cheers for her. The Senator then continued his speech.)

Governor Larrabee has been peculiarly fortunate in choosing his heroes. It is a difficult thing to pick out, especially from a list of men of our own time, appropriate subjects to be perpetuated in bronze or marble. It has been said that the sculptor's art is the most helpless of all the efforts of the human mind to express itself. Therefore the statue of a man seldom does more than to record the accepted estimate of his character and his achievements. It adds nothing to what he is and little to the reputation of what he has done. There is a sense in which a statue is a thing sacred and set apart so that men and women looking upon it may be made better, wiser, stronger, by considering the manner of man he actually was. "Show me the man you honor;" said Thomas Carlyle, "I know by that symptom better than any other what kind of a man you yourself are." This conclusion of the whole matter of statue making the blunt old Scotchman writes down in the midst of his fierce philippic on the subject of a proposed statue to a successful railroad promoter of 1850, a now entirely forgotten multi-millionaire by the name of Hudson, and incidentally against "that extraordinary population of brazen and other images" which at the time dominated the market places of towns and solicited worship from the English people.

A statue of Lincoln, while it adds nothing to him, is in itself a worthy commentary upon the national character, for it brings us face to face with the grandest, simplest, purest life that was ever lived by a man among the children of men. It stands for an epoch in human affairs in which were blended all the heroisms, all the sublime aspirations, all the pathetic sacrifices which have made the national life worth living. Yet there is a meaning which takes even a stronger hold upon our hearts, in the other figure standing there on crutches and looking down upon us with the benignity of an old neighbor and an old friend. Abraham Lincoln has already become one of the legends of our heroic age. All the rugged lines have been smoothed out of that care-worn face; while the man himself, who once sat upon store boxes and entertained villagers with curious narratives drawn from the homely experiences of his own life, or the quaint resources of his imagination, has been lifted up by the common consent of mankind above all thrones and has taken his august rank in the midst of the ages.

A statue of David B. Henderson brings back to us in a more intimate way the events of that period without taking us very far from home. It is fitting that this monument should stand here near the pioneer farmhouse from which Colonel Henderson and his two brothers went out as soldiers of the republic, and that these ceremonies should be conducted by those who remain of the regiment in which he served with such gallantry and renown. Not very far from this spot is the prairie upon which his parents established their homestead in 1849. They had come from a foreign land, but from a country so like our own in its inheritance of freedom that its scattered children have had little difficulty in making themselves at home everywhere in the United States.

I heard Colonel Henderson once in the midst of a gay social assembly at our capital, in answer to the question of a fashionable lady, relate the story of their long journey from Old Deer, Scotland, to America. He told of the injustice of the landlord's son who had come into the estate; of the anger of his old Scotch father, and of his resolution to take his little family, David being the youngest, and make his way to a new land to find better opportunities for his children; a land where "a man is a man for a that." He related also his visit to his old home a year or two ago, passing modestly over his audience with Kings and noblemen, to tell of his effort to discover among those who were acquainted with his family in Scotland, some one who had known his mother; and of finding only one who could tell him anything about her, an aged woman who only remembered that she was kind to the poor and was often seen going about carrying in a basket some delicacy for the sick.

The way he told of the privations of his boyhood and the gentle tone with which he spoke of his mother threw a true light upon his inner life, so that when he had finished, tears were in the eyes of the whole company which listened to his simple manly words.

I have known Colonel Henderson now for more than a quarter of a century, and whether I think of him as a farmer's lad following the furrow on the prairie yonder, or lying helpless on the battlefield at Corinth, or holding his own in the tumultuous encounters of the House of Representatives, or weilding the authority of the second office in the government of the United States, I confess that he has always seemed to me an admirable example of what is best and strongest in the life of the

American people.

In every aspect of his career he has been a representative of Iowa; though not born upon our soil, he came into contact with it before he was ten years old, and until he was twenty-one kept close enough to it to get the physical, intellectual and moral strength which comes up into a man out of plowed ground through his bare feet. To a young man like Colonel Henderson the call of his country for soldiers to defend her in the time of need, came as a command to be obeyed at once; and so the awkward country boy just turned twenty-one years of age, finds himself a member of Company C of the Twelfth Iowa Infantry, and entered with you upon that eventful experience which has given to the survivors of the regiment a heritage of honor and glory for all time to come.

He was with you in the camp of preparation while you made ready for the war; he was with you through the long winter at St. Louis when disease wasted your numbers, before yet you had seen your enemy in the field. He was with you at Cairo where you met for the first time your great commander, then holding a humble assignment in the national service; he was with you at Donelson where you won everlasting honor by bloody work well done; he was with you on the historic field of Shiloh where not even the bravery of the bravest could stand against the overwhelming disaster which befell you; he was with the little remnant of the regiment at Corinth where he fell in the thick of the fight under wounds which left him maimed and crippled and filled much of his after life with misery and pain. He has been with you in the blessed years of peace, and has entered with a perfect sympathy into the joys and sorrows of your daily lives. He is with you today, and all others seem like intruders upon the rites of a ceremony which belongs to you and to your comrades living and dead.

Colonel Henderson received in an extraordinary measure the recognition which the American people have always been prompt to give to those who have served their country in war. When he retired from public life, he had enjoyed for an unusual period the distinction which belongs to the House of Representatives, crowned at last by two unanimous elections to the office which more than ever embodies the influence and dignity of that great popular assembly. But no eminence of his career in civil life, can overshadow the service which he rendered when with willing heart and eager enthusiasm he offered his name to the Twelfth Iowa and with you have himself without reserve to the national defense.

For over twenty years Col. Henderson has been a notable figure in the arena of American public life. His record in the House of Representatives was remarkable not only for its length, but almost from the beginning, for the unique personal leadership which was accorded him by his colleagues.

It is a body which never fails to judge with infallible accuracy the qualifications of the men who aspire to direct the great affairs of legislation. It is considerate of the weak, inexorable in its dealings with the vain and presumptuous, proud of the valiant and successful, losing no time in according the full measure of appreciation to ability and strength. It is a fighting arena in which no intellectual gift is worth anything unless it is kept always ready for the fray. It is a forum of debate, of hand to hand combat, always ready to listen to words spoken in season, willing to give new men a chance and generous with its applause for the humblest member who takes occasion by the hand.

Into the midst of these restless and stormy activities Col. Henderson came in the Forty-eighth Congress after a brief but brilliant career at the Iowa bar; and he had not been there very long before the House had learned that he could be counted upon not only for wise counsel but in all the sudden emergencies of controversy and discussion. His opportunity came early in the session of the Forty-ninth Congress. He had been active and earnest in securing the legislation which provided for the increase of the pensions of widows from $8.00 to $12.00, and when the general pension appropriation bill was under discussion, he ventured to make some comments upon the attitude of members from the South towards that legislation. Almost immediately, as so often happens, without warning, acrimonious debate sprang up which raged for several days, involving nearly all the important party leaders on both sides of the House. Everything, as usual, was discussed except the matter under consideration, and while Colonel Henderson was supported adequately on his own side of the House, it is obvious from the Record that he had to bear the brunt of the battle himself. All the weapons of partisan warfare were directed against him; epithets and offensive personalities filled the chamber, through all of which Col. Henderson maintained a calm and cheerful temper. At length a gentleman from Georgia, Mr. Norwood, in a speech bristling with irritating satire and evil insinuations, sneered at his "expansive patriotism," and with malice ill concealed, tried to make a jest of his foreign nativity. When the Georgian had finished, so complete was his apparent victory that Mr. Allen, the quaint humorist from Mississippi, suggested "that business be suspended for a moment while the gentleman from Iowa receives the sympathy of his friends."

It was an important hour for Col. Henderson. If he had tried to answer wit with wit, ridicule with ridicule, he would have failed altogether. But Mr. Norwood's contemptuous allusions to the fatherland, to Ben Lomond and the thistle, made it appropriate for the Iowa orator to pass by in silence the words of levity and banter and to take his position upon higher ground where his antagonist was easily outclassed.

Straight from the shoulder came Colonel Henderson's reply: "It is thrown in my teeth that I first drew breath in sight of Ben Lomond. That is true, Mr. Chairman, but while it is true that I represent in my birth the land of the thistle, I want to tell the gentleman that 'from lowland moor to highland pass, treason never found birth in a Scottish heart. True it is that I was born in Scotland. True it is that a little child I came to America. Does it remain for a simple Scottish boy of twenty-one, not born under the folds of the beautiful flag of America, to teach patriotism to a gentleman who was born upon American soil?

Mr. Chairman, I recognize with pleasure the gentlemanly and manly character of some of my opponents in this debate. I take pleasure in recognizing in that way the gentleman from West Virginia (Mr. Wilson), and the cultivated and eloquent gentleman from Kentucky (Mr. Breckinridge), who spent four years of his life in the Confederate service. That gentleman drew a picture, beautiful, touching and instructive, of three brothers, all nursed at the same breast, fighting on opposing fields, and yet no barrier between their hearts.

I too, Mr. Chairman, will attempt to draw a "family picture." If I may have the same permission. Three brothers of us met together one night in 1861, under the old family roof, and agreed that in this great land of our adoption the hour had come for us to lay our lives at the feet of our common country. We slept none that night; all sat up. In the morning before parting, the old father (turning to Mr. Norwood) born in Scotland, too, took down the old family Bible (again turning to Mr. Norwood) brought from Scotland, and after reading it, knelt among his little group of Scottish-American children, prayed to the God of nations to guard us and make us brave for the right, finished the prayer and said amen.

The parting you gentlemen have nothing to do with; but those three brothers, 'all nursed at the same breast,' and 'with no barrier between their hearts,' went side by side to the war, all, however, fighting on the same side--the side of their country. The eldest, Thomas, fell, shot through the heart in the deadly "Hornet's Nest" of Shiloh, and he now sleeps in an unmarked grave by the quiet waters of the Tennessee. The next, serving four years and veteranizing, lives, but is almost a physical wreck, his health laid upon the altar of his country. The third and youngest is still pretty well, I thank you; but Mr. Chairman, I want it distinctly understood that so long as I have a memory to remember what Thomas fought for, so long as I know that for nearly a quarter of a century his widow and children have struggled without that gallant prop, (turning to Mr. Norwood) Scottish though he was in origin, I feel not called upon to get down on my bended knee in the Capitol of my country (with all due respect to the gentleman from Georgia) and apologize for Thomas' death, for William's ruined health, or for myself."

The blood of the Twelfth Iowa was evidently up once more and nobody came within his reach, who did not feel the stroke of the old Iowa soldier's wrath. That speech illustrating in the most effective way his ability to take care of himself in the rough and tumble engagements which have always been common in the House of Representatives was the beginning of a long series of parliamentary achievements which have given him a permanent place among the popular leaders of our times. Few men of this generation have made a more profound impression upon the national life. He has been identified with the business of the government for so many years that his departure from the House of Representatives has been everywhere deplored as a grevious loss to the public service; for leaving out of consideration altogether his abilities to do the work so long entrusted to him by his district, it has never happened to any other citizen of Iowa, and to few others in any state, to secure the training in public affairs which comes from an uninterrupted activity of more than twenty years in the House of Representatives.

I had the opportunity of knowing Colonel Henderson with a special degree of intimacy for the twelve years beginning with the administration of General Harrison, during which we served together in the House. He was already counted among the old members when I first entered, and in the memorable contest for the Speakership of the Fifty-first Congress he had a most flattering support drawn from all sections of the country. Mr. Reed won the prize and Colonel Henderson at once became a member of the little group of experienced legislators to whom the management of the business of the House was committed. And from that time, whether in the council chamber or upon the floor, he remained one of the chief supporters and defenders of the policies and program of the party to which he was attached.

When Mr. Reed retired from public life, Colonel Henderson was so generally looked upon as his natural successor that one after another the able men who were selected by the partiality of the community in which they lived, to contest the honor with him, withdrew in his favor, leaving him in possession of the field without a dissenting voice. A good many people were disturbed by the fear that no one could fill Mr. Reed's place; yet after four years in the chair it was the testimony of friends and foes alike that the office had suffered no disparagement during the period of Colonel Henderson's administration. He exhibited all of Mr. Reed's masterful talent for controlling the House, and with it a suavity of manner, a kindly sympathy, a thoughtful regard for the feelings of others, which were sometimes wanting in the cruder methods of his predecessor.

He put aside the honors of that office at a time when he enjoyed the confidence of both sides of the House, and might have looked forward to a future undisturbed by the ordinary vicissitudes of politics. Those of us who have come here today are not thinking so much as we look upon this statue, of the gavel which he holds in his hand as of the crutch he is leaning upon. The blaze and glare of official station seem dull and commonplace; the personal contentions which sometimes add to the cares of the public service, a burden too heavy to be borne, are all forgotten; the mistakes, the failings and mischances which are a part of our poor human frailty, are left to the charity which remembereth that we are dust. The presence here of these bent and white-haired men, whatever the artist may have intended, makes this a soldier's monument. When you look upon it you will think of a worn and faded uniform of blue, and when those who come after you, your children and grandchildren, stand about this spot with curious interest, they may have to ask what the gavel in the uplifted hand is for, but they will know without asking anybody what the crutch means: for they will hear the echo of Lincoln's solemn call for troops and Kirkwood's stern demand that Iowa should do her duty. And right well were all the proclamations answered, though they followed one after another like alarm bells in the night; for from her sparse and meager population, there marched into the field, eighty thousand fighting men, one in eight of all who lived within her borders, men, women, and children. More than 2,000 of them fell in battle. Over 10,000 died in the hospitals and the prisons. Your comrade, there on that pedestal, is only one of 10,000 more who came home disabled by wounds or stricken by disease; so that over one quarter of the whole enlisted force of Iowa was literally a sacrifice upon the altar of the Republic.

The years which have gone since your last battle was fought, have made sad havoc with the broken ranks, as your own roll call shows; but a goodly number still survive; and throughout the land wherever an Iowa veteran lives, from thousands of humble homes, there has today gone up to Heaven a soldier's blessing upon the name and fame of David B. Henderson.

DAVID B. HENDERSON.

IN WAR A HERO, IN PEACE A STATESMAN, A TRUE IOWAN. HE VOLUNTARILY LAID
DOWN THE SCEPTER OF POWER WHEN HE STOOD CONSPICUOUSLY THE
UNCHALLENGED LEADER OF THE AMERICAN CONGRESS.

Reunion Proceedings.

Assemble in pavilion at 7 p. m.

After entertaining music by Fayette drum corps and band, which was inspiring, and, for the time carried us back again to 61-5, the reunion was called to order by the president, Lieutenant Dunham, and Mr. A. H. Loomis proceeded to deliver his address of welcome and was followed by Hon. R. W. Tirrill of the 12th.

Mr. President and Friends, members of Twelfth Iowa:—

In bidding you welcome to Clermont it is with a realization, that no words can fully express the pleasure we feel in having you with us upon this occasion. We appreciate the great honor it is to our little city to have so large and distinguished an assembly for its guests and we greet you, old and young; soldiers of war and citizens of peace, we greet you and bid you a most cordial welcome.

And especially to you members of the 12th Iowa, who have seen fit to honor us by holding your quadrennial reunion where at this time, in behalf of the citizens of Clermont we bid you a most hearty welcome. Clermont feels greatly honored in having you as her guest; noted as your regiment is for its many acts of valor upon the field of battle, to which our distinguished Senator paid such eloquent tribute this afternoon.

We welcome you the more heartily because of the special interest Clermont has always had in the 12th Iowa, in which so many of the noble sons of Fayette county served, with credit to themselves and the honor of their State. Yes, Clermont is proud to entertain such a Company and long will this day be remembered as one in which we were privileged to bivouac with one of the bravest regiments that ever marched beneath the stars and stripes. (Why bless you Col. Henderson, if you could have had these veterans down at Dubuque yesterday or the day before, you would have quelled that riot among the car strike men so quickly, Senator Allison would probably never have known that there was trouble in his city and would have been with us at this time.)

Realizing that such an occasion as this may not offer itself to Clermont again, we ask you, members of the 12th, to surrender, unconditionally, as prisoners of our charge, not even asking for a parole, before the time of your exchange to the better accomodations of your own homes.

It is a happy thought, my friends, that so long as patriotism and reverence for our country exists the Nation need have no fear from external foes, or internal problems, and those monuments will serve to inspire the highest sentiments of patriotism in the hearts of the young, and perpetuate the memory of the men I have the honor to welcome and whose presence adds a sacredness to those blocks of marble and tablets of bronze.

God bless you, and may the teachings of this day lead us to a greater love of friends, of home, of country, and of God.

A. H. LOOMIS,
Secretary of Clermont Soldiers' Monumentary Association.

Mr. A. H. Loomis, and Citizens of Clermont:—

Individually I have some knowledge of the generous hospitality of some of the good people of your little city and I know that a large number of the comrades of the Twelfth Iowa Infantry, whom I represent here this evening, and in whose behalf I now speak, have been recipients of the bounteous hospitality of your people in times past, but today, the welcome that we have received by your kind and forceful words, has been even now, already fully verified by the realities this day experienced; and in behalf of my comrades, whose sentiments I voice, I now heartily thank you, and your people through you, for these manifestations of good cheer and loyal fellowship, as well as your generous hospitality so kindly proffered.

While perhaps, we are right in believing, that as soldiers of the late rebellion, we are entitled to the generous hospitality accorded us by your citizens, yet we must not, and I trust we do not, lose sight of the fact, that the great civil war of 61 to 65 was not crushed out wholly by us, but by the aid and assistance of the great loyal heart of Americans, meaning the soldiery and the loyal men and women of this country, typical examples of whom you find in your own little city in the persons of Gov. and Mrs. Larrabee.

I have known Governor Larrabee quite well ever since we met at West Union in 1863 and nominated our own Wm. B. Allison for his first term in Congress, and since that day it has pleased us both, to labor together in his interest and in the interest of this District, as well as in the interest of this great commonwealth and nation, until we have seen him grow from that small beginning in 1863, to a position in the affairs of the Nation, and in the hearts of his countrymen, never before excelled by any man or statesman in this or any other country.

At another convention, we joined forces to nominate another man for congress, who after many years of faithful service, during which time he battled with southern chivalry for the right, until he was recognized as the leader of his associates in the lower House of Congress, and finally elevated to the Speakership in that great body, by reason of his untiring zeal; acknowledged executive ability, and honest devotion to principles.

Col. D. B. Henderson was one of the boys of the Twelfth Iowa Infantry, and he is the conspicuous figure, whom we delight to honor here today, through the generosity of your worthy citizens, Governor and Mrs. Larrabee.

But after all, Allison and Henderson are only our boys, in a sense; they do our bidding, subject to the criticisms of their constituency, for or against, right or wrong, not a bed of roses after all; yet we have always been proud of them, glad to hear them spoken of in foreign lands as among the greatest statesmen of the Nation; and yet they are in our keeping and in a measure, subject to our dictations.

Col. Henderson could not if he would, prevent Gov. Larrabee from erecting that statue yonder, he must submit in this, as in many other things; of course, he has to some extent blocked the wheels of his future political progress to which he has so long been attached, but we will soon have him back in line and put him on double duty.

Mr. Mayor and Citizens of Clermont: In a sense, we meet you here on common grounds, to commemorate the stirring events of 61 to 65 in which we all had a common interest.

The loyalty and patriotic devotion of your citizenship furnished the banner company of our regiment, and proudly did your boys maintain the honor of that starry emblem.

That old flag handed down to us by the fathers of the revolution, preserved in its purity by the comrades of the Grand Army of the Republic and the loyal men and women of this great country of ours, has been carried by our boys across the mighty waters of the deep, to the far away islands of the sea, planting it upon the ramparts of universal brotherhood, and in the mighty presence of the nations of the world, have unfurled its silken folds, to human freedom and constitutional liberty.

R. W. TIRRILL.

Another pleasing feature following the address of Comrade Tirrill was a very beautiful song, artistically rendered by Miss Stella Spears, a daughter of Comrade Hart Spears of the 12th, which received hearty applause.

A reading, "The Man Without a Country," was then listened to with rapt attention by Miss Beulah Wright who held her audience spellbound from first to last, receiving a storm of applause upon retiring.

Shiloh as seen today by Comrade P. R. Woods, of Co. C, and W. F. McCarron of Co. I, as follows:

Shiloh Battlefield.

P. R. Woods.

When a camp fire is called, every old soldier who attends, is expected to bring a rail, to help keep the fire burning. I thought I would try to bring one that had not been too much charred. So I have selected for a short talk, our recent visit to Shiloh battlefield.

My wife accompanied me on the trip. I assure you it was a very enjoyable occasion. We avoided the crowd and had a most excellent opportunity of looking over the grounds, and studying the positions and movements of both armies.

We arrived at Paducah, Ky., by rail, May 16th, and took passage on a steamer for our trip of two hundred and twenty-seven miles up the Tennessee River, to Pittsburg Landing. There is much travel and traffic on these steamers, and our progress was slow. We were two days and most of three nights on the boat, reaching Pittsburg Landing at 2 o'lock on the morning of the 19th. I saw nothing especially familiar along the river, only that it is a beautiful stream. We passed old Ft. Henry, the objective point of our first campaign. Little could be seen, but the outlines of the old earthworks. On the boat, both up the river and on our return, we met many people of all ages, natives of Kentucky and Tennessee. They were kind and courteous, and we talked freely of the events of the war, and of conditions in the South. We learned much of the state of society in the border states, after the close of the war; of the hatred, the treachery and brutality. But time and a wise administration of public affairs, have greatly mollified these conditions.

When we reached Pittsburg Landing, my old college friend and army comrade, Major Reed, was there to greet us. The Major had a team at his disposal, and we spent the greater part of the fine days we were at the park, driving over the field, to the various points of interest.

The National Park and Cemetery contains about four thousand acres, and more will be purchased. Much has been done to beautify the grounds, but the work is not completed. The underbrush, old logs and rail fences have been removed and about twenty-five miles of road, running throughout the park, have been graveled. Otherwise, the grounds are left, as far as possible, unchanged. Some of the old trees, badly scarred by shells and bullets, are still standing. But the greater number have fallen to decay, and others grown up in their places; so that the general appearance of the field is much as it was at the time of the battle.

There are iron tablets marking the locations of the lines of battle, of both union and rebel armies, during both days; markers showing locations of camps, also, historical tablets. Each division headquarters is indicated by a pyramid of shell, on a base of granite; and where a general officer, either Federal or Confederate, was killed or mortally wounded, a monument is erected, consisting of a thirty-two pound Parrot gun, surrounded by four pyramids of shells, all on a base of granite. Two mounted cannon mark the position of each battery.

The states of Iowa, Illinois, Indiana, Ohio, and Pennsylvania, have erected monuments for their regiments engaged in the battle. Other states will probably follow their example. Most of the monuments are of granite with bronze tablets. Each regimental monument is erected where the regiment held its position in the battle. That of the Twelfth Iowa stands where the colors were located, during the day. Iowa and Illinois have also, each erected a state monument; the former being by far, the finer. The bronze work is not yet placed in position on the Iowa monument, owing to a dispute as to the quality of the bronze. When completed, it will stand seventy-four and a half feet to the top of the spread eagle, that is perched on top of the globe that surmounts the column. This will cost $25,000, while each of the eleven regimental monuments will cost about $2,000.

The cemetery, located on a beautiful site, near the river, contains about four thousand dead, many of them unknown; each grave being marked by a marble slab. It is inclosed with a stone wall and iron gates, and is beautifully ornamented by a variety of native trees, and others transplanted; and by a profusion of roses, flowering plants and shrubs. There are a number of magnolia trees, all bearing their rich, cream colored flowers. Over the stone walls, climb here and there, the honeysuckle and trailing vines. On the river front are two cannon mounted, as though standing guard over the "bivouac of the dead," while the stars and stripes floats from a staff near by. At convenient intervals along the graveled walks, are iron tablets, bearing poetical quotations from that beautiful patriotic poem by O'Hara.

IOWA STATE MONUMENT ON SHILOH BATTLEFIELD.

We visited our Twelfth Iowa camping ground, and stood at the edge of the bluff, overlooking the little spring branch where Reed and I were performing our Sunday morning ablutions, when the long roll rang out upon the air, on the morning of that fateful day. We drove out along the road where we had marched that morning, to the place where we took our position in the line of battle along the edge of the Duncan field, a mile and a half to the front. Here we stood, where we had stood forty-one years before, and looked out over the field. In my imagination, I fought over again, my part of that fearful conflict. I could see the rebels marching along in the edge of the woods at the farther side of the field, and take position behind the rail fence. I could see them charge across the field, three times, as far as the ravine near the middle, where we always stopped them by our fire. Then, as they advanced through the woods at our left, we drove them back in the same way. In every charge, we repulsed them with fearful slaughter. Then as we turned from our position in this "Hornet's Nest," and walked back over our line of retreat, the whole panorama was before me. I could see the rebel force directly in our rear, as we drove them back. Then I could see the rebel lines advancing on both sides, our own forces falling back before them. Then, as we attempted, by double-quick, to get out at the gap, that we could see was rapidly closing, the retreating soldiers on either side broke into our ranks, and our line was completely disorganized, and we were practically surrounded. It was impossible to fire, without shooting each other. The rebels were pouring in a murderous fire upon us, and men were falling by the score. I remember many incidents connected with this terrible scene; comrades falling all around me, bullets whizzing by, like so many bees, and of efforts to rally the men. Here, is where we surrendered. I recall, very distinctly, the circumstance of Capt. Edgington surrendering his sword to Gen. Polk. At this point, a tablet is placed, commemorating our surrender, which occurred at about half past five o'clock in the evening.

I will not attempt, and would fail if I did to describe my emotions, as I stood on that old battlefield, on the line of battle, where we held our position during that fearful conflict; my wife standing by my side, as interested as though she had passed through all these experiences with me; and later, as we stood on the very spot where the surrender took place, and still later, as we visited the field where we were first held as prisoners, during that night of terror and of storm. No one who has not passed through such an experience, can understand or realize what it means.

It will be worth the while of any comrade, who can do so, to visit the Shiloh National Park and Cemetery, and take his wife with him. Go when the secretary, Major Reed, is there. For some years he has made a thorough and systematic study of the battle, and is better informed as to all its details, both from a Federal and Confederate standpoint, than any other man. You will find him a comrade, and a competent and obliging guide.

The battle of Shiloh was one of the most sanguinary of the Civil War. The percentage of killed and wounded was greater than at any other battle of that great conflict.

PHILO R. WOODS,
Co. C. 12th Iowa.

W. F. McCarron.

A visit to the battlefield of Shiloh for the first time, after an absence therefrom of forty-one years by a man who, just leaving his 'teens, had been a soldier in that awful struggle of young American valor, calls vividly to mind the scenes that then and there transpired.

T. J. Lindsay, a soldier in an Ohio regiment, who was desperately wounded in the face on Sunday, and left for dead, and who suffered eight days after before he received proper attention, four of which he had nothing to eat, and whose regiment lost fifty per cent of the number engaged, speaking of his first visit to that field in later years says: "There is an epoch in the life of every man whether it be of misfortune or otherwise, the vivid recollection of which time cannot mar. "Shiloh," he says, "was my life epoch. I can see every thing as though it were yesterday. The great gray columns as they came chasing and cheering through the open woods and fields, upon an army preparing for inspection and review, and listening to the sweet southern song birds, as they welcomed the rising sun, but were soon hushed by the whizzing, murderous 'Minnie'".

Further describing the scene on Sunday night after the two armies, exhausted by a day of bloody work, rested on their arms, or maneuvered for new positions, this soldier who heard it all, describes the scene as follows: "Sunday night was more terrible than can possibly be pictured. The air was filled with pleading cries for help and water, and to add to the horror, the gunboats were throwing their heavy shells all night among the helpless wounded of both sides, setting fire to the woods in many places, and burning to death many helpless men who might have been saved. Heaven seemed to take pity, for before midnight a heavy deluge of rain came and put out the fires." I have quoted from this soldier because it so fully corroborates my own recollections. The present generation can scarcely realize what the feelings of an old soldier are on recalling scenes like these in which he was a participant.

May 30, 1903 was the first time I had found it convenient to re-visit the Shiloh battle field, and this was in response to an invitation by the G. A. R. Department of Tennessee, that being the occasion of the annual decoration of the graves of the Nation's dead. The route from Chattanooga is by way of Corinth, Miss., the battle field being about twenty-two miles from Corinth, by private conveyance, over the same route taken by Major-General Albert Sidney Johnson when he deliberately marched his 43,960 veterans of the Army of the Mississippi on April 4th and 5th, 1862 to attack Maj. Gen. U. S. Grant, with his Army of the Tennessee, 39,830 strong, then just camped and resting in repose on the bank of the Tennessee, at Pittsburg Landing.

I would not dare venture in the limited space here at command, even though it was desirable to do so, to give an extended account of the impressions now upon my mind of the scenes of that awful conflict, or even attempt a description of the battle as I saw it, though of the 80,000 men engaged, there are no doubt several thousand yet living, many of whom together with their descendants, are within the boundaries of this vicinity, who would be interested in any additional account that might be written. There have been volumes written about the battle of Shiloh, and considerable criticism indulged against Gen. Grant, much of which was unjust, but some of which was deserved, but suffice to say, the battle opened before daylight on the morning of April 6, 1862, with an attack upon the federal army, amounting to a surprise, and raged with unabated fury until dusk. The command to which I belonged at the time, the 12th Iowa Infantry, was stationed in front of what was known as the "Duncan field," and with several other Iowa regiments, was in Gen. W. H. L. Wallace's division. As the day's onslaught closed, my regiment with several others, found themselves surrounded, and were captured, our immediate captor being Gen. Polk. I remember, also, very distinctly of seeing Gen. Hardee who came among us commanding us to throw down our arms. Some of us instead of doing so, broke our guns as best we could, across the roots of trees. It is interesting to me to know that I easily recognized the exact spot where my regiment lay, aided in doing so by a monument of the regiment erected on the exact line we fought all day and with terrible effect repulsed charge after charge made across that field by the enemy. A tree pierced with cannon balls which stood upon our line, stands there yet, scarred as many veterans are, with old age and the wounds it received. It is needless to say that I eagerly secured relics from these spots, one of which is a piece of rotten wood from the stump of a tree which I am satisfied is the one against which I broke my gun.

In short, except that the undergrowth is removed, and other trees have grown up, Shiloh battle field looks as familiar to me today as it did forty one years ago.

The forces engaged, or present for duty, on April 6, were, "Army of the Tennessee," under General Grant—39,830, Army of the Mississippi under General Albert Sidney Johnson--43,968.

There arrived on the night of April 6, and reinforced General Grant in the battle of the next day, Gen. Lew Wallace, with 5,000 and the "Army of the Ohio," under Gen. Buell, about 18,000.

The casualties were as follows: Army of the Tennessee, killed, 1513; wounded, 6,601; missing, 2,830; total, 10,944. Army of the Ohio, killed, 241; wounded, 1807; missing 55; total 2103; making total killed of 1754; wounded, 8,408; and missing, 2,885; or grand total loss 13,047. The confederate losses were, killed 1728; wounded 8,012; missing, 959; total, 10,699; total losses, both sides, 23,746. It will here be observed that the aggregate losses of the two armies at Shiloh were exceeded by very few of the heaviest battles of the war, notably Gettysburg, where the losses were over 40,000, Wilderness, 25,000, Chickamauga nearly 27,000.

The park embraces about 4000 acres, and is beautifully preserved, in charge of commissioners as follows: Colonel Cornelius Cadle, formerly of the Eleventh Iowa, now residing in Ohio, chairman; Major J. H. Ashcroft, of the Twenty-sixth Kentucky, of Kentucky; Colonel Josiah Patterson, of the First Alabama, confederate, now of Memphis, Tennessee; and Major D W. Reed of the Twelfth Iowa, historian of the park, now living in Evanston, Illinois. Two other Twelfth Iowa men are employed, F. A. Large, guardian, and L. J. Lewis, in charge of the masonry. Mr. Atwell Thompson, formerly connected with the Chickamauga park, is resident engineer, and Mr. W. S. Keller is his assistant.

There are about twenty-five miles of splendidly graveled roads built along the lines occupied by mainroad, during the battle. There are over 400 tablets and markers to designate all important positions of troops of both armies, the "Army of the Tennessee" being designated by markers painted blue, the "Army of the Ohio," yellow and the confederates red.

MONUMENTS ERECTED.

There are monuments erected by the several states as follows:— Illinois, 39; Ohio, 34; Indiana, 21; Iowa, 11; and Pennsylvania, 1. The government has erected monuments to mark where general officers were killed, including that to Gen. Albert Sidney Johnson.

Iowa had in this battle her Second, Third, Sixth, Seventh, Eighth, Eleventh, Twelfth, Thirteenth, Fourteenth, Fifteenth and Sixteenth regiments, to all of which handsome monuments mark the most conspicuous positions occupied. In addition, Iowa has erected a magnificent monument 74 feet high with a base 34x34 feet, on the most conspicuous spot on the field.

THE NATIONAL CEMETERY.

The most beautiful spot in all these 4,000 acres, is the ten acres on the high bluff overlooking the river where sleep the remains of over 3,600 of the heroes who gave up their lives for the preservation of the union. The thoughts that came to my mind of scenes which had their termination in this silent city of the dead, crowd upon me, but I can only stop to say, that on these memorial occasions, this cemetery is visited by thousands of people. There were fully 4,000 people at the park on this year's memorial day, notwithstanding heavy rains. They came in wagons, buggies, horseback, by boat, on foot, many of them from 50 miles distant— men, women and children. The cemetery is in charge of Capt. Shaw, to whom with his excellent wife, Maj. Ashcraft, and to Capt. N. M. Kemp, Commander of Fielding Hurst Post No. 7, G. A. R., at Adamsville, I am particularly indebted for courtesies shown.

I regret very much the unavoidable absence at the time, of Major Reed, to whom the country is indebted for reliable data connected with the park, and to whom I am indebted for the reliable statistics given in this letter. Maj. Ashcraft was the only one of the commissioners who was present at Shiloh on this occasion, but they all bear the reputation of efficient men, and the result of their labors will soon make of the Shiloh National Military Park, one of the most delightful memorials of American valor on the continent.

It needs very little previous preparation by a participant in one of the great battles of the civil war, for a speech on an occasion like that at Shiloh on Memorial day, and the people who attend are good listeners. There are plenty of "both sides" represented in an audience at Shiloh, but I think, from the enthusiasm displayed for the "Stars and Stripes," they all appreciate the spirit of the words,

"The blue and the gray
In fierce array
No local hates dissever,
Strike hands once more
From shore to shore,
The North and South forever."

W. F. McCARRON,
Co. I, 12th Iowa.

FRONT OF SHILOH MONUMENT

BACK OF SHILOH MONUMENT

List of Casualties.

KILLED.

Co. A—Lt. Geo. W. Moir, Whitcomb Fairbanks, Barton H. Johnson, Reuben G. King, William Stotsen. Co C.--Corp. Thomas Henderson, Charles Larson, Charles Pendleton. Co. D—Lt. Jason D. Ferguson, James P. Ayers, Daniel Luther. Co. E—Israel W. Fuller, William L. Pauley. Co. F—Corp. Aborn D. Campbell. Co. G—Ole G. Olson. Co. I—Thomas H. Wilson. Co K—Lewellyn Larrabee. Total 17.

DIED OF WOUNDS.

Co. B—Charles King. Co. C—Henry George. Co. E—Jacob Howrey Charles Johnson, Samuel J. Lichty, Thomas Porter, John P. Thompson. Co. F—Aborn Crippen, David Clark, John A. McCullouch, Joseph Pate, Allen Ware. Orry Wood. Co. H—Edgar A. Ward. Co. K—Sylvester Griffin, John Moulton. Total 16.

MISSING IN ACTION AND NEVER FOUND.

Co. A—John Moran, William Lefier. Co. C--Geo. W. Grannis. Co., K--W. H. H. Fuller. Total 4.

DIED IN PRISON.

Co. A—Israel Hall, Roswell F. Quivey. Co. B—Lt. Lyman H. Merrill, Sergt. Daniel Harbaugh, Corp. Frank E. Hancock, Corp. Madison J. Roe, John L. Bryant, Jens. Hanson, Ole Hanson, Leem Kleven, Henry Kuck, Chas. H. Noyes, Edwin R. Perry, Ira E. Peck, Simeon Peck, Knud Thronson, William M. White. Co. C—Corp. Samuel F. Brush, Corp. Daniel D. Warner, James L. Ayers, Henry Beadle, John Quivey, Willard E. Simer, Samuel Stone, Charles Sigman. Co. D—Robt. McClain, Warren A. Flint, Lewis Snell. Co. E—Corp. John I. Smith, John Ahrens, William O. Bird, John F. Koch, Hiram Hoisington, Elias Moon, Washington Richmond, Milton Rood, Stephen Story, Joseph W. Johnson. Co. F—William H. Barney, William Koltonbach, David N. Lillibridge, William H. Mason, Elijah M. Overocker, Thomas Otis, George Parks, Ira W. Roberts, Charles P. Toney. Co. G—Lt. Joseph F. Nickerson, Henry Johnson. Co. H—Lt. Luther W. Jackson, John H. Byrns, William H. Collins, Thomas Clendenin, James E. Nichols, Royal F. Nutting, Henry L. Richardson, Charles E. Richardson, William J. Slack, Julius Ward. Co. I—Lt. John J. Marks, Jesse W. Dean, Charles W. Sackett. Co. K—Corp. Benj. E. Nash, Corp. John Fulton, Corp. Merriam Lathrop, Daniel Downer, William T. Johnson, Geo. Lande, Thomas Sover, Chas. W. Smith, Philander Wilson. Total 71.

STATE OF IOWA.
ADJUTANT GENERAL'S OFFICE.

Des Moines, June 15th, 1901.

I, Melvin H. Byers, Adjutant General of the State of Iowa, do hereby certify that I have made careful examination of the records of my office with respect to the 12th Regiment of Iowa Volunteer Infantry. That the records of my office show that the foregoing lists of the casualties of said regiment at the battle of Shiloh, Tenn., April 6th, 1862, as regards the killed in action, died of wounds, missing and never found, and died in prison, are true and correct and a complete record of such casualties in said regiment at said battle, as shown by the records in this office.

MELVIN H. BYERS,
Adjutant General.

Love Feast.

After this commenced the "Love Feast" proper. Our inimitable Col. Jack Stibbs, always doing the unexpected thing and doing it correctly, led off with a reading "The Man Who Carried a Gun", followed by selections of a similar nature, carrying his audience with him in laughter and tears. He was followed by Capt. Soper, Co. D's historian, and Col. Rood, a visiting comrade. It was a jolly good time we had of it, till midnight tattoo sounded, "lights out".

Comrade Soper's Remarks.

He began by telling a somewhat amusing goat story and applied it as connected with himself and the evening program.

He then proceeded to speak of the ties formed by life in the barracks, the camp, the march and upon the field of battle, as being incomparably more intimate and lasting than any other, and declared that the only ones in any manner approaching this comradeship, are the years of association in school and at college, in the class room, the athletic field and society halls; but even these associations are not to be compared to those gained by four years of active service in actual war.

The speaker, who is chairman of the Iowa commission appointed by the Governor, under the provision of the act appropriating $50,000 for the erection of monuments upon the Battlefield of Shiloh, then proceeded to explain why the dedication of the Shiloh monuments, which had previously been set by the commission for May 30th, 1903, had been indefinitely postponed.

He stated that the monuments were constructed of Barre granite, but ornamented with various bronze figures; that the commission had made a careful study of bronze before letting the contracts and provided therein that all bronze should be of the character and quality known as United States standard bronze, the alloy of which is composed of 90 per cent copper, 7 per cent tin and 3 per cent zinc; that important pieces of the bronze, including the ball and eagle surmounting the same, weighing several tons, had been cast in Italy; that when the bronze was delivered at Pittsburg Landing to be erected, careful borings were taken under the supervision of the United States Engineer and they were transmitted to a responsible firm of chemists and assayers in Chicago, who analyzed the alloy, from which the figures were cast, and ascertained that there was only from 78 to 82 per cent of copper in that portion of the bronze which had been cast in Italy, and a very much larger per cent of zinc than the contract provided for; that the commission, by reason of the failure of the contractor to furnish the bronze called for by the contract, had felt themselves compelled to reject the bronze, which left the state monument incomplete and the National Park commission did not permit of the dedication of unfinished or incomplete monuments. That also there had been some controversy as to the inscriptions to be placed upon the regimental monuments for the 15th and 16th Iowa, and the matter had been appealed to the Secretary of War, which had delayed the completion of those two regimental monuments, the others being complete. That it was impossible to tell when the monuments would be ready for dedication, by reason of the controversies between the contractor and the commission; but that proper notice would be given of the time fixed for the dedication

GEN. J. H. STIBBS.

and everybody, and particularly the survivors of the 12th Iowa, would be expected to attend; that a favorable season would be selected and a low rate of fare would be secured; that the Iowa monuments would be the finest on the field, and that it would well repay a visit to the Park.

Gen. Stibbs' Readings.

Since the war, Gen. Stibbs, has become quite prominent as an entertainer, and there has been a continual demand for his services, at reunions and camp fires, where his stories and readings are always received with favor. He tells the boys he is proud of the commissions he held, and especially proud of the fact that he commanded the 12th Iowa, but it is his chief delight to tell of his services as an enlisted man, or to recite some poem which pays tribute to the worth of the man who served in the ranks. Below we publish a poem by Comrade C. H. Robinson, of Marion county Indiana, which Gen. Stibbs recited for us at our last reunion, and which he says describes the man who put down the rebellion.

THE MAN WHO CARRIED A GUN.

When grim-visaged war raised his front in the land,
    And the smoke of the fight hid the sun,
Who was it left home to defend the old flag?
    'Twas the man who carried a gun.

When a long day's march was ended at last;
    Though he'd tramped from the rising of the sun;
Who was it stood guard all night o'er the camp?
    'Twas the man who carried a gun.

And when we'd invested the enemy's works,
    And had sapping and mining begun;
Who was it wielded the pick and the spade?
    'Twas the man who carried a gun.

When the enemy charged on our lines in full force,
    And his victory almost seemed won;
Who was it hurled back his masses at length?
    'Twas the man who carried a gun.

And when in retreat, though sullen and grim,
    We were pressed by the rebs on the run;
Who was it that turned and checked their advance?
    'Twas the man who carried a gun.

Who was it, I ask, at the end of the fray,
    When the hotly fought field had been won,
That succored the wounded men left on the field?
    'Twas the man who carried a gun.

While the officers ate all the hospital stores,
    And had all the whisky and fun;
Who was it lived on what he could steal?
    The man who carried a gun.

Let all honors due to our officers brave
    Be given for what they have done;
But never forget that the country was saved
    By the hero who carried a gun.

EIGHTH REUNION

BLUE AND GRAY.

"O, mother, what do they mean by blue?
    And what do they mean by gray?"
Was heard from the lips of a little child
    As she bounded in from play.
The mother's eyes filled up with tears;
    She turned to her darling fair,
And smoothed away from the sunny brow
    Its treasures of golden hair.

"Why, mother's eyes, are blue, my sweet,
    And grandpa's hair is gray,
And the love we bear our darling child
    Grows stronger every day."
"But what did they mean?" persisted the child,
    "For I saw two cripples today,
And one of them said he fought for the blue,
    The other one, he fought for the gray."

"Now, he of the blue had lost a leg,
    The other had but one arm.
And both seemed worn and weary and sad,
    Yet their greeting was kind and warm.
They told of battles in days gone by,
    Till it made my young blood thrill;
The leg was lost in the Wilderness fight,
    And the arm on Malvern Hill."

"They sat on the stone by the farm yard gate
    And talked for an hour or more,
Till their eyes grew bright, and their hearts seemed warm,
    With fighting their battles o'er.
And, parting at last, with a friendly grasp,
    In a kindly brotherly way,
Each called on God to speed the time
    Uniting the blue and gray."

Then the mother thought of other days—
    Two stalwart boys from her riven;
How they knelt at her side and lisping, prayed,
    "Our father, which art in heaven."
How one wore the gray, and the other the blue,
    How they passed away from sight;
And had gone to the land where gray and blue
    Are merged in colors of light.

And she answered her darling with golden hair,
    While her heart was sadly wrung
With the thoughts awakened in that sad hour
    By her innocent, prattling tongue;
"The blue and the gray are the colors of God;
    They are seen in the sky at even,
And, many a noble, gallant soul
    Has found them passports to heaven."

                    ANON.

Saturday Morning.

Sunrise salute, with booming of cannon. At eight o'clock we assemble at pavilion. After music by our drum corps and band, meeting is called to order, Col. Stibbs in the chair. Our president, Lieutenant Abner Dunham, proceeded to deliver his address, as follows:

President Dunham.

Comrades: Once more we meet in reunion, this time at the instance of our esteemed fellow citizen, Gov. Larrabee, who invited us to assist in the dedicatory exercises of a most beautiful statue erected by him to our beloved comrade, Col. D. B. Henderson.

The occasion is an inspiring one, it will be the bright spot in the lives of all present. Those of our comrades unable to be with us, send good cheer and join in paying tribute to the comrade whose life has made it possible for this reunion, while the spirits of the departed ones hover over, cheering on the good work and inviting us to that beautiful realm where war is unknown and sickness and death does not enter.

My comrades, the occasion is one of more than usual interest, we not only live over again the more than four years of solder's life and renew the associations formed during the most trying and thrilling events in the history of our country, but this statue leads us to new thoughts. We naturally look over our past life and ask what have been the lives of each other, a searching investigation reveals the fact that all have been good citizens, a very large majority have been reasonably successful in their chosen vocations, some have accumulated their full share of this world's goods; while one whom this occasion is to honor, has through his great ability, kindness of heart and true courage attained a position second only in importance to that of the President of the United States, and birth alone prevents his aspiring to that exalted position, his career as a statesman has been eminently successful and to him many an old soldier is indebted for the adjustment of claims long deferred, to him many if not all of us are under obligations for courtesies and favors shown. The day is far distant when the old soldier will have the true friend and indefatigable worker for his rights that he has had in the person of Col. Henderson, the old, the crippled, the rich, the poor receive the same cordial greeting, the same careful attention. His voluntary retirement from public life is our loss, we hope his gain and we bespeak for him the same success in his new undertaking whatever it may be, as has attended him during his public career.

My comrades it is a grand .... we have been permitted to exist .... greater part of the 19th century. We have seen our country advance from a fourth and third rate power to that of the first nation on the face of the globe and it is a satisfaction to feel that each has in a greater or less degree contributed to that end. As I look over this assemblage of veterans and see the halting step, the wrinkled brow, the silvered locks, I realize that our race is nearly run, and that to our children must be left the work so well begun and it is a great satisfaction that already we have evidences that the charge is to be left in good hands.

Our early boyhood days were passed during a terribly exciting period in the political history of our country, questions agitated the public mind which divided the sections, the halls of congress had for years been a seething cauldron of impassionate utterances. The newspapers contributed to excite the public mind, the officers of government then in power were crippling its resources preparatory to the grand struggle, and not until the flag was assaulted at Sumpter did the north awake from the sleep of security and peace to find our country engulfed in the throes of terrible war. Awoke to find our navy scattered to all parts of the earth, our forts and munitions of war in the hands of the conspirators, a bankrupt treasury, a very large proportion of those trained to the art of war by the government arrayed against it, in fact the administration of Lincoln found the government practically with bare hands to begin the subjugation of that traitorous band who had for years been preparing for this very move. The voice of Lincoln called for the first 75,000 men, afterwards for hundreds of thousands, and hundreds of thousands, until our ranks numbered into the millions who, under the guiding hand of Grant, retook the forts, retook the arsenals, retook the arms, retook the munitions of war, reset in the azure folds the stars stolen from our flag. Where, never again shall an enemy's hand dare pluck them out.

My comrades, you were a part of that immense host, for four long years your rallying point was that flag, borne by that grand soldier, Henry Grannis, who seemingly impervious to shot and shell, planted it on the front line, and upon it your alignments were promptly made.

You saw suffering, too awful to describe, in the camp, on the march, on the battlefield. You saw death in its most awful forms, you saw starvation in the prison hells of the south, you saw war in all its terrible details, yet this did not deter you when after three years service, and the loss of over one half your number, you re-enlisted, determined to see it through. Why follow your footsteps for those long dreary years? History is being corrected, and time will yet give to each his true measure. Suffice to say that soon rays of light began to appear, followed soon after by the unfurling of the flag of surrender, then we knew our country was saved.

Comrades, it was an awful experience, but it was worth all it cost. For years the result trembled on a balance, but right prevailed and God has seen fit to preserve us to see the fruits of victory.

To my young friends who are visiting with us, let me say that upon you will soon rest the fate of our country, the preservation of that flag; upon you the fate of future generations, largely depend. You may not be called upon to engage in the conflict of arms as your fathers have been, but you will have battles to fight no less serious. Every generation must fight its own battles. It is still true as ever it was that

> "We are living, we are dwelling
> In a grand and awful time—
> In an age on ages telling
> To be living is sublime."

This, my young friends, is our country. That flag is our flag. Think what it has cost to defend it. That flag has been bathed in the blood of heroes. It is the emblem of our liberty, the symbol of national unity and power. It represents home and friends, freedom and country. Many of us have seen it floating above the smoke of battle.

"Many an eye hath glanced to see
That banner in the sky."

Stand by the old flag, boys, stand by the old flag, girls. It is our flag handed down to us unimpaired by our ancestors. Let it be transmitted to posterity in the same unimpaired condition.

Flag of Co. "K."

Resolved, That the Twelfth Iowa association accept with gratitude the dear old flag of Co. K, that was carried by the Twelfth Iowa Infantry at the battle of Corinth, Miss., Oct. 3 and 4, 1862, and presented to the association by the widow of a dear comrade, Charles E. Merriam, and the sympathy of the association is unanimously tendered to Mrs. Merriam on account of the great loss she sustained in the death of a noble husband.

Resolved, That the president and secretary of the association cause to be prepared a careful and authentic history of the flag of Co. K, carried by the regiment at Corinth and certify the same and transmit the same with the flag to the governor of the state of Iowa with the request that both be deposited with other battle flags of the Twelfth Iowa Infantry in the archives of the state.

This flag was presented to Company "K", 12th Iowa by the ladies of Hopkinton, Delaware, Co., Iowa, in November 1861. Upon the organization of the Union Brigade after the battle of Shiloh, it became the regimental flag of that organization and was used as such during the siege of Corinth, at the battle of Corinth, and until December 1862 when the Union Brigade was disolved.

At the battle of Corinth the Union Brigade was attached to Hackleman's brigade of Davies' division, and on October 4th occupied a position on the Purdy road between the railroad depot and battery Powell. It was fiercely attacked by the confederates and in a hand to hand conflict lost, in a few minutes, one third of the men engaged. Every officer but three of the Union Brigade was killed or wounded. Among the wounded were Lt. Col. Coulter and Lt. D. B. Henderson. Three color bearers in succession went down and the flag was for a moment in the hands of the enemy, but its defenders rallied and drove the assailants back and Act. Serg't. Maj. J. D. Cole recovered the flag and raised it to its place but was almost immediately shot through the breast and crawled to the rear carrying the flag with him. The stains on the flag were made by the blood of Serg't Cole, and perhaps others of its gallant defenders.

Gen. Davies in his official report commends the Union Brigade for its gallant rescue of its flag and for its assistance in recovering battery Powell.

Surgeon Finley, of the 12th Iowa, says he saw the flag go down three times in that "Pot-Metal Hell" and as often come up again; that the staff was shot away and replaced, in the midst of the battle, by a staff captured from the enemy; that nearly half of the Union Brigade was piled up, dead or wounded, around the flag when Serg't. Major. J. D. Cole received what was supposed to be his death wound, and carried the flag to the rear. Serg't. J. D. Cole, in a privater letter in answer to a question recently asked of him, tells in his modest way the part he took in the action as follows:

"I can remember but little of the fight until I saw the colors fall. One of the 14th Iowa, I think, carried the colors when the battle commenced. I took the colors and advanced to the front and alligned myself with the colors to the right and the General and his Aids rallied the men to the colors, they fell back again and left me between the two fires. The General then waved his sword for me to fall back and the men were again formed on the colors. As I stood there I was wounded and when I saw the blood pouring from my breast I carried the colors back and when I was looking for water, an ambulance man of the 8th Iowa told me that he would get me water if I would lie down. I placed the flag on the porch of a house and laid down on the floor. When the water came I gave the man my watch and chain and told him to save himself as the bullets were coming through the house. He told me afterwards that the General sent to know my name but he could not tell him. Col. Coulter and Lt. Henderson were wounded about the same time. I have little remembrance of what occurred after that time."

ABNER DUNHAM, Pres.

G. E. COMSTOCK, Sec.

EXECUTIVE CHAMBER, Sept. 23, 1903.

ABNER DUNHAM, President 12th Iowa Vet. Vol.
Infantry Reunion Ass'n, Manchester, Iowa:

MY DEAR SIR:—I beg to acknowledge the receipt, at the hands of Richard P. Clarkson, Esq., of the flag of Company K, 12th Iowa Infantry, and the resolutions reciting its history and directing that the flag be transmitted to the Governor of the State of Iowa, and that both flag and resolutions be deposited with other battle flags of the 12th Iowa Infantry in the archives of the State.

I cannot permit this formal acknowledgment to leave me without adding a word that seems appropriate to the occasion. This flag, although faded and torn, is rich with the most sacred memories of American courage and patriotism. So long as it shall endure it will teach to this and coming generations the noblest lesson of citizenship, and I profoundly hope that those who look upon it in future years may be worthy of the men of 1861. It shall be placed with its fellow flags, and shall be given all the care and honor the State can bestow upon it.

With high regard, I am

Yours very truly,
ALBERT B. CUMMINS.

The Stars on the Flag.

Count the stars on the flag as it passes by,
And then number the stars in yon distant sky—
 The number would be the brave hearts that would die
For the stars on the flag.

Count the stripes on the flag—we weave into one,
The tears and the sighs for the lives that are done,
But out of the shadows of each setting sun
 Shine the stars on the flag.

Count the tears for the flag! Were they shed in vain?
What now seemeth loss even yet will seem gain,
For the nation's great heart will suffer no strain
 On the stars of the flag.

Hats off to the flag! For its life breathe a prayer
That brave hearts and brave hands its love folds may bear,
Till the stars in their courses, their glory shall share
 With the stars on the flag.

Business Meeting.

In the election of officers Col. Henderson moved and put the question, calling for rising vote, that the present officers be re-elected by acclamation. The vote was unanimous.

Gen. Stibbs discussed the question of completing a regimental history. He said the matter had been under consideration for nearly 20 years, and that Maj. D. W. Reed had finally compiled a very creditable work, but that it would cost about $1000 to issue an edition of 500 copies, and he appealed to the comrades to advance the sum required, to insure the publication of the work. As a result, Col. D. B. Henderson agreed to advance $200 of the amount required, H. C. Curtis agreed to advance $200, E. B. Soper $100 and J. W. Gift $100. With these pledges covering over one-half the sum required, J. H. Stibbs and D. W. Reed agreed that they would, if necessary, advance the remaining $400, and that the book would be published as soon as practicable.

This history will contain about 350 pages, showing fully what was done and accomplished by the regiment, from date of original muster in, until final discharge. In addition to this, it will contain a complete roster of all the companies, together with two official colored maps of the battlefield of Shiloh. The book will be a valuable one, worthy a place in any library, and every survivor of the regiment and the families of the deceased should have a copy.

It will be sent post paid on receipt of price, two dollars, and we would suggest that any who are not already subscribers, write at once to Maj. D. W. Reed No. 2008 Sherman Ave., Evanston. Ill.

The book will not be stereotyped, only five hundred copies are to be printed.

A committee on resolutions was appointed: Capt. Soper, chairman; John Steen, Wahoo, Neb.; Maj. G. H. Morrisey, Washington, D. C. The resolutions presented and adopted were as follows:

First. We tender to Ex-Governor Larrabee, the Clermont Soldiers' Monument Association and the citizens of Clermont our heartfelt thanks for this most happy reunion, and for the occasion that made it possible and for the honor conferred upon the most conspicuous and best known member of our organization. We appreciate the labor that was necessary to prepare for, and the trouble and inconvenience occassioned by, our presence in the homes, and city, and beg leave to assure them that this occasion in many ways so notable, will remain with us to our latest day, one of the happiest and most delightful experiences of our lives.

Second. The Twelfth Iowa Regimental Association hereby unanimously tenders its grateful thanks to Mrs. Gov. Larrabee for her affectionate and untiring efforts to make this meeting a success in every way and to provide for the comfort and pleasure of our members and the members of our families.

We also tender our loving thanks to Mrs. Loomis for her untiring efforts to add to our comfort. She is the sister of Capt. W. W. Warner, and has ever been a sister to all the members of the Twelfth Iowa Infantry.

Third. That the Twelfth Iowa Veteran Volunteer Infantry Association take great pleasure in unanimously tendering our hearty thanks to Senator J. P. Dolliver for his very able and scholarly address, that by it our hearts have been made to rejoice and further that we are happy in the fact that we made no mistake in extending to him the invitation to be with us on this happy occasion.

Fourth. That we tender to Miss Beulah Wright of the Department of Oratorical Expression, U. I. U., a tribute of praise for the assistance she has contributed to help make this occasion so pleasant. For her reading at our dedicatory services of the D. B. Henderson statue. Her soul stirring eloquence filled our hearts with admiration and for the time it seemed we were young again.

Resolved: That a message be sent to Miss E. A. Sorin of Pasadena, Cal., "In token of her undying love and devotion to the members of Co. C and the Twelfth Regt.

Resolved: That it is the sense of this association that the bill pending in congress pensioning all soldiers and sailors who served for ninety days or more in the civil war at the rate of $12 per month and all widows of such soldiers and sailors who were married prior to June 30, 1890, should become a law and that our Senators and Representatives in Congress be requested to support the same and use their influence to secure its enactment.

Resolved:—That the Twelfth Iowa Association accept with gratitude the dear old flag of Co. K, that was carried by the Twelfth Iowa Infantry at the battle of Corinth, Miss., Oct. 3 and 4, 1862, and presented to the association by the widow of a dear comrade, Charles E. Merriam, and the sympathy of the association is unanimously tendered to Mrs. Merriam on account of the great loss she sustained in the death of a noble husband.

Resolved: That the President and Secretary of the Association cause to be prepared a careful and authentic history of the flag of Co. K, carried by the regiment at Corinth and certify the same and transmit the same with the flag to the Governor of the State of Iowa with the request that

REUNION GROUP AT "MONTAUK" HOME OF GOV. LARRABEE

both be deposited with other battle flags of the Twelfth Iowa Infantry in the archives of the state.

Resolved: That the proceedings of this reunion, with the names of all members of the Twelfth Iowa and also an account of dedicatory exercises of the Lincoln and Henderson statues be printed in pamplet form and distributed to all survivors and the President, Secretary and Major D. W. Reed be made a committee to prepare and publish the same.

ABNER DUNHAM, President.

G. E. COMSTOCK, Secretary.

A telegram from Senator Allison, expressing his regrets at not being able to be with us, congratulating and wishing us a happy time on this occasion, received and read before the association.

"Montauk Home."

A special invitation extended to all the 12th Iowa and their families, by Mr. and Mrs. Larrabee, to Luncheon on the lawn, at their "Montauk" home.

This capped the climax, and another such a time as we did have on that hill will never be repeated by this generation (nor forgotten by those present). The day was perfect, the lawn was perfect, the company perfect, and from the way the luncheon disappeared, that must have been perfect too. Everybody was as happy as they ever will be in this world, singing songs, telling stories. The Fayette band was with us, and it was in a perfect mood, rendering most beautiful music, until finally the luncheon struck them, and they surrendered. "We'll all feel gay when Johnnie comes marching home".

If any organization on earth was ever tendered an ovation, it was the Twelfth and their friends at that beautiful home on the hill, where Gov. Larrabee and his wife dwell. "May they never grow old and their shadows never grow less." When we add to this the personal presence of that Colonel, after his voluntary retirement from the second post of influence in the nation, the services of an orator like Senator Dolliver, the princely hospitality of the best Governor Iowa ever had, whose well directed munificence alone, has made this great occasion possible, we, the boys of the Twelfth, doff our hats, make our best salute, extend our hands, and with the hand the heart, and surrender unconditionally, and quietly say, we never thought it would be so. Goodbye.

Historical Vicksburg.

To the Survivors of the Vicksburg Campaign and Siege:

It was none other than General Ulysses S. Grant who, soon after the surrender at Appomatox, gave expression to the following sentiment: "If there is one event connected with the civil war that, more than another, is worthy of commemoration because of the importance of the event, and the valor and courage displayed by both armies, it is the campaign and siege of Vicksburg."

That this event is to be commemorated by the construction of a National Military Park at Vicksburg, in which the old forts and fortifications and the trenches and earth-works are to be restored, is not only gratifying to the family of General Grant, but to thousands of surviving veterans who followed the great General on that memorable campaign, and were participants with him in that awful siege.

To the Iowa soldier there clusters about historic Vicksburg an interest not applicable, perhaps, to any other point of the civil war. This will be clearly understood when we recall the fact that the great struggle of the Vicksburg campaign was participated in by no less than thirty-two organizations from the Hawkeye state, viz: The 3d, 4th, 5th, 6th, 8th, 9th, 10th, 11th, 12th, 13th, 15th, 16th, 17th, 19th, 20th, 21st, 22d, 23d, 24th, 25th, 26th, 28th, 30th, 31st, 34th, 35th, 38th and 40th regiments of Infantry; the 3d and 4th Cavalry, and the 1st and 2d batteries of Artillery.

The surviving members of the above regiments, and their children and children's children, will be intensely interested in the information contained in this article; for it is not extravagant to say that every soldier in the Vicksburg campaign, and every member of his family, has a burning desire to visit those historic battle grounds and the beautiful National Cemetery, containing the remains of nearly 17,000 of our heroic dead; and witness what the Government is doing for those who died, and to establish, at Vicksburg, a National Military Park that shall fittingly commemorate, for all time to come, the bravery of every man who participated in that greatest military achievement of the civil war.

Four grand National Military Parks, each located upon the scene of one of the desperate conflicts of the Civil War, have been authorized by the Congress of the United States—not in honor of victory or of defeat, but to commemorate a crucial epoch in the history of the Republic and the fortitude and heroism of her soldiers on both sides. The last bill to this end was approved by President McKinley, February 21, 1899, and is entitled "An Act to establish a National Military Park to commemorate the campaign, siege, and defense of Vicksburg." Following the enacting clause the act says: "That, in order to commemorate the campaign, siege, and defense of Vicksburg, and to preserve the history of the battle and operations of the siege and defense on the ground where they were fought and were carried on, the batttlefield of Vicksburg, in the State of Mississippi, is declared to be a National Military Park whenever the title to the same shall have been acquired by the United States," etc. Then follows a proximate description of the area to be acquired, provision for the appointment of three commissioners to establish the Park under the direction of the Secretary of War, and some general directions for the work.

IOWA MEMORIAL

To her Soldiers who served in the Campaign and Siege of Vicksburg, March 29-July 4, 1863. Henry H. Kitson, Sculptor.

The campaign that was signalized by the establishment of this Park was one of the most notable during the entire war, both as to details and results. Military critics unite in declaring it the most brilliant operation initiated and conducted by General Grant. As for General Pemberton, while he was clearly out-generaled in strategy, his army made a magnificent fight.

The capture of Vicksburg was the crowning and most important event in the great struggle for the control of the Mississippi River which began at St. Louis in May, 1861. With varying fortunes the Federal lines swept slowly southward past Cape Girardeau, Bird's Point, New Madrid and Island No. 10, until the capture of Memphis June 6, 1862. New Orleans had fallen in April and all eyes were now turned to Vicksburg, with its double sweep of the great river along miles of high bluffs, as the scene of the next act in the drama. The 12th Mississippi regiment had been sent to Vicksburg in February. In March a few guns with ammunition were sent from Pensacola, and early in April General Beauregard drew a project of fortification requiring about 40 guns and a garrison of 3,000 men. The work was begun April 21, 1862, by Captain D. B Harris with a force of negro laborers.

Upon the capture of New Orleans, General Martin L. Smith was dispatched to Vicksburg with five regiments, under orders to complete the fortification with the utmost dispatch. He arrived May 12, and by working day and night had six batteries finished and armed when the advance division of Farragut's fleet arrived, May 18. The fleet was accompanied by no land forces, and after giving Vicksburg its first baptism of fire in a desultory bombardment, returned to New Orleans about June 1. Here Farragut found the most urgent demand from the navy department that he should at once capture the up-river city, then the only point on the river remaining in Confederate control. July 22, reinforcements bringing the garrison to about 15,000 began arriving at Vicksburg, and, June 28, the city and its defenders were placed under command of General Van Dorn. June 25 Farragut again arrived at Vicksburg with his fleet, accompanied by a mortar flotilla and by General Williams and his brigade of about 3,000 men. Collecting a force of some 12,000 blacks, General Williams began work on the celebrated canal across the peninsula, locating it upon the line as laid out several years before when the states of Louisiana and Mississippi were in dispute as to their boundaries and the former state determined to dig a canal which should cut Vicksburg off from the river. After passing the batteries and getting into position, Farragut bombarded the city pretty steadily for seven days, stating in his official report of the attack that "while the forts can be passed as often as required, I am satisfied it is impossible to take Vicksburg without an army of twelve to fifteen thousand men." The fleet, however, remained in the vicinity until July 27—the principal event of this period being the brilliant dash into and through the Union vessels by the Confederate ram Arkansas, which caused Farragut great chagrin.

Vicksburg now had a period of respite, Grant's attempt late that fall to march south from his distant base at Memphis being frustrated by the capture of the supplies at Holly Springs without his getting far enough to excite serious alarm. Then came Sherman's December attack on the Chickasaw Bluffs, where he was seriously worsted by General

Stephen D. Lee. Two months of the succeeding winter and early spring Grant devoted to the "bayou expeditions," vainly trying every conceivable plan to find a way to cross the low land of the Yazoo delta and reach the high ground beyond the right flank of the enemy, now commanded by General Pemberton. Then followed Grant's last and winning effort, which is briefly outlined in the "Record," compiled for the Park Commission by its secretary and historian, General J. S. Kountz.

The Vicksburg campaign opened March 29, 1863, with General Grant's order for the advance of General Osterhaus' division from Milliken's Bend, and closed July 4, 1863, with the surrender of Pemberton's army and the City of Vicksburg. Its course was determined by General Grant's plan of campaign. This plan contemplated the march of his active army from Millikin's Bend, La., to a point on the river below Vicksburg, the running of the batteries at Vicksburg by a sufficient number of gunboats and transports, and the transfer of his army to the Mississippi side. These points were successfully accomplished and, May 1, the first battle of the campaign was fought near Port Gibson. Up to this time General Grant had contemplated the probability of uniting the army of General Banks to his. He then decided not to wait the arrival of Banks, but to make the campaign with his own army. May 12, at Raymond, Logan's division of Grant's army with Crocker's division in reserve, was engaged with Gregg's brigade of Pemberton's army. Gregg was largely outnumbered and, after a stout fight, fell back to Jackson. The same day the left of Grant's army, under McClernand, skirmished at Fourteen Mile Creek with the cavalry and mounted infantry of Pemberton's army supported by Bowen's division and two brigades of Loring's division. After the battle of Raymond, Sherman's and McPherson's corps of Grant's army moved toward Jackson. They reached that city May 14, and occupied it after a brief and spirited engagement with the small force there under General Joseph E. Johnston, who reached that place the night of May 13. General Grant had now interposed his army between the armies of General Johnston and General Pemberton. He left Sherman's corp one day at Jackson to complete the destruction of the stores and as much as possible of the railroads there. McPherson's corps marched from Jackson, May 15, towards Vicksburg. May 16, McClernand's and McPherson's corps of Grant's army engaged three divisions of Pemberton's army at Champion's Hill. Pemberton's forces were driven from the field in some confusion and with severe loss in killed, wounded prisoners and guns. Two divisions fell back towards Vicksburg. One division (Loring's) was cut off from the others and did not fall back to Vicksburg, but marched to Crystal Springs and a little later united with Johnston's army at Jackson. May 17, a part of Pemberton's army attempted to hold the works on the east side of Big Black river, but was driven from its intrenchments with considerable loss in prisoners and guns by the 13th corps of Grant's army. May 18, Pemberton's army took position in the defensive works around Vicksburg, Stevenson's division on right, Forney's in the center and M. L. Smith's on the left. Bowen's division and Waul's Texas Legion were held in reserve, but later Green's brigade of Bowen's division was placed in the line of defense. Late in the afternoon of the same day Grant's army began taking position in the line of investment. Sherman's corps on the right resting its right on the Mississippi river above the city, McPherson's corps in the center and McClernand's corps on the left of McPherson. May 24, Lauman's (fourth) division, sixteenth army corps, took position on the left of McClernand, and June 15, the investment was completed by Herron's division from the Department of Missouri, taking position on the left of Lauman and resting its left on the Mississippi river below Vicksburg. May 19 and again May 22, assaults were made by Grant's army but were repulsed with severe loss to the assailants. From May 22 to July 4, regular siege operations were carried on by Grant and opposed by Pemberton. During this time Admiral Porter's fleet rendered valuable assistance, and Grant was reinforced by three divisions of the sixteenth corps, two divisions of the ninth corps and Herron's division. With the exception of Lauman's and Herron's divisions, which took position in the line of investment as above noted, all these reinforcements and a part of the army with which he began the campaign were employed by Grant against the army of General Johnston. This last named army, with headquarters at Jackson, was assembled with the hope of raising the siege or assisting Pemberton to break through Grant's line. No force of Johnston's army crossed the Big Black river during the siege and defense. At the surrender. July 4, it was close to and on the east side of that river."

This great struggle was participated in upon the Federal side by organizations (regiments or parts of regiments and batteries) representing states as follows: Illinois—infantry 52, cavalry 10, artillery 15; total 77. Indiana—infantry 24, cavalry 2, artillery 2; total 28. Iowa—infantry 28, cavalry 2, artillery 2; total 32. (The Iowa regimentsengaged were: Infantry, 3, 4, 5, 6, 8, 9, 10, 11, 12, 13, 15, 16, 17, 19, 20, 21, 22, 23, 24, 25, 26, 28, 30, 31, 35, 38; cavalry 3, 4; artillery 1, 2. Kansas-infantry 1. Kentucky-infantry 3, pioneers 1; total 4. Massachusetts—infantry 3. Michigan—infantry 7, artillery 2; total 9. Minnesota—infantry 3, artillery 1; total 4. Missouri—infantry 17, cavalry 3, artillery 7; total 27. New Hampshire—infantry 3. New York—infantry 3, artillery 1; total 4. Ohio—infantry 26, cavalry 1, artillery 11; total 38. Pennsylvania—infantry 4, artillery 1; total 5. Rhode Island—infantry 1; Regulars—infantry 2, artillery 1; total 3. West Virginia—infantry 1. Wisconsin—infantry 13, cavalry 1, artillery 3; total 17. (The Wisconsin commands were the 8th, 11th, 12th, 14th, 16th, 17th, 18th, 20th, 23rd 25th, 27th, 29th, and 33rd infantry regiments; the 2nd cavalry regiment: and the 1st, 6th and 12th batteries of light artillery.)

This makes an aggregate of 192 regiments or parts of regiments of infantry, 19 regiments of cavalry and 46 batteries of artillery—257 organizations, not including eight regiments of negroes in process of enlistment. This means that General Grant had approximately 45,000 rank and file when he began the campaign, 40,000 when the siege opened and 70,000 at its close—about two-fifths of whom were on the Big Black river line to oppose the threatened advance of General J. E. Johnston. The casualties in his force, as summarized in the Official Records (Vol. 24, Part 2, p. 167), were 98 officers and 1416 enlisted men killed, 474 officers and 6921 enlisted men wounded, 10 officers and 443 enlisted men captured or missing—total 9,362. About one-half of this loss was sustained in the battles preceding the siege and the remainder after Vicksburg was invested. The army

comrade of the Grand Army from Dubuque, Iowa, well known throughout the west and south as Assistant General Passenger Agent of the Illinois Central railroad, that belongs the high honor of finally taking the initiative in the matter, as well as of lending most valuable aid in carrying it to success.

The Confederate line of defense in 1863, consisting of redoubts, redans and lunettes on the higher points, connected by curtains of trenches or rifle-pits, followed a high, rugged and almost unbroken ridge from the river below, having an extension of eight miles. From this main ridge spurs set out frequently, separated the one from the other by, and ending abruptly in, deep and sharp ravines. No continuous ridge confronted the one occupied by the Confederate line, the investment line of the Union army was compelled to cross the steep ridges and deep ravines above described. The roughness and ruggedness of this area cannot be appreciated without being seen. This tended to make the place impregnable against Grant's assaults in 1863.

As the line or ridge held by the Confederates and assaulted and beseiged by the Federals was the battle-ground, it will be readily understood that it is closely followed by the Park boundaries. These have been established by the purchase for the United States of 1,232 acres of land, including the entire Confederate line upon the one side and also, for three and one-half miles in the center, the main Federal line of investment with all the ground between. This includes the points of greatest historical interest and importance, constitutes the main Park and is from one-third to one-half a mile in width throughout. Sufficient land to include the earthworks and to construct avenues behind them extends from this main Park to the river above the city along both lines, known respectively as the North Confederate and North Federal Wings. The South Confederate Wing is also continuous to the river below, but the Federal line will be shown by a series of loop roadways reaching the more important positions.

The plans of the commissioners include the construction of a macadamized Confederate avenue behind the Confederate works from river to river, of a Federal avenue from the east gate of the National Cemetery to Fort Garrott, the south end of the main Park, and of avenues along the loops which constitute the South Federal Wing—in all about twenty miles, not including the country roads, which radiate from the city through the Park like the spokes of a wheel, and which, within the Park limits, will be transferred to and improved by the government. When this shall have been done, the works that frown upon each other from the opposing hills restored with their artillery in position, and the whole beautified by memorial structures erected by the several states to the valor of their sons and illustrated by tablets showing the deployment of the armies and giving the history of each unit with its losses—when this shall have been accomplished, where can the American citizen, young or old, find so interesting or inspiring a scene or one better calculated to stir every patriotic impulse?

The Lincoln Monument.

The Monument occupies the center of a pretty little park, opposite the railroad depot and faces west. At the four corners are mounted massive pieces of ordnance relics of the Civil War secured through the efforts of Congressman Haugen of the Fourth District of Iowa. The figure of Lincoln bears the unmistakable features of the great man. It is truly Lincoln. In his right hand he bears the scroll, representing the "Emancipation Proclamation."

On the four sides are beautiful bronze designs in bass-relief, viz:

On west side. The "Surrender at Appomatox", "scene in the McLean House". Generals Grant and Lee in front, Sheridan on extreme right, Rawlins, Porter, Williams and Ord standing, Col. Marshall of Lee's staff, Col. Parker of Grant's staff. (See cut, "The Surrender", in this book.)

On the east side, "Battle of Shiloh". Old log church as it was at the time of the battle. Gen'l Sherman on horseback. Color Bearer H. J. Grannis, with colors in front. Capt. W. W. Warner of Co. C, cheering on his men who have captured a piece of artillery. Surgeon C. C. Parker, attending wounded soldier.

South side, "Soldiers Leaving Home". Soldiers marching, church spire in the distance, figure of Thomas Henderson (brother of Col. Henderson) of Co. C, the first soldier from Clermont township killed in battle, taking leave of wife and children.

On north side, "Battle of Mobile". Admiral Farragut in the rigging of his flagship, Hartford. Other officers peering through the smoke. Admiral Dewey, then a Lieutenant on the extreme left in charge of "Jackies" working a gun. On base below is the inscription—"Erected in 1902 in Memory of the Soldiers and Sailors of the Civil War. 1861-1865."

LINCOLN MONUMENT.

Erected at Clermont, Iowa, in 1903 in memory of the soldiers and sailors of the Civil War, by ex-Governor William Larrabee.

HENDERSON STATUE.

Statue of Col. Henderson.

The statue of Col. Henderson is wonderfully striking and is a masterpiece of sculptor's art in every detail. The figure is of heroic size, seven feet, six inches high. The sculptor caught the Colonel's best and strongest expression. He is represented as about to call to order the House of Representatives, over which he presided for four years, with a gavel in his left hand. Under his left arm he supports a crutch. In this way both the military and civil life of Col. Henderson is perpetuated in bronze. The gavel stands for Hon. D. B. Henderson, the statesman, and the crutch for Col. Henderson, the soldier. The whole monument is very striking and the friends of Col. Henderson as well as those who look upon his statue as a work of art, are both pleased.

The following inscription is on the pedestal of the Henderson statue:

David B. Henderson
Speaker of
the House of Representatives
of the United States, 1899-1903.

Lieutenant of Company C, Twelfth
Regiment, Iowa Infantry
Volunteers, 1861.

Colonel of the Forty-Sixth
Regiment Iowa Infantry
Volunteers 1864.

Member of Congress of the
United States from the Third
District of Iowa, 1883-1903.

Columbia's Flag.

By a Comrade on
"The New Ironsides" in Mobile Bay, 1864.

Of all the flags that proudly float o'er
    Neptune's gallant tars,
Or waves on high in victory, above the
    Sons of Mars,
Give us that flag—Columbia's flag—pure
    Emblem of the free,
Whose brilliant stars flashed through our
    Wars for truth and liberty.

Beneath its folds we fear no foe—our
    Hearts shall never quail,
With bosoms bare the storms we dare and
    Brave the battle's hail,
E'en when our decks of boats were ploughed,
    And their planks with gore dyed red,
Our gallant tars, firm at their guns, ne'er
    Paused to count their dead.

Far o'er the sea to every clime this
    Honored flag shall go,
And through all time its fame sublime
    With brighter hues shall glow;
For freedom's own that flag is now—
    Its guardians, freedom's sons.

Its enemies dispersed shall be
    Upon the land and main,
It's stars so bright 'mid storm and night
    Shall never shine in vain;
No foreign power nor treason rife
    Shall shake our courage keen,
We'll give our life to hold that flag—supreme.

Not honor we seek, nor life's shallow fame,
    Nor glory, nor hope of renown;
We'll battle for God, and our
    Country's fair name,
And the flag that will never come down.

Regrets and Reminiscences.

DUBUQUE, IOWA., JUNE 18, 1903.

MR. GEO. E. COMSTOCK, SEC.

DEAR COMRADE:—Your kind invitation to attend the reunion of the gallant old Twelfth was received several days ago; but I did not answer, hoping that I would be able to attend. I promised Col. Henderson this morning that, if possible, I would attend; but now I find at the last moment that I cannot get away. The strike which has prevailed here for six weeks has kept newspaper men on the jump. No one can possibly regret this more than I. I had hoped to be present and once more shake the hands and look into the eyes of my old comrades, with whom I went out in the long ago, to fight for the best country and the best flag in the world.

I had also looked forward with pleasure to a gathering where I should see four of Iowa's distinguished sons and statesmen—Allison, Henderson, Larrabee and Dolliver—men who have won honor and fame for their state and for themselves, and who have never been found wanting in sympathy when the interests of the men who preserved a nation are at stake.

It is eminently fitting that a monument to the Immortal Emancipator should be erected at Clermont, for in no other section of this grand state did he have more royal supporters during the dark days of the war than in Clermont. Gov. Larrabee was one of them. He fed the soldier's widow and the soldier's orphan, and in other ways gave of his substance for their support.

It is eminently fitting also that a statue should be erected to Col. Henderson, for whom the heart of every old soldier of the 12th will ever remain as steadfast and true as is his friendship for them. It was from Fayette county that three farmer boys went down to the Southland and fought on fields of blood and death, where one of them found a brave and honored soldier's grave. Another, wrecked physically because of the hardships he endured, is now sleeping in the bosom of the land he fought to save, and the third is with you today, with shattered limb, but whose heart is whole and strong and as full of the patriotic fire of the day, when with his two brothers, he knelt at his mother's knee, to receive her blessing before departing for the field of battle. I trust that the reunion may be the grand success we all wish it to be and that joy and good fellowship may reign supreme.

The shadows of the long night of silence are fast enveloping all of us. Only a short time and we shall all have passed from the scenes of life. Our monument will be a preserved and mighty nation—the greatest of all nations—and we will beqeath it to a nation of intelligent, liberty-loving freemen.

Yours in F. C. and L.

M. D. NAGLE,
Co. I, 12th Iowa V. I.

PORTLAND, ORE., JUNE 15, 1903.

G. E. COMSTOCK, SEC.

DEAR COMRADE:—My heart was made to thrill with gladness, when my good friend Dr. James Barr of this city informed me, that a reunion of the 12th Iowa Inft. would soon be held, and that a few lines from me for the noted occasion were earnestly solicited. Comrades, I assure you it is a gratifying privilege, which brings me at this remote time into touch with the memorable 12th Iowa, the regiment of my boyhood days, when we all went to war in '61. It may be I am unknown to you, as I was early in the war striken down by disease and discharged by reason of Surgeons Certificate of Disability, March 13, 1862. Though my experience as a soldier was cut short, yet a long and painful illness which followed, worked in me a soldier's fellowship and kindred feeling, so real that I feel I am one of you, as much so, as though I had fought on with you to the end of the war. I do not know that my love for you could be deeper, for I am in soul, mind and spirit with you and for you. There has been during the coming and passing of the years, a lingering and living memory of the 12th in my heart and affections, and it would be a happy event to me to attend the reunion and take my comrades by the hand, and enjoy the exercises of the excellent program which I have before me. But I must not take too much time in expressing my warm regard for you all, which is a holy exhibition of my soul. I was one of five brothers who responded to the calls of President Lincoln. Three of the brothers were at one time in the famous 2nd Iowa Cavalry, which Iowans remember with pride. I am the only male survivor of my family, which with your families, and the many thousands of others stood for the Union and "Old Glory" during the dark days of the rebellion. We have with our people in all the (coming) years since the war entered into the war-fruits, that have come from the sacrifices made by our dead, and by our living comrades. It is a legacy enriched by the heriosm and lives of our comrades that has made our Nation in growth and glory to be what it is today. Who is more elated to see this day, or can be, than the old soldiers of the Union Army? Who knows more, by what sacrifices and heroic efforts, our national greatness, prosperity and peace has come, than the ones who made personal denial, and gave up all for native country, to save the union and to hold the flag? Surely, Comrades we know, not in part, but fully. And who should share bountifully of the governments benefits, and of the peoples' gratitude more than the old soldiers of 61 to 5? We have perhaps little cause for complaint but much to rejoice over, and be thankful for.

May God keep you true in Fraternity, Charity and Loyalty. No grander principles could be spoken and lived. In conclusion: You may desire to know my home and age when I enlisted. My home was Hopkinton, Del. Co., and age 18, and Co. K my company.

I am very respectfully your Comrade,

271 College St. HENRY A. BARDEN.

MEMPHIS, TENN., JUNE 13, 1903.

G. E. COMSTOCK, SEC.

My Dear Comrade:—It is a source of profound regret to me that I shall be unable to join my comrades at the Reunion at Clermont, Iowa, June 19th, 1903, on the occasion of the dedication of the statue to Col. D. B. Henderson and the Lincoln monument. I should be pleased to join my comrades in their celebration, but the imperative demands of business require my presence here.

Hoping to be kindly remembered to Col. Henderson and my other comrades of the 12th Iowa Infantry and especially to the surviving members of Company A, who were with me in the "Hornet's Nest" at Shiloh, and previously in the assault upon the enemy's right at Fort Donelson, where the gallant Col. Henderson, then a lieutenant, was slightly wounded only a few feet from me in that terrific shower of grape and shrapnel which came down upon us from the fortifications, I am

Your Truly,

T. B. EDGINGTON,
Co. A.

NIAGARA FALLS, N. Y. JUNE 15, 1903.

G. E. COMSTOCK, Sec.

DEAR COMRADE:—I am in receipt of your favor of the 15th ult., inviting me to join in the Reunion of the Twelfth Iowa Veteran Volunteer Infantry to be held at Clermont on the 19th of the present month. More than I can express, I regret my inability to be present. My 66 years, distance and imperative duties forbid.

To me, who lived for years in Fayette County, and enlisted from there, even the name of the county is a sweet and pleasant memory. It was there that I early learned to vote the Republican ticket and curse the Democrats for short crops and rainy harvests. It was there that I piously voted each year in the County Convention and at the polls for Joe Hobson for County Clerk. It was there that I did myself and my locality great honor by casting in a Nominating Convention the vote of Jefferson Township for that prince among men, that real statesman, that genuine patriot, William Larrabee. It was, I believe, the first state office he ever held. It was there, too, that I once bought a pair of stogy boots for four dollars and fifty cents, and paid for them in corn at eight cents per bushel. However, that incident isn't in any way connected with the sweet and pleasant memory referred to above.

But none of that has anything to do with the Immortal Twelfth. In your program I note names that are dear me. I remember one whose name appears there, R. W. Tirrill, who with a bullet hole through him needed and got the little help I could give him on the battle field of Shiloh: and another, Abner Dunham, who with others, a select few, brothers all, when I was sick unto death, stood over and nursed me and bore with me as only a best man in the world could. And there, too, is D. B. Henderson. How fast he grew, how high he climbed, and still stands. And Jack Stibbs! Do we not all remember the snap and the percussion he used to put into his Company drills? I knew to a certainty that Company F, the one I belonged to, was the best Company in Grant's

Army, but I always thought that if there was no Company F I would like to to be with Jack Stibbs.

But we can not particularize short of calling the roll. The Twelfth Iowa was always a good, a hardy and a thrifty sort. You never heard, did you, of a Twelfth man catching cold from sleeping in a room with a damp tumbler? You can't recall, can you, that ever one of those fellows let his chum or his chum's chum go hungry when there was a chicken in easy reach? You remember, don't you, when that ill-advised order against foraging was read to us at Smithland on the Cumberland? And you remember how we all stood up and took a vow that, order or no order, if any cow, sheep, chicken, goose, lamb, duck or other ferocious animal should bite a member of the Twelfth Iowa, it should surely die. And yon remember how faithfully we kept that vow. I don't believe that you can recall a case when any edible animal was allowed to escape that vow on a technicality, or for want of evidence.

But stern and hardy and patriotic men they were, and only because they and their kind were so, have we now the privilege of belonging to a united country, and the most powerful nation that the glad sun of heaven in all its daily course shines upon.

I can not help wondering how many of the one thousand and ten men commanded by Col. Wood that broke camp at Eagle Point and crossed the icy river for the south on that cold November day are now alive; how many will be present to partake of the welcome and the hospitality of Wm. Larrabee, his excellent wife and their good friends and neighbors of Clermont. Few, very few, for they wasted rapidly away, and are still going in constant procession to join the great majority. In 18 months from the crossing of the river, we had buried our members in the soil of Missouri, Kentucky, Tennessee, Mississipi, Alabama, Georgia and Maryland, and numbers had also gone home to Iowa, the sick and the wounded, only to lay down and die. And constantly they have been going ever since, and the end of the processioc is only a little way back.

The War of the Rebellion was the most expensive, in human lives and treasure, of any war of modern times, but its results were unique in the history of wars, for it not only gave strength and stability to the greatest of nations, but it freed 3,000,000 slaves, freed their masters and conferred the blessings and beneficence of victory alike upon the victors and the vanquished.

Not many of us can leave much of this world's goods to our posterity, but each of us will leave not only to his own children but to all the children of the nation, even to all the coming generations of the world, a share of blessings, richer as a heritage, in all that goes to make for peace, security and prosperity, than all the accumulations of material that have been inherited.

Comrades of the Twelfth Iowa Volunteer Infantry,
  Hail and Farewell.

           R. C. ELDRIDGE,
            Sargeant Co. F.

POMONA, MO., JUNE 10, 1903.

DEAR COMRADES:—Nothing would please me better than to be with you on this occasion, but under the circumstances I cannot. Owing to the grate distance my physical strength will not permit. I am not able to stand the worry of the trip.

Thanks to Ex-Governor Larrabee, for conferring on our regiment the honor of dedicating the Henderson statue. My good wishes are with you at this reunion. My eyes grow dim when I think that it will be impossible for me to be with you on this occasion. I would like to be there and hear three cheers for Robert Light, the man in Co. H, who cut the burning fuse off the shell that the "Johnnies" had thrown in our camp, while we were at the Spanish Fort in Mobile Bay, Ala. Bob was too fast for the fuse. He cut it off with his knife, and threw the shell in the water. I suggest three cheers for the hero of the brave deed. He risked his life to save that of others.

Thanks to Mr. and Mrs. Larrabee and citizens of Clermont for their kind invitation to entertain the 12th at their reunion.

Wishing you all success in life and a pleasant time at this reunion, and may you live to meet together for many years yet to come, I am yours very truly, DAVID BRYAN.
Howell Co. Co. H.

CRAB ORCHARD, TENN., JUNE 1, 1903.

G. E. COMSTOCK, SEC.

DEAR COMRADE:—I received your letter stating that there would be a reunion of the 12th Iowa at Clermont, June 19 and 20. I am glad to hear that the old boys are to meet once more but I feel sad to think I can not be with them. I am so far away, my age and my physical condition, as well as financial, will not permit me. I am not able to do much. You know that time is telling on some of us old boys I want you to go and meet the boys and shake hands with them for me and tell them I often think of them and that I can see them as they loooked in line of battle at Shiloh; how we looked and felt when we had to surrender, as prisoners of war; and how we suffered that night out in that cornfield, with rain coming down on us, and how my leg pained me the next morning, with a bullet hole through it. I can feel a queer feeling in that leg every time I think of that day, the 7th of April, 1862; but it will not be long before our names will all be called, for the Angel is calling the roll now, I'm listening to hear my name. He has called my dear wife that I left behind me when I enlisted. Just before she passed away she said to me, "Oh it wont be long until you will come, and I shall be looking for you."

Are you ready comrades? Are you every whit made whole? May we all enter the blessed mansions when the Angel calls the roll. May the good Lord be with you all is my prayer, God bless you all.

JAS. W. TARPENNING,
Cumberland Co. Co. D, 12th and Co. C, 47th.

JERSEY CITY, JUNE 14, 1903.

DEAR COMRADES:—It is with sincere regret that I cannot be with you at your reunion, but I will be with you in spirit if not in person. I am living in New Jersey, the land of Mosquitoes. I am always glad to hear from any of the old boys of the 12th, though it has been many years since I have seen any of you, yet I can never forget you, and would welcome you with wide open arms, should any of you ever come within hailing distance. So I can only send you my sincere regards and hope you will have a good time. Your old Comrade,

AUGUSTUS W. HATFIELD.
Co. I.

CHETEK, WIS., JUNE 5, 1903.

G. E. COMSTOCK, SEC.

DEAR COMRADE:—Received yours May 15, with your kind invitation. I would so gladly be with you, but it is impossible. My health is so poorly I could not stand the trip and my hearing is very bad, I can scarcely hear any thing, at times I am totally deaf. In a few months I will be 79 years old. It is with the deepest regret that I can not be with you. I hope you will have a good time. Remember me to all the old boys.

Yours Truly,

JOHN J. WYATT, Co. D.

SAN ANTONIO, TEXAS, JUNE 10, 1903.

DEAR COMRADES:—Happy greeting to one and all. I can not be with you at your happy gathering, only in spirit. To once more grasp the hand of comrades who marched side by side with me, in those dark days of '61 to '5, in defense of the flag, would do my soul good, and fill a place in my heart, that nothing else can. Hoping you will have a grand good time, I am Truly Yours, ALVIN MOSHER, Co. K.

NEW ERA, OREGON, CLACKAMAS CO., JUNE 7, 1903.

DEAR COMRADES:—I have just received an invitation to meet with you in reunion at Clermont. It will be impossible, but my love and best wishes I send herewith. Oh how I would like to clasp the old comrades by their hands once more and have a jolly old visit; nothing on earth would please me better.

I am so far away that I cannot attend. In this respect I have been unfortunate, missing so many reunions. So many of my own company I have not seen since discharge in '66. There is only one of Co. C here, Dr. Jas. Barr. I met him at reunion at Astoria, Wash. The state will hold one this year at Portland. We have a good time but nothing to be compared with the old Twelfth.

I like the country here very much. My health is not very good. I live six miles from city, sixteen miles from Portland. I can stand in my yard and see Mt. Hood, covered with snow the year round, about sixty miles away. My wife joins me in anticipation of the great time you will have. We send our kindest regards. "God be with you till we meet again." Yours,

JASON L. MATTOCKS, Co. C.

FRANKLIN, NEB., JUNE 12, 1903.

G. F. COMSTOCK, SECY.

DEAR COMRADE:—Yours of the 12th Inst., informing me of the reunion of our old regiment on the 19th and 20th Inst. is received. I will not be able to be present. I know that it would be a great pleasure and satisfaction to meet you all once more, and I hope to do so at some future time if my life is spared,

I am proud of the 12th Iowa and glad that I belonged to it and proud of the great state that sent it to the field and committed in some manner its honor to our keeping, during those dark days and years.

Gen'l Tuttle said to us at Shiloh, Sunday morning, "Boys remember that you are from Iowa". Those words meant a great deal. I have been a citizen of another state for over twenty-one years, but on occasions like this my heart, as it were, returns to its first love. This letter is to convey through you my kindly greeting to the boys of the old regiment, with the hope that the reunion will be a success in every way, that all may enjoy themselves as old soldiers only can, and that they may return home in health and safety and that there may be another reunion.

Your Comrade,
JAS. L. THOMPSON, Co. I.

NAPANN, NEB., JUNE 16, 1903.

GEO. E. COMSTOCK, SEC.

DEAR COMRADE:—Rec'd reunion program, and sorry that circumstances are such that it will be impossible for me to meet with you. Otherwise I would pack my knapsack, draw on the commissary and take up my line of march for Clermont. I would enjoy grasping the old boys by the hand. By the way, we are getting to be pretty old boys, speaking for myself. My hair is getting pretty light, both in color and quantity. My wife calls it gray, but you will remember it always inclined toward a beautiful blonde. If Co. I should be represented please say to them that I would be pleased to hear from them, or for that matter any member of the old 12th. What has become of our regimental history? The delay is liable to deprive many of us the pleasure of reading it.

"Old Glory" was very much in evidence here Monday, Flag Day. The ladies made it the occasion of presenting the old soldiers with as beautiful a silk flag as it has ever been my pleasure to look upon. Possibly it is from force of habit, or it may be to humor us in our dotage, but the ladies, God bless them, continue to shower their sweetest smiles on us old boys. (May their shadows never grow less.) I send regards to all. Hoping that you may have a pleasant reunion, I remain your comrade,

JOHN S. RAY, Co. I.

ST. LOUIS, JUNE 8, '03.

MR. G. E. COMSTOCK.

DEAR SIR:—I received your favor of 15th Inst., advising me of the reunion of the 12th Iowa at Clermont. It will be an impossibility for me to meet you. I am not well enough to be out. I have been a semi-invalid for the past nine years. It would be a great treat and do me more good than medicine.

.. However, I would like to hear of Joe Linker, who was a transfer, also the following: John Crain, Giles Hall (Hall was a transfer from Co. G 27th Iowa Infantry, July 15, 1865) Henry Stein, and in fact all of Co. G, who's names I cannot remember. Wishing you all many reunions and advanced old age, I am ever your well wisher and comrade.

V. W. MONTGOMERY, Co. G.

4359 Cozens Ave.

SOLDIERS' HOME, MARSHALLTOWN, JUNE 14, 1903.

Dear Comrades of the 12th, in Reunion Assembled:—I am very sorry I cannot be with you, but I am glad so many of you can attend. I shall miss that warm, friendly greeting, shaking hands, talking over the past, present and future. Victories of the past have perched upon our banner. As a result, you dedicate at this reunion a statue to the memory of our First Lieut. D. B. Henderson, and a nobler young man never wore the straps than he. I would so like to be with you on this occasion. Please extend to Mr. and Mrs. Larrabee my sincere regards for the part they have taken in honor of our beloved comrade, statesman and friend. Three cheers for the flag, Henderson and Larrabee.

Sincerely Yours,

A. H. BARTON, Co. C.

CHATTANOOGA, TENN.

G. E. COMSTOCK, SEC.

DEAR COMRADE:—I regret that I cannot go to the reunion at Clermont. But I would be glad to be counted in the roll of thanks to Mr. and Mrs. Larrabee, for the splendid testimonial they are giving to the memory of a splendid Iowa soldier, and Iowa citizen.

To any of the boys who remember me, I would be glad to be remembered. I am now a pretty full fledged Tennessean, having been here nearly 30 years, during which time I have published a sound Republican newspaper, been a member of the State Senate twice, on the electorial ticket three times, Commander of my home post eight times, Senior Vice Commander Dept. of Tenn. G. A. R. twice, a delegate to the National Encampment two or three times, and am now teaching the gospel of McKinley and Roosevelt as editor of the only Republican newspaper in Chattanooga. So you see as an Iowa Soldier I have not let the banner of our dear old state trail in the dust. Fraternally Yours,

W. F. McCARRON, Co. I.

MT. PLEASANT, TENN., JUNE 10, 1903.

G. E. COMSTOCK, SEC.

DEAR SIR:—Your letter of the 15th received and will say in reply, that I would like very much to be present once more with the boys of the 12th. But my health will not permit me to make the trip. Remember me kindly to all of my old comrades, please write me, or send me an outline of the business done and what kind of a time the dear old boys of the 12th had. Very Truly Yours,

R. F. D. No. 1.   WINCHESTER WOOLEY, Co. I.

GILA BEND, Ariz., May 28, 1903.

MR. G. E. COMSTOCK, Fayette, Iowa.

Esteemed Comrade:—I am in receipt of your favor of the 15th, with enclosed program of the dear old 12th Iowa reunion at Clermont, Iowa.

To say that I regret very much not to be able to attend is to put it mildly. For when I read the names of Henderson, Stibbs, Dunham, Terrill and such, whose letters have been so great a help and solace to many of us in later years, some of which I have and treasure with the same jealous care as were the bean-pot and coffee-can of dear old company F at Donaldson or Shiloh. I long to be with you. I have the pleasure of meeting Captains Gift and Hale frequently, and in this way get a real taste of a love-feast; but to be able to meet you all would indeed be a feast of love which is to my great sorrow denied me.

With best wishes for a happy and successful reunion and until taps sound I am fraternally and sincerely yours,

LUTHER KALTENBACH, Co. F.

DENVER, Colo., June 14, 1903.

G. E. COMSTOCK, SEC.

My Dear Comrade:—I have your very kind invitation to the reunion before me, and after reading the program for the dozenth time and each time "slopping over," I am seated to write a letter that is in my mind. I can't be with you. How much I regret it you can never know. I realize that time is passing rapidly and in all probability many will attend this reunion for the last time, and the chance to look into your eyes and clasp your hands as memory travels backward to the days of "Auld Lang Syne" will more than likely never come to me again. My heart is in the right place and is doing business right now the same as ever when I think of the old 12th. Have a good time, boys; God knows you deserve it; and on the 19th and 20th I will play the reveille with my face toward Iowa. Now with a handshake for all, a hug for yourself and a kiss for Col. Stibbs, I bid you Godspeed.

Your old fife major, S. M. FRENCH.

3205 West 26th ave. Co. F.

REA, MICH., June 6, 1903.

G. E. COMSTOCK, SEC.,

Dear Comrade:—Through you I wish to send greetings and a "God bless you" to the "boys of the Twelfth Iowa."

Distance and ill health will not permit what I so earnestly wish, that of meeting with you.

The letter announcing this reunion took me back to those dark days of '61 and '62, whose hardships are nearly forgotten by the lapse of years, but whose friendships and victories will never be forgotten.

I prize today as my dearest treasure the old drum that went with me through the service, and would enjoy beating it for Co. C to fall in line (those who are left).

Thanking you for remembering and sending me this announcement,

From Comrade SUMNER HARTSHORN, Co. C.

Per daughter Mabel.

CHEROKEE, Iowa, June 15, 1903.

G. E. COMSTOCK, SEC.

Dear Comrade:—Your kind invitation to meet with the members of the old 12th Iowa V. V. Inft. for a reunion at Clermont, Ia., on the 19th is received, and "Barkis is willin'," yes! more than willing, delighted at the prospect. The arrangement is an excellent one. There is no question about the success of the meeting, as it might rain pitchforks and the boys would be there. Owing to poor health my wife will not be able to be there; but my brother Howard and brother-in-law Frank Thomas will be with me. They are not Vets, but they are going to take in the circus and visit at Postville.

As I write the thought comes to me, of how great Uncle Wm. L. Henderson's enjoyment, could he have been with us to attend this reunion. He would have done his full share to make the day one long to be remembered. Well! The boys are dropping away fast at Death's "lights out." The end of these reunions is very near now, but I believe that no one of the little fragment that is left of the grand old regiment ever regrets for one moment the sacrifices made, the pain endured, the toil of the weary marchings, the longing for home with its love and comforts. These were cheerfully endured that the principles of equality before the law, liberty, and government by the people, might be preserved and handed down to their children, and the union of the states as a nation be crystallized into a perpetuity. Clermont is a small place, but around it and the old home near by cluster many of the pleasant recollections of my life. Neither Clermont nor Fayette county need ever blush for their part in helping to make the history of the Nation. Every hamlet in the North had its William Warner; but no one of them all was purer, braver, nobler than our gallant Warner, who though dead these many years, yet lives enshrined amid a halo of proud and tender memories in our every heart. And coupled with the thoughts of the brave comrades who went forth to do and dare for the cause of right, and who came not home with us again, we must not forget the not less gallant few who would but could not go, but who with unceasing thoughtfulness and noble generosity cared for the loved ones left behind, and in this way and by act and word at all times and places where needed, encouraged and held up the hands of the men at the front As I write this to you, old comrade, the first thought in your mind, as in mine, is William Larrabee.

> There be heroes who die in war,
> And whose names we speak with pride,
>   As we think of their brave deeds done:
> But other heroes there are
> Who may rank with them side by side,
>   Though they never fired a gun.

And William Larrabee, of Clermont, to those who understand how he longed to go, but could not be accepted, and of his tireless energy and generosity in doing all that a man could do, both to encourage and help the boys at the front and their dear ones left behind, it will not be necessary to say that he and men like him, ought always to be remembered and revered side by side with those who marched to bugle note or tap of drum. Our grateful hearts ought to impel all of us to do honor on the 19th of June to our beloved and generous host of that day. And while on that day many words will be spoken in the endeavor to kindle and keep burning the fires of patriotism in the hearts of the generation who are to follow us when we pass into the dark valley, and gray-haired fathers and mothers of the boys of '61 to 65, who will be there, must not be forgotten among the glad greetings. Theirs was the greater sacrifice, theirs the harder part to play. Harder than our weary marching which was made easier by thoughts of the cause we did it for, was the wearier waiting of fathers and mothers for news of the absent boy. Harder to bear than the cravings of hunger in camp and field, was the gnawing fear which ate out the heart of the doting mother and the tender wife and sweetheart. The feverish exhileration of the frenzy of battle was an antidote against all fear of harm, amid the roar of cannon and the scream of the deadly shell; but what antidote had the loving ones at home for the fear that was eating their hearts away, while they waited for the smoke of battle to lift, and its echoes to die away, that they might learn what they yet dreaded to know, the fate of the dearest on earth to them?

All honor must be given on June 19th, in thought and speech, to the gray-haired fathers, mothers and widows of our comrades living and dead, who will gather with us there. It must be borne home to them in kindly words that sharing as they did so deeply with us the self-sacrifices of those old times, we cheerfully accord to them an equal share in all the achievements of those fateful years, in which we today take pride.

There is a possibility that I may not be able to be with you on the 19th, and if such be the case, friend Comstock, you are at liberty to read such portions of this letter as you may see fit.

Hoping to be with you, I remain

Your comrade, J. A. HENDERSON,
Transfer from 27th Iowa to Co. C. 12th Iowa.

PEORIA, ILL., June 13, 1903.

MR. G. E. COMSTOCK, Fayette, Iowa.

DEAR COMRADE:—I have yours of May 15th. Nothing would please me more than to be with you at Clermont on the 19th inst., but it will be impossible for me to be there. I desire to be remembered to all comrades. If General Stibbs is with you he can tell you something about me, as he spent a year or more in our city and we often lived over the old war days.

Sincerely yours.
J. W. GIFT, Co. F.

HIGHMORE, S. D, June 15, 1903.

G. E. COMSTOCK, SEC.

Dear Comrade:—It is with sorrow and regret that I cannot meet with the comrades. I have been chosen delegate to our state encampment and they come almost the same time. I hope you will have a good time. If spared, will try and answer roll call next time. Hoping to hear from you soon after the close of the reunion, I still remain

Your comrade,
HAMILTON CRAMER, Co. A.

DEP'T OF THE INTERIOR, U. S. PENSION AGENCY,
Des Moines, Iowa, May 29, 1903.

MR. G. E. COMSTOCK,
   Sec. 12th Iowa Reunion Association,
     Fayette, Iowa.

MY DEAR COMRADE:—Your favor, dated May 15, but postmarked May 28, arrived this morning. I will not be present at the regimental reunion next month. My hearing has become so deficient that I cannot hear the proceedings, therefore it would only be torture to myself to be present. Besides, while the regimental reunion is in session the whole force of this pension agency will be preparing for the July payment of pensions, in which the 12th Iowa comrades are nearly all interested. Every comrade hopes to receive his pension check by return mail, but all of them should remember that this agency pays 55,000 pensioners, and that they cannot all be paid at once. About twelve days are required to pay that number of pensioners.

I hope that the regimental reunion will pass a resolution endorsing the bill introduced by Hemenway of Indiana last February, which provides for the pensioning of all soldiers and sailors who served at least ninety days in the Civil war, at the rate of $12 per month; and all widows of such soldiers and sailors who were married prior to June 27, 1900. I have letters from Speaker Henderson and Congressman Hull stating that they are in favor of the Hemenway bill, and I think that it can be safely said that the entire Iowa congressional delegation will vote for it, and work for its enactment. The laws now provide for the pensioning of all Mexican war soldiers who served sixty days and are 62 years of age, or are disabled and dependent. That has been the law ever since January 29, 1887, and it is a discrimination against the soldiers of the Civil war, for that law has been in existence for sixteen years, while the Mexican war began but fourteen years prior to the Civil war. It is time for the comrades of the Civil war to make themselves heard against that discrimination, and I hope that the reunion of the 12th Iowa at Fayette will pass a resolution endorsing the Hemenway bill and asking that it be promptly enacted into law.

With the kindest regards to yourself, and to the comrades of the 12th Iowa at the reunion at Clermont, I am
              Always sincerely yours,
Co. A.   R. P. CLARKSON.

ELWOOD, IOWA, June 16, '03.

G. E. COMSTOCK,
   DEAR COMRADE:—I received your invitation in due time and I worked and expected to meet with my old comrades of '61 once more, especially as we were to be honored by the presence of Hon. D. B. Henderson. But the past weather and events have so changed my calculations that it will be impossible for me to attend, and with regret I send this word to you. Give love and greeting to all comrades of the 12th for me.
              Your comrade,
                            GEO. TESKEY, Co. I.

PORTLAND, OREGON, June 13, 1903.

My Dear Comrade Comstock:—Your circular letter and program reached me the 8th inst and am sure you cannot conceive the tumult of emotion it stirred in my breast. And then to know I could not join you and the comrades of the Old Regiment—comrades who are dearer to me than my kin. I need not explain to you why. You all know, comrades, just to look in your faces, grasp your hand, shed a few tears together, as the past would come up and drive away the present, and the white hairs of the present be lost sight of in the dark hairs of our boyhood days, we would live them over again. Can we grasp the meaning of such a meeting here? Can it be a foretaste of the hereafter? How strange and satisfying it is that we can look into each other's eyes—into the very soul, and see you in the bygone days—the days of trial, days when there were scarcely enough well men to stand guard and picket.

Then to talk of meeting Rogers, Co. B, Coolidge and Jim Taylor, Co. F, Stewart, Co. D, Jason Mattocks, Co. C, Barden, Co. K, Captain Williams, Co. E, and our old major, Brodtbeck, whom I helped lay away, and our good comrade, Col. Henderson, so sorely crippled, and so patient and cheerful. And then to be denied all this, and at Clermont, where I began my life work. But just remember, comrades, and friends of Clermont, I am with you in spirit.

And just let me say here, the Star of Empire is moving West and the Barr latch string is out for the 12th Iowa.

Comrades, give me a place in your thoughts. I do want to be with you. Your comrade,

JAMES BARR, Co. C.

RANDALL, KAN., June 14, 1903.

MR. G. E. COMSTOCK, Fayette, Iowa.

Dear Comrade and Friend:—Yours of May 15th just received, delay I suppose caused by the floods. I am sorry to state that I cannot be with you at Clermont June 19. I have not the time to spare on so short notice and I am so banged up with rheumatism that I would hardly dare to make the trip if I had the time.

This is indeed a disappointment to me. I continually live in hopes that I will some day greet my old comrades of the 12th at campfire reunion. Memory always dwells fondly and pleasantly in thinking of the boys of our old regiment. I hope you are all on the pleasant paths of life, contented and hopeful. As for me, don't worry on my account. I don't. I haven't a kick to make on anything, and in looking back over life's journey so far, I see more to feel thankful for than to regret, and some of the pleasantest and most cherished gems in my memory-box are of our old regiment as a regiment and of the many warm and true friends I had while with it.

And now in conclusion, boys, have as good time as possible while together. It won't last long and may be the last. I will be with you in desire and thought. Hoping that I will some day see each and all of you, I will close. In comradship,

N. G. PRICE, Co. D.

BULL RUN BATTLEFIELD, Henry House, Va., June 16.

COMRADES OF THE TWELFTH IOWA:

When I say to you that I am sorry that I cannot be with you on this happy day, it is a feeble expression of my feelings. But boys, you see I am too far out on the picket-line, here in Old Virginia, to be able to come home to Iowa on short notice; but remember my thoughts are with you and my thanks to the good people of Clermont for the honor conferred on our regiment on this happy occasion. I remember you well, and the lively times we had down in Dixie in 1861-5. God bless you, boys. Good bye. HENRY STEEN, Co. G.

BIRDSEYE, MONTANA, June 7, 1903.

G. E. COMSTOCK, SEC.,
  Fayette, Iowa.

Dear Sir and Comrade:—Your favor just received. I would like very much to attend reunion of old 12th Iowa on 19th, but it is just impossible for me to do so. This is the busy season with mining people and I cannot make the trip and do justice to myself, although I promised Capt. Soper that I would attend next reunion. I must disappoint him again—*at the risk of a reprimand.*

I wish to be kindly remembered to all comrades of 37 years ago.

Yours truly,
  WM. L. LEE, Co. D.

BARRON, WIS., June 17 '03.

G. E. COMSTOCK, SEC.

Received notice of our reunion and dedication of Lincoln monument and Col. Henderson statue, the gracious gift of that noble-souled man, Ex-Gov. Larrabee. It is with a sad heart of regret that I pen these lines of my inability to be with you at Clermont June 19th and 20th, to enjoy once more the greetings of the "boys" I love so well. I greet you one and all, far and near and hope you will have the best time of your life. Yours,
  WM. A. KENT, Co. C.

KEOKUK, IOWA, June 5, 1903.

G. E. COMSTOCK, SEC.

DEAR COMRADE:—I received your letter and program. Am very sorry, indeed, that I cannot be present at the reunion of the 12th Iowa. I have been very ill for the past month and will have to forego this pleasure. It comes as a double disappointment, as I was unable to meet you at last reunion. Remember me very kindly to all the boys. Express my thanks to Mr. and Mrs. Larrabee for their loving testimony. They surely have left a monument to their memory and a lesson of patriotism to the rising generation. Very truly yours,
  EDGAR C. COBB, Co. I.

LANARK, ILL., June 30, 1903.

Dear Comrades of the 12th Iowa:—One of the greatest disappointments of my life was when I received the invitation to Clermont that I was unable to meet you at that time. I have been bed-ridden for a long time with very poor prospects of getting well. I would have died content could I have met you, my dear comrades, and have had one more look into your faces.

My love for Old Glory has never cooled, and I am so sorry that I was unable to rally round the flag with the Dear Old Twelfth.

If the Great Commander shall see fit to gather me home and I never see any of you again on earth, I hope you will all meet me in Heaven.

Yours affectionately,

GEO. W. ANNIS, Co. F.

GEORGETOWN, Custer County, Neb., June 15, '03.

MR. G. E. COMSTOCK, Fayette, Iowa.

DEAR COMRADE:—I just received the notice of the reunion of the 12th Iowa at Clermont, Iowa, Saturday evening, and it increased that longing desire to meet my old comrades at a reunion, a pleasure I have never enjoyed. I did resolve last winter that I would attend the first or next reunion of the old 12th Iowa and enjoy once more a good handshake; but I regret to say that after all my resolves, I am unable to attend on account of poor health. But I will try again.

I hope that I will be the only one that cannot attend, and I hope that you will have a good time and that the reunion will be a success. I remember all the old comrades and I think of them often; and if I cannot see them, I would like to hear from any or all of them.

I would like to write more, but it is with much difficulty that I write this, on account of my eyes.

Fraternally,

FRANK MORROW, Co. D.

ABSAROKEE, Montana, June 4, 1903.

MR. G. E. COMSTOCK, Fayette, Iowa.

Dear Comrades of the 12th Iowa:—Just received notice of our reunion. It found me out here among the hills of Montana and in such shape that I cannot meet with you this time. I came out to this country a year ago for my health and took up a ranch, and as luck would have it, I have advertised to prove up June 20. So comrades, you can see it is impossible for me to be there; but my mind and well wishes are with you all, hoping you will have a good old time. Think of me while you are having it. I will have to close, hoping if there is another reunion of the 12th Iowa I will be able to attend. Love to the boys of the old 12th Iowa. So good bye, one and all.

R. L. BIRD, Co. E.

WASHINGTON, D C., June 12, 1903.

MR. G. E. COMSTOCK, Fayette, Iowa.

DEAR COMRADE:—I received your kind invitation to be present at a reunion of the 12th Iowa Veteran Volunteers on June 19 at Clermont, at which time and place a statue of Col. D. B. Henderson is to be unveiled and dedicated by our regiment through the courtesy of Governor Larrabee—a very plesant privilege, for Col. Henderson was one of us on the bloody field of Shiloh, and is one of us still, whom we are very proud to claim and honor. His name and fame have gone far beyond the confines of the State and Nation, not only as a military hero but as the peer of any statesman in the land.

I am proud to have been a humble member of the famous old 12th regiment, and I regret exceedingly that I shall not be able to be present at the unveiling, as I personally would receive more honor and pleasure than my presence could impart to the occasion.

My heart and thoughts are with you one and all for evermore.

Fraternally yours,

S. R. BURCH, Late Adjutant.

PITTSBURG LANDING, TENN., July 15, 1903.

JOHN STEEN, Wahoo, Neb.

Dear Comrade:--Enclosed find postoffice order for four dollars, the balance I agreed to give for expenses of our regimental association at Clermont, Iowa.

Didn't we have a jolly time, and when will we have another? Echo answers when, and should we have one in four years, how many that we took by the hand will have gone to join the final muster, no one can tell.

I am getting along here on the park nicely, except at times I am lonesome. All my partners are away at present on their annual leave of absence. I generally take mine in winter time, for the reason that the line of work I do, I can be better spared from it in winter than at this time of year. Please acknowledge receipt of the order and believe me,

Your ever true comrade,

T. J. LEWIS, Co. D.

BURWELL, NEB., June 18, 1903.

DEAR COMRADES OF THE TWELFTH IOWA:

No pen of mine can portray my regret at not being able to answer "here" at roll call tomorrow. But owing to the fact that my aged father of Maquoketa, Ia., is visiting me and I realize that his visits are numbered; therefore, I am unable to leave home. I desire, however, to join the boys in extending hearty thanks to Mr. and Mrs. Larrabee for their kind consideration of us, and especially ask my comrades that when they gather around the campfire they will throw on a rail for me. And I trust our Supreme Commander may permit us to "Rally round the Flag" and enjoy a few more campfires. I commend you all to His care, and remain   Yours truly in F., C. and L.,

MELLVILLE B. GOODENOW, Co. I.

SEATTLE, WASH., June 2, '03.

Dear Comrades of the 12th Iowa:--Your secretary's letter of May 15, telling of your reunion at Clermont June 19, and inclosing program, received yesterday. Yes, I'll be there, *in spirit*. My body, about that time, will probably be at or near Juneau, Alaska. I'll sing the "Star-Spangled Banner" and I wan't all "you'n's" to "jine in" the chorus.

Do you remember "Pontotoc to Tupelo?" I do not forget it. Some of you will remember my experience as a nurse, remaining behind to look after the wounded and being afterwards held as prisoner, instead of being returned to our lines, as a nurse should have been.

I am now postal clerk on the steamship, "Cottage City," between Seattle and Skagway. Mrs. Andrews joins in mourning our inability to go to the "banks of the Turkey" to eat turkey with you, also in sending greetings. She also wishes me to add further that she does not forget to remember to scold me occasionally for bringing her so far away from the 12th Iowa reunions. However, we have hopes for the future.

Yours in F. C. & L.,

Box 1401 Seattle. Wash   HIRAM R. ANDREWS, Co. B.

ADA, KANSAS, June 10, '03.

Dear Comrade Comstock:—Yours of 14th just received, having been delayed by our Kansas flood. I thank you for your kindness in sending me the notice of the reunion. I have a deep interest in Iowa where my home was for twelve years. The members of the old 12th have a warm place in my heart. God bless them. How I would like to see you all.

My soldier life was short. When we returned from acting as Jeff Davis' menagerie, and got back to St. Louis, there was just enough left of me to discharge. Reached home at Sand Springs Christmas, '62. The boys as they were before the Shiloh fight are photographed on my memory, and although I have met most of you since, having been twice at Manchester, I remember you best as you were in '61-2. I think that I never loved a man (a man I had never spoken to) as I loved Col. Stibbs, for taking us from Annapolis, Md., as prisoners, to our homes. May his shadow never grow less! Love to all of the boys and especially to any of Co. K. Accept the same for yourself, whom I well remember.

Yours in F., C. & L..

N. H. BALDWIN, Co. K.

GRANT'S PASS, Ore., June —, 1903.

G. E. COMSTOCK, Sec.

Dear Comrades:—It is with regret that I can't be with you this year—I am too far away. I think I shall work back east; Oregon doesn't suit me. I will try to be with you next time.

My health is good. I wish you were all here to eat bear-meat with me today. We got a fine cinnamon yesterday only four miles from town.

With love and best wishes to all, I remain   Yours, &c.,

J. H. ROSS, Co. D.

PRESTON, MINN., June 16, 1903.

G. E. COMSTOCK, SEC.

Dear Comrade:—I received your notice of reunion and program. I am very sorry to say that it will be impossible for me to be there, but with this I send greeting to all "the boys." I know you will have a jolly good time. My best wishes to all who may be there.

Ever yours.   GEORGE IBACH, Co. B.

SIOUX CITY, IOWA, June 16, 1903.
G. E. COMSTOCK, SEC.
Fayette, Iowa.

MY DEAR COMRADE:—It is with profound regret that I am compelled to say in response to your cordial and urgent request in your favor of the 15th that it will be impossible for me to attend at the dedication of Lincoln monument, Henderson statue and Reunion of the old 12th Iowa, at Clermont. I have had the extreme pleasure of being present at every reunion of the regiment except that in 1884, and I look back with the highest degree of satisfaction that it has been my good fortune to attend so many of these grand and pleasurable occasions. I only regret that I could not attend all of them, including the one this week. Hope you may have a successful and glorious reunion. Please express my undying devotion and love to every old friend and comrade of the "old 12th," and while we know that all of us are getting far down the westward slope of life, yet so long as we shall travel that way to the great unknown, we will linger and love each other still. May heaven bless all the "old boys" whether able or unable to be at Clermont.

Yours in F. C. & L.,
J. N. WEAVER, Co. D

DWIGHT, Kansas, June 16, 1903.

Dear Comrades:—Received your notice of our next reunion. Am sorry to say it will be impossible for me to be with you this time. Circumstances over which I had no control hinder me. I had my house burned and had to rebuild, and the terrible floods in this country washed out the crops and drowned our stock. Were it not for this double misfortune I would be with you. Nothing would give me more pleasure than to meet with the old boys once more before the last roll call. I hope you will have a good time. I know I would were it so I could be with you. If any of the 12th Iowa boys ever come to our county, be sure to come and see me. I live in Morris county near the Rock Island railroad.

Fraternally yours,
J. F. LEE, Co. F.

LINTON, N. D., June 19, '03.
MR. G. E. COMSTOCK, Fayette, Iowa.

Dear Comrade:—This, the first day of the reunion of the 12th Iowa at Clermont, I am away off in North Dakota, but my heart is with you, and I regret that I cannot be with you. I am up here holding down a claim. Will prove up on my claim next spring, then will go back to Plankinton, S. D., to spend the rest of my life.

I hope you are having a good time. Give my best wishes to all the boys of the 12th and especially those of Co. D. I hope that we may live to have lots of reunions yet. With thanks to you for the kind invitation to the reunion, I remain, Yours in F. C. & L.,

R. C. COWELL, Co. D.

LAWTON, OKLA., June 21, 1903.

Dear Comrades:—I received your very kind letter inviting me to your reunion, and was glad you had not forgotten "the little red wagon," as the boys used to call me. Comrades, I am well and hearty and chuck full of fun, for that is what will prolong our lives. I feel as young as I used to be. Yes, dear comrades, be cheerful.

I did think that I would be with you at the reunion, but I am so busy in my shop that it is too much of a sacrifice to leave just now. I would have to be out at least $100. Now, comrades, you will have to excuse me. I send you these few lines to let you know that my heart is with you and that I have not forgotten one of the dear boys, God bless them. I have lived here two years. The first year I was sick about all the time, but since I got acclimated I have had good health. I did not draw a claim, I came too late. I am doing very well running a wagon shop. Boys, write to me and tell me how you are getting along. I have been a widower eighteen years, but as soon as I get old enough I think I shall marry again; so if you come across some dashing widow, send her this way. Comrades, this is all and I remain as ever your friend,

ISAAC JOHNSON, "The Little Red Wagon" of Co. I.

MAQUOKETA, IA., June 16, 1903.

Dear Comrades:—I am sorry to say that I cannot be with you all at the reunion; but as circumstances are, it is impossible for me to attend. I send my best regards to all and wish you all a jolly good time.

Respectfully,

MARION ROLLF, Co. I.

TRIPP, S. D., June 17, 1903.

G. E. COMSTOCK, SEC.

Dear Comrade:—I have your announcement of the reunion of the 12th Iowa at Clermont, and am reminded by it that "Again the shadow passes o'er the dial-plate of time." I wish I could be with you once more, but business holds me here. Please convey my warmest wishes to all the members of the gallant Twelfth for a most enjoyable reunion.

Yours fraternally,

JOHN BREMNER, Co. F.

ST. PAUL, MINN., June 14, '03.

MR. G. E. COMSTOCK, Fayette, Iowa.

Dear Comrades of the 12th and Co. D in particular:—I am still on earth and drawing rations. I came to you at Eastport, Miss., as a "raw recruit" for one year and was assigned to Co. D. I went with the regiment one year and was with you at Spanish Fort, marched with you to Montgomery and Selma, Ala. Now, comrades, I said I came to you as a raw recruit; but I had served three years before in what I believed the best regiment ever mustered into the service (the fifth Iowa Inf.). But I found also that comrades of the 12th Iowa were good and true and stood right up on the battle line, always ready for duty. It would give me great pleasure to meet with you at Clermont, but cannot. My wife is an invalid and I cannot leave her. May an all-wise Providence bless and comfort you in your declining years, is the wish of your comrade,

959 Reaney st.   W. H. HOWARD, Co. D.

SPECIAL.

To stir up your pure minds by way of remembrance, and to refreshen the memories of us all, as well as to enliven the patriotic zeal of all who may chance to read this book, I herewith insert a part of Lieut.-Col. S. B. Edgington's address given at our third reunion held at Waterloo, Iowa, in 1888.—(G. E. C., Sec.)

When we think of who is most entitled to praise for saving the union, we do not think of our great generals and brilliant commanders—all honor to them and their noble deeds—but rather do we think of the brave men who carried their muskets, that stormed the trenches of Donelson and Vicksburg, who stood like walls of living flame at Shiloh and Gettysburg; and of the men who carried their muskets and one hundred rounds of cartridges and marched under Sherman from Atlanta to the sea.

These old veterans we have with us here to the gratitude of every American citizen. The men who carried and the men who followed that dear old flag. These are the men who, in 1861, put pleading love aside, unclasped the dimpled hands of prattling babes fast locked about their necks, parted from wife and child because their country called. Boys who forced back their tears, forsook a father's house and the happy home group, the loved maiden and the joys of youth, and with mother's kisses warm on their lips went to the field of battle, following their flag.

When in my dreams, or when my mind dwells on army days and I think of those killed in battle or died in hospital, or were starved to death in southern prison hells, I seem to hear something saying, "Comrade, we are in a fairer land than earth; we are in and enjoy a realm where the rainbow shines brightly evermore; where the sun, moon and stars are spread out before us like islands, great and small, on the great ocean of eternity; here traitors never come and treason is unknown. We leave robes of blue, for robes of gray are not used here."

Men who left home and loved ones and endured without a murmur the privations of camp and field; men who stood unmoved amid the storms of leaden hail—yes, brave, honorable and true men who never turned their backs on friend or foe—these are the men who saved our country and flag.

No other country on the face of the earth could have survived and come through so fierce a war with her territory intact, with the rights and liberties of all her people maintained; none other but this our own Columbia, "the land of the brave and the free."

These veterans of the 12th Iowa Infantry were in twenty-three battles. They were under the rebel fire 112 days. They marched during their term of service—four years and three months—2,670 miles. They traveled by water and land 13,809 miles. Total number of casualties 582. Total number killed in battle, 95. Total number died of disease, 217. Total number discharged for disease and wounds, 247. They were first in the fight and last to leave the field. They suffered in southern prison hells for more than six months, and some for more than a year.

This short historical sketch is given for the benefit of those who have grown up since the war, that they may better know what the old veterans did to save our country and flag from the traitors' grasp.

Comrades of the grand old 12th Iowa, veterans of twenty-three hard fought battles, behold that dear old flag again,

> With its stars and its stripes, and the red white and blue,
> So dear to the heart of all loyal and true;
> The banner of our Union, the flag of the brave and the free,
> On hilltop or in valley, or down by the sea.

In peace or in war, all hail to the flag of our country wherever it waves!

THE SURRENDER AT APPOMATTOX.

INSCRIPTION ON TABLET:

On the West Side, the Surrender at Appomattox—Scene in the McLean house, Gen Grant and Gen. Lee in front; Gen. Sheridan on extreme right; Gens. Rawlins, Porter, Williams and Ord standing; Col. Marshall of Lee's staff, Col. Parker of Grant's staff.

"With malice towards none, with charity for all, with firmness in the right as God gives us to see the right, let us strive to finish the work we are in."

In Memoriam.

To the living, Cheerful Praises: To the dead, Bright Flowers, Sweet Memories.

[As I recall these names, one by one, all of whom I remember so well, and one being my own brother, and think of the days when we were young, of prison pen, the awful carnage of battle, the march, the camp, I realize more than ever that these are the ties that bind us, the severance of which causes us to mourn when they depart. I find it impossible to publish lengthy obituaries, all of them good. It seems impossible to cut them down; it seems like mutilating a tablet to their memory.--G. E. C.]

HENRY SMITH, of Maquoketa, Iowa, and member of Co. I, died June 19, 1903 (day of our reunion) aged 70 years. He was engaged in the plumbing business and had been a resident of Maquoketa for 40 years. Comrade Smith was a man of the highest character and as a citizen and business man of Maquoketa was held in high regard. He was a man of even temperament, always courteous. One more old soldier of the 12th has passed over the line that divides time from eternity and is now with the silent Grand Army.

JOHN A. VAN ANDA, Fremont, Neb., was born in Mt. Vernon, Ohio, March 15, 1840, and died at his home in Fremont, Neb., July 10, 1903. In September, 1861 he enlisted in Co. H, 12th Iowa; taken prisoner at Shiloh and for over six months suffered in prison, resulting in shattered health; discharged in 1863. When recuperated in health, re-enlisted in 44th Iowa Inft. and served to the close of the war. One of his last requests was to be buried in his G. A R. uniform. He was a member of the M. E. church and for forty years an official member; belonged to the Centennial lodge I. O. O. F., and McPherson post G. A. R., to both of which he was greatly attached. Possessed of a glorious hope of immortality, he shrank not from a contemplation of death but conversed freely thereon with a serenity known only to such as are ripe for the Kingdom. His prayers, songs and testimonies all exhibited a fitness for the expected change. Toward the last he held up his hands to heaven, assisted by his devoted wife. And so, having served his generation as a christian, a soldier, a loving father and husband, and a citizen beloved by all, by the will of God he fell asleep.

CHARLES E. MERRIAM of Hopkinton, Iowa. Born in Princeton, Mass., Jan. 22, 1845; died Dec. 19, 1902. He enlisted when about seventeen, September 1861 re-enlisting, and serving faithfully to the end of the struggle. He was among the number captured in "Hell's Hollow" at Shiloh; confined in prison at Montgomery, Ala., Macon, Ga., and Libby prison. He was wounded at Vicksburg, and again severely at Tupelo, Miss., July 14, 1864.

In civil life Mr. Merriam had served his community in almost every capacity. He was postmaster for sixteen years, being appointed under Grant's first term and serving under Hayes, Garfield and Arthur until the election of Cleveland. He had served at various times on the council and as treasurer of the town, and was closely identified with the business interests and progress of Hopkinton.

RESOLUTIONS BY HOPKINTON STATE BANK.

Whereas, God in His providence has seen fit to remove by death Charles E. Merriam, our faithful and efficient cashier and member of the board of directors, now be it

Resolved, That we, the surviving directors of the Hopkinton State Bank, sincerely mourn his loss and deeply regret the untimely taking away of one so useful and one with whom all our relations have been most close and cordial.

Resolved, That we cherish the memory of his wise and conservative counsels as a valuable guide in the affairs of this institution.

Resolved, That a copy of these resolutions be spread upon the record books of the bank, a copy handed to Mrs. Merriam and a copy published in the Hopkinton Leader.
F. B. DOOLITTLE,
M. L. McGLADE,
R. G. BROOKS,
MARY R. DOOLITTLE,
W. H. THOMPSON,
FRANK E. WILLIAMSON.

Dated at Hopkinton, Iowa, December 20, 1902.

CAPT. W. L. HENDERSON.

Another veteran has gone to his reward, Captain Henderson of Cresco, Iowa, having been brought to Postville cemetery where his father, mother and other relatives are buried. The remains and friends were met at the depot by the G. A. R. of Postville and some of his own company, Co. C, 12th Iowa Inf. The following day funeral services took place at the Congregational church and were conducted by Rev. S. W. Pollard, who delivered a very fine address. "Gone to Rest," was very touchingly rendered. One of the most pathetic scenes, and one that would fill the soul with deepest emotion, was when his old comrades of Co. C surrounded the remains to take a last farewell, while the choir sang sweetly, "God be with you till we meet again." Co. C was the company that Col. D. B. Henderson, brother of deceased, recruited and also enlisted with in '61, and among the comrades of that company present, acting as pallbearers were Maj. D. W. Reed, Chicago; Hart Spears, Westgate; H. J. Grannis, of Randalia, and G. E. Comstock of Fayette, Iowa. Mr. Grannis was color bearer of the regiment and the only one it ever had serving in that capacity over four years and who was in every engagement and on every march of the regiment. The flag carried by Comrade Grannis was draped over the casket with beautiful flowers. At the grave, upon removing that beautiful old war-worn banner, Maj. Reed pronounced, in behalf of his comrades, an eulogy in a few well chosen words. They were thrice beautiful because of their coming from a comrade who knew the dead veteran so well.

Capt. W. L. Henderson was born in Old Deer, Aberdeenshire, Scotland, May 28, 1833. He came to America when 15 years old, and to Postville, Iowa, in 1850. He was married to Clara J. Durno March 27, 1856, and died at Riceville, Iowa, June 19, 1897, aged 64 years. He leaves a wife and four grown children, Frank H., of South St. Paul, Minn; Judson H., Riceville, Ia., Mrs. Maud Ramsey, of Racine, Wis., and and Mrs. Gussie Johnson, of Lime Springs, Iowa. Capt. Henderson was an exceptional man, "the noblest work of God," because he was a strictly honest man. He had a pleasant smile for everybody, and as a husband and father was kind hearted, true and good. As a soldier he was one of the best. He was modest, retiring, unpretentious, yet persistent and firm as the rocks when his mind was settled upon the right of any subject upon which he gave study and thought. He enlisted in Co. C, 12th Infantry, Sept. 15, 1861, re-enlisted Dec. 25, 1863, and was mustered out Jan. 20, '66. All these years he rendered faithful services, participating in most of the engagements in which the regiment took part, some of which were Fort Donaldson, Shiloh, Vicksburg, Jackson, Nashville, Tupelo, Spanish Fort and Fort Blakely.

And so they are "dropping from the ranks, one by one."

LIEUT.-COL. S G. KNEE, brevet colonel, was born in Martinsburg, Pa., March 11, 1834. Moved to Deleware Co., Ia., in 1855. Enlisted in Co H, 12th Iowa, Sept. 19, 1861. Mustered in as 1st Serg't; was promoted from time to time. Commanded the regiment from February, '65, to muster out, Jan. 20, 1866. He participated in the battles of Fort Henry, Fort Donaldson, Shiloh, Jackson, Vicksburg, Tupelo, Nashville, Spanish Fort; confined in prison at Montgomery, Macon and Libby, at one time six months. Upon muster out he returned to Colesburg, Iowa, where he engaged in mercantile pursuits, making a success of it. He died at his home August 13, 1896.

Colonel Knee was a prominent member of the Masonic and Odd Fellows fraternities. He was not a member of any church, but was an attendant upon the services of the Congregational society; was also a valued member of W. A. Morse post G. A. R., of Manchester, Iowa. He was a firm and loyal friend, as he had been a brave and faithful soldier.

FRANK W. COMSTOCK was born in Chicago, Ill., June 25, 1848. Enlisted in Co. C, 12th Iowa, as a recruit, April 27, 1864, at the age of fifteen years. He was with us in the Pontotoc raid and battle of Tupelo. The extreme hot weather and marching was too much for one so young. He was sick a long time in the hospital at Memphis, Tenn. He never fully recovered. It was during the exposure of the compaigns that the germs of the disease which finally resulted in his death first found lodgment in his system. He was present at the Clermont reunion, being the first he was ever able to attend. He said he never enjoyed anything equal to it. Little did he think then that in two months from that time he would be with the Grand Army above, where so many of our comrades have gone. Loving hands fought hard, but at 11 o'clock Monday morning August 10, 1903, from hemorrhage of the stomach, he died very suddenly. In October, 1888, he was married to Miss Teressa Keilhack, who cared for him as only a loving wife could, during his long illness, which continued with more or less severity for the past five years.

> "So let our heroes rest
> Upon your sunny breast:
> Keep them, O South, our tender hearts and true;
> Keep them, O South, and learn to hold them dear
> From year to year!
> Never forget,
> Dying for us they died for you.
> This hallowed dust should knit us closer yet."

A Faithful Soldier Gone to Rest.

SAMUEL C. BECK was born in Clarion county, Pa., Sept. 22, 1838. At the time of his death at Waverly, Iowa, May 27, 1904, he was in his 66th year. When but a young man the family moved west, settling in Fayette county, Iowa. In early life Mr. Beck purposed securing a thorough education. In keeping with this desire, he took advantage of the public school, and later became a student in the Upper Iowa University at Fayette. In 1861 he responded to the call of his country, and leaving college he enlisted in Co. C, 12th Iowa Inft. For three years he faced the dangers and endured the severe hardships of the civil strife. As a prisoner he spent seven months in Montgomery, Macon and Libby prisons. At the expiration of a term of three years service he was discharged on account of failing health. For a while the family and friends despaired of his life, but through the patient and unselfish efforts of his loved ones and friends, he was nursed back to health.

On the 11th of May, 1871, he was united in marriage to Mary Hursh of Waverly. They spent the first years of their married life on a farm in Fayette county. To them were born seven children; of these, Dor A., Cyrus, Bert, Elsie and Mrs. Patchin with the mother are left to mourn. Nineteen years ago Comrade Beck with his family moved to Waverly where they have since resided. Mr. Beck was converted at 17 years of age and united with the M. E. church. He has been a faithful and consistent member for nearly fifty years. The funeral was conducted by Rev. Frank Cole, assisted by Rev. W. W. Smith.

CAPT. HIEL HALL, of Co. D, was one of the original members of the company; was elected Second Lieutenant; promoted to First, and again to Captain, resigning Dec. 26, 1864.

I am without the details of his sickness and death. He died in March, 1903, in Tucson, Ariz., where I understand he had gone for his health. He was a model soldier and officer, one of superior dignity and commanding presence, beloved by all who had the pleasure of his acquaintance.

GEN. A. J. SMITH died, from the effects of a paralytic stroke, July 30, 1897, at St. Louis, Mo., at the advanced age of eighty-two years. The end came peacefully in the presence of his wife, his only son, William Beaumont Smith, Mrs. Edgar Miller and Mrs. W. T. Mason. The last named is a daughter of the late Col. Stephen Kearney, who was Gen. Smith's first commanding officer in the Mexican war. Mrs. Smith had stepped into the kitchen for a few minutes, and when she returned she found her husband unconscious. He never regained complete consciousness. At times he would have lucid periods during which he would talk about some of the battles in which he had participated. At other times he would repeatedly call out for his son.

Gen. Smith was born in Bucks county, Pa., April 21, 1815, and named in honor of Andrew Jackson, who afterward, when president, gave him an appointment to West Point. His father was Gen. Samuel Smith, who served with distinction in the war of 1812, and his grandfather was Gen. Hugh Smith, who served under Washington in the American revolution. He was educated in Philadelphia and at West Point, and came west at an early age. Gen. Smith was stationed where a young lieutenant at Jefferson barracks, and while there met, wooed and married Miss Ann Mason Simpson, who survives him. Mrs. Smith was a daughter of the late Dr. Robert Simpson, who at the time of his death was said to be the oldest American inhabitant at St. Louis.

Gen. Smith served in both the Mexican and civil wars. He was engaged in many battles, and was complimented and advanced in rank for valor at the battles of Pleasant Hill, La., and Tupelo, Miss., and other fierce engagements. In 1872 he was appointed postmaster at St. Louis, and five years later was elected city auditor. This position he filled for twelve years, being elected every time he ran. Congress placed him on the retired list of army generals in 1889.

Reminiscences of Our Army Nurse, Mrs. Rebecca Otis, of Manchester, Iowa.

The following is condensed from an article written and published as a souvenir by her friend, Mrs. H. Eaton, of Manchester, Iowa:

The virtues of men and women have been related in song and story through all time. It is a notable sacrifice to devote the best part of one's life to administering to the wants of those fallen in battle for their country's honor. While woman's mission as a military nurse is a development of later civilization, the success of a good woman in this trying and difficult position, only proves how entirely she is to the manor born. To this army of healers belongs the subject of this sketch, who was with us once more at our Clermont reunion to gladden the hearts and renew the lives of "her boys," as well as to receive the congratulations of all present, who were only too glad to do her honor.

Mrs. Rebecca Otis was a native of north Ireland, of Scotch descent. Born in 1826, she is now in her 78th year. Coming to America in her girlhood days, she drifted westward with the tide, finally settling in the little town of Manchester, Iowa. When the war broke out, Mrs. Otis enlisted as an army nurse and her devoted services were given until the close of the war. Her great sympathy for suffering humanity, her kind and gentle tenderness, soon made the soldier feel that she was his friend. After she had administered to them several weeks, some of them asked the privilege to call her mother. She replied that she would be proud to be a mother to so many brave boys. And mother she was to all during her service in the hospital. Hers to cheer and comfort the wounded and homesick ones as they were brought in bleeding from the battlefield, and many times unto death. She remained by each one as he passed over the river, giving him words of comfort and solace. As mother and friend her work was not finished until she had procured and prepared proper clothing for burial. When her day's work was ended and the other inmates of the hospital were preparing for rest, she was writing the home letters for "her boys", writing as many as eleven in one evening: writing from dictation if they were able, and if not, composing the message which was to convey intelligence to mother, sister or sweetheart, as to the whereabouts and condition of their boy. Soon the letters came in that cheered and comforted the surviving ones. When the doctor had a patient who was past help for his remedies he would turn him over to Mrs. Otis and say: "Here, mother, you may prescribe for this one:" and by her skillful nursing she often saved their lives.

That Mrs. Otis has lived so many years since the trying scenes in the hospital, is the wonder of her friends. She has been most patient and kind through all her suffering and is now patiently awaiting the summons, "come up higher."

Who then can soothe even as a mother? She who is indeed a heroine, with her tender ministration, her look so kind; her gentle voice; closing the eyes of those who wake no more; winning back to life and country those "half across the river."

> "Whom the wounded bless,
>   For her tender care,
> And name as a saint
>   In their evening prayer;
> Kissing her shadow, did it fall
>   Across their pillows from off the wall."

ROSTER OF SURVIVING MEMBERS OF THE TWELFTH IOWA VET. VOL. INFT.

FIELD AND STAFF.

Col. J. H. Stibbs, 160 Adams st., Chicago, Ill·
Major E. M. VanDuzee, Jackson and Fifth sts., St. Paul, Minn.
Major D. W. Reed, 2008, Sherman ave , Evanston, Ill.
Surgeon Charles C. Parker, Fayette, Iowa.
Assistant Surgeon, W. H. Finley, Coggan, Iowa.
"   "   James Barr, 554 Third st., Portland, Oregon.
Adjutant, N. E. Duncan, ————
"   S. R. Burch, Agricultural department, Washington, D. C.
Quartermaster Geo.H.Morisey,236 New Jersey ave,n.w.,Washington, D. C.
"   H. C. Morehead, Cedar Rapids, Iowa.
Chaplain Frederick Humphrey, ————
Serg't Major A. J. Rodgers, 1157 Fifty-seventh st., Chicago, Ill.
Q. M. Sergeant John Steen, Wahoo, Neb.
Hosp. Steward J. C. H. Hobbs, 1441 G st., Lincoln, Neb.
Hosp. Steward Samuel J. Walker, Oakwood, Mo.
Drum Major S. M. French, 3205 W. Twenty-sixth st., Denver, Col.
Color Sergeant H. J. Grannis, Fayette, Iowa.

COMPANY A.

Capt. J. R. C. Hunter, Webster City, Iowa.
Capt. John D. Congar, Eldora, Ia.
Lieut. Cyrus M. Runkle, Eldora, Ia.
" T. B. Edgington,Memphis,Tenn
Serg't Francis Fountain, Marshalltown, Ia. (Soldiers' Home)
" Geo. W. Rulow, South Bend, Ind.
" Geo. W. Reed, Yarkie, Mo.
" R. P. Clarkson, Des Moines, Ia.
" Eugene C. Combs, Hanover, Ill.
" Seth Macy, Des Moines, Ia.
" K. S. Sprague, Blair, Neb.
" R. F. Kellogg, Alden, Ia.
" Geo. H. Cobb, Eldora, Ia.
Corp'l S. B. Brown, Jewell City, Kan
" E. S. Sawin, Union, Iowa.
" Wm. W. Moore, Manchester, Ia
" Levi Dobbins, Eldora, Ia.
" W. G. McPherson, Milbank,S.D.
" T. H. Wilson, Robertson, Ia.

Armstrong, B. A., Liscomb, Ia.
Bell, Thomas R., Eldora, Ia.
Brothers, Ananias, Magnolia, Ohio.
Brown, S. B., Jewell City, Kan.
Cromwell, F. C., Oakland, Iowa.
Crist, Job, Marshalltown, Ia.
Cramer, Hamilton, Highmore, S. D.
Elsworth, D. V., Newman's Grove, Neb.
Ferree, S. R. Belle Plaine, Ia.
Glass, Carl, Dayton, O. (Mil. Home)
Hoskins, G. H., Maryville, Mo.
Kemp, Sumner, Alden, Iowa.
Mann, William, Steamboat Rock, Ia
Moore, G. W., Maryville, Mo.
Mitchell, G. W., Lawn Hill, Ia.
Richards, Jos. M., Ft. Dodge, Ia.
Wickham, A. J., Eagle City, Ia.
Zeigler, James W., Eldora, Iowa.
Zeiger, N. W., Buffalo Center, Ia.

COMPANY B.

Capt. W. C. Earle, Waukon, Ia.
Lieut. J. P. Jackson, Village Creek, Ia
Lieut. John D. Cole, Wauwatosa, Wis
Serg't John Upstrom, 403 Fourth st., Sioux Falls, S. D.
Serg't Geo. Ibach, Preston, Minn.
" Wm. P. Winter, Bancroft, Ia
Corp'l Stephen Thibedo, ———
" I. B. S. Isted, ——— ———
" W. B. Bort, Viroqua, Wis.
" Mathias Englehorn, ———
" L. D. Bearce, Onawa, Ia.
" John Dowling, Waukon, Ia.
" J. H. Butts, Cherokee, Ia.
" Robt. Wampler, Waukon, Ia.
" Fred Monk, Eitzen, Minn.
Andrews, H. R., Anacortes, Wash.
Bathen, Robert, Riceville, Ia.
Bort, A. K., Viroqua, Wis.
Bailey, W. F., St. Paul, Minn.
Bailey, George, St. Paul, Minn.
Burlingame, O. D., 193 So. Water st., Chicago, Ill.
Decker, Adam, Lansing, Iowa.
Dowling, Thomas, Rossville, Ia.
Erickson, E. A., Salem, S. D.
Ferguson, B., Akron; Iowa.
Goodykoontz, D. F., Boone, Ia.
Greenup, S. H., Motely, Minn.
Iverson, Knudt, Lansing, Ia.
Kloes, Frank, Rossville, Ia.
Larson, Aslack, Preston, Minn.
McCabe, Hugh, Waukon, Ia.
McClintock, James, Rossville, Ia.
McGuire, Bryan, Freeport, Ill.
Ogan, Chas. C., Sibley, Ia.
Oleson, John, Spring Grove, Minn.
Plank, Levi, DeFuniak Springs, Fla
Peck, John P., Plankinton, S. D.
Roe, Charles E., 320 East Eighth st., Waterloo, Ia.
Russell, Charles, Brooklyn, Mo.
Sanner, Michael F., Rossville, Ia.
Smith, Samuel C., N. McGregor, Ia
Wanberg, Ole, Spring Grove, Minn
Woodmansee, Isaac, Rossville, Ia.

COMPANY C.

Capt. Wm. W. Warner, died Memphis, Tenn, Dec. 12, 1863.
Capt. Geo. W. Cook, Huron, S. D.
Lieut. D. B. Henderson, (Col. 46th Iowa) Dubuque, Iowa.
Lieut. H. J. Grannis, Fayette, Ia.
Serg't G. Hazlet, Allison, Ia.
" Emery Clark, Woodbine, Ia.
" P. R. Woods, Sibley, Ia.
" P. R. Ketchum, New Plymouth, Idaho.
" F. W. Moine, Strawberry Point, Iowa.
Corp'l G. L. Durno, Springville, Ia.
" John E. Kent, Oelwein, Ia.
" Geo. E. Comstock, Fayette, Ia
" Henry C. Curtis, LeMars, Ia.
" W. H. Jordan, Cheney, Wash
" J. Wilson King, Newman's Grove, Neb.
" A. K. Ketchum, Clarion, Ia.
" John A. Delezene, Park Rapids, Minn.
" John W. Bysong, West Point, Neb.
Ballenger, John W., Lacey, Ia.
Brown, George, Woodstock, Ill.
Burroughs, Geo. A., Douglas, Ia.
Bowers, Wm. H., Limestoneville, Pa
Barton, A. H., Marshalltown, Iowa (Soldiers' Home)
Brant, Allen, (from 27th Iowa) Fairbanks, Iowa.
Clark, Henry, State Center, Ia.
Carmichael, James H., Volga, Ia.
Conner, Samuel, Maxfield, Iowa.
Davis, Andrew J., Berrien Springs, Mich.
Delezene, Benj., Republic City, Kan
Davis, J. C., Marshfield, Wis.
Forbs, David, Elgin, Ia.
Gifford, Simeon, Waucoma, Ia.
Hazlett, John B., Sioux Falls, S. D.
Hamlin, Wm. S., Crawford, Neb.
Hamlin, Lyman S., Oelwein, Ia.
Hendershot, Thos., Plainview, Neb.
Hinkle, E. H., Winfield, Ia.
Hartshorn, Sumner, Rea, Mich.
Henderson, J. A., (from 27th Iowa) Cherokee, Iowa.

Henselbecker, Henry, Blufton, Ia.
Jordan, I. L., Alton, Kansas.
Jordan, Wm., Cheney, Wash.
Jaques, Luther, Spokane, Wash.
Jones, Geo. M., Eugene, Oregon.
Jackway, G. H., (from 27th Iowa) Lamont, Iowa.
Kelley, A. L., Elm Grove, Mo.
Kent, William, Barron, Wis.
Kelsey, E. A., (from 27th Iowa) Tripoli, Iowa.
Lyons, Wm. A., Marshalltown, Ia. (Soldiers' Home)
Lott, Lawrence, Marshalltown, Ia. (Soldiers' Home)
Latimer, Robert Z., Fayette, Ia.
Latimer, George H., Westgate, Ia.
McCall, Daniel E., Culver, Kan.
McCall, John W., Nemaha, Neb.
Mattocks, Jason L., New Era, Ore.
Mattocks, Ross, Jennings, Okla.
Proctor, Geo. W., (from 27th Ia.) Laurens, Iowa.
Quivey, W. W., Pierce, Neb.
Rodgers, Reuben F., Waucoma, Ia.
Spears, N. Hart, Westgate, Ia.
Smith, Jacob R., Ft. Scott, Kan.
Stone, Daniel, Waucoma, Ia.
Sykes, Orvis, Freeport, Ill.
Strong, J. P., Olds, Alberta, Canada
Sprouls, John, Los Angeles, Calif. (Soldiers' Home)
Salsbury, John, Ivanhoe, Kan.
Tatro, Augustus, Clermont, Ia.
Utter, Albert W., McCook, Neb.
Williams, R. D., Fayette, Ia.

COMPANY D.

Capt. E. B. Soper, Emmetsburg, Ia
" John M. Clark, Cedar Rapids, Ia
Lieut. Eli King, Washington, Kan.
Sergt. N. G. Price, Randall, Kan.
" John W. Burch, Cedar Jct, Kan
" I. G. Clark, Cedar Rapids, Ia.
" R. C. Cowell, Plankinton, S. D.
Corp'l H. W. Ross, Campbell, Neb.
" Theo L. Prescott, 263 30th st. Chicago, Ill.
" Howard Pangborn, Clark, Wash
" Josiah Scott, Shellsburg, Ia.
" A. A. Stewart, Carthage, Mo.
" T. J. Lewis, Pittsburg Landing, Tenn.
Bailey, Edwin H., Fredonia, Kan.
Bailey, H. W., Manning, Ia.
Blanchard, A. M., Dayton, Ohio. (Soldiers' Home)
Bumgardner, Wm., Scranton, Ia.-R
Bunn, A. J., Lamar, Mo.
Butolph, E. A., Cedar Rapids, Ia.
Clark, Chas. W., Cedar Rapids, Ia.
Carson, John N., Pasadena, Calif.
Cooper, H. L., Littleport, Iowa. (from 27th Iowa)
Daley, James C., 512 W. 7th st., Grand Island, Neb.
Dubois, Ferd., Charter Oak, Iowa.
Darling, John H., Azusa, Calif.
Elgen, Harmon, Bolan, Iowa.
Flint, Sam'l H., 1000 Kansas ave., Leavenworth, Kan.
Ferner, James D., Nevada, Ia.
Grass, Harmon, 823 Seventh st. so., Fargo, North Dakota
Holler, Irdill W., Copay, Calif.
Howard, Wm. H., 959 Reany st., St. Paul, Minn.
Lee, William L., Bird's Eye, Mont.
Luse, Bentley, (from 27th Iowa) West Liberty, Ia.
Larimour, J. C., Mill Grove, Mo.
Minor, David W., Arcata, Calif.
Maryatt, O. H., Del Nort, Colo.
McElroy, M. H., Percival, Ia.
Morrow, Benj. F., Georgetown, Neb
Price, G. V., Mountain Grove, Mo.
Quigley, D. C., (from 27th Iowa) Mallard, Iowa.
Ross, Jesse H., Grant's Pass, Ore.
Soper, Roswell K., St. James, Minn
Sivets, Daniel, Fegley, Mo.
Thompson, Frank D., Nevada, Ia.
Trobridge, Wm. H., Des Moines, Ia. (Sub-station, E. D. M.)
Tapening, J. M., Crab Orchard, Tenn
VenEmmon, W. H., Chamberlain, S. D.
Whitneck, Wm. W., Waterloo, Ia.
Watrobeck, John, 1234 So. 8th st. St. Louis, Mo.
Wagner, Jasper, Kendallville, Ind.
Weaver, John N., Sioux City, Ia.
Wyatt, John J., Chetek, Wis.

COMPANY E.

Capt. Robt. Williams, Vancouver, Wash.
Lieut. Chas. R. Switzer, Lewis, Ia.
" John W. Shumaker, Waterloo, Iowa.
Sergt. Wm. H. Beckwith, Parkersburg, Iowa.
" Chas. P. Callins, Charles City, Iowa.
" Chas. V. Surfus, Bristow, Ia.
" J. S. Margretz, Kesley, Ia.
" Harvey Smith, Sibley, N. D.
" Allen E. Talbott, Dinsdale, Ia.
" Seth J. Crowhurst, Salem, S.D.
Corp'l J. W. Rich, Iowa City, Ia.
" Thos. Boylan, Stockton, Calif.
" Joel A. Stewart, Oregon City, Oregon.
" M.V.B. Sunderlin, Janesville, Ia
" Wm. Hamilton, Waterloo, Ia.
" C. D. Morris, Canton, S. D.
" David Creighton, Hampton, Iowa.
" Sylvester Cook, Newcastle, Neb
Bird, R. L., Hampton, Iowa.
Boone, R. G., Scott, Iowa.
Belton, James, Batavia, Minn.
Cook, Jas. P., box 114, Ponca, Neb
Church, Nathan, Renwick, Iowa.
DeMoss, Thos., Bristow, Iowa.
Eberhart, Benj. E., Laporte City, Ia
Early, Thos. M., Dumont, Iowa.
Fluent, George, Alma, Wash.
Graham, Jacob, Davenport, Iowa.
Hayward, C. B., Dysart, Iowa.
Harrison, H. J., Waterloo, Iowa.
Large, F. A., Pittsburg Landing, Tenn.
Ochs, Charles, Ackley, Iowa.
Pomeroy, R. L. Wausaukee, Wis.
Reed, Zeph, Fredonia, Iowa.
Seeber, G. L., Sabula, Iowa.
Schrack, David, Oelwein, Iowa.
Sharp, Oliver, Grand Island, Neb.
Strong, Ezra, Benecia, Calif. (Benecia Arsenal)
Shroger, Nathn'l, Laporte City, Ia.
Sellers, John, Davis City, Iowa.
West, D. F., Theon, Wash.
Sawyer, E., Sioux Falls, S. D.

COMPANY F.

Capt. J. E. Ainsworth, Omaha, Neb (Merchant's National Bank)
" J. W. Gift, 900 Main st., Peoria, Ill.
" John Bremner, Yankton, S. D.
Lieut. Abner Dunham, Manchester, Iowa.
Sergt. R. C. Eldridge, Niagara Falls, N. Y.
" R. W. Terrill, Manchester, Ia.
" Jas. F. Lee, Riverton, Oregon
" H. M. Preston, Ft. Dodge, Ia.
" C. F. Eldridge, Walnut, Kan.
" Luther Kaltenbach, Gila Bend, Arizona.
Corp'l Isaac Johnson, Lawton, Okl.
" W. A. Nelson, Hazleton, Ia.
" Frank W. Coolidge, Shoshone, Idaho.
" Justus Schneider, Rosewell, So. Dak.
" John F. Lee, Dwight, Kan.
" Geo. W. Woolridge, Edgewood, Iowa.
Annis, George W. Lanark, Ill.
Coolidge, C. L. Central City, Neb.
Eaton, John J., Edgewood, Ia.
Grice, A F., (from 27th Iowa) Doniphon, Neb.
Hafhill, Josiah, Wood Center, Ia.
Kaltenbach, Samuel, Manchester, Iowa.
Kint, George, Oelwein, Iowa.
Lyons, L. D., Marshalltown, Iowa. (Soldiers' Home)
Mackey, H. W., (transfer from 27th Iowa) Fayette, Iowa.
Olmsted, Henry, (from 27th Iowa) Independence, Iowa.
Potter, James W., Fredericksburg, Iowa.
Ralston, Nels, Canton, S. Dak.
Stribbling, C. C., Clifton, Tenn.
Tibbetts, W. F., Cheney, Kan.
Thorn, Christian, Waverly, Iowa.

TWELFTH IOWA 79

Taylor, James M., 49 E. Twelth st., Portland, Oregon.
Weeden, Robt. L., Coggen, Ia.
Widger, Josiah, Manchester, Ia.
Wandall, Alex, (from 27th Iowa) Volga, Iowa.

COMPANY G.

Lieut. Anton E. Anderson, (Soldiers' Home) Marshalltown, Iowa.
" Jas. E. Simpson, Norfolk, Neb.
Sergt. John O. Johnson, Hesper, Ia.
Corp'l Wm. L. Winsor, Clinton, Mo
" Anders Anderson, Albert Lea, Minn.
" Ole P. Rockswold, Thoten, Ia.
" Gilbert Anderson, Worden, Minn.
" Harvey E. Johnson, box 161 Evansville, Minn.
" Henry Steen, Manassa, Va.
" Guleck H. Houge, Albert Lea, Minn.
" Warren Wait, Ida, Mo.
" Alfred S. Fuller, Sioux Falls, So. Dak.
" Fred. Rachan, Skidmore, Mo.
Anderson, Peter, Lake Mills, Ia.
Aker, D. O., Ridgeway, Iowa.
Christopherson, C., Hartland, Minn.
Coon, Chas. A., Sabinal, Texas.
Dunn, Van R., DeWitt, Neb.
Engelbertson, Erick, Aastad, Minn.
Fuller, Alfred, Sioux Falls, S. D.
Gilbertson, Ole, Hot Springs, S. D.
Gulbronson, Anton, Rothsay, Minn.
Groves, A. H., Decorah, Iowa.
Hanson, Hans, Lake Park, Minn.
Hanson, Halver, Sheldon, N. Dak.
Hulverson, Andrew, Decorah, Ia.
Johnson, Nels O., Enderline, N. D.
Kittleson, Carl B., Norway Lake, Minn.
Kirkland, G. W., Freeport, Ia.
McCabe, Charles, Sherburne, Minn.
Meader, M. E., Hesper, Ia.
Moe, Peter, Springfield, Minn.
Montgomery, Wm. (from 27th Ia.) 4359 Cozen ave, St. Louis, Mo.
Nass, G. H., Washington Prairie, Ia
Oleson, Andrew H., Madison, S. D.
Ryerson, Finger, Ashby, Minn.
Smith, Israel K., Baraboo, Wis.
Smith, J. K., Hesper, Iowa.
Simmons, Roland, Lake Park, Minn
Stalim, Lars L., 208 Bluff street, Sioux City, Iowa.
Simmons, John, Flandreau, S. D.
Skinner, Frederick, Forest City, Ia.
Thompson, Thomas, Sedro, Wash.
Thoryson, Andrew, Aastad, Minn.
Tobiason, Andrew, Windom, Minn.
Wheeler, Horace, Algona, Ia.
West, Samuel, Red Cloud, Neb.
Young, A. S., Nashua, Ia.

COMPANY H.

Capt. H. J. Playter, 1921 6th st., n. w., Washington, D. C.
Lieut. Robt. Fishel, Manchester, Ia.
" David Moreland, Chicago, Ill.
Sergt. John B. Flenniken, Battle Creek, Neb.
" Ralph M. Grimes, Kearney, Neb
" Robt. W. Light, Ponca, Neb.
" John W. Ward, 608 S. Plane st., Burlington, Iowa.
" William H. Cox, Alta, Ia.
Corp'l B. A. Clark, Calhoun, Mo.
" Jos. Evans, box 195, Tipton, Mo
" Wm. H. McCune, Ruthven, Ia.
" Sam'l B. Sloan, Greeley, Ia.
Corp'l John S. Mason, Oak Park, Cal
" John W. Benedict, Lexington, Neb.
" Edward Winch, Arena, Wis.
" Alex S. McConnell, Hopkinton, Iowa. — R
Briggs, H. S., Marcus, Iowa.
Bryan, David, Pomona, Mo.
Crisman, William, Quincy, Ill. (Soldiers' Home)
Crist, John W., Central City, S. D.
Crosby, J. W., Fremont, Neb.
Fishel, S. K., Hot Springs, Wyo.
Frank, Joseph, Lamont, Iowa.
Garner, A. T., Farley, Iowa.

Hamblin, R. E., Arcadia, Ohio.
Henry, Phillip, Greeley, Ia.
Kuhnes, James C., R F D 6, Rockwell City, Iowa.
Jones, David, Monona, Iowa.
Light, Joseph A., Norfolk, Neb.
Nowman, Jno. G., North Platte, Neb
Shorter, James, Shell Rock, Ia.
Smith, Thos., box 97, Cassville, Mo.
Sloan, S. B., Greeley, Ia.
Stuthers, Andrew, Craig, Neb.
Wisegarber, Wm.S.,Walnut Hill,Ill.

COMPANY I.

Capt. Chas. L. Sumbardo, Houston, Texas.
" Jas. F. Zediker, North Yakima, Wash.
Lieut. Alfred L. Palmer, Seattle, Wash.
" Jas. L. Thompson, Franklin, Iowa.
Sergt. W. F. McCarron, (Times office) Chattanooga, Tenn.
" E. B. Campbell, Armstrong, Ia.
" J. Warren Cotes, Talcott, S.D.
" John S. Ray, Naponee, Neb.
" Wm. Starbuck, Oldham, S. D.
" Wm. L. Fry, Scranton, Ia.
" Wm. A. Cobb, Walla Walla, Wash.
Corp'l Marion Rolf, Maquoketa, Ia.
" Jas. Harding, Baldwin, Ia.
" J. F. Wilson, Fulton, Ia.
" Wm. H. Markham, Hawkeye, Kansas.
" Alonzo Wells, Vincent, Ia.
" Wm. Kohler, Dubuque, Ia.
" Mel. B. Goodnow, Burwell, Neb
" Michael D. Nagle, Dubuque, Ia
" Samuel L. Kennedy, Cedar Rapids, Iowa.
" N. F Austin, Andrew, Ia.
Austin, F. M., Staplehurst, Neb.
Allen, Eugene, Cedar Rapids, Ia.
Bitner, Albert, Brayton, Iowa.
Belknap, Albert, Fremont, Neb.
Buchanan, Jas. C., Cedar Rapids, Ia
Butters, John F., room 48, Bolton block, Sioux City, Ia.
Behnke, Frank, (from 27th Iowa) Guttenburg, Ia.
Campbell, John T., Unique, Ia.
Cobb, E. C., 1323 Timea st., Keokuk, Iowa.
Crane, I. K., Maquoketa, Ia.
Clark, Frank, (from 27th Iowa) Humboldt, Iowa.
Davenport, H. G., Superior, Neb.
Devine, John, 152½ N. High st., Columbus, Ohio.
Dupray, Wm. H., 2630 Adel st., Sioux City, Ia.
Eaton, Theophilus, Maquoketa, Ia.
Edie, T. C., Pueblo, Colorado.
Hatfield, Aug. W., 230 Whiton st., Jersey City, N. J.
Hendricks, Wm., Winterset, Ia.
Kickards, Jonas S., Memphis, Mo.
Kerns, Peter, Reubens, Kan.
Knudt, Carl, Postville, Iowa.
Lewis, Peter, (from 27 Ia)Lund,Wis.
Lewis, Lewis, (from 27th Iowa) Holmes City, Minn.
McDermott, Michael, Placid, Ia.
McKinley, James, Maquoketa, Ia.
Nims, Weed, Maquoketa, Ia.
Paup, David, Sac City, Ia.
Perkins, Henry, Seattle, Wash.
Peedch, Lorenzo, (from 27th Ia.) Postville, Iowa.
Ragen, James, Giard, Iowa.
Swank, John M., Muscatine, Iowa.
Schautz, John R., 766 Savier st., Portland, Oregon.
Schmidt, John, (from 27th Iowa) Lincoln, Neb.
Teskey, George. Elwood, Ia.
Thompson, Jas. L., Franklin, Neb.
Wilson, Thos. J., Maquoketa, Ia.
Wivinis, Michael, Dubuque, Ia.
Wooley, Winchester, Mt. Pleasant, Tenn.
Wolcott, Alden E., (from 27th Ia.) Lynixville, Wis.
Williams, Sidney, Atlantic, Ia.
Williams, S., Colfax, Ill.
Yeley, George, Clinton, Ia.

COMPANY K

Cpt O T Fuller, Webster Grove, Mo
Lieut L Webb, Cedar Rapids, Ia
" J J Brown, Bloomington, Neb
" J A Morgan, Davenport, Ia
" Henry C Merriam, Coggon, Ia
Sergt Richard Freeman, Spencer, O
" Wm R Mathis, Omaha, Neb
" T E Blanchard, LeMars, Kan
Corpl A Mosher, 520 Hays st., San Antonio, Tex
" P Church, Arborville, Neb
" E R Mathis, Omaha, Neb
" C Hickethier, Cedar Mills, Ore
" Aug Hickethier, Drain, Ore
" S N Bugby, 1012 N. Fifth st. Minneapolis, Minn.
" C D Billings, Bloomington, Neb
Blanchard, Ira D, Crookston. Minn
Billings, Abraham, Luzerne, N Y
Baldwin, Newton H, Ada, Kan
Barden, Henry A, 273 College st. Portland, Ore.
Beckner, J M, Charles City, Iowa
Davis, W H, Des Moines, Ia
Dolley, Godfrey, Coggon, Ia
Dutcher, Albert, Nat'l Home, Columbus, O.
Ellison, W H, St. Edward, Neb
Gilchrist, J N, Durham, Ia
Horn, Samuel, Colesburg, Ia
Kimp, William, Kirwin, Kan
Keith, W B, Prospect, Neb
Morehouse, P J, Los Angeles, Cal
Mickey, Isaac, Waukon, Ia
Morgan, Wm B, Bloomington, Neb
Willard, Porter H, Hopkinton, Ia
Waldroff, Henry, Laporte City, Ia

CORRECTIONS
In Roster from Addresses Given in this Book.
Letters returned unclaimed marked R.
Deceased Members, D.

Co A—F C Cromwell, Humbolt, Ia; Job Crist, R; D V Ellsworth, D; G W Reed, Tarkio, Mo.
Co B—Wesley B Bort, Foxboro, Wis instead of Viroqua; Samuel C Smith, Waukon Jct, Ia instead of N McGregor; E A Erickson, Center, So Dak.
Co C—Wm A Hamlin, Astoria, Ore instead of Crawford, Neb; Geo Brown R.
Co D—Theo L Prescott, 5702 Erie St, Austin, Ill.
Co E—Wm H Beckwith, R; R L Bird, Absarokee, Mont; Geo Fluent, R; Thomas D Moss, D.
Co F—T McGowan, Independence, Ia; C L Coolidge, Palmer, Neb. Josiah Halfhill, Wood, Ia.
Co G—D O Aker, D.
Co H—Thos Smith, Cassville, Wis; Samuel B and S B Sloan are the same; John B Fleniken, R.
Co I—Lt Jas L Thompson, Franklin, Neb instead of Iowa; James Ragan, R; F C Eddie, R; Wm A Cobb, R; Peter Kerns, R; Wm H Markham, D; I K Crane, D; Wm H Dupray, Hoquiam, Wash; John Devine, R; Weed Nims, Lyons, Ia, care of Capt. Geo A Schnider; J Warren Cotes, Clark So Dak instead of Talcott.

Los Angeles, Cal., Aug. 22, 1904.

Major D. W. Reed.

Dear Major:—Receive my thanks, and please tender them also to the other members of the "dear old Twelfth" for so kindly remembering me with a copy of the History of the Regiment.

Though I have grey hair now, I was but a little girl in those sad years of war, but I remember well, so many who came to see my dear father, and twice I had been in Camp Franklin.

You all appreciate my beloved father as he did you, and to hear of how he was loved by the men of the Twelfth, always gives me pleasure.

My cordial greetings to you and your dear ones. With thanks, yours respectfully,
Miss M. Brodtbeck.

354 Douglass st., Los Angeles, Cal.

Reminiscences of S. C. Beck in Prison Life.

By G. E. Comstock, Co. C. 12th Iowa Infantry.

We were schoolmates at college (Upper Iowa University) in 1861 when on that fatal day the first gun fired on Ft. Sumter went like an electric shock all through the North, firing the hearts of all loyal men to spring to the call of Our Father Abraham for three hundred thousand men. S. C. Beck, of Waverly, Iowa, was one of that number.

Here began the developement of the possibilities of stalwart young manhood as varied as the tints of the rainbow. It was while passing through the crucible of war that some noble characters came forth from the quiet, unassuming walks of life and were made to shine forth as the noonday sun. Not all the deeds of valor of true, noble manhood will ever be written. God alone will know. "To the man that carried a gun" all praise be given, with all due respect to the "Line" from the least to the greatest. Yet, the work to be done, the victory must be won by the man who carried the gun. The virtues of my friend were many, the defects few. He counted not his life dear to himself; he placed it a sacrifice on the altar of his country. What he has suffered no one but God can know. The following shows his unselfishness:

One of our comrades and one, too, of that same band of schoolmates that enlisted with us in Fayette, Iowa, was Hon. H. C. Curtis, now of LeMars. Dr. C. C. Parker, then surgeon of our regiment (12th Iowa Infantry) and still living, bless his memory, notified Capt. Warner, of our company, that Curtis, of his company, was down with the smallpox, that he must make a detail and carry him to the pest hospital. No sooner had this news come to Beck than he said to Capt. Warner, "Let me take him and take care of him." And this strong, brave, big-hearted man went to Curtis, took him in his arms and carried him to the hospital and there remained and nursed him through a long and severe sickness to health, and now Curtis says, "If it had not been for Beck's constant and tender care I would not have been alive today." And so I might enumerate many such instances which characterized, while in the army, as well as up to the last day of his life.

One incident of my army life seemed to cement our friendship in such a bond of love as time only can efface and causes me to mourn today as for a brother. We were prisoners of war and had been for two months. We had suffered from exposure to all kinds of weather, without blankets or shelter, hungry and sick at heart, receiving the jeers and taunts of our enemy instead of blankets and bread. Many sickened and died. Beck was on the sick list in Montgomery, Ala., prison.

The startling and joyous news came to us that we were to be exchanged and released from prison. Of course you can but imagine what emotions of joy filled all our hearts at the thought of once more being free. The cars couldn't run fast enough; time seemed to drag, we were so anxious.

Finally we found ourselves on a small island in the Tennesee river, some sixty miles from Chattanooga, some fifteen hundred in number, and from there we were sent down the river in small steamboats, the water being low. The boat could only take five hundred at a trip. It fell to our lot to be the last five hundred, after three days of waiting without a morsel of anything to eat save mulberries, and we lived in the trees. This was all borne without a murmur, because our hopes were high and our expectations so great we knew it would soon be over. Our time came to go and we boarded the boat in great glee. Even the sick counted not their sickness. We cut loose our boat and steamed down stream to what we supposed our liberty, friends and home. We arrived at the place of delivery: we saw the flag of truce; we saw "Old Glory"—how glorious it did look to us—and our boys in blue on the shore! I would that I could portray to your mind, dear reader, the undounded emotion that filled our very souls. My heart beats faster, my eyes fill with tears today, the 31st of May, 1904, as they did forty-two years ago, this very day. When at this extremely high state of emotion we were called to halt in midstream and not allowed to land. Still we did not dream of what was hanging over us. We supposed it to be the preliminary work of exchange, when lo! the word came to us that General Mitchell, who was then marching on to Chattanooga, could not receive us, and we must go back to prison and slowly starving death.

Remember the three days' fast had not prepared us to receive this with any good grace. The emaciated and enfeebled condition of "our men" made it one of the most distracting scenes it was ever my lot to witness. Up to this time Beck had never failed. Now his time had come. Weak, sick, discouraged, starvation staring us in the face, back to the prison dens our doom. The cloud was dark, "the sun did refuse to shine." Our die was cast, our fate was sealed, our trials had just begun. Four and one-half months more in Macon, Georgia, and Libby prison, brought the remnant that was left home, leaving our pathway strewn with our dead that had fallen by the way, and the remnant that survives to this day, have suffered, and will to the end of their lives suffer, from the effects of starvation and exposure while in prison.

The "bond of love" between Beck and I that we supposed had been so strong and great, really had its beginning right here. He was sick; I was well. It was my turn to minister; his to receive. What provision was on the boat, for the crew was meagre, was divided among our five hundred. Beck's share was a small greasy bone (no meat), mine a tablespoonful of cornmeal. I missed Beck. Upon looking about, I found he had crawled upon the brick encasement to the engine boiler where it was warm (evidently to die). Against his body lay this bone, as his share. I called to him but no reply. I took hold to arouse him only to find him almost gone. I saw at once it was for lack of nourishment and the bone would not suffice. I at once hastened to the engine room, procured a cup, took one-third of my precious spoonful of meal and drew from the boiler hot water, making a gruel (no salt). I roused him and almost forced him to take it, he seemingly unconscious of what I was doing. This I repeated three times and my precious meal was gone, but Beck was saved. The morning brought us to rations and back to life. These are the ties that bound us, the severance of which causes me to mourn as for a brother. The Father has said, it is enough, come up higher. Died at Waverly, Iowa, May 27, 1904; aged sixty-six years.

Obituary of Lieut. J. E. Simpson.

As we are about closing the publication of our pamplet comes the sad news of the death of Comrade Simpson, of Co. G., at Norfolk, Neb., Sept. 23, 1904, of cancer of the stomach. Interment at Decorah, Iowa, Sept. 26. Services befitting the occasion were held in the M. E. church attended by a large concourse of people. The last funeral rites were performed at the grave by the members of Col. Hughes Post of Decorah, of which Comrade Simpson was a charter member and to which he clung as his home post.

In the death of Lieut. Simpson the members of the 12th lose one of their most congenial comrades, his dear wife and son one of the kindest of husbands and fathers. His genial personality, generous good nature and sympathetic qualities made him a delightful companion and faithful father. His friendships were warm and lasting and he will be mourned by a far-reaching circle of loving friends and comrades.

G. E. COMSTOCK, Sec.

Later—Lieut. Simpson's wife died, a week later, of paralysis, brought on by care of her husband during his illness. G. E. C.

Special Mention.

I take this opportunity to make special mention and return thanks on behalf of the Regiment, to Henry H. Kitson, of Boston, Mass., designer and sculptor of the Iowa Memorial monument for Vicksburg Park for his kindness and courtesy in giving us the photograph of his beautiful work, (before its completion) to be erected in the near future. To Edmund H. Prior, of Postville, Iowa, designer, sculptor and contractor of the Regimental and Brigade monuments, at the Vicksburg Park, for the use of his half tone cut of our Brigade monument.

It is said "the rain falls on the just and on the unjust." Hence we would also return thanks to E. C. Kropp, of Milwaukee, Wis., for his selfish, penuriousness and unpatriotic cussedness, in refusing to loan us the use of his half tone cut of the Iowa State Monument at Shiloh, having been assisted to obtain the same by one of our own members: for, by so doing, by "eternal vigilance" "which is the price of liberty," we have secured one of our own.

To all the railroads in Iowa, and especially the Chicago Milwaukee & St. Paul and Rock Island System for rates and special accommodations.

To C. F. Paine & Co., publishers, and all the office force. Too much cannot be said of them for the interest manifested, kindness, courteous treatment, patience exercised (even beyond the limit); in the excellence of the work, as well as the very reasonable terms of their contract. We are fully satisfied.

G. E. COMSTOCK, Secretary.

Addenda.

COMRADES:—The long looked for and almost forgotten Reunion Pamphlet is about to appear. Thinking perhaps this might, and in all probability will be the last, I have spared no pains or expense to make it worthy of the cause it represents, as well as of one of the very best Regiments that went to the front in 61, returning in 66.

Victorious 'tis true, but all along through the years, our pathway is marked by the graves of our beloved comrades, on battlefield, in prison and hospital, many buried in unknown graves, all, that "our country might be one and inseparable."

My personal duties have been fully all that I should care for. The extra work this has brought me, has borne upon me heavily until at times, it has seemed impossible to finish. Being separated so far from the other members of the committee has made consultation almost impossible. Hence, whatever of criticism, defects or errors, appear, charge them up to the "Committee of the Whole House," your humble Secretary.

The embellishment of our phamplet with half tone cuts of our highly esteemed and honored friend and comrades, Gov. Larrabee, Speaker Henderson, and our beloved Col. "Jack" Stibbs, as well as the State, Regimental and Brigade monuments, on the Battlefields of Shiloh and Vicksburg, the Lincoln monument and Henderson statue make it, (for those interested,) a Souvenir and to us a cherished memory of the past, as well. By "eternal perseverance" mixed with good, honest toil, we have been able to bring forth this "Thing of beauty" and I hope "a joy forever."

It is the intention to send a pamphlet to every surviving member of our regiment. If you see this, and don't receive one, send me your address. To all who have contributed to the publishing fund, this is free. Also to all who feel they cannot afford it. To cover the extra expense of our cuts and postage, it will be necessary to charge forty cents per copy. We desire that widows, sons and daughters of deceased members shall have a copy. After these are served, if any remain, they will be on sale to the interested public, at same price. Order from

G. E. COMSTOCK, Secretary,

Fayette, Iowa.

Died Oct. 28, 1904, Christian Thorn, Co. F., at Waverly, Iowa.

On page 24, 6th line, five days instead of fine days.

www.ingramcontent.com/pod-product-compliance
Lightning Source LLC
Chambersburg PA
CBHW022148300426
44115CB00006B/393